Pan-Asian Integration

Linking East and South Asia

Edited by

Joseph Francois

Pradumna B. Rana

and

Ganeshan Wignaraja

First published 2009 by
PALGRAVE MACMILLAN

Palgrave Macmillan in the UK is an imprint of Macmillan Publishers Limited,
registered in England, company number 785998, of Houndmills, Basingstoke,
Hampshire RG21 6XS.

Palgrave Macmillan in the US is a division of St Martin's Press LLC,
175 Fifth Avenue, New York, NY 10010.

Palgrave Macmillan is the global academic imprint of the above companies
and has companies and representatives throughout the world.

Palgrave® and Macmillan® are registered trademarks in the United States,
the United Kingdom, Europe and other countries

ISBN-13: 978–0–230–22178–9   hardback
ISBN-10: 0–230–22178–5   hardback

This book is printed on paper suitable for recycling and made from fully
managed and sustained forest sources. Logging, pulping and manufacturing
processes are expected to conform to the environmental regulations of the
country of origin.

A catalogue record for this book is available from the British Library.

10   9   8   7   6   5   4   3   2   1
18   17   16   15   14   13   12   11   10   09

Printed and bound in Great Britain by
CPI Antony Rowe, Chippenham and Eastbourne

FOREWORD

There is growing policy interest in the pattern and effects of pan-Asian integration. East and South Asia—which include some of the world's largest and most dynamic economies—are forging closer economic ties than ever before. This process has been driven by the rise of the People's Republic of China and India as regional growth poles, deepening regional production networks, falling trade barriers and logistics costs, and the spread of free trade agreements (FTAs). The pace of pan-Asian integration seems set to accelerate in the next decade and underpin inclusive growth and prosperity in the Asia-Pacific.

The Asian Development Bank (ADB) has long recognized the importance of regional cooperation and integration for the region's economic development. ADB was mandated to support regional cooperation as a part of its Charter and a comprehensive *Regional Corporation and Integration Strategy* was adopted in 2006. Regional cooperation is also highlighted as one of ADB's core operational specializations in the *Strategy 2020: The Long Term Strategic Framework of the Asian Development Bank 2008–2020*.

Against this backdrop, ADB's Office of Regional Economic Integration conducted this study on deepening economic relations between East and South Asia. An international team of thematic and country experts participated in the exercise. The study aims to chart the pattern of economic linkages between these two subregions, analyze the factors underlying the growing ties, examine the benefits of closer integration and make recommendations for improving future East Asia–South Asia cooperation and integration.

The study finds that there has been a rapid growth in trade and investment linkages between the economies of East and South Asia, albeit from a low base. FTAs are playing a prominent role in fostering trade and investment within East and South Asia, with around 20 FTAs at different stages of implementation. Furthermore, the study estimates that a broad Pan-Asian agreement covering East and South Asian economies offers significant gains to regional incomes. Key impediments to realizing these gains include the persistence of trade barriers, a lack of trade-related infrastructure, and insufficient structural reforms.

The study makes five important recommendations at the regional level to foster closer East Asia–South Asia integration in the future. These include: (1) countries should continue lowering trade and non-tariff barriers, (2) investment in trade-related infrastructure and streamlining of cross-border procedures offers a direct path to lower trade costs, (3) South and East Asian countries need to consolidate their FTAs, (4) deregulation and policy reform in the services sector should be pursued, and (5) trade liberalization efforts need to be embedded in a wider program of economic reforms. It is hoped that the study will contribute to understanding and policy development for strengthening economic ties between East and South Asia.

Jong-Wha Lee
Head, Office of Regional Economic Integration
Asian Development Bank

ACKNOWLEDGMENTS

This book is a knowledge product of the Office of Regional Economic Integration (OREI) of the Asian Development Bank (ADB). It was financed by ADB's technical assistance funding program under Regional Technical Assistance 6282 (Study on Economic Cooperation between East Asia and South Asia) prepared by Sharad Bhandari. The book is the outcome of the efforts of a team of thematic and country experts led by Ganeshan Wignaraja (Principal Economist, OREI) and Joseph Francois (Principal Consultant). It was conducted under the overall supervision of Pradumna B. Rana (Senior Advisor, OREI) until his retirement in June 2007.

The thematic team consisted of John Arnold, Philippa Dee, J. Malcolm Dowling, Christopher Findlay, Miriam Manchin, Ryo Ochiai, Annette Pelkmans-Balaoing, Michael Plummer, and Robert Scollay. The country teams included Suthiphand Chirathivat, Ejaz Ghani, Binod Karmacharya, Nagesh Kumar, Nephil Maskay, Ramkishen Rajan, Mohammed Ali Rashid, Chayodom Sabhasri, Pooja Sharma, Shandre Mugan Thangavelu, Nadeem Ul Haque, Dushni Weerakoon, and Zhang Yunling.

Rosechin Olfindo provided excellent research assistance for Chapters 1 and 8, and organizational support for the project. Benjamin Endriga (Chapters 1 and 4), Fidelis Sadicon (Chapter 3), and Dorothea Lazaro (Chapter 3) also provided efficient research assistance. Annette Pelkmans-Balaoing and Erin Prelypchan have copy edited and improved the manuscript. Muriel Ordoñez organized publication of the book. Wilhelmina Paz, Ma. Rosario Razon, and Ma. Liza Cruz provided administrative support. We are most grateful to them all.

The book has benefited from valuable comments from many within ADB, including Rajat Nag, Masahiro Kawai, Jong-Wha Lee, Srinivasa Madhur, Giovanni Cappanelli, Jong Woo Kang, and Cuong Minh Nguyen.

Useful suggestions were provided by participants at several events, including an inception workshop in ADB Headquarters on 1–2 June 2006, a finalization workshop and policy seminar in Singapore on 27–30 November 2006 (jointly organized by ADB and Singapore Centre for Applied and Policy Economics, NUS; Institute of South Asian Studies; Institute of Southeast Asian Studies; and Research and Information System for Developing Countries), a seminar at ADB Headquarters on 5 June 2007, and a seminar in New Delhi on 10 March 2008 (jointly organized by ADB and

Indian Council for Research on International Economic Relations). This book has also been enriched through discussions with Richard Baldwin, Antoni Estevadeordal, Chia Siow Yue, Sundaram Pushpanathan, Sujiro Urata, among others.

The opinions expressed in the book are those of the authors and do not represent the views of ADB.

Joseph Francois
Pradumna B. Rana
Ganeshan Wignaraja

CONTRIBUTORS

John Arnold is a consultant at the Asian Development Bank.

Philippa Dee is Visiting Fellow at the Crawford School of Economics and Government, Australian National University, Canberra, Australia.

J. Malcolm Dowling is Visiting Professor at the University of Hawaii at Manoa, Hawaii, United States.

Christopher Findlay is Professor and Head of the School of Economics, University of Adelaide, Australia.

Joseph Francois is Professor at the Department of Economics, Johannes Kepler University, Linz, Austria, and the Principal Consultant for the study.

Miriam Manchin is Visiting Fellow at the Centro Studi Luca d'Agliano in Turin, Italy.

Ryo Ochiai is a Ph.D. candidate in economics at the Asian Pacific School of Economics and Government, Australian National University, Canberra, Australia.

Annette Pelkmans-Balaoing is Assistant Professor at Erasmus University, Rotterdam, the Netherlands.

Michael Plummer is Professor at the Paul H. Nitze School of Advanced International Studies, Johns Hopkins University, Bologna, Italy.

Pradumna B. Rana is Senior Fellow at the Division of Economics, School of Humanities and Social Sciences, Nanyang Technological University, Singapore.

Robert Scollay is Associate Professor at the Economics Department, University of Auckland Business School and Director of the New Zealand APEC Study Centre.

Ganeshan Wignaraja is Principal Economist at the Office of Regional Economic Integration, Asian Development Bank, and the Team Leader of the study.

Contents

ILLUSTRATIONS

Tables

Boxes

Appendix Figures

Appendix Tables

1

INTRODUCTION AND OVERVIEW

Joseph Francois, Pradumna B. Rana, and Ganeshan Wignaraja

Introduction

East and South Asia followed different economic strategies in the 1970s and 1980s. East Asia adopted outward-oriented strategies and witnessed remarkable economic prosperity while inward-oriented South Asia largely stagnated.[1] Not surprisingly, prior to 1990, East and South Asian economies were relatively isolated from one another and there was little talk of pan-Asian economic integration. The only trade agreement that covered the two subregions was the Bangkok Agreement signed in 1975 that included Bangladesh, India, Sri Lanka, Lao People's Democratic Republic (Lao PDR), Republic of Korea (henceforth Korea), and People's Republic of China (PRC) (see Box 1.1). There was very little bilateral trade and investment among these countries. The adoption of a "Look East" Policy in India in 1991 marked the start of a new era in East and South Asia economic relations. Since then, there has been heightened policy interest in the process of pan-Asian integration, and particular interest in evolving economic relationships between the two subregions.

Several reasons can be advanced for the gathering momentum. First, in the decade since the Asian financial crisis of 1997/98, East Asia has reemerged into the global economy with high growth rates and enviable flows of inward investment. Second, there has been a marked shift in Asia's export orientation and an increasing integration of regional markets. About half of all Asian exports are destined for regional consumption, and a further rise is widely expected given the high growth rates in intraregional trade. Third, the countries with the world's largest populations and most dynamic

---

[1] See Wignaraja (1991) for a comparison of the economic strategies and performance of the two subregions.

Box 1.1 East Asia–South Asia Economic Relations: Some Highlights

1975 • Signing of Bangkok Agreement by Bangladesh, India, Lao People's Democratic Republic (Lao PDR), Republic of Korea, Sri Lanka, and People's Republic of China (PRC).

1985 • Formation of the South Asian Association for Regional Cooperation (SAARC) by Bangladesh, Bhutan, India, Maldives, Nepal, Pakistan, and Sri Lanka. Afghanistan joined in 2007.

1991 • India adopted "Look East" Policy to strengthen economic relationships with East Asian countries.

1992 • Signing of the Association of Southeast Asian Nations (ASEAN) Free Trade Area (AFTA) by Brunei Darussalam, Indonesia, Malaysia, Philippines, Singapore, and Thailand. Other Southeast Asian countries joined later: Viet Nam (1995), Lao PDR and Myanmar (1997), and Cambodia (1999). AFTA became fully operational in 2003.
      • India became a sectoral dialogue partner of ASEAN.

1993 • Signing of Agreement on SAARC Preferential Trading Arrangement (SAPTA) by eight SAARC members. SAPTA entered into force in 1997.

1996 • India became a full dialogue partner of ASEAN.

1998 • Signing of Indo–Sri Lanka Free Trade Agreement, which came into force in 2000.

1997 • East Asian financial crisis, which highlighted the importance of regional cooperation among East Asian economies.

2000 • The PRC joined the World Trade Organization (WTO), starting with an early harvest program that liberalized 600 farm products. An agreement to trade in goods was signed in 2005, liberalizing 7,000 trading goods.

2002 • India–ASEAN partnership was upgraded to summit-level dialogue.
      • Signing of Framework Agreement between the PRC and ASEAN. Early Harvest Scheme came into force in 2005.

2003 • Signing of a Framework Agreement on Comprehensive Economic Cooperation between India and ASEAN, incorporating free trade agreement (FTA), at the Bali Summit.

2004 • Signing of an Agreement on South Asian Free Trade Area (SAFTA) during the 12th SAARC Summit in Islamabad. SAFTA came into force in 2006.
      • Signing of a Long-Term Partnership for Peace, Progress and Shared Prosperity by India and ASEAN at the Lao PDR Summit.

continued on next page...

Box 1.1 continued

2004	• Signing of Early Harvest Scheme for the India–Thailand Free Trade Framework Agreement under which preferential concessions have been exchanged on a specified set of commodities. • Signing of a Framework Agreement under the Bay of Bengal Initiative for Multi-Sectoral Technical and Economic Cooperation (BIMSTEC) by Bangladesh, Bhutan, India, Myanmar, Nepal, Sri Lanka, and Thailand.
2005	• Signing of a Comprehensive Economic Cooperation Agreement (CECA) between India and Singapore. • Renaming of the Bangkok Agreement as the Asia–Pacific Trade Agreement (APTA), which would offer up to 4,000 tariff concessions among members. • Signing of a Comprehensive Economic Framework Agreement between Pakistan and Indonesia.
2006	• The PRC became an observer of SAARC. • Ongoing Japanese proposal for a comprehensive agreement covering ASEAN+3, India, Australia, and New Zealand. • Signing of an FTA between PRC and Pakistan.
2007	• Signing of Pakistan–Malaysia Free Trade Agreement—Pakistan's first comprehensive FTA and Malaysia's first bilateral FTA with a South Asian country.
2008	• Conclusions of ASEAN—India FTA discussions in August 2008.

Sources: ADB's Asia Regional Integration Center website (www.aric.adb.org) and papers in Appendix Table A1.1. As of October 2008.

economies—the PRC and India—are in Asia. The evolution of these two economies, as well as the growing economic interrelations between them, has important implications for the region and global economy. Fourth, there are some concerns about whether the benefits of closer East–South Asia economic relations (particularly between the PRC and India) will reach poorer Asian countries and the poor within them. Fifth, there is a proliferation of free trade agreements (FTAs) involving the two subregions. These include the Asia–Pacific Free Trade Agreement (APTA) and ongoing negotiations on an FTA that would cover the Association of Southeast Asian Nations (ASEAN) plus Japan, Korea, and the PRC (ASEAN+3)[2] and India. A Japanese proposal also advocates a comprehensive FTA covering ASEAN+3, Australia, New Zealand, and India.

---

[2] Member countries of the Association of Southeast Asian Nations (ASEAN) are Brunei Darussalam, Cambodia, Indonesia, Lao People's Democratic Republic (Lao PDR), Malaysia, Myanmar, Philippines, Singapore, Thailand, and Viet Nam.

While there is growing policy interest in Asian economic integration schemes, there has been little systematic study of actual integration patterns, determinants, and potential. Interestingly, much of the literature on Asian regionalism focuses on either South Asia or East Asia. The few exceptions include studies focused mainly on India's economic relations with the PRC, ASEAN, or ASEAN+3.[3] Clearly, India accounts for about 80% of South Asia's gross national product (GNP) and has been the most active in pursuing enhanced economic relations with East Asia under its "Look East" Policy. However, other countries in South Asia (such as Pakistan and Sri Lanka) are also now initiating discussions toward FTAs with various East Asian countries; Bangladesh, Bhutan, Nepal, and Sri Lanka are members of the Bay of Bengal Initiative for Multi-Sectoral Technical and Economic Cooperation (BIMSTEC). Accordingly, there is a need for more comprehensive study of pan-Asian economic relations, and for a comparison of different options for regional integration.

Against this backdrop, as a part of its overall program to support regional cooperation and integration (RCI) in Asia, the Asian Development Bank (ADB) undertook this study, which addresses five interrelated questions:

- What is the extent of trade, investment, and other linkages between East and South Asia?
- What economic factors account for the pattern of linkages between East and South Asia?
- What are the potential benefits of enhanced East–South Asia cooperation and integration for member countries?
- What is the likely impact on countries outside the scope of East–South Asia economic cooperation and integration (i.e., third countries)?
- What recommendations at the regional and national levels can be made to improve future East–South Asia cooperation and integration?

Following the introduction and overview, the first chapters provide a regional perspective on current regional patterns of trade and investment and the state of regional infrastructure and logistics (chapters 2 to 4). There is also a chapter on ASEAN integration strategies focusing on trade and monetary cooperation. Another deals with economic integration in South Asia and lessons from East Asia. The next chapters then examine the scope for deeper regional integration in terms of services markets, goods mar-

---

[3] See, for instance, Asher and Sen (2005); Bchir and Fouquin (2006); Kumar, Sen, and Asher (2006); Mohanty, Pohit, and Roy (2004); Wignaraja and Nixson (2006); Kumar, Kesavapany, and Chaocheng (2007); and Kawai and Wignaraja (2008). Bay of Bengal Initiative for Multi-Sectoral Technical and Economic Cooperation (BIMSTEC) members are Bangladesh, Bhutan, India, Myanmar, Nepal, Sri Lanka, and Thailand.

kets, and scope for improved infrastructure and logistics. Thus, chapters 5 to 8 provide a regional perspective, and include a model-based analysis of trade and income effects of alternative integration schemes. Eight country papers from East and South Asia are compiled in the companion volume, *National Strategies for Regional Integration: South and East Asian Case Studies*. For a complete list of the papers, see Appendix Table A1.1.

This chapter also highlights the main findings and recommendations from the various papers and is organized as follows: section 2 examines patterns and trends in trade and investment linkages between East and South Asia; section 3 analyses trade policy, facilitation, and infrastructure; section 4 highlights potential benefits from closer integration between East and South Asian economies and impacts on these countries and others; and section 5 provides findings and recommendations at both regional and country levels.

Trade and Investment Linkages: Current Patterns and Recent Trends

Growth and Direction of Trade

In recent years, there has been rapid growth in trade linkages between the economies of East and South Asia, albeit from a relatively low base. As seen in Table 1.1, the dollar value of South Asian exports to East Asia grew dramatically between 1990 and 2007 from $5.2 billion to $45.3 billion. East Asian exports to South Asia have seen a comparable expansion, rising from $10.6 billion in 1990 to $93.6 billion in 2007. From the most recent data, trade between the two regions has increased by approximately $114.8 billion between 2000 and 2007 (Figure 1.1).[4] The most dramatic growth has involved the PRC's trade with South Asia. The growing trade volumes reflect strong underlying regional economic growth. While volumes have grown dramatically, relative trade shares have remained largely stable—except for the dramatic reorientation of India toward East Asia. India's experience highlights the point that closer economic linkages with East Asia offer South Asian economies a potentially dramatic enlargement of their economic horizons, making available a far greater regional market with which they can integrate. In contrast, closer economic integration with South Asia offers East Asia a relatively modest increase in market size.

---

[4] The figure represents the difference between South Asia's total trade with East Asia in 2000 ($33.0 billion) and 2007 ($147.8 billion).

Table 1.1 Value of Merchandise Trade between East Asia and South Asia, $ Mn

Reporting Economies	Exports						Imports					
	East Asia			South Asia			East Asia			South Asia		
	1990	2000	2007	1990	2000	2007	1990	2000	2007	1990	2000	2007
East Asia	282,256	799,170	1,870,435	10,559	25,575	93,571	283,951	796,806	1,778,418	6,747	14,592	49,275
PRC	40,956	121,031	460,315	950	3,775	34,667	25,590	100,558	421,570	213	1,881	15,941
Japan	86,154	195,315	335,577	3,482	4,096	8,779	64,294	153,423	259,129	2,825	3,260	4,804
Korea, Republic of	22,861	78,752	185,330	1,115	2,756	8,027	25,491	67,969	166,001	482	1,331	4,527
Brunei Darussalam	2,115	2,482	5,753	1	4	3	616	998	1,720	1	6	61
Cambodia	35	125	441	3	1	1	34	1,254	4,945	2	11	53
Indonesia	17,217	36,954	76,538	199	1,742	6,430	10,476	18,064	81,618	290	676	1,824
Lao PDR	54	188	729	0	0	0	130	613	1,898	0	7	8
Malaysia	17,086	54,877	97,890	870	2,765	8,044	15,583	49,850	90,852	261	800	2,209
Myanmar	217	729	3,207	63	202	791	454	2,754	4,627	3	58	197
Philippines	3,075	18,928	47,926	7	97	237	5,838	19,694	45,462	148	195	588
Singapore	23,219	74,322	185,135	2,154	4,696	12,899	30,652	77,376	143,707	550	1,275	6,080

continued on next page

Table 1.1 continued

Reporting Economies	Exports						Imports					
	East Asia			South Asia			East Asia			South Asia		
	1990	2000	2007	1990	2000	2007	1990	2000	2007	1990	2000	2007
Thailand	8,867	33,817	80,736	280	1,201	4,204	18,505	34,622	82,355	681	800	2,256
Viet Nam	1,022	7,868	17,639	20	84	280	1,026	12,166	49,396	4	209	1,038
South Asia	5,184	11,389	45,278	882	2,736	11,308	9,892	21,598	102,513	825	3,285	13,187
Afghanistan	3	9	9	19	60	155	315	195	572	70	169	2,045
Bangladesh	176	277	673	61	88	277	1,566	4,169	8,798	257	1,052	2,998
India	3,357	8,854	41,205	486	1,792	8,057	4,168	10,396	73,261	97	428	1,974
Maldives	17	14	61	7	14	26	101	195	530	17	90	198
Nepal	15	22	27	16	309	706	336	502	741	79	587	1,845
Pakistan	1,403	1,703	2,767	223	282	1,086	2,192	2,884	13,706	122	252	1,090
Sri Lanka	213	510	536	70	190	1,000	1,214	3,256	4,906	184	707	3,039

East Asia includes 10 countries of the Association of Southeast Asian Nations (ASEAN); Japan; Republic of Korea; People's Republic of China (PRC); Hong Kong, China; and Taipei,China. South Asia includes Afghanistan, Bangladesh, Bhutan, India, Maldives, Nepal, Pakistan, and Sri Lanka. No data for Bhutan. Lao PDR stands for Lao People's Democratic Republic.

Source: International Monetary Fund. Direction of Trade Statistics.

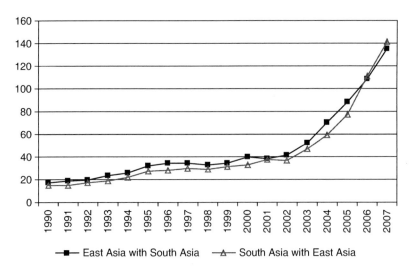

Figure 1.1   Total Trade between East and South Asia, $ Bn

Source: International Monetary Fund. *Direction of Trade Statistics.*

When we focus on individual country-pairs, it is clear from Table 1.1 that intraregional trade is highly developed within East Asia itself, and within the East Asian subregions of Northeast and Southeast Asia.[5] Intraregional trade has also been developing within South Asia, though not to the same extent as in East Asia.[6] Indeed, the relationship is unbalanced, reflecting the relative size of the two subregions' economies. East Asia's share of South Asia's trade is much higher than South Asia's share of East Asia's trade. In addition, East Asia accounts for a much larger share of South Asia's imports than of its exports. There is also a perception that South Asian exports perform poorly in the more open and dynamic markets of East Asia, and that East Asian exports perform well in the less open markets of South Asia. Even so, these markets account for a comparatively small share of East Asian exports.

On top of the PRC's rapid growth, several other East Asian economies have had growth of around 100% or more in their export and/or import trade with South Asia: Korea and Indonesia for both exports and imports; Thailand for exports; Singapore and Cambodia for imports. Hong Kong,

---

[5] For more details see Kawai (2005a), Petri (2006), Plummer (2007), Kawai and Wignaraja (2008), and Plummer and Wignaraja (2009).

[6] See World Bank (2006a and 2006e) and Panagariya (2007).

China; Malaysia; and the Philippines all recorded export and import increases over the period in the range of 60–90%. Of the economies in South Asia, India is the only one to have shown comparable growth in trade with East Asia over the same period. This implies, of course, that a very large share of the increased trade of East Asian economies with South Asia over the period has consisted of increased trade with India. The exports of Bangladesh to East Asia actually fell over the period, and export growth of Sri Lanka to East Asia was minimal. The imports of both the latter two economies from East Asia continued to grow modestly, despite a weak performance in exports traveling in the opposite direction.

Box 1.2 Intraregional Integration in East and South Asia

Intraregional trade is highly developed within East Asia and has also been developing within South Asia, although not to the same extent as in East Asia. East Asia's intraregional trade share in 2007 reached 53.9% and trade intensity indexes show that trade relations within East Asia are generally very intense. In other words, East Asian economies have much more trade with each other than would be expected on the basis of their shares of world trade. Within East Asia, intra-industry trade has expanded more rapidly than inter-industry trade.

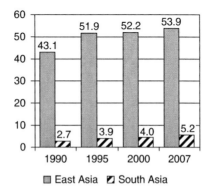

Figure 1.2 Intraregional Trade Shares in East and South Asia, %

Source: International Monetary Fund. *Direction of Trade Statistics.*

A large part of intra-industry trade is characterized as vertical, which has been driven by the diversity in the level of economic development among the East Asian economies and the emerging regional production networks through which parts and components of differing quality and characteristics are being actively traded for the production of final products.

Meanwhile, a significant share of South Asian exports and particularly imports takes the form of intra-South Asian trade, although the share of intraregional trade is clearly much lower in South Asia's case (5.2% in 2007) than in East Asia's. Trade intensity indexes are also predominantly above average for trade within South Asia, both at the aggregate regional level and at the individual country level, with the important exception of India's import intensity with South Asia as a whole, which in turn appears to reflect India's low import intensity with Pakistan. Trade costs and higher protection rates are among the factors behind the low intraregional trade within South Asia.

Box 1.3 Informal Trade in Nepal

Unrecorded or informal trade is an important aspect of Nepal's trade with India. This trade operates both through and outside legal channels. Informal trade through legal channels is carried out through false invoicing, which partially evades export and import tariffs, domestic taxes, and nontariff barriers (NTBs). Informal trade through unofficial channels totally evades tariffs, taxes, and NTBs. Such trade takes place along Nepal's border with India and the Tibet Autonomous Region (TAR) in the People's Republic of China. The following discussion concerns only the border crossing of goods between Nepal and India and is based on estimates from Indian and Nepalese territories (Karmacharya 2002a; Taneja and Pohit 2002; Taneja, Sarvananthan, Karmacharya, and Pohit 2004).

Estimates of India–Nepal Informal Trade: Contrary to the belief that informal trade between India and Nepal takes place largely from Nepal to India (Muni 1992), recent studies show that informal trade is two way. In fact, data suggests that informal exports from India to Nepal in 2000–2001 averaged $180 million while those from Nepal to India average $157 million, implying Nepal had a slight deficit in informal trade. Total two-way informal trade ranges between $368 million (Nepalese estimates) and $408 million (Indian estimates).

The conventional position is that informal trade is a response to trade and domestic policy distortions. This holds true for goods exported from Nepal to India that originated in third countries. The difference in tariffs prevailing between Nepal and India in third-country goods vis-à-vis rest of the world is wide-ranging (5–30%). Furthermore, Nepal's trade regime has few NTBs. Tariff differences might not be such a strong influence on informal imports from India, which consist mostly of rice and other unprocessed food products that face no tariff or NTBs in Nepal. Factors other than policy-related distortions are apparently more important in influencing informal trade. One survey by Taneja and Pohit (2000) showed that trade policy barriers, such as tariffs and quantitative restrictions between Nepal and India, were less significant than institutional factors—quick realization of payments, no paperwork, no procedural delays, and lower transport costs—in driving traders to informal channels. Taneja and Pohit (2000) also showed that informal traders bear relatively low transaction costs in comparison to formal traders. Most informal traders bear transaction costs of less than 10% of turnover, few bear costs of more than 20%, and none bear costs of more than 30%. Formal traders, by contrast, can bear total transaction costs of more than 30% of their turnover.

continued on next page...

Box 1.3 continued

Summary Estimates of Formal and Informal Trade Balance, 2000–2001, $ Mn [a]

	Exports (X)	Imports (M)	X+M	X−M
Indian Territory				
Formal	141	255	396	(114)
Informal	180	228	408	(48)
Share of informal trade to formal trade (%)	128	89	103	54
Nepalese Territory				
Formal	359	614	973	(255)
Informal	157	211	368	(54)
Share of informal trade to formal trade (%)	44	34	38	21

[a] The reference period for India (formal and informal) is April 2000–March 2001; for Nepal, June/July 2000–May/June 2001(formal), and April/May 2000–March/April 2001 (informal).
Values in parenthesis represent trade deficits; $ Mn stands for million of US dollars.

Sources: Karmacharya (2002); and Taneja, Sarvananthan, Karmacharya, and Pohit (2004).

Composition of Trade

The composition of trade between East and South Asian economies reflects differences in levels of technology, natural resources, and development. The leading exports from East Asia to South Asia are much more weighted toward finished and high-technology goods than the leading exports from South Asia to East Asia (see Table 1.2). Leading South Asian exports to East Asia include natural resource-intensive products such as iron ore, non-ferrous metals and ores, granite, leather, oil cake, beef, and crustaceans. In contrast, East Asia's leading exports to South Asia feature products such as computers and integrated circuits; TV, radio, and telecommunications equipment; motor vehicles and motor vehicle parts; and antibiotics. Where there is two-way trade in the same industry, East Asian exports tend to be at a higher level of processing. For the steel industry, South Asia's leading exports to East Asia including ferro-alloys, pig iron, and rolled steel; East Asia's leading exports to South Asia include rolled steel of a heavier grade.

Table 1.2   Commodity Composition of Merchandise Trade between East and South Asia, $ '000

East Asian Economies	Leading Exports	Exports to South Asia	
	Commodity Description	Annual Average	
		1999–2000	2004–2005
People's Republic of China (PRC)	Radio, television (TV) transmitters, and TV cameras	19	763
	Electric apparatus for line telephony and telegraphy	38	437
	Woven synthetic filament yarn and monofilament (>67 decitex)	31	382
	Automatic data processing machines (computers)	57	333
	Woven cotton fabric (>85% cotton, <200 grams per square meter)	142	320
Japan and Republic of Korea	Radio, TV transmitters, and TV cameras	21	1,075
	Parts and accessories for motor vehicles	312	898
	Motor vehicles for transport of persons (except buses)	292	449
	Hot-rolled products and iron/steel (width >600 millimeters, not clad)	73	240
	Motor vehicles for transport of goods	108	230
Hong Kong, China; and Singapore	Diamonds (not mounted or set)	466	1,218
	Parts and accessories (except covers) for office machines	386	865
	Automatic data-processing machines (computers)	457	632
	Oils, petroleum, bituminous, and distillates (except crude)	642	608
	Radio, TV transmitters, and TV cameras	37	419
Southeast Asia	Palm oil and its fractions (not chemically modified)		2,290
	Petroleum oils, oils from bituminous minerals, and crude		515
	Copper ores and concentrates		436
	Coal, briquettes, ovoids, etc. (made from coal)		372
	Automatic data-processing machines (computers)		348

continued on next page...

Table 1.2 continued

East Asian Economies	Leading Imports	Exports to South Asia	
	Commodity Description	Annual Average	
		1999–2000	2004–2005
PRC	Iron ores and concentrates and roasted iron pyrites	260	4,638
	Cotton yarn (not sewing thread, >85% cotton, not retail)	369	534
	Aluminum oxide, hydroxide, and artificial corundum	33	303
	Diamonds (not mounted or set)	52	254
	Chromium ores and concentrates	54	225
Japan and Republic of Korea	Oils, petroleum, bituminous, and distillates (except crude)	221	1,072
	Diamonds (not mounted or set)	476	503
	Cotton yarn (not sewing thread, >85% cotton, not retail)	593	478
	Iron ores and concentrates and roasted iron pyrites	413	478
	Crustaceans	624	269
Hong Kong, China; and Singapore	Diamonds (not mounted or set)	1,826	4,278
	Oils, petroleum, bituminous, and distillates (except crude)	75	1,218
	Cotton yarn (not sewing thread, >85% cotton, not retail)	491	471
	Bovine or equine leather (no hair, not chamois, patent)	97	221
	Jewelry and parts containing precious metals	61	149
Southeast Asia	Diamonds (not mounted or set)		293
	Soya bean, oil cake, and other solid residue		271
	Cyclic hydrocarbons		268
	Meat of bovine animals (frozen)		199
	Oils, petroleum, bituminous, and distillates (except crude)		178

East Asia includes 10 countries of the Association of Southeast Asian Nations; Japan; Republic of Korea; PRC; Hong Kong, China; and Taipei,China. South Asia includes Bangladesh, Bhutan, India, Maldives, Nepal, Pakistan, and Sri Lanka.

Source: Scollay and Pelkmans-Balaoing (2009).

Foreign Direct Investment (FDI)

Broadly speaking, investment flows mirror the regional bias seen in the pattern of trade flows. Focusing on the largest economies in the two sub-regions, the PRC's inward and outward Asian FDI flows are concentrated in East Asia (see Table 1.3). Indeed, in global terms East Asia is the most important source and destination for FDI. Japan is the single most important investor in the PRC, followed closely by Korea. In Asia, Korea is the most important destination for PRC firms. South Asia is an extremely small share of both inward and outward FDI. Less than one tenth of 1% of inward FDI comes from South Asia, while the region accounts for only 0.16% of the PRC's outward FDI. Consistent with the pattern of trade in goods, this suggests very little integration between the regional production chains in East Asia and the economies of South Asia.

Table 1.3   People's Republic of China's Foreign Direct Investment Inflows and Outflows

	Inflows (2003–2006)		Outflows (2003–2005)	
	In $ Mn	% Share	In $ Mn	% Share
East Asia	135,617	57.11	8,351	40.51
Japan	21,634	9.11	40	0.19
Korea, Republic of	15,906	6.70	638	3.09
ASEAN	12,415	5.23	476	2.31
Others [a]	85,662	36.07	7,197	34.91
South Asia	167	0.07	33	0.16
Bangladesh	26	0.01	2	0.01
India	109	0.05	12	0.06
Nepal	1	0.00	3	0.01
Pakistan	22	0.01	15	0.07
Sri Lanka	9	0.00	1	0.00
World	237,480	100.00	20,614	100.00

[a] Others include Hong Kong, China; and Taipei,China.
ASEAN = Association of Southeast Asian Nations, $ Mn = millions of US dollars, % = percent.

Source: Zhang (2009) and *China Statistics Yearbook*.

Turning to India, the largest economy in South Asia, we again see a bias toward East Asian rather than South Asian investment. East Asia accounts for approximately 14.0% of the stock of inward FDI into India, while also accounting for 12.4% of outward FDI (see Table 1.4). In this regard, Box 1.4 provides an example of Indian FDI into Thailand, influenced by the formation of the Thailand–India Free Trade Agreement, while Box 1.5 examines Singapore–India economic relations. In contrast, India's immediate neighbors account for less than one tenth of 1.0% of inward FDI and 1.6% of outward FDI. As discussed in the thematic and country chapters of this report, this reflects the relative openness of the two regions, in addition to relative income levels and levels of development.

Services Trade

Growth in all economies in South and East Asia has been associated with an expanding service sector. Not only has the sector been growing in absolute size but its share in output has also generally been rising with economic development. To varying degrees, these economies have been able to internationalize their services sector at the same time. They have reformed their

Table 1.4   India's Foreign Direct Investment Inflows and Outflows

	Inflows (Aug 1991–Apr 2006)		Outflows (Apr 1996–Jan 2006)	
	In $ Mn	% Share	In $ Mn	% Share
East Asia	4,642	14.08	1,838	12.35
Japan	2,126	6.45	6	0.04
Korea, Republic of	754	2.29	2	0.01
PRC	3	0.01	155	1.04
ASEAN	1,366	4.14	1,094	7.35
Others [a]	393	1.19	581	3.91
South Asia	15	0.04	241	1.62
World	32,966	100.00	14,878	100.00

[a] Others include Hong Kong, China; and Taipei,China. South Asia figure covers Bangladesh, India, Nepal, Pakistan, and Sri Lanka.
ASEAN = Association of Southeast Asian Nations, PRC = People's Republic of China, $ Mn = millions of US dollars, % = percent.

Source: Kumar and Sharma (2009).

Box 1.4 Thailand–India FTA: Encouraging Private Sector Investment

In September 2004, Thailand and India implemented an Early Harvest Scheme with a view to accelerating the benefits of a Thailand–India Free Trade Agreement that is still under official negotiation. The Early Harvest Scheme covers 82 items and will form an integral part of the free trade agreement (FTA). The scheme has increased trade between Thailand and India (Thailand's imports from India increased by 63% the following year) and has generated new Indian investments in manufacturing and services in Thailand.

For instance, Infosys Technologies Ltd. of India, EXIM Bank of Thailand, and Yip In Tsoi & Co. Ltd., Thailand, agreed to form a partnership to develop the core technology platform for the EXIM Bank using the universal banking solution developed by Infosys. EXIM Bank will deploy the program, Finacle, across its retail and corporate banking, trade finance, and treasury operations. According to Infosys vice president, the partnership is seen as a very important milestone for the Indian information technology (IT) industry as well as for Infosys to capture the market within the Association of Southeast Asian Nations (ASEAN) and marks the beginning of a highly competitive IT market in Thailand.

In June 2005, Tata Motors of India, the world's fifth largest medium and heavy truck manufacturer, and the second largest heavy bus manufacturer, entered a joint venture with Thailand's Thonburi Automotive Assembly Plant (TAAP) to produce a pick-up truck which is a niche product of the Thai automobile industry. The joint venture aims to export pickup trucks to the ASEAN and the People's Republic of China's (PRC) markets using the privilege of the tariff reduction under the ASEAN–PRC FTA. Similarly, Tata Steel took over the Thailand-based Millennium Steel Pcl. Ltd.

The latest foreign direct investment from India was in 2006 by the Tata Steel when it took over Millennium Steel Pcl. Ltd., a manufacturing company engaged in the production and distribution of steel products. The main products include deformed bars, round bars, angle channels, low-carbon wire rods, high-carbon wire rods, small sections, special bars, and rolled steel. The company changed its name to Tata Steel Thailand Public Company Limited. Tata Steel will also invest more in the mini blast furnace project and will inject more than $130 million into the Thai subsidiary.

Gems and jewelry is another area where Thailand and India have a strong possibility to deepen their investment relationship. Cooperation would stem from Thailand's well-known production of gems set in silver and gold, as well as its potential to become the trading center for colored stones, and India's abundant supply of rough precious stones and polished small diamonds.

Source: Chirathivat and Sabhasri (2009).

---

domestic policies to facilitate services imports in various modes. They have found success in exports as well, but the extent to which this has occurred varies between countries and over time. Services exports from members of ASEAN that had been growing rapidly in the 1990s were severely affected by the financial crisis. The PRC's services exports have grown steadily, including since accession to the World Trade Organization (WTO). South

Asian exports of services have also grown steadily but have been dominated by India.[7]

Patterns of services trade vary between countries, reflecting variations in comparative advantage:

- Members of ASEAN in general have a greater comparative advantage in travel and transport services than do members of the South Asian Association for Regional Cooperation (SAARC).
- Although ASEAN members had comparative advantages in computer, communications, and other services in the pre-crisis period, they lost that advantage after the late 1990s, just as the SAARC members (through India's contribution) gained an advantage in that area.
- ASEAN, like SAARC, does not show a comparative advantage in financial services.

Exports of information technology (IT) services from India to the PRC and Korea amounted to $24 million and $7 billion, respectively, together representing a mere 0.13% of total IT exports during 2004/05. In total, East Asia and South Asia accounted for around 5.9% and 0.9% of total IT exports from India during 2000/01. However, top Indian IT firms are currently attempting to diversify their markets using various strategies, such as setting up offices in the PRC to serve the local market and to attract Japanese outsourcing business by employing workers from the PRC and Japan to overcome the language barriers.

Contractual construction and labor service are the PRC's major service sectors, especially in Asia. In Asia, approximately 69% of construction exports (through 2004) have been to East Asia, with the remaining 31% destined for South Asia. In South Asia, Pakistan is one of the most important markets for contractual construction service exports from the PRC. Up to the end of 2004, companies in the PRC contracted 383 projects with Pakistan involving construction and exported machinery services with a total contractual value between 1992 and 2004 of more than $6.8 billion. Approximately 10.7% of this was in the area of construction services. The PRC also has some history of construction and labor exports to Sri Lanka and Bangladesh. However, its focus within Asia has generally been on its immediate East Asian neighbors.

Meanwhile, data shows the significance of remittances, especially for small developing countries such as Nepal and Bangladesh. South Asian and ASEAN countries tend to be exporters of labor services, but it is of interest that payments of remittances from these economies are also growing rapidly. Japan and Korea will face new challenges with respect to the movement of labor as their respective workforces age.

---

[7] See Findlay, Ochiai, and Dee (2009).

Box 1.5 Singapore's Growing Economic Relations with India

Given India's need for massive financial resources for development and Singapore's desire to expand its external wing, one would have expected significant synergies between the two countries. This is particularly so in view of the close geographical proximity of the two countries (particularly South India and Singapore). However, it was only since the mid-1990s as Singapore's political links with India improved under then prime minister Goh Chok Tong that Singapore started viewing India as a serious investment destination.

Singaporean companies have significant financial resources and expertise in urban planning, real estate, and infrastructure such as townships, industrial parks, airports, and seaports. More generally, Singapore is particularly strong in the logistics sector, an area of comparative weakness for India. There are many collaborative ventures between Singapore and various states in India. For instance, the Port of Singapore Authority (PSA) has been involved in the development and management of the Tuticorin Port in Tamil Nadu and the Pipavav Port in Gujarat, while Singapore's initial large-scale investment was in a multimillion dollar IT Park in Bangalore in 1994 (by Singapore-based Ascendas). Singapore's investments in India include infrastructure, banking, pharmaceuticals, and telecommunication. The Singapore government's holding company, the Government of Singapore Investment Corporation (SGIC), has emerged as a major foreign institutional investor in India, thus providing more equity capital to many Indian businesses.

Conversely, many Indian companies are increasingly viewing Singapore as a good secondary base to maintain some of their operations to service overseas clients (in the event that services out of India are disrupted by conflicts or natural disasters). Singapore is also seen as a good base from which Indian companies can service regional clients. Many Indian companies such as Satyam, Tata Consultancy Services, eSys, VSNL, and Bilcare have already established key regional operations in Singapore, and many more are likely to do so in the near future.

While Indian companies are finding it difficult to gain outsourcing contracts from Japanese and Korean firms because of language and cultural differences as well as a general reluctance of Japanese and Korean firms to move offshore, there is a belief that Singapore-owned and Singapore-based companies may be more willing and able to outsource in a large way to India. At the strategic and political levels, Singapore has been instrumental in helping India become more accepted into the broader East Asian community of nations. Aggregate trade between India and Singapore has been steadily growing since 1999. In fact, in recent years, Singapore's trade with India has outpaced its growth with other Asian neighbors.

Source: Rajan and Thangavelu (2009).

There are certainly complementarities between the regions, as these examples and the divergences in revealed comparative advantage (RCA) suggest. However, there is evidence of important impediments to trade and investment inhibiting integration between the regions. Data sets are incomplete, but reviews of country policy show significant impediments and other regulatory barriers affecting operations in many sectors. The treatment of services in FTAs varies, with little coverage in agreements operating within South Asia in particular but significant coverage in some recent agreements. Further, there is some concern about the treatment of services in FTAs since additions to competition, rather than preferential treatment of foreign firms, promise much larger gains.

Regional cooperation, more broadly defined, offers many benefits. These include the benefits of sharing the experience of domestic reform, the implementation of capacity-building programs, and joint efforts to develop new regulatory arrangements. Most of the specific suggestions for cooperation between East and South Asia concern the movement of people or the construction and operation of infrastructure linkages. Beyond trade facilitation, complementary packages of services and goods reforms also offer significant gains.

Policy, Facilitation, and Infrastructure

The rapid growth in intra-Asian trade, especially in the last couple of decades, represents both a marked shift in export orientation and an increasing integration of regional markets. In 2005, half of total Asian exports were destined for regional consumption, and a further rise can only be expected given the high growth rates of intraregional trade, peaking at 25% in 2004 (WTO 2006). Against such a backdrop, the surge of regionalism in Asia today comes as no surprise. Nowhere in the world is the proliferation of FTAs more evident than in Asia. As of January 2008, individual East and South Asian countries are involved in 20 FTAs that are either signed, under official negotiation, or proposed (see Appendix Table A1.3).[8] While political and security motives are also influential, the economic imperative to feed the market's appetite for more regional trade is clearly driving policy agents further along the FTA track.

FTAs are playing an increasingly prominent role in trade within East Asia and South Asia, and appear likely to also play a growing role in trade between the two regions. Existing FTAs range from partial preference agreements, generally following a positive list approach, to more comprehensive agreements designed to satisfy General Agreement on Tariffs and Trade (GATT) Article XXIV, usually following a negative-list approach. Partial preference agreements have tended to be more popular with the

---

[8] See ADB's Asia Regional Integration Center website (www.aric.adb.org) for more information.

South Asian countries; East Asian economies have shown a greater willingness to engage in more comprehensive agreements,[9] although not all East Asian FTAs are comprehensive. Defensive motivations for the establishment of FTAs are becoming increasingly important as countries seek to avoid being disadvantaged relative to their competitors in the markets of their trading partners.

Most South Asian agreements are less liberal than the ASEAN Framework Agreement on Services (AFAS). These agreements aim to liberalize trade in goods, particularly through reductions in tariffs. Although there are few agreements that have detailed services provisions, the intent of future negotiations are sometimes described in the text of agreements. Therefore, the increase in importance of trade in services seems to be recognized by many South Asian countries. According to the descriptions in the texts, there is a high possibility that future negotiations will include the provision that the degree of liberalization of trade in services should be no less liberal than in the member economies' commitments under the General Agreement on Trade in Services (GATS).

Bilateral agreements between AFTA and the PRC, between India and Singapore, and between India and Thailand liberalize services FDI under the framework of a more comprehensive investment agreement. For example, provisions on investment liberalization in the AFTA–PRC and the India–Thailand agreements are based on a broader and more independent agreement on investment. With regard to cross-border trade in services (modes 1 and 2), future negotiations are referred to in texts of the agreements, but in contrast to other Asian FTAs, no frameworks on investment liberalization have been proposed at this stage. With regard to mode 4 (movement of people), few agreements include any provisions on liberalization of movement of people.[10]

---

[9] For analysis of the features of East Asian free trade agreements (FTAs), see Kawai and Wignaraja (2008). They find that most of the 35 concluded FTAs in East Asia (i.e., 69%) as of October 2007 had World Trade Organization (WTO) plus elements. Such agreements cover the "Singapore issues" (trade facilitation, investment, government procurement, competition policy) and cooperation enhancement as well as goods and services. In general, developed countries seem to prefer this format of agreement with developed countries in the region.

[10] Mode 1 covers delivery of a service from the territory of one country into the territory of other country; Mode 2 covers supply of a service of one country to the service consumer of any other country; Mode 3 covers services provided by a service supplier of one country in the territory of any other country (i.e., foreign direct investment [FDI] undertaken by a service provider); and Mode 4 covers services provided by a service supplier of one country through the presence of natural persons in the territory of another economy.

Rules of origin (ROOs) are a critical determinant of the trade effects of FTAs. There is increasing concern over potential complications to the business environment as a result of proliferating FTAs whose ROOs are inconsistent with one other. Correspondingly, there have been growing calls to develop a common approach to ROOs across FTAs.[11] The choice between competing approaches to ROOs in important new trade agreements has potentially significant implications for the future trading environment within and between the two regions.

Any proposal for new arrangements or institutions to intensify trade linkages between East and South Asia will necessarily face major challenges. It is likely that countries that have so far restricted their involvement in preferential trade to "partial preference" agreements will have to accept deeper commitments on trade in goods than they have previously considered comfortable. If new arrangements do proceed, however, the alternative of being left out is likely to be even more unpalatable. The impact of any new preferential arrangements on trade patterns developed under existing preferential agreements will need to be carefully considered. Depending on the configuration of new arrangements, the impacts could stem both from preference erosion and from the creation of new patterns of discrimination and exclusion among the countries of the two regions. There is likely to be concern, especially in South Asia, over the possible adjustment costs arising from these impacts and from the likely deepening of liberalization commitments under any new arrangements. Strategies to address these adjustment costs will inevitably assume great importance. At the same time, any proposals for new trade arrangements in East and South Asia should take into account the need to develop sensible and efficient rules for the conduct of regional trade, where these are needed to supplement or rationalize existing rules, as in the case of ROOs.

While there is technically an increasingly complex web of bilateral and subregional agreements across Asia, levels of most-favored-nation (MFN) protection remain a basic determinant of trade costs between many countries in the region. In conjunction with infrastructure- and rules-based costs, the pattern of trade between East and South Asia reflects variations in tariffs. At present, MFN protection is much lower in East Asia than it is in South Asia. This is highlighted in Table 1.5. The average MFN tariff in India, for example, is 13.9%, while for the PRC (following accession to the WTO) it is now 4.9%. Bangladesh has an average MFN tariff of 55.8%, while Thailand's is one tenth of this. The pattern of trade between East and

---

[11] See Baldwin (2007), Scollay and Pelkmans-Balaoing (2009), and Kawai and Wignaraja (2008).

Table 1.5   MFN Protection, 2004/05, %

	Average MFN Tariff	MFN Tariff Rates (less energy)	Energy Share of Imports
PRC	4.9	5.3	0.1
Singapore	0.0	0.0	0.2
Thailand	5.4	6.5	0.2
Bangladesh	55.8	54.9	0.1
India	13.9	15.4	0.3
Nepal	14.6	14.7	0.2
Pakistan	12.2	13.1	0.2
Sri Lanka	7.3	7.9	0.1

MFN = most-favored-nation, PRC = People's Republic of China, % = percent.

Source: World Integrated Trade Solution (WITS) Database.

South Asia is driven, in part, by underlying rates of protection. East Asia is a more open destination, and hence serves as a preferred destination. It also benefits more from the potential for regional integration of industries.

At the same time, there has been widespread reduction of MFN tariffs in East Asia following unilateral liberalization in the 1990s. This means the trade-enhancing space for preferential tariff arrangements has narrowed. In ASEAN, for example, products with preferential margins above 5% constituted only 15% of total regional imports in 2001 and 13% in 2003.[12] Preferences are obviously more important among tariff-peak products, but the presence of nontariff barriers (NTBs) and complex ROOs have often proscribed bilateral concessions. This implies that the utility of FTAs without facilitating measures (such as streamlining of rules and infrastructure improvement) as a means of expanding intraregional trade may be fast approaching its limit.

For trade-related infrastructure, the dominant mode for freight transport between East and South Asia remains ocean transport and this situation is expected to continue for the foreseeable future (see Box 1.6). Land transport, both road and rail, will have an increasing role in bilateral trade within Asia. It may also facilitate trade between non-contiguous countries

---

[12] See Manchin and Pelkmans-Balaoing (2006).

within South and East Asia but this will require a significant improvement in border-crossing procedures. It is unlikely that land transport will attract a substantial share of trade flows between the two regions within the next decade, despite efforts to develop various links of the Asian Highway and the Inter-Asian Railway. Air transport is growing in importance as the value of commodities traded between the two regions increases; however, the growth in air freight has lagged behind that of ocean transport and is expected to continue to do so.

Box 1.6 Infrastructure and Trade Facilitation in Trade between East and South Asia

Trade among the countries of East and South Asia benefited from the dramatic improvements in both infrastructure and services over the last three decades. The effectiveness of the sea, land, and air routes in accommodating the expected increase in trade between East and South Asia depends not only on the quality of the infrastructure and transport services provided but also on the constraints introduced at the international borders through which these corridors pass.

Sea Transport. The Southern Ocean Corridor (see Appendix 1.1) has been the principal route for trade between East and South Asia for centuries, and this situation is expected to continue for the foreseeable future. The corridor forms part of the East–West trade route that circumnavigates the globe, connecting the Mediterranean Sea via the Suez Canal to the Persian Gulf, then continuing past South Asia through the Straits of Malacca to East Asia and on across the Pacific. Rapid growth in trade has been accommodated through the introduction of larger container vessels and the expansion and diversification of feeder services. Some bottlenecks, primarily in public ports, have delayed expansion of necessary infrastructure.

Land Transport. The Northern Land Corridor connecting East and South Asia includes the Asian Highway (see Appendix Figure A1.2), a 141,000-kilometer (km) standard roadway crisscrossing 32 Asian countries between Pakistan in the west and the People's Republlic of China (PRC) in the east, and the Trans-Asian Railway, a network of national rail lines that interconnects East and South Asia from Pakistan through to the PRC. However, neither the road nor rail routes are fully operational as there are missing links and problems with the conditions of other links. It is currently estimated that an investment of $18 billion would be required to create new roads and upgrade existing ones totaling 26,000 km of roads to complete the Asian Highway.

Air Transport. Unlike the other corridors, the Central Air Corridor has an unlimited set of potential direct routes between economic centers. The international freight hubs are used to transship cargoes moving between Europe, the Middle East, Southeast Asia, and East Asia. Collection and

continued on next page...

Box 1.6 continued

distribution activities are accomplished through feeder routes between the international hubs and the national gateway major airports and through domestic services connecting to the local airports. Air transport is growing in importance as the value of commodities traded between the two regions increases. However, the growth in airfreight has lagged behind that of ocean transport and is expected to continue to do so.

Logistics and Supply Chain Management. All the countries in South and East Asia have highly competitive transport services. Trucking services are privately operated and there is a large number of carriers. Likewise, there is strong competition in the ocean sector. The volume of traffic, however, is the principal constraint on the number of lines calling at the major ports and the frequency of services. There is a similar situation for air transport, but access to international operators is generally limited by bilateral agreements that restrict flights and limit the use of fifth and sixth freedoms (see note below). The different requirements of time and cost in trading goods are met by using different transport modes. Air freight is the most costly, with a range of $0.25–$0.50 per ton-km, and the fastest requiring 2–4 hours per 1,000 km. Road and rail transport have similar characteristics in terms of speed, but road transport is more costly at about $.025–$.050 per ton-km. Ocean transport is both the cheapest ($0.010–$0.015) and the slowest.

Trade Facilitation. There are three major initiatives directed at reducing the time and improving the transparency and consistency of cargo clearance procedures at the border: 1) introduction of a harmonized system for cargo classification; 2) implementation of the provisions for trade facilitation as part of accession to the World Trade Organization (WTO) (e.g., customs valuation); and 3) implementation of the customs reforms included in the Revised Kyoto Convention. The countries in South and East Asia are well advanced in adopting these initiatives but still have need to make progress to achieve full implementation.

Taking into account customs, infrastructure, ease of shipment, logistics services, ease of tracking, internal logistics costs, and timeliness, the PRC is perceived as having the best logistics, followed by Thailand. This is despite the fact that Thailand, Bangladesh, and India have the lowest internal logistics costs. The PRC and Thailand are at the top of the list while Bangladesh, Sri Lanka, and Myanmar are at the bottom because of quality of supporting infrastructure, ease of shipment, and problems with meeting schedules.

Note: The fifth freedom refers to the right to carry passengers from one's own country to a second country, and from that country to a third country. The sixth freedom refers to the right to carry passengers or cargo from a second country to a third country by stopping in one's own country.

Sources: Arnold (2009)

The changing structure of supply chains used for international trade is expected to have a more profound effect on trade between East and South Asia than any change in transport infrastructure. Improvements in logistics services will decrease transit time and cost while they increase reliability, allowing manufacturers to change their modes of production and retailers their methods of distribution. Integrated production activities are being replaced with extensive subcontracting of the different stages of production. Subcontractors locate either in a cluster around the primary manufacturer, so as to operate in a manner similar to that of an integrated industry, or they spread out in different locations where the factors of production are most favorable.

The Potential Benefits of Pan-Asian Integration

Directions of trade, trends in import protection, and scope for trade facilitation all suggest potential benefits from a regional (rather than bilateral or more limited) approach to integration in Asia. This study provides estimates of potential gains to trade volumes and real incomes under such an approach, in the context of a projected baseline of the Asian and major global economies to 2017.

There is a growing body of literature on the impact of FTAs in Asia using a type of economic model known as a global computable general equilibrium (CGE) model. By relying on these models to analyze the economic effects of policy changes due to the formation of FTAs, such studies shed light on the economic implications of regional integration. The interest in a CGE approach to this question can be attributed to the proliferation of bilateral and multilateral FTAs in Asia in recent years; to the controversies over the desirability of FTAs with overlapping country membership; to advances in CGE models and computing power; and to improvements in modeling capabilities, particularly in Asia. The bulk of the research in this area has been devoted to FTAs covering East Asian economies, while the literature on FTAs involving South Asian economies or pan-Asian FTAs between East and South Asian economies is limited. The findings of recent studies on Asian FTAs are reviewed in Francois and Wignaraja (2009).

Because the existing literature is limited to subregional experiments, in this study we have explored the implications of a pan-Asian approach to FTA formation by employing our own global CGE model. We summarize the main findings here.[13] The model used for this study offers many improvements over the existing literature. Working from a dataset with

---

[13] More details are provided in Francois and Wignaraja (2009).

35 regions and 36 sectors and benchmarked to 2017, we examine scenarios that include not only regional tariff elimination for goods but also services trade liberalization, trade facilitation, and the likely impact of improvements in trade-related infrastructure. While tariffs are important, NTBs are also crucial. Indeed, the thematic chapters of this report highlight NTBs to regional trade and investment in services, and the importance of infrastructure for interaction between regional economies. Furthermore, there is strong evidence that rules and procedures have also circumscribed potential market access benefits linked to regional tariff preference schemes. All of these factors point toward potential cost savings from a regional approach linked to subsuming existing bilateral initiatives into a comprehensive agreement that streamlines trade rules, promotes improvement of infrastructure, and furthers a loosening of restrictions on services trade and FDI. By construction, our scenarios therefore reflect this ambitious regional approach to tariff elimination, trade cost reduction (partly through infrastructure improvement), and services liberalization. We focus on four broad FTA scenarios: (i) a South Asia FTA; (ii) an ASEAN+3 FTA scenario where Japan, Korea, and the PRC reach an agreement with the members of ASEAN; (iii) an extension of the ASEAN+3 FTA to include India; and (iv) a further extension to include all of South Asia as well. The last scenario offers a pan-Asian scenario spanning the bulk of East and South Asia.

The estimated impacts on national income of the scenarios are summarized in Table 1.6 below. (More details on trade, production, and labor market effects are provided in chapter 8 of this volume.) From Table 1.6, the broad pan-Asian experiment offers significant gains to regional incomes (roughly $260 billion, measured in constant 2001 dollars). Reflecting the relative size of the regional economies, most of these gains are concentrated in East Asia. However, as a percentage of income, the impact is comparable (averaging 2.0–2.3%) across the East and South Asian subregions. For some countries, the projected gains as percentage change from 2017 baseline income are substantial. These include Thailand (12.9%), Viet Nam (7.5%), Malaysia (6.6%), Korea (6.5%), Singapore (5.7%), other South Asian countries (primarily Nepal, 3.7%), Indonesia (3.0%), Philippines (2.9%), India (2.3%), and Sri Lanka (2.0%).

The pattern of results in the scenarios studied follow from the underlying patterns of Asian trade and trade protection discussed elsewhere in the volume. What matters most for East Asia is that the PRC, Japan, and Korea be brought into any scheme for deeper regional integration. The inclusion of these three countries drives most of the income and trade effects in East Asia in all scenarios. Next in importance is then the inclusion of India, as this brings some gains—especially to the countries that share the Malay Peninsula—and effectively bridges East and South Asia. Because of higher incomes and greater absolute size of export markets in East Asia, deeper integration with the region could potentially allow South Asia to reap substantive income gains (roughly 2–4% of gross domestic product [GDP]) along with associated export growth. Interestingly, the one regional player in South Asia that seems to matter most for East Asian exporters in terms of benefits of improved market access is India. Most of the East Asian gains from a South Asian initiative would follow directly from Indian participation. The other players in the region have only a limited impact on East Asia. For the South Asian economies themselves, it is clear that if India looks East, they need to be part of the program as well. The politics of any regional scheme will therefore be complex; East Asian countries gain the most from access to India, while the South Asian economies stand to gain only if India's initiatives directed toward East Asia involve them as well.

The scenario modeling also examines the impacts on South Asia of alternative bilateral agreements between ASEAN and the PRC, Japan, and Korea. This exercise demonstrates the point that, depending on trade orientation, a subregional scheme is not necessarily in the interest of all economies in the subregion. These results are summarized in Figure 1.3. For Sri Lanka and Nepal (Other South Asia), for example, it is indeed subregional integration, or the subregional component of broad agreements, that matters most. In contrast, ties to East Asia matter more to India. The varied regional impacts in Table 1.6 illustrate why, overall, it is the broader approach that leads to the most balanced result across countries. This is so because the different countries in the region have different trade orientations vis-à-vis East and South Asia.

What happens to third countries under the various scenarios? Overall, the results provide a useful lesson on the impact of a pan-Asian FTA or subregional FTAs on countries that are inside and outside such agreements. In Asia itself, insiders benefit while outsiders will be hurt. Hence, an ASEAN+3 scenario will depress incomes in South Asia unless the scheme is broadened to include the economies in this region. However, as long as we throw a broad net and aim to include all countries in the various subregions, a pan-Asian FTA then has the potential to actually boost regional trade and incomes without substantive adverse trade effects on third countries. For individual countries there is a varied pattern of trade reorientation, but there is not a consistent, discernable global drop in trade and incomes. Rather, the widest of our FTA scenarios implies broad-based trade and income growth in Asia, with little effect in aggregate, positive or negative,

Table 1.6 Income Effects of Alternative Scenarios, change relative to 2017 baseline (at constant 2001 prices)

	South Asia FTA		ASEAN+3 FTA		ASEAN+3 and India FTA		ASEAN+3 and South Asia FTA	
	Value ($ Mn)	% change	Value ($ Mn)	% change	Value ($ Mn)	% change	Value ($ Mn)	% change
East Asia	(540)	(0.01)	226,855	2.17	239,097	2.29	241,485	2.31
PRC	(157)	0.00	41,502	1.26	43,289	1.32	43,454	1.32
Hong Kong, China	39	0.01	(1,051)	(0.33)	(1,713)	(0.53)	(1,811)	(0.56)
Japan	(9)	0.00	74,825	1.54	78,080	1.61	78,650	1.62
Korea, Republic of	(115)	(0.01)	49,393	6.19	51,545	6.46	52,100	6.53
Cambodia	0	0.00	107	1.20	106	1.18	79	0.88
Indonesia	(117)	(0.04)	7,884	2.62	8,818	2.93	9,090	3.02
Malaysia	(24)	(0.01)	10,391	5.54	12,014	6.40	12,376	6.60
Philippines	(7)	(0.01)	3,177	2.64	3,521	2.93	3,495	2.91
Singapore	(41)	(0.02)	7,943	4.79	9,285	5.60	9,717	5.86
Thailand	(101)	(0.05)	26,728	12.10	28,220	12.78	28,534	12.92
Viet Nam	(8)	(0.01)	5,293	7.35	5,449	7.57	5,428	7.54
Others	0	0.00	661	0.59	483	0.43	374	0.33

continued on next page...

Table 1.6 continued

	South Asia FTA		ASEAN+3 FTA		ASEAN+3 and India FTA		ASEAN+3 and South Asia FTA	
	Value ($ Mn)	% change	Value ($ Mn)	% change	Value ($ Mn)	% change	Value ($ Mn)	% change
South Asia	3,695	0.33	(3,620)	(0.32)	16,199	1.44	22,423	1.99
Bangladesh	351	0.31	(297)	(0.26)	(355)	(0.31)	1,874	1.66
India	1,138	0.14	(2,371)	(0.30)	17,779	2.23	18,240	2.29
Pakistan	625	0.42	(824)	(0.55)	(862)	(0.58)	298	0.20
Sri Lanka	335	1.08	(117)	(0.38)	(123)	(0.40)	631	2.03
Others	1,246	3.37	(12)	(0.03)	(240)	(0.65)	1,380	3.73
Rest of the World	361	0.00	(9,316)	(0.03)	(3,934)	(0.01)	(3,001)	(0.01)
World	3,516	0.01	213,919	0.45	251,363	0.52	260,907	0.54

ASEAN+3 = Assocation of Southeast Asian Nations plus People's Republic of China, Japan, and Republic of Korea; FTA = free trade agreement; $ Mn = millions of US dollars; % = percent; ( ) = negative value.
All values are relative to baseline income. Other countries in East Asia includes Brunei Darussalam, Lao People's Democratic Republic, and Myanmar; Other countries in South Asia includes Bhutan, Maldives, and Nepal; and Rest of the World includes all other countries not mentioned and not shown on the table.

Source: Estimates from Francois and Wignaraja (2009).

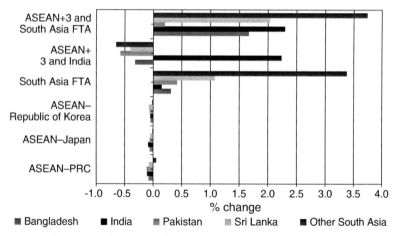

Figure 1.3   Impact of Subregional Schemes on South Asia, % change relative to baseline income

ASEAN+3 = Assocation of Southeast Asian Nations plus People's Republic of China (PRC), Japan, and Republic of Korea; FTA = free trade agreement.

Source: Francois and Wignaraja (2009).

for the rest of the world. Indeed, exports from some middle- and low-income countries and regions (Africa, Turkey, and Russian Federation) may benefit slightly, supplying third-country markets while Asia turns inward.

A broader regional scheme also witnesses more distributional gains to members than does a narrower arrangement. The estimated wage effects for unskilled workers (see Table 1.7) can be taken as a rough measure of the distributional impacts of the three scenarios. In the ASEAN+3 FTA scenario, Korea, Malaysia, and Thailand—with relatively large income effects—witness relatively large increases in wages for unskilled workers. For fast-growing poor countries such as Cambodia and Viet Nam, the effects are mixed (gains for Viet Nam, losses for Cambodia). As a mature developed economy with limited unskilled labor, Japan experiences an increase in unskilled worker wages in line with income effects. The inclusion of India in the basic scenario sees a significant increase in the wages for unskilled Indian workers (in excess of 2.5%) compared to the ASEAN+3 scenario. In the ASEAN+3 and South Asia FTA scenario, India sees an improvement in wages for unskilled workers while Pakistan and Sri Lanka record drops. This is reversed in the broadest FTA scenario. As the membership base widens, we have gains for unskilled workers in Bangladesh, India, Pakistan, and Sri Lanka. These increases range from 2% to 3% of real wages. Workers in other South Asian countries (i.e., Nepal) lose with the increased orientation of South Asia toward East Asia.

Table 1.7 Labor Wage Effects for Unskilled Workers, % change from baseline

	ASEAN+3 FTA	ASEAN+3 and India FTA	ASEAN+3 and South Asia FTA
East Asia			
China, People's Republic of (PRC)	1.8	1.8	1.8
Hong Kong, China	(0.6)	(0.8)	(0.9)
Japan	1.8	1.9	1.9
Korea, Republic of	9.3	9.7	9.7
Cambodia	(1.1)	(1.1)	(1.1)
Indonesia	1.7	1.5	1.4
Malaysia	4.9	5.0	5.1
Philippines	0.6	0.7	0.6
Singapore	4.6	5.4	5.7
Thailand	11.1	11.8	12.0
Viet Nam	8.0	8.2	8.3
South Asia			
Bangladesh	0.4	0.2	3.0
India	(0.2)	2.7	2.8
Pakistan	(0.1)	(0.2)	0.7
Sri Lanka	(0.3)	(0.4)	1.9

ASEAN+3 = Assocation of Southeast Asian Nations plus PRC, Japan, and Republic of Korea; FTA = free trade agreement; ( ) = negative value.

Source: Estimates from Francois and Wignaraja (2009).

Broadly speaking, an Asian regional agreement would appear to cover enough countries, with a great enough diversity in production and incomes, to actually allow for regional gains without a price measured in substantive third-country losses. Realizing such potential, however, requires overcoming a proven tendency in Asia to circumscribe trade concessions with rules of origin, NTBs, and exclusion lists. As reviewed in chapter 2 of this volume, recent experience suggests that the institutional barriers to any real progress (such as ROOs, failure to implement trade facilitation agreements that have already been agreed, substandard infrastructure, and NTBs) can be substantial. They pose formidable challenges, although the potential benefits in their defeat appear to be substantial.

Findings and Recommendations[14]

Regional Level

Countries Should Continue Lowering Trade and Nontariff Barriers. The relatively weak integration of South Asia with East Asia reflects to an important extent the general lack of openness of South Asian economies. Formal trade barriers are an important factor contributing to this situation. To benefit from closer integration with East Asia as well as from international trade more generally, South Asian countries should continue the steps they have begun to lower their trade barriers. The levels of tariffs and NTBs are low in many East Asian countries, but there is further room for reductions, especially in NTBs. Trade restrictiveness indices from the World Bank note that the average ad valorem tariff is about 26% in South Asia and 18% in East Asia. For East Asia, these are still high in Malaysia and Viet Nam—at about 26%—as well as in the PRC and Thailand, where they reach 19%.

Investment in Trade-Related Infrastructure and Streamlining of Cross-Border Procedures Offers a Direct Path to Lower Trade Costs. Lower trade costs can follow from improvements to trade-related infrastructure. Recent estimates of the impact of physical infrastructure suggest that for North–South trade, variations in trade-related infrastructure explain more of the variation in volumes of goods trade than do trade policy.[15] In this study, model estimates of the gains from regional integration reflect estimates that a 5% improvement in the general quality of trade-related infrastructure would yield 2.5% trade cost savings (as a share of cost of good traded) on average. For manufactured goods, transport and logistics costs could outpace tariff costs to be the highest cost of trading in developing countries. Most cargo between South and East Asia moves by water and air because no land transport services are operational at present. Land transit through Myanmar is not currently possible, but this will eventually change as the volume of South–East Asia trade is expected to increase. Additional

---

[14] This section draws on the papers in this volume as well as the country papers in the companion volume (see Appendix Table A1.1).

[15] See Francois and Manchin (2007); and Francois, Manchin, and Pelkmans-Balaoing (2008).

corridors between India and the PRC through Bhutan and Nepal will have to be developed. Land access to ports is also important for landlocked countries. In addition, international shipping lines serving the South–East Asia region operate on the equatorial route connecting East Asia and the Persian Gulf and Mediterranean. These shipping lines call at the major transshipment hubs of Singapore and Colombo and use feeder vessels to move cargo to other ports in the region. There are some ships that call at secondary hubs such as Malaysia's Port Kelang and India's Nhava Sheva, but these are relatively few. There is a need to develop regional shipping lines so that ships call in various regional ports. The reduction of freight and inland transport costs could significantly increase the level of trade between South and East Asia.

Trade cost reductions can also follow from trade facilitation measures that streamline the administrative cost of clearing goods across borders. Recent estimates place administrative costs at 6–30% of the costs of goods traded.[16] Substantially greater cost-reduction benefits may also follow from a simple streamlining of administrative barriers in the region. Countries should thus make efforts to reduce logistic constraints to facilitate movement of goods between East and South Asia. These include delays in customs inspection, cargo handling and transfer, and processing of documents. Customs procedures could be modernized by aligning the customs code to international standards, simplifying and harmonizing procedures, making tariff structures consistent with the international harmonized tariff classification, and adopting the WTO's Customs Valuation Agreement. The World Bank estimates that the number of days to complete processing of import documents at the preshipment and arrival stage is an average of 47 days in South Asia and 28 days in East Asia, compared to 14 days in countries that belong to the Organisation for Economic Co-operation and Development (OECD). Improved trade facilitation with greater attention to technical barriers to trade and "behind the border" impediments to trade could contribute to increasing economic openness and thus the capacity to benefit from greater interregional integration. A reduction of the scope for rules of origin to prove a barrier is also important. Overall, the region would benefit greatly from a concerted effort to reduce physical and administrative trade costs.

---

[16] See Francois, Hoekman, and Manchin (2006); and Manchin and Pekmans-Balaoing (2006).

South and East Asian Countries Need to Consolidate Their FTAs. Recently, there has been a proliferation of FTAs between South and East Asia. Asia should pursue a geographically broad scheme, instead of an expanding web of bilateral and subregional agreements. Against a backdrop of slow progress in global trade talks, FTAs can promote continuing liberalization, induce structural reforms in the countries concerned, and widen market access across the region. With a view to making the proliferation of FTAs between South and East Asia "stepping stones" rather than stumbling blocks to multilateralism and to reduce inefficiencies beacuse of overlapping rules of origin and others, policy makers in the region may wish to adopt the concept of "open regionalism" and broaden FTAs by creating as large and as wide a market as possible. Deepening FTAs by extending coverage beyond trade in goods into services, investment, and technology, may also reduce the problem of trade diversion. Our quantitative estimates suggest that a broad regional approach will largely preclude adverse effects on individual Asian economies that may follow when countries and subregions are otherwise left out. Basically, as Asia throws a broad net and aims to include all countries in the various subregions, an Asian FTA has the potential to actually boost regional trade and incomes without substantive adverse effects on outside countries.

Deregulation and Policy Reform in the Service Sectors Should be Pursued. This has the potential to greatly boost productivity and export performance. India provides an excellent example for other countries. The policy reforms initiated in the services sector since the early 1990s have been wide-ranging and phased-in with significant variations in progress across different subsectors. The telecommunications sector has been at the forefront of the process in terms of opening up activities to domestic private and foreign investment, privatizing government providers, establishing and strengthening an independent regulator, and changing associated legislation. Private-sector entry was also permitted in power generation, civil aviation, and oil and gas exploration during the early 1990s. Private-sector entry into insurance was permitted at the end of the 1990s and an independent regulator gained status in 2000. The government is currently contemplating setting up regulatory authorities for petroleum, civil aviation, and railways. The turnaround in railways' performance and recent policy initiatives—such as the permission accorded to private operators to run container traffic and the inauguration of a separate freight corridor between Mumbai and Delhi—have been acknowledged as unprecedented and valuable measures in relaxing infrastructure constraints on India's growth and development. In particular, domestic deregulation and liberalization in general and telecommunications reforms were key to the observed growth in services, especially IT and IT-enabled services (ITeS) during the 1990s.[17] International trade and investment reforms also appear to have contributed to growth in services. This can be surmised from the observed increase in service sector exports and FDI inflows in the telecommunications and IT sectors.

Trade Liberalization Efforts Need to be Embedded in a Wider Program of Economic Reforms. These efforts may include monetary, fiscal, and labor market policies; competition; deregulation; and other structural reforms. South Asian countries exhibit a relatively narrow range of comparative advantages compared to the economies of East Asia. They also face formidable competition from East Asia in all of the products in which they have comparative advantage. There is evidence that they are lagging in manufacturing competitiveness with their East Asian competitors.[18] Increases in South Asian exports to East Asia have tended to be concentrated in the natural resources sectors rather than in manufacturing. In parallel to trade liberalization, South Asian economies should thus take steps to boost the international competitiveness of the industries in which they have comparative advantages. This would require efforts to attract FDI; promote the development of small and medium-sized enterprises (SMEs); improve metrology standards and quality management; and increase spending on research and development.[19] South Asian countries and several East Asian countries also need to make progress in implementing the so-called second generation reforms to enhance transparency, good governance, and the quality of fiscal adjustment. These include reforms to the civil service and delivery of public goods; creation of an environment conducive to private sector opportunities; and reforms to institutions that create human capital, such as health and education. Comparative data from East and South Asian economies suggests that increasing education and skill levels should be a particular priority in South Asia.

---

[17] See Gordon and Gupta (2003) and Murthy (2004). According to Gordon and Gupta, the communications subsector grew rapidly in the 1990s coincident with deregulation. The private sector share in the service sector grew in this period, and FDI was positively correlated with services growth.

[18] A recent ranking of manufacturing competitiveness performance in 80 developing and transition economies reported that seven East Asian countries were in the top 10. Meanwhile, Sri Lanka was 28th; India, 37th; Nepal, 42nd; Bangladesh, 44th; and Pakistan, 49th. See Wignaraja and Taylor (2003).

[19] For more on this point see Wignaraja (2003 and 2008 a and b).

Country Level

In addition to our broad, regional assessment of trade in goods and services and their relationship to FDI and infrastructure across the region, this study also provides assessments based on country studies. The case studies both provide insight into the unique experience of various countries across the region and draw lessons for other countries in the region from this experience.[20] We summarize some of the main points from these studies here (see Table 1.8).

The PRC. The PRC—the region's largest and fastest growing economy—has successfully forged close economic relations with the rest of East Asia since liberalization. East Asia now accounts for half of the PRC's foreign trade and more than 60% of its FDI inflows. Forty percent of the PRC's considerable FDI outflows also go to other East Asian countries. Policy reforms, accession to the WTO, the PRC's emphasis on FTAs with regional partners, the government's FDI promotion strategy, and infrastructure investments are all associated with this regional orientation. More recently, the PRC has witnessed growing economic relations with South Asia. For instance, its total trade with South Asia has increased fivefold since 2000 to reach $26.6 billion in 2005 (equivalent to 1.9% of total trade). Furthermore, the PRC's cumulative FDI outflows to South Asia are small (amounting to $33 million in 2003–2005) but have grown steadily. With the emergence of India, trade and services between the PRC and India lie at the forefront of the PRC's economic relations with South Asia. There is considerable potential for large-scale FDI and financial flows to South Asia given the PRC's significant foreign exchange reserves. Three noteworthy policy imperatives in the PRC underlie growing economic relations between the PRC and South Asian economies: (i) new efforts at trade diplomacy to improve economic relations with South Asian economies, such as the signing of an FTA with Pakistan in 2005 and a feasibility study of a PRC–India FTA; (ii) the adoption of an invest abroad strategy to support overseas investments by PRC firms; and (iii) large investments in coastal harbors such as Shanghai, Ningbo, and Guangzhou to reduce transactions costs on sea freight. The size and sustained rapid growth of the PRC's economy can help the country play a pivotal role in strengthening economic relations between East and South Asia. In this regard, closer economic ties between the PRC and India could enable India to act as a gateway to South Asia. The following measures are suggested to strengthen such economies

---

[20] For a full list of the country study authors, see Appendix Table A1.1.

ties: (i) a comprehensive economic cooperation package under the likely PRC–India FTA; (ii) the development of an energy corridor between the PRC and Pakistan; (iii) closer engagement of the PRC in SAARC, building on its initial status as an observer; (iv) continued modernization of the PRC's seaports that are closest to South Asia; and (v) improvements to the Karakoram Highway, which links the PRC's western and southern regions with Pakistan, as well as reconstruction of the Stilwell Road which could link the PRC and India.

Singapore. Singapore, a high-income city-state, occupies a strategic location in Asia. Its geographic location; outward-oriented, business-friendly policies; world-class logistics and infrastructure; membership in AFTA; and high level of educational attainment have made Singapore a natural hub for strong economic relations with East Asia (which accounted for 53% of the city-state's total exports in 2005). Economic relations with South Asia are growing from a small base—Singapore's export share to South Asia amounted to 3.5% in 2005, of which India alone made up 2.6%. Likewise, the bulk of Singaporean FDI in South Asia goes to India (1.1% of total FDI outflows in 2000–2003). Singapore's investments in India encompass a wide spectrum of activities, notably infrastructure, logistics services, banking, pharmaceuticals, and telecommunications. Singapore could further strengthen its economic relationships with East Asia through (i) harmonizing the rules of origin (ROOs) in existing FTAs with those under negotiation; (ii) strengthening its competition policy framework; (iii) emphasizing intellectual property rights protection through comprehensive legislation and surveillance mechanisms; (iv) enhancing support for the development of Singaporean SMEs as independent exporters and overseas investors; and (v) upgrading human capital and training, particularly for the services sector. Additional measures are also required to support the growth of economic relations with South Asia, particularly India: (i) economic diplomacy to promote the East Asia Summit process and lobbying for inclusion of India and other South Asian economies in the Asia-Pacific Economic Cooperation (APEC) forum; (ii) expansion of Singapore's FTA strategy to cover more South Asian economies; and (iii) facilitation of Singaporean investment in South Asian economies.

Through an outward-oriented strategy led by FDI, Thailand has experienced impressive economic growth and increasing economic ties with East Asia. The share of Thailand's exports destined for East Asia increased from 45.0% to 51.3% between 2000 and 2005. Meanwhile, exports to South Asia are small but have increased (2.5% of exports in 2005). Interestingly, there is also evidence of FDI inflows from South Asia (mainly India) into

Thailand amounting to $37.1 million in 1998–2005. Indian investment into Thailand has taken place in IT services, motor vehicles, steel, gems, and jewelry. The direction of Thailand's trade and investment linkages has been influenced by several aspects of its export-oriented FDI-led strategy, including: (i) longstanding membership in AFTA and negotiations for a Thailand–India FTA (with an early harvest program), (ii) liberalization of investment regulations and investment promotion by the Thai Board of Investment, (iii) liberalization of regulations governing the services sector, (iv) development of export processing zones (EPZs), and (v) upgrading of the main seaport at Laem Chabang. There is growing recognition in multinational and regional policy circles that Thailand can build on its early achievements and become a corridor linking its Asian neighbors with one another. Suggestions in this vein are: (i) greater focus by the Thai Board of Investment on attracting FDI inflows from the PRC and India, including provision of detailed information on cost conditions and market opportunities; (ii) emphasis on lowering logistics costs and improving logistics systems to world class levels; (iii) development of transport corridors linking Thailand with East and South Asia including the Asian Highway; and (iv) improvement in the competition policy framework (including revision of the 1999 Competition Policy Law).

India. South Asia's largest and most dynamic economy, India, has long pursued the development of economic relations with South and East Asia. India has significant potential to play the role of a regional hub in South Asia that also connects the region with East Asia. In 1990/91 and 2004/05, the share of Indian exports to South Asia has grown from 2.9% to 5.2% and that to East Asia from 19.7% to 26.7%. India's export growth is being led by sectors including healthcare and IT services, pharmaceuticals, and automobiles. FDI inflows into India from East Asia (14% of FDI total inflows) are significant and India has also emerged as an outward investor in East Asia (12% of FDI outflows). India's FDI outflows to South Asia are growing but still relatively small. Policies adopted which help improve economic relations with East and South Asian economies include: (i) a phased and calibrated liberalization of the trade policy regime; (ii) the adoption of the "Look East" policy in 1991 to strengthen economic relationships with ASEAN and East Asian countries (where India became a Full Dialogue Partner of ASEAN in 1996 and a Framework Agreement was signed in 2003); (iii) a liberalized FDI policy (1991 Industrial Policy and 2006 FDI Policy) which has been accompanied by increasing FDI inflows; (iv) liberalization of policy governing outward FDI (Indian enterprises are now permitted to invest with automatic approval abroad up to 100%); (v) new legislation on Special Economic Zones in 2005 to systematically promote exports (including relaxation of rules pertaining to Industrial Licensing and Small Scale Industry reservation); (vi) priority given to infrastructure development, including the adoption of an integrated corridor approach, corporatization of management, Model Concession Agreement for public–private partnership in national highway development and establishment of independent regulatory authorities; and (vii) signing of trade and transit agreements with Bangladesh, Bhutan, and Nepal (currently linked with India through its rail network), as well as provision of transit facilities to its Nepal trade links (Radhikapur and Phulbari) to trade and transit through Bangladesh. Recommendations to improve economic relations with East and South Asia include (i) providing better information to exporters (Indian food exporters face problems with Japan import regulations and face frequent changes in rules and regulations in Southeast Asia); (ii) addressing physical infrastructure bottlenecks and delays at land border customs stations with Bangladesh and Nepal; (iii) enhancing supply capabilities in Bangladesh and Nepal by encouraging Indian investments on their export platforms (e.g., $3 billion investment of Tata Group in Bangladesh); (iv) providing education and training could be areas for greater cooperation and increased trade flows with South and East Asian nations; (v) exploiting synergies in services through regional economic integration in East and South Asia; (vi) adopting a coordinated approach in addressing issues related to sanitary and phytosanitary measures, as well as technical barriers to trade, in East and South Asia with the aim of reaching mutual recognition agreements; and (vii) developing a common transport policy for South Asia.

Pakistan. Pakistan is presently emphasizing a policy of improving economic ties with East and South Asian countries. Economic relations with neighboring South Asia are limited for historical and political reasons. For instance, South Asia accounts for 3.0% of Pakistan's exports and 2.4% of imports. Those with East Asia are more significant—East Asia accounts for 34.0% of Pakistan's imports, 14.0% of exports, and 2.3% of FDI inflows. The PRC is Pakistan's biggest trading partner in East Asia. Several policy initiatives underpin the economic ties between Pakistan and East Asia: (i) the "Strategic Vision East Asia" policy to help stimulate ties with Southeast Asia; (ii) an investment policy that opened up all economic sectors to FDI and allowed full foreign ownership (leading to intensive investment in Japanese joint ventures and independent power producer projects); (iii) elimination of state enterprises control over imports and exports of certain products; (iv) conversion of Saindak Project into an

EPZ allowed Pakistan's entry into the world market for metal exports; (v) private-sector involvement in economic activities at Port Qasim (Pakistan's second deep seaport) and establishment of a modern terminal complex at Lahore airport to improve port efficiency; and (vi) construction of a new international airport in Sialkot to be a hub for the leather and surgical goods industries. Many policies are suggested to bolster economic relations between Pakistan and East Asia, including (i) conclusion of an FTA with the PRC to widen the Silk Road between the two, reducing Pakistan's production costs; (ii) attainment of full dialogue partnership with ASEAN, which could strengthen Pakistan's overall economic relationship with ASEAN, establish joint ventures, and attract more investments; (iii) improvements to transport logistics to enhance Pakistan's export competitiveness, including the widening of the Karachi–Lahore highway and the promotion of rail transport for containers moving between Karachi and Lahore; (iv) a coherent regulatory framework for goods and services that promotes competition; (v) strengthening of the Monopoly Control Authority's enforcement capacity; (vi) upgrading of telecommunications infrastructure; and (vii) enhancing business services and technological support for the development of SMEs. Policies to improve ties with South Asia include implementation of the South Asian Free Trade Agreement (SAFTA) which came into force in July 2006, investments in infrastructure (especially road and rail links), streamlining of bureaucratic controls governing regional trade, and improving political relations with India.

Bangladesh. Since economic liberalization, Bangladesh has established significant economic relations with East Asia, which is the source of 83% of FDI inflows and around 40% of imports. However, Bangladesh's share of exports to East Asia (6.8%) and South Asia (1.6%) remains small as a result of a narrow export base, few complementarities with other countries in the region, and inadequate infrastructure. Bangladesh's trade with South Asia may be understated because of significant illegal imports from India. Some policies that have contributed toward Bangladesh's external orientation toward East and South Asia include (i) memberships in APTA, BIMSTEC, and SAFTA; (ii) improvement of operation and security of Chittagong Port (part of $31 million financed by ADB); (iii) simplification and improvement of customs procedures including processing of customs declaration and payment through the Automated System for Customs Data (ASYCUDA) system; and (iv) bilateral investment treaties signed with most East and Southeast Asian countries. Continuation of policy reforms, improvements to the investment climate, and liberalization of policies toward services imports will steadily increase integration with East Asia.

Additional measures are suggested to improve economic relations with South Asia: (i) improvement of the Dhaka–Chittagong corridor, especially the Chittagong Port facilities (Bangladesh's principal transport corridor, which provides potential subregional linkages to the northeastern states of India as well as to West Bengal, Bhutan, and Nepal); (ii) signing of a transit agreement between India and Bangladesh (to facilitate the Bangladesh–Nepal Corridor via Phulbari–Banglabandha Transit Route); (iii) development of an electronic monitoring system and risk-management and post-clearance audit procedures for customs clearance facilitation; (iv) implementation of SAFTA and removal of nontariff and paratariff barriers to intraregional trade; (v) promotion of investment cooperation under SAFTA to enhance Bangladesh's export supply capability; and (vi) upgrades to metrology testing and standards infrastructure, bringing them to international levels.

Nepal. Nepal has particularly close economic ties with neighboring India because of its landlocked, mountainous nature and narrow economic base. Much of Nepal's trade transits through Indian ports. Accordingly, a high concentration of Nepal's trade is with India (67% of exports and 57% of imports, according to official estimates that fail to account for illegal trade). Indian inward investment in Nepal is also significant. Other South Asian economies account for less than 1% of Nepal's total trade. East Asian economies are an important source of Nepal's imports (26%) but exports to East Asia are small (less than 5%). Some policy actions aimed to improve economic relations with East and South Asian economies are: (i) development of an air cargo complex to facilitate cargo movement; (ii) adoption of the Customs Reform and Modernization Action Plan and facilitation measures including systematic customs clearance procedures (at the border points of Birgunj, Biratnagar, and Bairahawa) and automated customs data software; and (iii) the establishment of the One Window Committee and Investment Promotion Board, as well as broad investment incentives and tax concessions. Measures to enhance economic relations with East and South Asia include: (i) promoting Nepal as a transit route between India and the PRC (including amendments to the India–Nepal Transit Treaty) and as an air corridor for countries in SAARC and ASEAN+3; (ii) implementing a comprehensive strategy to attract FDI, including strengthening of Investment Promotion Board and One Window Committee; (iii) amending the Industrial Enterprises and Foreign Investment Acts; (iv) establishing an EPZ and external investment agency; (v) enacting effective economic diplomacy to create investment links and enhance investments from SAARC and ASEAN+3; (vi) promoting potential services sectors for FDI, including hydropower (improving production and enhancing transmission links with India) and offshore service center for regional countries; and (vii) establishing an electronic data interchange and a road-based inland clearance depot in Birgunj.

Sri Lanka. Sri Lanka, the earliest economy in South Asia to adopt economic reforms, has notable economic relations with East Asia, which accounts for 55% of FDI inflows and absorbs 10% of Sri Lanka's exports. Meanwhile, Sri Lanka's economic relations with South Asian economies have been growing. For instance, Sri Lanka's exports to South Asia rose fivefold to 10% between 1998 and 2005, in a large part because of expanding India–Sri Lanka trade. Inward investment from India to Sri Lanka has also increased, with India accounting for 6.2% of FDI inflows to Sri Lanka. Closer ties with East and South Asian economies can be attributed to the following policy factors: (i) the implementation of an Indo–Sri Lanka Free Trade Agreement, which has encouraged exports and inward investment from India; (ii) a liberal export-oriented FDI regime which has attracted some investment in the services sector; (iii) the adoption of customs reforms and trade facilitation measures, such as the introduction of ASYCUDA, electronic data systems, and the Sri Lanka Automated Cargo Clearance System; (iv) the development of the Southern Highway, which has improved road access from production centers to ports; and (v) private sector participation in terminal operations to improve efficiency at Sri Lanka ports including Colombo, Sri Lanka's key link to international sea routes. Some recommendations to strengthen economic relations with East and South Asia include (i) promoting a more strategic FDI partnership with the PRC and Malaysia; (ii) implementing new ports projects, particularly completion of a new South Harbor (in 2009) and construction of a new port in Hambantota (funded by the PRC); (iii) restructuring the Sri Lanka Ports Authority to unbundle port management and improve the efficiency of port operations; (iv) undertaking a proposed 4-hectare offshore shopping complex and airport-related business process outsourcing zone as an investment opportunity for Indian entrepreneurs; (v) implementing further structural reforms to address domestic export supply constraints and fully benefit from the enhanced market access opportunities provided by regional agreements; and (vi) continuing deregulation of barriers to inward investment in services and exports.

Table 1.8 Summary of Recommendations from Country Chapters on Thematic Areas

Country	Merchandise Trade and Investment	Services	Infrastructure and Trade Facilitation	Other Areas
People's Republic of China (PRC)	• Promoting a comprehensive economic cooperation package under the likely PRC–India Free Trade Agreement (FTA) that is inclusive of other South Asian countries • Expanding coverage (energy and manufacturing) and speeding up implementation of a PRC–Pakistan FTA • Strengthening economic cooperation among the PRC, Bangladesh, and Sri Lanka • Initiating feasibility studies on FTAs		• Developing an energy corridor between the PRC and Pakistan • Continuing modernization of the PRC's seaports closest to South Asia • Improving the Karakoram Highway, which links the PRC's western and southern regions with Pakistan, and rebuilding the Stilwell Road, which could link the PRC and India	• Promoting closer engagement in the South Asian Association for Regional Cooperation (SAARC), building on its initial status as an observer

continued on next page…

Table 1.8 continued

Country	Merchandise Trade and Investment	Services	Infrastructure and Trade Facilitation	Other Areas
Singapore	• Harmonizing rules of origin in existing FTAs and those under negotiation • Expanding FTA strategy to cover more South Asian economies • Facilitating Singaporean investment in South Asian economies	• Upgrading human capital and training, particularly for the services sector • Developing a cohesive, coordinated, common framework for the Association of Southeast Asian Nations (ASEAN) to engage in bilateral agreements with major trading partners on services sector • Promoting mutual recognition of foreign degrees, especially from selected institutes in South Asia	• Ensuring greater transparency in government tendering procedures so as to ensure openness, fairness, and efficiency in business operations and procedures	• Strengthening the competition policy framework • Emphasizing intellectual property rights protection through comprehensive legislation and surveillance mechanisms • Enhancing support for the development of Singaporean small- and medium-sized enterprises (SMEs) as independent exporters and overseas investors • Observing economic diplomacy to promote the East Asia Summit process and lobbying for inclusion of India and other South Asian economies in the Asia-Pacific Economic Cooperation (APEC)

continued on next page...

Table 1.8 continued

Country	Merchandise Trade and Investment	Services	Infrastructure and Trade Facilitation	Other Areas
Thailand	• Thai Board of Investment focusing on attracting foreign direct investment (FDI) inflows from the PRC and India, including provision of detailed information on cost conditions and market opportunities • Harmonizing rules of origin in Asian FTAs and reducing nontariff barriers to trade between East and South Asia	• Liberalizing services trade, including the removal of nontariff measures, to improve linkages between the services sectors in Thailand and South Asia	• Lowering logistics costs while improving logistics systems to world-class levels • Developing transport corridors, including the Asian Highway, that link Thailand with East and South Asia	• Improving the competition policy framework (including revision of the 1999 Competition Policy Law)

continued on next page...

Table 1.8 continued

Country	Merchandise Trade and Investment	Services	Infrastructure and Trade Facilitation	Other Areas
India	• Promoting a broader scheme for regional economic integration that involves East Asian countries such as Japan, the PRC, and Republic of Korea, building on India's closer links with ASEAN • Enhancing supply capabilities in Bangladesh and Nepal by encouraging Indian investments in these countries' export platforms (e.g., a $3-billion investment by the Tata Group in Bangladesh)	• Exploiting synergies in services through regional economic integration in East and South Asia	• Making information available to exporters (Indian food exporters face problems with Japan import regulations and face frequent changes in rules and regulations in Southeast Asia) • Addressing physical infrastructure bottlenecks and delays at land border customs stations with Bangladesh and Nepal • Developing a common transport Policy for South Asia	• Promoting education and training as areas for greater cooperation and increased flows with South and East Asian nations • Adopting a coordinated approach to addressing issues related to sanitary and phytosanitary measures and technical barriers to trade in East and South Asia with the aim of reaching mutual recognition agreements.

continued on next page...

Table 1.8 continued

Country	Merchandise Trade and Investment	Services	Infrastructure and Trade Facilitation	Other Areas
Pakistan	• Implementing the South Asian Free-trade agreement which came into force in July 2006 • Speeding up implementation of a PRC–Pakistan FTA to widen the Silk Road between the two countries and to reduce Pakistan's production costs	• Enhancing business services and technological support for SME development • Liberalizing service sectors— including financial, telecommunications, transport, and professional services—accompanied by measures to strengthen the domestic services sector	• Improving transport logistics to enhance Pakistan's export competitiveness (including widening the Karachi–Lahore highway and promoting rail transport for containers moving between Karachi and Lahore) • Upgrading telecommunications infrastructure • Promoting investments in infrastructure (especially road and rail links) in South Asia • Streamlining bureaucratic controls governing regional trade and improving political relations with India.	• Becoming a full dialogue partner with ASEAN, with a view to strengthening Pakistan's overall economic relationship with ASEAN, as well as establishing joint ventures and attracting more investments • Developing a coherent pro-competitive regulatory framework for goods and services and strengthening the Monopoly Control Authority's enforcement capacity.

continued on next page...

Table 1.8 continued

Country	Merchandise Trade and Investment	Services	Infrastructure and Trade Facilitation	Other Areas
Bangladesh	• Implementing the South Asian Free Trade Agreement (SAFTA) and removing nontariff and paratariff barriers to intraregional trade • Promoting investment cooperation under SAFTA to enhance export supply capability in Bangladesh • Strengthening investment cooperation under the Bay of Bengal Initiative for Multi-Sectoral Technical and Economic Cooperation (BIMSTEC) and the Asia-Pacific Trade Agreement (APTA)	• Selectively opening up the service sector to foreign participation under the General Agreement on Trade in Services (GATS) to attract more FDI from East and South Asia.	• Improving the Dhaka–Chittagong corridor, especially facilities at the Chittagong Port, Bangladesh's principal transport corridor which has potential subregional linkages to the northeastern states of India, as well as to West Bengal, Bhutan, and Nepal • Implementing a transit agreement between India and Bangladesh to facilitate the Bangladesh–Nepal Corridor via the Phulbari–Banglabandha transit route • Developing an electronic monitoring system, as well as procedures for risk management and post-clearance audit to facilitate customs clearance	• Considering providing special incentives to foreign investors from East and South Asia

continued on next page…

Table 1.8 continued

Country	Merchandise Trade and Investment	Services	Infrastructure and Trade Facilitation	Other Areas
Bangladesh			• Upgrading metrology testing and standards infrastructure to international levels	
Nepal	• Promoting a comprehensive FDI strategy that includes strengthening the Investment Promotion Board and the One Window Committee • Amending the Industrial Enterprises and Foreign Investment Acts • Establishing an export processing zone and external investment agency • Promoting effective economic diplomacy to create investment links and enhance investments from SAARC and ASEAN+3	• Promoting potential services sectors for FDI, including hydropower and offshore services for regional countries	• Promoting Nepal as a transit route between India and the PRC (including amendment of India–Nepal Transit Treaty) and as an air corridor for SAARC and ASEAN+3 countries • Establishing an electronic data interchange and a road-based inland clearance depot in Birgunj	• Emphasizing economic diplomacy to initiate effective cooperation and linkages, particularly with SAARC and ASEAN+3 • Restructuring the Ministry of Industry, Commerce and Supply to facilitate trade and investment • Liberalizing the capital account

continued on next page...

Table 1.8 continued

Country	Merchandise Trade and Investment	Services	Infrastructure and Trade Facilitation	Other Areas
Sri Lanka	• Promoting more strategic FDI partnerships with the PRC and Malaysia • Undertaking a proposed 4-hectare offshore shopping complex and airport-related business process outsourcing zone as an investment opportunity for Indian entrepreneurs	• Continuing to deregulate barriers to inward investment in services and exports	• Implementing new ports projects particularly completion of a new South Harbor (in 2009) and construction of a new port in Hambantota (funded by the PRC) • Restructuring the Sri Lanka Ports Authority to unbundle port management and improve the efficiency of port operations	• Implementing further structural reforms to address domestic export supply constraints, helping Sri Lanka to fully benefit from the enhanced market access opportunities that are provided under regional agreements

Source: Based on country studies listed in Appendix Table A1.1.

Appendix

Table A1.1 Complete List of Papers

Pan-Asian Integration: Linking East and South Asia

1   Introduction and Overview
    Joseph Francois, Pradumna B. Rana, and Ganeshan Wignaraja

Perspectives on Current Integration

2   Current Patterns of Trade and Investment
    Robert Scollay and Annette Pelkmans-Balaoing

3   Integration Strategies for ASEAN: Alone, Together, or Together
    with Neighbors?
    Michael Plummer and Ganeshan Wignaraja

4   Economic Integration in South Asia and Lessons from East Asia
    Pradumna B. Rana and J. Malcolm Dowling

Regional Perspectives on Deeper Regional Integration

5   Integrating Services Markets
    Christopher Findlay, Ryo Ochiai, and Philippa Dee

6   The Role of Logistics Infrastructure and Trade Facilitation
    in Asian Trade
    John Arnold

7   Regional Integration in Asia: The Role of Infrastructure
    *Joseph Francois, Miriam Manchin, and Annette Pelkmans-
    Balaoing*

8   Pan-Asian Integration: Economic Implications
    of Integration Scenarios
    Joseph Francois and Ganeshan Wignaraja

National Strategies for Regional Integration:
South and East Asian Case Studies

Table A1.2   Country Profiles, 2006

Country	GDP per capita (in constant 2000 $)	Population (Mn)	Openness[a] (% of GDP)	Manufac-turing value added (% of GDP)	Poverty Headcount Ratio (PPP, at $1/day)
Bangladesh	453.6	144.3	42.1	17.2	41.3 (2000)
PRC	1,594.9	1,311.8	69.7	30.9	9.9 (2004)
India	633.7	1,109.8	43.6[b]	16.1	34.3 (2004)
Nepal	233.8	27.6	56.3	7.7	24.1 (2004)
Pakistan	622.8	159.0	39.9	18.3	17.0 (2002)
Singapore	27,685.2	4.4	473.5	29.2	...
Sri Lanka	1,075.9	19.8	75.6	15.1	5.6 (2002)
Thailand	2,548.5	141.6	141.6	34.6	2.0 (2002)

... = no data, GDP = gross domestic product, Mn = million, PPP = purchasing power parity, PRC = People's Republic of China, $ = US dollar.
[a] Exports and imports of goods and services as % of GDP (current $).
[b] 2005 data.

Source: World Bank, *World Development Indicators*, accessed February 2008.

Table A1.3   FTAs Involving East and South Asian Countries[a]

Free Trade Agreements (FTAs) Signed and Under Implementation

- Asia-Pacific Trade Agreement (APTA, formerly known as the Bangkok Agreement)
    - o FTA under implementation since 1976
- India–Singapore Comprehensive Economic Cooperation Agreement (CECA)
    - o Under CECA (signed June 2005 and effective August 2005), India will remove duties on 506 products from Singapore immediately, remove duties on 2,202 items by April 2009, and cut duties on another 2,407 products to 50% by the same date
    - o The pact also covers services, investments, and cooperation in technology, education, air services, and human resources
    - o Revised tariff concessions with India liberalizing additional 539 products, protocol signed in December 2007 and in effect in January 2008
- People's Republic of China (PRC)–Pakistan Free Trade Agreement
    - o Agreement signed at Islamabad on 24 November 2006 and in effect as of 1 July 2007
    - o Agreement on Early Harvest Program (EHP) was also signed
    - o EHP includes a common list of items whose tariffs will be removed and a separate list by country of items whose duties will also be scrapped
- Malaysia–Pakistan Closer Economic Partnership
    - o Early Harvest Program signed October 2005 for implementation January 2006
    - o FTA signed in November 2007 and took effect in January 2008
    - o Comprehensive FTA covering goods, services, investments, intellectual property rights (IPR) and cooperation provisions
- Preferential Tariff Arrangement–Group of Eight Developing Countries (D-8 PTA)[b]
    - o Negotiation was concluded at the 6th D-8 High-Level Trade Officials Meeting on 3–4 April 2006 in Bali, Indonesia
    - o Malaysia ratified the D-8 on 20 July 2006 and is so far the only member to have done so (ratification by at least four member countries is needed for the PTA to come into force)

---

[a] Source: ADB FTA Database (www.aric.adb.org) and official documents; status as of October 2008.

[b] D-8 PTA members are Bangladesh, Egypt, Iran, Malaysia, Nigeria, Pakistan, Indonesia, and Turkey.

o Negotiation on the rules of origin commenced on 18–19 December 2006 at the 7th D-8 High Level Trade Officials Meeting in Islamabad, Pakistan. Negotiation on the draft text of ROO provided by Pakistan is ongoing

Framework Agreements Signed and FTAs Under Negotiation

- Association of Southeast Asian Nations (ASEAN)–India Free Trade Agreement
  - o Framework Agreement signed October 2003
  - o Negotiations on agreement in trade in goods concluded in 28 August 2008 (FTA expected to be signed in December 2008)
  - o Reduction or elimination of tariffs will start January 2009
  - o For India and the ASEAN+6,^{c} excluding the Philippines, they have until 2011 to reduce or eliminate tariffs
  - o Between India and the Philippines, the schedule runs to 2016
  - o For India and new ASEAN members, India will reduce or eliminate tariffs before January 2011, while new ASEAN members will reduce or eliminate tariffs before 2016
- India–Thailand Free Trade Area
  - o The Framework Agreement for India–Thailand Free Trade Agreement (signed October 2003 and effective September 2004) reduces tariffs on 82 early harvest items by 50% in the first year, by 75% in the second year, and 100% thereafter
  - o The second phase hopes to have a comprehensive FTA covering all items by 2010
  - o Agreement contains a provision on emergency measures to protect domestic producers in case of sudden surges in imports
- Bay of Bengal Initiative for Multi-Sectoral Technical and Economic Cooperation (BIMSTEC) Free Trade Area
  - o The Framework Agreement on BIMSTEC FTA (signed February 2004 and effective June 2004) involves reducing and eliminating tariffs starting July 2006 up to 2010 for India, Sri Lanka, and Thailand and up to 2017 for Bhutan, Myanmar, and Nepal
  - o Negotiations began in September 2004
  - o FTA will have two phases (for fast track and normal track products)
  - o Member countries were scheduled to provide their sensitive lists to the trade negotiating committee meeting in June 2005
- India–Korea Comprehensive Economic Partnership Agreement (CEPA)
  - o A joint study group was set up on 6 October 2004 and its concluding report was signed on January 2006. It was recommended that a comprehensive

---

^{c} ASEAN+6 includes the 10 ASEAN members, Japan, Republic of Korea, People's Republic of China, India, Australia, and New Zealand.

economic partnership agreement (CEPA) would exploit the existing bilateral economic relations between the two countries and provide significant benefits for both

o Following the recommendations of the joint study group, a joint task force composed of government officials from both countries was constituted for the development of CEPA

o FTA negotiation launched in March 2006

- Pakistan–Singapore Free Trade Agreement

o FTA negotiation launched August 2005

- Pakistan–Indonesia Free Trade Agreement

o In November 2005, Pakistan and Indonesia signed the Framework Agreement on Comprehensive Economic Partnership and expressed willingness to conclude an FTA

o Both parties decided to negotiate a preferential trade agreement and move toward the goal of an FTA

- Trade Preferential System of the Organization of the Islamic Conference (TPS-OIC)

o Entered into force in 2002 after 10 OIC member states[d] ratified it

o Covers all commodity groups, including agricultural products; also eliminates paratariff and nontariff barriers

o Ministers of Commerce set 1 January 2009 as target date for making the TPS-OIC operational

o Malaysia–India Comprehensive Economic Cooperation

o FTA proposed January 2005

o Formal negotiations commenced on February 2008

Proposed Free Trade Agreements

- Pakistan–Brunei Darussalam Free Trade Agreement

o Joint study group established and met in August 2007

- PRC–India Regional Trading Arrangement

o In June 2003, India and the PRC agreed to set up a joint study group to present a report and recommendations for comprehensive trade and economic cooperation

o In March 2005, report of the joint study group was finalized, recommending a PRC–India Regional Trading Arrangement to cover trade in goods and services, as well as investments

- India–Indonesia Comprehensive Economic Cooperation Arrangement

o Goal of increasing trade to $10 billion in 2010 between the two countries; includes cooperation in defense development

o Joint Study Group set up in 2007

---

[d]   See http://www.oic-oci.org/oicnew/member_states.asp for list of member states.

- Japan–India Economic Partnership Agreement
  - o On 29 November 2004, Japan and India agreed to establish a Japan–India joint study group that would produce a comprehensive study that would serve as a framework for reviewing their economic relationship
  - o On 29 April 2005, both parties directed the joint study group to submit a report within a year, focusing on requirements for comprehensive expansion of trade in goods and services, as well as investment flows and other areas of economic cooperation
  - o FTA proposed August 2005
- Pakistan–Philippines Free Trade Agreement
  - o FTA proposed 2004
- Pakistan–Thailand Free Trade Agreement
  - o FTA proposed April 2004
- Singapore–Sri Lanka Comprehensive Economic Partnership Agreement
  - o FTA proposed October 2003

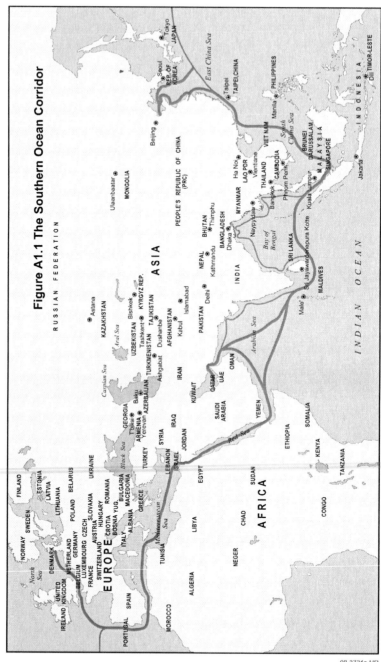

08-3731a HR

Figure A1.1   The Southern Ocean Corridor

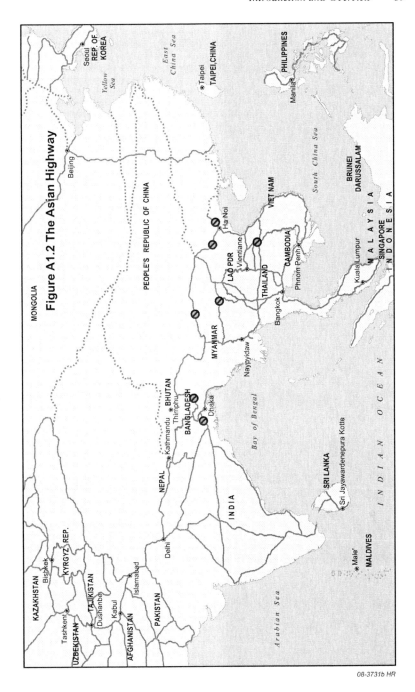

Figure A1.2   The Asian Highway

Perspectives on Current Integration

2

CURRENT PATTERNS OF TRADE AND INVESTMENT

Robert Scollay and Annette Pelkmans-Balaoing

Introduction

Until recently, economic integration in East and South Asia were essentially separate processes. The closing decades of the 20th century saw the economies of East Asia increasingly integrated through expanding trade and investment linkages that were important both in the region's impressive growth and in its rapid recovery from the deep economic crisis of 1997/98. South Asia presented a contrasting picture of slow and halting progress in economic integration, impeded by political conflicts and inward-looking economic policies. Trade and investment linkages between the two regions remained at a low level.

Since the turn of the century, preferential trading arrangements (PTAs) between the East Asian economies have been proliferating rapidly, and a proposal to create an East Asian Free Trade Agreement (EAFTA) encompassing 13 of the East Asian economies has also been on the table. At the same time, economic liberalization and the associated emergence of rapid economic growth in India has led to an upsurge of interest in the expansion of economic linkages between East and South Asia. Recognition of India's potential to emulate the People's Republic of China (PRC) as a rapidly expanding economic giant has been a key factor in this upsurge of interest. The implications for countries in both regions of increasing economic interaction between these two dynamic "growth poles," as well as between India and other East Asian countries, has accordingly commanded growing attention. Reflecting this growing interest, consideration has begun to be given to the potential for, and implications of, formally linking East and South Asia together as a single integrated region.

This paper sets out to examine the trade and investment issues relevant to the potential for future economic integration between East and South Asia. The paper is organized as follows. The next section presents summary data on the economic characteristics of the two regions that would be expected to have some bearing on the patterns of trade relations between them. These include the scale of economic activity in the countries of the regions as well as some crude proxy indicators of openness and potential comparative advantage. This section is followed by a detailed examination of patterns of trade flows, highlighting the varying extents to which the potential for integration has been exploited both between and within the two regions. A further section then briefly discusses aspects of PTAs that should be taken into account in any investigation of the possibility of new trading arrangements linking East and South Asia. Investment linkages between and within East and South Asia are then examined. The paper concludes with a set of policy recommendations.

For purposes of analysis, the East Asian region is initially divided into two subregions: Northeast Asia, comprising the PRC; Japan; Republic of Korea (henceforth Korea); Taipei,China; and Hong Kong, China; and Southeast Asia, comprising the 10 members of the Association of Southeast Asian Nations (ASEAN), namely, Brunei Darussalam, Cambodia, Indonesia, Lao People's Democratic Republic (Lao PDR), Malaysia, Myanmar, Philippines, Singapore, Thailand, and Viet Nam. This subdivision is subsequently modified when considered appropriate for the particular issues being discussed, for example to bring Hong Kong, China and Singapore together as a group of countries with common characteristics, or to separate the Southeast Asian countries into smaller groupings, again based on common characteristics. In South Asia, it is often useful to separate India from the other South Asian economies, since its trade structure is quite different from the other four. Likewise, in East Asia it often makes sense to separate the PRC from other countries of the region for the purposes of analysis.

Selected Economic Indicators and Their Implications

The data in Table 2.1 on the sizes of the East and South Asian economies is useful in establishing the focal points of economic activity in the two regions. When gross domestic product (GDP) is measured at official exchange rates—the rates used in most international trade and investment transactions—the leading economic role of Northeast Asia is very clear. The combined GDP of the Northeast Asian economies comprises 18% of world GDP, nine times the combined GDP of the Southeast Asian

Table 2.1   East and South Asian Economies Share of World GDP in 2005, in %

	At Official Exchange Rates (current $)	At Purchasing Power Parity (current international $)
Northeast Asia	18.0	23.4
China, People's Republic of	5.0	14.1
Hong Kong, China	0.4	0.3
Japan	10.2	6.5
Korea, Republic of	1.8	1.7
Taipei, China	0.6	0.9
Southeast Asia	2.0	4.2
Brunei Darussalam*	0.0	0.0
Cambodia	0.0	0.1
Indonesia	0.6	1.4
Lao People's Democratic Republic	0.0	0.0
Malaysia	0.3	0.5
Myanmar*	0.0	0.1
Philippines	0.2	0.7
Singapore	0.3	0.2
Thailand	0.4	0.9
Viet Nam	0.1	0.4
South Asia	2.2	7.5
Bangladesh	0.1	0.5
India	1.8	6.3
Nepal	0.0	0.1
Pakistan	0.2	0.6
Sri Lanka	0.1	0.1

* 2003 data, $ = US dollar, GDP = gross domestic product, % = percent.

Sources: World Bank, *World Development Indicators* (except Taipei,China); International Monetary Fund, *World Economic Outlook* (Taipei,China).

economies, and eight times the combined GDP of the South Asian economies. Japan remains the largest economy in the combined region, accounting for 10% of world GDP, while at 5% of world GDP the PRC's economy easily outranks in size all the other economies of the combined region. India dominates economic activity in South Asia, with 1.8% of world GDP, or around 80% of the combined GDP of the South Asian economies. India's GDP is just over one third of that of the PRC, the other emerging giant, and approximately the same as that of Korea. By contrast with South Asia, economic activity in Southeast Asia is more widely dispersed, with Indonesia, Malaysia, Philippines, Singapore, and Thailand all accounting for a significant share of the subregion's economic activity.

GDP measured at purchasing power parity (PPP) exchange rates emphasizes the economic weight of the two emerging giants, the PRC and India. On this basis, the PRC is easily the largest economy in the two regions, while the Indian economy is comparable in size to that of Japan, although still less than half the size of the PRC economy. Although the shares of world GDP of South and Southeast Asia on a PPP basis are respectively treble and double their shares, measured at official exchange rates, they are still far outranked in economic size by the economies of Northeast Asia, by a factor of over three in the case of South Asia and over five and a half in the case of Southeast Asia.

A key point highlighted by this data is that the rapid development of economic linkages within East Asia has offered the economies of the region the benefits of closer integration within one of the three major poles of economic activity in the global economy, and in particular has allowed the Southeast Asian economies the opportunities provided by integration into the greater East Asian economy. South Asia has lacked a center of activity of comparable magnitude, and its links with the East Asian growth pole lacked dynamism until recently, as noted earlier. Closer economic linkages with East Asia thus offers South Asian economies a dramatic enlargement in the size of the regional market with which they can become integrated. By contrast, closer economic integration with South Asia offers East Asia a relatively modest increase in market size, although the future potential of the rapidly growing Indian market is clearly greater than indicated by its current GDP levels.

The information in Table 2.2 further highlights the greater scope for beneficial integration that has existed in East Asia. The economies of the region exhibit a wide range of levels of development and factor endowments, and a corresponding diversity in comparative advantages. Per capita income levels range from $35,202 in Japan to $170 in Myanmar—a ratio of more than 200:1—and there is a wide dispersion of per capita incomes within that range. Natural resource endowments vary from Hong Kong, China and Singapore, where the endowments are virtually negligible, to resource-rich *Brunei Darussalam* and *Indonesia*.

Table 2.2   GDP per Capita and Population Densities of East and South Asian Economies

	2005 GDP per capita (current $)	Population density (people per sq. km)
China, People's Republic of	1,709	140
Hong Kong, China	25,389	6,541
Japan	35,202	351
Korea, Republic of	16,409	489
Taipei,China	12,662	623
Brunei Darussalam*	13,245	68
Cambodia	385	80
Indonesia	1,300	122
Lao People's Democratic Republic	476	26
Malaysia	5,206	77
Myanmar*	170	77
Philippines	1,184	279
Singapore	29,191	5,882
Thailand	2,759	126
Viet Nam	631	255
Bangladesh	422	1,090
India	717	368
Nepal	272	190
Pakistan	710	202
Sri Lanka	1,174	303

* 2003 data, $ = US dollar, sq. km = square kilometer, GDP = gross domestic product.

Sources: World Bank, *World Development Indicators* (except Taipei,China); International Monetary Fund, *World Economic Outlook* (Taipei,China).

Population densities are very high in the resource-poor industrialized economies of Northeast Asia and in Viet Nam, but significantly lower in the Southeast Asian economies that enjoy substantial endowments of natural resources, as well as in the PRC. East Asian economies have thus been able to exploit the enormous potential for beneficial specialization that exists within their region.

By contrast, South Asian economies exhibit a much narrower range of development levels and factor endowments. Without exception, they are low-income developing countries, with per capita incomes ranging from $1,090 in Sri Lanka to $272 in Nepal. Population densities are uniformly high, ranging from 1090 persons per square kilometer (km^2) in Bangladesh to 190 persons per km^2 in Nepal. Among the lower-income developing economies in East Asia, only the Philippines and Viet Nam have population densities higher than Nepal, and both these economies have lower population densities than Bangladesh, India, and Sri Lanka. Natural resource endowments in South Asian economies range from substantial to meager.

A qualification that needs to be noted is that India, like the PRC, contains a number of large regions that vary from one another in terms of factor endowments and, therefore, in comparative advantages. Nevertheless, the range of comparative advantages on which specialization can be based is clearly much narrower in South Asia than in East Asia. Integration with East Asia could thus allow South Asian economies to engage in specialization within their region and thus enjoy a much more complete range of comparative advantages. Within this wider region, the data suggests that South Asia would specialize in labor-intensive manufacturing, supplemented by country-specific specializations in some agricultural and other natural-resource products and possibly also by somewhat more capital-intensive manufacturing in more advanced regions of India. Among East Asian economies, the closest matches for the South Asian economies in terms of income levels and population densities are found in Indonesia, Philippines, and Viet Nam. Cambodia, Lao PDR, and Myanmar resemble Bangladesh and Nepal in income levels but not in population density.

The data in Table 2.3 provides some further indications as to the segment of the manufacturing spectrum likely to be occupied by South Asian economies if trade with East Asia occurs on the basis of comparative advantage. The selected indicators of educational attainment (literacy rates, secondary and tertiary school enrolment) and access to information (internet usage rate) for Southeast Asian economies other than Sri Lanka are significantly lower than those for the PRC and the larger Southeast Asian developing economies. This suggests that average skill levels in South Asian work forces are also likely to be lower, pointing toward specialization in manufacturing characterized by lower technology levels as well as lower labor intensity. This seems to be borne out by the figures for the share of high-technology products in total manufacturing exports—which are much lower even for India than for the PRC and the

Table 2.3   Indicators of Technology Levels, Education Levels, and Access to Information in East and South Asian Economies, 2004

	High-technology exports	Literacy rate, adult total	School enrollment, secondary	School enrollment, tertiary	Internet users
	(% of manufactured exports)	(% of people ages 15 and above)	(% gross)	(% gross)	(per 1,000 people)
PRC	30	91	73	19	73
Hong Kong, China	32		85	32	506
Japan	24		102	54	587
Korea, Rep. of	33		91	89	657
Cambodia		74	29	3	3
Indonesia	16	90	64	17	67
Lao PDR		69	46	6	4
Malaysia	55	89			397
Myanmar		90	40		1
Philippines	55	93	86	29	54
Singapore	59	93			571
Thailand		93	77	41	109
Viet Nam		90	73	10	71
Bangladesh	0				2
India	5	61	54	12	32
Nepal		49		6	7
Pakistan	1	50	27	3	13
Sri Lanka	1	91	83		14

Lao PDR = Lao People's Democratic Republic, PRC = People's Republic of China, % = percent.

Source: World Bank, *World Development Indicators*.

larger Southeast Asian developing economies—and very low indeed for Bangladesh, Pakistan, and Sri Lanka.

To realize the potential benefits of specialization countries must of course be open to international trade. Table 2.4 indicates that the South Asian economies generally lag far behind East Asia in terms of openness.

In East Asia—even in economies with relatively lower openness indicators, such as Indonesia, Philippines, and Viet Nam—openness indicators are uniformly higher than for all South Asian economies, with the exception that the value for Sri Lanka is higher than for Indonesia.

Another summary indication of the degree of engagement in international trade is obtained by comparing shares of world GDP with shares of world imports and exports, as is done in Table 2.5, showing the shares of world imports and exports of the East and South Asian economies over the 3-year period 2002–2004, along with their shares of world GDP for 2003, the midpoint in that period. The closest correspondence between

Table 2.4   Openness of East and South Asian Economies, 2005

	Merchandise trade (% of GDP)
China, People's Republic of China	64
Hong Kong, China	334
Japan	25
Korea, Republic of	69
Cambodia	126
Indonesia	54
Lao People's Democratic Republic	36
Malaysia	196
Philippines	89
Singapore	368
Thailand	129
Viet Nam	132
Bangladesh	38
India	28
Nepal	37
Pakistan	37
Sri Lanka	65

GDP = gross domestic product, % = percent.

Source: World Bank, *World Development Indicators*.

Table 2.5   East and South Asian Countries' Percentages of World Exports, World Imports, and World GDP, %

	Percentage of		
	World Exports 2002–2004	World Imports 2002–2004	World GDP 2003
Northeast Asia	**19.8**	**17.4**	**18.5**
China, People's Republic of	6.0	5.4	3.9
Hong Kong, China	3.0	3.0	0.4
Japan	6.3	4.9	11.8
Korea, Republic of	2.6	2.4	1.7
Taipei,China	1.9	1.7	0.8
Southeast Asia	**6.2**	**5.2**	**1.9**
Brunei Darussalam	0.1	0.0	0.1
Cambodia	0.0	0.0	0.0
Indonesia	0.8	0.5	0.6
Lao People's Democratic Republic	0.0	0.0	0.0
Malaysia	1.4	1.1	0.3
Myanmar	0.0	0.0	0.0
Philippines	0.5	0.5	0.2
Singapore	1.9	1.7	0.3
Thailand	1.1	1.0	0.4
Viet Nam	0.3	0.3	0.1
South Asia	**1.4**	**1.4**	**2.1**
Bangladesh	0.1	0.1	0.1
India	0.8	1.0	1.6
Nepal	0.0	0.0	0.0
Pakistan	0.2	0.2	0.2
Sri Lanka	0.1	0.1	0.0

GDP = gross domestic product.

Source: World Bank, World Development Indicators online.

shares of world GDP and shares of world exports and imports is in North-east Asia, although within that subregion there is considerable diversity between Japan (whose shares of world exports and imports are much smaller than its share of world GDP) and the other four Northeast Asian economies (whose shares in world exports and imports are much larger than their shares of world GDP). There is a marked difference between Southeast and South Asia. Southeast Asia's share of world exports and imports is a multiple of its share of world GDP, and this is true also of individual Southeast Asian countries. By contrast, South Asia's share of world exports and imports is about two thirds of its share of world GDP, reflecting a lower degree of overall engagement in international trade. Among the South Asian countries, this pattern is especially marked for India, and less marked for Sri Lanka.

The fact that South Asian economies are less engaged in international trade is likely to have a significant bearing on their trade performance relative to the East Asian economies and on trade between the two regions. South Asian countries will need to make continued progress in opening their economies if they are to realize the potential benefits of closer integration with East Asia.

East Asia–South Asia Trade and Its Future Potential and Implications

Recent Growth in East Asia–South Asia Trade

It has been correctly observed that recent years have seen a surge in trade between East and South Asia, albeit from a very low base (Rana 2006). When this trade is disaggregated by economy, as is done in Table 2.6, it is clear that the aggregate trade flow masks considerable variations across the interregional trade flows of individual economies.

Table 2.6 summarizes the recent growth in trade of East Asian economies with South Asia, and of South Asian economies with East Asia, over the period 1999/2000 to 2004/05 (or the nearest period for which comparable data was available). Trade between East Asian economies and South Asia has grown rapidly, albeit from a relatively low base, with Japan being the conspicuous exception. The most dramatic growth is obviously observed in the PRC's trade with South Asia, but several other East Asian economies have had growth of around 100% or more in their export and/or import trade with South Asia: Indonesia and Korea for both exports and imports, Thailand for exports, and Cambodia and Singapore for imports. Hong Kong, China; Malaysia; and Philippines all recorded export and import increases over the period in the range of 60% to 90%.

Table 2.6   Growth of East Asia–South Asia Trade, % increases from 1999/2000 to 2004/05 unless otherwise indicated

	Exports	Imports
(1) East Asia Trade with South Asia		
Cambodia (2000–2004)	36	157
China, People's Republic of	305	509
Hong Kong, China	68	60
Indonesia	130	113
Japan	11	12
Korea, Republic of	109	98
Malaysia	78	84
Philippines	70	87
Singapore	65	237
Thailand	129	89
(2) South Asia Trade with East Asia		
India (1999/2000–2004)	145	132
Bangladesh (1999/2000–2004)	(17)	13
Sri Lanka (2000–2004)	4	25

( ) = negative value.

Source: Calculated from Comtrade data.

India is the only one of the South Asian economies listed to have shown comparable growth in trade with East Asia over the same period. This implies, of course, that a very large share of the increased trade of East Asian economies with South Asia over the period has consisted of increased trade with India. The exports of Bangladesh to East Asia actually fell over the period, and export growth of Sri Lanka to East Asia was minimal. Imports of both the latter two economies from East Asia continued to grow modestly, despite the weak performance of exports in the opposite direction.

It seems clear that generalizations about trade between East and South Asia are likely to be misleading, or at least provide only a partial view. The following sections of the paper provide analysis of the trade of the two regions from a variety of angles, including analyses disaggregated by economy and by commodity. A range of approaches is used, including trade shares, trade intensity and complementarity indexes, revealed comparative advantage (RCA) index, and more detailed analysis of recent trade trends.

The discussion makes extensive use of an alternative classification of the economies of the two regions, designed to reflect certain common-alities in trade structure. In this classification, four Northeast Asian economies (PRC, Japan, Korea, and Taipei,China) are grouped together as the Northeast Asian-4. Hong Kong, China and Singapore are treated as a separate group. The five principal developing countries of Southeast Asia (Indonesia, Malaysia, Philippines, Thailand, and Viet Nam) are also grouped together under the label ASEAN-5, separated both from Singapore and from the smaller Southeast Asian economies (Brunei Darussalam, Cambodia, Lao PDR, and Myanmar). The latter group is labeled ASEAN-BCLM.[1]

Trade Shares

Table 2.7 provides summary information on the share of each region or subregion in each other's trade. In places, the following discussion refers to the more detailed information at the individual country level provided in Appendix 2.1, where data is presented separately by subregion.

The most obvious feature of Table 2.7 is the heavy concentration of trade within East Asia. Only under 50% of the exports and imports of the Northeast Asia 4 group are directed to and sourced from other East Asian economies. Intra-East Asia trade accounts for an even higher share of the trade of other East Asian economies: three-quarters of the imports of Hong Kong, China and Singapore and a slightly lower share of the imports of the two groupings within ASEAN, as well as comfortably over 50% of the exports of both Hong Kong, China and Singapore and the two groupings within ASEAN.

Northeast Asia predictably dominates intra-East Asian trade, account-ing for 35–43% of the imports and exports of both Northeast Asia itself and the ASEAN-5 grouping, and a higher percentage of the trade of Hong Kong, China and Singapore.

---

[1] Although Brunei Darussalam is at a different level of development from the other three economies in the Association of Southeast Asian Nations-Brunei Darus-salam, Cambodia, Lao People's Democratic Republic [Lao PDR], and Myanmar (ASEAN-BCLM) group, it shares with them a tendency for its trade to be heavily concentrated on its regional neighbors. Viet Nam (which is often convention-ally grouped together with Cambodia, Lao PDR, and Myanmar under the label CLMV) is in this classification grouped with the four larger developing coun-tries in ASEAN under the label ASEAN-5 (Indonesia, Malaysia, Philippines, Thailand, and Viet Nam), on the basis of greater similarity in trade structure.

Table 2.7   Shares in the Trade of Subregional Groupings in East and South Asia, 2002–2004 (%)

	Northeast Asia-4		Singapore and Hong Kong, China		ASEAN-5		ASEAN-BCLM		South Asia	
	Imports	Exports	Imports	Exports	Imports	Exports	Imports	Exports	Imports	Exports
North-east Asia	34.7	36.7	57.6	42.5	40.2	36.6	26.1	38.3	24.1	7.2
South-east Asia	12.5	10.4	17.7	14.9	21.7	20.1	39.7	33.4	14.1	2.4
East Asia	47.2	47.1	75.4	57.4	62.0	56.8	65.7	71.7	38.2	9.6
South Asia	0.9	1.4	1.6	2.1	1.3	2.4	1.5	4.1	11.7	4.4

ASEAN-5 = Five member countries of the Association of Southeast Asian Nations (Indonesia, Malaysia, Philippines, Thailand, and Viet Nam).
ASEAN-BCLM = Member countries of ASEAN-Brunei Darussalam, Cambodia, Lao People's Democratic Republic, and Myanmar.
East Asia = includes ASEAN and Northeast Asian economies (People's Republic of China [PRC]; Hong Kong, China; Japan; Republic of Korea; and Taipei,China).
Northeast Asia-4 = PRC, Japan, Republic of Korea, and Taipei,China.
South Asia = Bangladesh, India, Nepal, Pakistan, and Sri Lanka.

Source: International Monetary Fund, *Direction of Trade Statistics*.

Southeast Asia commands a larger share of trade within Southeast Asia itself than of the trade of Northeast Asia. Over 20% of the exports and imports of the ASEAN-5 grouping are conducted within Southeast Asia. Southeast Asia is especially prominent in the trade of the smaller economies grouped under the ASEAN-BCLM label. The individual country data in Appendix 2.1 shows that the trade of these four economies is heavily oriented toward their larger immediate neighbors: especially Thailand in the case of the Lao PDR, Myanmar, and the import trade (although not the export trade) of Cambodia; and Singapore in the case of the import trade of Brunei Darussalam, Cambodia, and Myanmar. In South Asia, the trade of Nepal is dominated in similar but even more pronounced fashion by India.

For the purposes of this study, the comparison between the figures for South and East Asia in Table 2.7 is of particular interest. A significant share of South Asian imports (particularly) and exports takes the form of intra-South Asian trade, but the share of intraregional trade is clearly much lower in South Asia's case than in East Asia's. The 12% share of intraregional trade in South Asian imports is due mainly to the share of India in imports of Bangladesh (15%), Nepal (43%), and Sri Lanka (16%). India's share of recorded exports is 47% for Nepal and 5% for Sri Lanka but negligible in the case of Bangladesh. South Asia's two largest economies—India and Pakistan— account for a very small proportion of one another's trade.

East Asia's share of South Asia's imports, although lower than the corresponding intraregional shares for East Asia, is a robust 24% for Northeast Asia and 14% for Southeast Asia, giving a total of 38% for East Asia as a whole. This is well above the share of East Asia in world exports indicated in Table 2.5. South Asia's shares of the exports of the East Asian groupings are very low by comparison, although generally higher than the share of South Asia in world imports indicated in Table 2.5. By contrast, the shares of Northeast and Southeast Asia in South Asian exports are much lower at 7.0% and 2.4% respectively, well below the respective shares of Northeast Asia and Southeast Asia in world imports. South Asia's shares in the imports of the East Asian subgroups are very modest, with its shares in the imports of the Northeast Asia-4 and ASEAN-5 subgroups in particular being below the shares of South Asia in world exports.

For the purposes of this study, key points to note from the analysis of trade shares are:

- While intraregional trade is highly developed within East Asia, and within the East Asian subregions of Northeast and Southeast Asia, intraregional trade has not developed within South Asia to the same extent.
- East Asia's share of South Asia's trade is very much higher than South Asia's share of East Asia's trade.
- East Asia accounts for a much higher share of South Asia's imports than of its exports.
- South Asian exports perform relatively poorly in the more open and dynamic markets of East Asia.
- East Asian exports perform relatively well in the less open markets of South Asia, although these markets account for a comparatively small share of East Asian exports.

Trade Intensities

The observation that the share of countries in each other's trade may be greater than or less than their corresponding shares of world trade highlights that other factors may influence these trade shares besides their overall level of engagement in global trade. Countries or regions accounting for a low share of their partners' trade, for example, may nevertheless be trading intensely with those same partners, in the sense that the low trade share might still be higher than might be expected on the basis of their share in world trade. Import and export trade with the same partners need not be of equal intensity; the intensity of one flow can be considerably greater or less than the other.

Measures of trade intensity are used to capture the propensity of countries to trade more or less with partners than would be expected on the basis of the corresponding shares of world trade. Various trade intensity indexes are used here to capture the dimensions of trade intensity. Details of the formulation of the indexes are given in Appendix 2.2.

The bilateral trade intensity index measures the intensity of a country or a region's trade—both imports and exports—with a partner country or region, in the sense of whether the partner's share in its overall trade is greater or less than would be expected on the basis of the partner's share in world trade. An index value of greater than one indicates the extent to which the partner's weight in the trade of the country or region concerned exceeds its weight in world trade. An index value of less than one indicates a less-than-expected intensity of trade, interpreted in the same way. In the discussion that follows, for the sake of brevity, index values of greater than or less than one are respectively described as above average or below average.[2]

Separate import and export intensity indexes focus respectively on the export and import sides of the bilateral trade flow, allowing the influence of each on the overall bilateral trade intensity to be identified. The export intensity index measures the extent to which a partner accounts for a larger or smaller share of the exports of a country or region, compared to the partner's share of world imports. An index value of one again provides the threshold; a value greater than one indicates the extent to which exports are more focused on the partner than would be expected on the basis of the partner's share in world imports, while a value of less than one indicates a lower-than-expected share of exports going to the partner.

In exactly the same way, the import intensity index measures the extent to which the share of imports sourced from the partner is greater or less than would be expected on the basis of the partner's share of world exports. An index value of one again provides the threshold.

The ratio of market share index measures whether an exporting country or region's share of a partner's export market is greater or less than its share of the world market.

---

[2] This convention is also followed in describing the values of other indexes that are above or below their threshold value.

Table 2.8 Trade Intensity Indexes for Northeast Asia-4

	Japan				Korea, Republic of				PRC				Taipei,China			
	Bilateral Trade Intensity	Import Intensity	Export Intensity	Market Share	Bilateral Trade Intensity	Import Intensity	Export Intensity	Market Share	Bilateral Trade Intensity	Import Intensity	Export Intensity	Market Share	Bilateral Trade Intensity	Import Intensity	Export Intensity	Market Share
Japan					2.51	3.18	1.74	1.69	2.79	2.68	3.02	2.34	2.84	3.97	1.62	1.65
Korea, Rep. of	2.69	1.82	3.66	2.92					3.30	4.52	2.04	1.45	1.96	2.65	1.28	1.28
PRC	2.42	3.31	2.36	2.43	2.37	1.94	3.64	3.73					1.74	1.37	2.64	2.65
Hong Kong, China	1.93	0.12	2.18	1.68	2.12	0.62	2.04	1.71	7.96	2.64	9.23	5.20	6.13	0.44	7.25	6.54
Taipei, China	3.24	1.62	5.21	3.62	1.99	1.24	2.83	2.47	2.17	2.81	1.53	1.04				
Northeast Asia	1.39	1.12	1.67	1.80	1.72	1.51	0.90	2.18	1.75	1.63	1.97	1.86	2.00	1.73	2.24	2.59
Brunei Darussalam	8.09	12.49	2.04	1.87	4.24	5.87	0.84	0.79	0.92	1.12	0.38	0.37	0.11	0.00	0.43	0.42
Cambodia	0.05	0.78	0.36	0.35	0.95	0.09	1.56	1.51	1.25	0.21	2.04	1.42	2.53	0.12	4.21	3.90
Indonesia	4.39	6.05	3.65	1.90	2.88	3.42	3.06	1.66	1.59	1.59	2.14	1.02	2.34	2.93	2.39	2.30
Lao PDR	0.34	0.30	0.28	0.28	0.27	0.05	0.33	0.33	1.53	0.42	1.79	1.27	0.27	0.47	0.11	0.00
Malaysia	2.01	2.36	2.43	2.42	1.50	1.65	1.81	1.89	1.55	2.12	1.29	1.06	2.01	2.52	2.07	2.01
Myanmar	0.78	0.96	0.58	0.56	1.42	0.54	2.10	2.00	3.55	1.05	6.14	3.48	1.37	0.69	1.84	1.84
Philippines	3.39	3.97	4.30	2.88	2.21	2.10	3.18	2.38	1.75	2.80	1.33	0.65	3.53	4.96	3.72	3.49

continued on next page...

Table 2.8 continued

	Japan				Korea, Republic of				PRC				Taipei,China			
	Bilateral Trade Intensity	Import Intensity	Export Intensity	Market Share	Bilateral Trade Intensity	Import Intensity	Export Intensity	Market Share	Bilateral Trade Intensity	Import Intensity	Export Intensity	Market Share	Bilateral Trade Intensity	Import Intensity	Export Intensity	Market Share
Singapore	1.61	0.72	2.01	1.72	1.73	1.42	1.49	1.43	1.52	1.29	1.25	1.05	2.09	1.45	2.06	2.02
Thailand	3.58	3.13	2.24	3.37	1.14	0.92	1.38	1.37	1.38	1.81	0.96	0.97	1.74	1.67	1.84	1.79
Viet Nam	2.41	3.17	1.76	1.60	3.00	1.06	4.51	3.94	1.89	1.43	2.20	1.55	4.11	1.34	6.18	5.54
Southeast Asia (ASEAN)	2.28	2.44	2.67	2.28	1.61	1.63	1.95	2.18	1.37	1.64	1.32	1.05	2.00	2.06	2.36	2.37
East Asia	1.44	1.22	1.69	1.91	1.54	1.36	1.73	2.18	1.51	1.44	1.65	1.67	1.83	1.60	2.05	2.54
Bangladesh	0.58	0.37	0.74	0.87	1.42	0.19	2.31	1.38	1.56	0.11	2.38	0.06	1.38	0.16	2.25	2.16
India	0.62	0.69	0.50	0.45	1.25	0.93	1.35	1.08	1.15	1.31	0.86	0.63	0.62	0.60	0.56	0.56
Nepal	0.23	0.22	0.20	0.20	0.55	0.07	0.68	68.00	1.37	0.18	1.73	1.24	0.10	0.07	0.10	1.00
Pakistan	0.72	0.24	1.13	0.91	1.11	0.90	1.37	94.00	1.61	0.86	2.15	0.11	0.62	0.32	0.91	0.89
Sri Lanka	0.76	0.67	0.80	0.84	1.07	0.29	1.64	1.44	0.76	0.06	1.26	0.60	1.28	0.14	2.09	2.01
South Asia	0.63	0.60	0.61	0.57	1.22	0.82	1.43	1.11	1.22	1.07	1.20	0.52	0.72	0.50	0.83	0.83

ASEAN = Association of Southeast Asian Nations, Lao PDR = Lao People's Democratic Republic, PRC = People's Republic of China.

Source: International Monetary Fund, *Direction of Trade Statistics*.

Northeast Asia-4. Table 2.8 shows the trade intensity indexes for the Northeast Asia-4 group. As might be expected on the basis of the information on trade shares, bilateral trade intensity of each country in the group is high with other Northeast Asian economies, and import and export intensity is also invariably high. The values for the bilateral intensity, export intensity, and import intensity indexes are also generally high with the ASEAN-5 group, with some exceptions where the value of the index is below average (Japan's import intensity with Singapore, Korea's import intensity with Thailand and Viet Nam, and the PRC's export intensity with Thailand). The picture is much more mixed with the countries in the ASEAN-BCLM grouping. At the regional aggregate level, all trade intensity indexes of the countries in the Northeast Asia-4 group are above the averages in Northeast, Southeast, and East Asia as a whole.

The picture of the Northeast Asia-4 group's trade intensity with South Asia exhibits some consistent patterns as well as some variations across the individual Northeast Asian-4 economies. One consistent pattern is that, with only one exception, import intensity indexes are below average with all individual South Asian economies and with South Asia as a region. The one exception is the PRC's above-average import intensity with India, which outweighs the PRC's below-average import intensity with other South Asian economies, so that the PRC's import intensity with South Asia as a region is also above average.

There is more variation across the Northeast Asian economies in the other indexes of trade intensity with South Asia:

- For Korea, the bilateral trade intensity, export intensity, and market share ratio indexes with Bangladesh, India, Pakistan, and Sri Lanka are all above average, except for the export intensity index with Pakistan. Each of Korea's intensity indexes are also above the average with South Asia as a region.
- The PRC also has above-average export intensity with all South Asian economies except India, where the export intensity index breaks the pattern by being below average, just as the import intensity index breaks the pattern by being above average. At the regional level, all of the PRC's intensity indexes with South Asia are above average except the market share ratio index.
- All intensity indexes for Japan's trade with South Asian economies are below average, except Japan's index of export intensity with Pakistan. All Japan's intensity indexes with South Asia as a region are also below average.
- For Taipei,China, the bilateral trade intensity and export intensity indexes are below average for India, Nepal, and Pakistan, but above

one for Bangladesh and Sri Lanka. All intensity indexes with South Asia as a region are below average.

On balance, the general picture is that the Northeast Asia-4 economies tend to export more to and import less from South Asian economies than would be expected on the basis of the corresponding shares of world trade. The PRC and Korea have the most intense trade relations with South Asia among the Northeast Asia-4 economies, with bilateral trade intensity index values that are almost uniformly above average. Japan has the least intensive trade relations, with bilateral trade intensity index values uniformly below average and all other trade intensity index values almost uniformly below average as well. Taipei,China has more intensive trade relations with South Asia than Japan does, but less intensive relations than either the PRC or Korea does.

It can be observed that the PRC and Korea are linked with Bangladesh, India, and Sri Lanka through the Asia-Pacific Trade Agreement (APTA), formerly known as the Bangkok Agreement. It might be hypothesized that the greater intensity of the trade of the PRC and Korea with South Asia, compared to the other Northeast Asia-4 economies, may be related to their participation in this agreement, but it is not possible to quantify this possible effect. It could also very well be that the PRC's already intense trade relations with the original members of the APTA prompted its decision to accede to the Bangkok Agreement in 2001.

Hong Kong, China and Singapore. Trade intensity indexes for Hong Kong, China and Singapore are shown in Table 2.9. As in the case of the Northeast Asia-4 group, at the regional aggregate level all trade-intensity indexes for both Hong Kong, China and Singapore are above average with Northeast, Southeast Asia, and with East as a whole. All Singapore's indexes for trade with individual Northeast Asian partners are above average—generally strongly so—except for the import intensity index with Hong Kong, China. The same is true of Hong Kong, China's indexes, with the exception of the export intensity indexes for Korea and Taipei,China.

On the other hand, Hong Kong, China exhibits strongly above-average export intensity with all South Asian economies and of course with South Asia as a whole, such that its bilateral trade intensity with these countries is also strongly above average.

Hong Kong, China has above-average import intensity with Pakistan as well as with India, and South Asia as a whole, but below-average import intensity with Bangladesh, Sri Lanka, and especially Nepal. With export intensities the pattern is largely reversed, with below-average export intensity with India and Pakistan and with South Asia as a whole and

Table 2.9   Trade Intensity Indexes for Hong Kong, China and Singapore

	Hong Kong, China				Singapore			
	Bilateral Trade Intensity	Import Intensity	Export Intensity	Market Share	Bilateral Trade Intensity	Import Intensity	Export Intensity	Market Share
Japan	1.47	1.81	1.01	0.44	1.56	1.81	1.30	0.99
Korea, Rep. of	1.38	1.85	0.85	2.22	1.63	1.50	1.74	1.93
PRC	7.55	7.96	7.54	5.82	1.17	1.39	1.27	1.75
Hong Kong, China					3.28	0.77	0.03	3.47
Taipei, China	3.97	7.61	0.46	1.59	1.74	1.97	1.52	1.99
Northeast Asia	2.94	3.14	2.36	2.39	1.38	1.26	1.46	1.88
Brunei Darussalam	0.32	0.01	1.30	5.40	6.64	2.49	22.27	19.62
Cambodia	2.74	0.12	5.08	16.56	4.63	1.83	6.63	8.49
Indonesia	0.75	0.81	0.92	0.77	5.30	5.32	7.70	9.00
Lao PDR	0.20	0.00	0.27	1.01	1.41	0.06	1.79	2.51
Malaysia	1.18	1.78	0.81	3.26	13.93	13.53	15.79	8.07
Myanmar	0.47	0.34	0.54	2.03	7.31	1.72	12.51	14.43
Philippines	2.14	3.10	2.04	5.47	3.91	4.78	4.67	5.02
Singapore	2.38	2.71	1.19	2.75				
Thailand	1.39	1.72	1.03	1.64	4.42	4.24	4.51	3.03
Viet Nam	0.53	0.35	0.68	4.77	4.61	3.04	5.68	7.60
Southeast Asia (ASEAN)	1.36	1.82	1.07	2.97	4.63	4.56	5.42	4.32
East Asia	2.34	2.53	7.90	2.53	1.90	1.71	2.06	2.44
Bangladesh	1.11	0.43	1.71	5.51	2.76	0.87	4.29	6.67
India	1.27	1.66	0.80	1.98	2.16	1.64	2.26	1.72
Nepal	0.58	0.05	0.77	2.84	2.07	0.32	2.53	3.50
Pakistan	0.79	1.50	0.27	1.04	1.05	0.24	1.80	2.02
Sri Lanka	1.30	0.37	2.11	9.41	2.57	0.63	3.99	5.52
South Asia	1.18	1.44	0.88	2.65	2.06	1.31	2.46	2.46

ASEAN = Association of Southeast Asian Nations, Lao PDR = Lao People's Democratic Republic, PRC = People's Republic of China.

Source: International Monetary Fund, *Direction of Trade Statistics*.

above-average export intensity with Bangladesh and Sri Lanka. With Nepal, the export intensity as well as the import intensity is below average. Bilateral trade intensities are above average with India, Bangladesh, and Sri Lanka, but below average with Pakistan and Nepal.

Singapore thus appears to have been somewhat more successful than Hong Kong, China in establishing itself as a focal point for trade with both Southeast and South Asia. The weak import intensity of East Asian economies with South Asia is once again in evidence in the case of Hong Kong, China and Singapore except in the case of India (and of Pakistan in the case of Hong Kong, China).

However, Hong Kong, China and Singapore present somewhat contrasting pictures of trade intensity with Southeast Asia. At the regional aggregate level, all trade-intensity indexes of both economies are above average, but much more strongly so in the case of Singapore. At the individual economy level, except for import intensity with the Lao PDR, all indexes of Singapore for trade intensity with Southeast Asia are above average, exceptionally so in the case of Malaysia, and strongly so in the case of the other Southeast Asian countries except the Lao PDR. Hong Kong, China has uniformly above-average trade intensity indexes only with Philippines, Singapore, and Thailand, although not as strongly so as in Singapore's case. Hong Kong, China's export intensity index with Malaysia is below average, while the other three indexes are all below average. With Indonesia on the other hand, all of Hong Kong's trade intensity indexes are below average, and all indexes except the market share ratio index are below average with Lao PDR, Myanmar, and Viet Nam, while Hong Kong, China appears to have an exceptionally intense export trade as well as a very low import intensity with Cambodia.

Singapore's import intensity index with India is above average, as is its import intensity with South Asia as a whole, but its import intensity with the other South Asian countries follows the pattern of the Northeast Asia-4 in being below average.

ASEAN-5. Table 2.10 gives the trade intensity indexes for the ASEAN-5 group. At the regional aggregate level, once again above-average index values are uniformly observed for the trade intensity of each of the five group members with Northeast, Southeast, and with East Asia as a whole. At the individual economy level, the main divergence from the pattern in Northeast Asia is the below-average values of all intensity indexes for Indonesia's trade with Hong Kong, China. There are other isolated examples as well.

The picture with Southeast Asia at the individual economy level is, as usual, more mixed. The intensity indexes for trade of the ASEAN-5

Table 2.10 Trade Intensity Indexes for ASEAN-5

	Indonesia				Malaysia				Philippines				Thailand				Viet Nam			
	Bilateral Trade Intensity	Import Intensity	Export Intensity	Market Share	Bilateral Trade Intensity	Import Intensity	Export Intensity	Market Share	Bilateral Trade Intensity	Import Intensity	Export Intensity	Market Share	Bilateral Trade Intensity	Import Intensity	Export Intensity	Market Share	Bilateral Trade Intensity	Import Intensity	Export Intensity	Market Share
Japan	3.18	1.99	4.40	4.49	2.29	2.54	2.10	1.86	3.02	3.03	3.04	2.82	3.21	3.58	2.79	2.70	2.07	1.67	2.68	2.86
Korea, Rep. of	2.44	1.75	2.97	2.91	1.66	1.99	1.37	1.35	2.03	2.51	1.48	1.64	1.14	1.44	0.81	0.87	2.85	4.17	1.01	1.04
PRC	1.01	1.34	1.05	1.42	1.09	1.39	1.13	1.75	0.94	0.86	1.33	2.17	1.07	1.27	1.17	1.69	1.58	2.05	1.41	1.37
Hong Kong, China	0.77	0.22	0.66	0.73	2.36	0.91	1.99	1.42	3.20	1.54	2.58	2.31	1.72	0.46	1.73	1.58	1.53	1.33	0.54	0.35
Taipei,China	2.62	2.21	2.98	2.53	2.27	1.95	2.60	2.03	4.07	3.40	4.85	3.65	1.73	1.74	1.72	1.56	3.76	5.42	1.36	1.31
Northeast Asia	1.70	1.28	2.03	2.48	1.52	1.53	1.48	1.70	1.93	1.78	2.05	2.45	1.59	1.64	1.49	1.83	1.80	2.03	1.35	1.57
Brunei Darussalam	4.89	7.59	2.62	2.46	4.39	0.34	17.46	11.23	0.37	0.37	0.41	0.31	7.67	9.92	2.97	3.01	0.10	0.05	0.27	0.00
Cambodia	2.30	0.11	3.14	2.88	1.25	0.49	1.67	1.43	0.31	0.14	0.44	0.36	14.25	0.77	26.64	20.34	21.86	12.03	32.16	34.33
Indonesia					3.96	4.49	4.76	2.02	2.04	2.84	1.36	0.72	3.70	2.93	6.53	4.46	2.51	2.35	3.73	3.50
Lao PDR	0.29	0.53	0.14	0.13	0.21	0.04	0.24	0.21	0.03	0.01	0.03	0.03	103.50	27.91	137.47	53.14	56.89	60.53	39.93	27.77
Malaysia	2.62	2.48	3.57	3.90					3.31	2.74	5.13	4.86	3.78	4.21	4.49	4.16	1.97	2.53	1.69	1.69
Myanmar	2.02	1.54	2.12	1.96	3.72	2.67	4.23	3.48	0.24	0.14	0.31	0.26	33.30	51.76	16.11	13.55	0.96	0.78	1.09	1.46
Philippines	1.88	0.92	3.09	2.51	3.73	6.46	2.89	2.24					2.97	3.33	3.82	3.04	2.27	2.47	3.05	2.84
Singapore	6.89	6.70	5.28	4.41	9.97	6.88	10.82	9.60	4.71	3.71	4.21	3.56	3.94	2.28	4.46	3.76	5.38	5.61	2.85	2.88
Thailand	3.32	4.85	2.48	2.58	4.63	4.59	4.74	3.36	3.19	3.29	3.13	2.57					3.61	5.22	1.47	1.52

continued on next page...

Table 2.10 continued

	Indonesia				Malaysia				Philippines				Thailand				Viet Nam			
	Bilateral Trade Intensity	Import Intensity	Export Intensity	Market Share	Bilateral Trade Intensity	Import Intensity	Export Intensity	Market Share	Bilateral Trade Intensity	Import Intensity	Export Intensity	Market Share	Bilateral Trade Intensity	Import Intensity	Export Intensity	Market Share	Bilateral Trade Intensity	Import Intensity	Export Intensity	Market Share
Viet Nam	2.90	3.61	2.35	2.09	2.26	1.74	2.50	2.08	1.98	2.93	1.09	1.94	3.66	1.56	5.23	4.84				
Southeast Asia (ASEAN)	3.06	3.63	3.30	3.19	3.89	3.85	4.90	4.38	2.66	2.74	3.11	2.88	2.91	2.60	3.89	3.49	2.93	3.69	2.39	2.50
East Asia	1.84	1.57	2.09	2.64	1.87	1.77	1.97	2.32	1.91	1.76	2.06	2.55	1.73	1.64	1.80	2.22	1.88	2.11	1.42	1.78
Bangladesh	2.53	0.18	3.47	2.35	1.52	0.23	2.31	1.26	0.10	0.04	0.16	0.00	1.83	0.34	2.93	1.87	0.48	0.59	0.45	0.14
India	3.04	2.69	2.85	2.60	2.00	1.19	2.31	1.35	0.63	1.01	0.24	0.03	1.17	1.45	0.81	0.64	1.28	2.13	0.26	0.20
Nepal	0.51	0.01	0.53	0.50	0.31	0.04	0.36	0.31	0.15	0.04	0.18	0.15	1.64	0.19	2.07	2.01	0.12	0.03	0.15	0.16
Pakistan	2.19	1.08	2.88	2.61	2.03	0.38	3.41	2.40	0.20	0.23	0.20	0.10	1.49	0.67	2.32	1.62	0.65	0.62	0.75	0.33
Sri Lanka	2.61	0.20	3.56	2.51	2.02	0.10	3.21	2.24	0.23	0.21	0.24	0.16	1.41	0.15	2.34	1.86	0.55	0.48	0.63	0.38
South Asia	2.80	2.10	2.90	2.55	1.94	0.93	2.46	1.52	0.49	0.77	0.22	0.05	1.28	1.17	1.29	0.97	1.05	1.69	0.36	0.22

ASEAN = Association of Southeast Asian Nations, Lao PDR = Lao People's Democratic Republic, PRC = People's Republic of China.

Source: International Monetary Fund, *Direction of Trade Statistics*.

group with each other are almost uniformly above average—in many cases very strongly so—indicating that the ASEAN-5 economies are trading very intensively with each other. The only exceptions to this pattern are the below-average values for Indonesia's import intensity index with the Philippines, and the Philippines' market share ratio index with Indonesia. The values of the ASEAN-5 group's trade intensity indexes with the ASEAN-BCLM group on the other hand display much greater diversity, seemingly depending on the existence of special trade relationships based on contiguous borders. Thus, there are extraordinarily high values for all trade intensity indexes of Thailand and Viet Nam with Cambodia and the Lao PDR (except Viet Nam's import intensity index with Cambodia), and for all Thailand's trade intensity indexes with Myanmar. Outside of these special relationships, trade intensity of the ASEAN-5 economies with the ASEAN-BCLM economies is highly variable, ranging from above average to very low.

The intensity of the trade with South Asia of the ASEAN-5 group tends to be higher than that of the Northeast Asia-4. At the individual economy level, Indonesia, Malaysia, and Thailand have above-average export intensity with all South Asian economies except Nepal. Indonesia and Malaysia also have above-average bilateral trade intensity with all South Asian economies except Nepal, while Thailand has above-average bilateral trade intensity with all South Asian economies including Nepal. On the other hand, the Philippines and Viet Nam have below-average export intensity with all South Asian economies. On the import intensity side, the tendency is for the ASEAN-5 economies to have above-average import intensity only with India in South Asia, and to have below-average import intensity with the others. This is the case with Malaysia, Philippines, Thailand, and Viet Nam, while Indonesia has above-average import intensity also with Pakistan.

ASEAN-BCLM. The trade-intensity indexes of the ASEAN-BCLM group are presented in Table 2.11. As might be expected, the pattern is highly varied. With Northeast Asia, at the regional aggregate level all intensity indexes of the Lao PDR are below average. Cambodia and Myanmar have below-average export intensity and market-share ratio indexes, but above-average import intensity and bilateral trade intensity indexes. With Southeast Asia, the trade intensity indexes at the regional aggregate level are uniformly above average, indicating that these ASEAN-BCLM economies trade intensively within Southeast Asia but there is wide variation at the individual economy level. The trade intensity indexes with South Asia show that the intensity of trade with South Asia of the ASEAN-BCLM economies, with the exception of Myanmar, is very low.

Table 2.11 Trade Intensity Indexes for ASEAN-BCLM

	Brunei Darussalam				Cambodia				Lao PDR				Myanmar			
	Bilateral Trade Intensity	Import Intensity	Export Intensity	Market Share	Bilateral Trade Intensity	Import Intensity	Export Intensity	Market Share	Bilateral Trade Intensity	Import Intensity	Export Intensity	Market Share	Bilateral Trade Intensity	Import Intensity	Export Intensity	Market Share
Japan	5.36	1.94	7.56	8.13	0.50	0.37	0.72	0.75	0.30	0.29	0.28	0.42	0.70	0.58	0.87	1.00
Korea, Rep. of	3.83	0.83	5.17	5.27	1.01	1.59	0.08	0.08	0.25	0.34	0.05	0.06	1.39	2.10	0.50	0.56
PRC	0.79	0.49	1.10	1.18	1.08	1.87	0.20	0.21	1.13	1.67	0.39	0.58	2.62	4.58	0.94	1.09
Hong Kong, China	0.64	1.51	0.01	0.01	4.26	4.64	0.11	0.11	0.29	0.28	0.01	0.01	0.70	0.57	0.32	0.36
Taipei, China	0.12	0.41	0.00	0.00	2.39	3.76	0.12	0.11	0.23	0.10	0.49	0.64	1.27	1.71	0.70	0.71
Northeast Asia	2.16	0.96	2.75	3.39	1.15	1.63	0.27	0.32	0.50	0.59	0.22	0.37	1.31	1.78	0.63	0.83
Brunei Darussalam	0.00	0.00	0.00	0.00	0.12	0.06	0.33	0.34	0.00	0.00	0.01	0.00	0.09	0.01	0.34	0.37
Cambodia	0.13	0.36	0.06	0.06	0.00	0.00	0.00	0.00	2.96	5.17	0.15	0.22	0.05	0.00	0.08	0.09
Indonesia	4.08	2.76	7.09	7.39	2.14	3.23	0.10	0.10	0.21	0.14	0.50	0.71	1.73	2.20	1.44	1.59
Lao PDR	0.00	0.00	0.00	0.00	3.13	0.17	4.87	4.87	0.00	0.00	0.00	0.00	0.00	0.00	0.00	0.00
Malaysia	4.31	13.62	1.26	0.34	1.14	1.73	0.46	0.46	0.17	0.25	0.04	0.06	3.10	4.22	2.45	2.72
Myanmar	0.10	0.36	0.01	0.01	0.05	0.09	0.00	0.00	0.00	0.00	0.00	0.00	0.00	0.00	0.00	0.00
Philippines	0.31	0.39	0.36	0.37	0.27	0.46	0.13	0.13	0.02	0.03	0.01	0.01	0.20	0.33	0.13	0.15
Singapore	6.86	14.30	2.44	2.43	5.37	6.18	1.68	1.71	1.54	1.82	0.05	0.08	7.89	10.53	1.58	1.77

continued on next page....

Table 2.11 continued

	Brunei Darussalam				Cambodia				Lao PDR				Myanmar			
	Bilateral Trade Intensity	Import Intensity	Export Intensity	Market Share	Bilateral Trade Intensity	Import Intensity	Export Intensity	Market Share	Bilateral Trade Intensity	Import Intensity	Export Intensity	Market Share	Bilateral Trade Intensity	Import Intensity	Export Intensity	Market Share
Thailand	7.51	3.21	9.50	9.07	13.40	21.81	0.72	0.73	45.34	56.88	20.87	29.40	22.86	14.49	33.27	36.30
Viet Nam	0.00	0.00	0.00	0.05	24.87	35.45	12.08	10.91	33.14	28.48	40.86	69.07	1.54	1.49	1.53	0.80
Southeast Asia (ASEAN)	4.25	8.19	3.37	3.28	5.03	7.74	1.51	1.52	9.12	11.16	6.30	10.04	6.45	6.84	7.19	8.23
East Asia	2.41	2.21	2.62	3.36	1.85	2.59	0.48	0.60	2.24	2.50	1.35	2.61	2.26	2.53	1.81	2.54
Bangladesh	0.07	0.33	0.00	0.00	0.00	0.00	0.00	0.00	0.05	0.00	0.13	0.18	4.18	0.73	7.23	7.90
India	0.74	0.45	0.73	0.01	0.00	0.00	0.00	0.02	0.17	0.25	0.02	0.03	8.56	3.66	12.18	13.40
Nepal	0.38	0.03	0.34	0.36	0.00	0.00	0.00	0.00	0.00	0.00	0.00	1.61	0.00	0.00	0.00	0.00
Pakistan	0.15	0.55	0.03	0.08	0.00	0.00	0.00	0.16	0.10	0.09	0.14	0.20	1.85	1.17	2.71	2.96
Sri Lanka	0.04	0.16	0.01	0.01	0.12	0.05	0.21	0.21	0.00	0.00	0.00	0.00	0.41	0.12	0.66	0.73
South Asia	0.54	0.43	0.52	0.02	0.01	0.00	0.05	0.05	0.13	19.00	0.04	0.08	6.58	2.85	9.59	10.61

ASEAN = Association of Southeast Asian Nations, Lao PDR = Lao People's Democratic Republic, PRC = People's Republic of China.

Source: International Monetary Fund, *Direction of Trade Statistics*.

The values of the trade intensity indexes of Myanmar on the other hand are uniformly above average, generally strongly so, with India, Bangladesh, and Sri Lanka (except for the import intensity index with Bangladesh), as are the values of the indexes for Myanmar's trade with South Asia as a region.

South Asia. The trade intensity indexes for South Asia in Table 2.12 present a sharply different picture from those presented for the East Asian economies in Tables 2.7 to 2.10. In general, the South Asian countries as a group have below-average trade intensities with the major markets of Northeast Asia. In particular, the export intensities of the South Asian countries are uniformly well below average with Northeast Asia as a whole, and are almost uniformly below average also with individual Northeast Asian economies. The only exceptions are the above-average export intensities and market-share ratios associated with above-average bilateral trade intensities for India, Pakistan, and Hong Kong, China. India has an above-average market share ratio, although not an above-average export intensity index, with the PRC. Import intensities are also uniformly below average with Northeast Asia as a region, although they are more variable with individual Northeast Asian economies. Bangladesh and Sri Lanka each have above-average import intensities with Hong Kong, China and with Taipei,China as does Nepal with the PRC, and in each of these case the bilateral trade intensity is also above average. India and Sri Lanka have above-average import intensities with Korea, as does Pakistan with the PRC, but in these cases the bilateral trade intensity remains below average.

The picture of South Asian trade intensity with Southeast Asia is more mixed but with some clear patterns. At the aggregate regional level, all of India's trade intensity indexes with Southeast Asia are above average. The other four South Asian countries—Bangladesh, Nepal, Pakistan, and Sri Lanka—all have above-average import intensities with Southeast Asia, associated with above-average bilateral trade intensities, but below-average export intensities and market share ratios. In other words, Southeast Asia has a larger share of the imports of these four South Asian countries than its share of world imports, but accounts for a smaller share of their exports. The former effect dominates the latter so that the bilateral trade intensity is above average.

At the individual country level, all trade intensity indexes are above average for India with Indonesia, Malaysia, and Myanmar, and for Pakistan with Indonesia. Above-average import intensities associated with above-average bilateral trade intensities are observed for Bangladesh with Indonesia, Myanmar, Singapore, and Thailand; for Pakistan with Malaysia,

Table 2.12   Trade Intensity Indexes for South Asia

	Bangladesh				India				Nepal				Pakistan				Sri Lanka			
	Bilateral Trade Intensity	Import Intensity	Export Intensity	Market Share	Bilateral Trade Intensity	Import Intensity	Export Intensity	Market Share	Bilateral Trade Intensity	Import Intensity	Export Intensity	Market Share	Bilateral Trade Intensity	Import Intensity	Export Intensity	Market Share	Bilateral Trade Intensity	Import Intensity	Export Intensity	Market Share
Japan	0.67	0.90	0.17	0.33	0.50	0.46	0.56	0.65	0.22	0.21	0.21	0.23	0.68	0.95	0.24	0.26	0.77	0.87	0.57	0.71
Korea, Rep. of	0.96	1.45	0.12	0.17	0.87	1.14	0.50	0.85	0.54	0.71	0.06	0.07	0.89	0.98	0.75	0.94	0.99	1.51	0.22	0.31
PRC	0.06	0.08	0.05	0.10	0.73	0.83	0.81	1.21	1.11	1.63	0.15	0.18	0.75	1.18	0.40	0.91	0.44	0.78	0.06	0.06
Hong Kong, China	1.73	1.54	0.48	0.38	1.59	0.55	1.61	1.47	0.88	0.79	0.05	0.05	1.30	0.29	1.50	1.53	2.61	2.63	0.42	0.39
Taipei, China	1.40	2.08	0.17	0.14	0.58	0.54	0.62	0.55	0.10	0.10	0.07	0.07	0.64	0.86	0.33	0.34	1.24	1.94	0.14	0.14
Northeast Asia	0.46	0.61	0.14	0.21	0.59	0.53	0.65	0.93	0.53	0.65	0.11	0.14	0.62	0.70	0.47	0.75	0.68	0.93	0.24	0.33
Brunei Darussalam	0.09	0.00	0.43	0.28	0.09	0.01	0.37	0.41	0.37	0.36	0.03	0.03	0.33	0.08	1.16	0.57	0.04	0.01	0.15	0.16
Cambodia	0.06	0.00	0.13	0.00	0.01	0.02	0.00	0.00	0.00	0.00	0.00	0.00	1.06	0.17	1.86	0.00	0.13	0.22	0.04	0.05
Indonesia	1.86	2.65	0.27	0.16	2.85	2.98	3.57	2.42	0.44	0.56	0.02	0.01	2.13	2.94	1.14	1.13	1.90	2.83	0.35	0.20
Lao PDR	0.07	0.14	0.00	0.00	0.17	0.02	0.23	0.22	0.70	1.22	0.00	0.00	0.12	0.15	0.08	0.09	0.00	0.00	0.00	0.00
Malaysia	0.93	1.53	0.08	0.50	1.32	1.66	1.22	1.08	0.27	0.38	0.04	0.04	1.76	2.91	0.56	0.39	1.58	2.71	0.17	0.11
Myanmar	4.98	7.72	0.68	0.62	9.65	14.63	3.54	3.31	0.00	0.00	0.00	0.00	2.13	2.88	1.10	1.21	0.46	0.71	0.11	0.12
Philippines	0.18	0.30	0.11	0.04	0.60	0.34	1.19	0.92	0.12	0.19	0.04	0.04	0.22	0.13	0.43	0.24	0.17	0.20	0.22	0.22

continued on next page....

Table 2.12 continued

	Bangladesh				India				Nepal				Pakistan				Sri Lanka			
	Bilateral Trade Intensity	Import Intensity	Export Intensity	Market Share	Bilateral Trade Intensity	Import Intensity	Export Intensity	Market Share	Bilateral Trade Intensity	Import Intensity	Export Intensity	Market Share	Bilateral Trade Intensity	Import Intensity	Export Intensity	Market Share	Bilateral Trade Intensity	Import Intensity	Export Intensity	Market Share
Singapore	3.86	4.87	0.29	0.76	1.91	1.27	2.05	1.47	2.37	2.54	0.30	0.32	1.25	1.47	0.44	0.25	3.31	4.02	0.83	0.65
Thailand	1.31	2.00	0.17	0.29	0.92	0.68	1.26	1.31	1.60	2.14	0.18	0.19	1.22	1.73	0.56	0.69	1.28	1.98	0.29	0.16
Viet Nam	0.32	0.14	0.54	0.50	1.07	0.21	1.94	1.93	0.12	0.16	0.03	0.03	0.53	0.34	0.71	0.64	0.43	0.39	0.46	0.49
Southeast Asia (ASEAN)	1.60	2.54	0.21	0.40	1.36	1.34	1.68	1.41	0.95	1.30	0.14	0.15	1.18	1.78	0.56	0.47	1.59	2.52	0.43	0.34
East Asia	0.65	0.90	0.14	0.26	0.70	0.62	0.78	1.04	0.57	0.70	0.10	0.14	0.68	0.83	0.45	0.68	0.81	1.12	0.25	0.33
Bangladesh					10.93	1.01	22.11	16.59	3.75	3.65	5.20	5.35	7.11	3.41	10.94	6.41	1.34	0.99	1.84	1.30
India	11.19	18.72	0.85	0.86					52.59	52.99	47.94	49.52	1.74	2.46	0.84	0.55	13.62	20.07	5.25	3.72
Nepal	4.29	5.57	3.45	3.12	97.65	95.86	86.74	47.64					1.89	2.09	1.66	1.82	0.74	0.17	1.04	1.13
Pakistan	4.62	6.27	3.26	2.90	1.52	0.53	2.78	2.22	1.68	1.76	1.96	2.01					5.56	7.78	3.81	4.35
Sri Lanka	1.15	1.27	1.04	0.85	13.86	3.81	24.78	17.88	0.74	1.10	0.16	0.16	7.03	4.27	9.57	8.00				
South Asia	8.49	14.39	1.11	1.07	2.40	0.71	4.03	3.49	36.94	38.66	34.47	35.78	2.28	2.29	2.16	1.49	10.32	15.53	4.35	3.32

ASEAN = Association of Southeast Asian Nations, Lao PDR = Lao People's Democratic Republic, PRC = People's Republic of China.

Source: International Monetary Fund, *Direction of Trade Statistics*.

Myanmar, Singapore, and Thailand; and for Sri Lanka with Indonesia, Singapore, and Thailand. Above-average export intensities are largely confined to India. In addition to Indonesia, Malaysia, and Myanmar, India has above-average export intensity associated with an above-average market share ratio and bilateral trade intensity with Thailand, and without an above-average bilateral trade intensity with Viet Nam. The only above-average export intensities for South Asian countries other than India are those of Pakistan with Brunei Darussalam and Cambodia.

In intra-South Asian trade, trade-intensity indexes are predominantly above average, both at the aggregate regional and the individual country levels. The one index that is well below average at the aggregate regional level is, however, an important one: India's import intensity with South Asia as a whole. This appears to be a reflection of India's low import intensity with Pakistan, since its import intensities are well above average with Sri Lanka, exceptionally high with Nepal, and almost average with Bangladesh. India's export intensity is strongly positive with Pakistan and very strongly above average with Bangladesh and Sri Lanka. Correspondingly, Bangladesh, Pakistan, and Sri Lanka have above-average import intensities with India, which are exceptionally high for both Bangladesh and Sri Lanka, and these import intensities account also for above-average bilateral trade intensities, but their export intensities and market share ratios with India are all well below average. Unsurprisingly, the intensity of trade between Nepal and Sri Lanka is also generally low. Trade intensity is exceptionally high between India and Nepal, and is also high between Pakistan and Sri Lanka, between Bangladesh and Nepal, and between Bangladesh and Pakistan.

Commodity Composition of Trade

The commodity composition of trade also has an important bearing on actual and potential trade levels. Here, again, different measures are used to capture different dimensions of the influence of the commodity composition of trade.

The export similarity index is a way of comparing the export profiles of two countries or regions. The value of the index can vary between zero and 100, with a value of 100 indicating identical export profiles and a value of zero indicating a complete absence of overlap in the export profiles. A high value for the export similarity index could indicate that the countries concerned are intense competitors in overseas markets, or it could also indicate that there is a significant potential for growth of intra-industry trade between them.

The index of RCA measures the extent to which the share of a product in a country's exports exceeds or falls short of the share of the same product in world exports. The threshold value of the RCA index is one, which indicates that the product concerned accounts for an identical share of both the exports of the country in question and of world exports. RCA is generally taken as a measure of the competitiveness of a country in exporting the product in question. The higher (lower) the value of the index, the more (less) competitive the country is as an exporter of the product in question.[3] Changes in the range of the products with an RCA above the threshold level, together with changes in the average RCA of those products, can also be taken as an indication of whether a country is extending the range of products in which it is an international exporter. RCA is not a measure of true comparative advantage, since while the trade flows on which it is based reflect the underlying comparative advantage albeit to an unknown degree, they also reflect the distortions of the underlying comparative advantage created by whatever trade barriers are in place.

Comparisons of RCAs between countries can indicate the extent to which they are likely to be competitors in world markets. Countries with a high RCA value for the same product are likely to be leading competitors in the export markets for that product. The potential for bilateral trade based on specialization will be higher the more two countries' RCA profiles differ from one another. Similar RCA profiles do not, however, rule out bilateral trade if intra-industry trade is involved.

Another measure indicating the potential for beneficial specialization is the commodity complementarity index. This index measures the degree of "matching" in the commodity profile of the trade of two countries or regions. In other words, the extent to which a high RCA value for products in one country or region is "matched" by a low RCA value for the same products in the partner country or region, and vice versa. The index has a threshold value of one, indicating a degree of matching that is "average" for the global economy. The higher the value of the index above one, the higher the complementarity between the two countries or regions. The lower the index value, the lower the complementarity.

Export Similarity

Table 2.13 summarizes the export similarity index readings for subgroups of East and South Asian countries, with the PRC and India each taken as

---

[3] Here the original version of the revealed comparative advantage (RCA) index is used. This has a threshold value if one, a lower limit of zero, and no upper limit. An alternative is the symmetrical RCA index, which takes a value between -1 and 1 and has a threshold value of zero.

Table 2.13   Export Similarity Index for Selected Country Groupings in East and South Asia

	India	Other South Asia	Japan/ Rep. of Korea	PRC	Hong Kong, China/ Singapore	Southeast Asia
India		37.6	34.8	45.7	41.8	45.6
Other South Asia	37.6		15.7	32.2	23.7	23.8
Japan/Rep. of Korea	34.8	15.7		66.6	66.0	66.2
PRC	45.7	32.2	66.6		72.5	69.1
Hong Kong, China/Singapore	41.8	12.3	66.0	72.5		68.9
Southeast Asia	45.6	11.7	66.2	69.1	68.9	

PRC = People's Republic of China.

Source: Calculated from Comtrade data for 2004.

a single group. The index used here was calculated from data at the 2-digit level of the Harmonized Commodity Description and Coding System (HS).

The results show a low degree of export similarity between India and each of the other groups, and a similarly low degree of similarity between the rest of South Asia[4] and both the PRC and India. The degree of similarity between the exports of the rest of South Asia and the exports of Japan; Korea; Hong Kong, China; Singapore; and Southeast Asia is even lower. In particular, the degree of export similarity between the rest of South Asia and each of the East Asian groups is lower than the export similarity between rest of South Asia and India. The degree of export similarity between the East Asian groupings is much higher than any of the export similarity index values involving South Asian economies. These results show that the overlap between the export specializations of East Asian and South Asian economies is relatively low.

Revealed Comparative Advantage

Tables 2.14 to 2.18 present a mapping of RCAs of East and South Asian economies at the HS 2-digit level, grouped according to HS

---

[4]   Nepal is not included because of unavailability of comparable data. Southeast Asia here comprises Indonesia, Malaysia, Philippines, and Thailand.

section.[5] Only RCAs that are greater than or equal to one (i.e., "above-average RCAs") are shown, allowing easy identification of overlaps in above-average RCAs.

In Table 2.14, for agricultural and other food products (HS Chapters I–XXIV), RCAs are unsurprisingly concentrated almost exclusively in Southeast Asia, South Asia, and PRC. The most extensive overlaps in RCA between South and Southeast Asia or the PRC occur in Sections I and II (animal and vegetable products). The most complete overlaps are for fish products (HS Chapter 3), where all South Asian countries as well as Indonesia, Philippines, Thailand, and PRC have above-average RCAs, and plant products (HS Chapter 14), where again all South Asian countries have above-average RCAs, as do Indonesia, Thailand, PRC, and Singapore. Other overlaps between East and South Asia in these two sections are for: vegetables, HS Chapter 7 (India with Thailand); fruit, HS Chapter 8 (India, Pakistan, and Sri Lanka with the Philippines); coffee and tea, HS Chapter 9 (India, Bangladesh, and Sri Lanka with Indonesia); milling products, HS Chapter 11 (Pakistan and Sri Lanka with Indonesia and Thailand); and lacs, gums and resins, HS Chapter 13 (India and Pakistan with Indonesia and the Philippines).

For Sections III (oils and fats) and IV (foodstuffs), above-average RCAs are largely confined to Southeast Asia and the PRC. Above-average RCAs in South Asia, with associated overlaps with Southeast Asian RCAs, are found only for sugar products (HS Chapter 17, Pakistan with Thailand and the Philippines) and tobacco products (HS Chapter 24, India, Bangladesh, and Sri Lanka with Indonesia and the Philippines).

Table 2.15, South Asian countries are without above-average RCAs in Section X (pulp and paper products). South Asian countries are almost devoid of above-average RCAs in Section IX (wood and wood products), where Bangladesh's above-average RCA for plaiting and basketwork products overlaps with PRC, Indonesia, Philippines, and Singapore; in Section V (minerals and fuels), where India's above-average RCA for ores, slag, and ash overlaps with Indonesia; and Section VII (rubber and plastic products), where Sri Lanka's above-average RCAs for rubber products overlaps with Japan, Korea, Indonesia, Malaysia, Thailand, and Cambodia.

The most extensive overlap in Table 2.15 is for Section VIII (hides, skins, and leather), where there are overlaps for: raw hides and skins, HS Chapter 41 (India, Bangladesh, and Pakistan with Korea; Hong Kong, China; and Thailand); and leather products, HS Chapter 42 (India, Pakistan, and Sri Lanka with the PRC and Hong Kong, China). In Section VI (chemical

[5] See Table A2.3 for descriptions of the sections in the Harmonized System.

Table 2.14 Above-Average RCAs for East and South Asian Economies in 2004: HS Sections I–IV

	JPN	KOR	HKG	SIN	INO	MAL	PHI	THA	CAM	PRC	IND	BAN	PAK	SRI
Section I: Animal Products, Animals														
H1-01 Live animals														
H1-02 Meat and edible meat offal														
H1-03 Fish, crustaceans, mollusks, aquatic invertebrates, n.e.s.					4.1		1.2	3.4		1.3	2.9	12.2	1.6	3.1
H1-04 Dairy products, eggs, honey, edible animal product, n.e.s.														
H1-05 Products of animal origin, n.e.s.										3.1			2.6	
Section II: Vegetable Products														
H1-06 Live trees, plants, bulbs, roots, cut flowers, etc.														1.1
H1-07 Edible vegetables and certain roots and tubers								1.7		1.2	1.3			
H1-08 Edible fruit, nuts, peel of citrus fruit, melons							3.0				1.9		1.7	2.5
H1-09 Coffee, tea, mate, and spices					5.7						6.3	1.8		93.6
H1-10 Cereals								5.8			4.9		10.0	
H1-11 Milling products, malt, starches, inulin, wheat gluten					1.0			3.2					4.4	2.6
H1-12 Oil seed, oleagic fruits, grain, seed, fruit, etc., n.e.s.											1.3			

continued on next page...

Table 2.14 continued

		JPN	KOR	HKG	SIN	INO	MAL	PHI	THA	CAM	PRC	IND	BAN	PAK	SRI
H1-13	Lac, gums, resins, vegetable saps and extracts, n.e.s.					1.1		3.9				11.4		5.5	
H1-14	Vegetable plaiting materials, vegetable products, n.e.s.				1.5	14.2			1.7		1.6	6.2	1.7	2.6	20.1
Section III: Oils and Fats															
H1-15	Animal, vegetable fats and oils, cleavage products, etc.					16.2	12.2	3.8							
Section IV: Foodstuffs															
H1-16	Meat, fish and seafood food preparations, n.e.s.					1.5		1.4	11.9		2.3				
H1-17	Sugars and sugar confectionery							1.2	4.4					3.6	
H1-18	Cocoa and cocoa preparations					4.2	1.7								
H1-19	Cereal, flour, starch, milk preparations, and products								1.1						
H1-20	Vegetable, fruit, nut, etc., food preparations							1.5	3.2		1.3				
H1-21	Miscellaneous edible preparations								1.7						
H1-22	Beverages, spirits, and vinegar														
H1-23	Residues, wastes of food industry, animal fodder								1.3			2.6			1.0
H1-24	Tobacco and manufactured tobacco substitutes					1.5		1.1				1.3	1.6		3.9

BAN = Bangladesh; CAM = Cambodia; HKG = Hong Kong, China; HS = harmonized system of tariff classification; IND = India; INO = Indonesia; JPN = Japan; KOR = Republic of Korea; MAL = Malaysia; n.e.s. = not elsewhere specified; PAK = Pakistan; PHI = Philippines; PRC = People's Republic of China; RCA = revealed comparative advantage; SIN = Singapore; SRI = Sri Lanka; THA = Thailand.

Source: Calculated from Comtrade 2004 Data.

Table 2.15   Above-Average RCAs for East and South Asian Economies in 2004: HS Sections V–X

	JPN	KOR	HKG	SIN	INO	MAL	PHI	THA	CAM	PRC	IND	BAN	PAK	SRI
Section V: Mineral Products and Fuels														
H1-25 Salt, sulphur, earth, stone, plaster, lime, and cement														
H1-26 Ores, slag, and ash					5.9						8.7			
H1-27 Mineral fuels, oils, distillation products, etc.				1.1	1.9	1.3								
Section VI: Chemical Products														
H1-28 Inorganic chemicals, precious metal compound, isoto	1.0									1.3				
H1-29 Organic chemicals		1.2		2.3							1.2			
H1-30 Pharmaceutical products											1.5			
H1-31 Fertilizers														
H1-32 Tanning dyeing extracts, tannins, derivs, pigments, etc.				1.2							1.4			
H1-33 Essential oils, perfumes, cosmetics, toiletries					1.5									
H1-34 Soaps, lubricants, waxes, candles, modeling pastes														
H1-35 Albuminoids, modified starches, glues, enzymes								1.8						
H1-36 Explosives, pyrotechnics, matches, pyrophorics, etc.										2.5	1.1		5.0	
H1-37 Photographic or cinematographic goods	3.3			2.0										
H1-38 Miscellaneous chemical products	1.3					1.4								

continued on next page…

Table 2.15 continued

Current Patterns of Trade and Investment 99

	JPN	KOR	HKG	SIN	INO	MAL	PHI	THA	CAM	PRC	IND	BAN	PAK	SRI
Section VII: Plastic and Rubber Products														
H1-39 Plastics and articles thereof		1.4						1.4						
H1-40 Rubber and articles thereof	1.4	1.2			4.6	2.4		5.7	1.4					6.1
Section VIII: Hides, Skins and Leathers														
H1-41 Raw hides and skins (other than fur skins) and leather		1.3	3.8					1.2			2.5	12.3	7.2	
H1-42 Articles of leather, animal gut, harness, travel goods			5.4							4.7	3.5		10.1	1.4
H1-43 Fur skins and artificial fur, manufactures thereof			6.2							4.2				
Section IX: Wood and Wood Products														
H1-44 Wood and articles of wood, wood charcoal					4.7	2.8								
H1-45 Cork and articles of cork														
H1-46 Manufactures of plaiting material, basketwork, etc.			1.1		6.2		5.2			9.9		4.3		
Section X: Pulp and Paper Products														
H1-47 Pulp of wood, fibrous cellulosic material, waste, etc.					3.2									
H1-48 Paper & paperboard, articles of pulp, paper, and board					2.2									
H1-49 Printed books, newspapers, pictures, etc.			1.3						55.2					

BAN = Bangladesh; CAM = Cambodia; HKG = Hong Kong, China; HS = harmonized system of tariff classification; IND = India; INO = Indonesia; JPN = Japan; KOR = Republic of Korea; MAL = Malaysia; PAK = Pakistan; PHI = Philippines; PRC = People's Republic of China; RCA = revealed comparative advantage; SIN = Singapore; SRI = Sri Lanka; THA = Thailand.

Source: Calculated from Comtrade 2004 Data.

products) there are overlaps for India alone in: inorganic chemicals, HS Chapter 28 (with the PRC); organic chemicals, HS Chapter 29 (with Japan, Korea, and Singapore); and tanning and dyeing extracts, HS Chapter 32 (with Singapore). There is also an overlap in explosives (HS Chapter 38) between India, Pakistan, and the PRC.

Table 2.16—covering textiles and clothing (Section XI) as well as footgear, headgear, and other related products (HS Section XII)—exhibits the most extensive overlap in above-average RCAs. In particular, there is a very extensive overlap between the PRC—with above-average RCAs in every chapter except HS Chapter 56 (wadding)—and India, with above average RCA in every HS chapter except 51 (wool), 56 (wadding, twine, and rope), 59 (impregnated, coated, or laminated fabrics), and 60 (knitted and crocheted fabrics). There are several chapters in which every South Asian economy has an above-average RCA. These are: Chapter 53, vegetable fibers (overlaps with the PRC and Hong Kong, China); Chapter 57, carpets etc (overlaps with the PRC); Chapter 58, special woven or tufted fabric (overlaps with the PRC; Hong Kong, China; Korea; and Thailand); and Chapters 61 to 63, clothing (overlap with the PRC and all Southeast Asian countries except Malaysia). There is also substantial overlap for: HS Chapter 52, cotton (India, Bangladesh, and Pakistan with the PRC; Indonesia; and Hong Kong, China); Chapter 54, man-made filaments (India and Pakistan with the PRC; Korea; Hong Kong, China; Indonesia; Malaysia; and Thailand); Chapter 56, wadding, twine, and rope (Bangladesh, Pakistan, and Sri Lanka with Korea, Philippines, and Thailand); and Chapter 60, knitted and crocheted fabrics (India, Pakistan, and Sri Lanka with the PRC; Korea; and Hong Kong, China). In general, above-average RCAs in clothing for East Asian economies are confined to the PRC; Hong Kong, China; and Southeast Asia. Korea also retains an above-average RCA for some textile products.

The picture for Section XII (footwear, headgear, etc.) is mixed. The PRC; Hong Kong, China; and Indonesia have above-average RCAs in each of Chapters 64 to 67, and there is a spread of above-average RCAs across the rest of Southeast and South Asia.

Table 2.17 presents RCA data for a range of HS sections covering manufactured goods. The PRC again has above-average RCAs for most of the chapters in these sections, but there is also a wide spread of above-average RCAs across other East Asian economies. Above-average RCAs are less prevalent for South Asian economies in these sections. There is a complete overlap in above-average RCAs between the PRC and Pakistan in the three chapters of Section 20 covering mainly labor-intensive light manufactures: Chapter 94 (furniture, lighting, and prefabricated buildings),

Chapter 95 (toys, games, and sports goods), and Chapter 96 (miscellaneous manufactures). Above-average RCAs in these chapters are also observed for Indonesia and Malaysia in Chapter 94; Hong Kong, China in Chapter 95; and Japan, Korea, Hong Kong, China, Indonesia, the Philippines, Thailand, and Sri Lanka in Chapter 96.

In metals and metal products, India has above-average RCA in: Chapter 72, iron and steel (overlapping with Japan and Korea); Chapter 73, iron and steel products (overlapping with the PRC); Chapter 74, copper and copper products (overlapping with Korea, Indonesia, and the Philippines); and Chapter 82, tools and implements (overlapping with Japan and the PRC). Sri Lanka also has an above-average RCA in copper and copper products and an above-average RCA in Chapter 78, lead and lead products (overlapping with the PRC and Malaysia).

Finally, Table 2.18 shows above-average RCAs in HS Sections XVI (machinery and electronics), XVII (transport equipment), and XVIII (instruments). It is striking that South Asia is almost completely devoid of above-average RCA in these sections, apart from Sri Lanka for aircraft and parts (HS Chapter 88) and Pakistan for ships and boats (HS Chapter 89). In East Asia, in contrast, above-average RCAs are very widely spread in machinery and electronics, two industries where extensive production networks have developed. Above-average RCAs in vehicles (HS Chapter 87) and ships and boats (HS Chapter 89) are confined to Japan and Korea in East Asia. Above-average RCAs in Section XVIII (Instruments) are observed for Japan and for Hong Kong, China in optical photographic and medical apparatus (HS Chapter 90); in Hong Kong, China and in the PRC for watches, clocks, and parts (HS Chapter 91); and Japan, Korea, Indonesia, and the PRC for musical instruments (HS Chapter 92).

For the purposes of this study, one conclusion to emerge from the analysis of RCAs is that there appears to be no sector (as defined under the HS sections) in which South Asia's above-average RCAs do not overlap to a significant degree with above-average RCAs in East Asia. In particular, in the textiles, clothing, and footwear sectors, where South Asia's above-average RCAs are most extensive, South Asian economies face head-on competition across the board from a number of East Asian economies, especially the PRC and Southeast Asia. It can be noted, as well, that Tables 2.14 to 2.18 do not include RCA data for the so-called CLMV countries of Southeast Asia (Cambodia, Lao PDR, Myanmar, and Viet Nam).[6] Their inclusion would undoubtedly increase the extent to which South Asia is shown to face overlapping Southeast Asian RCAs in the clothing

---

[6]   Taipei,China was not included in Tables 2.9 to 2.13.

Table 2.16   Above-Average RCAs for East and South Asian Economies in 2004: HS Sections XI–XII

	JPN	KOR	HKG	SIN	INO	MAL	PHI	THA	CAM	PRC	IND	BAN	PAK	SRI
Section XI: Textiles														
H1-50 Silk	1.6		2.0							5.6	13.7			
H1-51 Wool, animal hair, horsehair, yarn, and fabric thereof			1.5							1.9		1.1		
H1-52 Cotton			3.9		2.3					2.2	5.1	1.1	43.3	
H1-53 Vegetable textile fibers nes, paper yarn, woven fabric			3.2				1.0			2.2	4.9	85.4	1.2	17.3
H1-54 Man-made filaments		3.4	1.7		3.9			1.4		2.2	3.0		5.9	
H1-55 Man-made staple fibers		1.9	1.6		5.7	1.3		3.3		2.0	3.2		2.8	1.2
H1-56 Wadding, felt, nonwovens, yarns, twine, cordage, etc.		1.4					1.1	1.5	1.8			3.6	2.1	1.7
H1-57 Carpets and other textile floor coverings										1.1	8.4	1.2	16.4	1.4
H1-58 Special woven or tufted fabric, lace, tapestry, etc.		2.5	2.9					1.2		2.9	1.2	3.0	4.8	4.5
H1-59 Impregnated, coated, or laminated textile fabric		3.1	1.1		1.0					1.2				
H1-60 Knitted or crocheted fabric		5.3	5.4							2.5			6.6	1.6
H1-61 Articles of apparel, accessories, knit or crochet			3.6		1.8		1.1	1.5	52.5	3.4	2.4	32.4	9.8	13.8
H1-62 Articles of apparel, accessories, not knit or crochet			2.9		3.0		1.3	1.1	2.6	3.3	3.1	23.7	4.7	21.0

continued on next page....

Table 2.16 continued

	JPN	KOR	HKG	SIN	INO	MAL	PHI	THA	CAM	PRC	IND	BAN	PAK	SRI
H1-63 Other made textile articles, sets, worn clothing, etc.										4.0	7.0	8.3	53.6	2.1
Section XII: Footwear and Headgear														
H1-64 Footwear, gaiters and the like, parts thereof			3.3		3.1			1.2	2.2	3.9	1.6		1.2	
H1-65 Headgear and parts thereof		1.9	3.7		1.2		1.0		6.2	4.5		13.2		8.1
H1-66 Umbrellas, walking sticks, seat-sticks, whips, etc.			5.5		1.3					8.0				
H1-67 Bird skin, feathers, artificial flowers, human hair			10.8		3.2		1.3	1.8	6.3	6.3	3.0			1.7

BAN = Bangladesh; CAM = Cambodia; HKG = Hong Kong, China; HS = harmonized system of tariff classification; IND = India; INO = Indonesia; JPN = Japan; KOR = Republic of Korea; MAL = Malaysia; PAK = Pakistan; PHI = Philippines; PRC = People's Republic of China; RCA = revealed comparative advantage; SIN = Singapore; SRI = Sri Lanka; THA = Thailand.

Source: Calculated from Comtrade 2004 Data.

Table 2.17   Above-Average RCAs for East and South Asian Economies in 2004. HS Sections XIII–XV and XIX–XXI

	JPN	KOR	HKG	SIN	MAL	PHI	THA	CAM	PRC	IND	BAN	PAK	SRI
Section XIII: Stone and Glass Products													
H1-68 Stone, plaster, cement, asbestos, mica, etc. articles										1.2	1.7		
H1-69 Ceramic products					1.3			1.7		2.0			2.7
H1-70 Glass and glassware	1.2				1.2					1.1			
Section XIV: Gemstones													
H1-71 Pearls, precious stones, metals, coins, etc.			2.9					1.5			9.6		2.4
Section XV: Metals and Metal Products													
H1-72 Iron and steel	1.3	1.5									1.8		
H1-73 Articles of iron or steal										1.4	1.7		
H1-74 Copper and articles thereof		1.1			1.8		1.9				1.7		3.3
H1-75 Nickel and articles thereof					5.7								
H1-76 Aluminum and articles thereof													
H1-78 Lead and articles thereof						1.1				2.4			1.2
H1-79 Zinc and articles thereof		2.2	1.5	1.2									
H1-80 Tin and articles thereof				7.8	27.0	6.7		3.8		1.6			
H1-81 Other base metals, cements, articles thereof	1.3						2.2			2.7			
H1-82 Tools, implements, cutlery, etc. of base metal	1.3									1.8	1.1		
H1-83 Miscellaneous articles of base metal			1.2							1.6			

continued on next page....

Table 2.17 continued

	JPN	KOR	HKG	SIN	MAL	PHI	THA	CAM	PRC	IND	BAN	PAK	SRI
Section XIX: Arms and Ammunition													
H1-93 Arms and ammunition, parts and accessories thereof													
Section XX: Miscellaneous													
H1-94 Furniture, lighting, signs, prefabricated buildings					2.0	1.2		1.0		2.2		1.1	
H1-95 Toys, games, sports requisites			6.9							4.1		3.3	
H1-96 Miscellaneous manufactured articles	1.5	1.0	2.3		1.1		1.4	1.0		2.6		1.1	1.9
Section XXI: Art and Antiques													
H1-97 Works of art, collectors pieces and antiques									5.7		3.1		
H1-99 Commodities not elsewhere specified	1.8			1.3			15.0						

BAN = Bangladesh; CAM = Cambodia; HKG = Hong Kong, China; HS = harmonized system of tariff classification; IND = India; JPN = Japan; KOR = Republic of Korea; MAL = Malaysia; PAK = Pakistan; PHI = Philippines; PRC = People's Republic of China; RCA = revealed comparative advantage; SIN = Singapore; SRI = Sri Lanka; THA = Thailand.

Source: Calculated from Comtrade 2004 Data.

Table 2.18   Above-Average RCAs for East and South Asian Economies in 2004: HS Sections XVI–XVIII

	JPN	KOR	HKG	SIN	MAL	PHI	THA	CAM	PRC	IND	BAN	PAK	SRI
Section XVI: Machinery and Electronics													
H1-84 Machinery, boilers, nuclear reactors, etc.	1.4	1.1		1.4		1.3	1.2	1.1	1.4				
H1-85 Electrical, electronic equipment	1.6	2.1	2.5	2.8		2.5	1.7	1.5	1.6				
Section XVII: Transport Equipment													
H1-86 Railway, tramway locomotives, rolling stock, equipment									3.6				
H1-87 Vehicles other than railway, tramway	2.1	1.3											
H1-88 Aircraft, spacecraft, and parts thereof													1.5
H1-89 Ships, boats, and other floating structures	3.0	8.3										3.1	
Section XVIII: Instruments													
H1-90 Optical, photo, technical, medical, etc. apparatus	2.0		1.2										
H1-91 Clocks and watches and parts thereof			7.9					1.6	1.2				
H1-92 Musical instruments, parts and accessories	2.4	1.9			9.4				2.7				

BAN = Bangladesh; CAM = Cambodia; HKG = Hong Kong, China; HS = harmonized system of tariff classification; IND = India; JPN = Japan; KOR = Republic of Korea; MAL = Malaysia; PAK = Pakistan; PHI = Philippines; PRC = People's Republic of China; RCA = revealed comparative advantage; SIN = Singapore; SRI = Sri Lanka; THA = Thailand.

Source: Calculated from Comtrade 2004 Date.

and footwear industries. Viet Nam, in particular, is likely to be a formidable competitor for South Asia in a range of labor-intensive industries. In addition to textiles, clothing, and footwear, extensive overlaps in RCAs between South and East Asian economies, again mainly the PRC and Southeast Asia, are also found for animal and plant products; rubber products; and hides, skins, and leather products. Pakistan's RCAs in labor-intensive manufactures overlap with the RCAs of a number of East Asian economies.

The above-average RCAs of South Asian countries are found principally in the labor-intensive manufacturing sectors and the natural resource-based sectors, as would be expected on the basis of their resource endowments. The relatively weak performance of South Asian exports in Northeast Asian markets, and of exports from South Asia countries other than India in Southeast Asian markets, suggests that South Asian countries have struggled to maintain competitiveness with their direct competitors in these sectors among the East Asian economies.

Indian exports, unlike those of other South Asian countries, have performed relatively well in Southeast Asian markets at least. India stands out as having RCAs for a number of products that are not shared by other South Asian countries, such as ores, slag and ash, organic and inorganic chemicals, tanning and dyeing extracts, iron and steel, some other metal products, and tools and implements. In each case, however, there are substantial overlaps with RCAs in East Asia.

In contrast, there are a number of sectors where East Asian economies enjoy extensive above-average RCAs while above-average RCAs for South Asia are largely absent: machinery and electronics, transport equipment, instruments, pulp and paper products, wood and wood products, and foodstuffs. Many of these are sectors characterized by more advanced levels of technology. This may help to explain the findings of low export similarity between South Asian and East Asian economies despite an overlap in RCAs.

Commodity Complementarity

Table 2.19 summarizes the calculations of commodity complementarity indexes for the same East and South Asian country groupings that were used to calculate the export similarity indexes. One immediately striking feature of this table is the mismatch in commodity complementarity between India and the rest of South Asia. India has well-above-average commodity complementarity with the rest of South Asia, but the rest of South Asia has very low commodity complementarity with India. In other words, India's potential exports correspond closely with the rest of South

Table 2.19   Commodity Complementarity Indexes for East and South Asian Country Groupings, Indexes of Commodity Complementarity with Partners

Partners	India	Other South Asia	Japan/ Rep. of Korea	PRC	Hong Kong, China/ Singapore	Southeast Asia
India		0.5	0.8	0.7	1.0	1.1
Other South Asia	1.6		0.9	1.0	0.9	1.2
Japan/Rep. of Korea	1.1	1.1		1.0	1.0	1.0
PRC	0.9	0.7	1.1		1.3	1.1
Hong Kong, China/ Singapore	1.0	1.3	1.1	1.4		1.2
Southeast Asia	0.9	0.6	1.1	1.0	1.3	

PRC = People's Republic of China.

Source: Calculated from Comtrade data for 2004.

Asia's potential imports, but the rest of South Asia's potential exports do not correspond at all closely with India's potential imports.

Mismatches, albeit somewhat less pronounced, also characterize the trade of both India and the rest of South Asia with Japan, Korea, and Southeast Asia. The commodity complementarity of the South Asian countries with Southeast Asia is below average—strongly so in the case of the rest of South Asia—while the reverse complementarity of Southeast Asia with South Asia is above average. Southeast Asia's potential exports correspond significantly with South Asia's potential imports, but South Asia's potential exports do not correspond well with Southeast Asia's potential imports, especially in the case of the rest of South Asia. The opposite mismatch applies in the case of Japan and Korea. South Asia has above-average commodity complementarity with Japan and Korea, meaning that its potential exports correspond well with the potential imports of those two countries, but Japan and Korea have below-average commodity complementarity with South Asia, indicating that their potential exports are not so well matched with South Asia's potential imports. This is a surprising result, given the obvious divergence in comparative advantage that Japan and Korea enjoy vis-à-vis South Asia. A similar mismatch applies to the rest of South Asia's trade with Singapore and Hong Kong, China, where the rest of South Asia has well-above-average commodity complementarity with the two city-states, but Singapore and Hong Kong, China have below-average commodity complementarity with the rest of South Asia. India's trade with Singapore and Hong Kong, China, on the other hand, is characterized by average commodity complementarity in both directions. India's trade with the PRC exhibits somewhat below-average commodity complementarity in both directions, indicating that the potential exports of neither country correspond particularly well to the potential imports of the other. The rest of South Asia also has below-average complementarity with the PRC, but the PRC's commodity complementarity with South Asia is average.

In the case of trade within East Asia, there are no cases of below-average commodity complementarity. In the cases of trade of Hong Kong, China and Singapore with Southeast Asia and with the PRC, commodity complementarity is above average in both directions. Japan has slightly above average commodity complementarity with the PRC; Hong Kong, China; Singapore; and Southeast Asia, as does Southeast Asia with the PRC. In each case, however, the commodity complementarity in the reverse direction is only average.

To summarize the information available from the commodity complementarity indexes:

- India's export profile is well matched with the import profiles of the rest of South Asia, Japan, and Korea. Its import profile is well matched to the export profile of Southeast Asia. Its export profile is not well matched to the import profiles of the PRC or Southeast Asia, and its import profile is not well matched to the export profile of South Asia, Japan, Korea, or the PRC.

- The rest of South Asia has an export profile well matched to the import profiles of Japan; Korea; Hong Kong, China; and Singapore. Its import profile is well matched to the export profile of Southeast Asia. The export profile is not well matched with the import profiles of India, the PRC, or Southeast Asia. Its import profile is not well matched to the export profiles of Japan; Hong Kong, China; or Singapore.

- Southeast Asia's export profile is well matched to the import profiles of all other groups except Japan and Korea, for which it is neutral. Its import profile is well matched to the export profiles of Japan; Korea; Hong Kong, China; and Singapore. Its import profile is not well matched to the export profiles of India or the rest of South Asia.

- The PRC's export profile is well matched to the import profiles of Singapore and Hong Kong, China. Its import profile is well matched to the export profiles of Japan; Korea; Hong Kong, China; and Singapore. Its export profile is not well matched to the import profile of India and its import profile is not well matched to the export profiles of India or the rest of South Asia.

- Japan and Korea have export profiles that are well matched to the import profiles of all East Asian groups, and import profiles that are well matched to the export profiles of India and the rest of South Asia.
- Singapore and Hong Kong, China have export profiles that are well matched to the import profiles of Southeast Asia and the PRC, and import profiles that are well matched to the export profiles of the PRC, Japan, Korea, and the rest of Southeast Asia. Their import profiles are not well matched to the export profiles of the rest of South Asia.

In summary, commodity complementary has either a favorable or neutral influence on intra-East Asian flows, while its influence on South–East Asia trade is mixed, but with a predominance of unfavorable influences. There is also a mixed influence on intra-East Asian trade. Table 2.20 illustrates these points.

Changes in Trade in Leading Commodities, By Country

The following summary highlights some of the salient features at the commodity group level of each country's trade with countries in the other group in 1999/2000 and 2004/05:

The PRC

- Exports to South Asia are dominated by machinery and electrical and electronic goods, which recorded a 589% increase over the period, with especially rapid growth to India and strong growth also to Bangladesh and Pakistan.
- Exports of textiles to South Asia also grew strongly over the period, increasing by 230% over the period, with strong increases in exports to Bangladesh and Pakistan as well as to India. Exports of chemicals grew strongly to India, and by 224% to South Asia overall.
- Exports of other products also grew strongly, but from a much lower base.
- Imports from South Asia are dominated by a massive rise in imports from India in the minerals and fuels category. Imports from India of metals and metal products and also chemicals grew strongly from a much lower base. Thus a large part of the increase in the PRC's imports from India appears to be related to the PRC's quest for raw materials.
- Textiles imports grew sharply from Pakistan and to a lesser extent from India.

Japan

- Japan's exports grew more slowly than the PRC's. The largest category was machinery and electrical and electronic goods, exports of which grew significantly to India, Pakistan, and Bangladesh, but fell

Table 2.20 Influence of Commodity Complementarity on Trade Flows in East and South Asia: Summary

Commodity Complementarity	South Asia to East Asia	East Asia to South Asia	South Asia to South Asia	East Asia to East Asia
	Influence of trade flows (+ or -)			
India -> Rest of South Asia			+	
Rest of South Asia -> India			-	
India -> Japan and Republic of Korea	+			
Japan and Republic of Korea -> India		-		
India -> People's Republic of China (PRC)	-			
PRC -> India		-		
India -> Hong Kong, China and Singapore				
Hong Kong, China and Singapore -> India				
India -> Southeast Asia	-			
Southeast Asia -> India		+		
Rest of South Asia -> Japan and Republic of Korea	+			
Japan and Republic of Korea -> Rest of South Asia		-		
Rest of South Asia -> PRC	-			
PRC -> Rest of South Asia		+		
Rest of South Asia -> Hong Kong, China and Singapore		+		
Hong Kong, China and Singapore -> Rest of South Asia				
Rest of South Asia -> Southeast Asia		+		
Southeast Asia -> Rest of South Asia				
Japan and Republic of Korea -> PRC				+
PRC -> Japan and Republic of Korea				
Japan and Republic of Korea -> Hong Kong, China and Singapore				+
Hong Kong, China and Singapore -> Japan and Republic of Korea				
Japan and Republic of Korea -> Southeast Asia				+
Southeast Asia -> Japan and Republic of Korea				
PRC -> Hong Kong, China and Singapore				+
Hong Kong, China and Singapore -> PRC				+
PRC -> Southeast Asia				
Southeast Asia -> PRC				
Hong Kong, China and Singapore -> Southeast Asia				+
Southeast Asia -> Hong Kong, China and Singapore				+

PRC = People's Republic of China.
Source: Calculated from Comtrade 2004 data.

to Sri Lanka, with the overall increase in exports to South Asia only a modest 7%. Exports of transport equipment (i.e., mainly motor vehicles) were smaller but grew much more strongly, by 64% over the period, mainly to Bangladesh rather than to India.

- Like the PRC, Japan sharply increased its imports from South Asia in the minerals and fuels category over the period. The overall increase was 64%, almost entirely from India.
- Other major imports from South Asia were gemstones and textile products. Imports of the latter from South Asia fell, mainly because of a sharp drop in imports from Pakistan. Imports of marine and animal products from South Asia fell by 48%. On the other hand, imports of chemicals, machinery, and electrical and electronic goods, almost entirely from India, rose strongly from a low base.

Korea

- Korea's exports to South Asia were dominated by the export of machinery and electrical and electronic equipment to India, and these exports grew dramatically over the period. Exports to India of metals, metal products, and transport equipment also grew strongly from relatively low bases. Exports of these products to Pakistan and Bangladesh also grew but much less strongly and from a much lower base.
- Exports of textiles to Bangladesh and Sri Lanka fell over the period.
- Korea's imports from South Asia were sourced predominantly from India and to a much lesser extent from Pakistan and to an even lesser extent from Sri Lanka. Imports of minerals and fuels from India grew strongly to become easily Korea's largest imports from South Asia. Imports of textiles and clothing from India, formerly Korea's largest imports from South Asia, remained relatively stable over the period. Imports from India of metals and metal products, foodstuffs, and chemicals showed significant growth. Imports of textiles and clothing from Pakistan and Sri Lanka fell, while imports from Pakistan of mineral products and fuels rose strongly from a very low base.

Hong Kong, China

- Exports were dominated by exports of gemstones to India, which increased over the period by 126% to all South Asian destinations. Exports to South Asia of machinery and electronic goods, mainly to India, were also substantial and increased by 112% over the period. There were also significant but relatively slow-growing exports over the period of textile products to Bangladesh, Sri Lanka, and, a lesser extent, India.

- Imports are completely dominated by imports of gemstones from India, so that these products are the major item traded between South Asia and Hong Kong, China. Imports from all South Asian sources increased by 87% over the period. Imports in hides, skins, and leather—mainly from India and Pakistan—rose by 169%, but from a very low base. Imports of textile products from Pakistan were significant, but imports from all South Asian sources fell slightly, mainly because of a fall in imports from India.

Singapore

- Exports are dominated by machinery and electrical and electronic goods, mainly to India, which increased by 92% over the period to all South Asian destinations. Other significant exports to South Asia (particularly Pakistan and India) were chemical products, which increased by 78% over the period, and metals and metal products, which increased by 65%. Exports of fuels were significant but relatively static.
- Imports were heavily dominated by products from India in the categories of fuels, minerals, and gemstones. Imports from South Asia of products in these categories rose exceptionally strongly over the period, by 1,334% (fuels) and 702% (minerals and gemstones). Other significant imports, mainly from India, were in the categories of metals and metal products (up by 150%), machinery, electrical and electronic goods, and chemical products.

Indonesia

- Exports to South Asia were dominated by oils and fats (up 229%) and fuel and minerals (up 190%). Most of these exports went to India, but there were also significant exports to Pakistan and Bangladesh. Relatively small but growing exports of textile products were recorded to Bangladesh, India, Pakistan, and Sri Lanka. There were also significant exports to India of chemical products and vegetable products.
- Imports from South Asia came almost entirely from India and Pakistan. The largest imports from South Asia were chemical products and metals and metal products, up by 258% and 253% respectively. These were almost entirely from India. Imports of foodstuffs, again sourced mainly from India, increased by 36%, and vegetable products, minerals and fuels, and textile products all had minor roles.

Malaysia

- Exports were dominated by fuels and minerals, mainly to India. Exports of oils and fats were a significant item, but they fell over the period in the Japanese market, while rising to Pakistan and remaining fairly stable to Bangladesh. Exports of machinery, electrical and electronic goods, and chemical products showed strong growth over the period, mainly to India but also to Pakistan, Bangladesh, and Sri Lanka.

- Malaysia's imports from South Asia are sourced largely from India. The largest items were marine and animal products, metals and metal products, vegetable products, chemical products, and machinery and electrical and electronic goods, all of which were at similar levels in 2005. Imports of machinery and electrical and electronic goods fell over the period while imports in the other five product categories rose, especially metals and metal products (which rose by 140% over the period), vegetable products (128%), chemical products (233%), and animal and marine products (92%). Pakistan and Bangladesh were minor sources of marine and animal products, and Pakistan was also a source of vegetable products. Textile products were a significant but declining import from India and to a lesser extent from Pakistan.

Philippines

- Machinery and electrical and electronic goods were the Philippines' main exports to South Asia, having increased by 43% over the period. The trends, however, vary among South Asian markets. The largest share of these products goes to India, and these exports have been increasing strongly, as have exports to Bangladesh and Pakistan. Exports of these products to Nepal and Sri Lanka, on the other hand, have fallen.
- The Philippines has also developed substantial exports of transport equipment to South Asia. These exports increased by 185% over the period. In this case, Pakistan is the larger and faster-growing market, but exports to India were also substantial and growing strongly. Exports to South Asia of pulp and paper products, as well as metal and metal products, grew by 289% and 75%, respectively. These exports went mainly to India, although small but increasing exports were also made to Pakistan. Exports of these products to Bangladesh were low and falling, as were exports of metals and metal products to Sri Lanka. Textile products were a small but growing export to Bangladesh, India, and Pakistan, but a declining export to Sri Lanka.
- The Philippines' imports were sourced mainly from India. The leading imports were marine and animal products, metals and metal products, chemical products, vegetable products, and machinery and electrical and electronic goods, all of which increased substantially over the period. Imports from South Asia of metals and metal products and vegetable products rose especially strongly (by 350% and 166%,

respectively). India was far and away the main source of these imports. Textile products were a significant but declining import from India and Pakistan.

Thailand

- All of Thailand's main exports to South Asia increased strongly over the period: machinery and electrical and electronic goods (up by 152%), plastic and rubber products (173%), textile products (105%), chemicals (132%), metals and metal products (179%), and minerals and fuels (134%). Although India is a leading market—and especially dominant for machinery and electrical and electronic goods and plastic and rubber products—Thailand is distinctive among Southeast Asian economies in having developed levels and rates of increase in exports of a number of product categories to other South Asian markets that are comparable to its exports to India. Examples include textile products to Pakistan and Bangladesh and chemicals and metals and metal products to Pakistan alone. Significant exports of some of these products have also been developed to Sri Lanka.
- Thailand's leading imports from South Asia have also risen strongly, and are dominated to a much greater extent than its exports by India. Gemstones led the way, followed by metals and metal products, chemicals, minerals and fuels, foodstuffs, and machinery and electrical and electronic goods. Originally significant imports from Sri Lanka in the latter product category appear to have shrunk to negligible proportions over the period.

India

- The most striking feature of India's exports to East Asia was a dramatic increase in exports in the minerals and fuels category to the PRC. Taken together with substantial increases in exports to other East Asian countries, notably Japan and Singapore, exports in this product category rose by 1,331% over the period.
- Exports of gemstones rose by 62%, again principally to the PRC, but some stones also went to Japan, Singapore, and Thailand. Exports of chemicals and metals and metal products to East Asia also rose by 142% and 299% respectively over the period, principally again to the PRC but with contributions also from other East Asian markets including Malaysia and Singapore.
- Significant percentage increases from a relatively low base took place in exports of metals and metal products to Southeast Asian economies, notably Indonesia, Malaysia, Singapore, and Thailand. Similar

percentage increases (also off a low base) took place in exports of machinery, and electrical and electronic goods to Singapore.

- India's leading imports from East Asia were also relatively diverse by country. Imports of machinery and electrical and electronic goods were the largest, spread across the PRC; Japan; Malaysia; Singapore; Hong Kong, China; and Thailand.
- Chemical imports came next, also spread across a range of sources: the PRC; Hong Kong, China; Japan; Malaysia; and Singapore.
- It is interesting to note that transport equipment did not figure in India's leading imports from East Asia.

Bangladesh

- Bangladesh's most dynamic exports to East Asia were in the hides, skins, and leather category, which saw increases of 192% in exports over the period. The main market and biggest increase was for Hong Kong, China. Other significant markets for these products were Japan, Korea, and the PRC. A number of Bangladesh's other leading exports actually fell during the period, notably animal and marine products exports to Japan and Thailand. Exports of textile products also fell, the net result of rising exports to the PRC but declining exports to Japan; Korea; Hong Kong, China; Indonesia; and Thailand.
- Textile products are Bangladesh's leading import from East Asia, and were up 33% over the period, sourced principally from PRC; Hong Kong, China; Indonesia; and Korea. The sharpest increases were seen in fuels and minerals, mainly from Singapore; machinery and electrical and electronic goods, mainly from the PRC and Japan; transport equipment, mainly from Japan; and oils and fats sourced mainly from Malaysia, Indonesia, and Singapore. Imports of fuels and minerals actually fell slightly over the period, and there was a more substantial fall in imports of metals and metal products.

Sri Lanka

- Sri Lanka's main export markets in East Asia are Hong Kong, China; Japan; and, to a lesser extent, Singapore. With the exception of machinery and electrical and electronic goods, its leading exports to East Asia all showed modest increases over the period. The largest export—textile products—rose only slightly, however the net outcome of sharply reduced exports to Korea and increased exports to Japan; Hong Kong, China; Singapore; Thailand; and Indonesia. Exports of machinery and electrical and electronic goods to Thailand, Japan, and Korea fell sharply, but rose sharply to Singapore, resulting in a net fall in exports to East Asia of 47%. Exports of gemstones (directed mainly to Japan; Hong Kong, China; and Thailand), marine and animal products (mainly to Japan; Hong Kong, China; and Singapore), and vegetable products (mainly to Japan and Hong Kong, China) all rose modestly.

- There were very large increases in exports of foodstuffs and transport equipment.
- Sri Lanka's leading imports from East Asia were generally flat over the period. Textile imports from PRC; Hong Kong, China; and Thailand rose. At the same time, however, imports from Japan, Korea, and Singapore fell. Imports of transport equipment from Japan fell, offset by an increase in imports from Singapore. Imports of machinery and electrical and electronic goods rose from Hong Kong, China and from Singapore, but fell from Japan, Korea, and Thailand. Significant increases occurred in imports of fuels and minerals (mainly from Malaysia and Singapore) and metals and metal products (mainly from the PRC and Singapore).

Pakistan[7]

- Pakistan's exports to East Asia are dominated by textile products, which account for two thirds of the total. Pakistan's main markets are (in order of importance) Hong Kong, China; PRC; Korea; Japan; and Indonesia.
- Pakistan's main imports from Indonesia are machinery and electrical and electronic goods (mainly from the PRC, Japan, and Korea), transport equipment (mainly from Japan), chemicals (mainly from Japan and Korea), and oils and fats (mainly from Indonesia and Malaysia).

Nepal

- Nepal's exports are also dominated by textile products, accounting for only under half the total, mainly to Japan and to Hong Kong, China. Vegetable products and oils and fats, mainly to the PRC, are other significant exports.
- Leading imports are machinery and electrical and electronic goods, mainly from the PRC, Japan, Korea, and Singapore.

Disaggregating to 4-digit level of the Harmonized System (HS)

Finally in this section, Tables 2.21 and 2.22 present a tabulation of the leading exports and imports at the HS 4-digit level in East Asian economies'

---

[7] Data for Pakistan and Nepal was not available on a comparable basis for 1999/2000.

trade with South Asia. Also shown is the increase for each item over the most recent 5-year period.

Some general observations can be made from a comparison of Tables 2.21 and 2.22. There are examples of products that are traded in both directions between the two regions, particularly diamonds, which are exported from Hong Kong, China and from Singapore to South Asia as well as from South Asia to all four East Asian subregions. Petroleum products follow a similar pattern. Cyclic hydrocarbons and copper are traded in both directions between South and Southeast Asia.

The much more predominant impression, however, is that the leading exports from East Asia to South Asia are much more weighted toward finished and high technology goods than the leading exports from South Asia to East Asia. Leading South Asian exports to East Asia include iron ore, nonferrous metals and ores, granite, leather, oil cake, beef, and crustaceans. East Asian's leading exports to South Asia include computers and integrated circuits; TV, radio, and telecommunications equipment; motor vehicles and motor vehicle parts; and antibiotics. Where there is two-way trade in the same industry, the exports of East Asia tend to be at a higher level of processing; for example, East Asian leading exports feature fabric while South Asian exports feature yarn. For the steel industry, South Asia's leading exports to East Asia including ferro-alloys, pig iron, and rolled steel, while East Asia's leading exports to South Asia include rolled steel of a heavier grade.

Pattern of Protection in East and South Asia

What clearly distinguishes South from East Asia is its higher level of protection. As illustrated in Table 2.23, even the average applied most-favored-nation (MFN) tariffs of the most open economy in South Asia—Sri Lanka—are still higher than the average registered in East and Southeast Asian countries. It should likewise be stressed, however, that South Asia has experienced a progressive reduction of tariff barriers, especially in the last decade. Bangladesh, for instance, has brought down its protection level from 58% in 1992 to 15% in 2006; India from 35% (1997) to 19% (2005); and Pakistan from 39% (1991) to 14% (2006).

Southeast Asia mirrors the asymmetries in protection generally observed in the whole Asian region, as it brings together the most open economies of Singapore and Brunei Darussalam and the still relatively protected markets of Viet Nam, Cambodia, Thailand, and Lao PDR. East Asian countries, in turn, display higher levels of agricultural protection than most of Southeast Asia. In fact, as Table 2.24 shows, Korea's average MFN tariffs for agriculture, pegged at 48% in 2006, are higher than those in India (38% in 2005).

Table 2.21   East Asia's Leading Exports to South Asia in 2004–2005, HS 4-digit basis

Code	Commodity Description	Annual Averages ($ '000)		Change (%)
		2004/05	1999/2000	
People's Republic of China				
H1-8525	Radio and television (TV) transmitters, TV cameras	763,051	19,002	3,916
H1-8517	Electric apparatus for line telephony, telegraphy	436,783	38,435	1,036
H1-5407	Woven synthetic filament yarn, monofilament (>67 decitex [dtex])	381,781	31,035	1,130
H1-8471	Automatic data processing machines (computers)	333,280	57,397	481
H1-5208	Woven cotton fabric (>87% cotton, <200 grams per square meter [g/m^2])	320,470	142,472	125
H1-9999	Commodities not elsewhere specified	273,740	103,748	164
H1-2941	Antibiotics	257,612	82,202	213
H1-2704	Retort carbon, coke or semi-coke of coal, lignite, peat	252,052	109,069	131
H1-5209	Woven cotton n.e.s. (>85% cotton, >200 g/m^2)	239,310	66,567	260
Japan and The Republic of Korea				
H1-8525	Radio and TV transmitters, TV cameras	1,074,857	20,941	5,033
H1-8708	Parts and accessories for motor vehicles	897,699	312,318	187
H1-8703	Motor vehicles for transport of persons (except buses)	449,334	292,367	54
H1-7208	Hot-rolled products, iron/steel (width >600 millimeters [mm], not clad)	240,419	72,670	231
H1-8704	Motor vehicles for the transport of goods	229,639	107,579	113
H1-7210	Flat-rolled iron/steel (>600 mm, clad, plated or coated)	210,902	84,509	150
H1-2710	Oils petroleum, bituminous, distillates, except crude	204,403	113,483	80
H1-8409	Parts for internal combustion spark ignition engines	193,303	148,688	30
H1-8445	Machines for processing textile fibers	182,058	42,660	327

continued on next page…

Table 2.21 continued

Code	Commodity Description	Annual Averages ($ '000) 2004/05	Annual Averages ($ '000) 1999/2000	Change (%)
Hong Kong, China and Singapore				
H1-7102	Diamonds, not mounted or set	1,218,371	465,587	162
H1-8473	Parts, accessories, except covers, for office machines	865,077	386,324	124
H1-8471	Automatic data processing machines (computers)	631,773	456,797	38
H1-2710	Oils petroleum, bituminous, distillates, except crude	607,974	642,484	(5)
H1-8525	Radio and TV transmitters, TV cameras	419,225	37,270	1,025
H1-8542	Electronic integrated circuits and microassemblies	355,878	189,000	88
H1-2902	Cyclic hydrocarbons	248,965	64,923	283
H1-6002	Knit or crochet fabric, n.e.s.	216,193	144,230	50
H1-9999	Commodities n.e.s.	205,296	77,470	165
Southeast Asia				
H1-1511	Palm oil and its fractions, not chemically modified	2,289,662		
H1-2709	Petroleum oils, oils from bituminous minerals, crude	515,160		
H1-2603	Copper ores and concentrates	436,462		
H1-2701	Coal, briquettes, oviods etc., made from coal	371,509		
H1-8471	Automatic data processing machines (computers)	347,647		
H1-8542	Electronic integrated circuits and microassemblies	202,465		
H1-2902	Cyclic hydrocarbons	195,765		
H1-8708	Parts and accessories for motor vehicles	182,543		
H1-3823	Chemical industry products n.e.s.	138,783		

HS = Harmonized System of tariff classification, n.e.s. = not elsewhere specified, $ = US dollars, ( ) = negative value, % = percent.

Source: Calculated from Comtrade data.

Table 2.22 East Asia's Leading Imports from South Asia in 2004/05, HS 4-Digit Basis

Code	Commodity Description	Annual Averages ($ '000) 2004/05	Annual Averages ($ '000) 1999/2000	Change (%)
People's Republic of China				
H1-2601	Iron ores and concentrates, roasted iron pyrites	4,637,756	259,990	1,684
H1-5205	Cotton yarn not sewing thread >85% cotton, not retail	533,694	369,153	45
H1-2818	Aluminum oxide, hydroxide and artificial corundum	302,517	32,612	828
H1-7102	Diamonds, not mounted or set	253,709	52,403	384
H1-2610	Chromium ores and concentrates	225,106	54,378	314
H1-7219	Rolled stainless steel sheet (width > 600 millimeters [mm])	224,643	6,534	3,338
H1-3901	Polymers of ethylene, in primary forms	224,253	13,153	1,605
H1-7210	Flat-rolled iron/steel (> 600 mm, clad, plated or coated)	223,047	18	
H1-2516	Granite, porphyry, basalt, sandstone, etc.	170,461	59,810	185
Japan and The Republic of Korea				
H1-2710	Oils petroleum, bituminous, distillates, except crude	1,071,803	220,722	386
H1-7102	Diamonds, not mounted or set	503,001	475,636	6
H1-5205	Cotton yarn not sewing thread > 85% cotton, not retail	478,482	592,669	(19)
H1-2601	Iron ores and concentrates, roasted iron pyrites	478,034	413,133	16
H1-0306	Crustaceans	268,617	624,247	(57)
H1-2304	Diamonds, not mounted or set	226,901	154,162	47
H1-7202	Ferro-alloys	153,030	68,602	123

continued on next page...

Table 2.22 *continued*

Code	Commodity Description	Annual Averages ($ '000)		Change (%)
		2004/05	1999/2000	
H1-4104	Bovine or equine leather, not hair, not chamois, patent	78,420	45,778	71
H1-2306	Oil-cake other than soya-bean or groundnut	58,492	4,507	1,198
Hong Kong, China and Singapore				
H1-7102	Diamonds, not mounted or set	4,278,340	1,826,041	134
H1-2710	Oils petroleum, bituminous, distillates, except crude	1,217,556	75,183	1,519
H1-5205	Cotton yarn not sewing thread > 85% cotton, not retail	470,513	491,101	(4)
H1-4104	Bovine or equine leather, not hair, not chamois, patent	220,842	97,234	127
H1-7113	Jewellery and parts, containing precious metal	149,420	61,120	144
H1-4106	Goat or kid skin leather, without hair	134,780	38,960	246
H1-7601	Unwrought aluminum	130,425	71,494	82
H1-5209	Woven cotton n.e.s., (> 85% cotton, > 200 grams per square meter [g/m^2])	121,634	150,515	(19)
H1-2902	Cyclic hydrocarbons	65,235	131	49,791
Southeast Asia				
H1-7102	Diamonds, not mounted or set	292,889		
H1-2304	Soya-bean oil-cake and other solid residues	270,831		
H1-2902	Cyclic hydrocarbons	267,578		
H1-0202	Meat of bovine animals, frozen	198,910		
H1-2710	Oils petroleum, bituminous, distillates, except crude	177,566		
H1-7208	Hot-rolled products, iron/steel, width (> 600 mm, not clad)	132,867		
H1-7403	Refined copper and copper alloys, unwrought	126,519		
H1-7201	Pig iron and spiegeleisen in primary forms	95,873		
H1-1001	Wheat and meslin	82,600		

HS = Harmonized System of tariff classification, n.e.s. = not elsewhere specified, $ = US dollars, ( ) = negative value, % = percent.

Source: Calculated from Comtrade data.

The fact that tariffs still constitute important revenue sources, particularly for South Asian countries, could lead to some reluctance to further liberalize trade. Although the trend is toward reduced influence, trade taxes continue to take up more than 25% of total government revenues

Table 2.23   Applied MFN Tariffs in 2006, %

South Asia	MFN	Southeast Asia	MFN	East Asia	MFN
India	19.2	Viet Nam	16.8	Korea	12.1
Pakistan	14.3	Cambodia	14.3	PRC	9.9
Nepal	14.0	Thailand	10.0	Japan	5.6
Sri Lanka	11.2	Lao PDR	9.7	**East Asia**	**9.2**
Bangladesh	15.2	Malaysia	8.5		
South Asia	**14.8**	Indonesia	6.9		
		Philippines	6.3		
		Myanmar	5.6		
		Brunei Darussalam	3.3		
		Singapore	0.0		
		Southeast Asia	**8.4**		

MFN = most favored nation.
Source: World Trade Organization, Trade Profiles, 2006.

for Bangladesh, 19% for Nepal, 17% for Pakistan, and 14% for India (see Figure 2.1). In 1992, import tariffs contributed 19% to total Thai government earnings, but that has fallen to 10% at present.

Summary

Recent years have seen a surge in trade between East and South Asia, albeit from a very low base. Trends in the aggregate trade flow mask very considerable variations in the interregional trade flows of individual economies. A very large share of the increased trade of East Asian economies with South Asia over the period has consisted of increased trade with India. The exports of Bangladesh to East Asia actually fell between 1999–2000 and 2004–2005, and export growth of Sri Lanka to East Asia was minimal.

Table 2.24   Agriculture versus Non-Agriculture MFN Tariffs 2006, %

	Agricultural	Nonagricultural
Korea, Republic of	47.8	6.6
India	37.6	16.4
Japan	24.3	2.8
Viet Nam	24.2	15.7
Sri Lanka	23.8	9.2
Thailand	22.1	8.2
Lao People's Democratic Republic	19.5	8.5
Cambodia	18.1	13.7
Bangladesh	17.3	14.9
Pakistan	16.3	14.0
China, People's Republic of	15.7	9.0
Nepal	14.9	13.7
Malaysia	12.3	7.9
Philippines	9.6	5.8
Myanmar	8.7	5.1
Indonesia	8.2	6.8
Brunei Darussalam	5.2	3.0

MFN = most favored nation, % = percent.

Source: World Trade Organization, Trade Profiles, 2006.

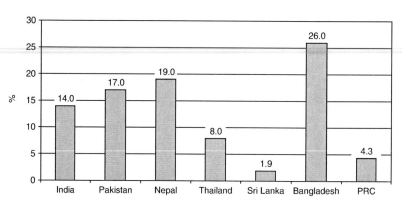

Figure 2.1   Importance of Tariff Revenues, % of total government revenues

PRC = People's Republic of China.
Source: ADB Country Studies (various), 2007.

"Stylized facts" on the intraregional and interregional trade of the two regions include the following:

- Intraregional trade is highly developed within East Asia, and within the East Asian subregions of Northeast and Southeast Asia. Intraregional trade has also been developing within South Asia, although not to the same extent as in East Asia.
- East Asia's share of South Asia's trade is very much higher than South Asia's share of East Asia's trade.
- East Asia accounts for a much higher share of South Asia's imports than of its exports.
- South Asian exports perform relatively poorly in the more open and dynamic markets of East Asia.
- East Asian exports perform relatively well in the less open markets of South Asia, although these markets account for a comparatively small share of East Asian exports.

South Asia's economies generally lag far behind East Asia's in terms of openness. South Asian economies' more limited engagement in international trade is likely to have a significant bearing on these economies' trade performance relative to East Asia and on trade between the two regions.

Trade intensity indexes show that trade relations within East Asia are generally very intense. In other words, East Asian economies have much more trade with each other than would be expected on the basis of their shares of world trade. Trade intensity indexes are also predominantly above average for trade within South Asia, both at the aggregate regional level and at the individual country level, with the important exception of India's import intensity with South Asia as a whole, which in turn appears to be a reflection of India's low import intensity with Pakistan.

Trade flows between East and South Asia exhibit considerable variations in intensity. The Northeast Asia-4 economies tend to export more to and import less from South Asian economies than would be expected on the basis of the corresponding shares of world trade. Korea and the PRC have the most intense trade relations with South Asia among the Northeast Asia-4 economies, with bilateral trade intensity index values that are almost uniformly above average. Japan has the least intensive trade relations of the Northeast Asia-4, with bilateral trade intensity index values uniformly below average. Taipei,China has more intensive trade relations with South Asia than Japan does, but less intensive relations than do Korea or the PRC.

Singapore appears to have been somewhat more successful than Hong Kong, China in establishing itself as a focal point for trade with both Southeast and South Asia.

The ASEAN-5 group of Southeast Asian countries has developed more intense trading relations with South Asia than has the Northeast Asian-4 group. From the South Asian side, all of India's trade intensity indexes with Southeast Asia are above average at the aggregate regional level. The other four South Asian countries (Bangladesh, Nepal, Pakistan, and Sri Lanka) all have above-average import intensities with Southeast Asia—associated with above-average bilateral trade intensities—but below-average export intensities and market share ratios. In other words, Southeast Asia has a larger share of the imports of these four South Asian countries than its share of world imports, but accounts for a smaller share of their exports. The former effect dominates the latter so that the bilateral trade intensity is above average.

South Asian countries as a group have below-average trade intensities with the major markets of Northeast Asia. In particular, the export intensities of the South Asian countries are uniformly well below average with Northeast Asia as a whole, and are almost uniformly below average also with individual Northeast Asian economies.

While export similarity indexes indicate that there is little overlap between the export specializations of East and South Asian economies, analysis of RCAs shows that South Asian countries generally face formidable competition from East Asian countries in all of the products in which they have above-average RCAs. For the most part, these are labor-intensive manufacturing and natural-resource-based sectors, although India also has above-average RCAs in sectors such as chemicals, metals, and metal products. Above-average RCAs are conspicuously lacking in South Asia in sectors characterized by more advanced technology. East Asian economies, by contrast, have considerable strength in the area of advanced technology.

Commodity complementarity indexes indicate that East Asian export profiles are well-matched to South Asian import profiles, but South Asian export profiles are not as consistently well-matched to East Asian import profiles. The relatively weak performance of South Asian exports in Northeast Asia, and of exports of South Asian countries other than India in Southeast Asia, suggests that South Asian countries have struggled to some extent to maintain competitiveness with their direct competitors among the East Asian economies. Analysis of the commodity composition of the interregional trade of South Asian economies suggests that to a significant extent the increase in South Asian exports to East Asia has been a response to increased East Asian demand for raw materials rather than an expression of South Asian manufacturing competitiveness in sectors of comparative advantage. Increased exports of raw materials has been one of the principal bright spots for South Asian exports to East Asia, along with the relatively strong performance in Southeast Asian markets of Indian exports, including manufactured exports as well as natural-resource-based products.

Free Trade Agreements in East and South Asia

Characteristics of Free Trade Agreements in East and South Asia

FTAs in East and South Asia can usefully be placed in three categories, each of which has three subcategories.

The first category distinguishes between those that are long established, those that are recently established, and those that are still under negotiation. The recently established initiatives belong to the new wave of PTAs that began around the turn of the century in both East and South Asia. In most cases, they have entered into force only recently so that a judgment on their effectiveness is not yet possible. Nevertheless, they have introduced new dimensions into approaches to preferential trade architecture, not least because of the presence in a number of the agreements of developed country partners that are required by the World Trade Organization's (WTO) rules to comply with the provisions of General Agreement on Tariffs and Trade's (GATT) Article XXIV, including the requirement for elimination of trade barriers on "substantially all the trade" between the parties. The presence of Japan as a developed economy in East Asia makes this a relevant consideration in discussing regional trade architecture.

A second three-way subdivision is between intra-East Asian FTAs, intra-South Asian FTAs, and FTAs that seek to link East and South Asia. The long-established FTA in East Asia is the ASEAN Free Trade Area (AFTA), launched in 1992, which superseded the earlier ASEAN preferential tariff regime. Since the turn of the century there has been an avalanche of new intra-East Asian FTAs, many of them involving ASEAN or its members as parties. Recently concluded FTAs include agreements between the following parties:
- Japan and Singapore
- Japan and Malaysia
- Japan and the Philippines
- ASEAN and the PRC
- ASEAN and Korea
- Korea and Singapore
- The PRC and Hong Kong, China
- The PRC and Macao, China

Agreements are still under negotiation between Japan and Indonesia and between Japan and Thailand, and negotiations between Japan and Korea, currently suspended, could reopen at some point in the future. Japan has recently begun to negotiate an FTA with ASEAN as a group, which would parallel FTAs between the ASEAN–PRC and ASEAN–Korea. A more ambitious proposal for an East Asian FTA (EAFTA), comprising the ASEAN+3 group of the PRC, Japan, and Korea with the 10 members of ASEAN, continues to be discussed and studied. In addition to these intra-East Asian initiatives, many East Asian countries are also actively pursuing FTAs with partners beyond the region, including the United States, Canada, Mexico, Chile, Peru, Australia, New Zealand, the Gulf States, the European Free Trade Association (EFTA) countries, and, perhaps in the near future, even the European Union.

South Asia also has a long-established PTA initiative, the South Asian Free Trade Agreement (SAFTA), which superseded the earlier South Asian Preferential Trade Agreement (SAPTA). More recently, separate agreements have been concluded between India and Sri Lanka, and between Pakistan and Sri Lanka.

The longest-established initiative seeking to link East and South Asia is the Asia-Pacific Trade Agreement (APTA), formerly called the Bangkok Agreement, which has been in operation since 1976. It now counts as members PRC, India, and Korea as well as Bangladesh, Lao PDR, and Sri Lanka. More recently, an agreement has been concluded between India and Singapore.

Linking initiatives still under way include negotiations for an FTA between ASEAN and India. Proposals also exist for FTAs between the PRC and India, the PRC and Pakistan, and Pakistan and Singapore. For several years the members of the Bay of Bengal Initiative for Multi-Sectoral Technical and Economic Cooperation (BIMSTEC) (Bangladesh, India, Myanmar, Sri Lanka, Thailand, Bhutan, and Nepal) have been in negotiations for establishment of a BIMSTEC FTA. Japan has recently proposed a Comprehensive Economic Partnership for East Asia (CEPEA), which broadens the concept of EAFTA to include as potential members India, Australia, and New Zealand.

This leads to the third of the proposed three-way classifications. Many of the early FTAs in all three contexts were "partial preference" agreements, involving reductions—sometime quite modest—of tariffs rather than their complete elimination, and covering a limited range of goods. Traditionally, the "partial preference" approach has been associated with "positive list" agreements, but it is clear that, as some recent initiatives demonstrate, a "negative list" agreement can also be a partial preference agreement. The experience with partial preference agreements is that they rarely, if ever, lead to comprehensive liberalization of trade between the members.

At the other end of the spectrum are agreements involving at least one developed country member, that are therefore required to comply with GATT Article XXIV. In these agreements, there are essentially two approaches to the treatment of sensitive products. One approach is to take full advantage of the looseness of the Article XXIV requirement for coverage of "substantially all trade" by simply excluding a minority of products from the provisions of the agreement. The other approach is to provide formally for the elimination of tariffs on all goods while building in mechanisms to ease the impact of the agreement in sensitive sectors. These mechanisms can include provisions for very lengthy periods for phasing out tariffs, and also for the use of tariff-rate quotas and special safeguards during the phase-out period. Typically the tariff-rate quotas are gradually expanded during the phase-out period, and they may be done away with completely, along with the special safeguard mechanisms, at the end of the phase-out period. In some agreements, however, there is provision for the tariff-rate quotas and special safeguards to continue to operate beyond the end of the phase-out period.

A number of modern agreements take this approach. Although the point is often obscured by the provision for gradual implementation, the provisions of these agreements may envisage that trade between the parties will become fully liberalized at the end of the implementation period, however far in the future that may be.

The third approach is intermediate between the first two, and is exemplified by AFTA. It involves dividing the universe of products into three lists: an inclusion list for products that are to become duty free at the end of the implementation period, a sensitive list for products that are to be subject to less stringent liberalization commitments, and an exclusion list for the products for which no commitments are to be made. In the case of AFTA, there have been successive rounds of negotiation that have provided a mechanism for transferring products from the exclusion list to the sensitive list and from the sensitive list to the inclusion list. At present, AFTA can be considered to be a fully fledged Article XXIV-compatible agreement as the liberalization scheme covers 99% of total intra-ASEAN trade, with only about 200 ASEAN tariff lines remaining on the exclusion list.

Free Trade Agreements: Opportunity or Threat?

Conventionally, FTAs have been viewed as opportunities to increase trade. As PTAs proliferate, however, they increasingly come to be viewed as defensive mechanisms, whereby countries seek to maintain market access parity with competitors that have already secured, or are actively pursuing, PTAs with partners of mutual interest.

Countries that are unable to participate in the rush to FTAs, for whatever reason, may find themselves increasingly disadvantaged as PTAs proliferate. The larger the group of countries involved in the PTAs, and the greater their importance as trade partners, the greater will be the likely cost of exclusion.

The costs of exclusion clearly depend on the margins of preference created in the FTAs in question for the products of export interest to the excluded country. If MFN tariffs in the members of the FTA are low for the products in question, the cost will be less. In the case of developed-country PTA members, the costs of exclusion for developing countries may be further reduced if the countries have access to favorable Generalized System of Preferences (GSP) rates. This will be especially the case for least-developed countries (LDCs) that have duty-free, quota-free access.

In the case of Japan, for example, while it is well known that tariffs are high for some sensitive products, MFN tariffs are low for most products, and a GSP scheme provides reduced-duty or duty-free access for some products, particularly for LDCs. The availability of duty-free access will expand further as Japan implements the decision of the 2005 Hong Kong WTO ministerial agreement.

Another example is provided by the case of the PRC. The early harvest provisions of the ASEAN–PRC Free Trade Agreement ensured that many of the earliest and deepest tariff cuts in that agreement occurred for the agricultural and other food products in HS Chapters 1 to 15. Preferential rates for some South Asian countries are available through APTA (for India, Bangladesh, and Sri Lanka) and for Pakistan and Bangladesh through separate arrangements for some products. These preferential rates do not, however, appear to be aligned with the preferences available to ASEAN members under AFTA. The PRC does not have a GSP scheme, although it has a policy of making duty-free access available to LDCs. The overall result can be that South Asian countries may face significant discrimination relative to Southeast Asian countries in the PRC market.

Purely as an example, Table 2.25 sets out the MFN, general, and various preferential duty rates applied by the PRC in 2006 to selected product in HS Chapter 3 (fish). This is a product category where there is considerable overlap in RCA between South and Southeast Asian countries. Members of ASEAN receive duty-free access under AFTA and in some cases under other arrangements as well, giving them a substantial margin of preference over the MFN rate. For South Asian countries partial preferences are provided under APTA, and also for Pakistan under a separate arrangement, but this leaves them at a considerable disadvantage relative to ASEAN countries, except in the case of certain products for which Bangladesh has also been granted duty-free access.

Table 2.25 is intended to be illustrative only. Much more work would be needed to establish how widespread situations like this are, and the extent of their significance for disadvantaged exporting countries, not only in relation to the PRC but also other East Asian countries. If the issue proves significant for South Asian exports to East Asia, the rapidly expanding range of FTAs being negotiated by East Asian countries will make it an urgent issue as well.

The information on the relative importance of the two regions in each other's trade suggests that this is a potentially much more significant concern for South Asia than for East Asia. Nevertheless, the issue may well turn out to be important in relation to South Asian imports as well as East Asian imports. In addition to the relatively low weight of South Asia in East Asia's trade, it is possible that East Asian exporters to South Asia have been sheltered for the time being from effects like these by the relatively modest nature of the preferences that South Asian countries have granted to each other, or indeed to other FTA partners. If, however, South Asian countries move toward deeper integration, granting each other fuller preferences, the discriminatory effect on nonpreferred exporters to their markets could be very large, given the relatively high level of South Asian MFN tariffs. On the other hand, these same high MFN tariffs mean that in cases where they are completely eliminated in intra-South Asia trade, very large margins of preference can be created, and the erosion of these preferences, for example by implementation of new preferential trading arrangements with East Asian countries, could have profound effects on the South Asian industries concerned. The impact of preference erosion could be especially severe on exports to India from other South Asian countries.

Rules of Origin

The proliferation of FTAs has also given rise to concerns that a "spaghetti bowl" of overlapping PTAs contains inconsistent rules, especially rules of origin (ROOs). When considering the possible future trade architecture of East and South Asia, one question that might usefully be considered is the possibility of achieving some rationalization of the ROOs being used in PTAs around the two regions.

ROOs are crucial to the structure of any FTA, and this fact is now well recognized as a crucial factor in determining the true degree of liberalization of trade in goods provided by any FTA. For example, the costs imposed on exporters by ROOs in record-keeping and documentation,

Table 2.25   Comparison of PRC's MFN General and Preferential Tariff Rates (%) for Selected Products

Goods Code	Description	MFN	ASEAN	APTA	PAK	HKG	MAC	GEN	BRU	INO	MAL	MYA	SIN	THA	CAM	LAO	PHI	VIE	BAN
0303.3200	Fish, fresh or chilled - yellow	12	0	9	9	0		40							0	0	0	0	
0303.3900	Fish, fresh or chilled - other	12	0	8	8	0		40				0			0	0	0	0	
0302.6500	Fish, fresh or chilled - shaker	12	0	9	9	0		40							0	0	0	0	
0303.3900	Fish, frozen, other	10	0	8	8			40				0			0	0		0	
0303.4200	Fish, frozen, yellowfin tuna	12	0	9	9			40							0	0		0	0
0303.4300	Fish, frozen, skipjack tuna	12	0	9	9			40							0	0	0	0	
0303.4900	Fish, froze, excluding fish fillet	12	0	9	9			40							0	0	0	0	
0303.7400	Fish, frozen, mackerel	10	0	6.7	6.7			40							0	0	0	0	
0303.7900	Fish, frozen, other	10	0	6.7	5	0		40				0			0	0	0	0	
0304.2000	Frozen fillets	10	0			0		70				0			0	0		0	0
0304.9000	Frozen fillets, other	10	0			0		70							0	0		0	
0305.5920	Shark fins	15	0				0	80							0	0		0	0
0305.5990	Fish, dried, smoked, in meals	16	0			0		80				0			0	0		0	0
0305.1311	Shelled shrimps	8	0	5	4	0		70				0			0	0		0	
0306.1312	Shrimps - northern pandalu	5	0		2.5	0		70				0			0	0		0	0
0306.1319	Shrimps - frozen in shell	5	0	4	2.5	0		70				0			0		0	0	
0307.9910	Abalone, sea cucumbers	10	0			0		80				0			0	0	0	0	
0307.9930	Clams, etc.	10	0					70							0	0	0	0	

APTA = Asia-Pacific Trade Agreement; ASEAN = Association of Southeast Asian Nations; BAN = Bangladesh; BRU = Brunei Darussalam; CAM = Cambodia; GEN = General; HKG = Hong Kong, China; INO = Indonesia; LAO = Lao People's Democratic Republic; MAC = Macao, China; MAL = Malaysia; MFN = most favored nation; MYA = Myanmar; PAK = Pakistan; PHI = Philippines; PRC = People's Republic of China; SIN = Singapore; THA = Thailand; VIE = Viet Nam.

Source: Customs Tariff of Import and Export of the People's Republic of China 2006.

production down-time, and switches to more expensive input mixes count as an offset to the cost advantages provided by tariff preferences. ROOs can often be more important than tariff preferences in determining the degree of market access provided by an FTA. One indication of this is the extent to which exporters choose not to use the tariff preferences available under FTAs, and prefer to continue to incur the MFN tariff when exporting to the partner country. Empirical simulations performed by Manchin and Pelkmans-Balaoing (2007), for instance, show that in the case of AFTA, preferential tariffs affect intraregional imports only at very high margins (around 25 percentage points). This indicates the likelihood of high administrative costs attached to the exploitation of preferences, particularly with regard to ROO compliance.

ROOs can vary enormously in the extent to which they restrict or facilitate trade. Some rules are deliberately restrictive, responding to pressures from import-competing producers demanding to be sheltered from the additional competition that would otherwise result from the tariff preferences under an FTA. A sufficiently restrictive ROO can completely nullify the effect of the tariff preferences. In other cases, restrictive ROOs may simply reflect poor design. ROOs perceived by one partner in an FTA as unduly restrictive can be an ongoing source of friction between the partners.

There is widespread consensus on the desirable features of ROOs that are intended to facilitate trade. These rules should be as straightforward as possible, and should be transparent, clear and consistent, and should not impose unnecessary compliance costs (easy to understand and to comply with," and "simple, consistent and flexible").

Regional value content (RVC) rules are often preferred because of their apparent simplicity. It is now widely understood however that the simplicity of RVC rules is largely illusory. LDCs that are also exporters are particularly burdened by high compliance costs, not to mention the more fundamental difficulty of local sourcing to meet whatever RVC requirements are imposed. Implementation is particularly problematic in the absence of automation; clear, harmonized rules; and readily accessible conciliation or contest procedures. The actual valuation of costs, thus, heavily depends on the judgment of individual customs officials, and this even more in an environment where contesting the rulings would imply more delays without any certainty of neutral arbitration.

In the case of AFTA, one key explanation for the underutilization of ASEAN preferences lies in the nature of the regional production chains where non-ASEAN content could be very high (Manchin and Pelkmans-Balaoing 2007). Although the ROOs of AFTA requiring at least 40%

regional content could be considered relatively liberal, electronics and electrical products, for instance, which make up approximately 40% of intra-ASEAN trade, typically have an ASEAN value-added component of only 8–15% (Dennis and Yusof 2003).

The potentially cumbersome procedures involved in the valuation and certification of declared costs under the RVC rule may have prodded ASEAN to increasingly shift to the change of tariff classification (CTC) criteria for all products. The advantage of a CTC rule is that it provides greater certainty to exporters than an RVC rule. Exporters know the tariff classification of their inputs and their final products, and this knowledge is all that is required for complete certainty as to whether their products will satisfy the ROOs. The same ROOs in AFTA are applied to its FTA with the PRC. The more recent agreement with Korea now carries the CTC as an alternative criteria for all products, which results in the rather strange scenario of the ASEAN–Korea FTA now being potentially more flexible than AFTA itself.[8] In the case of the ASEAN–Japan FTA, however, the more restrictive product specific rules of the various bilateral FTAs between Japan and the individual ASEAN countries will most likely define the parameters of the ASEAN–Japan agreement.

Another problem is that the Harmonized System (HS) of tariff classification was not designed with ROOs in mind, with the result that a single CTC rule will not be suitable for every product. As a consequence, comprehensive application of the CTC approach typically requires that the ROO for each tariff category be specified. This results in extremely lengthy ROO schedules. The complexity of these schedules is, however, more apparent than real. Exporters are generally interested only in a small number of products. They will therefore be interested in the small sections of the schedules that deal with those products, and these sections will provide them with precise guidance as to the requirements for meeting the ROOs on the products they wish to export.

On the other hand, the effect of CTC rules for particular products will be understood only by the firms involved in the production and export of those products. The limited extent of understanding of the effect of a particular ROO can assist special interests in taking advantage of this nontransparency to press for ROOs that will severely restrict the ability of competitors in the partner country to export under the preferences.

---

[8] For products where the preferential tariffs under the free trade agreement (FTA) between ASEAN and The Republic of Korea approximate the levels found in the ASEAN Free Trade Area (AFTA), then preferences in the latter will be eroded by the more liberal rules offered by the former.

The resulting ROOs may be both restrictive and complex. The success of automotive and textile interests in securing restrictive ROOs for their sectors under the North American Free Trade Agreement (NAFTA) has given CTC rules a bad name in some quarters. Vigilance on the part of exporters and their supporting officials is needed to counter attempts to introduce restrictive CTC ROOs.[9] The ROOs for textile clothing in the Thailand–Australia FTA (TAFTA), which require exporters to meet both the CTC rule and a 55% RVC rule, provide a classic example of how introduction of CTC rules can be manipulated to restrict rather than facilitate trade.

Important new FTAs have the potential to simplify or further complicate the ROO environment in which international business operates. The choice of ROO in such PTAs is thus a very important matter, so that it becomes really important to know which ROO is most effective in facilitating trade. A rigorous study to assess the effect on trade of each type of ROO is urgently needed to assist in resolving this issue.

Policy Implications of Free Trade Agreements in East and South Asia

Any proposal for new arrangements or institutions to intensify trade linkages between East and South Asia will necessarily face major challenges. It is likely that countries that have so far restricted their involvement in preferential trade to partial preference agreements will have to consider deeper commitments on trade in goods than they have previously considered comfortable. If new arrangements do proceed, however, the alternative of being left out is likely to be even more unpalatable.

Analysis of trade flows between the two regions suggests that there are underlying issues that will need to be addressed if potential benefits of new trade arrangements are to be realized.

The impact of any new preferential arrangements on trade patterns developed under existing preferential agreements will need to be carefully considered. Depending on the configuration of new arrangements, the impacts could stem from both preference erosion and the creation of new patterns of discrimination and exclusion among the countries of the two regions. There is likely to be concern, especially in South Asia, over the possible adjustment costs arising from these impacts as well as from the likely deepening of liberalization commitments under any new arrangements. Strategies to address these adjustment costs will inevitably assume great importance.

---

[9] This can be done by excluding inputs from certain tariff headings, attaching an essential process in the transformation of the product, or turning the regional value content into an additional, instead of an alternative, rule to satisfy origin.

At the same time, any proposals for new trade arrangements in East Asia and South Asia should take into account the need to develop sensible and efficient rules for the conduct of regional trade, where these are needed to supplement or rationalize existing rules, as in the case of ROOs.

Investment

As is the case with trade, investment links between East and South Asian economies need to be seen in the context of the overall investment performance and involvement in international investment flows of the economies of both regions.

Table 2.26 highlights important differences between the economies of the two regions. At the regional aggregate level, the ratio of gross fixed capital formation (GFCF) to GDP is similar in Southeast and South Asia. In Southeast Asia, Viet Nam is an outlier, with a substantially higher ratio, and Singapore and Thailand are also significantly above the regional average. In South Asia, Pakistan and Nepal have ratios significantly below the regional average. In Northeast Asia, GFCF/GDP ratios in Japan; Hong Kong, China; and Taipei,China are comparable to the regional averages for Southeast and South Asia, but the ratio is dramatically higher for the PRC and substantially higher for Korea as well. The combined ratio for the developing economies of Northeast Asia, therefore, is more than 50% higher than the ratios for Southeast and South Asia.

Where South and Southeast Asia differ dramatically is in the share of GFCF accounted for by foreign direct investment (FDI), and correspondingly in the ratio of FDI to GDP. Both of these ratios in Southeast Asia are approximately four times as high as in South Asia. The figures for Southeast Asia are clearly heavily influenced by Singapore, where FDI at 15% of GDP accounts for almost two thirds of GFCF. At the individual economy level, the figures for Southeast Asia are in fact highly variable. The ratios of FDI to GFCF and GDP in Malaysia, Viet Nam, and Cambodia are much higher than in any South Asian economy, but in Indonesia and Thailand they are lower than in any South Asian economy except Nepal. In the Philippines and the Lao PDR these ratios are comparable to India and Bangladesh but lower than in Pakistan and Sri Lanka. Northeast Asia also exhibits considerable variation in these ratios, which are very high in Hong Kong, China as they are in Singapore. The PRC ratios are comparable to those for Viet Nam and Cambodia, whereas those for Korea and Taipei,China are comparable to those of India and Bangladesh. The region's most developed economy, Japan, is an outlier in terms of these ratios, with FDI accounting for an exceptionally small share of GFCF (less than 1%).

Table 2.26 Selected Aggregate Investment Indicators for Northeast, Southeast, and South Asian Economies 2004

	Gross Fixed Capital Formation	Inward FDI		Outward FDI	Mergers and Acquisitions	
	% of GDP	% of GFCF	% of GDP	$ million	Purchases $ million	Sales $ million
Northeast Asia	**37.0**	**10.1**	**3.7**	**53,521**	**5,207**	**445**
Japan	23.8	0.7	0.2	30,951	3,787	82
China, People's Republic of	45.0	8.2	3.7	1,805	1,125	217
Hong Kong, China	22.5	92.1	20.7	39,753	2,963	143
Korea, Republic of	29.4	3.8	1.1	4,792	409	55
Taipei,China	20.1	3.1	0.6	7,145	710	23
Southeast Asia	**22.4**	**14.3**	**3.2**	**13,620**	**13,235**	**285**
Brunei Darussalam						1
Cambodia	23.5	12.6	3.0	10		2
Indonesia	21.0	1.9	0.4	107	491	45
Lao People's Democratic Republic	20.2	3.5	0.7			1
Malaysia	20.5	19.1	3.9	2,061	816	57
Philippines	16.8	3.3	0.6	412	105	24
Singapore	24.0	62.7	15.0	10,667	11,638	91
Thailand	25.8	2.5	0.7	362	185	54
Viet Nam	32.3	11.3	3.7			
South Asia	**22.9**	**3.7**	**0.8**	**2,288**	**877**	**89**
Bangladesh	23.7	3.5	0.8	4		
India	23.4	3.4	0.8	2,222	863	80
Nepal	19.9	0.8	0.2			
Pakistan	18.5	6.2	1.2	56	14	5
Sri Lanka	22.7	5.1	1.2	6		2

FDI = foreign direct investment, GDP = gross domestic product, GFCF = global fixed capital formation, $ = US dollar, % = percent.

Notes: Figures for Northeast Asia include Macao, China; Mongolia; and Democratic People's Republic of Korea.
Figures for Southeast Asia include Timor Leste but exclude Myanmar.
Figures for South Asia include Afghanistan, Bhutan, and the Maldives.

Source: United Nations Conference on Trade and Development (UNCTAD), *World Investment Report 2005*.

Outflows of FDI from the combined regions are dominated by Japan and Hong Kong, China in Northeast Asia, and by Singapore in Southeast Asia. The outflow from South Asia is approximately one sixth of that of Southeast Asia, and is sourced almost exclusively from India. India's outflow of FDI is comparable to that of Malaysia and is much lower than those of Korea and Taipei,China as well as Hong Kong, China; Japan; and Singapore. Interestingly, however, it is slightly higher than the FDI outflow from the PRC.

The impression of South Asia's relatively low degree of engagement in international investment flows is reinforced by the data on mergers and acquisitions (M&As) in Table 2.26. South Asian involvement in M&As is at a relatively low level compared to East Asia, were M&A activity is dominated by Singapore, followed at substantially lower levels by Japan; Hong Kong, China; and the PRC. The much lower level of involvement in M&A activity in South Asia is completely dominated by India.

Table 2.27 indicates the distribution across countries of the FDI inflows and outflows of the combined East and South Asian regions. Predictably, the inflows are dominated by the PRC, accounting for over 40% of the total, while the PRC and Hong Kong, China together account for almost two thirds of the total. Singapore accounts for 10% of the total, so that over three quarters of the FDI inflow into the combined regions is directed to these three economies alone. East Asia accounts for over 95% of the FDI inflows of the combined regions. India is the only South Asian country accounting for more than 1% of the inflow into the combined regions, with 3.7% of the total, behind Japan and Korea as well as the PRC; Hong Kong, China; and Singapore.

The FDI outflows of the combined regions are also dominated by three economies: Hong Kong, China and Singapore this time together with Japan. India is again the only South Asian economy to register flows of any significance, accounting for only 2.2% of the total. Almost 98% of the FDI outflows of the combined regions come from East Asia.

Tables 2.28 to 2.30 show the sources of FDI inflows, and in some cases destinations of FDI outflows, between selected East and South Asian economies and the rest of the combined regions, based on data from the Japan External Trade Organization (JETRO) in the case of Japan and from the country studies in the case of the other economies. It is clear from these tables that South Asia plays only a very minor role in the FDI flows of East Asian economies. Thus over 25% of Japan's FDI outflows are directed to other East Asian economies, as against only 0.3% directed to India, the only South Asian economy to register. East Asia accounts for only a tiny fraction of FDI inflows into Japan, but the share from South Asia (India)

Table 2.27   Distribution of Involvement in FDI by East and South Asian Economies, 2004

	Outward FDI			Inward FDI	
	$ Mn	% of NE/ SE/S Asia		$ Mn	% of NE/ SE/S Asia
Hong Kong, China	39,753	39.6	PRC	60,630	41.7
Japan	30,951	30.8	Hong Kong, China	34,035	23.4
Singapore	10,667	10.6	Singapore	16,060	11.1
Taipei, China	7,145	7.1	Japan	7,816	5.4
Korea, Rep. of	4,792	4.8	Korea, Rep. of	7,687	5.3
India	2,222	2.2	India	5,335	3.7
Malaysia	2,061	2.1	Malaysia	4,624	3.2
PRC	1,805	1.8	Taipei,China	1,888	1.3
Philippines	412	0.4	Viet Nam	1,610	1.1
Thailand	362	0.4	Thailand	1,064	0.7
Indonesia	107	0.1	Indonesia	1,023	0.7
Other	103	0.1	Pakistan	952	0.7
Total	**100,380**		Macao, China	600	0.4
			Myanmar	556	0.4
			Philippines	469	0.3
			Bangladesh	460	0.3
			Other	702	0.5
			Total	**145,511**	

FDI = foreign direct investment, NE/SE/S Asia = Northeast/Southeast/South Asia, PRC = People's Republic of China, $ Mn = millions of US dollars, % = percent.

Source: United Nations Conference on Trade and Development (UNCTAD), *World Investment Report 2005.*

is negligible. East Asia accounts for almost two thirds of the massive FDI inflows into the PRC, but the share of India and other South Asian economies is again negligible. East Asia figures prominently in the FDI inflows of Thailand and outflows of Singapore, and somewhat less prominently in the inflows of Singapore, but in all of these cases the share of India in these flows is very small.

While South Asia is only a very minor factor in the FDI flows from East Asian economies, Tables 2.30 and 2.31, providing data on FDI flows of South Asian countries for a variety of years or periods, indicate that

Table 2.28   Selected Foreign Direct Investment (FDI) Data for Northeast Asian Economies

(a) Japan

FDI Outflows to East and South Asian Economies (2004) (% of total FDI Outflows)		FDI Inflows from East and South Asian Economies (2004) (% of total FDI Inflows)	
PRC	12.8	Singapore	1.4
Thailand	3.3	Korea, Republic of	0.6
Korea, Republic of	2.4	Hong Kong, China	0.1
Singapore	2.0	PRC	0.0
Hong Kong, China	1.8	Taipei,China	0.0
Taipei,China	1.3	Malaysia	0.0
Philippines	0.9	Thailand	0.0
Indonesia	0.9	Pakistan	0.0
Malaysia	0.4	Indonesia	0.0
Viet Nam	0.3	Philippines	0.0
India	0.3	India	0.0

Source: Japan External Trade Organization.

(b) People's Republic of China (PRC)

FDI Inflows from East and South Asian Economies (2004) (% of total FDI Inflows)	
Hong Kong, China	31.3
Korea, Republic of	10.3
Japan	9.0
Taipei,China	5.1
Singapore	3.3
Rest of Southeast Asia	1.7
India	0.0
Rest of South Asia	0.0

Source: Zhang (2008).

East Asia plays a somewhat more prominent (although not necessarily dominant) role in the FDI flows of India, and some but not all of the other South Asian economies. East Asia accounts for about 12.0% of the FDI inflows into India. The share of India's FDI outflows directed to East Asia is rather smaller at 8.4%, but over 5 times higher than the 1.6% share

Table 2.29   Selected Foreign Direct Investment (FDI) Data for Southeast Asian Economies

(a) Singapore

FDI Inflows from East and South Asian Economies (2000–2003) (% of total FDI Inflows)		FDI Outflows to East and South Asian Economies (2000–2003) (% of total FDI Inflows)	
Japan	13.8	People's Republic of China (PRC)	13.2
Malaysia	2.7	Malaysia	8.3
		Hong Kong, China	8.2
		Japan	2.4
		Taipei,China	2.4
		Korea, Republic of	1.8
		India	1.1

(b) Thailand

Investment Promotion Certificate Issues (2005) (% of total certificates issued)	
Japan	43.2
Hong Kong, China	2.5
Taipei,China	1.5
Korea, Republic of	0.4
PRC	0.4
Singapore	4.6
Malaysia	1.7
Indonesia	0.1
Philippines	0.1
India	0.2

Source: Rajan and Thangavelu (2008) and Chirathivat and Sabhasri (2008).

Table 2.30   Selected Foreign Direct Investment (FDI) Data for India

FDI Inflows from East and South Asian Economies (1991–2006) (% of actual FDI Inflows)		FDI Outflows to East and South Asian Economies (1996–2006) (% of approved investment)	
Japan	6.4	ASEAN	7.4
ASEAN	4.1	PRC	1.0
Korea, Republic of	2.1	Japan	0.0
PRC	0.0	Korea, Republic of	0.0
South Asia	0.0	South Asia	1.6

ASEAN = Association of Southeast Asian Nations, PRC = People's Republic of China.
Source: Kumar and Sharma (2008).

directed to other South Asian countries. It is notable that ASEAN features strongly in FDI flows between India and East Asia, accounting for about a third of FDI inflows into India from East Asia and almost 90% of India's FDI outflows to East Asia.

The shares of East Asia in FDI inflows into other South Asian economies, as indicated in Table 2.31, are only over 50% for Sri Lanka, only over 26% for Bangladesh, and only over 21% for Nepal. Malaysia and Singapore as well as the Northeast Asian economies are prominent among the source of East Asian inflows into Bangladesh and Sri Lanka in particular. India accounts for a relatively minor share (only over 6%) of Sri Lanka's FDI inflows and a negligible share of the FDI inflows of Bangladesh, although other South Asian countries account for 3.5% of inflows into the latter country. On the other hand, India is the dominant source of FDI inflows into Nepal, accounting for almost 40% of the total, with the share rising to only over 41% for South Asia as a whole when inflows from other South Asian countries are included. Pakistan is the outlier in Table 2.31 with only over 2% of FDI inflows sourced from East Asia and inflows from India and other South Asian countries that do not register in the data.

Summing up, East Asian economies generally have a high level of involvement in international FDI flows, and the FDI flows within East Asia are much larger than the FDI flows between East and South Asia or within South Asia. Measured by the ratios of FDI to GFCF and GDP, the involvement in international FDI flows of several East Asian economies is higher than for any South Asian economy, although South Asian

Table 2.31   Selected Foreign Direct Investment (FDI) Data for Other South
Asian Economies

(a) Pakistan		(b) Sri Lanka	
FDI Inflows from East and South Asian Economies (1991–2006) (% of total FDI Inflows)		**FDI Inflows from East and South Asian Economies (2005) (% of total FDI Inflows)**	
Japan	1.2	Malaysia	34.7
Hong Kong, China	0.7	Singapore	10.7
Singapore	0.3	Hong Kong, China	5.4
People's Republic of China (PRC)	0.1	India	6.2
Korea, Republic of	0.0		
(c) Bangladesh		(d) Nepal	
FDI Inflows from East and South Asian Economies (2005) (% of total FDI Inflows)		**FDI Inflows from East and South Asian Economies (to 2005) (% of total FDI Inflows)**	
Singapore	11.5	PRC	10.6
Hong Kong, China	6.3	Japan	3.5
Malaysia	3.9	Korea, Republic of	3.5
Korea, Republic of	3.5	Hong Kong, China	1.9
Taipei,China	1.4	Singapore	1.3
PRC	0.2	Thailand	0.3
India	0.3	Philippines	0.2
Rest of South Asia	3.5	Malaysia	0.1
		India	39.8
		Bangladesh	0.8
		Pakistan	0.5
		Sri Lanka	0.1

Source: Ul Haque and Ghani (2008) and Rashid (2008).

economies other than Nepal do have a slightly higher level of involvement
than the East Asian economies that are least engaged in international FDI
flows, such as Indonesia, Philippines, and Thailand. Only India among
South Asian economies is a significant source of outflows of FDI. India's
FDI outflows are broadly comparable with (although slightly higher than)

the PRC's and Malaysia's, but well below those of Hong Kong, China; Japan; Korea; Singapore; and Taipei,China. This latter group comprises the East Asian economies with the largest FDI outflows. It follows that India is also the only South Asian country to have invested substantially in East Asia, which as a region accounts for a modest share of Indian outward FDI, although Indian FDI represents only a tiny fraction of the FDI inflows into East Asia. Southeast Asia has been a particular focus for Indian FDI in East Asia. FDI flows from East Asia into South Asia are a very minor component of outward FDI flows of East Asian economies. They are, however, a very significant component of the FDI inflows into Bangladesh, Nepal, and Sri Lanka, and to a lesser extent of India. Pakistan sees little FDI from East Asia.

Table 2.32 shows the rankings of East and South Asian economies in the World Bank's "ease of doing business" index and also for the 10 characteristics from which the overall score for ease of doing business is derived. While it is natural to think that success in attracting FDI should be correlated with a high ranking for ease of doing business, Table 2.32 suggests that the relationship is by no means straightforward.

It is true that Singapore and Hong Kong, China—two of the most popular destinations for FDI in East Asia—rank first and fifth respectively on the ease of doing business index. On the other hand, the PRC has a very low ranking on the index, below all East Asian economies except Viet Nam, Philippines, Indonesia, Cambodia, and Lao PDR. Among the latter, Cambodia and Viet Nam also have a relatively high ratio of FDI to GFCF. India ranks behind the other four South Asian economies for ease of doing business. The low rankings of the PRC and India on the "ease of doing business" index might suggest that market size and potential may compensate for a relatively difficult business environment. By contrast, in Japan—the most developed and, on the official exchange rate measure, the largest economy in East or South Asia—FDI plays a very minor role, despite a high ranking on the ease of doing business index. Thailand, too, has a relatively low share of FDI in GFCF despite a comparatively high ranking on the ease of doing business index. Korea and Malaysia have very similar rankings for ease of doing business but differ considerably in the contribution of FDI to GFCF.

Nor does there appear to be any simple correlation between attractiveness as a destination for FDI and rankings for the individual components of the ease of doing business index. For example, Singapore; Hong Kong, China; and Malaysia are all relatively attractive destinations for FDI and all rank highly for investor protections. So, however, does Japan. India too has a comparatively high ranking for investor protection, despite a low

Table 2.32 Rankings of East and South Asian Economies in World Bank's Ease of Doing Business Survey for 2006

Economy	Ease of Doing Business Rank	Starting a Business	Protecting Investors	Enforcing Contracts	Dealing with Licenses	Employing Workers	Registering Property	Getting Credit	Paying Taxes	Trading Across Borders	Closing a business
Singapore	1	11	2	23	8	3	12	7	8	4	2
Hong Kong, China	5	5	3	10	64	16	60	2	5	1	14
Japan	11	18	12	5	2	36	39	13	98	19	1
Thailand	18	28	33	44	3	46	18	33	57	103	38
Korea, Rep. of	23	116	60	17	28	110	67	21	48	28	11
Malaysia	25	71	4	81	137	38	66	3	49	46	51
Taipei,China	47	94	60	62	148	154	24	48	78	42	4
Pakistan	74	54	19	163	89	126	68	65	140	98	46
Bangladesh	88	68	15	174	67	75	167	48	72	134	93
Sri Lanka	89	44	60	90	71	98	125	101	157	99	59
PRC	93	128	83	63	153	78	21	101	168	38	75
Nepal	100	49	60	105	127	150	25	101	88	136	95
Viet Nam	104	97	170	94	25	104	34	83	120	75	116
Philippines	126	108	151	59	113	118	98	101	106	63	147
India	134	88	33	173	155	112	110	65	158	139	133
Indonesia	135	161	60	145	131	140	120	83	133	60	136
Cambodia	143	159	60	118	159	124	100	174	16	114	151
Lao PDR	159	73	170	146	130	71	148	173	36	161	151

Lao PDR = Lao People's Democratic Republic, PRC = People's Republic of China.

Source: World Bank.

ranking for ease of doing business. Registering a property is comparatively easy in Singapore; PRC; Taipei,China; and Nepal, but much more difficult in Hong Kong, China and Korea.

These observations suggest caution in reaching firm conclusions on current and potential future investment flows between East and South Asia. Further research on this topic would be useful.

Policy Recommendations

1. While increased economic integration between East and South Asia can in principle be expected to benefit all countries of both regions, the impact will be much greater on the South Asian economies than on the East Asian ones. The form that increased integration between East and South Asia takes will have an important bearing on the impact on individual South Asian countries. India has been expanding its trade with East Asia much more rapidly than other South Asia countries. Integration with East Asia by India alone is likely to have significant adverse impacts on other South Asian countries. To avoid this, the other South Asian countries must open their economies to trade with East Asia in parallel with India. It is also important that more complete integration within South Asia should be pursued in parallel with the pursuit of greater integration with East Asia.

2. The relatively weak integration of South Asia with East Asia reflects to an important extent South Asian economies' general lack of openness. Formal trade barriers are an important factor contributing to this situation. To benefit from closer integration with East Asia, as well as from international trade more generally, it is important that South Asian countries consolidate and continue the steps they have begun to take to lower their trade barriers. Whereas progress in lowering trade barriers has hitherto tended to be uneven across South Asian economies, it is important that all South Asian economies move forward together in this endeavor. It goes without saying that East Asian economies should also continue to lower their trade barriers, which are still high in some East Asian economies.

3. Improved trade facilitation, together with greater attention to technical barriers to trade and "behind the border" impediments to trade, can also contribute to increasing economic openness and thus to the capacity to benefit from greater interregional integration. Bringing the costs of international trade more closely into line with best international practice is an important objective for the economies of both regions, especially the economies of South Asia.

4. The countries of the South Asian region exhibit a relatively narrow range of comparative advantages compared to the economies of East Asia. Furthermore, they generally face formidable competition from East Asian countries in all of the products in which they have comparative advantage. There are signs—such as for example the generally low export intensities found in their trade with East Asia—that they are lagging in competitiveness with their East Asian competitors. Increases in South Asian exports to East Asia, especially to the PRC, have tended to be concentrated in the natural resources sectors rather than manufacturing. These observations lead to the recommendation that in parallel to trade liberalization South Asian economies should take steps to boost the international competitiveness of the industries in which they have comparative advantage. This is best achieved by measures designed to increase the overall efficiency of the economy and improve the business environment.

5. It follows that trade liberalization efforts need to be embedded in a wider program of economic reforms that embrace monetary, fiscal, and labor market policies; competition, deregulation, and other measures of structural reform; and transparency and governance issues. This recommendation is applicable to most economies in South and East Asia, but it applies with particular force to the South Asian economies. Comparative data from East and South Asian economies suggests that increasing education and skill levels should be a particular priority in South Asia.

6. Steps should be taken to rationalize the "spaghetti bowl" of preferential trade agreements covering East and South Asia. Achieving consistency in rules of origin in the various preferential trade agreements in the regions is an especially important objective.

7. Further research should be undertaken to assess the current and potential future investment flows between East and South Asia.

APPENDIX

Appendix 2.1 Trade Shares of East and South Asian Countries, %

Shares in the Trade of Northeast Asia-4

	Japan Imports 2002–2004	Japan Exports 2002–2004	Korea, Republic of Imports 2002–2004	Korea, Republic of Exports 2002–2004	PRC Imports 2002–2004	PRC Exports 2002–2004	Taipei,China Imports 2002–2004	Taipei,China Exports 2002–2004	Northeast Asia-4 Imports 2002–2004	Northeast Asia-4 Exports 2002–2004
WORLD	100.0	100.0	100.0	100.0	100.0	100.0	100.0	100.0	100.0	100.0
Japan	0.0	0.0	20.4	8.8	17.0	13.3	25.4	8.3	12.8	7.0
Korea, Rep. of	4.7	7.4	0.0	0.0	10.4	4.6	6.9	3.1	6.3	4.8
PRC	19.7	11.8	12.2	19.1	0.0	0.0	8.7	14.6	9.8	9.0
Hong Kong, China	0.4	6.2	1.9	6.1	5.0	16.9	1.4	19.8	2.5	11.6
Taipei,China	3.2	7.1	2.5	4.7	5.1	2.6	0.0	0.0	3.4	4.3
Northeast Asia	28.0	32.5	37.0	38.7	37.5	37.3	42.4	45.7	34.7	36.7
Brunei Darussalam	0.5	0.0	0.3	0.0	0.1	0.0	0.0	0.0	0.2	0.0
Cambodia	0.0	0.0	0.0	0.1	0.0	0.1	0.0	0.2	0.0	0.1
Indonesia	4.2	1.5	2.7	1.4	1.3	1.0	2.4	1.1	2.7	1.3
Lao PDR	0.0	0.0	0.0	0.0	0.0	0.0	0.0	0.0	0.0	0.0
Malaysia	3.2	2.4	2.3	2.0	3.0	1.4	3.5	2.3	3.0	2.0
Myanmar	0.0	0.0	0.0	0.1	0.0	0.2	0.0	0.1	0.0	0.1
Philippines	1.9	1.9	1.1	1.6	1.4	0.7	2.4	1.8	1.6	1.4
Singapore	1.4	3.2	2.8	2.5	2.5	2.1	2.9	3.5	2.2	2.8

Lao PDR = Lao People's Democratic Republic, PRC = People's Republic of China.

continued on next page...

Continued

Shares in the Trade of Northeast Asia-4

	Japan		Korea, Republic of		PRC		Taipei,China		Northeast Asia-4	
	Imports 2002–2004	Exports 2002–2004	Imports 2002–2004	Exports 2002–2004	Imports 2002–2004	Exports 2002–2004	Imports 2002–2004	Exports 2002–2004	Imports 2002–2004	Exports 2002–2004
Thailand	3.1	3.4	1.0	1.4	2.0	0.9	1.8	1.8	2.2	2.0
Viet Nam	0.8	0.6	0.3	1.4	0.4	0.7	0.4	1.9	0.5	0.9
Southeast Asia	15.1	13.1	10.5	10.4	10.7	7.0	13.3	12.6	12.5	10.4
East Asia	43.1	45.6	47.5	49.0	48.2	44.4	55.7	58.3	47.2	47.1
Bangladesh	0.0	0.1	0.0	0.3	0.0	0.3	0.0	0.3	0.0	0.2
India	0.6	0.5	0.8	1.3	1.1	0.9	0.5	0.6	0.8	0.8
Nepal	0.0	0.0	0.0	0.0	0.0	0.0	0.0	0.0	0.0	0.0
Pakistan	0.0	0.2	0.1	0.2	0.1	0.4	0.0	0.2	0.1	0.3
Sri Lanka	0.0	0.1	0.0	0.1	0.0	0.1	0.0	0.2	0.0	0.1
South Asia	0.7	0.9	0.9	2.0	1.2	1.7	0.6	1.2	0.9	1.4

continued on next page....

Continued

Shares in the Trade of Hong Kong, China and Singapore

	Hong Kong, China		Singapore		Combined	
	Imports 2002–2004	Exports 2002–2004	Imports 2002–2004	Exports 2002–2004	Imports 2002–2004	Exports 2002–2004
WORLD	100.0	100.0	100.0	100.0	100.0	100.0
Japan	11.8	5.4	12.0	6.7	11.9	5.9
Korea, Republic of	4.8	2.1	4.0	4.2	4.5	2.9
China, People's Republic of	43.7	42.2	8.9	7.2	31.0	28.3
Hong Kong, China			2.4	9.7	0.9	3.8
Taipei,China	12.5	0.8	3.9	2.6	9.4	1.5
Northeast Asia	**72.8**	**50.4**	**31.1**	**30.4**	**57.6**	**42.5**
Brunei Darussalam	0.0	0.0	0.1	0.3	0.0	0.1
Cambodia	0.0	0.2	0.1	0.2	0.0	0.2
Indonesia	0.7	0.4	4.1	3.2	1.9	1.5
Lao People's Democratic Republic	0.0	0.0	0.0	0.0	0.0	0.0
Malaysia	2.5	0.9	16.6	16.0	7.6	6.9
Myanmar	0.0	0.0	0.1	0.4	0.0	0.2
Philippines	1.5	1.0	2.3	2.3	1.8	1.5

continued on next page...

Continued

Shares in the Trade of Hong Kong, China and Singapore

	Hong Kong, China		Singapore		Combined	
	Imports 2002–2004	Exports 2002–2004	Imports 2002–2004	Exports 2002–2004	Imports 2002–2004	Exports 2002–2004
Singapore	5.0	2.1	0.0	0.0	3.2	1.3
Thailand	1.8	1.0	4.3	4.4	2.7	2.4
Viet Nam	0.1	0.2	0.8	1.7	0.4	0.8
Southeast Asia	**11.6**	**6.0**	**28.5**	**28.5**	**17.7**	**14.9**
East Asia	**84.4**	**56.4**	**59.6**	**59.0**	**75.4**	**57.4**
Bangladesh	0.0	0.2	0.1	0.5	0.1	0.3
India	1.3	0.8	1.3	2.2	1.3	1.4
Nepal	0.0	0.0	0.0	0.0	0.0	0.0
Pakistan	0.2	0.0	0.0	0.3	0.2	0.2
Sri Lanka	0.0	0.2	0.0	0.3	0.0	0.2
South Asia	**1.6**	**1.2**	**1.5**	**3.4**	**1.6**	**2.1**

continued on next page....

Continued

Shares in the Trade of Northeast Asia-5

	Indonesia		Malaysia		Philippines		Thailand		Viet Nam		ASEAN-5	
	Imports 2002–2004	Exports 2002–2004	Imports 2002–2004	Exports 2002–2004	Imports 2002–2004	Exports 2002–2004	Imports 2002–2004	Exports 2002–2004	Imports 2002–2004	Exports 2002–2004	Imports 2002–2004	Exports 2002–2004
WORLD	100.0	100.0	100.0	100.0	100.0	100.0	100.0	100.0	100.0	100.0	100.0	100.0
Japan	13.3	21.9	17.0	10.6	20.2	15.5	23.6	14.2	11.2	13.8	16.9	14.9
Korea, Republic of	4.6	7.0	5.3	3.3	6.6	3.6	3.8	2.0	11.0	2.4	6.3	4.2
PRC	8.6	6.0	8.9	6.3	5.5	7.5	8.1	6.6	13.1	8.0	8.1	6.7
Hong Kong, China	0.7	2.0	2.8	6.0	4.7	7.9	1.4	5.3	4.1	1.7	3.3	5.3
Taipei, China	4.4	5.1	3.8	4.4	6.7	8.3	3.4	3.0	10.6	2.4	5.7	5.5
Northeast Asia	31.6	42.0	37.8	30.7	43.7	42.7	40.4	31.0	50.0	28.3	40.2	36.6
Brunei Darussalam	0.4	0.0	0.0	0.3	0.0	0.0	0.5	0.1	0.0	0.0	0.1	0.1
Cambodia	0.0	0.1	0.0	0.1	0.0	0.0	0.0	0.8	0.3	1.1	0.0	0.1
Indonesia	0.0	0.0	3.6	2.2	2.3	0.6	2.4	2.9	1.9	1.7	2.4	1.2
Lao PDR	0.0	0.0	0.0	0.0	0.0	0.0	0.1	0.6	0.3	0.4	0.0	0.0
Malaysia	3.5	3.9	0.0	0.0	3.9	5.6	5.8	4.9	3.6	1.9	2.3	2.7
Myanmar	0.1	0.1	0.1	0.2	0.0	0.0	1.3	0.6	0.0	0.0	0.1	0.1
Philippines	0.5	1.6	3.2	1.4	0.0	0.0	1.7	1.9	1.3	1.6	1.4	1.1
Singapore	13.0	8.8	11.7	15.8	7.3	7.2	4.4	7.5	11.0	4.9	10.2	10.8

ASEAN = Association of Southeast Asian Nations, Lao PDR = Lao People's Democratic Republic, PRC = People's Republic of China.

continued on next page…

Continued

Shares in the Trade of Northeast Asia-5

	Indonesia		Malaysia		Philippines		Thailand		Viet Nam		ASEAN-5	
	Imports 2002–2004	Exports 2002–2004	Imports 2002–2004	Exports 2002–2004	Imports 2002–2004	Exports 2002–2004	Imports 2002–2004	Exports 2002–2004	Imports 2002–2004	Exports 2002–2004	Imports 2002–2004	Exports 2002–2004
Thailand	5.1	2.4	4.8	4.5	3.5	3.1	0.0	0.0	5.6	1.5	4.5	3.4
Viet Nam	1.0	0.8	0.5	0.8	0.8	0.4	0.4	1.7	0.0	0.0	0.6	0.6
Southeast Asia	23.6	17.7	23.9	25.3	17.8	16.9	16.7	20.8	24.0	13.1	21.7	20.1
East Asia	55.2	59.7	61.7	55.9	61.5	59.6	57.1	51.8	74.0	41.4	62.0	56.8
Bangladesh	0.0	0.4	0.0	0.3	0.0	0.0	0.0	0.4	0.0	0.1	0.0	0.2
India	2.2	2.7	1.0	2.2	0.8	0.2	1.2	0.8	1.7	0.3	1.2	1.6
Nepal	0.0	0.0	0.0	0.0	0.0	0.0	0.0	0.0	0.0	0.0	0.0	0.0
Pakistan	0.2	0.5	0.1	0.6	0.0	0.0	0.1	0.4	0.1	0.1	0.1	0.4
Sri Lanka	0.0	0.3	0.0	0.3	0.0	0.0	0.0	0.2	0.0	0.1	0.0	0.2
South Asia	2.4	4.0	1.1	3.4	0.9	0.3	1.3	1.8	1.9	0.5	1.3	2.4

ASEAN = Association of Southeast Asian Nations, Lao PDR = Lao People's Democratic Republic, PRC = People's Republic of China.

Continued

Shares in the Trade of ASEAN-BCLM

	Brunei Darussalam		Cambodia		Lao PDR		Myanmar		ASEAN-BCLM	
	Imports 2002–2004	Exports 2002–2004	Imports 2002–2004	Exports 2002–2004	Imports 2002–2004	Exports 2002–2004	Imports 2002–2004	Exports 2002–2004	Imports 2002–2004	Exports 2002–2004
WORLD	100.0	100.0	100.0	100.0	100.0	100.0	100.0	100.0	100.0	100.0
Japan	13.1	39.0	2.5	3.7	1.9	1.5	3.9	4.5	5.5	18.3
Korea, Republic of	2.2	12.4	4.2	0.2	0.9	0.1	5.6	1.2	2.9	6.8
PRC	3.1	6.2	12.0	1.1	10.7	2.2	29.3	5.4	14.2	7.0
Hong Kong, China	4.6	0.0	14.2	0.3	0.9	0.0	1.7	1.0	1.8	4.0
Taipei,China	0.8	0.0	7.5	0.2	0.2	0.9	3.4	1.2	1.6	2.3
Northeast Asia	23.8	57.7	40.3	5.6	14.6	4.7	43.9	13.3	26.1	38.3
Brunei Darussalam	0.0	0.0	0.0	0.0	0.0	0.0	0.0	0.0	0.0	0.0
Cambodia	0.0	0.0	0.0	0.0	0.1	0.0	0.0	0.0	0.0	0.0
Indonesia	2.3	3.3	2.7	0.0	0.1	0.2	1.8	0.7	1.2	2.3
Lao PDR	0.0	0.0	0.0	0.1	0.0	0.0	0.0	0.0	0.0	0.0
Malaysia	19.4	1.4	2.5	0.5	0.4	0.0	6.0	2.8	6.5	2.0
Myanmar	0.0	0.0	0.0	0.0	0.0	0.0	0.0	0.0	0.0	0.0
Philippines	0.2	0.2	0.2	0.1	0.0	0.0	0.2	0.1	0.1	0.2
Singapore	28.3	4.2	12.3	2.9	3.6	0.1	20.8	2.8	15.4	6.4

ASEAN = Association of Southeast Asian Nations, Lao PDR = Lao People's Democratic Republic, PRC = People's Republic of China.

continued on next page....

Continued

Shares in the Trade of ASEAN-BCLM

	Brunei Darussalam		Cambodia		Lao PDR		Myanmar		ASEAN-BCLM	
	Imports 2002–2004	Exports 2002–2004	Imports 2002–2004	Exports 2002–2004	Imports 2002–2004	Exports 2002–2004	Imports 2002–2004	Exports 2002–2004	Imports 2002–2004	Exports 2002–2004
Thailand	3.5	9.4	23.4	0.7	61.2	20.8	15.6	32.8	14.1	19.8
Viet Nam	0.0	0.0	9.7	4.0	7.8	13.5	0.4	0.5	2.2	2.7
Southeast Asia	53.8	18.6	50.8	8.3	73.3	34.7	44.9	39.5	39.7	33.4
East Asia	77.6	76.2	91.0	13.9	87.9	39.4	88.8	52.8	65.7	71.7
Bangladesh	0.0	0.0	0.0	0.0	0.0	0.0	0.1	0.9	0.0	0.3
India	0.4	0.7	0.0	0.0	0.2	0.0	3.0	11.9	1.3	3.7
Nepal	0.0	0.0	0.0	0.0	0.0	0.0	0.0	0.0	0.0	0.0
Pakistan	0.1	0.0	0.0	0.0	0.0	0.0	0.2	0.5	0.1	0.1
Sri Lanka	0.0	0.0	0.0	0.0	0.0	0.0	0.0	0.1	0.0	0.0
South Asia	0.5	0.7	0.0	0.0	0.2	0.1	3.2	13.4	1.5	4.1

ASEAN = Association of Southeast Asian Nations, Lao PDR = Lao People's Democratic Republic.

continued on next page…

Continued

Shares in the Trade of South Asia

	Bangladesh		India		Nepal		Pakistan		Sri Lanka		South Asia	
	Imports 2002–2004	Exports 2002–2004	Imports 2002–2004	Exports 2002–2004	Imports 2002–2004	Exports 2002–2004	Imports 2002–2004	Exports 2002–2004	Imports 2002–2004	Exports 2002–2004	Imports 2002–2004	Exports 2002–2004
WORLD	100.0	100.0	100.0	100.0	100.0	100.0	100.0	100.0	100.0	100.0	100.0	100.0
Japan	6.1	0.9	3.1	2.9	1.4	1.1	6.4	1.3	5.9	2.9	6.0	1.5
Korea, Republic of	3.8	0.3	3.0	1.2	1.9	0.2	2.6	1.8	4.0	0.5	3.3	1.1
PRC	11.8	0.3	5.3	4.6	10.5	0.9	7.5	2.3	5.0	0.3	8.4	1.3
Hong Kong, China	4.7	1.5	1.7	4.9	2.4	0.1	0.9	4.6	8.0	1.3	3.7	2.9
Taipei,China	4.1	0.3	1.1	1.1	0.2	0.1	1.7	0.6	3.8	0.2	2.8	0.4
Northeast Asia	30.5	3.2	14.2	14.7	16.4	2.4	19.1	10.5	26.8	5.3	24.1	7.2
Brunei Darussalam	0.0	0.0	0.0	0.0	0.0	0.0	0.0	0.0	0.0	0.0	0.0	0.0
Cambodia	0.0	0.0	0.0	0.0	0.0	0.0	0.0	0.0	0.0	0.0	0.0	0.0
Indonesia	2.2	0.1	2.4	1.6	0.5	0.0	2.4	0.5	2.3	0.2	2.3	0.3
Lao PDR	0.0	0.0	0.0	0.0	0.0	0.0	0.0	0.0	0.0	0.0	0.0	0.0
Malaysia	2.2	0.1	2.3	1.4	0.5	0.0	4.1	0.6	3.9	0.2	3.3	0.4
Myanmar	0.3	0.0	0.5	0.1	0.0	0.0	0.1	0.0	0.0	0.0	0.1	0.0
Philippines	0.2	0.1	0.2	0.6	0.1	0.0	0.1	0.2	0.1	0.1	0.1	0.1
Singapore	9.6	0.5	2.5	3.5	5.1	0.5	2.9	0.8	8.0	1.4	6.1	0.8

Lao PDR = Lao People's Democratic Republic, PRC = People's Republic of China.

continued on next page…

Continued

Shares in the Trade of South Asia

	Bangladesh		India		Nepal		Pakistan		Sri Lanka		South Asia	
	Imports 2002–2004	Exports 2002–2004	Imports 2002–2004	Exports 2002–2004	Imports 2002–2004	Exports 2002–2004	Imports 2002–2004	Exports 2002–2004	Imports 2002–2004	Exports 2002–2004	Imports 2002–2004	Exports 2002–2004
Thailand	2.2	0.2	0.7	1.3	2.3	0.2	1.9	0.6	2.1	0.3	2.0	0.4
Viet Nam	0.0	0.2	0.1	0.6	0.0	0.0	0.1	0.2	0.1	0.2	0.1	0.2
Southeast Asia	**16.6**	**1.2**	**8.7**	**9.2**	**8.5**	**0.8**	**11.7**	**3.1**	**16.6**	**2.4**	**14.1**	**2.4**
East Asia	**47.2**	**4.4**	**23.0**	**23.9**	**24.9**	**3.2**	**30.8**	**13.6**	**43.3**	**7.7**	**38.2**	**9.6**
Bangladesh			0.1	2.3	0.3	0.6	0.3	1.3	0.1	0.2	0.2	0.7
India	15.0	0.8	0.0	0.0	43.0	47.0	2.0	0.8	16.1	5.2	10.8	2.9
Nepal	0.0	0.1	0.4	0.9	0.0	0.0	0.0	0.0	0.0	0.0	0.0	0.0
Pakistan	0.9	0.6	0.1	0.5	0.3	0.3			1.2	0.7	0.6	0.3
Sri Lanka	0.1	0.1	0.2	1.8	0.1	0.0	0.3	0.8			0.2	0.4
South Asia	**16.1**	**1.6**	**0.8**	**5.5**	**43.7**	**48.0**	**2.6**	**3.0**	**17.4**	**6.1**	**11.7**	**4.4**

Source: International Monetary Fund, *Direction of Trade Statistics.*

Appendix 2.2 Index Formulas

Bilateral Trade Intensity Index

Intensity of Country i's bilateral trade with Country j

$$Tij = [(Xij+Mij)/(Xi+Mi)]/\{[Xwj+Mwj)-(Xij+Mij)]/[(Xw+Mw)-(Xi+Mi)]\}$$

where

Tij = Total trade intensity index of Country i with Country j
Xij = Exports of Country i to j
Mij = Imports of Country i from j
Xi = Total exports of Country i
Mi = Total imports of Country i
Xwj = Total world exports to Country j
Mwj = Total world imports from Country j
Xw = Total world exports
Mw = Total world imports

Import Intensity Index

$$Mija = [Mij/Mi]/[(Xj-Xji)/(Xw-Xi)]$$

where

Mija = Intensity of Country i's imports from Country j
Mij = Imports of Country i from Country j
Mi = Total imports of Country i
Xj = Total exports of Country j
Xji = Exports of Country j to Country i
Xw = Total world exports
Xi = Total exports of Country i

Export Intensity Index

$$Xija = [Xij/Xi]/[(Mj-Mji)/(Mw-Mi)]$$

where

Xija = Intensity of Country i's exports to Country j
Xij = Exports of Country i to j
Xi = Total exports of Country i
Mj = Total imports of Country j
Mji = Imports of Country j from Country i
Mw = Total world imports
Mi = Total imports of Country i

Market Share Ratio (MSR) Index

$$MSR = (Mji/Mjw)/(Mwi/Mww)$$

where

Mji = Country j's imports from Country i
Mjw = Country j's imports from the world
Mwi = World imports from Country i
Mww = Total world imports

Export Similarity Index

$$XS\ j,k = \Sigma\ [min\ (Xij, Xik) * 100]$$

where

XS j,k = Degree of similarity between export profiles of Countries j and k
Xij = Industry i's export shares in Country j's exports
Xik = Industry i's export shares in Country k's exports

Revealed Comparative Advantage (RCA) Index

RCAij = (xij/Xit) / (xwj/Xwt)

where

RCAij = Country i's RCA in Product j
Xij = Country i's exports of Product j
Xwj = World exports of Product j
Xit = Country i's total exports
Xwt = World total exports

Commodity Complementarity (CC) Index

CCij = Σ{Xwk/Xwt)*[(Xik/Xit) / (Xwk/Xwt)]/[(Mjk/Mjt) / (Mwk/Mw)]

CCij = Commodity complementarity of Countries i and j
Xwj = World exports of Product k
Xwt = World total exports
Xik = Country i's exports of Product k
Xit = Country i's total exports
Xwk = World exports of Product k
Xwt = World total exports
Mjk = Country j's imports of Product k
Mjt = Country j's total imports
Mwk = World imports of Product k
Mwt = World total imports

Appendix 2.3 Summary of Harmonized System (HS) Nomenclature

Section	Chapters	Description
I	01–05	Animals and animal products (includes fish)
II	06–14	Vegetable products
III	15	Fats and oils
IV	16–24	Foodstuffs
V	25–27	Mineral products, fuels
VI	28–38	Chemicals and allied industries
VII	39–40	Plastics/rubbers
VIII	41–43	Raw hides, skins, leather, and furs
IX	44–46	Wood and wood products
X	47–49	Pulp and paper products
XI	50–63	Textiles
XII	64–67	Footwear, headgear, etc.
XIII	68–70	Stone and glass products
XIV	71	Gemstones, etc.
XV	72–83	Metals and metal products
XVI	83–84	Machinery, electrical, and electronic goods
XVII	85–89	Transport equipment
XVIII	90–92	Instruments (optical, photographic, medical, musical)
XIX	93	Arms and ammunition
XX	94–96	Miscellaneous
XXI	97	Art and antiques

3

INTEGRATION STRATEGIES FOR ASEAN: ALONE, TOGETHER, OR TOGETHER WITH NEIGHBORS?

Michael Plummer and Ganeshan Wignaraja[1]

Introduction

Internationalization of the economies in the Association of Southeast Asian Nations (ASEAN) has been proceeding at a rapid pace. Moreover, the direction of this internationalization is clearly in favor of East Asia. To complement and facilitate this regionalization, ASEAN has been pursuing a multi-pronged approach, from deeper economic integration in ASEAN itself to bilateral and regional free trade agreements (FTAs) and national policy reform. While the subject of monetary union continues to be a popular topic, in practical terms little has been done in the direction of its realization. There have been a number of initiatives (discussed below) in terms of financial cooperation but to date the most important accords have been in the real sector. In fact, although there were few formal FTAs in place in East Asia outside of the ASEAN Free Trade Area (AFTA) at the turn of the century, the Asian Development Bank (ADB) estimates that 42 concluded FTAs exist today, with another 66 being either negotiated or proposed.[2]

Is there a case for wider FTAs and closer financial and monetary integration, perhaps even monetary union? This paper attempts to address this question through institutional, theoretical, and empirical analysis. The next section considers the trade side of ASEAN integration, including a

---

[1] An earlier version of this paper was presented at the East-West Center in August 2007 and the authors are grateful to seminar participants for suggestions, particularly Seiji Naya and Dieter Ernst. Thanks are due to Fan Zhai for running the computational general equilibrium (CGE) simulations.

[2] As of October 2008. Concluded free trade agreements (FTAs) are those either signed or under implementation. For list of FTAs involving East Asian countries, see ADB's Asia Regional Integration Center (ARIC) website at www.aric.adb.org.

review of the motivations behind the rapid rise in the number of FTAs and a survey of the status quo and emerging initiatives. In addition, this paper uses a computational general equilibrium (CGE) model to estimate the welfare implications of various FTA scenarios. We find that, while the current wave of integration accords will generate positive results, the region would gain more from a wider ASEAN+3, which includes the 10 ASEAN countries plus Japan, the People's Republic of China (PRC), and Republic of Korea (henceforth Korea), or an FTA that covers all member nations in the Asia-Pacific Economic Cooperation (APEC) that has come to be known as the Free Trade Agreement of Asia-Pacific (FTAAP). In the third section, we analyze financial and monetary integration, including recent initiatives and their prospects. This is followed by an in-depth investigation as to whether or not closer monetary integration (e.g., through monetary union) would make sense from an economic perspective in the long run. We conclude that, while there are no easy answers to this question, ASEAN+3 does meet the criteria for an optimum currency area (OCA) as well as Europe did before its monetary union; in fact, ASEAN+3 is exhibiting increasing convergence and growing symmetry since the Asian financial crisis of 1997/98. Nevertheless, the political momentum to create a monetary union, which is an essential variable in the equation, does not exist at present in Asia. In addition, we consider possible policy convergence issues, using the European Union's (EU) Maastricht Treaty as a benchmark. While we conclude that ASEAN and ASEAN+3 actually come quite close to meeting the European criteria in most cases, these criteria are insufficient given the institutional differences that exist across the region. We propose instead some additional considerations that would be required beyond mere policy indicators should ASEAN or ASEAN+3 decide to deepen monetary integration. This chapter ends with concluding remarks.

ASEAN Trade Integration in the Asian Regional Context

In the first decade following its creation with the Bangkok Declaration in 1967, ASEAN as an organization accomplished little in terms of economic cooperation. Perhaps that was for the better, as several of its member countries were pursuing inward-looking industrialization plans. More aggressive action may have put ASEAN on a very different track, perhaps condemning it to the same fate as the Free Trade Area of the Americas (FTAA), whose members also favored import substitution.

Today, ASEAN's situation could hardly be different; it has doubled in size from its original five member countries to its current 10, and almost all of its member countries would be counted among the model reformers in the developing world. ASEAN's approach to formal economic integration changed drastically in the early 1990s with the creation of the AFTA and has built momentum ever since. One indicator of closer regional economic integration is ASEAN intraregional trade shares; between 1980 and 1990, they rose modestly from 17.9% to 18.8%, according to ADB estimates.[3] The impact of the creation of AFTA and closer economic cooperation among members is reflected in a significant rise in ASEAN's intraregional trade share to 26.9% by 2007. While ASEAN's figure is lower than that of the North American Free Trade Agreement (NAFTA, at 43%) and the EU (67.2%) in 2006, its recent progress is commendable. In this section, we consider the motivations behind the deeper economic cooperation programs in ASEAN and ASEAN+3 contexts, followed by a brief review of ASEAN, ASEAN+3, and extra-regional initiatives. Finally, we survey the literature regarding the ex ante economic effects of various integration accords and estimate the welfare gains that would accrue from several scenarios of regional configurations. We conclude that the existing initiatives would yield generally positive effects on the member countries and on global welfare, but that it is inferior to an approach that covered ASEAN+3 or APEC. Indeed, for the ASEAN member countries, the gains from an ASEAN+3 FTA or APEC-wide FTA (FTAAP) are on par with that of global free trade.

Motivations for the New Regionalism in Asia

There are a number of factors behind the regionalism trend in Southeast Asia and the rest of the region.

The Asian Crisis. The potential for "contagion" in which a crisis in one country could quickly be transmitted to another was revealed to be an important reality of closer integration and dynamic economic growth in ASEAN, where a perceived regional identity on the part of economic actors has been increasingly prominent. It is also the case that the real-sector-related contagion causes of the Asian financial crisis of 1997/98 continue to exist and in most cases have accentuated over time. Clearly, the policy externalities that emerged in the region are higher than ever before and this enhances the case to internalize them through greater cooperation at the regional level in both macroeconomic and microeconomic areas.

---

[3] The intraregional trade share is the percentage of intraregional trade to total trade of the region, calculated using export data. For time series data on intraregional trade shares and technical details, see www.aric.adb.org.

Regionalism in Developed Countries. At the turn of this century, essentially all developed countries were embracing discriminatory trading arrangements with potential trade- and investment-diverting implications for Asia. Europe had been implementing deeper regional integration between its member states and former colonies for about 50 years; however, the "deepening" of integration had increased substantially in the 1990s (from the Single Market to monetary union between 12 of its members, with Slovenia [January 2007] and Cyprus and Malta [January 2008] joining later and bringing the members of the monetary union to 13). The EU's membership had now expanded to include transitional economies that could potentially compete with the ASEAN in terms of trade and investment. The United States (US) had few preferential trading arrangements before 2000 but bilateral FTAs become an important part of its commercial policy in subsequent years and continue to be a major force today.

Particularly with a World Trade Organization (WTO) that has not been able to reach a multilateral agreement in the Doha Development Agenda negotiations, discriminatory trading arrangements giving preferential treatment to Asia's competitors increased the need to use regional integration to enhance efficiency in order to prevent loss of market share ("defensive" FTAs).

Another effect of this trend regards the perceived success of deeper integration, particularly "behind the border" liberalization and facilitation that can improve competitiveness and reduce transaction costs associated with production fragmentation. This was especially evident in the case of the EU Single Market but also in the case of the NAFTA, which was only an FTA but had extensive innovative aspects, including national treatment for investment.

Bilateral FTAs by ASEAN Member Countries. As ASEAN itself is only an FTA, individual members have the right to pursue their own FTAs with non-ASEAN partners. This poses a threat to ASEAN solidarity and even integration, since some of these FTAs are even deeper than existing accords in the ASEAN framework. Arguably, this need to prevent a dilution of ASEAN integration becomes even more important in the context of greater East Asian integration, e.g., through various ASEAN+3 initiatives. If ASEAN can act increasingly as a bloc in ASEAN+3 initiatives, it can influence the evolution of such accords, which currently include mainly "soft" financial initiatives but with aspirations for much deeper cooperation, perhaps even in the form of an East Asia Free Trade Area (EAFTA), East Asian Economic Community, or FTAAP. Moreover, through deeper integration it can ensure the integrity of ASEAN even in the face of deeper East Asian integration.

In addition, the political economy of FTAs is such that ASEAN will create better outcomes in negotiations as a group rather than individually. But to negotiate as a group, deep integration is necessary.

The People's Republic of China (PRC). The PRC has become a formidable competitor with the ASEAN for foreign direct investment (FDI) and is competing increasingly with the region in third markets. Concerns associated with the emergence of the PRC—and other major economies such as India have become increasingly acute since the Asian financial crisis of 1997/98. In fact, a key motivation for creating an ASEAN Economic Community (AEC) by 2015 is to compete with the PRC: by creating one market ASEAN will be less at a disadvantage in terms of size, allowing the region to enjoy economies of scale in production fragmentation, a more efficient regional division of labor, and other "dynamic" features of integration that will enhance the attractiveness of ASEAN to foreign investors and its competitiveness in local and third markets. After all, the business environment in the PRC is no more attractive—and, in some cases, significantly less—than it is in most of the ASEAN countries.[4]

Doha Once Again. An incentive for FTAs in Asia is the need for the type of deep integration that the WTO has yet to deliver (and probably won't be able to do in the short-to-medium term). To facilitate the construction of production networks and profit from the process of production fragmentation, it is critical to remove as many obstacles to trade and investment as possible, and FTAs between two (or a small group) of like-minded countries is easier to achieve than in the context of a 150-member WTO. While a successful Doha would reduce the potential negative effects of regionalism (at the margin), generate important welfare benefits, and help to knit the global economy together, it would not stem the growth in the FTA movement, especially in Asia. The economic development strategy of Asia is predicated on outward orientation, and the deep integration measures associated with FTAs appear to be a more effective means of advancing globalization.

The PRC enters the debate once again in the context of Doha. The PRC's accession to the WTO in 2002 was a major event for the country and for the global trading system as a whole. The PRC is now one of the most important trading countries in the world and has emerged as a formidable global trade presence in a relatively short period of time. That, coupled with the sheer size and potential of the country, has created considerable

---

[4] Plummer (2007).

nervousness in developed and developing countries alike. This has important implications for the WTO as well. Although as a WTO member the PRC has had to enact many rules-based policies to open up its market and create more opportunities for FDI and trade (and has reduced its trade barriers significantly), it would appear that its membership has caused some members to be cautious about offering up too much in terms of trade liberalization at the WTO out of fear of increasing PRC competition in domestic markets. For example, this was explicitly noted as a motivation for Brazil's initiation of FTA negotiations with the EU.[5] This could be one reason why there is less effort being devoted to ensuring a successful Doha outcome.

Overview of ASEAN Initiatives

A brief review of the evolution of regional trading agreements in Asia, focusing on ASEAN and ASEAN+3 initiatives, is presented in Appendix Table A3.1. An in-depth review of these accords would be beyond the scope of this paper as well as being somewhat redundant, given that many excellent surveys already exist[6] and the ADB's Asia Regional Integration Center (ARIC) website gives regular updates of FTAs and news.[7] But note that the pace of ASEAN integration has quickened considerably over the past decade, as AFTA was being implemented and member countries began to establish their own FTAs. The culmination of this process has been the AEC, which endeavors to create a region of free trade in goods and services, and freer capital and skilled-labor flows. As noted in Appendix Table A3.1, the deadline to establish the AEC has been pushed up to 2015 (for the original ASEAN countries and Brunei Darussalam), which, given the diversity of ASEAN, is highly ambitious. The reasons behind the decision to create the AEC are many, including: (i) a desire to create a post-AFTA agenda that would be comprehensive; (ii) a perceived need to deepen economic integration in ASEAN in light of the new international commercial environment, especially the dominance of FTAs; (iii) as noted above, the possibility that bilateral FTAs could actually jeopardize ASEAN integration since all member states were free to pursue their own commercial-policy agenda; and (iv) the recognition since the Asian financial crisis that cooperation in the real and financial sectors must be

---

[5] Wall Street Journal Online. 5 July 2007.

[6] For example, ADB (2006), Feridhanusatyawan (2005), Hew ed. (2005), Kawai (2005a), and Kawai and Wignaraja (2008), but there are many.

[7] See the ARIC website at www.aric.adb.org for more information.

extended concomitantly, and that free flows of skilled labor will be necessary to do this.[8]

Moreover, given that the ASEAN initiatives are explicitly or implicitly outward oriented in nature, it is only natural that attempts to integrate these accords at the regional level, as well as to adopt best practices in regional trading agreements, would emerge. We consider extra-ASEAN accords in the next subsection, but in Appendix Table A3.1 we include the fledgling ASEAN+3 meetings and the East Asian Summits. While little concrete progress has been made, the fact that these forums are being established is significant. Such initiatives may even extend outside of Asia to include the Asia–Pacific as a whole, either under the rubric of APEC or independently. Indeed, there have been recent proposals to establish FTAAP, a concept that is being advocated by the APEC Business Advisory Council (ABAC), the voice of the private sector in APEC.

These initiatives are designed to advance globalization, rather than to build strong yet isolated economies. Arguably, Asian accords—particularly related to ASEAN—are somewhat unique in that open regionalism and/or nondiscrimination is actually codified in the agreement. For example, the ASEAN Investment Area (AIA) has three pillars: investment liberalization, facilitation, and promotion. With respect to the first pillar, the goal is national treatment, which is to be accorded to ASEAN investors by 2010 and to non-ASEAN investors by 2020. In other words, any discrimination that would emerge from the process would only be transitional. Moreover, as countries reform their national investment policies to conform with AIA exigencies, they are often erecting nondiscriminatory measures from the start, thereby unambiguously strengthening the international marketplace rather than weakening it.

Extraregional Accords of ASEAN and Its Members

Table 3.1 summarizes the FTAs that members in ASEAN have proposed, concluded, or are negotiating as of October 2008. These agreements are separated into intraregional (within the Asia–Pacific) and cross-regional categories. Moreover, it considers the same units of analysis for ASEAN as a regional organization, i.e., ASEAN+1 initiatives. Some details of ASEAN's FTAs are shown in Table 3.2.

Clearly, by every reasonable measure, member countries in ASEAN have been extremely active in the regionalism movement; almost none of

---

[8] The free flow of all labor, including unskilled labor, was deemed too politically difficult to consider in the ASEAN Economic Community (AEC).

these agreements were in existence prior to 2000. Typically, the richer ASEAN countries have been more active in negotiating FTAs than poorer ones. This may reflect factors like differences in economic interests, outward orientation, industrialization, and negotiating capacity. Singapore has been the most active, with 16 concluded agreements and another 9 under negotiation, followed by Thailand with 9 concluded agreements and 9 under negotiation. Malaysia is also somewhat active with 7 concluded FTAs. In addition, Singapore has by far the largest number of FTAs with extraregional countries (six), whereas Brunei Darussalam, Indonesia, and Malaysia each have one and the others do not have any. Thus, most ASEAN members still rely on the regional organization for their FTA strategy.

ASEAN itself has four accords in place (all within the Asia–Pacific) and three are under negotiation. The former represent a process of securing market access to the region's largest economies, particularly, Japan, the PRC and Korea. The latter includes the ASEAN–EU FTA, which when concluded will be the regional organization's first cross-regional FTA with a major traditional export market. An FTA between ASEAN and the US is neither under negotiation nor proposed at present. But the Enterprise for ASEAN Initiative (EAI), which was announced in 2002, lays the foundation for a future ASEAN–US FTA. The US also has an FTA with Singapore and is negotiating FTAs with Malaysia and Thailand. In 2006, it negotiated a Trade and Investment Framework Agreement (TIFA) with the region.

ASEAN's FTAs are becoming more complex in their scope and increasingly going beyond the WTO regulatory framework to include provisions on the Singapore issues (trade facilitation, investment, government procurement, and competition policy). ASEAN itself has put in place an ASEAN Investment Area and trade facilitation agreements. Negotiations on investment are ongoing in the ASEAN–PRC FTA and the ASEAN–Korea FTA. The bilateral FTAs of ASEAN members are even more comprehensive in scope and deal with the other Singapore issues as well as issues such as the environment and intellectual property.[9]

In sum, tables 3.1 and 3.2 show us that (i) bilateral FTAs have become increasingly popular in the region and ASEAN itself has started to become active, with more accords under negotiation or proposed than it has finished, (ii) there is some revealed preference for Asia–Pacific-centered FTAs as a means of consolidating intraregional trade and investment flows, and (iii) "WTO Plus" provisions are increasingly common in FTAs involving ASEAN and its members.

---

[9] Kawai and Wignaraja (2008) find that the majority of the 39 concluded FTAs in East Asia (i.e., 72%) had "WTO Plus" provisions in addition to goods and services provisions. Furthermore, they note that developed countries seem to prefer this format of agreement with developing countries in the region.

Table 3.1   ASEAN's and ASEAN Member Countries' FTA Status, January 2008

Country	A Total (A = B+C)			B Within Asia and the Pacific			C Cross-Regional		
	Concluded	Under Negotiation	Proposed	Concluded	Under Negotiation	Proposed	Concluded	Under Negotiation	Proposed
Brunei Darussalam	6	3	4	5	2	3	1	1	1
Cambodia	4	3	2	4	2	2	0	1	0
Indonesia	5	5	6	4	4	4	1	1	2
Lao People's Democratic Republic	6	3	2	6	2	2	0	1	0
Malaysia	7	8	4	6	4	4	1	4	0
Myanmar	4	4	2	4	3	2	0	1	0
Philippines	5	3	4	5	2	2	0	1	2
Singapore	16	9	3	10	3	3	6	6	0
Thailand	9	9	6	9	4	4	0	5	2
Viet Nam	4	5	2	4	3	2	0	2	0
ASEAN	4	3	2	4	2	2	0	1	0

ASEAN = Association of Southeast Asian Nations, FTA = free trade agreement.

Notes: Cross-regional = where one member of the FTA is outside Asia–Pacific; Proposed = parties are considering a free trade agreement, establishing joint study groups or joint task force, and conducting feasibility studies to determine the desirability of entering into an FTA; Concluded FTAs = signed FTAs and/or under implementation; FTAs under negotiation = those under negotiation with or without a signed Framework Agreement.

Source: Asia Regional Integration Center (ARIC) FTA database (www.aric.adb.org), data as of October 2008.

Table 3.2   Status of ASEAN FTA Agreements, October 2008

Status/Type	Within Asia and the Pacific	Cross-Regional
Concluded (4)	**ASEAN FTA** • Goods (CEPT scheme in effect 1993) • Services (Framework Agreement [FA] signed 1995) • ASEAN Investment Area (FA signed 1998) • Trade facilitation (FA signed 1998) and Single Window Agreement (signed 2005) **ASEAN–PRC FTA (2005)** • FA on Comprehensive Economic Cooperation (signed November 2002) • Goods (in effect July 2005) • Services (in effect July 2007) • Investment (ongoing negotiations) **ASEAN– Republic of Korea FTA (2006)** • Goods (in effect June 2007) • Services (signed November 2007) • Investment (ongoing negotiations) **ASEAN–Japan FTA** • FA on Comprehensive Economic Partnership signed October 2003 • Signed April 2008 (in effect December 2008)	
Under Negotiation (3)	**ASEAN–Australia and New Zealand CER FTA** • Commemorative Summit November 2004 • Negotiations have been completed; FTA expected to be signed in December 2008 **ASEAN–India FTA** • Economic Cooperation FA signed October 2003 • Expected to be signed in December 2008	**ASEAN–EU FTA** • Joint Ministerial Statement to launch negotiations in May 2007

continued on next page...

Table 3.2 continued

Status/Type	Within Asia and the Pacific	Cross-Regional
Proposed (2)	ASEAN+3 FTA (Japan, PRC, and Republic of Korea) • ASEAN+3 process institutionalized 1999 • Kuala Lumpur Declaration December 2005 ASEAN+6 FTA (Japan, PRC, Republic of Korea, India, Australia, and New Zealand) • 1ˢᵗ East Asia Summit December 2005	

ASEAN = Association of Southeast Asian Nations, CER = Closer Economic Relations, CEPT = Common Effective Preferential Tariff, EU = European Union, FTA = free trade agreement, PRC = People's Republic of China.

Source: ADB Asia Regional Integration Center FTA Database (www.aric.adb.org).

What would be the economic costs of these fragmented FTAs? Which would be the optimal configuration for ASEAN? We turn to these and associated questions in the next subsection.

FTA Scenarios

The ultimate implications of formal trade accords for the welfare of participating countries are complicated; they include (i) the static effects of integration (i.e., trade creation and diversion), (ii) dynamic effects (e.g., creation and diversion of FDI, productivity effects, and economies of scale), and (iii) various political-economy implications of preferential trading arrangements. To the extent that FTAs change intraregional real-sector integration, all else being equal the FTA movement will be important in determining whether or not the FTA trend is consistent with the ultimate goal of outward-oriented policy reform.

Even before the many FTAs in Asia have had any discernable effect, the process of real integration in Asia is increasing the potential gains from monetary union (discussed below) and appears to be driving at least in part the symmetry of economic structure in the region (Rana 2006). To the extent that FTAs serve to reinforce this process ("flag following trade"), benefits will be magnified. In the remainder of this section, we consider the aggregate economic effects of a series of possible scenarios in the region. In sum, we find that the ASEAN offshoot ASEAN+3 and

FTAAP scenarios would generate a far better outcome for the region than the existing mix of bilateral FTAs.

There is increasing academic interest in examining the economic effects of EAFTA using global CGE models. This interest stems from advances in CGE model development and computing power as well as strong international policy attention to the implications of EAFTA. Policy makers are particularly interested in understanding the magnitude of the benefits of EAFTA for member countries, the possible losses to nonmembers, and sector-level gains and losses for members and nonmembers alike. But they are also important to the analysis of the future of economic integration in the region, including proposals related to the AEC and, of course, Asian monetary union, discussed later in the paper.

By relying on a simulation approach to analyze the economic effects of policy changes due to the formation of EAFTA, CGE models can shed light on these effects. The CGE models used in empirical studies have varied somewhat in their underlying economic structure, behavior of agents, and focus but commonly use the Global Trade Analysis Project (GTAP) database to examine an ASEAN+3 FTA policy scenario, an FTAAP policy scenario or alternative hub and spoke FTA arrangements. The primary focus of such policy scenarios is on the removal of price distortions against imports that arise from existing trade barriers and other sources. Most studies have used the standard GTAP model[10] with constant returns to scale in production, perfect competition, and the Armington assumption (or some variant of GTAP) while a few have adopted CGE models with firm-level imperfect competition.

Four major findings from the formation of EAFTA are indicated by CGE studies (e.g., Ballard and Cheong [1997], Urata and Kyota [2003], Gilbert et al [2004], Lee et al [2004], and Mohanty and Pohit [2007]):

(i)   all the countries involved would collect welfare gains;

(ii)   the countries that are excluded are likely to suffer welfare losses;

(iii)   production of sectors with a comparative advantage increases; and

(iv)   an East Asian FTA is a step toward multilateral liberalization which, as expected, provides larger global welfare gains than an East Asia FTA.

Depending on factors such as the CGE model and data sources used, studies differ in their estimates of welfare gains to members and losses to nonmembers from EAFTA. An optimistic view is suggested by Urata and Kyota (2003). This study estimates from GTAP simulations that an ASEAN+3 FTA will generate welfare gains for members from the highest of 12.5% of gross domestic product (GDP) for Thailand and 6.6% for Viet Nam to the lowest

---

[10] See Hertel (1997). For more details about the current standard Global Trade Analysis Project (GTAP) model, see www.gtap.agecon.purdue.edu.

of 0.19% for Japan and 0.64% for the PRC. Urata and Kyota find modest welfare loses for nonmembers of -0.02% for the EU, -0.09% for the US, and -0.29% for Australia and New Zealand. Also using GTAP, Gilbert et al (2004) find that an ASEAN+3 FTA will produce higher welfare gains for members than a PRC–Japan–Korea FTA indicating that broadening FTAs brings benefits. However, Gilbert et al report lower welfare gains from an ASEAN+3 FTA for Viet Nam (3.1%) and Thailand (1.6%) than Urata and Kyota (2003). In a scenario of only tariff liberalization, Mohanty and Pohit (2007) using GTAP, report even more modest gains (from 0.5% to 2.3%) for members of an ASEAN+3 FTA and loses of -0.1% for non-members. Interestingly, the inclusion of India (i.e., the formation of an ASEAN+3 and India FTA) results in an increase in gains for members.

Meanwhile, from their Linkage CGE model, Lee et al (2004) show significantly higher welfare gains from an ASEAN+3 FTA for the PRC plus Hong Kong, China (4%) and Japan (1.6%), notable gains for Korea (3.7%) and ASEAN as a group (4%), and welfare losses for the rest of the world of under -0.2%. Using a CGE model with firm-level imperfect competition, Ballard and Cheong (1997) indicate that both FTAAP and EAFTA would generate gains for all members even without the participation of the US and Japan. They go on to show that developing nations of Asia are expected to gain more when the US joins the FTA than when Japan joins.

Furthermore, some studies point to how regional trade and country specializations could evolve in the future. One might expect, for example, that EAFTA would increase the share of intraregional trade as well as the degree of specialization of each country according to comparative advantage. In part, this effect might arise from an enlarged regional market resulting from elimination of trade barriers that gives more scope for differentiated products. Nonetheless, the available CGE simulation studies indicate a mixed and inconclusive picture of the likely effects of EAFTA on regional trade and country specializations. For instance, Urata and Kyota (2003) suggest that such effects may be small in the case of an ASEAN+3 FTA. They argue that "the results show that the impact of EAFTA is not large enough to change the composition of each country's exports and imports substantially" (2003, 12–13). They suggest that 5% changes in exports are indicated for a few sectors like mining and textiles in Viet Nam and food and beverages in Korea and Thailand. For other sectors and countries, the changes in exports are found to be mostly less than 1% (with some less than 5%). Likewise, Urata and Kyota argue that an ASEAN+3 FTA may not significantly expand intra-industry trade. In contrast, Gilbert et al (2004) looking at production effects (rather than exports) of an ASEAN+3 FTA find large changes in value added, including declines of between 13% and 42% in the automobile sector in most member countries, rises in the textile sector of 5–10% in many member countries, and increases in electronics of 2–8% in some member countries. If the changes in value added indicated by Gilbert et al (2004) mirror changes in exports, then it is likely that an ASEAN+3 FTA may have notable impacts on intra-industry trade and country specialization. Further work is needed on this important issue using a combination of CGE analysis and industry-level studies. Such an exercise is beyond the scope of the current study.

The effects of alternative hub and spoke arrangements in East Asia has attracted recent attention in the literature. Bchir and Fouquin (2006) use the Mirage model to create several scenarios of economic integration based on hub-and-spoke (ASEAN+1 agreements) and Asian regional approaches, as well as whether or not the agreements will be all-inclusive or would exclude sensitive products. They find that ASEAN countries, for example, would be better off with a series of bilateral agreements than with an Asian-inclusive approach, as this would allow them to better exploit their comparative advantage in agriculture, which is characterized by much higher levels of protection in the region than manufactures. Using ADB's General Equilibrium Model for Asia's Trade (GEMAT) with imperfect competition, Zhai (2006) examines the effects of alternative hub-and-spoke configurations with ASEAN, the PRC and Japan competing as regional hubs of bilateral FTAs. He reports that an Asian hub centered around the PRC will produce net welfare gains for the world as a whole of $18.5 billion, which is significantly more than that of either an ASEAN hub or a Japan hub.

Previous CGE studies provide valuable insights on the likely economic effects of an ASEAN+3 FTA, an APEC FTA and different hub and spoke arrangements. There is a need to build on this literature and adopt a more comprehensive approach that incorporates the new reality of multiple FTA initiatives in East Asia, new data sources, and recent modeling developments. Accordingly, the following four policy scenarios are considered in the CGE modeling exercise.

(i)   *Fragmentation scenario.* A continuation of the current wave of bilateralism, including AFTA, where the region is fragmented by several bilateral or small regional FTAs.

(ii)   *ASEAN+3 FTA scenario.* Free trade among ASEAN members, PRC (includes Hong Kong, China), Japan, and Korea, (or EAFTA).

(iii)   *FTAAP scenario.* Free trade among all APEC members (or an APEC-wide FTA).

(iv)   *Global free trade scenario.* Complete abolition of import tariffs and export subsidies.

Some comments on these scenarios are appropriate. Scenario (i) represents the current reality of multiple and overlapping bilateral or regional

FTAs involving East Asian countries in general and ASEAN in particular. Scenario (ii) is included because this seems to be gradually taking shape with ASEAN having concluded liberalization of goods and services agreements with both the PRC and Korea while negotiations with Japan are still ongoing. Scenario (iii) is provided to represent the discussions among APEC economic ministers on ways to improve trade relations and has received considerable attention on the part of the private sector and academics.[11] Scenario (iv) is included to enable comparisons of gains and losses relative to global free trade (our benchmark).

The estimates of the economic impacts of FTA scenarios were prepared using ADB's GEMAT (an applied general equilibrium model of the global economy with a focus on Asia), which extends the Linkage model developed at the World Bank (see ADB 2006 for details of GEMAT). The model has strong micro-foundations and captures detailed interactions among industries, consumers, and governments, across the global economy. It is ideally suited for the analysis of structural changes over periods that are sufficiently long to allow markets to adjust and rigidities to work themselves out. Among other assumptions, GEMAT incorporates firm heterogeneity, fixed trade costs, and imperfect competition.

Table 3.3 summarizes the results for GDP and welfare in terms of equivalent variation for the four policy scenarios. It comes as little surprise that scenario (i), which is a fragmented reality of multiple bilateral and regional FTAs, is the least attractive for regions and most countries. Among others, this scenario may give rise to the "spaghetti bowl" effect, which refers to higher transactions costs from multiple rules of origin and standards in the growing number of FTAs in East Asia. Global free trade (scenario iv) is the most attractive for most countries. This scenario, however, remains unrealistic; even the WTO process has been beset by uncertainties regarding the timing and depth of multilateral agreement to reduce trade barriers.

The FTAAP brings gains to Northeast Asia and the US, but ASEAN witnesses fewer gains than it does under scenario (i), with the exceptions of Malaysia and Viet Nam. The rest of Asia and Europe, which would be outside a FTAAP, also lose relative to scenario (i).

---

[11] A particularly powerful case for the Free Trade Agreement of Asia-Pacific (FTAAP) can be found in Bergsten (2007). He points out that Asia-Pacific Economic Cooperation (APEC) members account for more than half the world economy and about half of world trade. Accordingly, an FTAAP approaching free trade would be even more far-reaching in terms of global benefits than the European Union (EU) and the North American Free Trade Agreement. He concludes that FTAAP would be the best "Plan B" to restart widespread trade liberalization if the Doha Round fails to proceed.

Table 3.3   Impact of Four Scenarios, Real Income (Equivalent Variation)

	(i) Fragmentation Scenario	(ii) ASEAN+3 FTA	(iii) FTAAP	(iv) Global Free Trade
In $ Mn 2001 prices				
ASEAN	8,869	10,375	8,341	11,319
Indonesia	712	523	702	1,206
Malaysia	1,753	3,941	3,084	3,712
Philippines	481	350	(5)	(136)
Singapore	1,833	1,240	747	1,409
Thailand	3,545	3,305	2,707	3,866
Viet Nam	564	1,016	1,106	1,263
Northeast Asia	(1,219)	21,724	56,734	72,944
Rest of Asia	(101)	(425)	(1,560)	4,288
United States	(1,371)	(2,362)	12,035	22,884
Europe	(1,021)	(904)	(3,047)	25,325
Rest of the World	(555)	(464)	280	14,861
World	4,401	27,546	74,689	153,718
In % of GDP				
ASEAN	1.72	2.02	1.62	2.20
Indonesia	0.51	0.38	0.50	0.87
Malaysia	2.04	4.62	3.62	4.36
Philippines	0.71	0.52	(0.01)	(0.20)
Singapore	2.25	1.52	0.92	1.73
Thailand	3.22	3.00	2.46	3.51
Viet Nam	1.81	3.27	3.55	4.06
Northeast Asia	(0.02)	0.37	0.96	1.23
Rest of Asia	(0.01)	(0.06)	(0.22)	0.61
United States	(0.01)	(0.02)	0.12	0.24
Europe	(0.01)	(0.01)	(0.04)	0.30
Rest of the World	(0.01)	(0.01)	0.01	0.34
World	0.01	0.09	0.25	0.51

ASEAN+3 = Association of Southeast Asian Nations plus People's Republic of China, Japan, and Republic of Korea; FTAAP = Free Trade Agreement of Asia-Pacific, GDP = gross domestic product; $ Mn = millions of US dollars; % = percent; ( ) = negative value.

Source: ADB staff estimates based on General Equilibrium Model for Asia's Trade (GEMAT).

Under scenario (ii), the welfare of members increases, with Northeast Asia and ASEAN witnessing gains of 0.37% and 2.02%, respectively. In fact, for ASEAN there is very little difference between the ASEAN+3 FTA scenario and global free trade (0.18% of GDP). The difference between the ASEAN+3 FTA scenario and the FTAAP is slightly more (0.40%) but global gains from the FTAAP are (slightly) greater than the ASEAN+3 (0.16% of global GDP).[12]

Note that CGE simulation studies are useful in indicating the channels by which the formation of an FTA translates into changes in the economy. Existing studies have focused on liberalization of import tariffs on goods trade. A major shortcoming of such studies is their inability to incorporate rules of origin and nontariff measures such as sanitary and phytosanitary (SPS) measures and technical barriers to trade (TBT), which are likely to afford more protection for domestic industries than tariffs. In addition, there are no CGE studies on liberalization of barriers to services trade. Furthermore, in these approaches, it is unclear whether the members of an FTA ultimately realize potential effects. Nevertheless, there is also a strong incentive for economies in these agreements to embrace best practices, which in turn could have a strong positive effect on not only members but also non-member countries (Plummer 2007). Thus, CGE studies are best when used in conjunction with other empirical tools—notably analysis of the complex structure of FTAs and enterprise perception studies of the benefits of FTAs (Francois, McQueen, and Wignaraja 2005).

Financial and Monetary Cooperation

Initiatives related to trade have by far the longest tradition in ASEAN and have been much more comprehensive than any measures related to cooperation in financial or monetary matters. Moreover, economists have much better tools in analyzing the welfare implications of trade accords. Hence, the bias in the literature has heretofore been in the direction of trade analysis. However, as argued above, since the Asian financial crisis of 1997/98 the need to move forward on financial and monetary matters has assumed greater policy importance. The *Ministerial Understanding on ASEAN Cooperation in Finance* (March 1997) sets out the broad goals of cooperation in diverse

---

[12] These CGE estimates are based on welfare gains that could arise from tariff liberalization. Larger estimates for the ASEAN+3 (Association of Southeast Asian Nations plus People's Republic of China [PRC], Japan, and Republic of Korea) scenario are presented in Francois and Wignaraja (2008) from a CGE exercise which allows for medium-to-long run investment effects and a more comprehensive FTA (encompassing services liberalization, trade costs, and tariff reduction).

areas of finance and macroeconomics, including banking, capital markets, insurance matters, taxation, and public finance, as well as in exchanging information on developments affecting ASEAN countries in various multilateral and regional organizations. Realizing the importance of developing capital markets in the region, the ASEAN Finance Ministers endorsed a Finance Work Program designed to deepen capital markets in ASEAN. In the Joint Ministerial Statement of the Fourth ASEAN Finance Ministers Meeting (25–26 March 2000), the ministers agreed that ASEAN should "...further strengthen corporate governance practices, including transparency and disclosure, and establish a regional framework for the development of the ASEAN bond market. Our aim is to develop and deepen ASEAN's capital markets, particularly bond markets." In December 1999, the ASEAN heads of government focused on the need to move toward greater regional cohesion and economic integration, as expressed in the ASEAN Vision 2020 statement. In this document, they pledge, among other things, to maintain regional macroeconomic and financial stability through closer cooperation in terms of monetary and financial policies. The next year in Viet Nam they agreed to the Ha Noi Plan of Action, which calls for (i) maintaining financial and macroeconomic stability; (ii) strengthening financial systems; (iii) liberalizing financial services; (iv) intensifying cooperative efforts in monetary, tax, and insurance matters; and (v) developing ASEAN capital markets.

As countries in ASEAN endeavor to deepen their national capital markets, they have been using both ASEAN-based and ASEAN+3 approaches. In effect, most significant financial initiatives have been thus far at the ASEAN+3 level. Hence, in what follows, we consider exchange rate management and financial and monetary cooperation mainly from an ASEAN+3 perspective. This section considers whether or not the region would be a good candidate for very deep integration in the area (i.e., monetary union) over the long term.

Exchange Rate Management

Exchange rate regimes in Asia differ widely, from various degrees of managed floats (e.g., most countries in ASEAN, Japan, and Korea) to hard pegs (e.g., the PRC and Hong Kong, China). There are many excellent reviews of exchange rate regimes in the region (see, for example, ADB 2006). However, they all have one common characteristic: the US dollar as the (explicit or implicit) reference currency or anchor. In reviewing the evolution of the roles of the US dollar, yen, and euro in East Asia, Kawai (2002) notes that the US dollar was either the de facto or de jure anchor in the region's economies prior to the 1997/98 Asian financial crisis. The role of the US dollar declined during the crisis, but in its aftermath the US dollar generally assumed its traditional role as anchor. Still, its importance diminished in certain countries (e.g., Indonesia) and there has been greater flexibility in exchange rate management. As of early 2007, the US dollar remained prevalent in its importance, but there are some indications of certain strains and a desire to diversify is in evidence. Weakness in the US dollar appears to have led some countries (e.g., the PRC) to announce explicit reserve diversification strategies. Thailand in December 2006 even (briefly) imposed capital controls to prevent further appreciation of the baht against the dollar, reflecting problems associated with continued sterilization of foreign exchange interventions over a long period of time (holdings of US dollars by the region's central banks are at historical highs).

Numerous studies in the literature evaluate alternative exchange rate regimes in the ASEAN grouping with the PRC, Japan, and Korea (ASEAN+3). Kwan (2001), for example, considers from an institutional/political-economy perspective the case for closer exchange rate management in Asia, with a focus on the potential role of the Japanese yen in future arrangements. McKibbin (2004) evaluates the performance of several potential Asian exchange rate arrangements with respect to their effects on output and inflation variability in the presence of various shocks. McKibbin finds that no regime dominates in the presence of all shocks, but that a currency regime featuring a full float or a peg against a basket of currencies that includes the US dollar, euro, and yen generally perform better than would an Asian currency union or yen-zone regime.

There continues to be a strong appetite in the region for various proposals regarding future exchange rate management and cooperation, even if there has been little or no concrete progress in this regard at the policy level (as will be discussed below, various forms of monetary union in Asia have been tabled by academics but these have not been considered seriously in policy discussion). Arguably, this desire relates to the problems associated with the Asian financial crisis of 1997/98. The contagion effects of the crisis, which began in Thailand on 2 July 1997 and quickly spread to Malaysia, Indonesia, Philippines, and ultimately Korea and even Hong Kong, China took the region by surprise, particularly since the potential for real contagion was thought to be small given the relatively low levels of trade integration between the affected economies at the time. The contagion effect was devastating, however. Kim et al (2002) separate contagion into several separate categories, with bilateral real integration just being one (and a small part of it). [13] The

---

[13] Glick and Rose (1999), for example, examine five currency crisis episodes and find that countries affected by crisis have strong trade relations with the country that was the first victim of the crisis episode. But this effect is not important relative to other channels. Moreover, in the case of the Asian financial crisis, Thailand accounted for 1.0–4.5% of the exports of the affected Asian economies.

others would include competition in third markets;[14] "financial contagion," which relates to international investors' behavior during a crisis; and "pure contagion," which could be "herd behavior" such as informational cascades. Kim et al (2002) argue that all these channels played a role in the crisis and survey the relevant literature.

For Asian policy makers, this contagion effect clearly underscored the policy externalities associated with macroeconomic and financial policies in an increasingly integrated region, which in turn has given birth to a variety of approaches geared to endogenize at least in part these externalities. We discuss these initiatives below. Suffice it to note that the presence of contagion at higher levels of integration (see, for example, Candelon, Piplack, and Straetmans 2006; and Dungey et al 2004) reinforces arguments in favor of a monetary union.

Financial and Monetary Integration

One might trace the first initiative in favor of monetary/financial cooperation in ASEAN+3 to be the original Miyazawa Plan, which was initiated by Japan during the Asian financial crisis to create an Asian Monetary Fund to supplement the International Monetary Fund (IMF). It was opposed by the IMF and the US, but the desire for cooperation eventually led to the establishment of currency swap arrangements among East Asian countries (basically bilateral swaps between Japan and individual countries) during the annual meeting of ADB in May 2000 (the Chiang Mai Initiative). These swaps have grown in terms of nominal values to approximately $75 billion (May 2006).

There have also been proposals to integrate capital markets in the region, from modest proposals to coordinate more closely existing national capital markets to more ambitious proposals such as the creation of supranational regional bond and stock exchanges. The main issues relate to integration as opposed to capital market development more generally, although one motivation for integration is typically to foster development of the market.

Interest in stock market integration arises primarily because financial theory suggests that an integrated regional stock market is more efficient than are segmented national capital markets. Capital market efficiency in Southeast

---

[14] That is, if a crisis hits Thailand, and Malaysia and Thailand compete significantly in the United States (US) market, a strong devaluation of the baht would impact the competitiveness of Malaysia, which would lead investors to sell short the Malaysian ringgit. For analysis of this type of competitiveness effect in the Asian crisis context, see Kochar, Loungani, and Stone (1998), who find that this phenomenon played an important role in the crisis.

Asia has become even more important after the Asian financial crisis. Southeast Asian countries are specifically seeking to reduce the traditional dependence of firms on bank loans rather than bond and stock issuances, and at the same time are seeking new capital from outside the region.

With an integrated regional stock market, investors from all member countries will be able to allocate capital to the locations in the region where it will be put to the most productive use. With more cross-border flows of funds, additional trading in individual securities will improve the liquidity of the stock markets, which will in turn lower the cost of capital for firms seeking capital and lower the transaction costs for investors. These suggest a more efficient allocation of capital within the region.

From the perspective of a portfolio investor outside the region, stock market integration suggests that separate markets move together and have high correlations, so there is less benefit from portfolio diversification across countries. However, an integrated regional stock exchange will be more appealing to investors from outside the region who would find investment in the region easier or more justifiable. As shares become more liquid and transaction costs fall, fund managers become increasingly willing to take positions in the stocks. In addition, outside investors may take notice of the regional stock exchange instead of dismissing a collection of small national exchanges; the whole (one regional stock exchange) might be greater than the sum of the parts (individual country exchanges). Click and Plummer (2005) find evidence of co-integration of the original ASEAN-5 (namely, Indonesia, Malaysia, Philippines, Singapore, and Thailand) stock markets, which would bode well for the creation of a regional market. Candelon, Piplack, and Straetmans (2006) come to the same conclusion; they consider five different Asian economies (Malaysia; Thailand; Taipei,China; Singapore; and Korea) and find an increased co-movement of these stock markets during periods of boom and bust, with a common break in 1997 (which can only be interpreted as an "Asian flu" effect).

The need to finance emerging government deficits in the region, the robust demand for infrastructure projects, and the ambitious business plans of many private sector companies make the development of bond markets a natural priority, although a major challenge. Fixed-income instruments are important not only as an additional financial vehicle but also as a complement to equity markets. Firms may wish to raise medium- and long-term financial capital without relinquishing more control of the firm, or possibly as a complement to equity issuances (or vice versa; major corporate bond issues are often accompanied by warrants). Moreover, governments in ASEAN countries in particular have recognized that a stronger and more extensive local bond market can be strong protection against maturity and currency mismatches. While ASEAN launched a study on the possibility of creating an ASEAN bond market in 2002–2003, the idea was deferred in favor of an ASEAN+3 framework, which would include the major financial players in Asia. For example, the December 2002 Asian Bond Markets Initiative established a (small but growing) bond pool under the auspices of the Bank for International Settlements.

Nevertheless, financial and monetary cooperation in Asia remains at the conceptual stage. Even its most successful cooperative effect, the Chiang Mai Initiative, lacks ambition if one considers that its swaps totaling $75 billion (May 2006) will be drawn from reserves that are currently at about $2.5 trillion. The economics seem to support such initiatives, however.

Do Macroeconomic and Policy Trends in Asia Support Monetary Union?

Ever since the World Bank's publication of *East Asian Miracle* (World Bank 1993), the successful, export-oriented approach to economic development has been a model for developing countries. Of course, the region's remarkable trade performance has been made possible by general political stability, stable macroeconomic policies, and market-oriented microeconomic reforms (see, for example, World Bank 1993, World Bank 2006, and ADB 2006). While an exhaustive review of the determinants of the "East Asian Miracle" would go beyond the scope of this paper, suffice it to note that more than any other region in the developing world, Asia has been able to exploit to its advantage the global marketplace and globalization.

As has been well documented,[15] over the past 20 years the region has been highly successful in raising living standards, reducing poverty, and maintaining healthy macroeconomic indicators. Moreover, the region exhibits a classic process of structural change as economic development proceeds apace, with agriculture falling in importance while services (and, usually, manufactures) rise.[16]

There has also been a process of convergence at work. As Barro and Sala-i-Martin (2004) show, while the hypothesis of global economic convergence ("beta" convergence) can be rejected with reasonable degrees

---

[15] ADB (2006) and World Bank (2006) each give excellent reviews of these processes, but the literature is large.

[16] The exception in terms of services is Thailand, whose share actually falls slightly. However, this reflects a problem with collection of services data in Thailand; in short, laborers who work only part-time in agriculture are included as agricultural workers, even if they generally rely on employment in services as their most important source of income.

of confidence, there is evidence of "conditional convergence."[17] But East Asia is the only region where economies are catching up unambiguously with each other and with countries in the Organisation for Economic Co-operation and Development (OECD) (World Bank 2006). For example, while the per capita incomes of Singapore and Taipei,China were about half that of Japan in 1985, by 2004 they had almost caught up to Japan. Hong Kong, China's per capita income had actually surpassed Japan's by that time.[18] Korea's per capita GDP was still one-third lower than that of Japan in 2004 but its rate of growth in improving this indicator has been impressive. Per capita GDP virtually quadrupled from 1985 to 2004.[19] Most countries in ASEAN also narrowed the gap between their per capita incomes and Japan's (as well as those of other OECD countries). The most remarkable story, however, is that of the PRC, which has been transformed from a poor, isolated, autarkic economy into an economic powerhouse in a generation. This dramatic transformation is attributable to a major overhaul of economic policy that has embraced (and, in some ways, is now leading) globalization, rather than resisting it as it had done in the past.

This outward-oriented approach to economic development, which has been a key engine of growth in Asia, has made it a natural candidate for regional economic integration initiatives in a world that is increasingly eschewing a multilateral approach to trade policy in favor of bilateralism and regionalism. In addition to the need to reclaim most-favored-nation (MFN) status in key markets ("defensive" regionalism), FTAs in Asia are being used as a means to address key areas that have been hitherto excluded in the WTO talks.

The Economics of Monetary Union: Is Asia an Optimum Currency Area?

There exist several studies in the literature that attempt to address the question of whether or not some sort of Asian currency area would make sense, often using the experience of monetary union in Europe as a yardstick. Such comparisons are only natural. The theory of optimum currency areas (OCAs) does not provide us with an optimal threshold; however, if it is assumed that the EU makes sense as a currency area, comparisons of indicators between what the EU was like prior to monetary union and what Asia is now would be appropriate.

---

[17] In calculating "conditional convergence," the authors only include countries that meet certain criteria, that is, countries with hyperinflation, political instability, and the like are excluded from the database.

[18] World Bank's *World Development Indicators* database; CEIC database.

[19] Ibid.

Perhaps the most comprehensive work on the subject was undertaken by Bayoumi and Eichengreen (1999) and by Bayoumi, Eichengreen, and Mauro (1999). They use a variety of indicators consistent with the OCA litera-ture, from analysis of intraregional trade to correlations of aggregate sup-ply shocks, to compare the EU prior to Maastricht with Asia and ASEAN today.[20] They find that, in general, Asia comes as close to meeting OCA criteria as Europe did. However, they note that historically the essential preconditions for a durable regional monetary arrangement depend criti-cally on politics rather than economics. In this sense, Asia looks much less like an OCA. Nicolas (1999) essentially comes to the same conclusion in terms of political limitations but is less sanguine with respect to the eco-nomics of a currency area in ASEAN. Tang (2006) focuses on symmetry of supply and demand shocks and speed of adjustment in evaluating pos-sible configurations of monetary union across major Asian economies. He finds that smaller subgroupings of economies in Asia (e.g., Malaysia and Singapore; ASEAN more generally; Hong Kong, China and Taipei,China) fit the OCA criteria better than does Asia as a whole.

One way to evaluate the OCA symmetry criterion is to estimate correla-tions of macroeconomic variables between members of a proposed currency group over time using high-frequency data. The more highly correlated these variables are throughout the business cycle, the greater the implied symme-try of economic structures of the component members of the group, and the more likely the group would constitute an OCA. Kose et al (2003) use overall output (real GDP) as the key macroeconomic variable for ASEAN-5, Korea, and Taipei,China. The results show fairly high, positive cross-correlations of output between most members of the ASEAN countries and between individ-ual countries and the Asian aggregates. For example, correlations between the ASEAN-5 countries and the Asia Cycle 2 aggregate fall in the range of 0.36 (the Philippines) and 0.49 (Singapore). Moreover, with the exception of Indonesia, correlation coefficients have generally been rising over time. Excluding Indonesia, they increased over time in all cases except that of Malaysia–Philippines. The highest correlations in period 2 were found between Malaysia and Indonesia (0.73), Singapore and Thailand (0.63), and Singapore and Malaysia (0.58). In general, correlations between ASEAN countries are often higher than with the general Asia group aggregates.

---

[20] One problem with the Bayoumi, Eichengreen, and Mauro (1999) paper is that they define ASEAN to include all of its official member states, including the most recent members, i.e., Cambodia, Lao People's Democratic Republic (Lao PDR), Myanmar, and Viet Nam. None of these countries would be a candidate for mon-etary integration in the short or medium run, given their low level of economic and financial development, closed financial markets, and inconvertible currencies.

In short, it would be difficult to state unequivocally that East Asia constitutes an OCA. However, macroeconomic trends and symmetry analysis would suggest that at least it is moving in that direction, and if the EU is used as the benchmark, it already may be there. Moreover, the "endogeneity" process noted by Frankel and Rose (1998) would suggest that, should Asia join in monetary union, the convergence indicators would be reinforced. Nevertheless, the political status quo, particularly in Northeast Asia, would preclude such an arrangement...at least in the short term. But the confluence of closer trade integration and the emergence of an "Asian identity" could well enhance the potential for a removal of existing political obstacles.

The Maastricht Treaty created considerable excitement in the discipline of international economics regarding the economic logic behind monetary union. Since then, there have been hundreds of studies estimating the economic effects of monetary union. Grubel (2006) gives an excellent survey of the economics of monetary union, using a framework that is highly relevant to the Asian case. In this section, we review both the convergence of financial indicators and survey the literature on monetary union in Asia, with a focus on studies related to symmetry of economic structure.

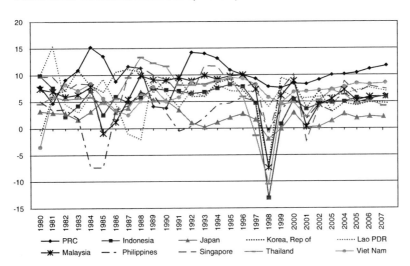

Figure 3.1a   GDP Growth (%) of ASEAN+3, 1980–2007

ASEAN+3 = Association of Southeast Asian Nations plus People's Republic of China (PRC), Japan, and Republic of Korea; GDP = gross domestic product; Lao PDR = Lao People's Democratic Republic; % = percent.

Sources: International Monetary Fund, *World Economic Outlook* database; and World Bank, *World Development Indicators* (WDI) Online.

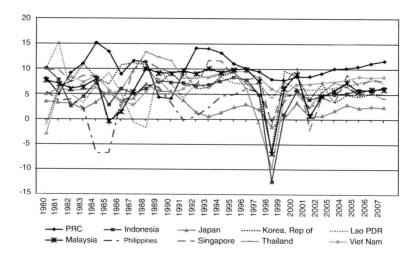

Figure 3.1b   GDP Growth (%) of ASEAN+3, Q1 1994 to Q4 2007

ASEAN5+3 = five members of the Association of Southeast Asian Nations (Indonesia, Malaysia, Philippines, Singapore, and Thailand) plus People's Republic of China (PRC), Japan, and Republic of Korea; GDP = gross domestic product; Q1 = first quarter; Q3 = third quarter; % = percent.

Sources: CEIC; World Bank, *World Development Indicators* (WDI) Online; and national sources.

Figures 3.1a and 3.1b show GDP growth rates for ASEAN+3, both individually and as a group. Figure 3.1a is based on annual data for the period 1980–2007, whereas figure 3.1b employs quarterly data for the first quarter (Q1) of 1994 to the third quarter (Q4) of 2007.[21] Clearly, the ASEAN+3 economic performance has been impressive; growth has been strong for only about all countries (Japan and the Philippines are exceptions) outside the Q3 1997–Q4 1998 period of the Asian financial crisis.

A process of convergence also appears to be in evidence. To capture this process, we calculate correlation coefficients between individual country growth and ASEAN+3 for pre- and post-crisis periods using annual (1980–2006, Table 3.4a) and quarterly (Q1 1994 to Q4 2007, Table 3.4b) data. The results are illuminating. Table 3.4a shows that while in the pre-crisis period only Japan and Thailand were statistically significant (and many were negative), in the post-crisis period all but one (Korea) were, and the magnitudes are positive and high (i.e., in the range of 0.7606

---

[21] Data for Brunei Darussalam, Myanmar, and Cambodia were not available for the annual data calculations; data for Brunei Darussalam, Myanmar, Cambodia, and the Lao PDR were unavailable for the quarterly-based calculations.

Table 3.4a Pairwise Correlation of GDP Growth Rates between Individual Countries and ASEAN+3: 1980–2007[a]

	1980–1997	1998–2007
PRC	(0.1330)	0.7956*
Indonesia	(0.0552)	0.8946*
Japan	0.9463*	0.9441*
Korea, Republic of	0.4119	0.6244
Lao People's Democratic Republic	(0.3758)	0.7680*
Malaysia	(0.1685)	0.8556*
Philippines	(0.1433)	0.9591*
Singapore	(0.1321)	0.7810*
Thailand	0.4953*	0.8311*
Viet Nam	(0.2286)	0.7606*

ASEAN+3 = Association of Southeast Asian Nations plus People's Republic of China (PRC), Japan, and Republic of Korea; GDP = gross domestic product; ( ) = negative value.
* Significant at 5% level.
[a] Computation for ASEAN+3 excludes Brunei Darussalam, Cambodia, and Myanmar. Regional GDP growth is weighted by gross national income (atlas method, current $).

Sources: Extracted from International Monetary Fund, *World Economic Outlook* Database; World Bank, *World Development Indicators* Online.

Table 3.4b Pairwise Correlation of GDP Growth Rates between Individual Countries and ASEAN5+3: Q1 1994–Q4 2007[a]

	Q1 1994–Q4 1997	Q1 1998–Q4 2007
PRC	(0.1349)	0.7356*
Indonesia	0.3810	0.7921*
Japan	0.9789*	0.9254*
Korea, Republic of	0.1806	0.6074*
Malaysia	0.3617	0.7842*
Philippines	0.3317	0.8657*
Singapore	(0.2859)	0.7525*
Thailand	0.1457	0.7722*

ASEAN5+3 = five members of the Association of Southeast Asian Nations (Indonesia, Malaysia, Philippines, Singapore, and Thailand) plus People's Republic of China (PRC), Japan, and Republic of Korea; GDP = gross domestic product; Q1 = first quarter; Q4 = fourth quarter.
* Significant at 5% level.
[a] Regional GDP growth is weighted by gross national income (atlas method, current $).

Sources: Extracted from CEIC; World Bank, *World Development Indicators* Online; and national sources.

to 0.9591 for the statistically significant coefficients). The same results generally obtain using quarterly data (Table 3.4b), with lower estimated coefficients (range 0.6074–0.9254) but all estimated coefficients are statistically significant.

In combination with the existing literature summarized above, these results give strong support to the view that, while we do not know if East Asia constitutes an OCA, we can be confident that symmetry in the region is increasing and is high for only about every country. But the literature points to two other possible criteria: factor flows and degree of interdependence. With respect to the former, the prognosis is less optimistic; intraregional labor flows are very small even by international standards (World Bank 2006b) and intraregional flows of FDI are relatively low.[22] On the other hand, intraregional trade shares are relatively high and growing. As can be seen from figures 3.2a and 3.2b, while the share of subregional trade in ASEAN is relatively low for most countries except the transitional economies (figure 3.2a), ASEAN+3 is becoming increasingly important in the trade of only about all regional economies since 2001, although the trend is not generally monotonic. In fact, with few exceptions, all economies undertake more than 40% of their total trade with other East Asian partners, and for most the share is 60% or more. This is especially impressive when one remembers from the above discussion that, unlike the EU, no preferential trading arrangements were really in place to influence these trade shares with the (theoretical) exception of AFTA.

As Rana (2006) argues, intra-industry trade is leading this process of rising intraregional trade. He uses a gravity model to show that the rise in economic symmetry in the region derives from this increase in intraregional trade. The literature would suggest that this process would bode well for a continuing "endogenous" process of increasing symmetry.

Macroeconomic Policy Diversity in East Asia: Would Maastricht Criteria be Possible?

As part of the monetary union process in Europe, it became clear that some policy harmonization was necessary to ensure a stable regime. The

---

[22] United Nations Conference on Trade and Development (UNCTAD), foreign direct investment (FDI) Statistics online. For example, intraregional FDI in ASEAN comes to only 13% of the total. Singapore is an FDI hub in ASEAN (accounting for two-thirds of FDI in the region) but its major sources are from outside the region, particularly the EU and the US. Japan and Republic of Korea only account for about 1% of global flows of FDI each. Only the PRC stands out as a major recipient of FDI flows from the region (mainly from Hong Kong, China; Japan; and Taipei,China).

famous Maastricht Criteria, later reinforced by the Stability and Growth Pact, had four principal requirements: (i) debt compared to GDP should be no greater than 60% (though this indicator was downplayed given the greater than 100% shares in Belgium and Italy), (ii) any deficit to GDP ratio should be no more than 3%, (iii) inflation and the nominal interest rate of a country should be no greater than 1.5% higher than the average of the lowest three countries, and (iv) there should be no realignment of a country's exchange rate peg in the Exchange Rate Mechanism (ERM) of the European Monetary System (EMS) for 2 years prior to acceding to monetary union. Thus, the main goal was macroeconomic policy harmonization and stability.

There has been considerable debate on the economic logic of the Maastricht Criteria in general, and the actual numeric criteria in particular. But if we were to subject East Asia to the same test, how would it fare?

First, fiscal policy would generally receive high marks, especially relative to the EU. The share of government spending in GDP in the newly industrialized economies (NIEs) (less than 25%), ASEAN (11–30% range, save the peculiar cases of Brunei Darussalam and Myanmar), and the PRC (18%) are low relative to the EU average, even though as developing countries

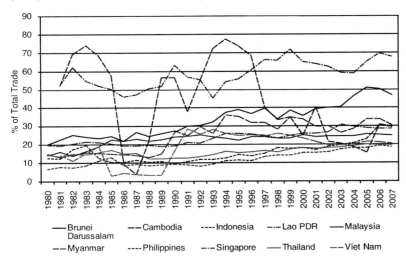

Figure 3.2a Intraregional Trade Share of East Asian Economies – ASEAN, % of total trade (1980–2007)

ASEAN = Association of Southeast Asian Nations, Lao PDR = Lao People's Democratic Republic.

Source: International Monetary Fund, *Direction of Trade Statistics.*

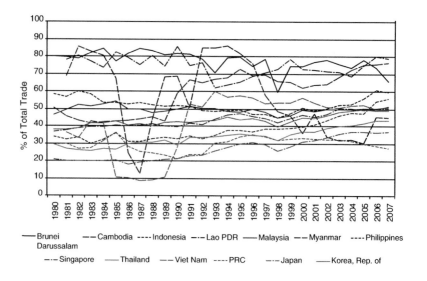

Figure 3.2b   Intraregional Trade Share of East Asian Economies – ASEAN+3, % of total trade (1980–2007)

ASEAN+3 = Association of Southeast Asian Nations plus People's Republic of China (PRC), Japan, and Republic of Korea; Lao PDR = Lao People's Democratic Republic.

Source: International Monetary Fund, *Direction of Trade Statistics.*

this is not a surprising outcome.[23, 24] Japan's share is somewhat higher (37%) but this is among the lowest in the OECD (although, of course, its debt-GDP ratio of more than 165% is the highest in the OECD). With respect to budget deficits, Table 3.5 shows that there is a good deal of variability across East Asia. Deficit-GDP ratios of the ASEAN countries were less than 3% for all original ASEAN countries, but only Cambodia among the transitional economies would meet the Maastricht budget deficit criterion. Singapore actually had a surplus of 10% of GDP. It is interesting to note that the crisis-affected ASEAN countries had surpluses or essentially balanced budgets on the eve of the crisis. Since then, they have tended to have modest deficits, with the occasional exception of Thailand. The deficits of the PRC and Taipei,China

---

[23] With a smaller tax base, potential fiscal burdens are less.

[24] All data for this section not included in Table 3.5 are taken from the International Monetary Fund's *World Economic Outlook* Database; World Bank's *World Development Indicators* Database; ADB *Key Economic Indicators;* or the Organisation for Economic Co-operation and Development Statistics Database.

(2005) were approximately in balance, while Korea had a 2% deficit and Hong Kong, China had a surplus. Only Japan, which currently has a deficit-GDP ratio of about 4% and has not met the Maastricht Criteria since 1993, and some of the transitional ASEAN countries would fail the test outright. Hence, besides these latter countries, reaching a 3% target would not be particularly difficult for East Asia.

By developing-country standards, East Asia has been characterized by conservative monetary policies and price stability. Inflation rates in ASEAN countries are in the 0.5–13.1% range (with Indonesia defining the upper boundary); the PRC and the NIEs have inflation rates of less than 3.0%; and Japan's inflation rate is only 0.2% in 2006. Thus, while inflation in the region is generally under control, there exists considerable disparity in terms of inflation rates. It is worth noting, however, that the inflation criterion for Maastricht has been a source of major disagreement: for example, if Luxembourg, the Netherlands, and Sweden were experiencing deflation, would it make sense to use their average as a reference point, given their relative sizes and falling prices? If we did the same for East Asia, we would calculate an average 0.3% (Brunei Darussalam, Japan, and Singapore), meaning that all countries with inflation rates above 1.8% would be ineligible. While this would seem normal to the European Central Bank, whose inflation target is 2% or less, it would mean that 12 out of 15 countries would fail to meet the criteria. In any event, it would take some effort to force relative convergence of inflation rates, although this would not be a task that would be much more difficult than it was in Europe. The same story generally applies to interest rates, although divergence on this indicator is much less than it is for inflation. However, as most East Asian countries have underdeveloped bond markets, it is unclear if economy-wide interest rates reflect the true price of risk in the economy, due to factors including lack of liquidity in the market. In addition, there is no doubt a far greater spread of risk across bonds in East Asia than there was in the case of the EU.

Finally, regarding exchange rates, Japan and the NIEs have been characterized by high-trend volatility relative to each other and, particularly, compared to countries in ASEAN. This is a reflection of both institutional arrangements (e.g., peg, managed float, or float) and underlying macroeconomic variables. ASEAN exchange rates, however, pretty much seem to move in step with each other since the early 1990s, reflecting in large part the implicit or explicit peg to the US dollar. In any event, these regimes have been developed in an independent context; certainly, prior to any movement toward monetary union the regime would require an exchange rate mechanism (such as the ERM or EMS prior to monetary union).

Table 3.5   Divergence in East Asian Macroeconomic Indicators, 2006

	Public Sector Debt (% of GDP)[a]	Fiscal Balance of Central Government (% of GDP)	Inflation Rate (%)	Interest Rate (%)[b]
Japan	...	(4.0)	0.2	0.56
PRC	17.3	(0.4)	1.5	3.20
NIEs 3				
Hong Kong, China	...	0.4	2.0	1.96
Korea, Republic of	32.2	(2.4)	2.2	5.23
Taipei,China	30.3[c]	0.0	0.6	2.22
ASEAN				
Brunei Darussalam	...	26.5	0.5	...
Cambodia	...	(1.5)	4.7	...
Indonesia	38.6	(1.0)	13.1	8.01
Lao PDR	...	(5.7)	6.8	...
Malaysia	56.5	(2.6)	3.6	3.36
Myanmar	...	(4.0)	10.7	...
Philippines	77.4	(1.0)	6.2	4.19
Singapore	...	10.0	1.0	1.97
Thailand	42.3	0.1	4.6	3.18
Viet Nam	45.5	(5.0)	7.5	...

ASEAN = Association of Southeast Asian Nations, GDP = gross domestic product,
Lao PDR = Lao People's Democratic Republic, NIE = newly industrialized economy,
PRC = People's Republic of China, ... = no data, ( ) = negative value.
[a] Refers to consolidated government debt except for: (a) Indonesia and Republic of Korea
which refers to central government debt, and (b) the Philippines which refers to nonfinan-
cial public sector debt.
[b] 3-month local currency sovereign yields.
[c] 2005 data.

Sources: *Asia Economic Monitor* (December 2007); *Asian Development Outlook 2007;*
Article IV Consultations, International Monetary Fund; and Bloomberg.

In short, while there is no magic number that one could assign to the
degree of economic symmetry across these countries in terms of basic
macroeconomic variables, empirical assessments would support the view
that ASEAN+3 countries are increasingly symmetrical, and the share of
intraregional trade in total trade is relatively high and rising. The process

of increasing symmetry and increased interdependence in terms of trade is being bolstered by increasing shares of intra-industry trade. Moreover, with respect to policy harmonization, the conclusion is mixed: fiscal policies could be fairly easily harmonized, whereas the monetary variables might take more effort. In any event, any policy decision to move toward monetary union in Asia would require a transitional period, as was the case in Europe.

Toward an Asian Maastricht

The Maastricht Criteria were set up for a group of developed countries that had some of the world's most sophisticated economic and financial superstructure. Given that institutional best practices were generally already in place in the countries determining the framework for monetary union, the choice for convergence criteria based on policy variables alone is understandable. However, this is not at all the case in the ASEAN+3 region; while there are a few economies with sophisticated infrastructure, the region is highly diverse in terms of its financial and monetary-related institutions, including some countries with only elementary infrastructure and institutions. Hence, before moving in the direction of closer monetary integration, it will be necessary to come up with a set of policy, institutional, and governance criteria, which we might call the "Manila Criteria."

Concluding Remarks

In this paper, we evaluated the economic prospects of economic integration in Asia. We reviewed the current evolution of trade and financial accords in the region and surveyed the literature on the economic viability of these accords, including some fresh simulations on the correlation of business cycles and the economic effects of potential trade groupings being considered. In general, the paper suggests that the economic potential for closer economic integration is strong. In terms of trade, we noted that there would be positive gains from integration within ASEAN and the current wave of bilateral agreements, but that these gains are much less significant for ASEAN than would be the case of other scenarios, such as an ASEAN+3 FTA or FTAAP. We also argued that the case for deepening financial and monetary integration in Asia is strong, even though the political underpinnings of such an accord are not yet in place.

In a related study (Plummer and Wignaraja 2006), we argue that real integration has been taking place at the bilateral, multilateral, and regional levels, and note that the economic implications of these emerging agreements will actually reinforce the economic case for monetary union in

Asia, in a similar way that real-sector integration did so in Europe. Hence, we conclude that, at present, the post-sequencing of economic integration in Asia is developing such that trade agreements, which are dominating the formal accords in Asia, will ultimately complement the movement toward financial and monetary integration, which will take a great deal more time and political will.

As a final point, we should note that the process of creating FTAs at various levels has an important political effect on cementing a regional identity and in bringing the region closer together. The proliferation of superficial FTAs in the world testifies to the political usefulness of such agreements. Indeed, it would be impossible to understand the unfolding of regionalism in Asia (or in Europe, for that matter) from a merely economic perspective: there exist strong political and strategic motivations behind this movement. Given that many see the chief problem of monetary union in Asia as being political (unlike in Europe), the "endogeneity" effect noted by Frankel and Rose (1998) could very well have its counterpart in the political realm. In this sense, the FTAs are serving as a political, as well as economic, complement, to monetary union.

APPENDIX TABLES

Table A3.1   Chronology of Major Decisions of ASEAN and ASEAN+3 Summits

ASEAN Summit Main Points	Asia-Pacific Telecommunity (APT) Summit Main Points
1st - Bali 1976 (Association of Southeast Asian Nations [ASEAN] Concord) • Established ASEAN Secretariat • Treaty of Amity signed, pledging mutual respect for independence, sovereignty, equality, territorial integrity, and identity of nations (i.e., noninterference) • establishment of a zone of peace, freedom, and neutrality	
2nd - Kuala Lumpur 1977 • ASEAN Industrial Project agreed upon • Preferential Trading Agreement (PTA) signed	
3rd - Manila 1987 • Accelerate implementation of PTA • Accelerate and make more flexible ASEAN Industrial Joint Venture (AIJV)	
4th - Singapore 1992 • ASEAN Free Trade Area (AFTA) agreed • Common Effective Preferential Tariff (CEPT) agreed	
5th - Bangkok 1995 • Pledge to actively participate in ASEAN–Europe Meeting (ASEM) in 1996	
1st - Informal - Jakarta 1996 • Proposal for ASEAN Vision 2020	

continued on next page...

Table A3.1 continued

ASEAN Summit Main Points	Asia-Pacific Telecommunity (APT) Summit Main Points
2nd - Informal - Kuala Lumpur 1997 • ASEAN 2020 presented, a broad, long-term vision for ASEAN in 2020 (with ASEAN Economic Community [AEC] in mind)	1st - Kuala Lumpur 1997 • 1st ASEAN+3 (adds People's Republic of China [PRC], Republic of Korea, and Japan)
6th - Ha Noi 1998 • Hanoi Plan of Action adopted to move toward Vision 2020: 1. Advance AFTA to 2002, 90% intra-trade subject to 0–5% tariff 2. ASEAN Investment Area (AIA)—Goal to liberalize investment within ASEAN by 2010, outside ASEAN by 2020 3. Increase Secretariat staff from 64 to 99 4. ASEAN Surveillance (Revolutionary Idea) 5. Eminent Persons' Group (EPG) proposed to come up with plan for ASEAN Vision 2020	2nd - Ha Noi 1998 • East Asian Vision Group (EAVG) proposed by Kim Dae Jung, President of the Republic of Korea, to look into East Asian Integration
3rd - Informal - Manila 1999 EPG develops plan for Vision 2020: • Concern that ASEAN not effective in responding to Asian financial crisis, so proposed financial cooperation • Speed up AFTA • Accelerate AIA • Respond to economic surge in the PRC, as well as the need to become more competitive, to attract investment, to speed up integration, and to promote information technology (IT)	3rd - Manila 1999
4th - Informal - Singapore 2000 Adopted Initiative for ASEAN Integration (IAI): • Framework for more developed ASEAN members to assist those less-developed members in need	4th - Singapore 2000 • East Asian Study Group (EASG) to consider East Asia Free Trade Area (EAFTA) and agreement to hold East Asian Summit

continued on next page...

Table A3.1 *continued*

ASEAN Summit Main Points	Asia-Pacific Telecommunity (APT) Summit Main Points
• Focus on factors to enhance competitiveness for new economy: education, skills development, and work training	• Two big ideas: (i) Development of institutional link between Southeast and East Asia, and (ii) Study group for merit of an EAFTA and investment area • Begin financial cooperation, e.g., Chiang Mai Initiative May 2000 (swap arrangements) • Propose expert group study on the PRC–ASEAN Free Trade Area
7th- Brunei Darussalam 2001 • Challenges facing ASEAN: Declining foreign direct investment (FDI), erosion of competitiveness • Road map for Integration for ASEAN to achieve by 2020 • Go beyond AFTA and AIA by deepening market liberalization for both trade and investment	**5th - Brunei Darussalam 2001** • Endorse EAVG recommendation for EAFTA but overshadowed by the PRC–ASEAN Free Trade Area proposal within 10 years, with the adoption of an early harvest provision to speed up FTA • Prompted by the PRC–ASEAN Free Trade Area proposal, Prime Minister Koizumi proposed Japan–ASEAN Economic Partnership in reaction to the PRC–ASEAN proposal • Japan–Singapore Agreement for a New Age partnership signed January 2002 and enforced summer 2002
8th - Phnom Penh 2002 • AEC end goal of Vision 2020 • Japan–Singapore Free Trade Agreement effective in November	**6th- Phnom Penh 2002** Adopt EASG recommendations of deepening and broadening of East Asian integration
9th - Bali 2003	**7th - Bali 2003** • Japan–ASEAN Free Trade Agreement study undertaken • Korea–ASEAN Free Trade Agreement study undertaken
10th- Vientiane 2004 Vientiane Action Plan, which in part: 1. Accelerated complete implementation of AFTA from 2010 to 2007, although excluded some sensitive sectors, such as rice.	**8th - Vientiane 2004** • Australia, New Zealand, and India also attended along with original APT countries. • Extra-regional deals dominated proceedings

continued on next page...

Table A3.1 continued

ASEAN Summit Main Points	Asia-Pacific Telecommunity (APT) Summit Main Points
2. Began discussion on effective dispute settlement mechanism for AFTA	• The PRC, after only 2 years of negotiation over early harvest agreements, signed FTA with ASEAN to become completed by 2010, but excludes number of sensitive goods, i.e., iron, steel, automobiles, and sugar. It also lacks agreement on services and dispute settlement mechanism. • Japan and the Philippines agreed in principle on FTA that will cover some services sectors and Japan will open up labor market to Filipino nurses and caregivers. • ASEAN–Japan Comprehensive Economic Partnership Agreement will commence negotiation from 2006 with completion date set for 2012. • FTA plans with Republic of Korea, India, Australia, and New Zealand unveiled; India by 2016, Australia, and New Zealand by 2017 • ASEAN set plans to improve institutional capacity to negotiate FTA with external partners • This summit reflected the PRC's desire to expedite trade liberalization with ASEAN and its East Asian partners toward the formation of an East Asian trading bloc, like the European Union (EU) or North American Free Trade Agreement (NAFTA) • Malaysia proposed to host first East Asia Summit

continued on next page...

Table A3.1 continued

ASEAN Summit Main Points	Asia-Pacific Telecommunity (APT) Summit Main Points
	Meeting of Asian Foreign Ministers in Cebu - April 2005 The PRC and Malaysia come to agreement with Indonesia, Singapore, and Viet Nam to include outside participants in the East Asian Summit, provided they agree to the Treaty of Amity and Cooperation and two other conditions. These participants will include India, Australia, and New Zealand.
11th- Kuala Lumpur 2005 • Major agreement is the Kuala Lumpur Declaration, establishing charter to make ASEAN a legal institutional framework, strengthening competitiveness and deepening economic integration • Transfer ASEAN from loosely associated organization into rule-based legal regime • Created high-level EPG and is assigned to prepare charter documents	**9th- ASEAN+3** • Signed the Kuala Lumpur Declaration on the ASEAN Plus Three Summit reaffirming annual meetings in conjunction with the ASEAN Summit **First East Asian Summit (EAS) - December 2005** • Members: ASEAN+3, Australia, New Zealand, and India • Discussion focused on strategic dialogue and promoting cooperation in security, energy security, financial stability, economic integration, eradication of poverty, and narrowing of development gaps, as well as promoting deeper cultural understanding • Little concrete discussion of East Asian integration; therefore, objectives, agenda, and modalities of EAS are difficult to assess • EAS is a development of, not a successor to, ASEAN+3 • EAS will be held annually in conjunction with ASEAN summit at same location, chaired by ASEAN country chairs at ASEAN summit. This assures ASEAN as the driving force.

continued on next page...

Table A3.1 continued

ASEAN Summit Main Points	Asia-Pacific Telecommunity (APT) Summit Main Points
12th - Cebu 2007 • Signed the Cebu Declaration on the Establishment of the ASEAN Economic Community by 2015 • Directed the High Level Task Force to complete the drafting of the ASEAN Charter in time for the 13th summit in Singapore in 2007 • Issued the ASEAN Declaration on the Protection and Promotion of the Rights of Migrant Workers • Adopted the Third ASEAN Work Program on HIV/AIDS (AWP III) for 2006–2010 • Signed the ASEAN Convention on Counter Terrorism	**10th - ASEAN+3** • Agreed to putting ASEAN community building at the center, according priority to the successful implementation of the Vientiane Action Programme (VAP), narrowing the development gap and facilitating ASEAN integration **2nd - EAS** • Signed the Cebu Declaration on East Asian Energy Security • Stressed openness of EAS and close coordination with ASEAN

Source: Authors' compilation.

Table A3.2a Correlation of GDP Growth Rates of East Asian Economies: 1980 to 1997

	PRC	Indonesia	Japan	Korea, Rep. of	Lao PDR	Malaysia	Philippines	Singapore	Thailand	Viet Nam	ASEAN+3
PRC	1.0000										
Indonesia	(0.2499)	1.0000									
Japan	(0.4003)	(0.0996)	1.0000								
Korea, Rep. of	0.1305	(0.3604)	0.1976	1.0000							
Lao PDR	(0.3573)	0.3736	(0.2112)	(0.6025)*	1.0000						
Malaysia	(0.0795)	0.6011*	(0.1782)	(0.0715)	(0.0502)	1.0000					
Philippines	(0.4984)*	0.3079	0.0049	(0.0522)	(0.1214)	0.4361	1.0000				
Singapore	(0.1452)	0.4819*	(0.1361)	(0.0692)	(0.1057)	0.8029*	0.5709*	1.0000			
Thailand	(0.1327)	0.2805	0.4528	0.4350	(0.3015)	0.4237	0.2334	0.3928	1.0000		
Viet Nam	0.2860	(0.2063)	(0.3574)	0.3537	0.0510	0.3245	(0.1159)	0.0459	0.0286	1.0000	
ASEAN+3	(0.1316)	(0.1541)	0.9488*	0.3553	(0.3828)	(0.1675)	(0.1267)	(0.1315)	0.4864*	(0.2491)	1.0000

ASEAN+3 = Association of Southeast Asian Nations plus People's Republic of China (PRC), Japan, and Republic of Korea; GDP = gross domestic product; Lao PDR = Lao People's Democratic Republic; ( ) = negative value.
* Significant at 5% level.

Source: World Development Indicators, various years.

Table A3.2b Correlation of GDP Growth Rates of East Asian Economies: 1998 to 2007

	PRC	Indonesia	Japan	Korea, Rep. of	Lao PDR	Malaysia	Philippines	Singapore	Thailand	Viet Nam	ASEAN+3
PRC	1.0000										
Indonesia	0.5774	1.0000									
Japan	0.6466*	0.8296*	1.0000								
Korea, Rep. of	0.1129	0.7871*	0.5778	1.0000							
Lao PDR	0.5961	0.7472*	0.6010	0.7071*	1.0000						
Malaysia	0.4097	0.8685*	0.8521*	0.8810*	0.7443*	1.0000					
Philippines	0.7134*	0.8380*	0.9144*	0.6520*	0.6830	0.8872*	1.0000				
Singapore	0.4799	0.5729	0.7846*	0.6467*	0.6806	0.8327*	0.8319*	1.0000			
Thailand	0.4666	0.9511*	0.7711*	0.8422*	0.7544*	0.9248*	0.8231*	0.6137	1.0000		
Viet Nam	0.8952*	0.6246	0.6968*	0.0671	0.4070	0.3560	0.6524*	0.3414	0.4452	1.0000	
ASEAN+3	0.7965*	0.8946*	0.9441*	0.6244	0.7680*	0.8556*	0.9591*	0.7810*	0.8311*	0.7606*	1.0000

ASEAN+3 = Association of Southeast Asian Nations plus People's Republic of China (PRC), Japan, and Republic of Korea; GDP = gross domestic product;
Lao PDR = Lao People's Democratic Republic.
* Significant at 5% level.

Source: World Development Indicators, various years.

Table A3.3 Country Profiles, 2007

	GDP Growth (annual average)		GDP per capita (constant 2000 $)	Openness[a] (% of GDP)	Manufacturing value added (% of GDP)	Poverty Head-count Ratio[b] (PPP, at $1/day, % of population)	
	1990–2000	2001–2007					
Japan	1.6	1.5	40,655.7	27.3[d]	21.0[d]	...	
PRC	9.8	10.2	1,791.3	72.0[c]	33.5[d]	9.9	(2004)
Hong Kong, China	4.0	4.9	34,036.5	404.1	3.2[c]	...	
Korea, Republic of	6.5	4.7	14,540.3	90.4	27.9	...	
Brunei Darussalam	2.2	2.6	18,304.4[c]	96.2[c]	10.5	...	
Cambodia	7.5	9.7	482.3	144.6[c]	18.6[c]	66.0	(2004)
Indonesia	4.8	5.1	1,033.6	54.7	27.0	7.5	(2002)
Lao PDR	6.3	6.6	461.5	78.2[c]	20.9[c]	27.0	(2002)
Malaysia	7.4	4.8	4,715.2	210.0	29.8[c]	2.0	(1997)
Myanmar	6.5	9.0	...	...	...	...	
Philippines	3.1	5.0	1,216.2	83.3	22.0	14.8	(2003)

continued on next page...

Table A3.3 continued

	GDP Growth (annual average)		GDP per capita (constant 2000 $)	Openness[a] (% of GDP)	Manufacturing value added (% of GDP)	Poverty Head-count Ratio[b] (PPP, at $1/day, % of population)	
	1990–2000	2001–2007					
Singapore	7.8	5.3	28,964.2	433.0	25.5	...	
Thailand	5.2	5.1	2,712.7	132.5	34.5	2.0	(2002)
Viet Nam	7.4	7.7	617.0	159.3	21.3[c]	...	

... = no data from the same source, GDP = gross domestic product, Lao PDR = Lao People's Democratic Republic, PRC = People's Republic of China, PPP = purchasing power parity, $ = US dollar, % = percent.
[a] Exports and imports of goods and services as % of GDP (current $).
[b] Year of latest available data in parenthesis.
[c] 2006 data.
[d] 2005 data.

Source: World Bank, *World Development Indicators*, accessed November 2008.

4

ECONOMIC INTEGRATION IN SOUTH ASIA AND LESSONS FROM EAST ASIA OF TRADE AND INVESTMENT

Pradumna B. Rana and J. Malcolm Dowling

Introduction

South Asia was a well-integrated region within the British Empire during the 19th century and the early 20th century before World War II. In 1947, when Pakistan (which then included Bangladesh) and India became independent, more than half of Pakistan's imports and nearly two thirds of its exports were traded with India. Similar trade relations existed between India and Sri Lanka, which was settled by immigrants from South India much earlier. Nepal also had a relatively open border with India. After partition, tensions between India and Pakistan increased over the issues of water rights, territory, and currency valuation. In the 1950s and 1960s, all the countries in South Asia pursued import substitution strategies and eschewed export promotion. South Asian economies pursued self-finance and bootstrap development according to the Soviet model and exports were directed at developed countries in Europe and North America. Trade among the South Asian countries diminished dramatically. Eventually, the United States (US) became the most important trading partner of all South Asian economies (US Agency for International Development [USAID] 2005).

Total trade volumes among the countries of the region before partition were estimated at around 20% of total trade (World Bank 2004). Twenty years later, this figure had fallen to 2%. The share of intraregional trade began to increase only after the countries in the region abandoned import substitution and began to liberalize trade. In recent years, the level of intraregional trade has increased to around 4% of total trade—still quite small compared with trade in other developing regions in Asia and the rest of the world. Within South Asia, India's share of intraregional trade is the smallest at 2.4%, while smaller countries' shares are much larger. Nepal's share

is close to 50.0% because of its extensive trade with India. Sri Lanka's
share is also much larger than the average (14.4%) followed by the share of
Bangladesh (10.3%). Intraregional trade shares are much larger in regions
where trade agreements have been in force for some time. For example,
in the European Community, 67% of trade takes place within the region,
and the comparable figure for the Association of Southeast Asian Nations
(ASEAN) is 26% (Table 4.1).

There were many reasons for the dramatic fall in trade within South
Asia. The most obvious was the hostility between India and Pakistan that
emerged after the British partitioned colonial India in 1947. The hostility
arose from a series of disagreements resulting from Partition. The first was
the apportionment of water from the Indus River, which flows primarily
through Pakistan and provides irrigation for arid lands in Sind Province.
The river has a number of tributaries and, while it flows through Pakistan,
its headwaters are in India. After much negotiation over more than a
decade, an agreement was reached to assign the Ravi, Beas, and Sutlej
tributaries to India, and the Indus, Jelum, and Chenais to Pakistan. There
were also conflicts over Kashmir, which still persist. Surplus food grain
was produced in the Punjab and Sind and this surplus had to transported
to other food-deficit parts of the country. The British developed roads and
other infrastructure to implement this trade. It was stopped after Partition
as differences between the two countries were exacerbated by disagreements over exchange rates. Pakistan refused to follow the other countries

Table 4.1   Share of South Asia Intraregional Trade in World Trade, %

Country	1980	1985	1990	1995	2000	2005
Bangladesh	4.8	4.7	6.0	12.8	7.9	10.3
Bhutan	n.a.	n.a.	n.a.	n.a.	n.a.	n.a.
India	1.9	1.6	1.4	2.7	2.4	2.4
Maldives	n.a.	12.5	12.7	14.3	22.2	18.3
Nepal	n.a.	34.3	11.9	14.8	22.3	49.0
Pakistan	3.6	2.8	2.7	2.2	2.7	2.7
Sri Lanka	6.7	5.5	5.6	7.8	7.4	14.4
South Asia	**2.9**	**2.8**	**2.5**	**4.1**	**3.8**	**4.1**

n.a. = not available.

Source: International Monetary Fund. 2006. *Direction of Trade Statistics* CD-ROM, July.

in the "sterling area" (including India and Sri Lanka) and devalued its currency. India refused to honor the new exchange rate and stopped all trade with Pakistan. This created havoc in Pakistan, which overnight was deprived of the consumption and investment goods that it had relied on for many years. To adjust, Pakistan began an industrialization program of its own to become self-sufficient. It steered clear of its comparative advantage in agriculture (Burki 1980). Trade between Pakistan and India never returned to pre-Partition levels, despite the previous successful trade relationships and the extensive infrastructure built by the British to connect these two parts of colonial India.

South Asia generally embarked on a development model that drew widely on the Soviet experience, stressing import substitution and self-sufficiency rather than export promotion and openness. Soviet-style heavy industry development was also stressed along with the importation of capital goods from the Soviet Union. Believing in the ability of the public sector to increase incomes, the Nehru government developed a wide range of public-sector companies to achieve this objective. At the same time, the private sector was overregulated with a web of licenses, taxes, and price and production controls that shackled economic activity and discouraged foreign direct investment (FDI) in this license permit–quota Raj. This system dated from World War II, when public sector enterprises were set up to produce and procure supplies to support the British in the war effort while ensuring adequate domestic supplies. An elaborate system of rationing and price controls developed, as it did in many other countries involved in the war. Subsequently, India set up a series of import and export monopolies for agricultural products and imposed a de facto import ban on consumer goods.

Higher education was reserved for the elites, and widespread education and health were not a priority for the rest of the population. Low literacy, low life expectancy, and the spread of disease persisted for decades (Das 2002).

Pakistan, the other major economy in the region, followed a slightly different strategy after Partition. It had to develop a private sector that could produce consumer goods quickly to offset the shortages created by the shutdown in trade with India. To protect this fledgling consumer goods industry, it set up tariff protection for domestic industry. In the early 1970s, all this changed when Pakistan's former Prime Minister Bhutto began to nationalize large-scale industry, the banking system, and eventually small-scale agriculture-based industries. Within a few years, state control in Pakistan was as pervasive as that in India and extended to Bangladesh, as East Pakistan had recently been renamed, under its first prime minister, Mujibur Rahman.

In the 1980s, the region began to undergo fundamental change. First, Sri Lanka (in the 1970s) and then the other countries began to open their

Table 4.2   Exports of Goods and Services, % of GDP

Country	1978	1991	2000	2005
Bangladesh	5.6	6.7	14.0	16.8
Bhutan	–	32.1	29.4	27.2
PRC	6.6	21.0	23.3	37.5
India	6.2	8.6	13.8	20.5
Maldives	–	–	89.5	62.1
Nepal	10.6	11.5	23.3	16.1
Pakistan	9.2	17.0	13.6	15.3
Sri Lanka	34.8	28.2	39.0	34.0

GDP = gross domestic product, PRC = People's Republic of China, – = no data, % = percent.

Source: World Bank, *World Development Indicators* Online.

economies to international trade and dismantle industry regulations. International trade volumes began to increase, particularly following the Indian financial crisis of 1991 and the set of reforms that followed. Trade as a share of gross domestic product (GDP) generally rose in the 1990s and into the 21st century, especially for the larger economies (Table 4.2). The bulk of these exports was bound for industrial countries. With the exception of Bhutan and Nepal, which are landlocked and depend on India for most of their trade, the rest of South Asia did not share in the growth of trade in the region. Of the exports of Bangladesh in 2004, only 1% went to India, 4% to Sri Lanka, and 0.5% to Pakistan. On the import side, data showed a stronger performance. India's share of Bangladeshi imports was 19% while its share of Sri Lanka's was 14%. A simple gravity model suggests that trade should be much greater. Contiguous countries in the rest of the world have considerable trade with each other. Canada and Mexico, for instance, are the biggest trading partners in the US. All countries in Europe trade with each other, and 65% of trade in the European Union (EU) is intraregional. In South Asia, the share of intraregional trade in world trade has not increased much since the start of reforms in 1991. Bangladesh's share has increased from 5.5% to 10.3%, and Sri Lanka's from 6.5% to 14.4%. On the other hand, in the two biggest economies, Pakistan's share has fallen from 3.1% to 2.7%, and India's has increased from 1.8% to about 2.4%. It is not an understatement to say that there is wide scope for greater regional cooperation within South Asia.

Trade within South Asia is also lopsided and dominated by Indian exports to the rest of the region. The World Bank estimates that 85% of exports to the region are from India. Pakistan's share is quite small, reflecting continued political difficulties. Most of India's exports go to Bangladesh and Sri Lanka, which run large trade deficits with India. Smaller countries have not been able to penetrate the Indian market for several reasons. The smaller countries produce labor-intensive consumer goods, which are also produced by Indian competitors, while India supplies a variety of machinery and raw materials that are not available locally at competitive prices. The devaluation of the Indian rupee between the mid-1980s and 1992 resulted in large real devaluations of bilateral exchange rates with Bangladesh and Sri Lanka; it also provided a competitive advantage for Indian exporters even as they were lowering their tariff and nontariff barriers.

Economic Integration

There are several mechanisms and modalities for increasing intraregional trade and fostering regional cooperation. Generally there are three areas of greater economic integration. These are cross-border infrastructure, international trade and investment (including services), and financial sector cooperation. We explore each of these in turn.

Cross-Border Infrastructure

Major cross-border initiatives are now taking place through the South Asia Subregional Economic Cooperation (SASEC) program. This program was initiated by four of the seven South Asian Association for Regional Cooperation (SAARC) members (Bangladesh, Bhutan, India, and Nepal) that formed the South Asian Growth Quadrangle (SAGQ) in 1996. The aim of SAGQ was to accelerate economic development—a task that these countries believed was not being accomplished under SAARC. At the request of SAGQ, the SASEC program was launched in 2001 with support from the Asian Development Bank (ADB). The aim of SASEC was to accelerate economic cooperation within SAGQ. Six priority sectors were identified: transport; energy and power; tourism; environment; trade, investment, and private sector cooperation; and information and communications technology (ICT). Each of these areas was to be chaired by one of the four countries, with ADB providing facilitation and coordination. Working groups were set up in each sector. ADB has provided technical assistance to support these activities. There has been some progress in each of the sectors in identifying projects and undertaking some preliminary work. In transport, a framework was developed for regional connectivity; it involved

Table 4.3   Loans to SASEC

Project	Year	Sector	Amount ($ million)
West Bengal Corridor Development (India)	2001	Transport	210.0
Road Network Improvement (Bangladesh)	2003	Transport	126.0
Subregional Transport Facilitation (Nepal)	2004	Transport	20.0
Road Network (Bhutan)	2005	Transport	27.3
Total			383.3

SASEC = South Asia Subregional Economic Cooperation, $ = US dollar.

Source: South Asian Association for Regional Cooperation (SAARC).

a number of corridors, both actual and potential. Six of these corridors were further examined with the help of ADB technical assistance. ADB has also provided loans to the individual countries for upgrading key segments of the corridors in the subregion. Additional work will be carried out in the future, including the upgrading of logistical systems and coordination with the Greater Mekong Subregion (GMS) program of regional cooperation in the Mekong area. In trade and investment, the focus was on removing nontrade barriers and promoting private sector cooperation. Business facilitation has been promoted through the recently established South Asia Business Forum (SABF) and commissioned studies on private sector cooperation to lower trade barriers, boost human resources, and increase connectivity in ICT.

Other work to harmonize standards and simplify customs procedures is also being carried out by SASEC, and members of this group have been welcomed into other groups in tourism, ICT, and transport. In tourism, the plan is to focus on ecotourism and visits to Buddhist sites in the region. A website has been created and collaborative efforts have been made with various travel organizations; training sessions have also been held for those in the travel media. Sri Lanka has joined this group. Cooperation with the transport group is recommended to close the gap between tourist sites and main roads where necessary. ICT initiatives have been identified in enhancing high-bandwidth connectivity, establishing community information centers, strengthening ICT regulations, developing common software tools and information sharing, and developing human resources. As part of community information centers, distance learning and telemedicine could produce the biggest developmental impact. Less progress has been made in energy, power, and environment. Projects for the rural electrification of Assam based on the Bangladeshi model and the distribution of natural gas in Bangladesh with Indian assistance were started. Little progress has been reported, however. In the environment, problems of overlapping jurisdictions, lack of interest, and the complexity of cross-border environmental issues have hampered project formulation and implementation. Of the many projects proposed, only regional air quality management was implemented. The implementation of SASEC initiatives has been modest. Since 2001, four loans from ADB totaling $383 million, all in the transport sector, have been extended (Table 4.3).

Trade and Investment

SAARC and Its Trade Initiatives. SAARC, with its trade initiatives—the SAARC Preferential Trading Arrangement (SAPTA) and the South Asia Free Trade Agreement (SAFTA)—is the major institutional entity charged with promoting free trade in South Asia. Earlier, trade agreements had been reached between India and Nepal and between India and Bhutan, as well as trade and transit agreements between India and Bangladesh. The Bangkok Agreement was also signed in 1975 by India, Bangladesh, Sri Lanka, Republic of Korea (henceforth Korea), and Lao People's Democratic Republic (Lao PDR). Concessions under the Bangkok Agreement were minimal and quantitative restrictions were not reduced significantly. Hence, trade among the signatories to the agreement has been small, amounting to 2% of total trade. The accession of the People's Republic of China (PRC) to the agreement in 2001 has done little to expand trade, according to World Bank analysis. The booming trade between the PRC and India and also between Korea and India has very little to do with the concessions granted under the agreement but are rather induced by comparative advantage outside of any preferential agreement. The Bangkok Agreement has since been replaced by the Asia Pacific Forum.

SAARC is an association of seven countries in South Asia (Bangladesh, Bhutan, India, Maldives, Nepal, Pakistan, and Sri Lanka). Afghanistan has been accepted as a new member, but the membership procedures have not yet been completed. SAARC encourages cooperation in agriculture, rural development, science and technology, culture, health, population control, narcotics control, and antiterrorism. In 1993, SAARC countries signed an agreement to gradually lower tariffs within the region through SAPTA. Three rounds of preferential tariff reductions were implemented on a product by product basis. In 2004, SAARC countries framed the SAFTA, which sought to establish a free trade zone in South Asia. SAFTA became operational in 2006.

SAFTA set out a series of objectives in discussions that started in 1995 and continued into the next decade. The objectives were to (i) eliminate all tariffs and import restrictions; (ii) harmonize customs procedures; (iii) facilitate intraregional banking, and port and land transport facilities; (iv) develop a program to facilitate trade-related services; (v) establish a review and monitoring mechanism; (vi) ensure equitable benefits to all member countries; and (vii) remove structural impediments to regional trade. Representatives from the members of SAARC meet yearly to discuss progress and ensure that the benefits from trade expansion resulting from the implementation of the agreement are distributed equitably.

As in other agreements within SAARC, there are two groups of countries in this agreement: the least-developed countries (LDCs) in SAFTA (Bangladesh, Nepal, Bhutan, and Maldives) and the non-LDCs (India, Pakistan, and Sri Lanka). Tariff reductions are phased differently for the two groups. LDCs agree to reduce maximum tariffs to 30% and the non-LDCs to 20%, within 2 years. In the second phase, starting 1 January 2008, the non-LDCs agree to reduce tariffs to 0–5% within 5 years, while the LDCs agree to implement the same tariff range in 8 years. One caveat is that items on the "sensitive lists" are exempt from these schedules. The sensitive lists are to be negotiated by the members.

SAFTA puts more teeth into the trade agreement than SAPTA. The sensitive-list loophole still exists, however. It is unlikely that any agreement could have been reached without it. Perhaps this agreement will pave the way for progress in tariff reductions that were not possible previously. One reason for optimism is that there have been substantial tariff cuts on industrial products by India, and on both industrial and agricultural products by Pakistan. If these two countries, which dominate economic activity and trade in the region, were to make substantial tariff reductions, the rest of the region would very likely follow quickly. There should also be some synergy between trade liberalization and political rapprochement between Pakistan and India. An effective and vibrant SAFTA and SAARC will likewise enhance the region's ability to bargain in multilateral negotiations if and when they resume. Moreover, the implementation of this trade agreement will open the door for negotiations in trade facilitation dealing with so-called behind-the-border bottlenecks that go beyond harmonizing customs procedures.

Some weaknesses in the agreement could, however, undermine its effectiveness unless they are remedied in further negotiations. Only customs duties are addressed. A number of other protective arrangements (nontariff barriers) serve to reduce trade and increase costs. While nontariff barriers (NTBs) that are not compatible with the General Agreement on Tariffs and Trade (GATT) are to be removed, there is no effective mechanism in the agreement for removing other NTBs. Any reduction in agricultural tariffs is likely to be contentious, as these rates are high in Bangladesh, India, and Sri Lanka and will be complicated by subsidies, particularly in India. The successful implementation of the agreement faces other bottlenecks, such as the escape clause of sensitive lists, negotiation of rules of origin, and possible suspension of concessions for members with balance-of-payments difficulties. Given mixed experience in SAPTA achieving much in the past, these potential bottlenecks could well scuttle the agreement. The hope is that all countries will be more committed to free trade than they have been in the past and will be willing to make mutual concessions to make the agreement work. If the agreement is implemented, all countries in the region could benefit from scale economies and greater competition; this would also pave the way for greater trade with the rest of the world.

How successful have SAARC and its related trade initiatives been in raising the share of intraregional trade in total trade? Since we do not know what would have happened without them, a definitive answer is difficult. Gravity models have been used to estimate how much SAARC and its trade initiatives have contributed to the growth in trade. The gravity model suggests that trade between two countries will depend on the geographic distance between them and the relative size of their economies. Research using such a model suggests that SAFTA has had a positive effect on intra-bloc trade. In the case of SAPTA, it should be recognized that, despite membership in SAPTA and some positive impact of SAPTA on trade between members, India and Pakistan are trading at a 70% lower rate than would be expected given their relative size and geographic proximity (ADB 2002, Frankel and Wei 1998).

Bandara and Yu (2003) use the Global Trade Analysis Project (GTAP) computable general equilibrium (CGE) model to analyze the impact of SAFTA on the countries in South Asia. They find that India gains more than the other countries, but that the rest of the region also benefits. This is because India has a large manufacturing sector and high initial tariffs. They find that removing all tariffs increases the importation of cheaper goods and increases consumption as a result. They find that textile and apparel trade will increase. Increased intraregional trade possibilities will be created but will be small relative to gains from unilateral liberalization by all SAFTA countries. A study by Hirantha (2004) reports strong evidence of trade creation in the South Asian region under SAPTA and with no trade diversion on trade with nonmembers. Srinivasan (1994) uses a gravity model to show that complete removal of tariffs would result in a 3% increase in India's gross national product (GNP). Using an expanded gravity model—where bilateral trade is a function of distance, economic size, and common language—Batra (2004) finds positive trade potential in the SAARC, mainly from increased trade between India and Pakistan. The estimates of Frankel and Wei (1995) indicate that trade between India and Pakistan is 70% lower than that between two other economies that are otherwise identical.

Bilateral and Multilateral Free Trade Agreements. Two bilateral free trade agreements (FTAs) involve South Asian countries: those between Sri Lanka and India and between Nepal and India. The Sri Lanka–India FTA took effect in March 2000. The agreement provides for duty-free as well as duty-preference access for goods manufactured in the two countries. Both countries have prepared a list of products that will be duty-free and have agreed to phase out tariffs on a number of other items. The phase out will be implemented over 5 years for India and 8 years for Sri Lanka. There are also negative lists of products that will not be covered by duty concessions. These negative lists will be reduced in the future through mutual consultation. Rules-of-origin criteria for preference eligibility have been agreed on. Products that meet 35% or more of those criteria will qualify for preferential market access. Sri Lankan exports with a domestic value-added content of 25% will also qualify for entry into the Indian market if they have at least 10% Indian content.

The main features of the agreement are as follows (Mukherji, Jayawardhana, and Kelegama 2004). Garments are on India's negative list but will be given some tax concessions. There are 429 items on India's negative list and 1,180 products on Sri Lanka's. The import and export mix of both countries, as well as estimates of trade creation and trade diversion, were analyzed by Mukherji, Jayawardhana, and Kelegama (2004). India's preferential imports from Sri Lanka have increased in a number of products. If this increase is at lower or higher prices relative to the rest of the world, trade creation or trade diversion can occur. The authors also carried out a similar analysis of Sri Lanka's preferential imports from India. Data compiled for 1999 and 2000 showed that there was net trade creation in both cases, more so for Sri Lankan imports from India. A number of constraints on trade are not addressed by the agreement. The negative list and continued tariffs are a major impediment. There are also NTBs that constrain exporters in Sri Lanka, including required food sampling, which takes a long time to clear, and licensing and customs checks for food items. Sri Lankan exports are also permitted only through designated ports. Negotiations are under way to open other ports. There were complaints of arbitrary customs valuations and discriminatory sales taxes imposed by the Tamil Nadu government on Sri Lanka imports. The negative list exempts almost 10% of India's imports and more than a third of its exports from liberalization under the agreement. To qualify as a true FTA, the one between India and Sri Lanka should set a time frame for liberalizing all mutual trade, aside from a few sensitive items.

India and Nepal have had a trade treaty for many years. The current treaty was renegotiated in 2002 from a treaty signed in 1996. The treaty has a number of components. The major features are an emphasis on trade facilitation and the reciprocal grant of unconditional most-favored-nation (MFN) status. A unique feature not found in other trade agreements is a provision for refunds to Nepal for excise and other duties collected by India on goods produced in India and exported to Nepal. Nepalese primary products have full access to the Indian market, free of duties and quantitative restrictions. Indian exports to Nepal are similarly unencumbered. There is a clause where India agrees to promote industrial development in Nepal through the favorable treatment of industrial goods produced in Nepal. Whether this provision has been helpful to Nepal's industrial development depends on whether the local content of these industrial goods has been increasing, creating backward linkages to the Nepalese industrial sector. Unfortunately, there has been little research on this question. Whether the treaty is consistent with World Trade Organization (WTO) rules has been analyzed by Nath (2004), who argues that it is not. The treaty operates more like an FTA, Nath says, and would be compatible with GATT Article XXIV if free trade in industrial goods were also made reciprocal. If Nepal is considered a developing country and India a developed country then the treaty could be considered as a preferential trading arrangement (PTA). Further details of the treaty are provided in the Nath paper and in Shrestha (2003).

The Bay of Bengal Initiative for Multi-Sectoral Technical and Economic Cooperation (BIMSTEC) started in June 1997 at a meeting of the trade ministers of Bangladesh, India, Sri Lanka, and Thailand. In December 1997, Myanmar was added as a fifth member. Each member country has been assigned a lead role in different sectors, which include trade and investment, technology transfer, transportation and communication, energy, tourism, and fisheries. Ministerial meetings are held periodically, and at a meeting in November 2003 additional subsectors for cooperation were identified: textiles and clothing, drugs and pharmaceuticals, gems and jewelry, horticulture, processed foods, automotive parts, coconuts, spices, rubber, and tea and coffee. Thailand was the most active member and had the idea of using the initiative to establish a foothold in South

Asia. The emphasis on gems and jewelry and automotive parts reflects the commercial interests of Thailand (Bhattacharya and Bhattacharyay 2006; Inoue, Murayama, and Rahmatullah 2004).

An FTA between India and the other members of BIMSTEC is being discussed. A framework FTA was signed in February 2004; it stipulates preferential treatment and a time frame for tariff reductions. Subsequent meetings focused on agreeing on details on rules of origin, sensitive lists, and nontariff barriers so that an agreement could be concluded before the BIMSTEC summit in February 2007. Originally, the agreement was to be concluded in July 2006. The India–BIMSTEC FTA differs from SAFTA in that it has provisions for agreement in services and investment. These were not part of the package to be discussed at the BIMSTEC summit but will be negotiated later on. Talks between India and BIMSTEC are mired in disagreement over the number of products on the sensitive lists and rules of origin. India wants a short preferential list of items, but its BIM-STEC partners want to accommodate a large number of items. Other areas of discussion include the negative list of items to be excluded from tariff reduction commitments under the FTA and the removal of NTBs. India's intraregional trade with BIMSTEC countries has been increasing in the past few years, from 4.0% in 2001 to 6.6% in 2003.

Further increases are projected for 2006 and beyond. However, careful analysis of the agreement should be made to assess whether it will create or divert trade and what industries will be most affected. BIMSTEC has also agreed to work toward improved transport links between member countries. Setting up an energy center under the auspices of the initiative in India to strengthen energy sector cooperation is in the pipeline as well. Members have agreed to strengthen cooperation in grid connectivity, gas pipelines, hydropower, renewable sources of energy, energy efficiency, and access to energy in all areas.

Impact of Preferential Trade Agreements (PTAs): Some Historical Results. In addition to gravity models, several CGE models have also been constructed to investigate the impact of PTAs on trade. Robinson and Thierfelder (1999) conclude that PTAs create, rather than divert, trade. Several other studies suggest that larger PTAs like the EU and the North American Free Trade Agreement (NAFTA) have positive welfare effects, particularly if trade preference is liberalized in a nondiscriminatory manner by including those outside the agreement. These models also suggest that PTAs have trade creation effects that dominate trade diversion. The results of gravity and CGE modeling suggest that there are often negative impacts on nonmembers and smaller countries that are not part of a larger PTA.

Furthermore, there is the risk that PTAs do not confer the same benefits of the general reciprocity of MFN treatment and may therefore obscure the transmission of trade externalities to many countries, both inside and outside the agreement.

Compared with PTAs in other regions, PTAs in Asia have been limited in size and scope. ASEAN is the most visible and most active. Asia has therefore developed primarily as a region where trade barriers have been lowered by reciprocal agreement in accordance with MFN principles but without as much formal structure as in Europe or Latin America. Besides, the ASEAN Free Trade Area (AFTA) and SAPTA have not made much of a difference in the pattern of trade. This is particularly true of SAPTA, which has been handicapped by ongoing conflicts between Pakistan and India. BIMSTEC, which drops Pakistan and adds Thailand and Myanmar to SAARC, has been formed to sidestep this problem and to move forward with regional integration within South Asia and build bridges with Southeast Asia (Bhattacharya and Bhattacharyay 2006).

Trade Creation and Trade Diversion. There are a number of important perspectives when considering regional trading arrangements in a subregion such as South Asia. One of the principal objectives of countries in this context would be to divert imports from lower-cost suppliers outside the region to higher-cost local suppliers within the region. Other things being equal, an FTA in South Asia would induce buyers to switch from outside suppliers and domestic producers to producers within the region. This creates and diverts trade at the same time. Without knowledge of the costs of alternative supply and trade policy toward nonmember countries, the effects on welfare and income are not clear. In shaping policies, it is important to recognize these two effects and to evaluate the costs and benefits not only to the trading country but also to its partners within South Asia. There has been little work in this area aside from Mukherji (2000).

We can consider a framework for analyzing these issues as a matter of three different kinds of policies: (i) policies that discriminate in favor of trade with other South Asian economies and against the rest of the world; (ii) policies that do not discriminate against trade with neighboring countries but, in the final analysis, hurt neighboring countries more than the rest of the world; and (iii) policies that overtly discriminate against neighboring countries in South Asia. In analyzing these three kinds of policies, there is general agreement that (i) is better than (ii) or (iii), and that within (i) multilateral trade liberalization is the best solution. There are a number of possible alternatives under (i) which depend on the market power of the bloc and the relative effects of trade diversion and trade creation.

It is better to argue for free trade and, when that is not possible, to analyze the pros and cons of the alternative. Policies consistent with (ii) have been widespread in South Asia. Following import substitution, policies that combined import licenses with high tariffs resulted in excluding from imports unessential items that could not be obtained locally. These policies essentially excluded all imports from South Asia and confined imports to machinery and other intermediate products from developed countries outside the region. A general consumer goods import ban (phased out in 2001) was the most onerous of these restrictive practices. While other restrictive practices of this type have been modified or removed, India still protects many products that are potential exports of its neighbors, including textiles and garments as well as a range of agricultural products; imports of major agricultural commodities, including wheat and rice, are also controlled by quasi-state enterprises or public monopolies. The trade ban and general trade impasse between India and Pakistan is a glaring example of policy (iii) that overtly hurts a neighboring country. Pakistan bans most products from India at the same time that both countries restrict transport links and business contact with each other. As a result, trade between the two countries is very small. The removal of these restrictions on both sides would unequivocally benefit both Pakistan and India. Political rather than economic factors are behind these policies.

Trade before Partition was about 20% of total trade in the region. Since then, trade barriers have resulted in changes in comparative advantage, particularly in Pakistan where the most obvious result is the development of an industrial base to counter the cessation of trade with India. How much trade would occur if all trade barriers were removed is thus debatable. The World Bank (2004) argues that even with free trade the amount of trade within South Asia would be relatively small (although certainly bigger than current flows) because of limited complementarities. All countries in the region have comparative advantage in labor-intensive manufactured products, and the benefits of trading these products among themselves are limited. There is scope for trade between India and the smaller countries on its periphery, including Bangladesh, Nepal, and Sri Lanka, by taking advantage of the size and diversity of the Indian economy and the ability of smaller countries to fill niche markets. Nevertheless, SAFTA can provide a framework for the further expansion of Pakistan–India trade. The USAID (2005, p.197) suggests that with SAFTA in place "India should replace the US as the main market for Pakistan's exports ... In 2011 ... India should account for one-fourth of Pakistan's total export earnings. India should also replace Saudi Arabia as the single largest source of imports for Pakistan."

Table 4.4   Commodities in Which Various South Asian Countries Have
Comparative Advantage, 2004*

Country	Commodity
Bangladesh	Clothing and accessories, leather and leather goods, fish, textile fibers, textile yarn, fabric, tobacco and tobacco manufacturing (increase in RCA of clothing and accessories, tobacco and tobacco manufacturing; decline in RCA of leather and leather goods, textile fibers, textile yarn and fabrics)
India	Nonmetal mineral manufacturing, textile yarn, fabric, cereals, coffee, tea, animal feed stuff, iron and steel, footwear, organic chemicals, dyes, petroleum products, oil seed, tobacco and tobacco manufacturing, vegetables and fruits, animal and vegetable fats and oils, plastics in primary form, rubber manufactures (some decline in RCA of level 0 and 6 products except cereals, and iron and steel, which increased; increase in RCA of petroleum and petroleum products)
Pakistan	Textile yarn, fabric, leather and leather goods, clothing and accessories, cereals, animal and vegetable fats and oils, sugar, fish, furniture, beddings, footwear, other transport equipment, vegetables and fruits (some increase in RCA of level 8 products)
Sri Lanka	Coffee, tea, clothing and accessories, textile fibers, yarn, fabric, crude rubber, rubber manufactures, tobacco and tobacco manufacturing, animal and vegetable fats and oils, fish, travel goods, handbags, vegetables and fruits, nonferrous metals, crude animal or vegetable material, other transport equipment (increase in RCA of coffee, tea and spices, clothing and accessories, rubber manufacturing, nonferrous metals, other transport equipment; relatively no change for other products)

RCA = revealed comparative advantage.
*Changes since 1993 are in parentheses.

Source: Rana (Chapter 5 of this volume).

Revealed comparative advantage analysis based on more disaggregated data on international trade in goods and services suggests that there may be scope for greater trade within South Asia (Table 4.4). India has comparative advantage in capital-intensive products such as iron and steel, transport equipment, organic chemicals, and petroleum products, as well as some agricultural products. Bangladesh, Pakistan, and Sri Lanka have comparative advantage in clothing and accessories, leather goods, and

Table 4.5   Revealed Comparative Advantage in Services, 2004

Country	Services
Bangladesh	Communications
India	Computer and information, communications
Maldives	Travel
Nepal	Communications, travel
Pakistan	Communications, transportation
Sri Lanka	Transportation, insurance, communications, computer and information, construction, travel

Source: Computed from the International Monetary Fund. 2006. *Balance of Payments Statistics* CD-ROM, April, using Stata Package 9.0.

textile yarn and fabric, along with rubber in the case of Sri Lanka. In the services sector (Table 4.5), all the countries in the region have comparative advantage in communications services, so the scope for trade may be limited. Maldives, Nepal, and Sri Lanka have comparative advantage in travel, and these countries can be destinations for Indian tourists. India and Sri Lanka have comparative advantage in computers and information technology (IT), which could be imported by Pakistan and Bangladesh. Kemal, Abbas, and Kadir (2000) note that trade complementarity has increased between Bangladesh and India and that there is compatibility in the trade structures of Sri Lanka and India. Complementarities between India and the PRC are also higher than those between other countries in the region. Batra and Khan (2005) note that Pakistan imports cereals, milling products, malts, starches, sugar, and textiles—all products in which India has a high revealed comparative advantage in the global market. India does not export any of these products to Pakistan. They also note that intraindustry trade between Pakistan and India can expand in a number of products including paper, machinery and transport equipment, pharmaceuticals, and leather products. Furthermore, there is some scope for vertical integration in textiles, leather products, light engineering, rubber, transportation equipment, and bioresources.

While services are not part of the existing SAFTA framework, greater economic exchange between Pakistan and India will have some beneficial impacts on the service sector. It is possible that there will be some penetration of the Pakistan banking sector in India and for Indian IT into

Pakistan. It is also likely that the role of Pakistan as a conduit and energy hub between India and Central Asia and also between India and the PRC will be expanded. Generally there are additional opportunities for cooperation in the energy sector, where trade in energy is now quite low. Only Bhutan, India, and Nepal trade electricity. Pakistan and Nepal have considerable hydroelectric power-generating potential, and Pakistan and Bangladesh have gas reserves that could supply neighboring countries.

Tourism from India to Pakistan could also increase particularly among Muslim and Sikh communities. Labor migration is another possible benefit to further integration and better relations between India and Pakistan. Skill shortages in Pakistan could be met from India and Pakistan could provide labor in Punjab and Haryana states of India.

Intra-South Asian trade is, therefore, expected to increase in the future, especially if the political will to implement the various agreements can be sustained. While seeking to enhance regional trade, it is also important for South Asia to find economies of scale in the rest of the world. The region's Look East policies seem to reflect added emphasis on increasing trade with Southeast and East Asia. BIMSTEC reflects this orientation. South Asia can pursue such a strategy by lowering tariffs and other forms of protection on an MFN basis and by pursuing FTAs with East Asia. This would open their economies further and allow them to release comparative advantage. South Asia could also enhance linkages with Central Asia.

Sector Focus on Agriculture, Energy, and Textiles. Agricultural tariffs in Bangladesh, India, and Pakistan are subject to WTO rules. However, bound tariff rates are allowed as tariff rates resulting from the GATT negotiations or accessions that are incorporated in a country's schedule of concessions. Bound rates are enforceable under article II of GATT. If a GATT contracting party raises a tariff above the bound rate, the affected countries have the right to retaliate against an equivalent value of the offending country's exports or to receive compensation, usually in the form of reduced tariffs on other products exported to the offending country. Bound rates for agricultural products are 100% in Bangladesh, 200% in India, and 300% in Pakistan. These rates are so high that they can restrict all trade in agricultural products. Sri Lanka and Nepal have much lower tariffs (50% and 42% respectively) but still far higher than general tariffs on manufactured goods. State trading and export monopolies, however, have been abolished in all countries. Subsidies to agricultural producers have also resulted in distortions in the mix of products produced. The irrigation network, for example, could support higher-value-added crops. In addition, food exports have been discouraged, to keep prices to domestic consumers low, creating yet another distortion. The rationalization of agriculture could bring large net benefits to the entire region.

In the energy sector, the US oil company Unocal has proposed building oil and gas pipelines from Turkmenistan through Afghanistan to Pakistan and later to India. Afghanistan's long war has prevented this project from moving forward. If some degree of stability returns to Afghanistan, the project may be resurrected. Transboundary power sharing has been investigated by the United Nations Development Programme and the UN Economic and Social Commission for Asia and the Pacific. Nepal could develop power projects and sell hydropower to India. This trade could be further expanded in the future. Other possibilities are to link the Pakistan national electrical grid to the power-deficient Indian states of Punjab and Haryana, or to use Bangladeshi natural gas to supply industries in the Indian city of Kolkata. A more general approach to power sharing involving trading and investment could also be pursued for the region as a whole.

In the textile and apparel sectors, the end of the multi-fiber agreement has resulted in shifts in production to the PRC as well as stiffer competition among other suppliers. South Asia has maintained its competitive advantage through labor costs that are even lower than the PRC's. However, other costs including transport could more than compensate for a slight labor cost advantage. Nevertheless, South Asia kept pace with the PRC's world textile and apparel markets in 2005. There is no question that these export products, composing 83% of manufactured exports in Bangladesh, 51% in Nepal, 70% in Pakistan, and 51% in Sri Lanka (ADB 2006), are critical for South Asia. To increase efficiency and improve competitiveness, it would be useful for South Asia to develop an integrated textile and apparel industry based on comparative advantage. Bangladesh and Sri Lanka could then concentrate on garments, while India and Pakistan could concentrate more on capital-intensive spinning and weaving. Lower tariffs on textile, apparel, fabrics, and components would enable the region to compete even more effectively with the PRC and Egypt.

If we shift our focus to NTBs, antidumping, special (reserved) lists, tariffs, and the challenges of revenue collection as trade is liberalized, we can observe in more detail some of the issues facing SAARC, SAPTA, and SAFTA.

Nontariff and Other Barriers. Aside from tariffs and lists of excluded items, NTBs protect a variety of state-owned enterprises, which receive special subsidies. These firms and sectors are evidently inefficient and in need of extensive restructuring and upgrading if they are to compete internationally. In other industries, the removal of protectionist barriers would lead to restructuring and improved efficiency, and not necessarily to bankruptcy. Still other industries, despite operating efficiently, receive

Table 4.6 Sectors and Industries protected by NTBs, Subsidies, and Other Special Treatment

Bangladesh	Sugar, jute textiles, oilseeds, textile fabrics
India	Food grains, edible oils, sugar, milk and milk products, tea and coffee, natural rubber, basic steel, copper, lead and zinc, petrochemicals, fertilizers, synthetic fibers, automobiles, some auto components, textile fabrics, garments
Pakistan	Sugar, oilseeds, basic steel, fertilizers, automobiles, some auto components, some engineering industries
Sri Lanka	Rice and potatoes

NTB = nontariff barrier.

Source: World Bank (2004).

protection or subsidies in line with comparative advantage. Garments and textiles, for example, would be strengthened by the removal of protection and exposure to greater international competition. Finally, agriculture is protected for a variety of reasons, including a desire to insulate the sector from swings in supply and to promote self-sufficiency. All these industries are lumped together into a single list for each country in Table 4.6. India has the longest list, reflecting the size of its economy as well as the strength and extent of its regulatory apparatus.

While tariff rates have decreased, there was an accompanying increase in the number of NTBs imposed in South Asia in the late 1990s (Alburo 2004). The form of NTB most often imposed relates to sanitary and phytosanitary (SPS) measures, technical barriers to trade (TBTs), and related measures, which together account for about 86% of NTBs in the region. This group of NTBs is followed by tariff quotas (about 10%) and antidumping measures (about 7%). Despite tariff liberalization, the region has not seen commensurate increases in trade volumes and narrowing price differentials. Other forms of NTBs have also emerged in the region, such as restricted ports of entry, antidumping and countervailing measures, health and sanitary regulations, customs valuation, and SAPTA certification.

The reform of large public-sector firms requires labor shedding as part of efficiency enhancement and streamlining. Governments are unwilling to undertake such unpopular steps. After all, governments have lost elections and even been overthrown for less. Often, ministries support these inefficient state-owned enterprises since in a real sense their jobs depend on the continuation of the industries they regulate.

Antidumping Measures. India has used antidumping laws to erect artificial tariff barriers. These laws should be repealed and other measures used to address protectionist pressure. Companies that are victims of dumping can be allowed to use safeguard provisions as special tariffs until they adjust. More research needs to be done to determine the effects of antidumping measures in India as well as to close the loopholes in WTO rules that allow antidumping measures as a legitimate way of dealing with unfair foreign competition.

Tariffs. Customs duties that apply to most but not all products in South Asia are still high. These are 25% in Pakistan, Bangladesh, and Sri Lanka; 30% in India and Bhutan; and 40% in Nepal. There are also three to five tariff bands. These tariff regulations represent a significant improvement compared with a decade ago, when maximum rates were much higher and the tax structure was more complex. An agenda for lowering tariffs should contain a few key provisions. First, the maximum tariff should be reduced. Other rates will follow accordingly. Second, the reduction should then extend to agricultural tariffs, which are now substantially above duties on other products. Third, countries can move toward a uniform tariff structure with one low rate for all products. At first, this would involve reducing the variance in rates within the different tariff bands. Fourth, any exemptions from the standard tariff schedule can be removed or reduced. Aside from raising effective protection rates, the existing systems of exemptions are opaque, complex, and inefficient, as well as subject to abuse by officials, inviting bribery and other forms of corruption. India, Pakistan, and Bangladesh are the biggest offenders (World Bank 2004). Fifth, the high binding rate for agricultural tariffs can be reduced. Sixth, other taxes on imports that are being imposed in Bangladesh, India, Nepal, and Sri Lanka should be removed.

Revenue Collection. As tariffs have fallen, so have government tax revenues. The implications vary by country. In India, Pakistan, and Sri Lanka import duties now account for around 10% or less of consolidated government revenue, and other sources of finance, primarily value-added tax (VAT) or VAT-type and similar sales taxes, have been developed to offset these losses. In Bangladesh and Nepal, tax revenues from import duties are more than double the share of government revenue and nearer to 40% of indirect tax revenue. To offset losses from this revenue source, Bangladesh and Nepal will have to raise revenue from other sources such as sales taxes, and tighten tax administration.

Money and Finance

Several institutional developments in the past decade were designed to promote greater monetary and financial integration in South Asia. In 1998, SAARC heads of state agreed in principle to establish a network of central bank governors and finance secretaries of the SAARC region. Dubbed SAARCFINANCE, this network was established later that year. The basic objective of the network is to discuss macroeconomic policy issues and establish closer links among the members. This is achieved through semi-annual meetings of central bank governors and finance secretaries, staff visits and regular exchange of information, and harmonization of banking legislations and practices. In addition, the network will forge closer cooperation on macroeconomic policies; promote research on economic and financial issues; and train staff of the central banks, ministries of finance, and other financial institutions of SAARC members. The secretariat of the network rotates among the member countries and its chair moves with the SAARC chair. Each central bank has established a cell in its research department to coordinate the activities of SAARCFINANCE (Dasgupta and Maskay 2003).

In addition to SAARCFINANCE, at the Dhaka summit of November 2005 it was formally decided to initiate regular meetings of the South Asian finance ministers within the first quarter after the annual SAARC summits. The Dhaka summit also required the South Asian Finance Ministers (SAFM) to meet on the sidelines of ADB and World Bank annual meetings to take stock of the macroeconomic developments and outlook for South Asia; the achievement of SAARC development goals as correlated with the Millennium Development Goals; and the investment climate, foreign capital flows, financial sector reforms, and other areas of cooperation. While this effort is very useful in initiating regional policy dialogue in South Asia, a system of multi-tiered meetings based on the East Asian experience could also be considered. The meetings of SAFMs could be preceded by meetings of finance secretaries and central bank deputy governors, and by working-level meetings of mid-level officials. Issues could thus be reviewed and discussed at various levels before they are brought before the SAFMs for decision.

At the Dhaka summit, it was also decided to establish a SAARC development fund to be an umbrella funding mechanism for all SAARC projects. Accordingly, in 1996 the South Asia Development Fund was set up under the SAARC to identify regional projects in industry, energy, agriculture, and services, as well as projects in infrastructure and social development.

For further financial and monetary integration beyond these steps to take place within South Asia, additional work has to be done to assess whether a common currency is feasible and whether there is enough macroeconomic convergence and political will to entertain the idea of a common market. With this in mind, financial integration within South Asia can be studied from several points of view. Looking at the background conditions required for a monetary union similar to the EU, there are good prima facie reasons for moving forward with plans to pursue a monetary union. The region has begun to exhibit greater convergence for a number of macroeconomic indicators like inflation, interest and exchange rates, public debt, and the fiscal deficit (Saxena and Baig 2003, Jayasuriya et al 2003). The patterns of shocks experienced tend to be similar. Agricultural volatilities tend to be correlated since the monsoon patterns are similar across the region. The countries also have similar mixes of production, and a similar variety of agricultural products including sugar, wheat, and rice, and labor-intensive manufacturing including textiles, cotton fabrics, and garments. India is the exception. Its economy is more diverse and it produces a variety of manufactured goods. Because of its small share of international trade, the region has not been subject to strong external shocks as Southeast and East Asia have been. Exchange rates have tended to move together and the major currencies are closely aligned with the US dollar in a managed float while the small countries are tied to the Indian rupee. Pursuing a basis for a common currency could strengthen fiscal and monetary policy coordination and create more incentives for greater intraregional trade and the establishment of a single market. Labor mobility would be encouraged and fiscal transfers could provide insurance by diversifying risk among several countries.

Two further points can be considered. First, while a currency union may not have a strong basis at the start, its establishment would increase harmony. Second, a currency union is definitely beneficial for the economies that join. Rose and Engel (2002) find that members of a currency union trade more and have less volatile exchange rates. Frankel and Rose (2000) show that trade triples for each member of a currency union. They also find that every 1% increase in trade relative to GDP raises income per capita by 0.33% over a 20-year period. Furthermore, Glick and Rose (2001) show that bilateral trade doubles when a pair of countries forms a currency union.

The stumbling blocks to further monetary cooperation lie with the lack of political will, which is manifested in hostility between Pakistan and India, and the continued low level of internal trade in the region. Ironically, Saxena (2002) and Maskay (2003) both find, on the basis of the above

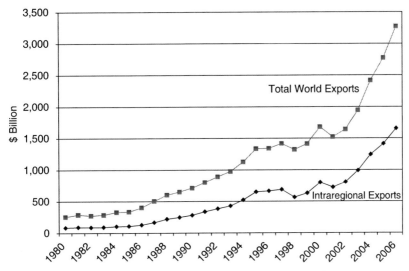

Figure 4.1   Total World and Intraregional Exports of East Asia, $ Bn

Source: International Monetary Fund. 2007. *Direction of Trade Statistics CD-ROM*, June.

criteria, that India and Pakistan are the most suitable candidates for a single currency. Until more trade occurs, either spontaneously or through regional agreements like SAARC, BIMSTEC, SAPTA, and SAFTA, the chances of a monetary union are unlikely. However, mutual cooperation toward more realistic opportunities such as currency swap arrangements and the use of surplus foreign exchange reserves to fund infrastructure development in the region can be effectively considered.

Lessons from East Asia

East Asia[1] has grown dramatically in the past three decades and in the 1990s was known as the Asian economic miracle. Much of this dynamism has been the result of openness to international trade and the pursuit of multilateralism within the GATT/WTO framework. Intraregional trade also grew in tandem with trade with the rest of the world (see Figure 4.1).

---

[1]   East Asia is defined as ASEAN+3 (Association of Southeast Asian Nations plus People's Republic of China, Japan, and Republic of Korea) plus Hong Kong, China and Taipei,China.

Since the Asian financial crisis of 1997/98, there has been a reorientation of development thinking in East Asia regarding the role of regionalism. The contagion effects of the Asia financial crisis were strong and unexpected and some of the initial policies under the International Monetary Fund (IMF) package were not fully appropriate, requiring a reassessment of the role of regional factors in growth and international trade. Slow progress in the Doha Round of multilateral trade negotiations was also partly responsible for renewed interest in regional trade arrangements.

As discussed in the Appendix, regionalism in East Asia has focused on these areas: trade and investment, money and finance, and infrastructure and trade facilitation.

What can South Asia learn from the experiences of East Asia? The most significant lesson is that regionalism can help maximize the benefits of globalization while minimizing its costs. South Asia should strengthen its efforts to enhance cooperation within the region and with East Asia. At the November 2005 SAARC summit, the leaders approved, among others, observer status for Japan and the PRC. SAARC ministers have also approved observer status for the US and Korea. The presence of the PRC, Japan, and Korea—which have broad experience in promoting regional cooperation in East Asia—should provide a catalyst for SAARC integration. The level of integration within ASEAN+3, which includes these three countries, has been increasing rapidly. Granting observer status to the East Asian countries should also have a positive impact on economic integration between South and East Asia for Asia-wide integration.

Trade and Investment. As mentioned above, although SAFTA has given more clout to the trade agreement than previously agreed on as part of the SAARC, the sensitive-list loophole still exists. Speedy implementation of SAFTA would certainly help. Trade in services and movement of labor could also be included in SAFTA. As noted in chapter 5, following the global trend, FTAs between South and East Asia have recently proliferated. While there is a risk that the proliferation of FTAs could raise administrative costs and divert trade, there seems to be no stopping the spread of these agreements, particularly after the stalling of the Doha Round of multilateral trade negotiations in the middle of 2006. Deepening the scope of FTAs beyond tariffs to include services and other facets of international exchange, as well as broadening membership, is one way of increasing the efficiency of these kinds of trade arrangements.

Money and Finance. As mentioned above, the recently established regular meetings of the South Asian finance ministers could be supplemented by meetings of deputy finance secretaries and central bank deputy governors to set the agenda for the ministerial meetings. Efforts could be made to develop consensus on topics of regional interest and to monitor short-term capital flows as part of an early warning system to detect potential currency and banking crises. East Asia has made good progress in establishing regional financing arrangements under the Chiang Mai Initiative. To date, 16 bilateral swaps agreements amounting to $75 billion have been signed. Encouraging progress is being made to "multilateralize" these bilateral swaps and to form a centralized reserve pool. South Asian countries may consider participating in these efforts for liquidity support in emergencies, in addition to funds from the IMF.

East Asia has also come up with initiatives to develop regional bond markets. These include the ASEAN+3 Asian Bond Market Initiative and the Asian Bond Funds I and II of the Executives' Meeting of East Asia-Pacific Central Banks (EMEAP). These efforts can serve as a template for local currency bond markets in South Asia.

Infrastructure. The SASEC initiative in South Asia can benefit from interaction with the Greater Mekong Subregion Initiative begun in 1992 and involving Cambodia, Lao PDR, Myanmar, Thailand, Viet Nam, and two southern provinces in the PRC. This program is well established and has overcome many of the handicaps that SASEC may encounter as it begins its programs of regional cooperation in infrastructure. Chapter 5 highlights the significant constraints posed by high transport and logistic costs on increased trade relations between South and East Asia. Land transit through Myanmar is not possible at present, but this situation will eventually change. Additional corridors between India and the PRC through Bhutan and Nepal will have to be developed. Logistic constraints will also have to be addressed to facilitate the movement of goods between the two regions.

International Financial Integration. One of the characteristics of the Asian financial crisis that most surprised economists and government officials was the power of capital movements to disrupt activity and cause large movements in exchange rates. There were many reasons for the large amount of speculation at that time, including the amount of international liquidity and the large amounts of short-term external debt held by Thailand and other countries whose currencies were under attack. Capital account convertibility certainly played a critical role as well. Where capital accounts were closed in South Asia and in the PRC, speculators could not mount an attack. This does not mean that the countries of South Asia should eschew capital account convertibility. To fully integrate into the global economy and to attract foreign investors into local stock and bond markets, currency convertibility is a must. However, South Asia should study the crisis carefully, particularly the bank and financial practices that sowed the seeds of the crisis. When South Asia feels it is ready and its financial sectors are strong, viable, and sufficiently well regulated (prudential regulations), it can begin to loosen the controls on capital movement, but not earlier.

Appendix:
Trends in Economic
Integration in East Asia

Introduction

E ast Asia's experience with outward-oriented development policies in the last four decades is well known. This outward-oriented
approach involved unilateral reforms and embraced multilateralism under the GATT/WTO framework and led to East Asia's
economic dynamism and global integration, in tandem with regional
integration in international trade and capital flows. Market-led regional
integration flourished under the multilateral framework of trade—driven
by increasing market access and the force of competition. It was only
after the Asian financial crisis of the late 1990s when a paradigm shift
occurred in East Asia's development strategy that it began to pursue
formal policy-led regionalism more actively.[2] This development can be
attributed, as Kawai (2005a) and others have mentioned, to various factors such as growing economic interdependence in the region, the slow
progress in multilateralism and popularity of regionalism elsewhere, and
various lessons learned from the 1997/98 financial crisis.

Regionalism in East Asia

East Asian regionalism, which began in the late 1990s, has two features.
First, in terms of scope, it covers three areas: (i) trade and investment,
(ii) money and finance, (iii) and infrastructure and associated software.
Second, in terms of geographic coverage, it has been mainly bilateral and

---

[2] In contrast, regionalism was popular in Latin America and Africa in the 1960s,
driven by the desire to consolidate import-substitution policies in a regional context. These efforts were highly protectionist and ineffective (later referred to as
"closed regionalism").

subregional, except for money and finance. More recently, bridges are being built across the subregions and proposals have also been made for establishing an ASEAN+3 free trade area.

Trade and Investment

As mentioned, East Asia basically adopted multilateralism in designing its trade policy. In this sense, AFTA, begun in 1992, was an exception. However, with the signing of the Japan–Singapore Economic Partnership Agreement in November 2002 and the Framework Agreement toward the ASEAN–PRC FTA that same month and year, the region's approach seems to have changed. At present, FTAs are proliferating in the region. Within East Asia, eight FTAs have been signed and are being implemented, six are under negotiation, and seven have been proposed. Similarly, between East and South Asia, two FTAs are under implementation, eight under negotiation, and six have been proposed. Many of the FTAs in East Asia go beyond just tariff reduction and encompass agreements that include trade facilitation measures for customs duties, partial movement of labor, or the opening up of government procurement. The India–Singapore Comprehensive Economic Cooperation Agreement covers not only trade in goods but also services, investments, and cooperation in technology, education, air services, and human resources.

The growing number of FTAs in the region is in part a response to the uncertain progress of multilateral trade liberalization under the WTO. There is also a precautionary motive behind them as countries seek to avoid being placed at a competitive disadvantage by the other regional trading arrangements that are taking shape in the rest of the world. Another factor behind the spread of FTAs is that many economies that are geographically close to each other have already established strong trade and investment relationships and now wish to deepen their economic cooperation. For example, ASEAN has established closer economic partnerships with the "+3" countries (PRC, Japan, and Korea) and other trading partners (Australia, New Zealand, and India). The outcome of these agreements has been the establishment of various FTAs between ASEAN and these countries.

The spread of FTAs in Asia has both positive and negative implications. On the positive side, the proliferation of FTAs can help countries to pursue their dynamic comparative advantage and allocate resources efficiently. Against a backdrop of slow progress in global trade negotiations, FTAs can promote continuing liberalization, induce domestic and structural reforms in the countries concerned, and widen market access across the region. Trade arrangements with dynamic, competitive partners can also encourage the spread of efficient production practices. On the negative side, FTAs can be trade-diverting and the demands of negotiating many trade agreements place increasing strains on the scarce trade negotiation resources of many countries, especially given the expanding scope and content, and increasing complexity, of recently negotiated FTAs in the region. Overlapping FTAs also increase the cost of international trade.

Also at the Bali summit in 2003, ASEAN leaders decided to establish an ASEAN community for economic, security, and sociocultural cooperation. The deadline for the establishment of the ASEAN economic community has been advanced from 2020 to 2015.

Money and Finance

In the aftermath of the Asian financial crisis, East Asian countries have sought to promote closer monetary and financial cooperation. There is an ascending order of intensity of these efforts in the sense that they involve progressively increasing constraints on the amount of discretion that individual countries can exercise in the design of macroeconomic policies. By level of intensity, these efforts have ranged from economic review and policy dialogue to the establishment of regional financing arrangements and, eventually, coordinated exchange rate policies.

There are two major ongoing initiatives in the area of economic review and policy dialogue. First, the ASEAN Surveillance Process was established in October 1998 to strengthen policy-making capacity within the group. Based on the principles of peer review and mutual interest, this process reviews global, regional, and individual country developments and monitors exchange rate and macroeconomic aggregates, as well as sectoral and social policies. Under this process, the ASEAN finance ministers meet yearly and the ministries of finance and central bank deputies meet twice a year to discuss issues of common interest. Second, with the formation of the ASEAN+3 Finance Ministers' Process in November 1999, the first ASEAN+3 Economic Review and Policy Dialogue (ERPD) was held in May 2000. Under the ERPD, ASEAN+3 finance ministers meet once a year and their deputies meet every 6 months. Steps have been taken to monitor short-term capital flows and develop early warning systems of currency and banking crises. Initially, deputies would meet for a couple of hours but now they meet for a full day and a half. The value added by regional monitoring is that countries tend to be more frank with each other in a regional forum as they tend to focus on issues of common interest. The ASEAN+3 Research Group, comprising about 30 think tanks from across the region, has also been established to support ERPD. Until its dissolution in December 2005, the Manila Framework Group was another forum that brought together deputies from a wide range of countries for policy dialogue.

Progress has also been made in establishing regional financing arrangements. At their May 2000 meeting in Chiang Mai, Thailand, the ASEAN+3 finance ministers agreed on the Chiang Mai Initiative (CMI) to expand the ASEAN Swap Arrangement (ASA) to all ASEAN members, and to set up a network of bilateral swap arrangements (BSAs) among ASEAN+3 countries. The ASA was expanded in November 2000, and its size increased from $200 million to $1 billion. In April 2005, the size of the ASA was again increased to $2 billion. At their May 2005 meeting, the ASEAN+3 finance ministers announced that the size of existing bilateral swaps would be doubled and that swaps would be signed among ASEAN countries as well.[3] To date, ASEAN+3 countries have signed 16 bilateral swaps amounting to $75 billion, almost double the amount a year ago. At the May 2005 meeting, the ministers decided to increase the percentage of swaps that can be disbursed without programs supported by the IMF from 10% to 20%. They also agreed on a collective decision-making system for BSAs. Although the latter agreement to some extent complicates the administration of the bilateral swaps, it is an important breakthrough for two reasons: as mentioned in the ministerial statement, it is the first step to the full multilateralization of bilateral swaps, and it is also the first time that the ASEAN+3 members agreed to sacrifice a certain amount of national sovereignty for the common regional good. There was further progress at the May 2006 meeting, where the ministers decided that "all swap-providing countries can simultaneously and promptly provide liquidity support to any parties involved in bilateral swap arrangements at times of emergency" and "set up a new task force to further study various possible options toward an advanced framework for the regional liquidity support arrangement (CMI multilateralization, or Post-CMI)."[4]

In the area of exchange rate coordination, aside from research under various forums such as the ASEAN Currency and Exchange Rate Mechanism Task Force, the Kobe Research Project of the Asia–Europe finance ministers, and the ASEAN+3 Research Group, there has yet to be a clear regional initiative. This situation will, however, undoubtedly change as integration moves forward, business cycles become more synchronized, and macroeconomic policy interdependence becomes stronger. In fact, at the May 2006 meeting, the ASEAN+3 finance ministers endorsed a study on "regional monetary units." On 21 July 2005, the PRC and Malaysia

---

[3] Joint Ministerial Statement of the 8th ASEAN+3 Finance Ministers' Meeting, 4 May 2005, Istanbul, Turkey.

[4] Joint Ministerial Statement of the 9th ASEAN+3 Finance Ministers' Meeting, 4 May 2006, Hyderabad, India.

joined Singapore in adopting a managed floating exchange rate regime based on a currency basket, suggesting that pegging one's currency to a basket of others is gaining popularity in the region and in due course could culminate in enhanced exchange rate coordination.

For other types of financial sector cooperation, East Asia has come up with several initiatives to develop regional bond markets. These include the Asia–Pacific Economic Cooperation (APEC) bond initiative, the Asian Bond Fund (ABF) initiative under the Executives' Meeting of East Asia–Pacific Central Banks (EMEAP), and the Asian Bond Market Initiative (ABMI) under the ASEAN+3 Finance Ministers Process. In 2003, EMEAP launched the first ABF with an initial $1 billion, and invested in US-dollar-denominated bonds issued by Asian sovereign and quasi-sovereign issuers. A $2-billion second ABF, which invests in bonds denominated in regional currencies, began implementation in April 2005. Under the ABMI, ASEAN+3 established several apex bodies—a focal group with an ad hoc support group and a technical assistance coordination group—and four working groups that meet regularly. The AsianBondsOnline website developed by ADB was launched in May 2005.[5] It has become a popular one-stop clearing house of information on sovereign and corporate bonds issued in ASEAN+3 countries.

Infrastructure and Associated Software

In Asia, most of the poor live in remote or isolated areas, especially in regions close to national borders. They need to be linked to commercial and industrial centers not only within their own countries but in other countries in the region and beyond as well—via highways, railways, ports, telecommunications, and other "hard" infrastructure. The "software" aspects of infrastructure development, including trade facilitation, are also important for the smooth flow of traffic. Greater connectivity enhances trade and investment integration by facilitating the movement of goods.

The most advanced program in Asia is the Greater Mekong Subregion—comprising Cambodia, Lao PDR, Myanmar, Thailand, Viet Nam, and Yunnan Province in the PRC. The six countries initiated the program of subregional cooperation in 1992. The Brunei Darussalam–Indonesia–Malaysia–Philippines East ASEAN Growth Area (BIMP-EAGA) initiative was also begun in 1992.

---

[5] This website tracks developments in East Asia's local currency bond markets and provides detailed progress reports on the various Asian Bond Market Initiatives, among others.

Measures of Integration

Trade Integration

Appendix Tables A4.1 and A4.2 update the various measures of trade integration developed by Kawai (2005b), among others, using data from the June 2006 IMF *Direction of Trade Statistics* CD-ROM. Appendix Table A4.1 shows that in 1980–2005, intraregional trade among ASEAN+3 members increased steadily from 30.2% to 38.2%.[6] This level is somewhat lower than NAFTA's (45.0%) and significantly lower than that for the EU-25[7] (66.2%). If, however, we include data from Hong Kong, China and Taipei,China, the intraregional trade ratio increases to 54.5%, well above NAFTA's and closer to the EU-25 level. Intraregional trade among ASEAN countries has remained unchanged since 1995, while among the South Asian countries it has increased somewhat.

Appendix Table A4.2 presents data on total trade intensity indexes. By adjusting for the country or region's relative size, this gives a better measure of economic interdependence. The data show that after a dip in the 1980s, total trade intensity index among the ASEAN+3 countries has remained relatively steady at about 2.0 since 1990. This level is higher than that for the EU-25 (1.7) and lower than NAFTA (2.6).

Financial Integration

Available price and quantity measures of financial integration in East Asia are presented in Figures A4.1 to A4.3. These indicate that in recent years, financial integration in East Asia has started to increase. Prime lending and many market rates are starting to converge and the share of intraregional portfolio investment is starting to rise.

---

[6] Country-level data suggest that trade ratios of the ASEAN countries were highest for Brunei Darussalam and the newer ASEAN member countries, and lowest for the PRC, Japan, and Korea, with other countries falling in between.

[7] EU-25 are Austria, Belgium, Cyprus, Czech Republic, Denmark, Estonia, Finland, France, Germany, Greece, Hungary, Ireland, Italy, Latvia, Lithuania, Luxembourg, Malta, Netherlands, Poland, Portugal, Slovakia, Slovenia, Spain, Sweden, and United Kingdom.

Table A4.1   Intraregional Trade, as % of total world trade[a]

Country	1980	1985	1990	1995	2000	2005
Brunei Darussalam	80.1	77.3	81.7	79.5	74.2	75.0
Cambodia	67.4	68.6	81.5	35.8	46.8	
Indonesia	58.3	53.3	51.7	49.5	50.6	54.6
Lao PDR	82.6	85.7	65.3	72.8	74.0	
Malaysia	46.7	54.1	49.6	48.2	49.4	54.7
Myanmar	50.6	42.9	58.7	72.5	62.2	74.9
Philippines	33.8	36.0	32.8	37.5	39.7	52.7
Singapore	36.8	40.6	39.5	47.2	46.5	45.4
Thailand	38.1	42.7	42.6	43.7	44.9	49.5
Viet Nam		10.5	27.8	57.6	56.4	52.7
PRC	29.4	36.2	21.3	33.7	33.1	30.0
Korea, Republic of	29.2	26.7	29.1	35.4	36.6	43.6
Japan	20.7	20.3	21.2	29.9	30.9	36.8
ASEAN+3	30.2	30.2	29.3	37.3	37.0	38.2
ASEAN	17.9	20.3	18.8	23.9	24.5	24.0
ASEAN+3 + Hong Kong, China + Taipei,China	34.6	37.1	43.0	51.7	51.9	54.5
South Asia	4.6	3.2	2.9	4.0	4.2	5.5
EU (EU-25)	61.3	59.8	67.0	67.4	66.8	66.2
NAFTA	33.8	38.7	37.9	43.1	48.8	45.0

ASEAN+3 = Association of Southeast Asian Nations plus People's Republic of China (PRC), Japan, and Republic of Korea; EU = European Union; Lao PDR = Lao People's Democratic Republic; NAFTA = North American Free Trade Agreement.
[a] For regional groupings, intraregional trade share is calculated using export data and the formula: Xii /{(Xiw + Xwi)/2}, where Xii is export of region i to region i; Xiw is export of region i to the world, and Xwi is export of world to region i.

Sources: International Monetary Fund, *Direction of Trade Statistics* CD-ROM (June 2006), and CEIC.

Table A4.2   Intraregional Trade Intensity Index[a]

Country	1980	1985	1990	1995	2000	2005
Brunei Darussalam	6.7	5.4	5.3	4.0	3.7	3.5
Cambodia		4.7	4.4	4.1	1.8	2.2
Indonesia	4.9	3.7	3.4	2.5	2.5	2.5
Lao PDR		5.8	5.6	3.3	3.7	0.1
Malaysia	3.9	3.8	3.2	2.4	2.5	2.5
Myanmar	4.2	3.0	3.8	3.6	3.1	3.5
Philippines	2.8	2.5	2.1	1.9	2.0	2.4
Singapore	3.1	2.8	2.6	2.4	2.3	2.1
Thailand	3.2	3.0	2.8	2.2	2.3	2.3
Viet Nam		0.7	1.8	2.9	2.8	2.4
PRC	2.5	2.5	1.4	1.7	1.7	1.4
Korea, Republic of	2.4	1.9	1.9	1.8	1.8	2.0
Japan	1.7	1.4	1.4	1.5	1.5	1.7
ASEAN+3	2.4	2.1	1.9	2.0	2.0	1.9
ASEAN	4.8	5.7	4.4	3.7	4.0	4.2
ASEAN+3 + Hong Kong, China + Taipei,China	2.5	2.3	2.2	2.1	2.2	2.2
South Asia	5.1	2.9	3.0	3.9	3.9	4.1
European Union (EU-25)	1.5	1.6	1.5	1.7	1.8	1.7
NAFTA	2.1	2.0	2.1	2.4	2.2	2.6

ASEAN+3 = Association of Southeast Asian Nations plus People's Republic of China (PRC), Japan, and Republic of Korea; EU = European Union; Lao PDR = Lao People's Democratic Republic; NAFTA = North American Free Trade Agreement.

[a] Intraregional trade intensity index is the ratio of intraregional trade share to the share of world's trade with the region. For regional groupings, trade intensity index is calculated using export data and the formula: $[Xii / \{(Xiw + Xwi)/2\}] / [\{(Xiw + Xwi)/2\}/Xww]$, where Xii is export of region i to region i; Xiw is export of region i to the world, Xwi is export of world to region i, and Xww is total world export.

Sources: International Monetary Fund, *Direction of Trade Statistics* CD-ROM (June 2006), and CEIC.

Financial Integration: Price and Quantity Indicators

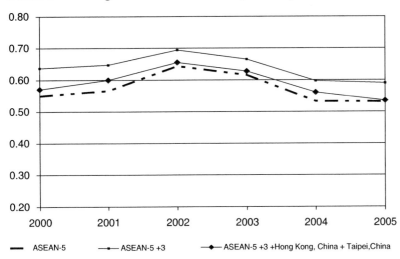

Figure A4.1   Coefficient of Variation of Prime Lending Markets

ASEAN-5+3 = Five members of the Association of Southeast Asian Nations (Indonesia, Malaysia, Philippines, Thailand, and Viet Nam) plus People's Republic of China, Japan, and Republic of Korea. Source: Computed from Bloomberg data.

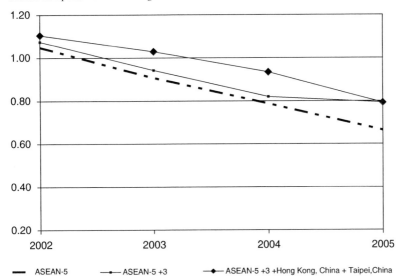

Figure A4.2   Coefficient of Variation of Money Market Rates

ASEAN-5+3 = Five members of the Association of Southeast Asian Nations (Indonesia, Malaysia, Philippines, Thailand, and Viet Nam) plus People's Republic of China, Japan, and Republic of Korea. Source: Computed from Bloomberg data.

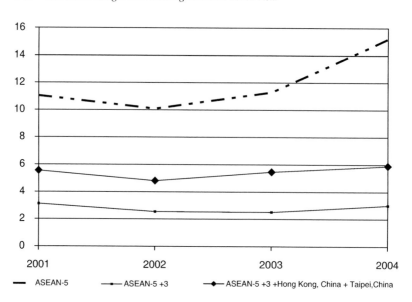

Figure A4.3   Share of Intraregional Portfolio Investment, as % of total

ASEAN-5+3 = Five members of the Association of Southeast Asian Nations (Indonesia, Malaysia, Philippines, Thailand, and Viet Nam) plus People's Republic of China, Japan, and Republic of Korea.
Source: International Monetary Fund, Coordinated Portfolio Investment Survey.

Regional Perspectives on Deeper Regional Integration

5

INTEGRATING SERVICES MARKETS

Christopher Findlay, Ryo Ochiai, and Philippa Dee

Introduction

F ew papers have examined trade in services in developing countries, and there are none on trade in services in South Asian countries and their relationship with other Asian countries. This paper aims to fill this gap. We find that (i) trade and investment flows in services among economies in South and East Asia are not yet widespread but that they could be greater, (ii) impediments to trade and investment can be identified, and (iii) reform agendas in both regions will contribute to their integration.

We begin with a discussion of the gains from market integration in the service sector. We note the nature of the gains from integration, both their similarities to and differences from those associated with integration in markets for goods.

We then map the existing relationships within and between East and South Asia in services trade and investment flows (relative to the relationships of the component countries or regions with the rest of the world). We find that services trade in both East and South Asia has been growing, but driven by developments in the People's Republic of China (PRC) and India. There are also some significant bilateral flows in movements of students and tourists between the regions. Overall, however, we find that trade in services tends to be concentrated within each of these regions, and that trade between them is relatively less intense compared to other regions.

Complementarities between the regions, however, are significant and lead the prospects for stronger growth in the trading and investment relationships. Barriers to integration of services markets within and between East and South Asia could be related to a number of distance factors (geographic and cultural, as well as those related to infrastructure) and to policy settings. In the third part of the paper, we explore the existing data on barriers to trade and investment in services, and find instances of significant impediments in particular countries.

How to remove policy barriers to integration is the topic of the final sections of the paper. We note the lack of progress in the treatment of services policy in South Asian regional agreements (within and between each region) but we also observe that a preferential path to reform is not a priority. We explain the basis of this argument and comment on the joint interests of developing countries, including those located in these two regions, in progress in the World Trade Organization (WTO) negotiations on services.

Gains for Integration in Markets for Services

The gains from integration of services markets include some already familiar from the integration of markets for goods and some peculiar to services. The gains include those from specialization and trade, from competition, from variety, and from increments to capacity, both physical and technological.

Services production is characterized by differences in factor intensities, and given differences in endowments of factors of production, countries can gain from specialization in different services activities. Further, some services activities have specific fixed inputs on which competitiveness is based (tourism for instance). The consequences of opening markets for trade in services are not fixed. A country may find its early export-oriented services businesses built on labor intensive processes, but as development proceeds, and the international competitiveness of various sectors shifts over time, then the pattern of trade and investment in services would also be expected to adjust to more capital- and technology-intensive activities.

Second, the introduction of new international suppliers into domestic markets as a result of reform adds to competition and to significant welfare gains through this channel as well. Services can also be supplied in a variety of modes:
- Exchanges without direct contact (mode 1)
- Consumers travel abroad (mode 2)
- Establishment of a new business by a foreign provider (mode 3)
- Movement of staff (mode 4)

Market reform should open all these modes of supply, thereby contributing to competition within each mode. Furthermore, openness affects competition. In one mode of supply, such as through commercial establishment, there may be opportunity for only one provider, but the provision via the other modes (such as the movement of people or cross-border transactions through telecommunications) can inject competition into the relevant market.

The conditions of entry in all modes depend on the policy environment. The scope of services policy (as referred to in the General Agreement on Trade in Services, or GATS) includes the treatment of all potential competitors, domestic and foreign—not just foreign suppliers. This perspective is important as we discuss below.

Findlay and Guo (2007) argue that there are important interactions between policy reform and the growth of trade in different modes. For example, in some scenarios, policy reform that opens domestic markets to commercial establishment by foreign supplies later stimulates growth in trade in other modes of supply. This sequence of reform, flows of foreign direct investment (FDI), and trade growth is evident in the experiences of India and the PRC, as discussed below.

The third benefit of integration relates to variety. Services are inherently highly differentiated, given (i) the nature of their production, (ii) their inability to be stored, and (iii) the direct contact between consumer and producer required in their delivery. This characteristic also provides the opportunity to tailor-make services to consumer interests. Market integration provides new options and methods for differentiation and contributes to the diversity of services offered in the marketplace. In some cases, market opening adds not only to variety of an existing type of service, but also contributes to the development of new sectors and new ways of doing business; the logistics sector is one example and the redefinition of what constitutes energy services is another.

The fourth contribution of market opening of services is to add to capacity. In some cases, the entrance of new suppliers may add literally to the physical capacity of the road, telecommunications, or other network sector systems. With foreign participation, this effect could also apply to transport corridors' linking economies. That is, the effects are not limited to domestic infrastructure. Participation of new local and foreign providers can also add to technological capacity, for example, leading to ways of better utilizing existing infrastructure through new management practices.

Technology transfer of more familiar forms is also associated with open markets for services. For example, open markets for professional services will facilitate the transfer of diagnostic, analytical, or design skills. There are, in addition, complementarities between movements of goods and services; the transfer of electronic or electrical products may be complemented by the provision of services related to their installation and application, and the bundle of goods and services then embodies the transfer of technology.

In summary, integrated and open markets for services offer gains from trade, competition, and capacity, as well as from services variety and technology transfer.

The effects of reform and market opening in one services sector will likely have significant effects on other sectors of the economy, given that many services are intermediate inputs to production of other sectors. A more efficient services sector therefore helps the adjustment that might be demanded of other internationally oriented sectors of the economy. For example, a more efficient transport sector aids the competitiveness of exporters of agricultural products.

Services reform supports the processes of shifting models for doing business. As development occurs, and as new technologies emerge for coordination of activities related to production or the transfer of information, firms tend to consider more options for external sourcing. This includes manufacturing firms, leading to the growth in the so-called producer services markets (Daniels 1998). These services are not only locally sourced but can also be internationally traded. Some services are more efficiently provided by the same partner as the client firm extends its international operations (e.g., logistics and banking).

More generally, services reform is an important complement to the trade facilitation agenda. The country papers prepared for this project point out, for example, the infrastructure constraints to the growth of trade. The Bangladesh paper, for example, points to the poor conditions of roads, railway, and inland water transport that have hindered trade. The paper refers to the returns to heavy investment in these sectors and mentions the scope of multilateral agencies to make a contribution. But depending on the investment policy regime, private investors may also provide the funds and management resources. An appropriate arrangement could be a public–private partnership (PPP).

Further, as noted in the Organisation for Economic Co-operation and Development (OECD) (2004) and in Dee, Hanslow, and Phamduc (2003), services themselves are also big consumers of other services. For example, many service providers consume telecommunications services. The India country paper prepared for this project makes a similar point, referring to analysis of input–output tables which found that not only agriculture and industrial sectors have become more intensive consumers of services, but also other services. Services reform therefore leads to significant effects on other services providers; air transport reform, for example, would support the international competitiveness of the tourism sector; while telecommunications reform would support the development of back-office business services or telemedicine.[1]

In the next section we review some features of world trade and investment in services, especially within East and South Asia in services markets. We then examine the revealed comparative advantage (RCA) in trade in services in these economies, and review the available on trade and investment flows between them. This includes some discussion of the experiences of specific countries. We then turn to issues concerning impediments to integration.

Features of Trade and Investment in Services[2]

In this section, we review data on trade in services (modes 1 and 2), FDI in services (mode 3), and movement of people (mode 4).

Trade in Services

Asia-Pacific's share of world trade in services (modes 1 and 2) remains small (Tables 5.1 and 5.2). Further, trade is concentrated within that region: trade in services in Asia and the Pacific is more likely to be intraregional trade, compared to countries in the OECD and other countries.

---

[1] There are instances of these effects in the country papers prepared for this project. The linkages between services sector and manufacturing as well as agriculture are stressed in the India country study. As also noted, the provision of more efficient services to finance international trade helps facilitate those transactions.

[2] Some qualifications to these data need to be made, particularly cross-border transactions and mode 3 transactions. For example, many Japanese services firms have been outsourcing labor-intensive tasks such as data processing to firms in the People's Republic of China (PRC) via the internet. These transactions are not captured in official trade statistics. The importance of trade in services through the internet is recently increasing (in business and professional services), so the actual amount of trade may be much larger than the published data. Services transactions associated with commercial establishment are not always identified and associated with the service sector. A study undertaken by the Australian Bureau of Statistics found that transactions via mode 3 had been significantly understated in Australian statistics. Another study by the Australian Services Roundtable indicate that Balance of Payments statistics might be capturing only about 36% of total actual services exports. See www.servicesaustralia. org.au/pdfFilesNewsletters/24May2005Newsletter.pdf and www.ausstats.abs. gov.au/ausstats/subscriber.nsf/0/17722D704FDAE92ECA256F3800756502/ $File/54950_2002-03.pdf

Table 5.1   Estimated Patterns of World and OECD Trade in Services in 2002, % of world exports

Country of origin	World	Total OECD	Country of destination				
				Non-OECD			
			Total	Africa non-OECD	America non-OECD	Asia and Oceania non-OECD	Europe non-OECD
World	100.0	75.8	24.0	2.6	4.4	14.7	2.3
Total OECD	76.9	62.6	14.3	1.5	3.6	7.3	1.9
Total non-OECD	22.9	13.2	9.7	1.1	0.8	7.4	0.4
Africa	2.0	1.6	0.4	0.3	0.0	0.1	0.0
America non-OECD	3.0	2.5	0.5	0.1	0.4	0.2	na
Asia and Oceania non-OECD	15.1	7.1	8.0	0.6	0.5	6.9	0.0
Europe non-OECD	2.8	2.0	0.8	0.1	na	0.2	0.6

na = not available, OECD = Organisation for Economic Co-operation and Development, % = percent.

Source: OECD. 2005. *South-South Service Trade: Interim Report*, November.

Balance of payments (BOP) data on trade in services are shown in Tables 5.3 and 5.4. In many Asian countries, the growth rates of trade in services have decreased since 1997, although the growth rates are generally positive (Table 5.4). Among the members of the Association of Southeast Asian Nations (ASEAN), however, services trade growth rates became negative after the Asian financial crisis. These results indicate that trade in services in Asian region that grew remarkably before 1997 was seriously discouraged by the crisis and the recovery may have been delayed relative to trade in goods.

On the other hand, trade in services has increased steadily among the members of South Asian Association for Regional Cooperation (SAARC).[3] This is mainly because of the remarkable growth of trade in services in India in the 1990s. India's exports and imports of trade in services in

---

[3] The changes in the availability of data on other services may also contribute to this result.

Table 5.2 Estimated Patterns of World and OECD Trade in Services in 2002, $ Mn and %

Country of origin	World ($ Mn)	Total OECD (%)	Country of destination				
			Non-OECD (%)				
			Total	Africa non-OECD	America non-OECD	Asia and Oceania non-OECD	Europe non-OECD
World	1,622,400	75.8	24.0	2.6	4.4	14.7	2.3
Total OECD	1,247,626	81.4	18.6	2.0	4.7	9.5	2.5
Total non-OECD	371,530	57.6	42.4	4.8	3.5	32.3	1.7
Africa	32,448	80.0	20.0	15.0	0.0	5.0	0.0
America non-OECD	48,672	83.3	16.7	3.3	13.3	6.7	0.0
Asia and Oceania non-OECD	244,982	47.0	53.0	4.0	3.3	45.7	0.0
Europe non-OECD	45,427	71.4	28.6	3.6	0.0	7.1	21.4

OECD = Organisation for Economic Co-operation and Development, % = percent, $ Mn = millions of US dollars.

Source: OECD. 2005. *South-South Service Trade: Interim Report*, November.

2003 are respectively 5.1 and 4.2 times those in 2003, which are significantly larger than other SAARC members (e.g., 2.6 and 2.4 times those in Bangladesh, 1.8 and 1.6 times those in Nepal, 2.1 and 1.6 times those in Pakistan, and 3.2 and 2.6 times those in Sri Lanka). The India country paper in this report notes some of the policy changes since the early 1990s that are associated with this result.

As was expected, the growth rates of trade in services in the PRC exceed 10% even after the crisis. Its total services exports after the crisis grew a little slower than those in SAARC but its services imports grew more rapidly. The implications of the PRC's entry into world markets are not only felt in goods trade. Further, the PRC's performance in this sector is of particular interest given the extent of its commitments in the process of its accession to the WTO (Mattoo 2003).

Table 5.3   Trade in Services (Balance of Payments Statistics), $ Mn

	Credit		Debit		Balance	
	1990–1996 Average	1997–2003 Average	1990–1996 Average	1997–2003 Average	1990–1996 Average	1997–2003 Average
SAARC						
Total	8,955	20,235	(12,647)	(24,271)	(3,692)	(4,037)
Transport	2,549	3,526	(7,119)	(11,432)	(4,570)	(7,906)
Travel	2,698	3,802	(1,559)	(3,328)	(1,139)	474
Other services	3,708	12,905	(3,969)	(9,511)	(262)	3,394
ASEAN						
Total	63,569	71,960	(32,655)	(26,251)	30,914	45,708
Transport	9,267	17,460	(12,186)	(7,499)	(2,920)	9,961
Travel	20,671	19,548	(2,026)	(1,968)	18,645	17,581
Other services	30,305	28,001	(16,101)	(15,499)	14,204	12,502
Japan						
Total	61,128	67,114	(113,813)	(113,574)	(52,685)	(46,460)
Transport	20,835	23,737	(32,530)	(31,904)	(11,695)	(8,167)
Travel	3,583	4,361	(32,840)	(31,231)	(29,258)	(26,870)
Other services	36,710	39,017	(48,440)	(51,880)	(11,730)	(12,863)
PRC						
Total	16,886	32,135	(19,036)	(37,480)	(2,150)	(5,345)
Transport	2,858	4,230	(8,235)	(11,168)	(5,377)	(6,938)
Travel	7,734	15,798	(3,496)	(12,258)	4,238	3,540
Other services	6,294	12,108	(7,303)	(14,197)	(1,008)	(2,089)
Korea, Republic of						
Total	18,999	28,476	(22,270)	(32,071)	(3,272)	(3,595)
Transport	7,711	12,848	(8,312)	(10,897)	(601)	1,951
Travel	4,084	6,142	(5,467)	(7,275)	(1,384)	(1,133)
Other services	7,205	9,485	(8,491)	(13,938)	(1,286)	(4,452)
Hong Kong, China						
Total	–	–	–	–	–	–
Transport	–	–	–	–	–	–
Travel	–	–	–	–	–	–
Other services	–	–	–	–	–	–

continued on next page

Table 5.3 continued

	Credit		Debit		Balance	
	1990–1996 Average	1997–2003 Average	1990–199 Average	1997–2003 Average	1990–1996 Average	1997–2003 Average
Taipei,China						
Total	11,928	19,397	(20,232)	(24,984)	(8,304)	(5,587)
Transport	3,335	3,826	(5,079)	(6,132)	(1,744)	(2,306)
Travel	2,755	3,711	(7,108)	(7,398)	(4,353)	(3,687)
Other services	5,838	11,860	(8,045)	(11,453)	(2,207)	407

ASEAN = Association of Southeast Asian Nations, PRC = People's Republic of China, SAARC = South Asian Association for Regional Cooperation, – = data not available, ( ) = negative value.

Sources: International Monetary Fund, *Balance of Payment Statistics Yearbook*, various issues; Central Bank of the PRC: www.cbc.gov.tw/Eng-Home/Economic/Statistis/BOP/hist/index.asp

Table 5.4   Trade in Services (Balance of Payments Statistics Average) Growth Rates, %

	Credit		Debit	
	1990–1996 Average	1997–2003 Average	1990–1996 Average	1997–2003 Average
SAARC				
Total	8.2	14.5	10.1	10.5
Transport	9.5	5.7	9.9	4.4
Travel	9.0	5.5	13.2	14.9
Other services	6.9	21.3	9.5	17.4
ASEAN				
Total	21.9	(2.8)	20.9	(9.0)
Transport	16.4	10.7	15.4	(7.3)
Travel	13.0	(4.5)	11.5	(6.4)
Other services	30.2	(7.4)	27.9	(14.1)
Japan				
Total	8.4	1.9	10.5	(1.7)
Transport	4.5	3.3	5.2	1.6
Travel	4.7	12.7	11.3	(2.2)
Other services	11.0	(0.3)	13.5	(3.3)

continued on next page

Table 5.4 continued

	Credit		Debit	
	1990–1996 Average	1997–2003 Average	1990–1996 Average	1997–2003 Average
PRC				
Total	22.6	11.3	23.3	12.0
Transport	16.7	17.8	23.5	10.6
Travel	29.6	6.3	17.1	11.0
Other services	17.0	14.4	27.5	14.2
Korea, Republic of				
Total	21.8	3.8	25.2	5.4
Transport	17.2	7.7	17.8	4.7
Travel	18.1	2.1	28.4	6.3
Other services	29.1	(0.2)	31.0	5.3
Hong Kong, China				
Total	–	–	–	–
Transport	–	–	–	–
Travel	–	–	–	–
Other services	–	–	–	–
Taipei,China				
Total	15.1	5.1	8.9	0.5
Transport	10.5	2.5	8.8	0.6
Travel	13.1	(2.2)	8.5	(3.8)
Other services	19.1	8.0	9.1	3.4

ASEAN = Association of Southeast Asian Nations, PRC = People's Republic of China, SAARC = South Asian Association for Regional Cooperation, – = data not available, ( ) = negative value.

Sources: International Monetary Fund, *Balance of Payment Statistics Yearbook*, various issues; Central Bank of the PRC: www.cbc.gov.tw/EngHome/Economic/Statistics/BOP/hist/index.asp

The link between reform and services trade performance (both exports and imports) as well as FDI performance in both India, as noted above, and in the PRC is an important observation for other economies at earlier stages of reform.

Data on exports of computer, communications, and other services and of insurance and financial services—components of the category "other services"—are shown in Table 5.5. Exports of computer, communications, and other services dramatically increased in SAARC after the late 1990s. Indian export growth was an important contributor to the rapid expansion of these sectors' exports from this region. On the other hand, in ASEAN, the growth rates of the exports of these services decreased following the financial crisis after having grown remarkably in the early 1990s. Similar results are obtained for the exports of insurance and financial services, where Indian exports have also grown more rapidly compared with the other SAARC members and ASEAN.

Table 5.5   Exports of Computer-Related and Financial Services

(a) Computer, communications and other services, exports				
	Average ($ Mn)		Growth rate (%)	
	1990–1996	1997–2003	1990–1996	1997–2003
SAARC	**2,924**	**10,735**	**4.4**	**20.9**
Bangladesh	290	130	(14.2)	15.4
India	1,856	9,681	1.4	25.8
Nepal	195	205	43.0	(30.6)
Pakistan	417	451	11.1	0.3
Sri Lanka	166	268	11.1	7.1
ASEAN	**19,959**	**24,312**	**23.4**	**(6.7)**
Brunei Darussalam	–	–	–	–
Cambodia	8	41	–	6.8
Indonesia	199	139	(0.9)	11.2
Lao PDR	1	1	–	–
Malaysia	3,189	5,737	43.7	(11.2)
Myanmar	104	243	20.6	(17.7)
Philippines	5,076	3,196	31.0	(37.2)
Singapore	8,555	10,938	10.6	6.1
Thailand	2,830	4,018	40.5	(4.2)
Viet Nam	–	–	–	–

continued on next page

Table 5.5 continued

(a) Computer, communications and other services, exports				
	Average ($ Mn)		Growth rate (%)	
	1990–1996	1997–2003	1990–1996	1997–2003
Japan	32,268	35,358	(1.8)	(1.3)
PRC	3,732	11,554	36.9	14.0
Korea, Rep. of	4,986	8,032	20.8	(2.0)
Hong Kong, China	–	17,274	–	–
Taipei,China	5,423	10,628	17.4	8.7

(b) Insurance and financial services, exports				
	Average ($ Mn)		Growth rate (%)	
	1990–1996	1997–2003	1990–1996	1997–2003
SAARC	**196**	**647**	**10.5**	**14.2**
Bangladesh	2	18	–	15.6
India	153	510	7.7	17.2
Nepal	0	0	–	–
Pakistan	16	24	25.0	(6.2)
Sri Lanka	25	95	9.7	3.4
ASEAN	**855**	**2,384**	**64.2**	**8.2**
Brunei Darussalam	–	–	–	–
Cambodia	0	–	–	–
Indonesia	0	0	–	–
Lao PDR	0	1	–	–
Malaysia	0	194	–	–
Myanmar	0	–	–	–
Philippines	25	68	–	–
Singapore	770	2,040	62.3	5.6
Thailand	60	82	–	–
Viet Nam	–	–	–	–

continued on next page

Table 5.5 continued

(b) Insurance and financial services, exports				
	Average ($ Mn)		Growth rate (%)	
	1990–1996	1997–2003	1990–1996	1997–2003
Japan	720	2,483	–	10.9
PRC	736	353	(1.8)	11.2
Korea, Rep. of	88	561	–	16.5
Hong Kong, China	–	4,286	–	–
Taipei,China	415	1,232	39.3	1.6

ASEAN = Association of Southeast Asian Nations, Lao PDR = Lao People's Democratic Republic, PRC = People's Republic of China, SAARC = South Asian Association for Regional Cooperation, $ Mn = millions of US dollars, % = percent, – = no data available.

Source: World Bank, *World Development Indicators*.

A number of studies have examined the origins of India's success in exports of information technology (IT) services (e.g., Balasubramanyam and Balasubramanyam 1997). A recent presentation by the National Association of Software and Services Companies (NASSCOM) (2006) identified some contributing factors. External factors include a shift in business models and the demand for services provided by external suppliers. Significant decisions by foreign firms, or "anchor clients," were then important to demonstrate India's competitiveness. Supply-side factors included the cost of skilled labor, the regulatory environment (including the openness to foreign investment), the quality of the telecommunications infrastructure, and the capacity within firms to provide security for information flows as well the support for that effort from regulators and standards-monitoring agencies.

Another feature of the Indian experience was the evolution of the services provided. The initial scope was described as "out-tasking," with the work contracted including such tasks as data entry. The scope then widened to include software support and customer contact, then later even more sophisticated services such as research analysis. The wider scope of services helped maintain the growth of exports.

Table 5.5 also includes data on exports of financial and insurance services. Countries in SAARC have maintained the growth of exports of these services, while growth in exports from ASEAN slowed after the financial crisis.

Foreign Direct Investment

Table 5.6 refers to mode 3 FDI transactions at a global level. Although the years to which these data refer to are not clear (since timing of collection varies between countries), they show that countries in the OECD account for nearly 75% of the world stock of services FDI and that OECD countries are much more likely to invest in other OECD countries.

Table 5.6   Services FDI Stock, %

	World	Total OECD	Non-OECD					
			Total	Africa and MENA	America non-OECD	Asia and Oceania non-OECD	Europe non-OECD	Non-OECD
World	100.0	76.4	23.6	0.9	2.1	17.4	0.1	3.1
Total OECD	54.5	50.5	4.0	0.4	1.4	1.1	0.1	1.1
Total non-OECD	45.5	25.9	19.6	0.5	0.8	16.3	0.0	2.0
Africa and MENA	11.2	10.6	0.6	0.2	0.0	0.1	0.0	0.2
America non-OECD	1.6	1.3	0.2	0.0	0.1	0.1	0.0	0.0
Asia and Oceania non-OECD	31.0	12.9	18.1	0.2	0.6	15.6	0.0	1.6
Europe non-OECD	0.5	0.5	0.1	0.0	0.0	0.0	0.0	0.0
Non-OECD	1.2	0.6	0.6	0.0	0.0	0.5	0.0	0.1

FDI = foreign direct investment, MENA = Middle East and North Africa,
OECD = Organisation for Economic Co-operation and Development, % = percent.

Source: OECD. 2005. *South-South Service Trade: Interim Report*, November.

Table 5.7 shows total FDI inflows by country and region of origin. Although the share of FDI to SAARC is increasing, this region is still a small FDI recipient relative to ASEAN and the PRC, and also to other Asian countries. FDI to India accounts for most of the FDI inflows to this region, and the share of other SAARC members is small.

Table 5.7   FDI Inflows by Country and Region

Region/ Economy	Total FDI Inflows ($ Mn)		Share of each country and region (%)	
	1990–1996	1997–2004	1990–1996	1997–2004
SAARC	10,892	35,459	**0.62**	**1.74**
Bangladesh	49	1,649	0.00	0.08
India	6,746	27,195	0.38	1.33
Nepal	52	79	0.00	0.00
Pakistan	3,253	4,750	0.18	0.23
Sri Lanka	792	1,787	0.05	0.09
ASEAN	134,677	184,708	7.65	9.06
Brunei Darussalam	1,270	6,246	0.07	0.31
Cambodia	600	1,302	0.03	0.06
Indonesia	18,995	(4,385)	1.08	(0.22)
Lao PDR	332	303	0.02	0.01
Malaysia	35,226	27,574	2.00	1.35
Myanmar	1,734	3,305	0.10	0.16
Philippines	7,690	9,578	0.44	0.47
Singapore	46,987	99,501	2.67	4.88
Thailand	14,359	28,664	0.82	1.41
Viet Nam	7,483	12,621	0.43	0.62
Japan	7,161	57,101	0.41	2.80
PRC	215,377	643,914	12.24	31.57
Korea, Rep. of	7,041	43,858	0.40	2.15
Hong Kong, China	39,615	193,752	2.25	9.50
Taipei,China	9,195	18,229	0.52	0.89
World	1,759,569	2,039,564	100.00	100.00

ASEAN = Association of Southeast Asian Nations, FDI = foreign direct investment, Lao PDR = Lao People's Democratic Republic, PRC = People's Republic of China, $ Mn = millions of US dollars, % = percent, ( ) = negative value.

Source: United Nations Conference on Trade and Development (UNCTAD), *World Investment Report 2004*.

Data on services inflows of FDI are reported in Table 5.8, which shows that, in SAARC, the services sectors account for about 50% of total inward investments. In ASEAN and the PRC, the share of services sectors decreased after the late 1990s (to about 30%) but in more advanced economies such as Hong Kong, China; Japan; Korea; and Taipei,China—in which these sectors have become more important in their industrial structures—the share of services industries is rising steadily.

Table 5.8   Services in FDI Inflows

Region/ economy	Average inward FDI in services ($ Mn)			Average share of services in total inward FDI (%)		
	1990–1994	1995–1999	2000–2002	1990–1994	1995–1999	2000–2002
SAARC	337	1,435	473	42.6	53.9	50.1
Bangladesh	–	81	165	–	28.5	45.7
India	52	725	–	10.5	28.3	–
Nepal	14	19	–	52.7	68.3	–
Pakistan	271	304	227	64.6	69.1	56.6
Sri Lanka	–	306	81	–	75.4	48.1
ASEAN	1,330	12,221	6,526	57.0	38.2	33.4
Brunei Darussalam	–	3	199	–	0.4	28.3
Cambodia	425	508	95	84.2	57.6	59.2
Indonesia	–	(726)	(699)	–	28.5	22.4
Lao PDR	–	25	10	–	48.9	34.6
Malaysia	–	115	12	–	3.0	0.6
Myanmar	–	26	50	–	8.7	28.3
Philippines	110	710	607	25.0	57.8	49.3
Singapore	–	9,067	5,716	–	70.7	58.2
Thailand	1,220	3,004	830	61.8	68.6	30.3
Viet Nam	–	561	291	–	37.8	23.0
Japan	2,005	6,073	18,442	53.3	63.4	78.6
PRC	–	15,760	12,805	–	36.1	27.4
Korea, Rep. of	289	1,708	2,232	38.4	41.9	44.2
Hong Kong, China	–	16,540	30,647	–	84.1	96.4
Taipei,China	662	1,565	3,176	39.4	44.4	59.5

ASEAN = Association of Southeast Asian Nations, FDI = foreign direct investment, Lao PDR = Lao People's Democratic Republic, PRC = People's Republic of China, $ Mn = millions of US dollars, % = percent, ( ) = negative value, – = no data available.

Source: United Nations Conference on Trade and Development (UNCTAD), *World Investment Report 2004*. The shift toward services.

The India country paper reports that share of services in the inward stock of FDI rose from 12% to 24% between 2000 and 2006. The share of services in FDI inflows in the PRC is similar to that of India (except the reported PRC data excludes investment in financial services). Services also accounts for a significant share of India's FDI outflows, mainly in software-related services and followed by media, broadcasting, and publishing; then hotels/tourism and financial services (Pradhan 2003). The PRC's FDI outflows in services have also been growing rapidly, but concentrated in sectors such as transportation, warehousing, wholesale and retail, and business services. The extent of these flows also highlights the point that BOP data captures only part of a country's international services business, since it ignores mode 3 transactions. On the other hand, the growth in services investment outflows, alongside the earlier data on growth in BOP services trade, suggests that reform in services is associated with some lags with growth in two-way trade in services in all modes of supply.

Movement of People

Reference to earnings from workers living offshore is a common theme in the papers in this project. In some cases, remittances are a significant part of total services exports. In Bangladesh, for example, remittances grew from $1.2 billion in 1994/95 to $3.8 billion in 2004/05 (a sum equal to 45% of the value of merchandise exports). The country paper on Nepal identifies the rapid growth in overseas workers, but also notes the data are likely to be underestimates because of the use of informal channels, and because a treaty with India eliminated restrictions on employment there. A large proportion of Nepalese working offshore, other than in India, are in Malaysia.

The data on remittances includes not only services workers but also manufacturing workers. Changes in restrictions on transfer of payments and tax policies will also affect the magnitude of remittances. In addition, even if there are no changes in the number of foreign workers, the changes in economic conditions in the recipient countries of foreign workers will directly influence the size of remittances. Furthermore, not all remittances are managed in formal channels where they can be observed and measured.

Table 5.9 reveals that, in the labor-exporting regions of SAARC and ASEAN, the receipts of workers' remittances and compensation of employees have been greater than the payments. This is entirely different from the situation in high-income countries in the OECD. On the other hand, the payments of the remittances have grown rapidly, implying that SAARC and ASEAN countries are also increasingly accepting foreign workers in association with their rapid economic growth. In addition, the dramatic inflows of FDI in the 1990s may also help explain the sharp rise in the outflows of workers' remittances.

Table 5.9 Workers' Remittances and Compensation of Employees

	Average value ($ Mn)		Average growth rate (%)	
	1990–1996	1997–2004	1990–1996	1997–2004
Workers' remittances and compensation of employees, paid				
SAARC	268	742	32.4	30.6
Bangladesh	na	5	na	21.2
India	256	585	31.1	29.8
Nepal	10[a]	30	81.7[a]	16.4
Pakistan	2	4	26.0	25.8
Sri Lanka	na	118	na	45.7
ASEAN	676	2,658	23.9	16.3
Brunei Darussalam	na	na	na	na
Cambodia[a]	39[a]	114	72.5[a]	19.9
Indonesia	na	na	na	na
Lao PDR	7	2	216.2	(31.4)
Malaysia	557	2,374	35.5	13.4
Myanmar	na	20	na	15.0
Philippines	52	40	50.0	(33.5)
Singapore	na	na	na	na
Thailand	na	na	na	na
Viet Nam	na	na	na	na
Japan	14	984	39.6	37.8
PRC	1,642	2,901	51.8	(12.6)
Korea, Rep. of	539	1,231	13.9	16.4
Hong Kong, China	na	259[b]	na	10.6[b]
Taipei,China	na	na	na	na

continued on next page

Table 5.9 continued

	Average value ($ Mn)		Average growth rate (%)	
	1990–1996	1997–2004	1990–1996	1997–2004
OECD	57,943	82,954	6.9	7.3
Latin America and Caribbean	1,245	1,805	5.0	5.6
World	84,199	121,570	7.5	7.1

Workers' remittances and computerization of employees, received

SAARC	8,004	20,551	14.1	10.8
Bangladesh	1,024	2,331	9.5	13.0
India	4,706	14,429	24.2	9.8
Nepal	34[a]	341	(7.2)[a]	49.6
Pakistan	1,617	2,234	(7.2)	12.7
Sri Lanka	628	1,216	13.4	7.8
ASEAN	5,324	12,879	19.4	9.4
Brunei Darussalam	na	na	na	na
Cambodia	11[a]	118	6.3[a]	46.9
Indonesia	395	1,205	29.9	14.5
Lao PDR	17	12	26.5	(41.2)
Malaysia	512	960	17.5	(1.2)
Myanmar	41	119	65.7	(3.4)
Philippines	3,161	7,626	22.2	8.0
Singapore	na	na	na	na
Thailand	1,190	1,513	10.9	(0.3)
Viet Nam	na	2,653	na	17.0
Japan	861	9,757	43.0	22.2
PRC	853	1,360	19.3	(5.1)
Korea, Rep. of	1,071	721	(1.5)	(0.3)
Hong Kong, China	na	151[b]	na	7.7[b]
Taipei,China	na	na	na	na
OECD	39,241	51,736	3.1	5.1

continued on next page

Table 5.9 continued

	Average value ($ Mn)		Average growth rate (%)	
	1990–1996	1997–2004	1990–1996	1997–2004
Latin America and Caribbean	9,701	24,583	15.4	16.0
World	86,355	155,641	7.8	9.7

ASEAN = Association of Southeast Asian Nations, Lao PDR = Lao People's Democratic Republic, OECD = Organisation for Economic Co-operation and Development, PRC = People's Republic of China, SAARC = South Asian Association for Regional Cooperation, na = no data available, $ Mn = millions of US dollars, % = percent, ( ) = negative value.

a 1993–1996 average.
b 1998–2004 average.

Source: World Bank, *World Development Indicators*.

The yearly average growth rate of the receipts of workers' remittances in SAARC was 10.8% after the late 1990s, and the same indicator for ASEAN was 9.4%. However, these rates are low relative to growth in the PRC (22.2%) and in Latin American and Caribbean countries (16.0%).

As Box 5.1 shows, Singapore changed its policies to make use of (skilled) foreign laborers. In many Asian countries where skilled workers are scarce in services sectors, the international mobility of these workers and the efficient use of these human resources are critical for the development of services industries. In particular, in most services industries, the technologies and skills are not separable from human resources and they are generally embodied in workers, so that the facilitation of movements of people will contribute to the development of local services industries.

Box 5.1 Open Labor Market Policies in Singapore

The Singaporean economy, with poor natural resources, is largely dependent on human resources. However, because the population in Singapore is only 4.2 million and its fertility rate has recently been decreasing, the government has adopted policies that not only improve the educational and skill level of the local workers, but also ones that encourage the inflows of foreign workers into Singapore.

The shortage of local laborers appeared in the late 1960s as a result of the export-oriented development policies and rapid economic growth. Consequently, immigration policies were adjusted, leading to large inflows of foreign unskilled workers, mainly in the manufacturing, construction, and

---

continued on next page

domestic services sectors. The upgrading of the industrial structures in the 1990s reinforced this policy stance to foreign workers, which is relevant to the restructuring of the industrial structures in Singapore. Singapore aims to satisfy the increasing demand for workers with higher skills as a consequence of the relocation of relatively resource-intensive productions overseas and of the concentration of more technology-intensive activities, such as headquarters, in Singapore. In order for foreign nationals to work in Singapore, both skilled and unskilled workers must obtain employment passes or work permits from the Ministry of Manpower. There are about 620,000 foreign workers who had these rights in 2005 (The Japan Institute for Labor Policy and Training 2006, see website on the next page). Distinctions among foreign workers are based on occupation and salary. Employment passes are issued to workers who engage in professional or managerial jobs, or to workers who earn at least S$1,800 a month. Work permits are issued mainly to unskilled workers who do not belong to the above category (mainly the workers seeking unskilled jobs in construction, finance and insurance, real estate, transportation, communications, community services, social services, hotels and restaurants, manufacturing and domestic work). The work permit lasts 2 years, but it is renewable up to a cumulative total of 4 years.[a] On the other hand, there is no upper limit of the duration of an employment pass and its holders can renew the pass every 3 years.

Except for a prohibition of change in employer and restrictions on duration of employment mentioned below, foreign workers who obtained the above permissions enjoy a status specified in the Labor Law that is equal to local workers[b]. In addition, they are also entitled to industrial accident compensation insurance and accident insurance, and are provided inexpensive housing. Singapore limits the countries from which it imports foreign workers to Non-Traditional Sources (NTS) consisting of India, Sri Lanka, Thailand, Bangladesh, Myanmar, the Philippines, Pakistan, and the PRC; it also takes workers from North Asian Sources (NAS) such as Hong Kong, China; Macao, China; Republic of Korea; and Taipei,China. Malaysia is another source of foreign workers for Singapore. Furthermore, services-related companies are allowed to recruit workers from Malaysia and NAS countries, but are, in principle, not permitted to import workers from NTS countries. The recruitment of foreign workers in manufacturing sectors is limited to workers from Malaysia and NAS countries, whereas construction and marine sectors are open to all workers from Malaysia, NAS, and NTS countries.

Although the inflows of unskilled foreign laborers are restricted, they are managed by the Dependency Ceiling system and Foreign Workers Levy system and there is no upper limit on total number of foreign workers employed. The Dependency Ceiling system limits the number of foreign workers that firms can employ based on the number of local workers employed in the firms and the ceiling rate differs across sectors. Under the Foreign Workers Levy system, the employers are obliged to pay a certain amount of employment levy per unskilled foreign worker employed to the government. Furthermore, to ensure the return of the foreign workers to their home country after termination of employment, the employers of foreign workers are mandated to put up a

continued on next page

S$5,000 security bond per worker. Therefore, in Singapore the inflows of foreign (unskilled) workers have been managed by a change in employers' incentive to hire foreign workers, rather than a direct control of entrants of foreign workers by the government.

S$ = Singapore dollar.

[a] If foreign workers return to their home country, they are unable to re-enter Singapore.
[b] However, because household workers are not covered in the Labor Law, the Ministry of Manpower proposed a guideline regarding employment conditions between employers and household workers.

Source: Japan Institute for Labor Policy and Training, www.jil.go.jp/foreign/labor_system/2006_3/singapore_01.htm

RCA Index in Services Industries

Before turning to data on trade and investment flows between the regions, we first establish some expectations about those flows by analyze the international competitive advantages of services sectors in East and South Asia. We do this by calculating an RCA index for those sectors. The RCA index in service sector i in country j is generally defined as:

$$RCA_{j,i} = \frac{x_{j,i}/\bar{x}_j}{x_{W,i}/\bar{x}_W}$$

where xj,i indicates country j's export of service i, $\bar{x}_j$ country j's export of goods and services, xW,i total world export of service i, and $\bar{x}_w$ total world export of goods and services. Therefore, if the index takes a value that exceeds one, the country has a greater comparative advantage in that sector.

To capture the comparative advantages in these sectors between East and South Asia, data on bilateral trade in services should be used. Unfortunately, these are not available and the analysis is thus forced to focus on the competitive powers of services industries in the countries of interest relative to the world averages. In addition, we should note that this index is an ex-post indicator, i.e., it may include the impacts of trade barriers, other policy influences, geographical distances, and cultural similarities on trade in services. Thus, this index may not always represent ex-ante or potential comparative advantages. Particularly in services sectors, policy impediments are more likely to affect the performance of trade, compared with trade in goods, as we discuss further below. The data used in this study were collected mainly from *World Development Indicators* published by the World Bank and *Balance of Payments Statistics Yearbook* published by the International Monetary Fund (IMF). Regarding the data on Taipei,China, this study used the BOP data that are available from the website of the central bank.[4] A final point to note is that these data are based on cross-border transactions; that is, modes 1 and 2, only.

The results of the RCA calculations for SAARC and ASEAN are shown in Figures 5.1 and 5.2, and more detailed results with broader coverage of countries are shown in Table 5.10. These results highlight some areas of complementarity between SAARC and ASEAN. They also demonstrate significant shifts in comparative advantage over time.

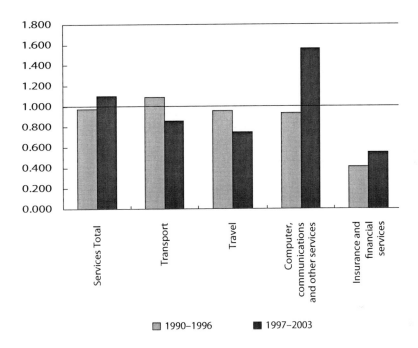

Figure 5.1 RCA Index in Services Sectors – SAARC

RCA = revealed comparative advantage, SAARC = South Asian Association for Regional Cooperation.

Sources: Computed from *World Development Indicators* and *Balance of Payments Statistics Yearbook.*

---

[4] Central Bank of China. Available at www.cbc.gov.tw/EngHome/Eeconomic/ Statistics/BOP/hist/index.asp

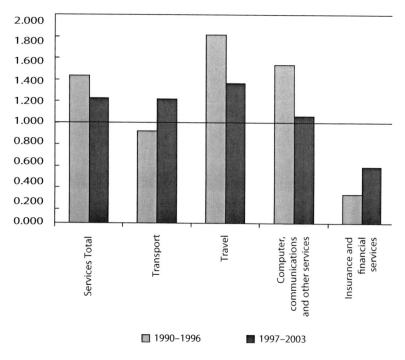

Figure 5.2 RCA Index in Services Sectors – ASEAN

ASEAN = Association of Southeast Asian Nations, RCA = revealed comparative advantage.

Sources: Computed from *World Development Indicators* and *Balance of Payments Statistics Yearbook*.

In SAARC, the overall services RCA index was less than one in the early 1990s but it exceeded one after 1997. However, this change was caused by the increase in exports of services in India. As Table 5.10 shows, only India increased its comparative advantages in these sectors after the Asian financial crisis, while the values of this index decreased in the other SAARC members in the same period.

ASEAN countries have shown significant comparative advantages in services, but the degree of that advantage has declined since 1997. Compared to members of SAARC, there are three key points to note about ASEAN's position:

- ASEAN countries in general have a greater comparative advantage in travel and transport services than do SAARC members.

Table 5.10 RCA Index in Services Sectors

	Services Total		Transport		Travel		Computer, communications, and other services		Insurance and financial services	
	1990–1996	1997–2003	1990–1996	1997–2003	1990–1996	1997–2003	1990–1996	1997–2003	1990–1996	1997–2003
SAARC	0.972	1.099	1.092	0.859	0.958	0.752	0.932	1.564	0.407	0.547
Bangladesh	0.695	0.228	0.334	0.283	0.134	0.142	1.523	0.255	0.036	0.211
India	1.007	1.275	0.906	0.734	1.215	0.902	0.924	1.960	0.492	0.596
Nepal	2.648	1.795	1.084	0.905	3.477	2.355	3.330	2.202	0.000	0.000
Pakistan	0.836	0.647	1.839	1.542	0.239	0.142	0.683	0.538	0.170	0.170
Sri Lanka	0.941	0.917	1.398	1.514	0.851	0.791	0.670	0.573	0.703	1.180
ASEAN	1.433	1.224	0.923	1.218	1.818	1.367	1.535	1.063	0.339	0.593
Brunei Darussalam	—	—	—	—	—	—	—	—	—	—
Cambodia	0.654	1.044	0.359	0.789	1.060	2.418	0.084	0.306	0.000	0.000
Indonesia	0.490	0.449	0.024	0.085	1.395	1.365	0.072	0.028	0.000	0.000
Lao PDR	0.814	1.153	1.067	0.609	1.504	2.173	0.086	0.012	0.168	0.072
Malaysia	0.661	0.678	0.629	0.542	0.753	0.793	0.671	0.744	0.000	0.132
Myanmar	—	—	—	—	—	—	—	—	—	—
Philippines	1.551	0.765	0.272	0.325	0.774	0.813	3.314	1.080	0.118	0.124
Singapore	—	—	—	—	—	—	—	—	—	—

continued on next page

Table 5.10 continued

	Services Total		Transport		Travel		Computer, communications, and other services		Insurance and financial services	
	1990–1996	1997–2003	1990–1996	1997–2003	1990–1996	1997–2003	1990–1996	1997–2003	1990–1996	1997–2003
Thailand	1.123	0.947	0.751	0.803	1.961	1.572	0.744	0.675	0.083	0.072
Viet Nam	1.147	0.875	–	–	–	–	–	–	–	–
Japan	0.685	0.725	0.804	1.061	0.119	0.155	1.155	0.982	0.141	0.401
PRC	0.536	0.558	0.458	0.287	0.688	0.930	0.431	0.505	0.557	0.097
Korea, Rep. of	0.690	0.746	1.058	1.406	0.533	0.557	0.627	0.554	0.070	0.216
Hong Kong, China	–	0.866	–	0.940	–	0.385	–	0.798	–	1.158
Taipei,China	0.592	0.647	0.622	0.523	0.419	0.411	0.732	0.888	0.345	0.624
Australia	1.071	1.113	1.271	1.108	1.532	1.818	0.470	0.578	1.057	0.908
East Asia and Pacific	0.746	0.654	0.547	0.412	1.069	1.113	0.637	0.546	0.368	0.078
OECD	1.078	1.088	1.101	1.090	0.959	0.934	1.121	1.149	1.222	1.251
Latin America and Caribbean	0.781	0.645	0.737	0.504	1.274	1.127	0.345	0.355	0.714	0.583

ASEAN = Association of Southeast Asian Nations, Lao PDR = Lao People's Democratic Republic, OECD = Organisation for Economic Co-operation and Development, PRC = People's Republic of China, RCA = revealed comparative advantage, SAARC = South Asian Association for Regional Cooperation, – = no index.

Source: Authors' own calculations.

- Although ASEAN members had comparative advantages in computer, communications, and other services in the pre-crisis period, they lost those advantages after the late 1990s, just as the SAARC members (through India's contribution) gained advantages in these areas.
- ASEAN, like SAARC, does not reveal a comparative advantage in financial services.

Results of interest for other countries include the following: (i) RCA index values for the PRC are all less than one; (ii) Japan has comparative disadvantages in services sectors, as do Korea and Taipei,China; (iii) Australia shows relatively high RCA index values in services, except in communications and computer services.

Trade and Investment Flows—East and South Asia

Data on bilateral flows of trade and investment in services are notoriously difficult to find. The country papers in this project provide one set of sources and some of the key points from those papers are now reviewed. Finally, we examine available data on student and tourist movements between the economies of interest.

Country Experience

The focus here is the features of each country's international transactions in services and of interregional linkages in services. This material highlights some significant links in certain bilateral relationships but, as already noted, not extensive links between the two regions. The main points of interest concern (i) the movement of people (workers, tourists, and students); (ii) FDI flows in some services sectors; and (iii) some trade in IT-related services. Box 5.2 summarizes the main examples and the following paragraphs provide more detail.

Bangladesh. Bangladesh's services trade volumes are small compared to that in manufacturing. Exports of services have increased from $3.4 million in 1990/91 to $165.5 million in 2004/05. Imports of services have grown from $185.3 million to $242.7 million during this time. Much more important are the remittance flows into Bangladesh, which have grown rapidly from $1.2 billion in 1994/95 to $3.8 billion in 2004/05. Bangladesh has mainly exported unskilled workers to the Middle East; there is little or no export of labor from Bangladesh to South Asian countries, and the export of labor from Bangladesh to East Asian countries has been comparatively small (only Malaysia and Singapore import some labor from Bangladesh). In FDI inflows, there has been a reorientation to services. The total inflow to the services sector during the period 1996–2001 was \$7.3 billion. The manufacturing sector received 73.4% of the registered FDI in 1991–1995, while the service sector absorbed 26.6%. In the second half of the 1990s, the share of the manufacturing sector in FDI inflow declined to 25% while the share of the services sector rose to about 75%. In 2005, the shares in FDI of the manufacturing and service sectors were 26% and 74%, respectively (services investment in that year was \$624 million). Important host sectors are power and gas, followed by telecommunications (where Malaysia has a significant share in cellular services) and container terminals.

Box 5.2 Examples of Interregional Transactions

- East Asia plays a small role as a destination of labor services exports from Bangladesh.
- Exports of construction and labor services from the People's Republic of China (PRC) to South Asia are significant.
- India's exports of information technology (IT) services to East Asia account for less than 5% of the total, although efforts are in progress to diversify markets for those services and Indian exports of health services may become significant in future (a number of Indian students have traveled to the PRC to study medicine).
- Japan and Singapore are significant services sector investors in India (however, India accounts for a very small share of Singapore's outbound foreign direct investment [FDI]) and India is a significant source of tourists in ASEAN (East Asia in total accounts for 56% of Indian tourist departures). East Asia is an important source of both students and tourists arriving in India.
- ASEAN companies are active in the Indian construction sector.
- East Asian countries are important investors in Nepal, particularly in tourism and East Asia accounts for about 20% of tourist arrivals.
- Of the Nepalese working offshore in countries other than India, half are in Malaysia.
- East Asia accounts for only a small share of worker remittances in Pakistan (although Japan ranks sixth).
- Pakistan hosts significant flows of FDI from East Asia (particularly from Japan) in telecommunications, financial services, and electric power.
- Japan is a significant investor in telecommunications, energy, port services, and construction in Sri Lanka.
- Exports of IT-related services are growing rapidly from Sri Lanka but not to East Asia; there has also been a sharp drop in remittance earnings from East Asia.
- There has been significant growth in tourist arrivals in Thailand from South Asia, especially from India.

ASEAN = Association of Southeast Asian Nations.

Source: Compiled by authors.

The PRC. The share of services in the PRC's total trade is relatively low (10%), but in recent years services trade has grown rapidly (since 2000, at more than 18% a year). Services exports and imports have more than doubled since accession to the WTO, at which time the PRC implemented significant policy reform. Exports and imports are mainly tourism and transport services. The PRC exports construction services and labor services, especially to Pakistan and India (a total of $1.8 billion in 2004) but also Bangladesh, Sri Lanka, and Nepal. Services accounted for 20–25% of FDI inflow since 2001 (excludes investment in financial services), although the volumes and share in total FDI have fallen slightly. Host sectors include computer services, construction, retail, hotel and catering, water transport, and warehousing. In 2005, services sector FDI was $11.7 billion. Official data on services FDI excludes the banking sector, which sees about the same proportion as flows to all other sectors (FDI data are discussed in more detail below). The PRC's FDI inflows other than in the financial sector are concentrated in real estate (which is included in the services data and which accounts in some years for nearly half the total) as well as in water transport, construction, hotels, retailing, and computer services, according to data from the PRC's Ministry of Commerce.

India. There has been rapid growth in India's services exports, led by IT-related and business process offshoring (BPO) services but with health services also making an important contribution. It is estimated that India accounts for 65% of the global offshoring in IT services and 46% of global BPO. India accounts for a large share of world trade in these services but East Asia accounts for a relatively small share of its exports. Exports of IT services to Japan, Singapore, the PRC, and Korea together represent 4.63% of total IT exports in 2004/05. However, India is attempting to diversify its markets for these services and have been targeting markets in the PRC and Japan, setting up offices in the PRC to supply services to both the PRC and Japan. Indian businesses have also employed PRC and Japanese workers to overcome their disadvantages in language. India's advantage in English was an important contributor to India success in penetrating the US (66.5% of IT and BPO exports) and United Kingdom (14%) markets.

India's exports of services grew at an average 20% a year during 1990/91 and 2005/06. The total value of services exports in 2005–06 was $61 billion. The share of services in India's total exports of goods and services rose from 20% to 37% between 1990/91 and 2005/06. India's share of world exports of commercial services more than quadrupled from 0.6% in 1990 to 2.8% in 2005. The composition of India's services exports has also changed.

The share of travel and transportation in total services exports fell from 53.6% in 1990/91 to 33.3% in 2005/06. The share of miscellaneous services (which includes IT services) rose from 43.6% to 74.6%. Software services account for over half of miscellaneous services exports.

Health services exports may become more important. India is already an important exporter of health services to Bangladesh, Nepal, and Bhutan. Success in these fields will depend on a number of factors, including access to accommodation packages that match the preferences of the various groups of visitors, quality assurance, and consumer confidence in suppliers (which may be linked to an accreditation system and to the impact of the regulatory regime).

The share of services in FDI has also grown rapidly. That share doubled from 12% to 24% between 2000 and 2006. Important hosts in the services sectors were telecommunications and financial services. Japan and Singapore were among the big investors. Chakraborty and Nunnenkamp (2006) (as reported by Findlay and Guo 2007) note that inflows of FDI are concentrated in the category of "other services," which they expect are information and communications services. They report data in which telecommunications accounts for 60% of approvals in 1991/2000 and that computer services and financing, insurance, real estate, and business services accounted for 30% of inflows in the period 2002/03 to 2004/05.

India has also become an important investor in service sectors offshore such as IT-related activities as well as health care, telecommunications, and financial services.

India is a booming market for many East and South Asian countries for tourism and construction and transport services. India is already the largest source of tourists to Sri Lanka and is one of the biggest sources of tourists in Singapore, Malaysia, Thailand, and other countries. East Asia accounts for 56% of Indian tourist departures, compared to only 6.6% to other destinations in South Asia.

Malaysian, Singaporean, and Thai companies participate in Indian infrastructure development and construction markets. There has been a rapid growth of Indian students going to the PRC to study medicine, but a combined 90% of Indian students abroad are in the US (76%), Europe, and Australia.

South Asia is an important source of tourists and students arriving in India (20–21% of each category, according to data in the first half of the 2000s). East Asia is almost as important as South Asia in markets for education (19% of student arrivals) but far less significant in tourism (12% of arrivals). Korea is the fastest-growing market for tourism arrivals; other important markets in East Asia are Japan, Malaysia, and Singapore.

Important sources of students are Nepal and Malaysia followed by Sri Lanka, Bangladesh, Thailand, and Viet Nam.

Nepal. Between 1990 and 2005, average annual FDI inflows to the services sector were $15.4 million (out of a total annual FDI inflow of $27 million). Significant destinations of this inflow were in tourism and energy. South Asia (India the most important) and East Asia (the PRC the most important) accounted for 35% and 24% of the total services FDI inflow respectively. East Asian investment is concentrated in tourism, but South Asian investment takes place in a range of other sectors. Services exports have not grown significantly since 2001 (in 2006, services credits were $370 million) but services imports have grown from $278 million in 2001 to $457 million in 2006. However, worker remittances are not included in these figures. In 2006, the total remittances were $1.4 billion, or about a third of total current account income. Tourism is the other significant source of services credit. Transport is the major source of services debit. Total tourist arrivals in 2005 were only over 375,000 of which about 96,000 were from India, 21,000 were from the PRC, and nearly 19,000 from Japan. South Asia accounted for 137,000 (37%) and East Asia for about 73,000 (20%).

India is the major destination for Nepalese workers offshore, but the number of workers traveling to other countries has grown rapidly. In 2005, according to official data, there were a total of 591,400 people working offshore of which 138,838 were not in India (the number in India is likely underestimated, possibly by as much as a factor of five). Of those not in India, nearly half were in Malaysia.

Pakistan. International trade in services is estimated to exceed $1 billion a year and account for over 20% of Pakistan's international trade. During the 1990s, the annual growth rate of trade in services was 12%; in telecommunications, financial, professional, and business services, growth averaged 16%. Worker remittances were $4.2 billion in 2004/05, an increase of 9% over the previous year. The US is the most important source and East Asian or other South Asian economies account for only a small share (Japan ranks about sixth). There has been a surge of investment in the service sector. Total inflows of FDI in 2005/06 were expected to reach $3.5 billion. The major host sector has been telecommunications. Energy, construction, and financial services are other important host sectors. There are now about 14 foreign banks operating in the country. In absolute terms, Japan is a major contributor to total FDI inflows, but East Asian economies account for a small share of that total. Of the inflows from East Asia, telecommunications is the most important destination, followed by financial services and electric power.

Singapore. Singapore is one of the world's top 20 exporters of services. Total export credits in 2005 were $45.1 billion. The composition of its services export credits is changing rapidly, however. The share earned from transport services is falling while that from financial services is rising. Around 65% of FDI inflows to Singapore have gone to the services sector; within that sector, financial and insurance services and commerce and business services account for the bulk of inflows. Singapore is also a significant external investor. Only a small share goes to South Asia (just over 1% to India) while nearly 29% goes to other East Asian economies. Of this investment, over half is related to finance and insurance.

Sri Lanka. The stock of realized foreign investment in Sri Lanka at the end of 2005 was $2.3 billion, of which services accounted for $1.3 billion (57%). Energy and telecommunications accounted for more than 60% of the cumulative FDI in the services sector during 2000/04. Japan has invested in telecommunications, energy, port services, and construction. India has concentrated on leisure, health, IT training, and other professional services. There are examples of outbound Sri Lankan FDI in tourism in India and the Maldives, as well as in banking in Bangladesh. Total services exports grew from $745 million in 1994 to $1.5 billion in 2005. Services account for 20% of total export earnings. The major credit items are travel and transport (70% of the total). Computer and information services exports are expected to grow, supported by investment from India. Sri Lanka does not appear to be exporting these services yet to East Asia. Sri Lanka has advantages such as language, literacy, and technical skills.

Remittances (not included in the services data) became the second largest source of total export earnings in the early 1990s, ranked after garments but overtaking tea. Remittances account for about 6–7% of GDP. The share from Asia has declined, from over 11% in 1990 to 7.5% in 2005. The share from South Asia is only 1%. The sharpest drop occurred in remittances from East Asia. Tourist arrivals have risen from 298,000 in 1990 to 550,000 in 2005. Earnings are estimated to be $513 million (2004) or 35% of total services credits. India is the major source country (21% of the total and 51% of those from Asia). Arrivals from India have been surging while those from Japan have been declining; about two thirds of arrivals are on holiday, where motivations include shopping and lifestyle. Contributors include the quality of the air transport linkages (based on a bilateral open skies policy) and the decision by Sri Lanka to extend visas on arrival to Indian nationals in 2003. This latter privilege was extended to all countries in SAARC in 2004.

Thailand. Thailand's services receipts reached more than $20 billion in 2005 (about twice the level of 1993) compared to debits of only over $15 billion. Travel is the more important credit and "other services" the most important debit. Tourism flows between South Asia and Thailand favor Thailand. The number of tourists visiting Thailand from South Asia increased by 226% between 1997 and 2005, rising to a share of 4.5% of the total. The absolute number increased from nearly 230,000 in 1997 to more than 500,000 in 2005. India is the most important source country, accounting for 70% of the arrivals from South Asia. East Asia accounts for 60% of total arrivals. South Asia accounts for less than 2% of Thailand's tourism departures, despite a doubling in that flow since 1997. The assessment of the country paper was that compared to East Asia, destinations in South Asia are less competitive because of the quality of the tourism infrastructure, pricing, and other personal services. Services account for 86% of total FDI inflows, with transport and travel dominating. Major investors are Japan and Singapore. There was little FDI flowing out of South Asia in any sector, services or otherwise (South Asia accounted for around $23 million of inflows to Thailand over the period 1998–2005).

Japan. Japan is one of the large investors in Asia and its role in particular countries was noted in the previous section. Table 5.11 shows the patterns of its outflows. Differing from its services FDI to other Asian economies, its FDI to South Asia increased after the financial crisis, but remains very small (less than 1%). In addition, services FDI to Sri Lanka and India accounted for about 57% and 36% respectively of Japanese total FDI to SAARC in 1997–2003, but in general, Japan's services FDI to South Asia is small relative to that to other regions.

Japanese firms' FDI in Hong Kong, China; Korea; and ASEAN is significant in the services sectors (about 40% of total FDI). Table 5.11 shows that the share of trading services and services (most likely business services) is relatively large. On the other hand, the share of financial services and transport is small, which may reflect restrictions applied in host economies.

The share of Asian countries in Japan's cross-border trade in services over the last decade (Table 5.12) is almost constant (about 34%), but the share of imports of services (as recorded in BOP data) from Asian countries is increasing. The share of trade (both exports and imports) with the PRC (and Taipei,China) is increasing, although the share of trade with other Asian economies remains almost constant or is decreasing.

Table 5.11 Services Foreign Direct Investment (FDI) Inflows from Japan

	South Asia*		ASEAN		Hong Kong, China		Taipei,China		PRC		Korea, Republic of		World	
	1990–1996	1997–2004	1990–1996	1997–2004	1990–1996	1997–2004	1990–1996	1997–2004	1990–1996	1997–2004	1990–1996	1997–2004	1990–1996	1997–2004
Share of each region, $ Mn														
Construction	0.5	3	553	438	55	19	34	38	250	280	5	24	2,629	1,728
Trading services	24	54	1,835	2,289	2,437	1,802	598	445	639	879	114	401	34,930	28,428
Financial and insurance services	45	54	3,013	2,342	2,404	1,177	33	49	46	488	17	790	44,013	88,677
Services	151	129	1,884	1,571	446	600	218	221	1,319	736	848	343	48,791	22,478
Transport	4	261	1,365	905	216	231	19	48	146	99	1	48	15,290	36,921
Real Estate	58	68	2,059	1,424	854	103	37	0.0	731	201	13	0.0	48,801	14,718
Service Total	282	569	10,707	8,969	6,413	3,932	938	800	3,131	2,683	998	1,606	194,453	192,950

continued on next page

Table 5.11 continued

	South Asia*		ASEAN		Hong Kong, China		Taipei, China		PRC		Korea, Republic of		World	
	1990–1996	1997–2004	1990–1996	1997–2004	1990–1996	1997–2004	1990–1996	1997–2004	1990–1996	1997–2004	1990–1996	1997–2004	1990–1996	1997–2004
Share of each region, %														
Construction	0.02	0.16	21.04	25.37	2.11	1.12	1.28	2.18	9.53	16.19	0.19	1.41	100.00	100.00
Trading services	0.07	0.19	5.25	8.05	6.98	6.34	1.71	1.57	1.83	3.09	0.33	1.41	100.00	100.00
Financial and insurance services	0.10	0.06	6.84	2.64	5.46	1.33	0.08	0.05	0.10	0.55	0.04	0.89	100.00	100.00
Services	0.31	0.57	3.86	6.99	0.92	2.67	0.45	0.98	2.70	3.28	1.74	1.52	100.00	100.00
Transport	0.02	0.71	8.93	2.45	1.41	0.63	0.12	0.13	0.96	0.27	0.01	0.13	100.00	100.00
Real Estate	0.12	0.46	4.22	9.67	1.75	0.70	0.08	0.00	1.50	1.37	0.03	0.00	100.00	100.00
Service Total	0.15	0.30	5.51	4.65	3.30	2.04	0.48	0.41	1.61	1.39	0.51	0.83	100.00	100.00
Share of services in total FDI	24.15	26.22	42.66	40.74	75.32	81.46	34.44	28.60	23.26	17.22	43.17	33.33	62.44	55.30

ASEAN = Association of Southeast Asian Nations, PRC = People's Republic of China, % = percent, $ Mn = millions of US dollars.

* Bangladesh, India, Nepal, Pakistan, and Sri Lanka.

Sources: Ministry of Finance, Japan, website (www.mof.go.jp/lc008.htm)

Table 5.12   Trade in Services by Country and Region, Japan

	Credit					Debit				
	1996	1998	2000	2002	2005	1996	1998	2000	2002	2005
Asia	37.2	34.3	34.5	31.8	34.8	26.4	27.3	27.2	26.7	30.2
PRC	3.0	3.1	3.4	4.2	6.4	3.2	3.4	3.6	4.0	6.0
Taipei,China	4.0	4.8	5.2	4.5	6.5	2.4	2.7	2.8	2.6	3.1
Korea, Republic of	6.0	3.8	4.9	4.8	5.8	3.7	4.5	5.4	4.9	5.5
Hong Kong, China	7.2	6.1	5.8	5.1	3.1	5.4	4.8	4.1	4.3	4.6
Singapore	6.9	5.9	6.2	5.3	5.7	4.3	4.4	4.2	4.3	4.5
Thailand	3.1	2.7	2.7	2.6	2.8	1.7	1.9	1.8	2.0	2.2
Malaysia	0.9	1.5	1.4	1.2	(0.3)	1.4	1.3	1.3	1.3	0.8
Indonesia	3.3	2.6	1.7	1.2	1.6	1.8	1.7	1.6	1.2	1.2
Philippines	1.3	1.7	1.6	1.2	1.6	1.1	1.2	1.2	1.2	1.1
India	0.5	0.6	0.5	0.5	0.7	0.4	0.4	0.4	0.3	0.3
North America	31.4	32.0	36.0	35.7	30.1	34.5	35.0	34.9	33.3	31.7
Central and South America	6.2	5.2	6.0	5.7	3.7	5.4	6.8	7.0	6.8	4.8
Oceania	2.9	2.7	2.4	2.4	2.4	3.9	4.9	4.7	5.2	5.1

continued on next page

Table 5.12 *continued*

	Credit					Debit				
	1996	1998	2000	2002	2005	1996	1998	2000	2002	2005
Western Europe	18.7	20.8	18.9	21.0	25.3	25.0	20.7	20.9	22.7	23.1
Easter Europe and Russia	0.7	0.8	0.6	0.6	1.0	0.7	0.8	0.6	0.7	1.3
Middle East	1.0	2.1	0.0	0.9	1.4	1.8	2.1	1.9	1.9	2.1
Africa	1.8	2.0	1.5	1.9	1.2	2.2	2.3	2.7	2.5	1.7
World (%)	100.0	100.0	100.0	100.0	100.0	100.0	100.0	100.0	100.0	100.0
($ Mn)	69,487	62,805	70,399	63,348	110,400	131,103	110,672	117,022	102,435	134,390

PRC = People's Republic of China, $ Mn = millions of US dollars, % = percent share, ( ) = negative value.

Source: Ministry of Finance, Japan, website (www.mof.go.jp/bpoffice/bparea.htm)

Student and Tourist Flows

As noted in the country reports, movements of students and tourists are important contributors to integration between South and East Asia. Data on flows of international students (mode 2 transactions) are reported in Table 5.13.[5] In SAARC; Japan; Korea; and Hong Kong, China the number of international students from Asia increased after 2000, but then sharply decreased in 2004. Intra-SAARC movements and the movements from SAARC to ASEAN dropped in that year,[6] while movements from ASEAN to SAARC have increased.

Tourist flows (also mode 2 transactions) are reported in Tables 5.14 to 5.16. Because the period for which the data is available is limited, the long-term trend in tourist flows is difficult to identify. Intra-Asia movements of tourists generally increased during the period, but it seems that entirely different patterns of tourist flows have also emerged in Asian region after 1999; visitors from the PRC to Asia are increasing rapidly, reflecting expanding regional business relationships and increasing in incomes in the PRC. In particular, visitors to SAARC from Korea and the PRC also increased during the period to a more significant extent. On the other hand, visitors from Japan to other Asian countries did not increase after 2001. Furthermore, intra-SAARC movements slightly decreased during the same period, although the number of SAARC tourists visiting other Asian countries increased (except for tourist flows to the PRC). The integration between SAARC and other Asian countries through tourist flows seems weaker than among other Asian countries. Tourists visiting SAARC are more likely to come from Europe and North America.

Table 5.17 shows that, in ASEAN countries, the receipts of international tourism exceed the expenditures to a significant extent. Meanwhile, receipts in SAARC are almost equal to expenditures, which may suggest that international tourism is still underdeveloped in this region. But these industries are growing rapidly in SAARC; after the late 1990s, the average growth rates in this period are more than 30% for both the receipts and expenditures.

In both ASEAN and SAARC, the growth rates of the receipts and expenditures of international tourism are higher than those in Latin American and Caribbean countries. The development of transport in the Asian region and the removal of policy impediments to international movement of people may have contributed to this result.

---

[5] Data on flows of international students to the PRC are not available in statistics from the United Nations Educational, Scientific, and Cultural Organization (UNESCO).

[6] The reason is not clear; one explanation could be the impact of severe acute respiratory syndrome (SARS) and bird flu.

Table 5.13   Flows of International Students

Country of Origin	Year	Host Country/Region						Asia Total
		SAARC	ASEAN	PRC	Japan	Korea, Republic of	Hong Kong, China	
Total World	2000	6,988	19,677	na	59,691	2,869	na	89,225
	2002	8,499	36,102	na	74,892	3,850	2,355	125,698
	2004	7,589	154,686	na	117,903	7,843	3,270	291,291
Asia (total)	2000	4,004	16,964	na	54,385	2,318	na	77,671
	2002	4,314	30,671	na	69,034	3,299	2,131	109,449
	2004	4,749	2,199	na	111,194	6,822	3,079	128,043
SAARC	2000	1,266	1,285	na	776	57	na	3,384
	2002	1,380	2,439	na	963	77	52	4,911
	2004	1,033	168	na	1,385	200	56	2,842
ASEAN	2000	724	7,310	na	5,533	168	na	13,735
	2002	586	8,633	na	6,045	205	60	15,529
	2004	1,363	670	na	7,646	624	68	10,371
PRC	2000	20	5,978	–	28,076	902	na	34,976
	2002	16	12,535	–	41,180	1,645	1,942	57,318
	2004	31	208	–	76,130	4,025	2,886	83,280

continued on next page

Table 5.13 continued

Country of Origin	Year	Host Country/Region						
		SAARC	ASEAN	PRC	Japan	Korea, Republic of	Hong Kong, China	Asia Total
Japan	2000	43	129	na	–	551	na	723
	2002	65	388	na	–	697	13	1,163
	2004	45	193	na	–	938	5	1,181
Korea, Republic of	2000	na	227	na	18,237	–	na	18,464
	2002	38	1,129	na	18,899	–	9	20,075
	2004	84	816	na	23,280	–	13	24,193
Hong Kong, China	2000	na	16	na	108	3	–	127
	2002	na	32	na	na	4	–	36
	2004	na	na	na	na	7	–	7

ASEAN = Association of SoutheastAsian Nations, PRC = People's Republic of China, SAARC = South Asian Association for Regional Cooperation, na = not applicable, – = not available.

Source: United Nations Educational, Scientific and Cultural Organization website (http://stats.uis.unesco.org/ReportFolders/ReportFolders.aspx?CS_referer=&CS_ChosenLang=en)

Table 5.14 Tourist Visitor Flows, Number

Country of Origin	Year	SAARC	ASEAN	Japan	PRC	Korea, Republic of	Hong Kong, China	Taipei;China
SAARC	1999	973,612	923,640	56,018	2,163	75,069	170,756	11,498
	2001	929,492	1,309,021	62,476	1,747	75,597	247,885	13,062
	2003	939,936	1,124,877	71,551	1,944	77,791	254,266	12,405
ASEAN	1999	198,018	13,403,327	326,070	1,507,312	479,026	1,338,756	498,601
	2001	193,122	17,479,965	393,204	1,984,763	521,018	1,493,445	474,965
	2003	246,498	15,804,568	448,705	1,947,975	585,634	1,088,057	447,395
Japan	1999	158,263	3,425,879	–	1,855,197	2,184,121	1,174,071	823,799
	2001	133,375	3,675,037	–	2,385,700	2,377,321	1,336,538	970,741
	2003	138,203	2,892,171	–	2,254,800	1,802,171	867,160	655,131
PRC	1999	26,997	1,959,551	294,937	–	316,639	3,206,453	na
	2001	38,999	2,554,398	391,384	–	482,227	4,448,583	na
	2003	53,170	2,349,375	448,782	–	513,236	8,467,211	na
Korea, Republic of	1999	33,641	1,063,847	942,674	991,979	–	291,015	74,411
	2001	52,896	1,501,165	1,133,971	1,678,836	–	425,732	82,081
	2003	62,680	1,712,062	1,459,333	1,945,484	–	368,176	90,174

continued on next page

Table 5.14 continued

Country of Origin	Year	SAARC	ASEAN	Japan	PRC	Korea, Republic of	Hong Kong, China	Taipei,China
					Host Country/Region			
	2001	4,385	686,232	262,229	na	204,959	–	80,752
	2003	3,713	771,943	260,214	na	156,373		56,076
Taipei,China	1999	12,049	1,703,776	931,411	na	110,563	2,063,027	–
	2001	8,868	1,926,839	807,202	na	129,410	2,418,827	–
	2003	17,558	1,492,583	785,379	na	194,681	1,852,378	–
Europe	1999	1,586,052	5,247,254	580,135	2,148,520	408,481	1,059,155	161,377
	2001	1,502,711	6,321,810	630,128	2,732,112	454,777	1,063,767	147,610
	2003	1,572,220	5,562,771	665,187	2,597,606	514,403	822,146	118,273
North America	1999	478,929	2,185,982	815,379	958,023	450,568	1,095,368	348,257
	2001	577,952	2,324,821	829,749	1,203,037	491,445	1,199,085	380,329
	2003	679,823	2,156,433	792,973	1,063,279	491,674	881,773	305,609
Total World	1999	4,014,870	34,262,477	4,437,863	8,432,050	4,659,785	11,328,272	2,411,248
	2001	3,942,231	41,837,642	4,771,555	11,226,384	5,147,204	13,725,352	2,831,035
	2003	4,288,549	37,126,020	5,211,725	11,402,855	4,753,664	15,536,839	2,248,117

ASEAN = Association of Southeast Asian Nations, PRC = People's Republic of China, SAARC = South Asian Association for Regional Cooperation, na = not applicable, – = no data available.

Source: World Tourism Organization, Yearbook of Tourism Statistics, various issues.

Table 5.15 Flows of Nonresident Visitors: Share of the Country of Origin, %

Country of Origin	Year	SAARC	ASEAN	Japan	PRC	Korea, Republic of	Hong Kong, China	Taipei;China
	2001	23.6	3.1	1.3	0.0	1.5	1.8	0.5
	2003	21.9	3.0	1.4	0.0	1.6	1.6	0.6
ASEAN	1999	4.9	39.1	7.3	17.9	10.3	11.8	20.7
	2001	4.9	41.8	8.2	17.7	10.1	10.9	16.8
	2003	5.7	42.6	8.6	17.1	12.3	7.0	19.9
Japan	1999	3.9	10.0	–	22.0	46.9	10.4	34.2
	2001	3.4	8.8	–	21.3	46.2	9.7	32.3
	2003	3.2	7.8	–	19.8	37.9	5.6	29.1
PRC	1999	0.7	5.7	6.6	–	6.8	28.3	na
	2001	1.0	6.1	8.2	–	9.4	32.4	na
	2003	1.2	6.3	8.6	–	10.8	54.5	na
Korea, Republic of	1999	0.8	3.1	21.2	11.8	–	2.6	3.1
	2001	1.3	3.6	23.8	15.0	–	3.1	2.9
	2003	1.5	4.6	28.0	17.1	–	2.4	4.0

continued on next page

Table 5.15 continued

Country of Origin	Year	Host Country/Region						
		SAARC	ASEAN	Japan	PRC	Korea, Republic of	Hong Kong, China	Taipei;China
	2001	0.1	1.6	5.5	na	4.0	–	2.9
	2003	0.1	2.1	5.0	na	3.3	–	2.5
Taipei,China	1999	0.3	5.0	21.0	na	2.4	18.2	–
	2001	0.2	4.6	16.9	na	2.5	17.6	–
	2003	0.4	4.0	15.1	na	4.1	11.9	–
Europe	1999	39.5	15.3	13.1	25.5	8.8	9.3	6.7
	2001	38.1	15.1	13.2	24.3	8.8	7.8	5.2
	2003	36.7	15.0	12.8	22.8	10.8	5.3	5.3
North America	1999	11.9	6.4	18.4	11.4	9.7	9.7	14.4
	2001	14.7	5.6	17.4	10.7	9.5	8.7	13.4
	2003	15.9	5.8	15.2	9.3	10.3	5.7	13.6
Total World	1999	100.0	100.0	100.0	100.0	100.0	100.0	100.0
	2001	100.0	100.0	100.0	100.0	100.0	100.0	100.0
	2003	100.0	100.0	100.0	100.0	100.0	100.0	100.0

ASEAN = Association of Southeast Asian Nations, PRC = People's Republic of China, SAARC = South Asian Association for Regional Cooperation, na = not applicable, – = no data available.

Source: World Tourism Organization, *Yearbook of Tourism Statistics*, various issues.

Table 5.16   Annual Growth Rate of Visitors 1999–2003, %

	Host Country/Region						
	SAARC	ASEAN	Japan	PRC	Korea, Rep. of	Hong Kong, China	Taipei, China
SAARC	(0.88)	5.05	6.31	(2.33)	0.89	10.47	1.92
ASEAN	5.63	4.21	8.31	6.62	5.15	(5.05)	(2.67)
Japan	(3.33)	(4.15)	–	5.00	(4.69)	(7.30)	(5.57)
PRC	18.46	4.64	11.06	–	12.83	27.48	na
Korea	16.83	12.63	11.54	18.34	–	6.06	1.92
Hong Kong, China	0.50	3.72	0.72	na	(9.59)	–	(2.99)
Taipei,China	9.87	(3.25)	(4.17)	na	15.19	(2.66)	–
Europe	(0.22)	1.47	3.48	4.86	5.93	(6.14)	(7.47)
North America	9.15	(0.34)	(0.69)	2.64	2.21	(5.28)	(3.21)
Total World	1.66	2.03	4.10	7.84	0.50	8.22	(1.74)

ASEAN = Association of Southeast Asian Nations, PRC = People's Republic of China,
SAARC = South Asian Association for Regional Cooperation, na = not applicable,
– = no data available, ( ) = negative value.

Source: World Tourism Organization, *Yearbook of Tourism Statistics*, various issues.

Table 5.17   Expenditures on the Receipts from International Tourism

	Average value ($ Mn) 1997–2003	Average growth rate (%) 1997–2003
Expenditures		
SAARC	3,770	31.6
Bangladesh	343[a]	3.6[a]
India	4,531	13.2
Nepal	123	(2.6)
Pakistan	676	11.9
Sri Lanka	363	8.7
ASEAN	9,182	6.2
Brunei Darussalam	na	na

continued on next page

Table 5.17 continued

	Average value ($ Mn) 1997–2003	Average growth rate (%) 1997–2003
Cambodia	46	13.5
Indonesia	na	na
Lao PDR	na	na
Malaysia	2,925	1.2
Myanmar	33	(0.9)
Philippines	1,538	(5.1)
Singapore	na	na
Thailand	3,448	(1.0)
Viet Nam	na	na
PRC	13,346	10.4
Japan	39,298	(2.1)
Korea, Republic of	8,089	5.5
Hong Kong, China	na	na
Taipei,China	na	na
OECD	393,001	3.3
Latin America and Caribbean	23,228	(1.3)
World	538,370	3.4
Receipts		
SAARC	3,076	30.4
Bangladesh	na	na
India	3,705	3.5
Nepal	212	2.5
Pakistan	565	0.1
Sri Lanka	432	12.4
ASEAN	19,200	6.3
Brunei Darussalam	na	na
Cambodia	289	28.3
Indonesia	na	na
Lao PDR	na	na

continued on next page

Table 5.17 continued

	Average value ($ Mn) 1997–2003	Average growth rate (%) 1997–2003
Malaysia	5,835	5.5
Myanmar	169	(14.8)
Philippines	1,968	(4.1)
Singapore	na	na
Thailand	9,619	2.4
Viet Nam	na	na
PRC	16,805	6.8
Japan	6,574	10.9
Korea, Republic of	7,542	1.7
Hong Kong, China	8,284[b]	4.3[b]
Taipei,China	na	na
OECD	382,882	2.1
Latin America and Caribbean	26,346	3.1
World	562,482	2.5

ASEAN = Association of Southeast Asian Nations, Lao PDR = Lao People's Democratic Republic, OECD = Organisation for Economic Co-operation and Development, PRC = People's Republic of China, SAARC = South Asian Association for Regional Cooperation, na = not applicable, $ Mn = millions of US dollars, % = percent, ( ) = negative value.

[a] 2000–2003 average; [b] 1998–2003 average.

Source: World Bank, *World Development Indicators*.

The shares of ASEAN and SAARC in the total world receipts of international tourism are small, about 3.4% and 0.5% respectively, and far lower than the share of the economies in the OECD (about 70%). We obtain a similar finding using the data on the numbers of the international tourists (Table 5.18) where the share of ASEAN in the world inflows of foreign tourists is about 5% and that of SAARC is less than 1%. These low shares suggest the scope for growth of this sector. The Nepal country paper identifies some factors constraining tourist arrivals, including entry processing and transport linkages (as well as marketing).

Table 5.18 International Tourism Arrivals and Departures

	Average number ('000) 1997–2003	Average growth rate (%) 1997–2003
Numbers of arrivals		
SAARC	3,917	2.5
Bangladesh	194	5.1
India	2,475	2.3
Nepal	401	(3.6)
Pakistan	458	4.9
Sri Lanka	390	5.4
ASEAN	35,057	3.0
Brunei Darussalam	873[a]	6.9[a]
Cambodia	462	21.4
Indonesia	4,909	(2.5)
Lao PDR	190	0.3
Malaysia	9,212	9.3
Myanmar	200	1.4
Philippines	2,028	(2.5)
Singapore	6,422	(2.2)
Thailand	8,962	5.5
Viet Nam	2,019	6.0
PRC	29,103	5.6
Japan	4,572	3.6
Korea, Republic of	4,634	3.3
Hong Kong, China	13,078	5.5
Taipei,China	na	na
OECD	361,847	2.0
Latin America and Caribbean	44,571	1.5
World	656,172	2.8
Number of departures		
SAARC	6,068	6.3
Bangladesh	1,081	8.5
India	4,298	6.2
Nepal	169	11.8
Pakistan	na	na
Sri Lanka	520	0.9

continued on next page

Table 5.18 continued

	Average number ('000) 1997–2003	Average growth rate (%) 1997–2003
ASEAN	36,813	3.2
Brunei Darussalam	na	na
Cambodia	45	4.9
Indonesia	na	na
Lao PDR	na	na
Malaysia	28,755	3.5
Myanmar	na	na
Philippines	1,856	(1.1)
Singapore	4,015	2.4
Thailand	1,862	4.4
Viet Nam	na	na
PRC	10,934	24.9
Japan	16,190	(3.8)
Korea, Republic of	5,300	7.7
Hong Kong, China	4,265	2.8
Taipei,China	na	na
OECD	340,940	2.9
Latin America and Caribbean	27,397	1.1
World	756,811	2.7

ASEAN = Association of Southeast Asian Nations, Lao PDR = Lao People's Democratic Republic, OECD = Organisation for Economic Co-operation and Development, PRC = People's Republic of China, SAARC = South Asian Association for Regional Cooperation, na = not applicable, % = percent, ( ) = negative value.

[a] 1997–2001 average.

Source: World Bank, *World Development Indicators*.

Impediments to Integration[7]

In this section, we follow two approaches to identifying impediments to trade and investment in services. One is comparative work on reform programs in the largest countries in this sample: the PRC and India. The second source is a series of sectoral studies regarding estimates of impediments to trade in services to analyze the barriers to trade in services in the

---

[7] This section uses material also reported in Centre for International Economic Studies (CIES) (2006).

selected Asian countries. The services sectors reviewed are air passenger transport, banking, distribution services, maritime (ports), professional services, and telecommunications.

Country Studies

The PRC made substantial commitments to liberalization of the service sector in accession to the WTO in 2001.[8] Mattoo (2003) reports a comparison of the extent of the PRC's commitments based on a representative sample of service sectors as defined in the GATS. The PRC, at the time of accession, made at least partial market access commitments of some kind in nearly all sectors sampled in the work reported by Mattoo for all modes (although less so for cross-border supply). But if the focus is the point in time when all the commitments are implemented (seven years after accession) then, according to Mattoo, the extent of the PRC's commitments is "much higher than the commitments offered in the Uruguay Round by any other group of countries (including high-income countries)."[9] The extent of commitments to full liberalization was also higher than that of any other group of developing economies.

A further important component of the PRC's commitments is the provision in its commitments to full national treatment. These are also wider (covering more sectors) and deeper (that is, fewer limitations are recorded) than those of all other country groups.

Findlay and Guo (2007) note that the impact of the PRC's accession to the WTO is apparent in the rise in services FDI inflows to $14 billion in 2002, but even before then inflows were significant, perhaps in expectation of accession. Inflows have since fallen back to their 2001 levels. As noted earlier, these data do not include foreign investment in the banking or financial services sector. These inflows vary from year to year. Findlay and Guo note that average total assets of foreign banks increased by about $7 billion a year between 1994 and 2005. Data from the PRC's Ministry of Commerce suggests that in 2005 the FDI inflow to financial services was $12 billion and in 2006 there were 12 new enterprises established in the financial services sector utilizing $6.5 billion of FDI. The more rapid inflow of FDI in financial services corresponds to the timing of implementation of the PRC's commitments to the WTO on financial services.

Mattoo (2003) noted how the PRC had retained significant degrees of freedom in the implementation of its commitments, and that the reform

---

[8] This review of the PRC's accession commitments on services is based on text in Pangestu and Findlay (2004) and in Findlay and Guo (2007).

[9] Mattoo (2003), p. 302.

process continues. For example, in a statement dated March 2007, the US Coalition of Service Industries (CSI) noted the following remaining issues.

- In financial services, CSI seeks 100% foreign ownership, to have all options available on the legal form of the business, to enjoy national treatment in all aspects of business operations, to be able to supply services cross-border, and to have greater regulatory transparency.
- Specific issues in insurance include the slow approval for new branches, the delay in the treatment of applications to convert branches to subsidiaries, large capitalization requirements, limitations on opportunities to invest foreign exchange capital in overseas funds or equities, limitations on the ability to establish insurance assets managements companies, and restrictions on reinsurance business.
- There is a 49% cap on foreign ownership in asset management firms, and a high level of paid-in capital is required of the foreign partner.
- Electronic payment cards cannot be issued unless they are co-branded with ChinaUnionPay, the only domestic electronic payments provider and processor.
- Foreign entry is being delayed for some value-added services in telecommunications. Foreign telecommunications service providers can only enter as a joint venture with an existing, state-owned provider. No independent telecommunications regulator has been established.
- There are concerns that plans for postal reform will not lift restrictions on express delivery services and about limits on the ability of freight forwarding firms to offer a full range of services.

India's reforms in services began earlier than the PRC's. Ahluwalia (2002) reviews the program of gradual reform, dating from the response to the economic crisis of 1991. Most important for services was the relaxation of controls on foreign investment, although banks, insurance companies, telecommunications, and airlines were among sectors excluded from the sectors where full or majority foreign ownership was possible. The Foreign Investment Promotion Board, however, "established a track record of speedy decisions"[10] where approval was required.

Ahluwalia reports good results from reform in telecommunications, more work to be done in civil aviation and ports, some progress in banking (although still a large government ownership share in that sector), some more recent reform in insurance, disappointment in electric power, and some private participation in road building. Railways remained untouched.[11]

---

[10] Ahluwalia, page 75.

[11] A summary of India's services sector reforms is available at www.indicus.net/fileadmin/Studies/Service_sector_reforms.pdf

Indicus Analytics (2006) provides further detail to a more recent date, as summarized in Box 5.3. The following shows the allocation of activities to stages of reform.

The sequence of policy changes appears to be connected, according to Findlay and Guo (2007) and their report on FDI inflows in the Indian services sector. They note the striking structural change evident from 2005, and they point out that the month of December 2006 alone accounts for Rs70 billion, more than twice that of any of previous year.

The lags (compared to the apparent linkages in the PRC, between policy reform in India and the apparent significant response of the FDI flows in recent years, is a topic for further work. However, comparing the chart with the sequence of policy changes discussed below, the structural change occurred just after significant reforms were announced in banking and telecommunications. Also of interest is the observation that despite significant reform in some sectors, there has not been significant growth in FDI inflows. One hypothesis is that there remain significant barriers associated with domestic regulation, as well as delays in processing applications or conflicts between local and central governments or competition policy concerns about entering markets where government-owned firms have large market shares. Critical sections of infrastructure are sometimes also missing.

Box 5.3 India's Services Reforms

Early movers:
Tourism (1991/92):
> Automatic approval to 51% foreign ownership for tourism projects was allowed in 1991/92 and up to 100% on application.

Information technology (1991/92):
> 100% foreign direct investment (FDI) in value-added services has been possible since 1991/92, while FDI in software was capped at 51%. Also relevant was the steady reduction in tariffs on all software to 10% by 1995/96 and reduction in tariffs on computers and peripherals in the following year. Reform of policy on access to complementary infrastructure was also important.

Health (1996):
> From 1996, automatic approval for FDI up to 51% was possible for hospitals and diagnostic centers.

Infrastructure (1996/97):
> Alongside tax concessions in 1996/97, automatic approval up to 74% was made available for construction of roads, bridges, railways, and ports; and automotive approval was made available up to 51% for support services such as the operation of infrastructure like toll roads and cargo handling.

---

continued on next page

Box 5.3 continued

Maritime services (1996/97) and ports (1997/98):
> Reform has opened the port sector for investment, along with related services. For example, from 1996/97, the private sector had options to lease out existing port assets, construct new assets, and construct complementary facilities. In 1997/98, automatic approval was made available for 74% foreign participation in construction of ports and harbors and 51% in supporting services. The cap applying in construction projects was lifted to 100% in 1998/99. There is currently no cap on investment in passenger or freight transportation services.

Road construction and transport (1997/98):
> Foreign investment in road construction lifted to 74% on construction and maintenance in 1997/98 and 51% in the operation of supporting services, the 74% cap was raised to 100% in the following year. There are few large trucking companies in India but there are no regulatory barriers to entry by Indian or local firms.

New century reforms:

Housing and township construction (2001/02):
> Any company that is incorporated in India (even if totally foreign owned) is regarded as an Indian company and can buy and sell property. However in construction no foreign entity has been allowed to set up an Indian company. Integrated contractors are operating in the country (without a local corporate structure). In 2001/02, 100% FDI was permitted in the development of integrated townships. This policy was replaced in 2005 to allow 100% FDI in townships, housing, built-up infrastructure, and construction-development projects under the automatic route. Rent control, stamp duty, property tax, and procedures for transferring agricultural land to urban use remain issues.

Banking (2003/04):
> The share of foreign banks in total deposits had risen from 4.5% in the early 1990s to 6% in 2000, while the domestic private sector share had risen from 5% to 14%. These changes were related to a series of reforms on privatization of government banks and the opportunity to set up private banks dating from 1991. Banking operations were also deregulated over the 1990s, but foreign ownership had been capped at 40%. This was raised to 49% under automatic clearance in 2002/03 and higher equity shares could be sought by application. This limit was then raised to 74% in the following year, finally allowing foreign control. In 2005, the government released a road map for the presence of foreign banks in India.

Telecommunications (2004):
> Private entry into valued-added services was permitted from 1992 to 1993 and basic telecommunications from 1994 to 1995. The cap on foreign participation was lifted to 51% in value-added services in 1994/95 but fixed at 49% in basic services as well as mobile and paging. A bill to deal with competition policy issues associated with private entry was passed

continued on next page

Box 5.3 continued

in 1996/97. The foreign ownership cap was lifted to 74% in 2004 (with approval case by case).

Wholesale and retail (2005):

This sector was generally closed. In 2006, the government allowed 100%-owned projects in the cash and carry (i.e., no credit) wholesale trade. In 2006, 51% FDI was also allowed in single-brand retailing. FDI is not allowed in multibrand retailing.

Slow to change:

Air transport (----) and airports (1999/2000):

Entry was opened to domestic firms on domestic routes in 1993/94 and with a cap on foreign ownership of 40% from 1997/98, which is now at 49% (there is restriction on investment by foreign airlines). From 1999 to 2000, foreign participation in airport projects at 74% was permitted with automatic approval and up to 100% on application. In 2002/03, the government sold down its shares in some airlines. In 2003/04 and 2004/05, various aspects of capacity controls under India's bilateral agreements were relaxed.

Railways (----):

This sector is dominated by public-sector firms with little scope for private participation, except some options for owning wagons or participating in build-operate-transfer projects.

Insurance (----):

A new regulation in 1999/2000 capped foreign participation at 26%, which was raised to 49% in 2005 (this has been announced, but not yet allowed, since the changes required in relevant legislation are being opposed by some political parties).

Professional services (----):

Audit and accounting sector was closed, but, in 2005, 26% foreign ownership was to be introduced (given the partnership structure of professional firms, it is not clear what this reform will mean). Reciprocal recognition agreements can be negotiated but the Council of Architecture has not entered into any such agreements.

Postal and courier services (----):

The Indian Post has a monopoly on letter delivery, but there is no cap on foreign investment in courier services. There are no restrictions on entry into markets for parcel services.

Source: Compiled by authors.

Sectoral Studies

According to Dee (2005a), in many studies estimating impediments to trade in services, the barriers are estimated by converting the qualitative information on regulatory regulations in services sectors to a quantitative index. Therefore, the definition of an impediment depends on the contents of the regulatory restrictions. In some studies, the restrictions are classified into those discriminatory against foreign firms and those applied to both foreign firms and domestic firms. This is an important distinction. Research results find that the gains from reform are larger when the measures reformed apply to all potential participants, not only foreign providers, because of the contribution of freer entry to competition.

The general technique for quantifying the impediments is to score the degree of each restriction on the basis of arbitrarily established criteria. Namely, a number that represents the degree of restrictiveness—for example, 1, 0.5, or 0—is allocated to each scoring item. See Dee (2005a) for details of scoring criteria for each sector. A larger value is given to a more restrictive measure. The overall index for individual sectors is generally computed using a weighted average of the restrictions.

There are a number of issues involved in the application of these index values. The first is how to form the weights, and different approaches have been adopted in the past studies. For example, some studies use the results of a factor analysis, while others arbitrarily set the weight values. Another source of the weight values could be the results of surveys of business people, according to their assessment of the significance of the impact of a measure. Second, comparison of the significance of impediments in different sectors is complicated by the different time periods of the data.

A further issue in the assessment of impediments is the nature of their welfare impact. Dee and Findlay (2006) review the nature of barriers to entry into markets for services. They stress their origin in regulatory processes that are designed primarily to resolve problems of market failure. Examples include market power, which is a feature of network industries, and a lack of information in professional services sectors. Barriers to trade are therefore associated with policies or processes that are more burdensome than necessary to solve the particular problem. These barriers can have two effects: one is to create rents, and the other is to add to costs. Rents could follow from restrictions on entry of competitor suppliers. Costs could be higher, for example, because of the processes of compliance. Reform of the measures will have different welfare effects depending on their effects. Reforms to the cost-creating barriers yield more welfare gains than do reforms to barriers whose main effect is to add to rents. The former generates real resource savings. The latter eliminates some transfers with smaller deadweight loss implications. However, the indicators of restrictiveness reported in this section at this stage are unable to distinguish between these effects on rents and costs. Developing measures which do so and which can be incorporated into modeling work is an important topic for further work.

The estimates of impediments for the above sectors are summarized in Tables 5.19 to 5.24. Unfortunately, in the reviewed studies estimates of restriction indexes are not available for most South Asian countries with the exception of India. In addition, the data for ASEAN members other than Indonesia, Malaysia, Philippines, and Thailand are not often available in most sectors. Furthermore, the years for which the estimations are undertaken differ across countries, and the estimates may be dated. For example, because many Asian countries have implemented many liberalization policies after the Asian financial crisis, the estimates in 1997 may not reflect the current trade barriers and trade regimes may have been liberalized to a more significant extent.

The results are summarized in the following remarks. Common themes are the significance of the restrictions on establishment and delivery via mode 3, and the presence of higher level of (discriminatory) restrictions applying to foreign suppliers. However, there is also significant variation among countries.

Air Passenger Services. Significant regulatory restraints on entry and capacity apply in many countries. The average scores of the restriction indexes, which were computed on the basis of the scoring results for each bilateral route, are reported in Table 5.19.[12] The total index scores are generally large (closer to 1) meaning that there exist large barriers to trade in this services sector in most countries in ASEAN. These results reveal that the regulatory system in Singapore is more liberal, while that in the Philippines is most restrictive. The impediments to trade in air passenger services are also very high in India even in comparison with ASEAN countries. On the other hand, the trade barriers in this sector are relatively low in more developed countries such as Singapore, Japan, and Korea.

Banking Services. Generally, impediments to mode 3 transactions are the higher barriers to trade in the banking sector. Also, restrictions on the businesses of foreign operators are generally larger than those on the businesses of domestic suppliers. Table 5.20 reports the overall degree of the restrictions for trade in banking services, classifying them into the restrictions discriminatory to foreign services suppliers and otherwise.[13] Compared with India and the countries in ASEAN, the barriers to trade in

---

[12] In Gonenc and Nicoletti (2000), the weights used for computing the overall restriction index are the results of a factor analysis (the squared factor loadings) in Doove et al (2001). More specifically, Doove et al (2001) extracted the factors indicating the above four regulations by a factor analysis. Gonenc and Nicoletti (2000) used the factor loadings to these factors as a weight.

[13] The weights were obtained from McGuire and Schuele (2000).

Table 5.19 Impediments to Trade in Air Passenger Services

	Authorization of carriers	Regulation of capacity	Regulation of prices	Authorization of charter flights	Total index score
Bangladesh	na	na	na	na	na
India	0.509	0.564	0.842	1.000	0.837
Nepal	na	na	na	na	na
Pakistan	na	na	na	na	na
Sri Lanka	na	na	na	na	na
SAARC Ave.	0.509	0.564	0.842	1.000	0.837
Brunei Darussalam	na	na	na	na	na
Cambodia	na	na	na	na	na
Indonesia	0.553	0.531	0.933	1.000	0.730
Lao PDR	na	na	na	na	na
Malaysia	0.482	0.635	0.955	1.000	0.744
Myanmar	na	na	na	na	na
Philippines	0.699	0.866	0.950	1.000	0.839
Singapore	0.589	0.611	0.806	1.000	0.717
Thailand	0.544	0.787	0.880	1.000	0.767
Viet Nam	0.330	1.000	1.000	1.000	0.808
ASEAN Ave.	0.533	0.738	0.921	1.000	0.768
Hong Kong, China	0.330	0.670	1.000	1.000	0.808
Taipei,China	na	na	na	na	na
Japan	0.521	0.498	1.000	1.000	0.735
PRC	0.948	1.000	0.615	0.615	0.769
Korea, Republic of	0.724	0.646	0.706	0.941	0.726

ASEAN = Association of Southeast Asian Nations, Lao PDR = Lao People's Democratic Republic, na = not available, PRC = People's Republic of China.

Source: Dee (2005a). *A Compendium of Barriers to Services Trade.* Paper prepared for the World Bank. November.

Hong Kong, China and Japan are much lower. The degree of discrimination is evident in the results for Malaysia and Indonesia. Singapore and Thailand have lower overall levels of restrictions.

Distribution Services. The level of barriers to trade in this sector appears to be generally lower than those in air passenger and banking services. Viet Nam provides an exception, while a particularly liberal regulatory system has been established in Singapore. Impediments are relatively low in Hong Kong, China. Table 5.21 summarizes the scoring results of the overall restrictiveness of trade in distribution services.[14] While the overall level of restrictions is lower, discriminatory restrictions to foreign operators are also observed in this sector. In addition, barriers to trade through mode 3 are significant.

Maritime Services. Restrictions on cargo handling services, a significant aspect of port services, are most severe in most members of ASEAN (Table 5.22). Among ASEAN members, a relatively liberal port environment has been built in Singapore and Malaysia, but large barriers that hinder the efficiency of ports exist in other member countries.[15]

Professional Services. Regulations in accountancy services and legal services are particularly high, mainly the result of the presence of large discriminatory restrictions to foreign firms with regard to commercial presence. The estimates of impediments to trade and investment are presented in Table 5.23.[16] The data show that in professional services barriers are high in both developed and developing economies.

Telecommunications Services. Market access in telecommunication services sectors (mode 3) has been severely restricted in many countries in ASEAN. Restrictiveness indexes derived in Dee (2004) and Warren (2000) are reported in Table 5.24. Investments in mobile phone services are highly regulated in most countries. Callback services have not been allowed in most ASEAN countries. Generally there are caps on foreign participation; for example, among ASEAN members except Cambodia, the participation rate of foreign capital has been limited to less than 50%. Although more liberal commitments have been made under the ASEAN

---

[14] The weights are same as those applied in Kalirajan (2000).

[15] The scoring results are reported in Appendix Table 5.22. Clark, Dollar, and Micco (2001) provide an assessment for each category but do not calculate an overall index. Data on port efficiency obtained from *The Global Competitiveness Report* (1996–2000) is also presented to complete the assessment.

[16] The same techniques and weights are applied to all of the four subsectors, although different weights should be given for different categories. But, because of the lack of the information at subsector level, the scoring was undertaken using the same weights in Dee (2005a).

Table 5.20 Impediments to Trade in Banking Services

Country	Year	Total Restrictiveness Index: Foreign			Total Restrictiveness Index: Domestic		
		Total	Commercial Presence	Other restrictions	Total	Commercial Presence	Other restrictions
Bangladesh	–	na	na	na	na	na	na
India	1997	0.5368	0.2850	0.2518	0.0475	0.0475	0.0000
Nepal	–	na	na	na	na	na	na
Pakistan	–	na	na	na	na	na	na
Sri Lanka	–	na	na	na	na	na	na
SAARC Average	1997	0.5368	0.2850	0.2518	0.0475	0.0475	0.0000
Brunei Darussalam	–	na	na	na	na	na	na
Cambodia	–	na	na	na	na	na	na
Indonesia	1997	0.4893	0.3420	0.1473	0.0713	0.0000	0.0713
Lao PDR	–	na	na	na	na	na	na
Malaysia	1997–2003	0.6104	0.3705	0.2399	0.2731	0.1900	0.0831
Myanmar	–	na	na	na	na	na	na
Philippines	1997	0.4802	0.3591	0.1211	0.1425	0.0950	0.0475
Singapore	1997	0.3420	0.1140	0.2280	0.1069	0.0000	0.1069

continued on next page

Table 5.20 *continued*

Country	Year	Total Restrictiveness Index: Foreign			Total Restrictiveness Index: Domestic		
		Total	Commercial Presence	Other restrictions	Total	Commercial Presence	Other restrictions
Thailand	2004	0.2119	0.1026	0.1093	0.0000	0.0000	0.0000
Viet Nam	2004	0.4731	0.1501	0.3230	0.1544	0.0475	0.1069
ASEAN Average		0.4345	0.2397	0.1948	0.1247	0.0554	0.0693
Hong Kong, China	1997	0.0380	0.0000	0.0380	0.0356	0.0000	0.0356
Taipei,China	–	na	na	na	na	na	na
Japan	2005	0.0024	0.0000	0.0024	0.0000	0.0000	0.0000
PRC	–	na	na	na	na	na	na
Korea, Republic of	1997	0.3900	0.1976	0.1924	0.1900	0.0000	0.1900

ASEAN = Association of Southeast Asian Nations, Lao PDR = Lao People's Democratic Republic, na = not applicable, PRC = People's Republic of China, SAARC = South Asian Association for Regional Cooperation, – = not available.

Source: Dee (2005).

Table 5.21 Impediments to Trade in Distribution Services

Country	Year	Total Restrictiveness Index: Foreign			Total Restrictiveness Index: Domestic		
		Total	Commercial Presence	Ongoing Operations	Total	Commercial Presence	Ongoing Operations
Bangladesh	–	na	na	na	na	na	na
India	1999	0.3983	0.1130	0.2033	0.0900	0.0000	0.1500
Nepal	–	na	na	na	na	na	na
Pakistan	–	na	na	na	na	na	na
Sri Lanka	–	na	na	na	na	na	na
SAARC Average	1999	0.3983	0.1130	0.2033	0.0900	0.0000	0.1500
Brunei Darussalam	–	na	na	na	na	na	na
Cambodia	–	na	na	na	na	na	na
Indonesia	1999	0.3106	0.1695	0.1412	0.0938	0	0.0938
Lao PDR	–	na	na	na	na	na	na
Malaysia	1999	0.3983	0.3075	0.0908	0.0900	0.0525	0.0375
Myanmar	–	na	na	na	na	na	na
Philippines	1999	0.3648	0.2865	0.0783	0.0500	0.0300	0.0250

continued on next page

Table 5.21 continued

Country	Year	Total Restrictiveness Index: Foreign			Total Restrictiveness Index: Domestic		
		Total	Commercial Presence	Ongoing Operations	Total	Commercial Presence	Ongoing Operations
Singapore	1999	0.0665	0.0000	0.0665	0.0250	0.0000	0.0250
Thailand	1999	0.3830	0.2610	0.1221	0.0563	0.0250	0.0313
Viet Nam	1999	0.5204	0.3290	0.1915	0.2144	0.1300	0.0844
ASEAN Average	1999	0.3406	0.2256	0.1151	0.0883	0.0396	0.0495
Hong Kong, China	1999	0.0428	0.0000	0.0428	0.0250	0.0000	0.0250
Taipei,China	1999	na	na	na	na	na	na
Japan	2005	0.1583	0.0300	0.1283	0.1050	0.0300	0.0750
PRC	–	na	na	na	na	na	na
Korea, Republic of	1999	0.3217	0.2540	0.0678	0.2550	0.2050	0.0500

ASEAN = Association of Southeast Asian Nations, Lao PDR = Lao People's Democratic Republic, na = not applicable, PRC = People's Republic of China, SAARC = South Asian Association for Regional Cooperation, – = not available.

Source: Dee (2005).

Table 5.22   Impediments to Trade in Distribution Services

	Year	Cargo handling restriction index	Mandatory services index	Lack of organized crime**	Port efficiency**
Bangladesh	–	na	na	na	na
India	2001	0.00	0.00	0.33	0.67
Nepal	–	na	na	na	na
Pakistan	–	na	na	na	na
Sri Lanka	–	na	na	na	na
SAARC Average	2001	0.00	0.00	0.33	0.67
Brunei Darussalam	2001	0.00	0.00	na	na
Cambodia	2001	na	na	na	na
Indonesia	2001	1.00	0.60	0.33	0.67
Lao PDR	2001	na	na	na	na
Malaysia	2001	0.00	0.25	0.33	0.33
Myanmar	2001	na	na	na	na
Philippines	2001	0.50	0.00	0.67	0.67
Singapore	2001	1.00	0.38	0.00	0.00
Thailand	2001	0.50	0.63	0.33	0.67
Viet Nam	2001	0.00	0.00	0.33	0.67
ASEAN Average	2001	0.43	0.27	0.33	0.50
Hong Kong, China	2001	0.00	0.25	0.33	0.00
Taipei,China	2001	0.50	0.00	0.33	0.33
Japan	2001	0.75	0.13	0.33	0.33
PRC	2001	0.50	0.00	0.33	0.67
Korea, Republic of	2001	0.00	0.38	0.33	0.33

**: These are a one-to-seven index ranking port efficiency and lack of organized crime available from *The World Competitiveness Report* (1996–2000). These data are based on surveys performed to representative firms of each country. The specific question is "Port facilities and inland waterways are extensive and efficient (1 = strongly disagree, 7 = strongly agree)," "Organized crime does not impose significant costs on business and is not a burden (1 = strongly disagree, 7 = strongly agree)." However, this study changed the indexes to the following ones: (i) less than 2 = 1, (ii) 2 to less than 4 = 0.67, (iii) 4 to less than 6 = 0.33, (iv) 6 to 7 = 0.

ASEAN = Association of Southeast Asian Nations, Lao PDR = Lao People's Democratic Republic, na = not applicable, PRC = People's Republic of China, SAARC = South Asian Association for Regional Cooperation, – = not available.

Source: Based on Dee (2005).

Table 5.23 Impediments to Trade in Professional Services

Country	Year	Total Restrictiveness Index: Foreign			Total Restrictiveness Index: Domestic		
		Total	Establishment	Ongoing Operations	Total	Establishment	Ongoing Operations
		(a) Accountancy Services					
Bangladesh	–	na	na	na	na	na	na
India	1999	0.4425	0.2600	0.1825	0.3050	0.1300	0.1750
Nepal	–	na	na	na	na	na	na
Pakistan	–	na	na	na	na	na	na
Sri Lanka	–	na	na	na	na	na	na
SAARC Average	–	0.4425	0.2600	0.1825	0.3050	0.1300	0.1750
Brunei Darussalam	–	na	na	na	na	na	na
Cambodia	–	na	na	na	na	na	na
Indonesia	1999	0.5640	0.5400	0.0100	0.0000	0.0000	0.0000
Lao PDR	–	na	na	na	na	na	na
Malaysia	1999	0.5137	0.4562	0.0575	0.0900	0.0400	0.0500
Myanmar	–	na	na	na	na	na	na
Philippines	1999	0.6302	0.4405	0.1897	0.2925	0.1175	0.1750

continued on next page

Table 5.23 continued

Country	Year	Total Restrictiveness Index: Foreign			Total Restrictiveness Index: Domestic		
		Total	Establishment	Ongoing Operations	Total	Establishment	Ongoing Operations
Singapore	1999	0.4124	0.2824	0.1300	0.1800	0.0800	0.1000
Thailand	1999	0.4885	0.3485	0.1400	0.1900	0.0775	0.1125
Viet Nam	1999	0.2896	0.2180	0.0716	0.0875	0.0250	0.0625
ASEAN Average		0.4831	0.3833	0.0998	0.1400	0.0567	0.0833
Hong Kong, China	1999	0.3159	0.1754	0.1405	0.2035	0.0705	0.1330
Taipei,China	–	na	na	na	na	na	na
Japan	1999	0.4313	0.2638	0.1675	0.2775	0.1275	0.1500
PRC	–	na	na	na	na	na	na
Korea, Republic of	1999	0.4768	0.3118	0.1650	0.2400	0.0775	0.1625
(b) Architectural Services							
Bangladesh	–	na	na	na	na	na	na
India	1999	0.0781	0.0690	0.0091	0.0245	0.0245	0.0000
Nepal	–	na	na	na	na	na	na
Pakistan	–	na	na	na	na	na	na
Sri Lanka	–	na	na	na	na	na	na

continued on next page

Table 5.23 continued

Country	Year	Total Restrictiveness Index: Foreign			Total Restrictiveness Index: Domestic		
		Total	Establishment	Ongoing Operations	Total	Establishment	Ongoing Operations
SAARC Average	–	0.0781	0.0690	0.0091	0.0245	0.0245	0.0000
Brunei Darussalam	–	na	na	na	na	na	na
Cambodia	–	na	na	na	na	na	na
Indonesia	1999	0.3018	0.2993	0.0025	0.0400	0.0400	0.0000
Lao PDR	–	na	na	na	na	na	na
Malaysia	1999	0.3325	0.3300	0.0025	0.0400	0.0400	0.0000
Myanmar	–	na	na	na	na	na	na
Philippines	1999	0.3300	0.2725	0.0575	0.0500	0.0000	0.0500
Singapore	1999	0.0900	0.0200	0.0700	0.0000	0.0000	0.0000
Thailand	1999	0.1320	0.0455	0.0865	0.0000	0.0000	0.0000
Viet Nam	1999	0.2330	0.2080	0.0250	0.0500	0.0375	0.0125
ASEAN Average.		0.2366	0.1959	0.0407	0.0300	0.0196	0.0104
Hong Kong, China	1999	0.2150	0.1750	0.0400	0.0875	0.0500	0.0375
Taipei,China	–	na	na	na	na	na	na
Japan	1999	0.1863	0.0938	0.0925	0.0750	0.0000	0.0750
PRC	–	na	na	na	na	na	na
Korea, Republic of	1999	0.1863	0.1538	0.0325	0.0000	0.0000	0.0000

continued on next page

Table 5.23 continued

Country	Year	Total Restrictiveness Index: Foreign			Total Restrictiveness Index: Domestic		
		Total	Establishment	Ongoing Operations	Total	Establishment	Ongoing Operations
		(c) Engineering services					
Bangladesh	–	na	na	na	na	na	na
India	1999	0.0965	0.0890	0.0075	0.0000	0.0000	0.0000
Nepal	–	na	na	na	na	na	na
Pakistan	–	na	na	na	na	na	na
Sri Lanka	–	na	na	na	na	na	na
SAARC Average		0.0965	0.0890	0.0075	0.0000	0.0000	0.0000
Brunei Darussalam	–	na	na	na	na	na	na
Cambodia	–	na	na	na	na	na	na
Indonesia	1999	0.2380	0.2280	0.0100	0.0525	0.0525	0.0000
Lao PDR	–	na	na	na	na	na	na
Malaysia	1999	0.2591	0.2400	0.0191	0.0825	0.0775	0.0050
Myanmar	–	na	na	na	na	na	na
Philippines	1999	0.1505	0.1430	0.0075	0.0000	0.0000	0.0000
Singapore	1999	0.1125	0.1075	0.0050	0.0125	0.0125	0.0000
Thailand	1999	0.1065	0.0990	0.0075	0.0400	0.0400	0.0000

continued on next page

Table 5.23 continued

Country	Year	Total Restrictiveness Index: Foreign			Total Restrictiveness Index: Domestic		
		Total	Establishment	Ongoing Operations	Total	Establishment	Ongoing Operations
Viet Nam	1999	0.0737	0.0480	0.0257	0.0000	0.0000	0.0000
ASEAN Average		0.1567	0.1443	0.0125	0.0313	0.0304	0.0008
Hong Kong, China	1999	0.1255	0.0805	0.0450	0.0750	0.0375	0.0375
Taipei,China	–	na	na	na	na	na	na
Japan	1999	0.1813	0.0738	0.1075	0.1375	0.0375	0.1000
PRC	–	na	na	na	na	na	na
Korea, Republic of	1999	0.1155	0.1080	0.0075	0.0000	0.0000	0.0000
(d) Legal Services							
Bangladesh	–	na	na	na	na	na	na
India	1999	0.3991	0.3350	0.0641	0.0875	0.0375	0.0500
Nepal	–	na	na	na	na	na	na
Pakistan	–	na	na	na	na	na	na
Sri Lanka	·	na	na	na	na	na	na
SAARC Average		0.3991	0.3350	0.0641	0.0875	0.0375	0.0500
Brunei Darussalam	–	na	na	na	na	na	na
Cambodia	–	na	na	na	na	na	na

continued on next page

Table 5.23 continued

Country	Year	Total Restrictiveness Index: Foreign			Total Restrictiveness Index: Domestic		
		Total	Establishment	Ongoing Operations	Total	Establishment	Ongoing Operations
Indonesia	1999	0.5696	0.5030	0.0666	0.1650	0.1150	0.0500
Lao PDR	–	na	na	na	na	na	na
Malaysia	1999	0.5375	0.4500	0.0875	0.1275	0.0400	0.0875
Myanmar	–	na	na	na	na	na	na
Philippines	1999	0.5366	0.4900	0.0466	0.1025	0.0650	0.0375
Singapore	1999	0.4156	0.3415	0.0741	0.0750	0.2500	0.0500
Thailand	1999	0.4381	0.3740	0.0641	0.1005	0.0505	0.0500
Viet Nam	1999	0.2568	0.1818	0.0750	0.1925	0.1300	0.0625
ASEAN Average		0.4590	0.3901	0.0690	0.1272	0.0709	0.0563
Hong Kong, China	1999	0.2670	0.2013	0.0657	0.0750	0.0250	0.0500
Taipei,China	–	na	na	na	na	na	na
Japan	1999	0.5220	0.3013	0.2207	0.3300	0.1300	0.2000
PRC	–	na	na	na	na	na	na
Korea, Republic of	1999	0.4446	0.3730	0.0716	0.1125	0.0500	0.0625

ASEAN = Association of Southeast Asian Nations, Lao PDR = Lao People's Democratic Republic, na = not applicable, PRC = People's Republic of China, SAARC = South Asian Association for Regional Cooperation, – = not available.

Source: Dee (2005).

continued on next page

Table 5.24 Impediments to Trade in Telecommunications Services

Variable	Details	Bangladesh		India		Nepal		Pakistan		Sri Lanka		SAARC Average	
		Domestic	Foreign	Domestic	Foreign	Domestic	Foreign	Domestic	Foreign	Domestic	Foreign	Domestic	Foreign
	Policy variables												
Market Access/Trade		0		0		4		2		0		1.2	
(Score of 1–6) Are the following operations allowed (both domestic and international)?													
	i) Leased lines or provide networks	na		na		na		na		na		–	
	ii) Third party resale	na		na		na		na		na		–	
	iii) Connections of leased lines and private networks to the PSTN	na		na		na		na		na		–	
Market Access/Investment (fixed) (0–1)		0.27		0.35		0.17		0.59		0.83		0.4389	
	i) Number of competitors in fixed market (maximum 3)	na		na		na		na		na			
	ii) Average policy score in the provision of fixed services in PSTN markets (local service,									na			

continued on next page

Table 5.24 *continued*

Variable	Details	Bangladesh	India	Nepal	Pakistan	Sri Lanka	SAARC Average
	domestic long distance, international, data, leased lines): monopoly (0), partial competition (0.5), full competition (1)	na	na	na	na	na	
	iii) % of incumbent that is privatized	na	na	na	na	na	–
Market Access/Investment (mobile)		0.83	0.72	0.17	0.35	0.89	0.5923
(0–1)	i) Number of competition in the mobile market (maximum 3)	na	na	na	na	na	–
	ii) Average policy score in the provision of mobile services (either analogue or digital mobile markets): monopoly (0), partial competition (0.5), full competition (1)						
	iii) % of incumbent that is privatized	na	na	na	na	na	–

continued on next page

Table 5.24 continued

Variable	Details	Bangladesh	India	Nepal	Pakistan	Sri Lanka	SAARC Average
National Treatment (NT)/Trade (1 or 0)	Are callback services allowed? (0: yes, 1: no)	1	1	1	1	1	1
NT/Foreign Direct Investment (FDI) (%)		1.00	0.49	0.00	1.00	1.00	0.698
NT/FDI fixed % of foreign investment allowed in competitive carriers		na	na	na	na	na	–
NT/FDI mobile		na	na	na	na	na	–

Variable	Details	Brunei Darussalam (1997)		Malaysia (2002)		Cambodia (1997)		Indonesia (1997)	
Policy variables									
Market Access/Trade		Domestic	Foreign	Domestic	Foreign	Domestic	Foreign	Domestic	Foreign
(Score of 1–6) Are the following operations allowed (both domestic and international)?		3		2		0		2	
i) Leased lines or provide networks		na*	na	na	na	na	na	1	1

continued *on next page*

Table 5.24 continued

Variable	Details	Bangladesh	India	Nepal	Pakistan	Sri Lanka	SAARC Average
	ii) Third-party resale	na	na	na	0		0
	iii) Connections of leased lines and private networks to the PSTN	na	na	na	0		0
Market Access/Investment (fixed)		0.20	0.23	0.57	0.88		
(0–1)	i) Number of competitors in fixed market (maximum 3)	na	na	na	3		
	ii) Average policy score in the provision of fixed services in PSTN markets (local service, domestic long distance, international, data, leased lines): monopoly (0), partial competition (0.5), full competition (1)	na	na	na	0.7		
	iii) % of incumbent that is privatized	na	na	na	0.2		

continued on next page

Table 5.24 continued

Market Access/Investment (mobile)	0.50	0.83	0.71	0.89
(0–1) i) Number of competitors in the mobile market (maximum 3)	na	na	na	3
ii) Average policy score in the provisions of mobile services (either analogue or digital mobile markets): monopoly (0), partial competition (0.5), full competition (1)	na	na	na	0.75
iii) % of incumbent that is privatized	na	na	na	0.2
NT/Trade Are call back services allowed? (0: yes, 1:no) (1 or 0)	1	1	1	1
NT/FDI (%)	0	1.00	0.35	0.49
NT/FDI fixed % of foreign investment allowed in competitive carriers	na	na	na	0.49
NT/FDI mobile	na	na	na	0.49

(fixed) = fixed market, na = not applicable, PSTN = Public Switched Telephone Network, SAARC = South Asian Association for Regional Cooperation, – = no data available.

* Data is not available.

Table 5.25   Selected Free Trade Agreements between South and Southeast Asia

	Date
India–Sri Lanka Free Trade Agreement	15 December 2001
South Asia Preferential Trading Agreement	7 December 1995
Asia-Pacific Trade Agreement (formerly known as the Bangkok Agreement)	17 June 1976
ASEAN–PRC Free Trade Agreement	1 July 2003
South Asia Free Trade Agreement	1 July 2006
India–Singapore Comprehensive Economic Cooperation Agreement	1 August 2005
India–Thailand Free Trade Area	3 October 2003
ASEAN–India Regional Trade and Investment Area	March 2004
Bay of Bengal Initiative for Multi-Sectoral Technical and Economic Cooperation Free Trade Area	September 2004
PRC–Pakistan Free Trade Agreement	5 April 2005
Malaysia–Pakistan Free Trade Agreement	April 2005
Pakistan–Sri Lanka Free Trade Agreement	15 June 2005
Indo–Nepal Treaty of Trade	6 March 2002

ASEAN= Association of Southeat Asian Nations, PRC = People's Republic of China.

Source: Compiled by authors.

Framework Agreement on Services (AFAS), there have, in reality, been significant trade barriers in this sector, which may be because of a large number of limitations imposed on the commitments. The treatment of services in preferential agreements is the topic of the next section.

Free Trade Agreements

We now investigate how trade in services has been liberalized in South Asian free trade agreements (FTAs). Qualitative information on services provisions in FTAs is collated on the content of each agreement and transformed into quantitative scores, according to the procedures outlined in Appendix Tables A5.1 to A5.3. A lower score is applied to an FTA that is regarded as less liberal, and a higher score is applied to more liberal arrangements. Scores range between zero and one. Appendix tables A5.1 to A5.3 contain the full set of scores organized by modes of supply for the various elements of the agreements, under subheadings of the form and content of the agreement. The scoring was undertaken for 13 South Asian FTAs listed in Table 5.25. For comparisons with the degree of services liberalization in other East Asian FTAs, the scoring results for AFTA (particularly AFAS), AFTA–PRC, and GATS are reported in Appendix Tables A5.4 to A5.6.

Most South Asian FTAs do not have services chapters and provisions. As a result, the scoring results for the above agreements are generally very low (i.e., less liberal). Only the India–Singapore agreement has elaborated services provisions and this agreement seems relatively liberal among Asian FTAs. This may be because services industries are very important in both countries and liberalization between them is more likely to bring about large benefits to both countries.

As Appendix Tables A5.4 to A5.6 also show, most South Asian agreements are less liberal than the AFAS. These agreements basically aim to liberalize trade in goods particularly through reductions in tariffs.

Although there are few agreements that have detailed services provisions, the intent of future negotiations are sometimes described in the text of agreement. Therefore, the increase in importance of trade in services seems to be recognized by many South Asian countries. According to the descriptions in the texts, there is a high possibility that an approach that goes somewhat beyond member countries' commitments under the GATS be taken in the future negotiations.

The AFTA–PRC, India–Singapore, and India–Thailand agreements liberalize services FDI under the framework of a more comprehensive investment agreement. For example, provisions on investment liberalization in AFTA–PRC and India–Thailand agreement are based on a broader and independent agreement on investment.

With regard to cross-border trade in services (mode 1 and 2), future negotiations are referred to in texts of the agreements, but in contrast to other Asian FTAs, no framework on investment liberalization has been proposed at this stage.

Few provisions on the liberalization of movement of people are included in the agreements listed in Table 5.25.

Regional Cooperation and Sectoral Priorities

The substantial gains from services sector reforms were discussed in the first section, particularly the linkages between the proper functioning of the service sector and the international competitiveness of the rest of the economy.

As shown in the second section, there are instances of deepening integration in services markets between East and South Asia, but the trend is not yet widespread. There are, however, significant transactions in FDI inflows in some sectors, in student and tourist movements, and in the movement of unskilled labor. There is also some important trade in IT-related services.

Two big economies, India and the PRC, are clearly driving the services transactions of the two subregions. The experiences of India and the PRC also highlighted the evolution of trade and investment flows following policy reform. Their experiences illustrate how reform leads to not only significant capital inflow into the services sector and to growth in services imports, but also to significant growth in services exports and to offshore investment by domestic services firms. The evolution of two-way trade in all modes of supply is similar to the patterns of intra-industry trade that tend to emerge following liberalization of markets for goods.

Opportunities are foregone because of barriers to integration, including those related to distance and policy. Our review of regional (and preferential) trading arrangements suggests that these impediments are not likely to be removed in the near future under the current South Asian FTAs. Programs of domestic reform, in line with the principles of the WTO, are more likely to make a significant contribution.

Dee and Findlay (2006) note that preferential trading arrangements tend to focus on restrictions that explicitly discriminate against foreigners. They argue that such restrictions are not likely to be those that matter most in economic terms. More valuable is attention to matters that affect the terms of access of all suppliers (that is, market access provisions in the language of the GATS and that contribute to competition). Focusing on measures directed at foreigners is more likely to have the effect of redistributing the rents available rather than significantly reducing their size. Dee and Findlay refer to results of Dee (2005b) which show that the gains from FTAs are small compared to a moderately successful completion of the Doha Round. And they are trivial compared to a comprehensive program of unilateral regulatory reform, one that targets nondiscriminatory behind-the-border restrictions on competition. For this reason, and since unilateral reforms might yield more significant returns, Dee and Findlay (2006) propose a refocusing on the WTO rather than on preferential agreements.

The focus on the WTO, however, is challenged by the lack of progress in the Doha Round. Drawing on Adlung's (2006) review of current issues in the GATS negotiations, the following priorities are suggested:

- cooperation on transparency and review,
- efforts to bind current policy,
- a focus on market access and domestic regulation in further liberalization,
- clarity on scheduling (in the GATS), and
- specification of paths of evolution of regulatory reform.

Dee and Findlay point out that these are primarily issues related to the design of domestic reform, rather than matters to be resolved through international negotiation on market access for foreign services providers. They are also not central to preferential agreements.

The experience of large economies of the PRC and India also show that the gains from regional cooperation could be substantial; they include the benefits of sharing reform experiences, the implementation of capacity building programs, and the joint efforts to develop new regulatory arrangements.

This analysis highlights the value of domestic reform, but also the scope for international cooperation in the manner just outlined. The country papers identify a number of specific areas in which this cooperation might be focused (see Box 5.4). Some are focused on domestic reform, and some require explicit international cooperation. In sectoral terms, these suggestions are particularly related to the movement of people and to infrastructure linkages, including air transport.

The GATS provides a framework for cooperation on issues related to professional or skilled labor but, as Stahl (1999) argues, there is no international cooperation regime for unskilled workers. The Nepal country study stresses the value of bilateral agreements between labor-sending and -receiving countries.

As also evident in Box 5.4, a key area for policy cooperation is the building of more infrastructure interconnections. Explicit cooperation and manifestation of political will are required to facilitate investment-intensive infrastructure linkages, such as those in road, rail, and air transport as well as in international telecommunications. Construction of grids that would facilitate trade in electricity is of special interest. Vucetic (2004) identified some of the opportunities for cooperation in regional electricity trade, particularly the potential for Nepal and Bhutan to export hydro-electric power to India.

Not shown in Box 5.4 is the possibility of cross-sectoral strategies that are not restricted to services. In some business areas, the efficient provision of services is a key to the attainment of competitiveness in goods production. These might be after-sales services, services that complement goods (medical services related to new medical technology), or cases in which goods are inputs into services production (IT hardware supporting software development). A region comprised of economies with varying degrees of competitiveness in these sectors could then decide to cooperate with each other to create new markets that could exploit these complementarities.

Box 5.4 Policy Suggestions

Domestic Reform
- Initiate or continue regulatory reform (Nepal, Thailand) and openness (Bangladesh)
- Restructure and liberalize infrastructure services (Singapore), especially those leading to improved port efficiency (Bangladesh, Sri Lanka)
- Increase transparency in government tendering (Singapore)
- Relax restrictions on foreign direct investment, including in education (Sri Lanka)

Regional Cooperation
- Improve transit rights and access to ports (Nepal)
- Expand road capacity and networks (Nepal, PRC)
- Link energy networks or build "energy corridors" (PRC, Nepal)
- Reform in air transport (including cargo [PRC]) and tourism [Singapore])
- New regulatory arrangements with labor importing countries (Nepal)
- Mutual recognition of qualifications (Singapore, Sri Lanka)

PRC = People's Republic of China.

Sources: Compiled by authors.

Box 5.5 Priorities for Services Trade and Investment Data Collection

- Information on policy according to the categories used in the modal templates reported in the paper by country, by sector, and over time (in sufficient detail to be able to develop quantitative indicators with respect to conditions facing both domestic firms and foreign suppliers, including degrees of preferential treatment).
- Inbound and outbound investment flows in services by sector, also including associated sales data as well as flows of earnings, both reinvested income

continued on next page

Box 5.5 continued

and that remitted as well as Foreign Affiliates Trade Statistics (FATS) more broadly, i.e., including the costs and sales "structures" of foreign affiliates, not just their total sales. (This would give information about the extent to which recipient countries buy inputs from parents, and sell output to other linked companies. This helps to identify whether foreign direct investment in services encourages structural change, and perhaps encourages additional trade indirectly, because the foreign affiliates have different costs and sales structures from domestic companies. It would also allow an assessment of whether the productivity of foreign affiliates differs from domestic firms.)

- Cross-border trade in services at higher levels of disaggregation than the categories now used in the Balance of Payments statistics; the United Nations' Manual on Statistics of International Trade in Services gives guidance in how to collect services trade and investment statistics.
- Inflows and outflows of worker remittances.
- Bilateral data on trade, investment, and remittance flows for each country by sector
- Data about the performance over time of individual services sectors in dimensions other than trade and investment (e.g., prices, costs, and profits). This will also provide information about the effects of services trade barriers and domestic regulatory impediments on things that affect economic well-being (trade volumes being a poor welfare proxy).

Source: Compiled by authors.

APPENDIX

Table A5.1   Scoring Results for Cross-Border Trade, Modes 1 and 2

	India–Sri Lanka FTA	South Asia PTA	Asia-Pacific Trade Agreement (Bangkok Agreement)	ASEAN–PRC FTA	South Asia FTA	India–Singapore CECA	India–Thailand FTA
Form of Agreement							
Scope	0	0	0	0.2	0	0.8	0.2
MFN	0	0	0	0.25	0	0.25	0
MFN exemptions	0	0	0	0	0	0	0
National treatment	0	0	0	0	0	0.5	0
Market access	0	0	0	0	0	0.5	0
Local presence not required	0	0	0	0	0	0	0
Domestic regulation	0	0	0	0	0	0.75	0
Transparency	0	0	0	0	0	0.7	0
Recognition	0	0	0	0	0	0.75	0
Monopolies and exclusive services providers	0	0	0	0	0	0.75	0
Business practices	0	0	0	0	0	0.75	0
Transfers and payments	0	0	0	0	0	1	0

continued on next page

Table A5.1 continued

	India–Sri Lanka FTA	South Asia PTA	Asia-Pacific Trade Agreement (Bangkok Agreement)	ASEAN–PRC FTA	South Asia FTA	India–Singapore CECA	India–Thailand FTA
Denial of benefits (i.e., rules of origin)	0	0	0	0	0	1	0
Safeguards	0	0	0	1	0	1	0
Subsidies	0	0	0	0	0	0.5	0
Government procurement in services	0	0	0	0	0	0	0
Ratchet mechanism	0	0	0	0	0	1	0
Telecommunications	0	0	0	0	0	0	0
Financial services	0	0	0	0	0	0	0
Content of Agreement							
Exclusion of modes	0	0	0	0	0	1	0
Exclusion of measures (MFN, MA, and NT)	0	0	0	0	0	0.5	0
Sectoral exclusions	0	0	0	0	0	0.25	0
Measures at regional level	0	0	0	0	0	1	0

continued on next page

Table A5.1 continued

	India–Sri Lanka FTA	South Asia PTA	Asia-Pacific Trade Agreement (Bangkok Agreement)	ASEAN–PRC FTA	South Asia FTA	India–Singapore CECA	India–Thailand FTA
Other general exclusions	0	0	0	0	0	1	0
Restrictions on land purchases	0	0	0	0	0	1	0
Reservations on Minority	0	0	0	0	0	1	0
Requirements on the number of domestic	0	0	0	0	0	1	0
Provisions asymmetric?	1	1	1	1	1	1	1

ASEAN = Association of Southeast Asian Nations, CECA = Comprehensive Economic Cooperation Agreement, FTA = Free Trade Agreement, MFN = most favored nation, NT = national treatment, MA = market access, PRC = People's Republic of China, PTA = Preferential Trading Agreement.

Source: Authors' own scoring.

continued on next page

Table A5.1 continued

Forms of Agreement	ASEAN–India RTIA	BIMSTEC FTA	PRC–Pakistan FTA	Malaysia–Pakistan FTA	Pakistan–Sri Lanka FTA	Indo–Nepal Treaty of Trade	GATS
Scope	0.2	0.2	0	0	0.2	0	0.75
MFN	0	0	0	0	0	0	1
MFN exemptions	0	0	0	0	0	0	na
National treatment	0	0	0	0	0	0	0.5
Market access	0	0	0	0	0	0	0.5
Local presence not required	0	0	0	0	0	0	0
Domestic regulation	0	0	0	0	0	0	0.75
Transparency	0	0	0	0	0	0	0.7
Recognition	0	0	0	0	0	0	0.5
Monopolies and exclusive services providers	0	0	0	0	0	0	0.75
Business practices	0	0	0	0	0	0	0.75
Transfers and payments	0	0	0	0	0	0	1
Denial of benefits (i.e., rules of origin)	0	0	0	0	0	0	1
Safeguards	0	0	0	0	0	0	0.5

continued on next page

Table A5.1 continued

	ASEAN–India RTIA	BIMSTEC FTA	PRC–Pakistan FTA	Malaysia–Pakistan FTA	Pakistan–Sri Lanka FTA	Indo–Nepal Treaty of Trade	GATS
Subsidies	0	0	0	0	0	0	0.25
Government procurement in services	0	0	0	0	0	0	0.5
Ratchet mechanism	0	0	0	0	0	0	0
Telecommunications	0	0	0	0	0	0	0.5
Financial services	0	0	0	0	0	0	0.6
Content of Agreement							
Exclusion of modes	0	0	0	0	0	0	na
Exclusion of measures (MFN, MA, and NT)	0	0	0	0	0	0	na
Sectoral exclusions	0	0	0	0	0	0	na
Subnational exclusions	0	0	0	0	0	0	na
Other general exclusions	0	0	0	0	0	0	na
Restrictions on land purchases	0	0	0	0	0	0	na

continued on next page

Table A5.1 continued

	ASEAN–India RTIA	BIMSTEC FTA	PRC–Pakistan FTA	Malaysia–Pakistan FTA	Pakistan–Sri Lanka FTA	Indo–Nepal Treaty of Trade	GATS
Reservations on Minority	0	0	0	0	0	0	na
Requirements on the number of domestic employees	0	0	0	0	0	0	na
Provisions asymmetric?	1	1	1	1	1	1	na

ASEAN = Association of Southeast Asian Nations, BIMSTEC = Bay of Bengal Initiative for Multi-Sectoral Technical and Economic Cooperation, FTA = Free Trade Agreement, GATS = General Agreement on Trade in Services, MA = market access, MFN = most favored nation, NT = national treatment, PRC = People's Republic of China, RTIA = Regional Trade and Investment Area.

Source: Authors' own scoring.

Table A5.2: Scoring Results for Investment, Mode 3

Form of Agreement	India–Sri Lanka FTA	South Asia PTA	Asia-Pacific Trade Agreement (Bangkok Agreement)	ASEAN–PRC FTA	South Asia FTA	India–Singapore CECA	India–Thailand FTA
Sectoral coverage	0	0	0	0.5	0	1	0.4
Scope of MFN, NT, etc. provision	0	0	0	0	0	1	0.8
MFN	0	0	0	0.25	0	0.25	1
MFN exemptions	0	0	0	0	0	0	1
National treatment	0	0	0	0	0	0.5	1
Nationality (residency) of management and board of directors	0	0	0	0	0	0.5	0
Performance requirements	0	0	0	0	0	0.75	0
Transparency (in services or investment chapter)	0	0	0	0	0	0.4	0
Denial of benefits (i.e., rules of origin)	0	0	0	0	0	1	0
Expropriation, etc.	0	0	0	0	0	0.4	0.4

continued on next page

Table A5.2 continued

	India–Sri Lanka FTA	South Asia PTA	Asia-Pacific Trade Agreement (Bangkok Agreement)	ASEAN–PRC FTA	South Asia FTA	India–Singapore CECA	India–Thailand FTA
Transfers and payments	0	0	0	0	0	1	1
Investor-State dispute settlement	0	0	0	0	0	1	1
Safeguards	0	0	0	0	0	0	1
Subsidies	0	0	0	0	0	0.5	0
Government procurement	0	0	0	0	0	0	0
Ratchet mechanism	0	0	0	0	0	1	0
Content of Agreement							
Exclusions of measures (MFN, MA, and NT)	0	0	0	0	0	0.5	1
Sectoral exclusions	0	0	0	0	0	0.25	1
Measures at regional level	0	0	0	0	0	1	1
Other general exclusions	0	0	0	0	0	1	1
Restriction on land purchases	0	0	0	0	0	1	1
Reservation on Minority	0	0	0	0	0	1	1

continued on next page

Table A5.2 continued

	India–Sri Lanka FTA	South Asia PTA	Asia-Pacific Trade Agreement (Bangkok Agreement)	ASEAN–PRC FTA	South Asia FTA	India–Singapore CECA	India–Thailand FTA
Requirement of prior residence for establishment	0	0	0	0	0	1	1
General restrictions on foreign capital participation	0	0	0	0	0	1	1
Review or approvals on large foreign investments (acquisition)	0	0	0	0	0	1	1
Provisions asymmetric?	1	1	1	1	1	1	1

ASEAN = Association of Southeast Asian Nations, CECA = Comprehensive Economic Cooperation Agreement, FTA = Free Trade Agreement, MA = market access, MFN = most favored nation, NT = national treatment, PRC = People's Republic of China, PTA = Preferential Trading Agreement.

Source: Author's own scoring.

Table A5.2 continued

Form of Agreement	ASEAN–India RTIA	BIMSTEC FTA	PRC–Pakistan FTA	Malaysia–Pakistan FTA	Pakistan–Sri Lanka FTA	Indo–Nepal Treaty of Trade	GATS
Sectoral coverage	0.25	0.25	0	0	0	0	0.5
Scope of MFN, NT, etc. provision	0	0	0	0	0	0	1
MFN	0	0	0	0	0	0	1
MFN exemptions	0	0	0	0	0	0	na
National treatment	0	0	0	0	0	0	0.5
Nationality (residency) of management and board of directors	0	0	0	0	0	0	0
Performance requirements	0	0	0	0	0	0	0.75
Transparency (in services or investment chapter)	0	0	0	0	0	0	0.7

continued on next page

Table A5.2 continued

	ASEAN–India RTIA	BIMSTEC FTA	PRC–Pakistan FTA	Malaysia–Pakistan FTA	Pakistan–Sri Lanka FTA	Indo–Nepal Treaty of Trade	GATS
Denial of benefits (i.e., rules of origin)	0	0	0	0	0	0	1
Expropriation, etc.	0	0	0	0	0	0	0
Transfers and payments	0	0	0	0	0	0	1
Investor-State dispute settlement	0	0	0	0	0	0	0
Safeguards	0	0	0	0	0	0	0.5
Subsidies	0	0	0	0	0	0	0.25
Government procurement	0	0	0	0	0	0	0.5
Ratchet mechanism	0	0	0	0	0	0	0
Content of Agreement							
Exclusions of measures (MFN, MA, and NT)	0	0	0	0	0	0	na
Sectoral exclusions	0	0	0	0	0	0	na
Subnational exclusions	0	0	0	0	0	0	na

continued on next page

Table AS.2 continued

	ASEAN–India RTIA	BIMSTEC FTA	PRC–Pakistan FTA	Malaysia–Pakistan FTA	Pakistan–Sri Lanka FTA	Indo–Nepal Treaty of Trade	GATS
Other general exclusions	0	0	0	0	0	0	na
Restriction on land purchases	0	0	0	0	0	0	na
Reservation on Minority	0	0	0	0	0	0	na
Requirement of prior residence for establishment	0	0	0	0	0	0	na
General restrictions on foreign capital participation	0	0	0	0	0	0	na
Review or approvals on large foreign investments (acquisition)	0	0	0	0	0	0	na
Provisions asymmetric?	1	1	1	1	1	1	na

ASEAN = Association of Southeast Asian Nations, BIMSTEC = Bay of Bengal Initiative for Multi-Sectoral Technical and Economic Cooperation, FTA = Free Trade Agreement, GATS = General Agreement on Trade in Services, MA = market access, MFN = most favored nation, NT = national treatment, PRC = People's Republic of China, RTIA = Regional Trade and Investment Area.

Source: Authors' own scoring.

continued on next page

Table A5.3 Scoring Results for Movements of People, Mode 4

	India–Sri Lanka FTA	South Asia PTA	Asia-Pacific Trade Agreement (Bangkok Agreement)	ASEAN-PRC FTA	South Asia FTA	India–Singapore CECA	India–Thailand FTA
Form of Agreement							
Sectoral coverage	0	0	0	0	0	1	0
Scope	0	0	0	0	0	0.5	0
Immigration	0	0	0	0	0	0	0
MFN for mode 4 delivery	0	0	0	0	0	0.25	0
MFN exemptions	0	0	0	0	0	0	0
National treatment for mode 4 delivery	0	0	0	0	0	0.5	0
Market access	0	0	0	0	0	0.5	0
Domestic regulation	0	0	0	0	0	0.75	0
Transparency of regulation governing service delivery via mode 4	0	0	0	0	0	0.7	0

continued on next page

Table A5.3 continued

	India–Sri Lanka FTA	South Asia PTA	Asia-Pacific Trade Agreement (Bangkok Agreement)	ASEAN–PRC FTA	South Asia FTA	India–Singapore CECA	India–Thailand FTA
Transparency of regulations governing temporary movement of persons	0	0	0	0	0	0.7	0
Recognition	0	0	0	0	0	0.75	0
Denial of benefits (i.e., rules of origin)	0	0	0	0	0	1	0
Ratchet mechanism	0	0	0	0	0	1	0
Content of Agreement							
Service Delivery							
Exclusions of measures (MFN, MA, and NT)	0	0	0	0	0	0.5	0
Sectoral exclusions	0	0	0	0	0	0	0

continued on next page

Table A5.3 *continued*

	India–Sri Lanka FTA	South Asia PTA	Asia-Pacific Trade Agreement (Bangkok Agreement)	ASEAN–PRC FTA	South Asia FTA	India–Singapore CECA	India–Thailand FTA
Measures at regional level	0	0	0	0	0	1	0
Other general exclusions	0	0	0	0	0	1	0
Content of Agreement - Facilitation							
Skill coverage	0	0	0	0	0	0.5	0
Short-term entry	0	0	0	0	0	0.75	0
Long-term entry	0	0	0	0	0	0.6	0
Quotas on numbers of entrants	0	0	0	0	0	1	0
Needs test	0	0	0	0	0	1	0
Local labor market testing or other criteria	0	0	0	0	0	1	0
Restrictions on land purchases	0	0	0	0	0	1	0
Considerations on Minority	0	0	0	0	0	1	0

continued on next page

Table A5.3 continued

	India–Sri Lanka FTA	South Asia PTA	Asia-Pacific Trade Agreement (Bangkok Agreement)	ASEAN–PRC FTA	South Asia FTA	India–Singapore CECA	India–Thailand FTA
Requirements on the number of domestic	0	0	0	0	0	1	0
Provisions asymmetric?	1	1	1	1	1	1	1

ASEAN = Association of Southeast Asian Nations, CECA = Comprehensive Economic Cooperation Agreement, FTA = Free Trade Agreement, MA = market access, MFN = most favored nation, NT = national treatment, PRC = People's Republic of China, PTA = Preferential Trading Agreement.

Source: Authors' own scoring.

continued on next page

Table A5.3 continued

Form of Agreement	ASEAN–India RTIA	BIMSTEC FTA	PRC–Pakistan FTA	Malaysia–Pakistan FTA	Pakistan–Sri Lanka FTA	Indo–Nepal Treaty of Trade	GATS
Sectoral coverage	0	0	0	0	0	0	0.5
Scope	0	0	0	0	0	0	0.5
Immigration	0	0	0	0	0	0	0
MFN for mode 4 delivery	0	0	0	0	0	0	1
MFN exemptions	0	0	0	0	0	0	na
National treatment for mode 4 delivery	0	0	0	0	0	0	0.5
Market access	0	0	0	0	0	0	0.5
Domestic regulation	0	0	0	0	0	0	0.75
Transparency of regulation governing service delivery via mode 4	0	0	0	0	0	0	0.75

continued on next page

Table A5.3 continued

	ASEAN–India RTIA	BIMSTEC FTA	PRC–Pakistan FTA	Malaysia–Pakistan FTA	Pakistan–Sri Lanka FTA	Indo–Nepal Treaty of Trade	GATS
Transparency of regulations governing temporary movement of persons	0	0	0	0	0	0	0
Recognition	0	0	0	0	0	0	0.5
Denial of benefits (i.e., rules of origin)	0	0	0	0	0	0	1
Ratchet mechanism	0	0	0	0	0	0	0
Content of Agreement							
Exclusions of measures (MFN, MA, and NT)	0	0	0	0	0	0	na
Sectoral exclusions	0	0	0	0	0	0	na
Subnational exclusions	0	0	0	0	0	0	na
Other general exclusions	0	0	0	0	0	0	na

continued on next page

Table A5.3 continued

	ASEAN– India RTIA	BIMSTEC FTA	PRC– Pakistan FTA	Malaysia– Pakistan FTA	Pakistan– Sri Lanka FTA	Indo–Nepal Treaty of Trade	GATS
Content of Agreement							
Skill coverage	0	0	0	0	0	0	na
Short-term entry	0	0	0	0	0	0	na
Long-term entry	0	0	0	0	0	0	na
Quotas on numbers of entrants	0	0	0	0	0	0	na
Needs test	0	0	0	0	0	0	na
Local labor market testing or other	0	0	0	0	0	0	na
Restrictions on land purchases	0	0	0	0	0	0	na
Considerations on Minority	0	0	0	0	0	0	na
Requirements on the number of domestic employees	0	0	0	0	0	0	na
Provision asymmetric?	1	1	1	1	1	1	na

ASEAN = Association of Southeast Asian Nations, BIMSTEC = Bay of Bengal Initiative for Multi-Sectoral Technical and Economic Cooperation, FTA = Free Trade Agreement, GATS = General Agreement on Trade in Services, MA = market access, MFN = most favored nation, NT = national treatment, PRC = People's Republic of China, RTIA = Regional Trade and Investment Area.

Source: Authors' own scoring.

continued on next page

Table A5.4   Cross-Border Trade

	GATS	AFTA (AFAS)	AFTA–PRC
Form of Agreement			
Scope	0.75	1	0.2
MFN	1	1	0.25
MFN exemptions	na	0	0
National treatment	0.5	0.5	0
Mark access (i.e., prohibition on QRs as in GATS)	0.5	0.5	0
Local presence not required	0	0	0
Domestic regulation	0.75	0	0
Transparency	0.7	0	0
Recognition	0.5	0.5	0
Monopolies and exclusive services providers	0.75	0	0
Business practices	0.75	0	0
Transfers and payments	1	0	0
Denial of benefits (i.e., rules of origin)	1	1	0
Safeguards	0.5	1	1
Subsidies	0.25	0	0
Government procurement in services	0.5	0	0
Ratchet mechanism	0	1	0
Telecommunications	0.5	0	0
Financial services	0.6	0	0
Content of Agreement			
Exclusion of modes: Modes 1, 2, 3, and 4	na	1	0
Exclusion of measures: MFN, NT, MA	na	1	0
Sectoral exclusions	na	0	0
Subnational exclusions	na	1	0

continued on next page

Table A5.4 continued

	GATS	AFTA (AFAS)	AFTA–PRC
Restrictions on land purchases	na	1	0
Reservations on Minority	na	1	0
Requirements on the number of domestic employees	na	1	0
Symmetry of provisions	na	1	1

AFAS = ASEAN Framework Agreement on Services, AFTA = ASEAN Free Trade Area, GATS = General Agreement on Trade in Services, MA = market access, MFN = most favored nation, na = not applicable, NT = national treatment, PRC = People's Republic of China, QRs = qualitative restrictions.

The services agreement between AFTA and PRC is under negotiation.

Source: Authors' own scoring.

Table A5.5:   Investment

	GATS	AFTA		
		AFAS	Investment Agreement	AFTA–PRC
Form of Agreement				
Sectoral coverage	0.5	0.5	1	0.5
Scope of MFN, NT, etc. provisions	1	1	1	0
MFN	1	1	1	0.25
MFN exemptions	na	0	0	0
National treatment	0.5	0.5	1	0
Nationality (residency) of management and board of directors	0	0	1	0
Performance requirements	0.75	0	0	0
Transparency	0.7	0	0.4	0
Denial of benefits (i.e., rules of origin)	1	1	0	0
Expropriation, etc.	0	0	0	0
Transfers and payments	1	0	1	0
Investor-State dispute settlement	0	0	0	0
Safeguards	0.5	1	1	1
Subsidies	0.25	0	0	0
Government procurement	0.5	0	0	0
Ratchet mechanism	0	1	0	0
Content of Agreement				
Exclusion of measures, MFN, NT, MA	na	1	1	0
Sectoral exclusions	na	0	0	0
Subnational exclusions	na	1	1	0

continued on next page

Table A5.5 continued

| | GATS | AFTA | | AFTA–PRC |
		AFAS	Investment Agreement	
Reservations on minority	na	1	1	0
General restrictions on foreign capital participation	na	0	1	0
Review or approvals on large foreign investments (acquisition)	na	1	1	0
Symmetry of provisions	na	1	1	1

AFAS = ASEAN Framework Agreement on Services, AFTA = ASEAN Free Trade Area, GATS = General Agreement on Trade in Services, MA = market access, MFN = most favored nation, na = not applicable, NT = national treatment, PRC = People's Republic of China.

Source: Authors' own scoring.

Table A5.6   Movement of People

	GATS	AFTA (AFAS)	ASEAN–PRC
Form of Agreement			
Sectoral coverage	0.5	0.5	0
Scope	0.5	0	0
Immigration	0	0	0
MFN for mode 4 delivery	1	1	0
MFN exemptions	na	0	0
National treatment for mode 4 delivery	0.5	0.5	0
Market access (i.e., prohibition on QRs as in GATS)	0.5	0.5	0
Domestic regulation	0.75	0	0
Transparency of regulations governing service delivery via mode 4	0.7	0	0
Transparency of regulations governing temporary movement of persons	0	0	0
Recognition	0.5	0.5	0
Denial of benefits (i.e., rules of origin)	1	1	0
Ratchet mechanism	0	1	0
Content of Agreement - Service Delivery			
General reservations/ exceptions	na	1	0
Sectoral exclusions	na	0	0
Subnational exclusions	na	1	0
Restrictions on land purchases	na	1	0
Considerations on Minority	na	1	0
Symmetry of provisions	na	0	1

continued on next page

Table A5.4 continued

	GATS	AFTA (AFAS)	ASEAN–PRC
Content of Agreement - Facilitation of Mobility			
Skill coverage	na	0.25	0
Short-term entry	na	0.75	0
Long-term entry	na	0	0
Quotas on numbers of entrants	na	1	0
Needs test	na	0	0
Local labor market testing or other criteria	na	0	0
Requirements on the number of domestic employees	na	1	0

AFAS = ASEAN Framework on Services, AFTA = ASEAN Free Trade Area, ASEAN = Association of Southeast Asian Nations, GATS = General Agreement on Trade in Services, MFN = most favored nation, na = not applicable, PRC = People's Republic of China, QRs = qualitative restrictions.

Source: Authors' own scoring.

6

THE ROLE OF TRANSPORT INFRASTRUCTURE, LOGISTICS, AND TRADE FACILITATION IN ASIAN TRADE

John Arnold

Introduction

The impact of the quality of transport infrastructure and logistics services on the level of trade among the countries of East and South Asia is less significant than it used to be. This is so because dramatic improvements have taken place in both infrastructure and services over the last three decades. The dominant mode for freight transport between these two regions remains ocean transport, and this situation is expected to continue for the foreseeable future. Land transport, both road and rail, will have an increasing role in bilateral trade within Asia. It may also facilitate trade between noncontiguous countries within South and East Asia, but this will require a significant improvement in border-crossing procedures. It is unlikely that land transport will attract a substantial share of trade flows between the two regions within the next decade, despite efforts to develop various links of the Asian Highway and the Inter-Asian Railway. Air transport is growing in importance as the value of commodities traded between the two regions increases. However, the growth in airfreight has lagged behind that of ocean transport and is expected to continue doing so.

The role of trade logistics and the demand for logistics services must be viewed within the context of global trade competition. Reductions in transit times and transport costs have allowed importers to select potential suppliers from a wider geographical area. The selection of a supplier depends on various factors, not the least of which is the quality of production and the delivered cost. However, for most manufactured goods, the issue of quality has diminished in importance as production technology and procedures for quality assurance have become increasingly standardized.

Advances in production technology have also allowed producers to adjust their mix of labor and capital so as to produce goods at a competitive price ex-factory. Since importing countries are able to select from an increasing number of countries able to provide similar quality goods, the selection of suppliers is increasingly based on delivered price and lead time (from initiating an order to delivery of the goods). To meet the contractual obligations for multiple shipments at a fixed price with specified delivery dates, exporters require logistics that are predictable in terms of costs (C) and delivery times (T). Some trade is more sensitive to cost, while other trade is more sensitive to transit time. Importers' demand for reliability (R) in terms of minimal delays in shipments and cost overruns varies. Therefore, in looking at the impact of logistics on trade, it is necessary to focus on these parameters, which are referred to collectively as C/T/R, which stands for cost/time/reliability.

C/T/R for the transport services connecting East and South Asia is affected by a number of factors. Some of these are inalterable, such as distance, topography, and the increasing importance of energy in determining the relative cost for different modes. Others can be and have been changed; most notably, the scale of shipments, the throughput of the infrastructure used by logistics services, the role of the private sector in the funding and operating logistics services and infrastructure, and the degree of competition among logistics service providers. The increase in scale has been most dramatic in ocean transport, where the size of container and the throughput or capacity of container berths have each increased by a factor of 20 over 40 years. While the sizes of trucks, rail wagons, and aircraft have not increased significantly, there has been an increase in size of larger trucks and aircraft and the length of trains used for freight transportation. The increase in competition has been dramatic as a result of deregulation of the transport sector and the elimination of public monopolies in all modes but rail. The role of the private sector, always strong in the provision of logistics services, has increased dramatically in the provision and operation of transport infrastructure. The countries of South and East Asia have benefited from these changes albeit to different degrees. They have also responded to the demand for substantial increases in transport infrastructure with varying degrees of success. Not surprisingly, their success in these areas is closely linked to their success in developing trade not only regionally but also globally.

Most of the trade between South and East Asia follows a southern ocean route that provides good connectivity to the extensive coast of the countries in the two regions where most of the population and the majority of production is located. There is now growing interest in establishing northern land routes that will provide access to those areas away far from the coast, in particular, the landlocked countries, the western People's Republic of China (PRC), and northern Southeast Asia. These routes are expected to follow the alignments set out for the Asian Highway. The transport services provided on these routes will face the same requirements in terms of C/T/R as ocean transport. While there are a number of origin-destination pairs for which a land route would offer a competitive advantage, there is negligible existing trade between these pairs and limited potential for growth in trade to stimulate the development of these routes.

With the exception of the pure truck movements, nearly all transport is multimodal. In the case of ocean transport, the complementary land connection to the cargo origins or destination introduces a significant increase in the cost and time for door-to-door movement. Where the inland origins or destination are far from the coast, the cost and time for the land movement can be similar to that of the ocean leg of the journey. In addition, land movement can have a significant impact on the reliability of movement. Much of the uncertainty with regard to transit time occurs during the transfer at intermodal connection (e.g., port, rail yard, and airport). The delays and associated uncertainty are caused by a number of factors, the most important of which are the frequency of vessel calls, the transactions required to transfer the cargo from one mode to the other, and the throughput rates of the cargo terminals.

A similar difficulty occurs for air cargo when it is transferred between the aircraft and road transport. While the time for this transfer is much shorter than for seaports, it is still significant relative to aircraft transit time.

International land routes have similar problems, but these occur primarily at the borders, where infrastructure or protocols mostly hinder the transport of goods into the adjoining country. The time lost and costs incurred in transferring cargo between the transport service providers on either side of the border can be substantial. This can create a significant competitive disadvantage for routes that transit several countries in which all these border procedures must be repeated. Even for borders where the transport units are allowed to cross, there will be protocols for clearing the cargo and securing the cargo for transport under customs bond.

Since the choke points for both the land and sea routes occur primarily at points of intermodal exchange and border crossings, considerable effort has been given to improving the performance of these facilities. With regard to seaports, there have been extensive efforts to improve cargo handling technology and the use of information technology (IT) to reduce the handling time in port. Efforts to improve the performance of land borders have been less successful because they are located in remote areas where it is difficult to monitor performance. While there have been substantial efforts in South and East Asia to reduce the time and cost for crossing borders, considerably more is expected. This will change not only the uses of different modes but also the way in which supply chains that use these routes are structured.

The changing structure of supply chains used for international trade is expected to have a more profound effect on trade between East and South Asia than any change in transport infrastructure. Improvements in logistics services will decrease transit time and cost and increase reliability, allowing manufacturers to change their mode of production and retailers their method of distribution. Integrated production activities are being replaced with extensive subcontracting of the different stages of production. The subcontractors locate either in a cluster around the primary manufacturer, so as to operate in a manner similar to that of an integrated industry, or they are spread out in different locations where the factors of production are most favorable to the specific processes.

Retailing has consolidated its warehousing activities into strategically located distribution centers that supply retail outlets throughout a wide area. For goods that are exported, buyers' warehouses are used to consolidate loads from different suppliers for shipment to specific market areas. For goods that are imported, distribution warehouses are used to deconsolidate shipments and reconsolidate them for specific markets. In both cases, the warehouses are either clustered near seaports where the goods are loaded or unloaded or are positioned slightly inland where there the cost for land and labor is lower.

Modern manufacturing is evolving toward a tiered structure similar to that pioneered by the automotive industry. Progression is from the lowest tier, where individual components are manufactured, to intermediate tiers, in which components are gradually integrated into larger subassemblies. The final tier is where products are assembled and customized to meet specific consumer demand.[1] Under this paradigm, trade between South and East Asian countries will evolve from the exchange of raw materials and final products to exchange of intermediate goods on eastbound supply chains destined for European markets and westbound supply chains destined for the North American markets.

---

[1]   In many ways this is similar to the earlier separation of processes for the manufacture of basic metal products, e.g., mining, refining, primary conversion, and finishing.

Characteristics of Potential Trade between East and South Asia

The development of international trade requires the capability not only to produce goods that are competitive in terms of cost and quality but also to deliver these goods efficiently. The logistics for efficient delivery differ depending on the type of cargo (e.g., dry and liquid bulk, loose, and unitized cargo). The countries in South and East Asia have made considerable investments to improve both transport infrastructure and logistic services through the increasing privatization of public transport companies and the reduction in the regulation of private service providers.

To understand what additional improvements in logistics are required, it is necessary to understand the type of cargo that is being traded. For this purpose, an analysis was made of the types of cargo that are traded among the countries in East and South Asia using data from United Nations Commodity Trade Statistics Database (UN Comtrade), specifically between three countries: India in South Asia, Thailand in Southeast Asia, and the PRC in East Asia. The volume of trade was estimated using the value of cargo by commodity group and applying an average price to each group of commodities (Table 6.1).

Table 6.1   Average Value by Commodity Classification

SITC 2 Code	Value $/ Metric ton	Description
0	2,500	Food and live animals
1	1,500	Beverages and tobacco
2	250	Crude materials, inedible, except fuels
3	500	Mineral fuels, lubricants, and related items
4	1,000	Animal and vegetable oils and fats
5	3,500	Chemicals
6	5,000	Manufactured goods classified chiefly by material
7	7,500	Machinery and transport equipment
8	5,000	Miscellaneous manufactured articles
9	10,000	Commodity and transactions, not classified accordingly

SITC = Standard International Trade Classification, $ = US dollar.

Source: United Nations Commodity Trade Statistics Database and consultant estimates.

The predominance of manufactured goods in global trade applies to the exports of the PRC, India, and Thailand but with important variations. India's largest exports are general manufactured goods, while both the PRC and Thailand derive the greatest value from exports of machinery and transport equipment. India has significant exports of ore and mineral fuels, while the others do not.

The trade between India, Thailand, and the PRC represents a relatively small portion of their total trade as shown in Table 6.2. The exceptions are the percentage of imports from the PRC for both India and Thailand, which account for 6.4% and 8.8%, respectively. The majority of the trade between these countries is found in three commodity groups:

- chemicals and related products (Standard International Trade Classification [SITC] 2 Code 5), including organic and inorganic chemicals, especially plastic resins and naturally occurring nonmetallic minerals;
- manufactured goods classified by materials (6), including textiles, leather, gems, and metal products; and
- machinery and transport equipment (7), including automobiles, automotive parts, telecommunications gear, and manufacturing equipment.

The first group is transported mostly as dry bulk or bagged cargo. The second and third groups are shipped primarily as unitized cargo. The shipments of crude materials (2) and mineral fuels (3) although less important in terms of value, are important in terms of volume.

Table 6.2   Percentage of Value of Trade by Country of Origin/Destination

From	To		
	India	Thailand	PRC
% of Exports			
India		1.2	7.2
Thailand	1.0		7.3
PRC	1.0	1.0	
% of Imports			
India		1.1	1.4
Thailand	0.8		2.1
PRC	6.4	8.8	

PRC = People's Republic of China.

Source: United Nations Commodity Trade Statistics Database (2004).

The relative concentration of trade between these countries in terms of commodities was examined based on value of trade for 2004. India has the highest concentration and the PRC the greatest diversity. For India, only 2% of the commodity categories (at the four-digit level) account for 73% of its exports, 82% in the case of trade with the PRC and 73% for its trade with Thailand. On the import side, 2% of commodity categories account for 85% of its total imports versus about half for its imports from Thailand and the PRC. The PRC has the greatest diversity for exports, although its imports from India and Thailand display high levels of concentration. For its exports, 2% of the categories account for only 35% of its trade with the world, and 47% for its exports to India and 40% to Thailand. Concentration of imports is much higher.

About 30% of India's export earnings come from jewelry including diamonds and about 10% from iron ore and related products. For exports to the PRC, nearly half the earnings are from iron ore and another 10% from related products. An additional 5.5% comes from resins associated with the manufacture of plastics. In contrast, about one third of the value of exports to Thailand is from diamonds and semiprecious stones and almost 12% from copper alloys.

For Thailand, the major exports by value are electronic components and circuits, data storage units, and other data processing equipment, which together account for about 14% of export value. In contrast, rubber and rice each account for a little less than 3% of the value. Key exports to the PRC are electronic equipment, which accounts for about one quarter of total value, and rubber for another 10%. For shipments to India, auto vehicle parts account for 7% and data processing equipment more than 7%.

PRC exports are more diversified, with data processing equipment accounting for 12% of total value and electronic components and circuits a bit more than 7%. For exports to India, about 10% of the value is for television (TV) and radio transmitters, 5% is data processing equipment and 5% is coke and coking coal. For shipments to Thailand, data processing equipment accounts for about 12% of the value, while TV and radio transmitters contribute 4% and semifinished iron and steel another 6%.

The linkage between the quality of logistics and type of commodities involves three factors:

- the value of the commodity per shipment unit, e.g., per metric ton or 20-foot equivalent units (TEU);
- the shelf life of the commodity due to physical deterioration or volatility of demand; and
- the scheduling requirements of the importer, e.g., just-in-time manufacturers, retailers with coordinated national sales programs.

If there are limitations in the quality of logistics, this should show up in terms of relatively small trade in those commodities most sensitive to the cost and transit time for shipment. These include fruits and vegetables, parts for automobiles and other equipment, apparel, and seafood. Exports of fresh fruits and vegetables have short shelf lives and require a protected environment from the field to the point of sale. The logistics for processed foods are less demanding, especially for the movement from the factories to the overseas point of sale. Of the three countries, only Thailand is a significant exporter of fruits and vegetables, which account for 4% of its exports to the PRC (Table 6.3). Only about 2% of the exports from the PRC to Thailand are fruits and vegetables but again this is twice the percentage for its total trade.

Table 6.3   Importance of Trade in Selected Commodities

	To (%)		
Exports from India	**PRC**	**Thailand**	**World**
Seafood	2.07	2.23	1.90
Fruits and Vegetables	0.01	0.22	1.62
Textiles	1.42	2.21	5.90
Motor Vehicle Parts	0.20	1.93	0.92
Apparel	0.04	0.20	8.56
Exports from the PRC	**India**	**Thailand**	**World**
Seafood	0.00	0.44	1.13
Fruits and Vegetables	0.42	2.12	1.07
Textiles	10.03	5.50	3.89
Motor Vehicle Parts	0.14	0.54	0.75
Apparel	0.23	0.45	9.35
Exports from Thailand	**PRC**	**India**	**World**
Seafood	0.75	0.15	4.28
Fruits and Vegetables	4.30	0.69	1.93
Textiles	2.11	3.75	1.95
Motor Vehicle Parts	0.65	7.10	1.51
Apparel	0.09	0.42	4.20

PRC = People's Republic of China.

Source: United Nations Commodity Trade Statistics, 2004. Export Data.

Motor vehicle parts are extremely time sensitive, especially where these are being supplied as inputs to an assembly process. Spare parts are less demanding although there has been increasing emphasis on reducing inventories to avoid overstocking. All three countries produce significant amounts of automotive parts but primarily for domestic manufacture. Thailand has the largest trade in automotive parts as a percentage of exports. About 7% of its trade with India is in automotive parts, while its shipments to the PRC amount to only 2% of its exports.

Exports of seafood require tight logistics from the source (fishing vessel or farm) to the factory to ensure freshness. From the factory to the markets, the logistics are less demanding since most seafood is shipped frozen and can be stored for several months. Nevertheless, it is necessary to maintain the cold chain from the factory to the final point of sale. Thailand has the largest percentage of exports in this category: about 4% of its total trade. However, the primary destinations are markets in the developed countries; very little is shipped to the PRC or India. In contrast, about 2% of India's exports are seafood and this commodity accounts for about the same percentage of its trade with the PRC and Thailand.

The increasing competition in the global trade of textiles and apparel has required all exporting nations to ramp up their logistics to cope with more exacting delivery schedules. These commodities account for a significant portion of the exports of the PRC (13.2%) and India (14.5%), but less so for Thailand (6.1%). All are well above the 4% of global trade accounted for by textiles and apparel. Very little of this trade is destined toward each other, although there is significant exchange in textiles, with India and the PRC providing cotton and Thailand synthetics. The PRC is a net exporter of textiles to India and Thailand, as these countries purchase about 10% and 6% of the PRC's total textile exports, respectively.

Southern Ocean Route

The Southern Ocean Corridor has been the principal route for trade between South and East Asia for centuries. As shown in Figure 6.1, it forms part of the east-west trade route that circumnavigates the globe. It connects the Mediterranean via the Suez Canal to the Persian Gulf then continues past South Asia through the straits of Malacca to East Asia and on across the Pacific. The corridor serves all mainline shipping services including round-the-world services; pendulum services between the Mediterranean and East Asia; interregional services between the Persian Gulf and East Asia; and regional services within the Arabian Ocean, Bay of Bengal, Gulf of Thailand, and along the coast of Viet Nam and the PRC.

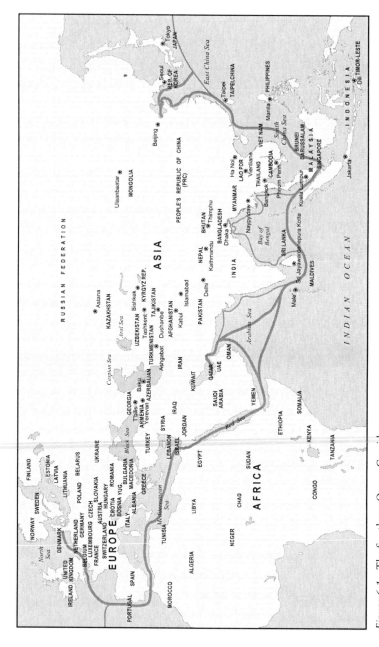

Figure 6.1   The Southern Ocean Corridor

Source: Asian Development Bank.

Table 6.4   2005 Container Traffic in 20 Largest Ports, Mn TEU

Hong Kong, China	21.9	Antwerp	6.1
Singapore	20.6	Long Beach	5.8
Shanghai	14.6	Port Kelang	5.2
Shenzhen	13.7	Qingdao	5.1
Busan	11.4	New York	4.4
Kaoshiung	9.7	Tanjung Pelepas	4.0
Rotterdam	8.3	Ningbo	4.0
Los Angeles	7.3	Tianjin	3.8
Hamburg	7.0	Laem Chabang	3.8
Dubai	6.4	Tokyo	3.6

Mn TEU = million of 20-foot equivalent unit.

Source: United Nations Conference on Trade and Development.

This route is served by a combination of mainline and feeder container shipping services that interconnect the major transshipment hubs. These hubs include the six largest container ports in the world in terms of container traffic: Hong Kong, China; Singapore; Shanghai; Shenzhen; Busan; and Kaoshiung (Table 6.4). These are supported by a series of regional hubs, many of which rank among the top 25 container ports and include Qingdao, Ningbo, and Tianjin in the PRC; Laem Chabang in Thailand; Tanjung Pelepas and Port Kelang in Malaysia; and Colombo in Sri Lanka. The regional hubs connect through a network of feeder services to the major national ports, including Karachi and Qasim in Pakistan; Nhava Sheva, Chennai, and Calcutta/Haldia in India; Chittagong in Bangladesh; Tanjung Priok in Indonesia; Ho Chi Minh City in Viet Nam; and the second-tier ports in the PRC. The largest of the regional ports, Nhava Sheva, currently handles more containers than Colombo but is unlikely to become a transshipment hub because of its location away from the main east-west route.

The hierarchy of ports is based on a hub-and-spoke strategy that allows the largest and most efficient vessels to operate on the main line haul routes where there are sufficient volumes to allow frequent sailings in each direction. The vessels serving the feeder ports are smaller and more costly to operate, but can offer more frequent service. In this way, the shipping lines can offer a balance between cost and frequency. The transshipment services compete with direct services on many of the medium-volume routes. The direct services offer port-to-port movements in medium-sized vessels. They can offer shorter sailing times even though they follow more circuitous routes with several port calls along the way. While there are fewer port calls in a hub-and-spoke strategy, the time for transshipment often results in a longer transit time.

The round-the-world and major pendulum services (e.g., Western Europe–Far East) typically use vessels in the 6,000–11,000 TEU range. Regional services that connect the international transshipment hubs to the regional hubs utilize vessels in the 2,500–6,000 TEU range. The local feeder services that shuttle between the regional hubs and the smaller container ports utilize 500–2000 TEUs.[2] This differentiation in size of vessels is important because of the significant economies of scale associated with vessel operations. The economies of scale associated with container terminal operations are less significant, except for very large transshipment ports for which there are significant savings in unit costs.

The scale economies associated with the larger vessels lead to transport costs that are nonlinear with distance. Larger vessels are used for longer distances, so that the marginal cost per ton-kilometer declines with distance, allowing exporters to compete in more distant markets with relatively little premium in terms of additional cost for delivery. This is important because, other things being equal, larger Asian traders will favor the bigger, more integrated markets in Europe and North America over the smaller, less organized markets in Asia even though the latter are much closer. For the same reason, the preference will gradually shift as the size of the markets in East Asia increases, access to these markets improves, and reduction in delivery times become more important.

The sailing times to Europe for the major ports on the western coast of South Asia are 15–22 days versus 22–32 days for Southeast and East Asia (Table 6.5). The sailing times from the smaller ports are longer. For example, the low volume ports in the Bay of Bengal, e.g., Kolkata and Chittagong, have transit times about 1 week longer because of their distance from the east-west route as well as long vessel turnaround times. In addition, the frequency of vessel calls is lower because of the small volumes handled.

Most of the ports within Asia are within a 2-week sail of each other (Table 6.6). These sailing times depend on the connection times at the transshipment hub. As volumes grow and there are more direct sailings, the transport duration should decrease to 10 days or less.

---

[2] Notable exceptions are the coastal services in the People's Republic of China (PRC) that use 4,000-twenty-foot-equivalent-unit (TEU) vessels to connect Shanghai with the other large ports.

Table 6.5 Typical Sailing Times to International Markets (Days)

Port	North Europe	US East Coast	US West Coast
Nhava Sheva	17–22	19–23	26
	15–21	19–22	22–29
Kolkata	23–28	30–35	27–30
Chittagong	22–30	27–35	19–28
Colombo	17–21	22–26	21–27
Laem Chabang	26	31	18
Singapore	22	27	15
Shanghai	26–32	26–35	12–18

US = United States.

Source: Author's estimates.

Table 6.6 Typical Scheduled Sailing Times, Days

Port	Singapore	Laem Chabang	Hong Kong, China	Shanghai	Chennai	Chittagong	Nhava Sheva	Colombo
Singapore		3	3	7	6	8	7	6
Laem Chabang	3		5	14	9	12		14
Hong Kong, China	3	11		2	15	16	10	7
Shanghai	6	15	2		18	19	12	10
Chennai	7	16	12	15		13		2
Chittagong	5	9	16	14	8			4
Nhava Sheva	6		14	14				6
Colombo	6	15	8	10	2	16		

Source: Author's estimates.

Container freight rates depend more on the relationship between supply and demand of transport capacity than on various underlying costs. As a result, fluctuations in freight rates are significant both over time and across trade routes. The period 2002 to the beginning of 2006 saw a significant rise in the worldwide freight rates as the growth in PRC exports created a significant shortage in shipping capacity. This was addressed through the introduction of additional capacity—most notably vessels of 10,000 TEU and more—on the major trade routes. This led to a moderation in freight rates in 2006 following by an increase with rising fuel prices.

Freight rates vary significantly by route, depending on both competition and load factor. They are particularly sensitive to imbalances in trade that cause a high proportion of empty backhauls. For example, the freight rates from Asia to the United States (US) in the first quarter of 2006 were about $1,680 per TEU versus $750 for the backhaul. From Asia to Europe the rates were about $1,770 versus $790 for the backhaul. In both cases, the rates for the loaded direction had been increasing while the backhaul rates had been declining. With the current pattern of trade, the rate for moving a container from Shanghai to Nhava Sheva is close to the full cost for the round trip, whereas, the rate from Nhava Sheva to Shanghai covers little more than the additional cost incurred in loading and unloading the container and transferring it at the transshipment port.

The Southern Ocean Corridor continues to offer the best transport alternative for trade between South and Southeast Asia. Rapid growth in trade has been accommodated through the introduction of larger container vessels and the expansion and diversification of feeder services. There have been some bottlenecks, primarily in public ports that have delayed the expansion of necessary infrastructure. This problem has decreased as more countries have shifted to private sector investment in container terminals and handling equipment and private operation has increased throughput at these terminals. India has traditionally suffered from limited capacity and poor throughput. While an increase in private-sector investment and operations has helped to ease some constraints, the Public Port Trusts still control the development of the infrastructure so that congestion problems and high port tariffs remain.

With the growth in trade between South and East Asia, there will be demand for additional port capacity. The investments that are needed to meet this expansion will benefit not only from private sector participation but also from an increase in berth productivity, measured in TEU/berth/year, which has averaged between 3% and 5% per year for the last 40 years. Currently, the capital cost for container terminal capacity averages about $150 million to $200 million per million TEU/year in existing ports and about $250 million to $450 million for greenfield ports.

While most of the governments have developed mechanisms for expanding port capacity, they have been less successful in providing the road and rail infrastructure needed to insure that the goods can be moved quickly in and out of the port. The result is an increase in congestion both in storage and at the berth. Efforts to develop multimodal corridors to serve the major ports are discussed in the following section.

There is significant competition on the Southern Ocean Corridor, and as a result of the expansion of domestic port systems, there is substantial interport competition at the national level as well. This is most notable in India, where the ports in Gujarat compete with those in Mumbai and the ports on the east coast from Visakhapatnam to Chennai compete to dominate the central Indian hinterland. The PRC also has a high density of ports but less interport competition because each serves the industrial zones in their immediate hinterlands. The most intense competition is between those ports handling transshipment. In the 1970s and 1980s, there was strong competition between Colombo and Singapore for South Asia transshipment cargoes, between Singapore and Hong Kong, China for Southeast Asian transshipment cargoes, and between Hong Kong, China and Kaoshiung for East Asia transshipment cargoes. This evolved into a much broader competition with the recent introduction of a new generation of transshipment ports including Port Kelang/Westport and Port of Tanjung Pelepas in the Malacca Straits; Salalah and Jebel Ali in the Persian Gulf; and Shanghai, Busan, and Keelung in the China Sea. In port operations, the challenge involves a large number of global players including PSA, Hutchinson Whampoa, DPW, and Maersk, as well as local operators. Despite the growth of the two major carriers, Maersk and MSC, the competition between container shipping lines on the major routes remains intense. On the feeder routes, local operators compete both under their own names and as designated feeders for the major lines. This competition is heightened by the practice of slot sharing and by widespread discounting. This has increased at the global level with the larger shippers entering into worldwide contracts at discounted rates and at the local level with non-vessel operating common carriers (NVOCCs) consolidating shipments to obtain lower rates from the carriers.

Northern Land Corridor

The Northern Land Corridor connecting South and East Asia includes both rail and road routes. The road route combines a number of national roads linked through various border crossings between Pakistan in the west and the PRC in the east. This road network is referred to as the Asian Highway, a concept developed through the efforts of the United Nations Economic and Social Commission for Asia and the Pacific (UNESCAP) and in collaboration with the countries through which the highway passes. A similar network of national rail lines and cross-border connections has been identified that interconnects South and East Asia from Pakistan through to the PRC. The concept of the Trans-Asian Railway was also developed by UNESCAP and approved by the participating countries. Neither the road nor rail routes are fully operational as there are missing links and problems with the conditions of other links.

Asian Highway

The Asian Highway (AH) was one of the early initiatives of the United Nations Economic Commission for Asia and the Far East (ECAFE). The concept was formally proposed in 1959 as a network of 65,000 kilometers (km) in 15 member countries. By the early 1970s, it had become the major activity of ECAFE, which was subsequently restructured to become UNESCAP. In the 1970s, progress was slowed down by lack of financing. The effort was restarted in the 1980s, and by 1992, it had become the major component of UNESCAP's Asian Land Transport Infrastructure Development Project. In 2005, an intergovernmental agreement on Asian Highway Network was formally ratified. The supporting border protocol is now being developed.

As the concept has evolved, the network has become a set of existing national highway links connecting the major cities in the transit countries. Currently, this network includes some 141,000 km of standard roadways crisscrossing 32 Asian countries and providing linkages to Europe. The sections of the network that connects South and East Asia include a cluster of routes in India and Southeast Asia, while a single connection through Bangladesh and Myanmar and three partially developed routes involve the PRC. There is generally only one designated border crossing for each country pair, as shown in Figure 6.2. Since these crossings are in remote areas, they are generally in poor condition and have problems with security and infrastructure. These pose significant constraints for the links connecting Pakistan, India, Bangladesh, and Myanmar. The road links within India have recently been upgraded as part of the development of the Golden Quadrilateral, but northeast India (nicknamed "the chicken's neck") leading to Myanmar still has two-lane roads in poor condition. The various routes through Bangladesh have similar problems and suffer from significant congestion at the border crossings. Most of the network in Southeast Asia is well developed having been upgraded through efforts at the national level, by the Association of Southeast Asian Nations (ASEAN) and Greater Mekong Subregion (GMS) initiatives. Most of the border

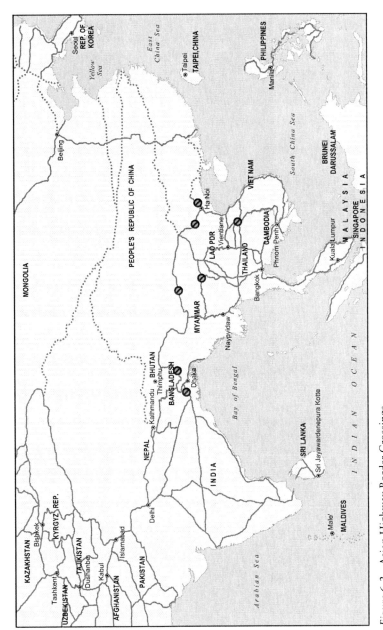

Figure 6.2   Asian Highway Border Crossings

Source: United Nations Economic and Social Commission for Asia and the Pacific.

crossings operate efficiently, despite the requirement for transshipping the cargo at the border.[3]

The four routes linking South Asia with the PRC, passing to the north of Southeast Asia, are:

- AH 42 through Nepal and Tibet and on into the central PRC;
- AH 3 through the Lao People's Democratic Republic (Lao PDR);
- AH 43 to Myanmar connecting to Kunming and from there to Shanghai; and
- AH 1 north through Viet Nam to Shenzhen and the southern PRC.

The first two are in poor condition while the latter two are in the process of being upgraded.

Of the 55,000 km of the existing road links in South, Southeast, and East Asia, about three quarters have two lanes or less. Nearly all of the links are asphalt, cement, or bitumen. About three fourths of the network is listed in good condition, but this refers to the configuration rather than the physical condition. The roads that are actually in good physical condition are limited to the primary links connecting the major cities, which are maintained to serve the high levels of domestic traffic.

There is very little international freight traffic on the Asian Highway, and nearly all of that is bilateral trade. The largest cross-border traffic is between India and Bangladesh at the Benapole/Petrapole crossing. There are very few instances of goods moving through transit countries to other destinations, although this should change with the opening of the transit link through the Lao PDR connecting the PRC and Thailand.

While efforts to develop the Asian Highway have produced little in the way of new physical infrastructure, they have produced agreements on designated transit routes, such as preliminary accords regarding border protocols. However, there are still no procedures that would allow trucks to cross these borders or to transit through third countries. Instead, cargo must be transferred between trucks registered on either side of the border. This transfer occurs either at the border or within a short distance of the border. There are some exceptions, such as the movement of Nepalese trucks through India and Thai trucks into the Lao PDR, but neither of these arrangements allows for movement in transit to third countries. The role of the Asian Highway in the future will very much depend on developing an effective transfer protocol such as the Transport Internationaux

---

[3] At present, the only borders that allow trucks to cross are those between Thailand and the Lao People's Democratic Republic (Lao PDR), Singapore and Malaysia, and Malaysia and Thailand. The latter has some limitations on border movements.

Routiers (TIR) system used in Europe. So far, such an arrangement has proved elusive despite lengthy efforts to develop a comparable system among countries in ASEAN and the GMS.

It is currently estimated that an investment of $18 billion would be required to develop and/or upgrade 26,000 km of roads to complete the Asian Highway network. For an efficient connection between South and East Asia, it will only be necessary to complete specific linkages in Myanmar to connect India and Bangladesh with Thailand as well as sections of AH 1 and AH 3 leading east from the border with the PRC. The cost for these would only be about $3 billion and would require 3–5 years to complete. The PRC government is expected to undertake the sections in that country at some time in the near future. In Myanmar, earlier efforts by the Indian and Thai governments to upgrade portions of these road connections and develop additional links were unsuccessful. Among the linkages that would be upgraded are:

- The 450-km section of AH 2 starting from the junction with AH 3 at Kyaington in Wa State to Taunggyi in Myanmar. This section is being improved and it is proposed to upgrade it to a standard double lane road meeting Asian Highway standards.
- The 211-km road link from Jinghong to Mohan (AH 3) in the south of the PRC's Yunnan Province is an important section of the corridor from Kunming to Bangkok. This is the only Asian Highway linkage between the PRC and the Lao PDR. Although a class II section, it is a rough road with long slopes and sharp turns.
- The 60-km road link from Menghun to Daluo (AH 3) in the south of Yunnan Province (PRC) is one of the two Asian Highway linkages between the PRC and Myanmar. It was constructed in 1960 and is a class II road.

The other option, the route north from Nepal through Lhasa (AH 42), would be much more costly to develop because the terrain there is rough. Also it would have very little traffic because of the low population density along the route.

Even with the completion of the Asian Highway and implementation of effective border protocols, it is unclear how much traffic there will be on the Asian Highway. There is very little trade along this northern route (even informal trade) since the route passes through the least developed areas of those countries, i.e., northeastern India, eastern Bangladesh, northern Myanmar, northeast Thailand, the northern part of the Lao PDR, and the southwestern part of the PRC. Most of the regional trade flows continue to be in a north-south direction connecting urban centers and major ports.

One possible source of traffic for the Asian Highway would be the diversion of goods that traditionally move by the ocean between India and the PRC. Although the land route is shorter, it will not provide significant savings in transport costs because of the higher ton-km of costs for trucking. The exception is goods moving between areas in northern India and the western PRC that are already far from the coast. The potential savings in transit time because of the shorter route and higher average speed of the trucks could be offset by delays at the border crossings. Without a regional transit protocol, the border crossings would quite likely add 2–5 days to the journey. As a result, for origins and destinations that are relatively near to the coast, there would be no advantage, although for inland origins and destinations there could be savings in the order of 5–10 days.

Table 6.7 provides an estimate of the difference in cost and time for an all-road movement by the Asian Highway versus a multimodal route including an ocean movement between Mumbai and Shanghai. These differentials were computed assuming that the average cost per truck-km was $1.[4] The average truck operating speed on a 24-hour basis was assumed to be 65 km per hour. Delays at each of the borders were optimistically assumed to be 12 hours. The ocean movement including terminal handling charges was assumed to cost $2,000 per TEU and require 4 days. As the results indicate, the Southern Ocean Corridor is preferable in terms of cost for most origin and destination pairs but has a significantly longer transit time. The imputed value of time ranges between $200 and $500 for most of these pairs, with the exceptions of those for which the Asian Highway would have a significant competitive advantage (i.e., Kunming, Chengdu, Chongqing, and Lanzhou).

Trans-Asian Railway

The proposal for the Trans-Asian Railway was initiated by ECAFE in 1960 as a 14,000-km rail link connecting Turkey and Singapore transiting Iran, Southeast Asia, and South Asia. UNESCAP commissioned two feasibility studies for the railway in 1995. One examined the northern route connecting Korean Peninsula, PRC, Mongolia, Kazakhstan, and Russian Federation. The other examined the route from the PRC through Southeast Asia to Singapore. In 2006, an intergovernmental agreement was prepared for construction of an enlarged Trans-Asian Railway network to connect 28 countries from Asia through to Europe, but this has yet to be signed.

---

[4] This assumes an average vehicle operating cost of $0.80 per kilometer (km) for an articulated truck and an average empty backhaul factor 40%.

Table 6.7 Comparison of All-Land and Multimodal Routes

City	Province	Land Distance (km)		Savings with AH	
		AH	Multimodal	$/TEU	Days
Beijing		7,380	1,220	$(4,170.00)	6.0
Changchun	Jilin	8,410	3,439	$(2,971.00)	6.8
Changsha	Hunan	5,810	2,320	$(1,490.00)	7.8
Chengdu	Sichuan	5,140	3,510	$370.00	9.0
Chongqing	Sichuan	5,240	3,250	$10.00	8.7
Dalian	Liaoning	8,280	1,100	$(5,180.00)	5.4
Fuzhou	Fujian	6,700	2,210	$(2,490.00)	7.1
Guangzhou	Quangdong	5,680	1,100	$(2,580.00)	7.1
Hangzhou	Zheijiang	6,720	1,290	$(3,430.00)	6.5
Hefei	Anhui	6,620	1,520	$(3,100.00)	6.7
Jilin	Jilin	8,520	3,609	$(2,911.00)	6.9
Jinan	Shandong	7,060	2,130	$(2,930.00)	6.8
Kunming	Yunnan	4,150	3,880	$1,730.00	9.8
Lanzhou	Gansu	6,130	3,290	$(840.00)	8.2
Nanjing	Anhui	6,780	1,380	$(3,400.00)	6.5
Qingdao	Shandong	7,310	2,106	$(3,204.00)	6.7
Shanghai		6,930	1,100	$(3,830.00)	6.3
Shenyang	Liaoning	7,640	3,180	$(2,460.00)	7.1
Shenzhen	Quangdong	5,970	1,100	$(2,870.00)	6.9
Shijiazhuang	Hebei	7,100	2,438	$(2,662.00)	7.0
Tianjin		7,430	1,100	$(4,330.00)	5.9
Urumqi	Xinjiang	8,360	5,220	$(1,140.00)	8.0
Wuhan	Hubei	6,160	2,020	$(2,140.00)	7.3
Xian	Shaaxi	6,150	2,600	$(1,550.00)	7.7
Zhengzhou	Henan	6,690	2,190	$(2,500.00)	7.1

AH = Asian Highway, km = kilometer, TEU = 20-foot equivalent unit, ( ) = negative value.

Multimodal distance computed using port of Shanghai except for those cities that have major ports.
Trucking cost $1 per TEU km; tolls $0.05/km, average trucking speed 65 km/hour.
Ocean shipping costs: $2,000; Time in port 4 days and at sea 8 days.
Time at land borders 12 hours each.

Source: Author's estimates.

In 1997, a study was made of the use of block trains for transport on the northern route through Central Asia. This led to four pilot operations conducted in 2003/04:

- Tianjin (PRC) to Ulaanbaatar (Mongolia) in 3 days (1,691 km);
- Lianyungang (PRC) to Almaty (Kazakhstan) in 7.25 days (5,020 km);
- Brest (Belarus) to Ulaanbaatar (Mongolia) in 9 days (7,180 km); and
- Nakhodka (Russian Federation) to Malacewicze (Poland) in 12.3 days (10,335 km).

These demonstrated the benefits from use of the northern trans-Asian route, and led to a growing interest in transit routes through Mongolia. At the same time efforts to integrate the Southeast Asian rail network are proceeding as part of the efforts to integrate the transport networks in the GMS and ASEAN.

One of the principal impediments to the development of the entire Trans-Asian Railway is a difference in rail gauges (Figure 6.3 and Table 6.8). The Indian and Pakistani networks are broad gauge whereas the Southeast Asian network is meter gauge and the network in the PRC is standard gauge. Bangladesh, which connects the South and Southeast Asia networks, has broad gauge in the western half of the country that connects to India and meter gauge in the eastern half so that it can connect to the Myanmar network. There are various measures to allow through-train movements including using wagons with dual-gauge bogies or adding a third rail, but none is practical for long hauls. A better solution would be to develop facilities located near the border to efficiently transfer cargo between trains of different gauges. This is most easily done for trains carrying containers. The transfer could be done in 4–6 hours using rubber-tire gantries assuming that there are efficient arrangements for clearing containers traveling under customs bond. Bulk cargo would be more difficult to transfer because of slower handling rates and cargo losses during handling.

The railways have significant operational problems that will limit opportunities for realization of an efficient rail connection between South and East Asia. The first is a dramatic difference in the size of their networks and scale of operations, which would cause problems when coordinating movements. The second is the lack of uniform standards for rolling stock in terms of size, brakes, coupling, etc. This is already a problem in South Asia; wagons from Bangladesh cannot operate efficiently on the Indian network (while the reverse is not necessarily true). The third is difficulty in integrating operations including the allocation of locomotives and track slots. The fourth is the lack of experience with procedures for controlling wagon movements across the border and through third countries including their timely return and the need to agree on a structure for trackage fees

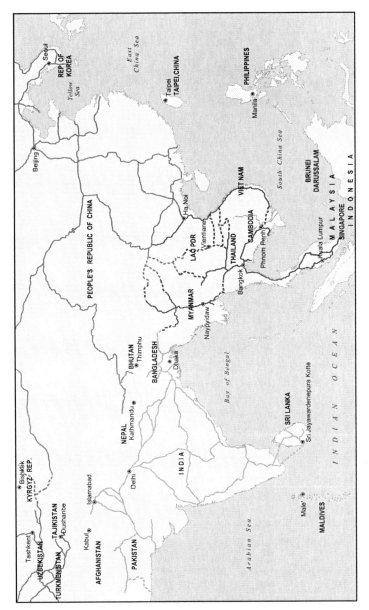

Figure 6.3   Trans-Asian Rail (TAR) Network

dotted lines on sea = ferry crossing, dotted lines on land = potential route or under construction, solid lines on land = existing tracks.

Source: United Nations Economic and Social Commission for Asia and the Pacific.

Table 6.8   Rail Network Characteristics

Country	Route Length ('000 km)	Gauge	Double Track (%)	Electrified (%)	Container Services	Container Traffic	
						'000 TEU	Market share (%)
Bangladesh	2.88	BG (23%), MG (77%)	54.0	–	Dhaka–Chittagong	35	5.0
PRC	58.80	Std Gauge	39.0	30.0	Throughout	3,000	7.5
India	63.12	BG (75%)	33.0	25.0	Throughout	1,450	35.0
Pakistan	7.36	BG	50.0	–	Lahore–Karachi		
Thailand	4.04	MG	0.2	–	Laem Chabang–Lat Krabang	432*	10.0

BG = broad gauge, km = kilometer, MG = meter gauge, PRC = People's Republic of China, Std = Standard, TEU = 20-foot equivalent unit, – = not applicable.

* 2004 data.

Source: Author's estimates.

and wagon per diem.[5] The fifth is the problem of developing balanced traffic to reduce the amount of empty wagon movements and to ensure a quick turnaround of wagons at both ends of the journey.

The problem of insufficient volume of traffic is more problematic for the Trans-Asian Railway than for the Asian Highway. Railways are most effective for carrying bulk cargoes such as coal and iron ore over long distances. This could apply to coal and iron ore traded between India and the PRC, but it is unclear if this would be a balanced flow. Unit container trains can be operated efficiently over long distances, as has been demonstrated in India and the PRC, but this requires a balanced flow. It also requires a better quality of service to compete with road transport.

So far, unit train operations have had limited success in capturing market share for container movements. The only country with a substantial volume of containers moving by rail is India, where about 30% of the containers moving between its ports and inland points (including the border with Nepal) are carried by Indian Railways. To serve this demand, Indian Railways has developed a national network of inland container

---

[5] Unlike trucks, where there are single vehicles with considerable flexibility in their operations and the driver retains responsibility for the return journey, the railways hand off a rake of wagons to another railroad which may or may not have the ability to control its movements and arrange a return movement.

depots (ICDs). In contrast, Pakistan has limited unit train service between Lahore and Karachi, which is not competitive with road movements and carries relatively few containers. Bangladesh Rail (BR) transports containers along the Chittagong–Dhaka corridor between the port and the ICDs in Dhaka and Tongi but this traffic represents a small portion of the country's container traffic (5%) and Bangladesh Rail is losing market share. Thai Railways (SRT) carries a large portion of its container traffic (10% of total seaborne container traffic), but the movement is limited to a shuttle between the port at Laem Chabang and the ICD at Lat Krabang. Thai Railways does not provide any other container train services. PRC railways carry a relatively small portion of container traffic despite an otherwise successful freight operation.

Finally, there are serious operational problems with freight operations in most of the countries involved in the Trans-Asian Railway. These include problems with financing capital improvements, lack of commercial management, shortages of rolling stock, and preference given to passenger operations over freight. The quality of railway management varies significantly among the countries.

Indian Railways has been able to operate an extensive network offering essential passenger and freight services. It has also developed a subsidiary, Concor, to operate unit container trains. As a result, there has been a significant increase in freight volumes. However, Indian Railways continues to suffer from the inefficiencies of overstaffing and excess routes that are common to public railroads, and it uses freight traffic to cross-subsidize passenger operations. While there are efforts to introduce private unit train services, there continue to be problems with availability of wagons for the movement of bulk and container cargoes. The rail systems in Pakistan and Bangladesh are less developed and have more severe operational problems despite the fact that both countries have smaller rail networks. In Southeast Asia, the lack of commercial management combined with relatively short travel distances and good road networks have severely limited the role of rail in freight transport. The PRC has an extensive rail network and relatively efficient operation for both passenger and freight services. As a result, it carries a large and increasing amount of freight. However, it is unclear whether the quality and availability of service in the coastal regions can be replicated in the interior.

Given the variance in quality of operations, differences in gauges and rolling stock, and lack of commercial management, it is difficult to imagine how an effective rail service between the PRC and India can be established. Even with an efficient service, there would still be strong competition in terms of transit time from road transport and in terms of cost from ocean transport. There may be some option for developing a multimodal service through the use of trailer on freight car services that could reduce transport costs without significantly increasing transit time. No such operations exist at present, however. Nevertheless, the best opportunity for successful operations along the route between South Asia and the PRC would involve movements between intermediate rail yards that function as dry ports for networks that have a common gauge. Otherwise the principal activities on the Trans-Asian Railways will be within Southeast Asia and between the PRC and Eastern Europe.

Even this operation will require the construction of missing segments, especially in Myanmar and the Lao PDR. Most of these require construction over extremely difficult terrain. There is also a proposal to extend the new rail link built by the PRC to Lhasa to Nepal and India, but this is even more difficult terrain and would be quite expensive. The only likely successes for the Trans-Asian Railway are an integration of the network in Southeast Asia and the establishment of through movements between the PRC and Eastern Europe.

Intermediate Corridors

South Asia

In Pakistan, India, and Bangladesh, the traditional centers for manufacturing have traditionally been located far inland from the major ports. In contrast, many of the fastest growing markets are located near the major ports. The corridors connecting the manufacturing centers to the seaports have had poor quality infrastructure because trade had been limited and most of the production was distributed locally. However, over the last two decades as trade has grown, a number of efforts to improve these corridors have taken place, most notably:

- N5 connecting Karachi with the northeastern centers of production;
- the Golden Quadrilateral, connecting the northwestern production centers around Delhi with the ports of Nhava Sheva and Kolkata; and
- the national highway connecting Dhaka, Naranganj, and Chittagong.

Many of the major corridors include rail lines (Table 6.9), but the railroads carry a relatively small share of freight traffic with the exception of the line connecting the area around New Delhi with Mumbai.[6]

Currently, the time and cost for shipments from major inland sources to the port of export are reasonable. The duration of a trip is typically 1–2 days and trucking costs for a 40-foot container range from \$120 in

---

[6] This reflects the important of rail transport in India where it carries about one third of the container traffic versus less than 5% in other South Asian countries.

Table 6.9 Typical Corridor Performance

Corridor	Road	Rail
Dhaka–Chittagong (Bangladesh)	220 km	298 km
One-way	7 hours	3.5 days
TEU, one way, factory-port	$100	$145
Kathmandu–Haldia (Nepal)	1,137 km	
One way, factory-port	6–8 days	4–5 days
TEU, round trip, factory-port	$1200	$750
Lahore–Karachi (Pakistan)	1,300 km	
One way, factory-port	48 hours	48 hours
TEU, round trip, factory-port	$450–600	$450-$500
Delhi–Mumbai (India)	1,408 km	
one way, factory-port	3 days	48 hours
TEU, one way, factory-port	$450	

km = kilometer, TEU = 20-foot equivalent unit, $ = US dollars.

Source: Author's estimates.

Bangladesh to $600 in Pakistan and India (because of longer distances). Transport that involves cross-border movements takes the most time because of border delays. This is most notable on the corridor between Dhaka and Kolkata.

Despite the improved connections to the inland production centers, there has been growth in production in the areas adjoining the ports, especially in India where the production of automobiles, automotive parts, and low-cost apparel requires tight logistics in order to be competitive.

Southeast Asia

In Southeast Asia, production activities have tended to be located close to the coast. The obvious exception is the Lao PDR, which is landlocked and requires a lengthy land connection to utilize Thailand's ports of Bangkok and Laem Chabang. Most of Thailand's production is concentrated around Bangkok and along the eastern seaboard. Production activities further inland are associated primarily with agriculture and food processing. Viet Nam is relatively narrow and the industrial activities are concentrated along the coast, primarily in the 105-km corridor connecting Ha Noi and Haiphong, and in the metropolitan areas of Da Nang and Ho Chi Minh City (Figure 6.4).

Cambodia has relatively little industrial production, but has direct access to the Mekong as well as road connections to the ports of Sihanoukville

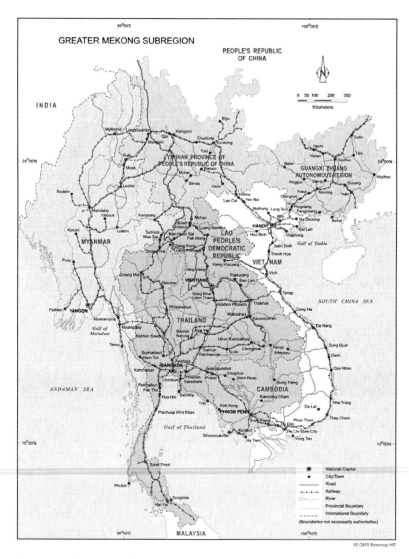

Figure 6.4   Inland Corridors for Southeast Asia

Source: International Bank for Reconstruction and Development (IBRD).

(230 km) and Ho Chi Minh City (250 km). As a result, there are very few corridors to the interior that carry significant traffic. There are various proposals for development of new corridors to improve connectivity within the GMS countries as shown by the dotted lines in Figure 6.4. However, it is unclear if these will attract significant traffic.

East Asia

The PRC's industrial production is concentrated along its coast. Its three major special economic zones have been developed around the ports of Shanghai, Guangzhou/Hong Kong, China, and Tianjin/Bohai. Additional zones have been developed near the second-tier ports of Shenzhen, Shantou, Xiamen, Dalian, Qingdao, Ningbo, and others. A large percentage of the import cargoes move relatively short distances because they are processed near the border and re-exported. This activity is supported by an extensive network of highways in the coastal area. There is also an extensive rail network. While there is a competitive trucking industry and an efficient rail operation, the costs for land transport is higher than in South Asia, even though the PRC has larger trucks operating at higher average speeds.

The corridor with greatest potential is that connecting Yunnan Province (which is far from the coast) to the Thai ports. This is part of the proposed North–South Corridor, which would carry cargo all the way to Singapore. Two others would connect Kunming and Nanning with Haiphong. All three are intended to provide alternatives to the major ports in the PRC, which are further away.

Movements of imports to the interior are facilitated by an extensive system of rail inland container depots located in the provincial capitals. There is also a network of highways connecting these capitals. However, so far few exports are produced in the interior and most of the movements are raw materials and agricultural production shipped from the interior to the coast for processing and manufactured goods moving inland for sale in the provincial markets. There is also a significant volume of coastal shipments of containers but these are primarily between the transshipment hubs of Shanghai and Hong Kong, China and the other ports in the PRC.

Future Development of Interior Corridors

Since the Southern Ocean Corridor will continue to serve most of the shipments between East and South Asia, it will be necessary to expand the capacity and number of these internal corridors to move the growing volume of trade to and from the ports. In South and Southeast Asia, these corridors are on a North–South axis. Most are multimodal corridors and it is anticipated that rail traffic will maintain or increase its market share. This will require integrated planning of the development of transport infrastructure as is being attempted in Pakistan and India. In the PRC, the demand for internal mobility has been limited but this is expected to change as production activities move away from the coast in search of more low-cost land and labor. This movement will require expansion of road and rail movements, primarily on an east-west axis. An extensive highway and rail network already exists but will have to be expanded if the movement of production inland is to be improved. However, it is unlikely that this shift in production will move so far inland as to generate the long distance movements typical of those in South Asia.

The development of these corridors will, like those for the Asian Highway, be undertaken as part of the public investment in basic infrastructure for the transport of passengers and freight. However, there is growing interest in constructing rail lines that are dedicated to freight (specifically container) movements. The most notable of these is the proposed Delhi–Mumbai rail corridor, which is projected to cost $2 billion to $4 billion for the double-track, 1,400-km electrified line.

Central Air Corridor

Unlike the other corridors, the Central Air Corridor has an unlimited set of potential direct routes between economic centers; however, the airlines have generally adopted a hub-and-spoke arrangement for their scheduled passenger and freight operations. The international freight hubs (Figure 6.5) are used for transshipment of cargoes moving between Europe, the Middle East, Southeast Asia, and East Asia. Collection and distribution activities are accomplished through feeder routes between the international hubs and the national gateway major airports and through domestic services connecting to the local airports.

Eleven of the top 30 freight airports are located in Asia, second only to North America, which has 12. However, five of the major gateways in North America are hub facilities for the global courier services such as Federal Express (FedEx) and the United Parcel Service (UPS). In contrast, most of the Asian and European hubs have been developed on the strength of the national carriers that center their operations there to meet the demands of the local market (Table 6.11). Thus, Paris acts as a hub for Air France's freight operation, Frankfurt for Lufthansa's operations, Dubai for Emirates, Singapore for Singapore Airlines, Shanghai for China Southern, and Seoul for Korean Airlines. The major exception is Bangkok, which has developed as a freight hub despite the fact that Thai Airways does not have a pure freight operation. South Asia has yet to develop a regional transshipment hub in part because of the lack of a national carrier with a strong freight operation and in part because of the lack of suitable airfreight facilities.

The freight services offered by the airline industry in South and East Asia are of five types (Table 6.12).

- *Express package, modeled on FedEx operations.* Next-day delivery services are now readily available in India, Thailand, and PRC.

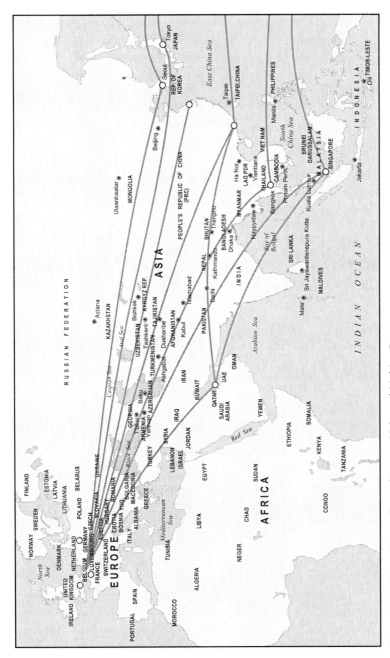

Figure 6.5 Major Airport Transshipment Hubs and Linking Routes

Table 6.10   South Asian Corridors

Corridor	Road	Rail	Distance (km)
India			
Mumbai–Pune	Expressway		163
Mumbai–Delhi*	4 lanes	Dual track	1,408
Gujarat Ports–Delhi*	2 lanes	1–2 tracks	1,096
Guwahati–Siliguri–Kolkata/Haldia	2 lanes	Single track	1,197
Chennai–Bangalore	4 lanes		331
Chennai–Hyderabad	2 lanes**	1–2 tracks	688
Tuticorin–Tirupur	2 lanes		400
Pakistan			
Karachi–Lahore/Sialkot/Peshawar	4 lanes	1–2 tracks	1,721
Bangladesh			
Chittagong–Naranganj/Dhaka/Tongi	2–4 lanes	Single track	320
Dhaka–Benapole/Kolkata	2 lanes	Single track	460
Nepal, Bhutan			
Thimpu–Phuentsoling–Kolkata			
Katmandu–Birgunj–Haldia	2 lanes	1–2 tracks	1,137

* Ludhiana–Agra, ** under construction, km = kilometer.

Source: Author's estimates.

In addition, these services provide international connections to global carriers such as FedEx, UPS, and DHL.

- *Cargo carried on regularly scheduled passenger flights.* This capacity is limited because priority is given to passenger baggage and mail. Internationally, this capacity has accounted for slightly more than half of total air freight.
- *Scheduled air freighter services.* Provided by the major passenger airlines such as British Airways, Air France, Lufthansa, Northwest, Emirates, Singapore Airlines, and China Southern as well as by pure freighter operators such as Cargolux, Martinair, DHL/Danzas/Airborne, UPS/Emory, and FedEx. Generally provide weekly services.

Table 6.11 Regional Air Freight

	Tonnage	Increment
International		
Africa	435.6	12.2
Asia-Pacific	17,420.5	5.9
Europe	8,346.0	4.9
Latin America	1,266.9	1.8
Middle East	2,609.3	10.8
North America	6,055.4	2.7
Total	**36,133.7**	**5.3**
Domestic		
Africa	40.1	(4.1)
Asia-Pacific	4,394.8	6.3
Europe	339.2	(4.0)
Latin America	682.5	(8.6)
Middle East		
North America	10,767.3	(2.1)
Total	**16,223.9**	**(0.3)**

( ) = negative value.

Source: Airports Council International.

Table 6.12 Typical Consignment Size for Airfreight Services

	Consignment Size
Express Package Services	<100 kg
Passenger Belly Cargo	<2 tons
Scheduled Air Freighter Service	<10 tons
Chartered Air Freighter	<50 tons
Sea-Air	5–20 tons

kg = kilogram.

Source: Author's estimates.

- *Chartered air freighters utilizing Antonov 124, Boeing 747 and 777, and Airbus 330 and 380.* Used especially during peak seasons, harvest time, and holidays, to handle surges in exports.
- *Hybrid air-sea and sea-air operations.* Sea-air combines scheduled airfreight and ocean services for delivering Asian cargo to Europe via Dubai and European cargo to South America via Miami. In South Asia, the air-sea service is used to connect with sea shipments when scheduled sailing dates have been missed.

All of these are scheduled services, except for charter services. They are differentiated partly by the size of shipments handed and partly by the speed of service. Charters offer direct service with the shortest air-transit time and can handle the largest consignments. Express services generally offer the shortest door-to-door time, but they can only handle packages and small consignments. Scheduled passenger services offer the greatest frequency of departures and often the shortest transit time, but have limited capacity because freight must compete with passenger baggage. The difference in typical consignment size is substantial, as shown in Table 6.12.

International airfreight traffic has been growing at an annual rate slightly less than the overall growth in volume of trade. International Air Transport Association (IATA) carriers recorded an average increase in international tonnage carried on scheduled services of about 5.7% over the last 10 years. The all-cargo segment grew much faster, however, with the result that the share of cargo carried in freighters increased to 50%. The growth in airfreight has been more rapid in Asia than in Europe and North America, making Asia the largest market for international airfreight where it accounts for almost half the total traffic. Although the highest percentage growth in 2005 was in the Middle East in absolute terms, the greatest increase in absolute terms was in Asia. IATA data indicates that much of the airfreight originating in Asia involves a movement within the region.

The market for airfreight is limited because of its relatively high cost; however, there are a number of important market niches that can be served. The largest is small consignments of high-value goods including documents, samples, jewelry, pharmaceuticals, and electronic components. Another important niche is for goods with short shelf lives because of their perishability or volatility of demand. The former include fresh fruits and vegetables, flowers, and crustaceans. The latter include fashion apparel and footwear. A third market niche is for critical goods requiring rapid resupply. This includes spare parts for machinery, vehicles, aircraft, etc. The fourth niche is for goods that have missed their ocean shipment date and must be shipped by air to meet their delivery date.

The cost of airfreight per kilogram (kg) depends on the type of service. Express services are the most costly. Freight rates are generally determined by total distance traveled. The cost for the long-distance flights has decreased along with the distance as a result of increased use of the polar routes. The rates are generally an order of magnitude greater than the cost of ocean freight. Table 6.13 presents typical rates for goods shipped out of Beijing. The rates from India are lower for westbound cargo, about $3.25 per kg to the US east coast and $3.0 per kg to Europe, but are higher westbound including to the US west coast.

In Asia, the vast majority of airfreight is handled at the major airports. Most of the countries have one or two airports that handle most of the airfreight. Even in the PRC, Beijing, Shanghai, and Guangzhou account for over half of the total cargo (Figure 6.6) while in India, Mumbai, and Delhi account for about two thirds (Figure 6.7).

The major airports all have at least two runways, each measuring 3,000 meters or more in length to accommodate the largest aircraft. They are equipped for year-round operation with relatively few days in which there are diversions due to weather. However, they vary in the quality of their air cargo facilities. The facilities in the PRC and Southeast Asia are far superior to those in South Asia, which reflects that slower development of air transport services in South Asia. This may be changing as the air transport markets in India and Pakistan are liberalized. Although India has some of the least developed air cargo facilities this could be rectified as

Table 6.13 Airfreight Rates and Times for Beijing

Beijing to	Rates ($/kg)	Time (days)
Mediterranean (Rome)	3.90	4
Northern Europe (Amsterdam)	3.96	4
East coast of the US (New York)	4.22	2
West coast of the US (Los Angeles)	4.15	2
Middle East (Dubai)	3.30	3
West coast of India (Mumbai)	3.18	2
East Asia (Tokyo)	2.54	1

kg = kilogram, US = United States, $ = US dollar.

Assumption: 5,000 kg/year.

Sources: Various.

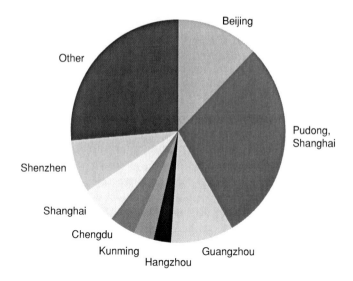

Figure 6.6   Market Share of Airfreight for PRC Airports

PRC = People's Republic of China.

Source: Civil Aviation Administration of China. Available: www.caac.gov.cn

a result of the transfer of operations, including air cargo, from the Airports Authority of India (AAI) to private operators.

So far there has been no airport developed solely for airfreight, which is generally handled as an adjunct to the main passenger operations. Although there have been some efforts to develop large airfreight terminals in South Asia and the PRC, there are no air cargo villages such as those existing in Dubai and Singapore.

Despite the growth in both freight and passenger traffic, there are relatively few direct passenger flights between South and East Asia, with the exception of those connecting the major passenger hubs of Hong Kong, China; Singapore; and Bangkok. Most of the indirect connections transit through one or more of these. For airfreight, there are some point-to-point movements, but most are indirect with the result that transit times for international shipments are typically 3–5 days. While the lack of direct connections increases the transit time, it also increases the freight capacity available since larger aircrafts are used in the hub-and-spoke operations.

Expected Improvements in the Airfreight System

While the Central Air Corridor handles a relatively small volume of the cargo (less than 1% of those moving among South, East, and Southeast Asia),

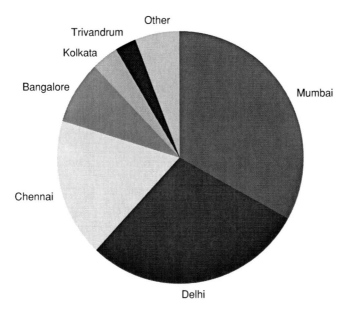

Figure 6.7   Market Share of Airfreight for Indian Airports

Source: Airports Authority of India (AAI).

the shipments represent a much higher proportion in terms of value, around 5% of the trade. By providing faster shipments, it allows regional producers to open new markets and supplement the range of products offered to existing markets. Equally importantly, it provides the critical pre-sales support including the shipment of documents and samples related to trade and after-sales support in terms of warranty and maintenance services. Most important, airfreight allows importers and exporters to guarantee shorter delivery times for their non-air shipments. This is done by allowing exporters to set delivery times consistent with a best-case scenario, and then providing them with compensation for unanticipated delays that occur in other parts of the supply chain. The volume of airfreight is expected to continue growing rapidly in Asia, including intra-Asian traffic, as a result of greater trade within the region.

The effectiveness of airfreight services depends on the connectivity between local collection and distribution flights, and line haul flights between major regional hubs. For scheduled services, it is important to have efficient interline movements utilizing a large number of carriers and an efficient system for cargo transfer at the airports. The former is being addressed through the introduction of "fifth and six freedoms" which allows airlines from one country to carry cargo between two other countries, and the expansion of open skies policies. India and Pakistan have already established open skies policies for airfreight airlines and many other countries have liberalized access to their air-cargo markets through bilateral agreements with the US and the European Union (EU). So far, new entrants to the airfreight market within Asia have been limited because volumes are small. Since most of the goods are for shipment to Europe and North America, the European and North American carriers have dominated the market. Both conditions are expected to change and it will become increasingly important to establish an open skies policy also for freight within the region.

Improvements in cargo handling are being addressed as part of the region's efforts to upgrade airport infrastructure. The new airports in Seoul, Bangkok, Shanghai, and Hong Kong, China all provide special facilities for freight. South Asia has lagged in this regard, but it is inevitable that major investments will occur within the next 10 years to meet the rapidly growing demand and to upgrade the facilities to international standards. Most of these capital costs for capacity expansion are incurred in developing new airports and passenger terminals. Greenfield airports costs range from $2 billion to $4 billion for a 60-million-passenger capacity, while passenger terminals typically cost $100 million to $300 million. In contrast, cargo facilities cost $10 million to $20 million.

Logistics and Supply Chain Management

Importance of Choice a Supply Chain

The ability to compete in international trade depends on the ability of the shipper to develop supply chains that can provide on-time delivery of inputs to production and deliver goods to the final market in a manner that meets the demands of the buyer. The performance of the supply chain can be specified in terms of delivered cost (includes cost of production and logistics), lead-time (order cycle from initial order to final delivery), reliability (measured in terms of order fulfillment), and flexibility (ability to adjust the routing of cargo), or C/T/R/F (cost/lead-time/reliability/flexibility).

Sensitivity to logistics cost is greatest where it represents a significant portion of the delivered cost and where there is significant competition based on delivered price. It is less important where non-price factors such as brand have a significant impact on demand. In other cases, an increase in logistics costs can reduce the perceived delivered cost. For example, packaging can be used to make smaller units, preparing shelf-ready products (labeled and packaged for sale), knock-down kits, etc.

Each traded item has a different requirement in terms of C/T/R/F. The trade-off between cost and time for logistics can be used to estimate the value of time. This value is higher for goods with a higher unit value or a short shelf life, due either to perishability or to product cycle. It is also higher where there is significant unpredictability because of fluctuation in demand, and where inventories must be adjusted to avoid shortages or overstocking. This fluctuation can result from a number of sources such as the seasonality of demand (apparel), inability to predict the level of demand with reasonable accuracy (consumer electronics), or volatility in demand over the product life (fashion goods).

Table 6.14 classifies goods according to their unit value and shelf life.[7] The highest value goods are those typically shipped by air, e.g., pharmaceuticals, fashion apparel and footwear, optical equipment, electronics, and machinery spare parts. Most of the commodity classification includes a mix of goods with varying shelf life. For example, crustaceans have very short shelf lives as they are generally served fresh; fish has a longer shelf life since it can be stored frozen.

There is also a trade-off between reliability and time. Where the supply chains are complex or activities within the chains are unpredictable (in terms of when they start and how long they last), it is necessary to add slack time to ensure on-time delivery. Reliability has become increasingly important for inputs to production manufacturers, as well as for larger retailers and manufacturers of branded goods as they seek to reduce their inventories.

The different requirements of time and cost are met by using different transport modes. Airfreight is the most costly, with a range of $0.25–0.50 per ton-km, and the fastest, requiring 2–4 hours per 1,000 km. Road and rail transport share similar characteristics in terms of speed but road is more costly at about $0.025–0.050 per ton-km. Ocean transport is both least cost ($0.010–0.015 per ton-km) and the slowest. Within these modes, there is considerable variation as shown in Figure 6.8.

The logistics industry allows the use of different modes and different levels of service. The result is a frontier of possibilities in terms of time and cost from which individual shippers can choose. Figure 6.8 presents a typical boundary of efficient options. The shipper would choose an option based on his trade-off between time and cost (the implicit value of time).[8]

---

[7] Shelf life is categorized as short (days or at most weeks), medium (months), or long (several months to years).

[8] The marginal cost is defined by the tangent to the supply curve at the selected combination of time and cost.

Table 6.14 Unit Prices and Shelf Life for Typical Exports

Export Items	CIF Price ($/kg)		Shelf Life
	Low	High	
Articles of apparel and clothing accessories	10.30	28.20	short–medium
Articles of leather, saddlery, harnesses	4.60	13.90	medium
Carpets and other textile floor covering	3.70	7.10	long
Cereals	0.10	0.60	medium
Coffee, tea, and spices	0.90	2.20	medium
Cotton	3.00	5.10	medium
Edible vegetables and roots	0.20	0.80	short
Fish, crustacean, mollusk, and other	2.70	5.20	short–medium
Footwear, gaiters, etc.	8.60	19.90	short
Furniture, bedding, mattresses, matt	2.40	4.90	medium
Knitted or crocheted fabrics	3.40	12.10	short–medium
Other made up textile articles (set)	4.00	6.80	short–medium
Pharmaceutical products	13.90	118.00	short–medium
Prep of vegetable, fruit, nuts	0.70	1.30	short–medium
Sugars and sugar confectionery	0.10	0.80	short–medium
Wood and articles of wood	0.60	2.80	medium–long

cif = cost, insurance, and freight; HS = Harmonized system for tariff classification; kg = kilogram; $ = US dollar.

Source: United Nations Commodity Trade database, HS 2000 code, 2004.

A typical international movement involves a number of sequential activities each of which adds to the time and cost for that movement. Table 6.15 shows typical time and costs for movement of a container by ocean. To reduce the time or cost or increase reliability, it is necessary to identify those activities that have the greatest impact on C/T/R/F and then select the subset of these activities that can be improved. The most important activity in terms of time and cost is the line-haul movement of ocean shipments, although there is usually little that can be done to reduce a shipment's cost or time other than to change to more costly direct services (that avoid the intramodal exchange at a transshipment port) or to less costly but more circuitous route. For distribution and collection activities, there is usually latitude to revise routes and relocate distribution centers. There

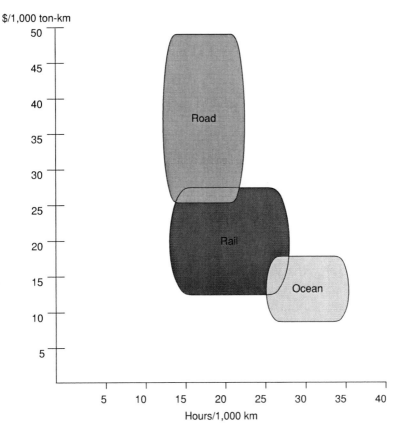

Figure 6.8 Relative Performance of Transport Modes

km = kilometer, $ = US dollar.

Source: Author's estimates.

is also the possibility for reducing the time and cost for the movement through the international gateways or between the line-haul and collection and distribution services.

Supply-chain management combines efficient transport with effective storage use. Efficient transport includes not only the choice of mode based on cost and transit time but also the coordination of the individual links of a multimodal trip where there is some variability in the departure and arrival times for each link. It also requires the efficient transfer of documents associated with transport and shipping, and the capability to track the cargo movements from origin to destination.

Table 6.15   Notional Time and Cost for Supply Chain Activities

	Time (days)	Cost ($)
Storage	3	20
Collection	1–5	100–1,000
Storage	4	40
Cargo Clearance	1–2	50–75
Intermodal Transfer	1–2	125–300
Line Haul	12–30	500–2,000
Intermodal Transfer	1–3	125–300
Storage	3–5	60–100
Cargo Clearance	2–3	100–250
Distribution	1–5	100–1,000

$ = US dollar.

Source: Author's compilation.

Initially, the effective use of storage implied efficient inventory management, which involved setting stocking levels that minimize the cost of inventory (carrying costs plus lost sales due to shortages and the write-offs for unused inventory). Since then, the concept of inventory costs has been broadened to incorporate the costs incurred throughout the supply chain (including in transit) and to the savings from consolidating loads at various points in the supply chain in order to maximize economies of scale in shipping. It also considers the location of storage facilities, specifically distribution warehouses, to optimize the trade-off between lead time and delivered costs. As a result, intermediate storage is introduced to serve various functions, but at the same time, the use of temporary storage is being decreased through cross-docking and transloading.[9] Storage-related functions include freight consolidation, container stuffing and unstuffing, positioning empty containers, supplier's inventory, wholesaler's inventory, retailer's distribution centers, cross-dock, and transloading. As real-time information on cargo location and destination has improved, it has been possible to shift from intermediate storage with pick and pack to real-time consolidation from one transport unit to another.

---

[9] The former refers to reconsolidating consignments from one set of inbound transport unit to another set of outbound transport units. The latter refers to the transfer of an entire load from a container to an enclosed truck or vice versa.

To take advantage of the efficiencies offered by supply-chain management, it is necessary to have an environment in which the logistics industry can thrive. This implies

- a regulatory environment that allows for the integration of logistics services and minimizes barriers to entry but, otherwise, supports economic regulation;
- modern information and communications technology systems that provide effective coordination between the different activities in the supply chain and speed the flow of information between the participants in these activities; and
- public-sector development logistics infrastructure where there are regulatory constraints (e.g., customs controls), or access to large tracts of land.

Competitiveness of Logistics Industry

Transport Services. To evaluate the level of competition, it is important to further classify the logistics industry based on the core activity of transport on one hand, and the complementary activities associated with supply-chain management on the other hand. All the countries in South and East Asia have highly competitive transport services. The trucking services are privately operated, and there are a large number of carriers. Fleet sizes vary from independent owners with a single truck to large trucking firms with several hundred trucks. The costs for trucking operations vary from country to country, as shown in Table 6.16, but this is primarily because of differing cost for inputs, especially labor and fuel. In addition there are higher capital costs in Thailand and the PRC, reflecting the use of more modern trucks for operating on the higher-speed road networks.

There is limited competition in the provision of rail services because these remain in the public domain. Container train operations in the PRC and India are relatively efficient. India's success in creating a government-owned corporation, Concor, to operate container trains and in granting concessions for individual rail services suggest that there is some scope for increasing competition in this mode.

The ocean transport market is highly competitive. The principal constraints as far as the number of lines calling at the major ports are concerned are the volume of traffic and the frequency of services. As shown in Table 6.17, the PRC has the best access to shipping services, while Bangladesh and Myanmar have the worst. A similar situation for air transport exists, but access to international operators is generally limited by bilateral agreements that restrict flights and that limit the use of fifth

Table 6.16   Trucking Costs

	Truck Type (No. of Wheels)	Load (Tons)	Cost ($/km)
Pakistan	6	10	0.23
	10	18	0.43
	14	27	0.50
India	6	9	0.26
	10	16	0.35
	14	27	0.56
Bangladesh	6	10	0.55
Thailand	14	35	0.65
PRC	18	40	1.00

km = kilometer, PRC = People's Republic of China, $ = US dollar.

Source: Various surveys.

Table 6.17   Line Shipping Connectivity 2005

	No. of lines calling
China, People's Republic of	1
India	18
Thailand	22
Pakistan	38
Viet Nam	54
Bangladesh	109
Myanmar	149

Source: Containerization International.

and sixth freedoms.[10] On the domestic front, India has active competition among a number of private carriers. It has also adopted an open-skies policy with regard to its airfreight operations but limits the landing

---

[10] The fifth freedom is the right to carry passengers from one's own country to a second country, and from that country to a third country. The sixth freedom is the right to carry passengers or cargo from a second country to a third country via one's own country.

rights for commercial aircraft operated by foreign carriers, affecting the availability of cargo capacity. The other countries in South Asia lack the domestic competition and have more limits on the international carriers. However, they are also more liberal in allowing foreign airfreight services. Thailand is the most open to international flights and to the use of fifth and sixth freedoms. It has also allowed increased competition for domestic services. The PRC, on the other hand, is less open to international carriers than Thailand but compensates for this through extensive code-sharing.

Non-Transport Services. There is a wide range of non-transport services provided by the logistics industry. These include services offered by both domestic and foreign third-party logistics firms (3PLs). In South and East Asia, the foreign providers act primarily as nominated forwarders for foreign buyers and suppliers. As such, they arrange for the ocean shipment, the clearance of goods, temporary storage of goods at the local port, and the inland movement in the foreign country. They are generally reluctant to become involved in domestic logistics activities because they generally have a higher cost base and no offsetting competitive advantage. In this situation, they allow the domestic importer and/or exporter to arrange for the domestic inland movement or arrange for these services from local 3PLs either through individual contracts of affreightment or through longer-term collaboration with specific providers. One notable exception to the role of foreign 3PLs is the effort by Exel (now part of DHL) to establish a national network of warehouses in India to offer a domestic distribution network for both local and foreign companies.

The extent of services provided by 3PLs depends on local regulations. Thailand is the most liberal economy, allowing foreign 3PLs to establish wholly owned subsidiaries and to provide a full range of services. The PRC and India have similar provisions, but most companies establish a joint venture to overcome difficulties with local bureaucracy as well as to rapidly develop a national presence. Bangladesh allows wholly owned subsidiaries but because of lack of volume many foreign 3PLs limit their presence to a joint venture or agency. The same applies to Sri Lanka. The other areas in which foreign companies have contributed to the logistics industry are the brand manufacturers (e.g., Nestlé and Pepsico) and hypermarkets (e.g., Carrefour, Wal-Mart, and Tesco). These have developed distribution and marketing networks including distribution centers, inbound-outbound supply chains, and integrated information systems linking points of production with points-of-sale, all as a means for establishing competitive advantage. Again, Thailand has been the most liberal in allowing major foreign retailers to enter the market. Both India and the

PRC have been more cautious in this area, but they have nonetheless begun to open up their markets. The smaller economies of South Asia have been more protective but they also present fewer opportunities for large-scale retail activities.

The domestic logistics industry in South and East Asia is composed primarily of providers of a transport service, a storage service, a cargo clearance service, or some combination of these. There are relatively few enterprises that provide multimodal service or an integrated fourth-party logistics (4PL) service. Some forwarders are involved in international shipments but primarily through the issue of combined bills of lading in partnership with an overseas 3PL. The domestic enterprises having the best capabilities in supply-chain management are the courier services. These provide overnight delivery of packages and documents. They also have linkages with the international courier services. They are now increasing the size of shipments they will transport by both land and air, and in some cases these firms are extending their service areas outside the country. There are other enterprises that have developed supply-chain management skills for specific sectors such as automotives and apparel.

The logistics industry is represented by international freight forwarding associations, many of them linked with the International Federation of Freight Forwarders Associations (FIATA). While most of these associations are active in political lobbying, few have developed an active program in training and/or technology dissemination aimed at strengthening capacity among member firms. One of these, Thai International Freight Forwarders Association (TIFFA), has been able to develop a substantial training program and is active in developing the capabilities of local 3PLs. TIFFA and some others are also making an effort to self-regulate by using accreditation as a mechanism to improve the quality of services among its members.

The contribution of the public sector to the logistics industry is generally limited to the provision of transport infrastructure and to facilities for storage of goods under customs bond. As shown in Table 6.18, the PRC has been the most successful in developing logistics infrastructure. The PRC and Thailand have been most effective in developing transport infrastructure for roads, airports, and seaports. India and Pakistan are in the process of upgrading their infrastructure, but both countries will require some years before they catch up with East and Southeast Asia. In terms of the provision of logistics hubs such as inland container depots (ICDs) and distribution hubs, the PRC and India have been able to develop national networks of ICDs, in contrast with other countries that have only one or two linked to a major seaport. The PRC is in the process of developing large-scale distribution hubs similar to those shown in Table 6.19, but other countries have yet to begin such initiatives.

The PRC has also led the way in developing industrial zones oriented toward external trade (special economic zones [SEZs], export processing zones [EPZs], and free-trade zones). India has also recently commenced a

Table 6.18   Ranking of Logistics Infrastructure

Country	Transport			Logistics	
	Roads	Gateways	Border Crossings	ICDs	Zones
PRC	1	1	1	1	1
Thailand	2	2	1	3	2
India	3	3	3	2	3
Pakistan	3	4	4	3	4
Bangladesh	5	5	2	4	3

ICD = inland container depot, PRC = People's Republic of China.

Source: Author's assessment.

Table 6.19   Typical Distribution Hubs Zones

	Transport	Direction	International Connection	Domestic Connection
Singapore ALPS	Air	Transship	Regional Airport Hub	Malaysian Corridor
Singapore Distripark	Sea	Transship	Regional Transship Port	
Jebel Ali	Both	Transship	Regional Transship Port	Dubai Corridor with link to GCC network
Freeport Bahamas	Sea	Transship	Regional Transship Port	
Rotterdam Distripark	Sea	Transship	Regional Transship Port	EU highway network and Rhine river

ALPS = Airport Logistics Park of Singapore, EU = European Union, GCC = Gulf Cooperation Council.

Source: Author's compilation.

large-scale program of SEZs that offers significant tax advantages, although the goals of this undertaking and its potential benefits have increasingly been questioned. Bangladesh has a large EPZ program but very few of these zones have been successful. Sri Lanka, in contrast, has seen more success with SEZs despite the small size of its economy. Thailand has yet to develop such a program.

As a result of the various factors discussed above, and taking into account the significant impact that customs has on the efficiency of trade logistics, the PRC is perceived as having the best logistics, followed by Thailand (Table 6.20). Thailand, Bangladesh, and India have the lowest internal logistics costs. The ranking is largely due to the quality of supporting infrastructure, ease of shipment, and problems with meeting schedules.

The quality of logistics has an important impact on the ability of a nation to trade. In many cases, the quality of logistics can compensate for a country's other handicaps as far as doing business is concerned. For instance, although both the PRC and India are ranked low in the World Bank's annual survey of doing business because of restrictions on and the procedures involved in setting up a business, both have rapidly growing export trade.

Table 6.20   Logistics Perception Index

Country	PRC	Thailand	India	Pakistan	Bangladesh	Sri Lanka	Myanmar
Overall	30	31	39	69	87	96	147
Customs	35	32	47	70	124	89	123
Infrastructure	30	31	40	71	81	105	145
Ease of Shipment	29	32	39	64	95	113	146
Logistics Services	26	29	31	61	100	93	128
Ease of Tracking	31	36	42	74	87	80	148
Internal Logistics Costs	75	27	49	92	44	54	79
Timeliness	35	28	45	90	54	116	146

PRC = People's Republic of China.

Source: International Bank for Reconstruction and Development, Draft Report – Measuring Global Connections: A New Set of Logistics Indicators.

Role of Information and Communications Technology in Logistics

Information systems remain at the heart of modern logistics and supply-chain management. A range of systems needs to be integrated to achieve efficiency in the individual cargo handling and transport activities. Moreover, the scheduling of these activities needs to be sufficiently synchronized. The most modern of these systems are those used by brand manufacturers and large retail chains to order goods for delivery from the distribution centers and restock the warehouses based on information from points of sale. Some of the critical pieces of this system are already in place in South and East Asia, primarily under the control of the global manufacturers and retailers from Europe and North America. However, parts of these systems are being replicated by larger local manufacturers and retailers in India, Thailand, and PRC. A similar sophistication has been introduced in the shipping, tracking, and tracing systems employed by the international courier services, which is now being introduced by domestic courier services as well. A similar process of dissemination is occurring in the forwarding and transport sectors, but their highly fragmented nature leads to a slower pace of innovation. In the public sector there have been widespread efforts at e-governance, although in some countries, the legislation providing for electronic signatures has not yet been drafted or ratified. In the area of trade regulation, the customs organizations have been the most progressive in introducing information and communications technology (ICT) systems for the processing of customs declaration and increasingly for controlling cargo inspection procedures. The other agencies involved at the borders have been much slower, and most transactions related to sanitary and phytosanitary standards, drug enforcement and security, continue to be enmeshed in red tape. Efforts to develop networks for facilitating trade that provide one-window access to the regulatory agencies, the terminal operators in the gateways, and the transport and logistics companies have yet to emerge, despite the increasing number of successful examples in Southeast Asia and the rapid growth in electronic data interchange (EDI) networks and in domestic software development firms. It is anticipated that the current decade will see a rapid growth in the use of ICT systems in supply chain activities.

Trade Facilitation

The effectiveness of the Northern, Southern, and Central corridors in accommodating the expected increase in trade between South and East Asia depends not only on the quality of the infrastructure and transport services provided but also on the constraints introduced at the international borders through which these corridors pass. Air transport is the fastest not only in terms of average speed in transit but also in terms of processing through the gateways. It does not require crossing borders since it involves direct movements between inland points where cargo can be cleared relatively efficiently. The processing of the cargo is also more rapid because of the realization that this cargo is time sensitive. Ocean transport is the slowest in terms of transit speed[11] and is also vulnerable to delays at the ports of call from port of loading to port of unloading. These delays at the ports of loading and unloading are because of inefficiencies in both cargo-handling operations at the berth and the procedures for clearing the cargo, both of which can significantly increase the time for the door-to-door movement. Road transport falls between the other two in terms of average travel speed, but can incur significant delays at the land borders. Because these border crossings tend to be in remote places, processing of cargo and vehicles is often slow and the performance is inconsistent. The Northern Road Corridor, for instance, involves multiple border crossings, so that these delays and costs can be quite significant.

Extensive efforts are underway throughout the world to facilitate cross-border movements through international conventions and bilateral agreements. Progress, however, has been slow. There are three major initiatives directed at reducing the time and improving the transparency and consistency of cargo clearance procedures at the border. These include the introduction of a harmonized system for cargo classification, implementation of the provisions for trade facilitation as part of accession to the WTO (e.g., customs valuation), and implementation of the customs reforms included in the Revised Kyoto Convention (Table 6.21). The countries in South and East Asia are well-advanced in adopting these initiatives but still need to make progress toward full implementation.

The overall objective is to simplify the procedures involved in moving goods through international gateways and across land borders. For the latter, the goal is to develop seamless borders. While this concept is well understood and current technology makes it possible, there have been difficulties in the initial stages of implementation even on borders between countries participating in regional agreements such as ASEAN, GMS, and the South Asia Free Trade Agreement (SAFTA). The various FTAs being implemented throughout South and East Asia have attempted to

---

[11] This assumes a comparison with highways and unit train operations. The speed of container vessels is comparable to that of trucks operating on state highways and roads and to normal freight train operations in terms of km per 24-hour period.

Table 6.21 Participation in Trade Reform Initiatives

	Membership		Revised Kyoto Convention	HS Codes
	WTO	WCO		
Bangladesh	1995	√		√
Bhutan		√		
India	1995	√	√	√
Nepal	2004	√		
Pakistan	1995	√	√	√
PRC	2001	√	√	
Sri Lanka	1995	√	√	√
Thailand	1995	√		√

HS = Harmonized system for tariff classification, PRC = People's Republic of China, WCO = World Customs Organization, WTO = World Trade Organization, √ = participant.

Sources: www.wcoomd.org; www.wto.org/English/thewto_e/whatis_e/tif_e/org6_e.htm; www.wcoomd.org/ie/En/Conventions/conventions.html

reduce these impediments by reducing duties and tariffs but they do not sufficiently address other aspects of trade facilitation and often introduce new barriers.

While considerable attention has been given to developing one-stop or single-window clearance facilities, these efforts are built on the premise of a single physical point for submission of customs information. This approach has been eclipsed through advances in IT. Initially these efforts focused on simplification of documents, i.e., reduction in the number of clearance forms and standardization of their format, but this has now advanced to online entry of customs information utilizing the internet, including pre-arrival submission of documents.

Efforts to establish single-window, single-inspection border crossings[12] at land borders remain at the pilot stage. While many of the outmoded procedures have been eliminated, others have only been modified. The application of integrated ICT systems and modern risk management practices continue to be limited to the major gateways. More troubling, many of the countries have difficulty making the transition from regulation to facilitation of trade. They continue to operate the borders with the intent

---

[12] "Single window" refers to a single point for submission of all documents, "single stop" refers to a single inspection, not one on each side of the border.

of imposing numerous administrative requirements, which in turn nurture the environment for corruption. This thwarts efforts to move the clearance procedures off the border to inland locations where they could be performed more efficiently.

Trade facilitation initiatives must be implemented at the national level but must eventually be subjected to regional coordination to achieve their full benefits. The most important initiatives currently underway include:

- simplification of cargo documentation,
- reforms in customs procedures,
- coordination of border management activities,
- provision for transit movements, and
- expansion of customs-bonded areas.

Underlying each of these is the need to improve the flow of information between public and private participants.

Cargo Documentation

Simplification of cargo documentation is the starting point for most efforts to facilitate the cross-border movement of goods. Most of the countries in South and East Asia have adopted a single administrative document for declaration of imports, exports, and goods entering under temporary admission. This reduction in the number of required documents reduces administrative costs, time required to prepare shipments, and opportunities for corruption.

The supporting documents that must accompany the cargo declaration have also been standardized. The essential documents include a transport document (bill of lading or consignment note), commercial invoice, packing list, and certificate of origin. Depending on the type of goods, additional documents may be required (e.g., insurance certificate, phytosanitary or other inspection certificate, Generalized System of Preferences [GSP] certificate, dangerous goods declaration). These documents are related to the shipper rather than the shipment (i.e., import and export licenses, company registrations, foreign and exchange authorization).

The simplification of tariffs has been proceeding at an uneven pace. While there has been progress in reducing the number of lines in the tariff codes and the number of bands used to assess duties, as well as an acceptance of the invoice value as a means to compute the duties, other problems have been introduced. These include negative or positive lists, surcharges, excise and value-added taxes, and new requirements for certification, particularly those related to health and safety.

Ironically, the result has been a gradual increase in the number of documents required because of the proliferation of bilateral and multilateral trade agreements and standards for both food products and manufactured goods. To take advantage of the lower duties offered in various trade agreements, it is necessary to comply with various rules of origin and complete specific forms documenting the local content of the goods and the eligibility for preferential rates.[13] Stiffer requirements for certification, especially in the case of trade with the EU, have increased the amount of inspection and testing of exports and the documentation associated with the certification process. The resulting increase in time and cost has caused smaller exporters to increase their shipments to less demanding regions such as the Middle East, although even there some tightening of requirements has been recently observed. Any effort to promote trade between South and East Asia must address the issue of harmonization and simplification of the related documents.

To facilitate cross-border movements, it is necessary to harmonize the data required concerning the cargo and transport used in a language that is understood on both sides of the border. International efforts to accomplish the former include the United Nations Key Layout for the format of the declaration and the World Customs Organization (WCO) data model for the format of the data. Efforts to introduce a common language have proven more difficult, but some countries now require a declaration in two languages, one of which is English.

Cargo moving in transit (under customs bond) through a country requires a transit permit. This is issued at the point of entry and closed out at the point of exit (or at an internal location where the cargo is cleared). The supporting documents for the permit are the same documents as for imports and exports, exclusive of the declaration form. Because these goods need to move across the border with minimum delays, it is important to harmonize the data requirements and format of the documents that must be submitted. It is also important to use EDI to submit the information used to prepare the permit prior to the arrival of the cargo at the border.

While most documentation problems are associated with the cargo, there is another problem associated with the cargo list for the transport vehicle, especially the Inward General Manifest for cargo carried on container vessels. Most customs systems utilize reconciliation between the manifest and the bills of lading submitted by the consignees as the first stage of document checking. This was relatively simple in the past because the manifest provided very little information on the cargo;

---

[13] Often the administrative time and cost, not to mention informal costs, associated with meeting these requirements exceeds the benefits and an increasing percentage of shippers are forgoing the potential savings in duties to reduce their administrative costs and shipping times.

however, as a result of new security requirements, these documents contain considerably more information so that reconciliation with the bills of lading is more problematic. The proliferation of trade agreements has also created problems as each has different requirements for cargo certification and different duties. This has led to an increase in documentation and more due diligence with regard to rules of origin. Food products and livestock have also been subjected to greater scrutiny as a result of the increasingly stringent health standards being introduced. This requires not only more documentation but also an increase in the amount of inspection and quarantine both prior to shipment and upon arrival at the country of destination. Continuing support for modernization and simplification of customs procedures remains an important component of trade policy.

Customs Procedures

The international effort to reform customs over the last decade has produced a substantial reduction in the time and cost to clear cargo. These efforts have now been formalized in the framework of the Revised Kyoto Convention, which entered into force in 2006.[14] This convention emphasizes the development of simple, effective, and predictable customs procedures. A common set of procedures is in various stages of implementation in the countries of South and East Asia which include introduction of harmonized tariff customs code and some form of single administrative document (Table 6.22). They have all automated the processing of customs data using the United Nations' Automated System for Customs Data (ASYCUDA) system or a locally designed system. However, the range of functions that has been automated varies depending on the number of ASYCUDA modules implemented and on the comprehensiveness of the local systems. All of these systems provide for the lodgment of customs declarations and accounting and back-office procedures, although the point of lodgment varies.

The more advanced systems, such as those in the PRC and Thailand, allow registered customs brokers to submit declarations over the internet. Other countries such as Bangladesh require that declarations be submitted at specific service centers operated by customs officials or customs brokers. Typically, 70–90% of the declarations are submitted electronically. However, the supporting documents and a hard copy of the declaration must be submitted and signed at some point during the cargo clearance procedure.

---

[14] International Convention on the Simplification and Harmonization of Customs Procedures.

Table 6.22   Customs Reforms and Objectives

Initiative	Objectives
Single Administrative Document	Simplification
Harmonized Code (HS)	
Electronic Data Processing Systems	Efficiency
Electronic Data Interchange	
Direct Trader Input	
Internet Input	
Green Channel	
Post-Clearance Audit	
Risk Management Systems	Transparency
Electronic Banking	
Electronic Signatures	
Inland Container Depots	Behind the Border
Private-Bonded Warehouses	
Bonded Factories	

Source: Author's compilation.

In all of these countries, customs has introduced some level of EDI to communicate with the other parties involved in the shipment of goods. Nearly all have a system for electronic submission of the Inward General Manifest of vessels and aircraft. However, there are no such systems for trucks crossing the international borders. Many of the EDI systems provide information to the consignee on the status of the cargo clearance process, but few have integrated this with information from the terminal operators regarding the status and location of the cargo in the airports and seaports.

All customs services rely on some form of risk management to determine the level of scrutiny to be applied for individual shipments. Traditionally this combines intelligence gathering with the subjective judgment of customs inspectors based on interaction with the shippers. Modern risk management systems (RMSs), as utilized in India, Thailand, and the PRC, employ statistical analysis to develop risk profiles, initiate queries, decide on the level of inspection and select inspectors. This enables a reduction in the percentage of cargoes that are inspected and the queries regarding the cargo declarations, while improving the rate of detection and amount of revenue collected. As a result, they significantly reduce both the clearance time and the level of corruption.

The effectiveness of RMS depends on the degree to which they have replaced traditional systems. An RMS is usually introduced at the major gateways first, and after an extended period of testing, they are then rolled out at other customs clearance facilities. The land borders are the last to receive these upgrade because of problems with the availability of power and communications as well as lack of training and supervision of the border personnel. Thailand has introduced the system at its major crossings with the Lao PDR and Malaysia but not with Myanmar. The PRC has recently introduced its E-Port system on its southern borders with Viet Nam and the Lao PDR but it is not fully operational. India and Bangladesh have begun rolling out their systems at major ports, but it will take some time for RMS to be installed at these countries' border crossings.

As for the payment infrastructure, the countries of South and East Asia have introduced electronic banking, although these are often limited to banks designated by customs. This permits efficient transfer of funds not only for payment of duties, but also for maintaining escrow accounts with customs as part of a scheme for clearance against documents (e.g., the gold card system). The introduction of electronic banking and signatures will further expedite clearance procedures, as it further lessens the need for submission of paper documents, and the face-to-face contact between the individual customs officers and representatives of the cargo owners.

Cross-Border Movements

One of the most difficult problems confronting the implementation of the Northern Route is reaching an agreement that would facilitate cross-border movements. The three basic issues to be addressed are as follows:

- the right of the vehicles from one country to operate within the boundaries of another country;
- the standards that these vehicles and their drivers must meet; and
- the mechanism for covering the potential liability for duties and taxes if the vehicle or its contents remain in the country.

With regard to the first, there is a generally agreed prohibition of vehicles transporting another country's domestic cargo. However, there are other activities in which these vehicles can be allowed to participate. These include

- bilateral trade between adjoining countries by trucks registered in one of those countries;
- transit through a third country of cargo originating in, or destined to, the country in which the truck is registered; and
- transport of cargo between two countries by a truck registered in a third country.

The first is covered under bilateral agreements, whereas the third is covered under a regional agreement as discussed below. The second requires either a policy in the transit country that allows but regulates transit movements and/or a regional agreement in which this right is granted to specified countries.

The first is relatively easy to negotiate. It requires agreements on mutual recognition of driver's licenses and certificates of roadworthiness, and on enforcement of local regulations regarding axle limits and traffic regulations. There are well-established conventions regarding road traffic and signage, which are generally used as a basis for these agreements.

The third has proven to be problematic despite the existence of appropriate international conventions, most notably the TIR system. The latter provides guarantees for the duties and taxes that a transit cargo is liable for if it does not exit the country; TIR carnets[15] exist to document this coverage. The TIR carnets have been effective in facilitating transit movements between EU, Eastern Europe, and Central Asia and there are efforts underway to extend the system further into Asia. However, this system has been met with resistance from countries seeking to introduce their own systems of guarantees.[16]

So far, there have been two regional attempts to address these and other cross-border-related issues on a regional basis. The first is the ASEAN Framework Agreement on the Facilitation of Goods in Transit, which was signed in 1998. It included nine protocols that were to be individually approved. It contained annexes 1, 2, and 6, which address the designation of routes and crossing points; annexes 3 and 4 the restrictions on type, quantity, and technical requirements of vehicles crossing the borders; and annex 7 the customs transit regime. While four of the protocols were approved within 3 years of the initial signing, those concerning the routes and border crossings and the customs transit regime continue to be negotiated.

The second regional agreement is the Cross-Border Transit Agreement (CBTA) that covers the GMS countries. The objective is similar to that of ASEAN in that it seeks to develop simplified and consistent procedures for vehicles, cargo, and people crossing the borders between the member countries. Concretely, it hopes to eliminate the prevailing practice of requiring transshipment of cargo between trucks at the borders. The CBTA eschews protocols in favor of annexes covering specific issues

---

[15] The Transport Internationaux Routiers (TIR) carnet is a customs transit document that is used in the international transit of goods.

[16] Efforts to introduce a local version in Africa have not been successful. Efforts to introduce an alternative system in Southeast Asia have so far failed.

for facilitating cross-border movements; however, the outcome has been similar. Although most of the annexes have been agreed to, the four that pertain specifically to the movement of trucks and containers across the border are still in negotiation 6 years after the initial signing and 3 years after the agreement was revised to include Cambodia, Myanmar, and PRC. While there is growing pressure to approve the remaining annexes, it will still require several years before they can be fully implemented.

Border Management

Another important area of trade facilitation that would have significant impact on trade between South and East Asia is the integration of activities of the regulatory agencies operating on the border. These include the agencies involved in customs, inspection, quarantine, and security, whose activities include enforcement of sanitary, phytosanitary, and other controls for agricultural and food products and livestock, as well as safety standards for consumer goods and industrial equipment. There are other regulations related to restricted goods including drugs, arms, and ammunition, and hazardous material. Since it is not possible for all of these agencies to have full representation at the borders, it is generally left to customs to act as the first line of defense and to contract the other agencies when more specific inspection of shipments is required. The principal difficulties arise from the delays involved in inspections, especially where laboratory tests are required and the laboratories are located far from the border.

Several options are available to minimize the delays associated with these inspection activities. The CBTA has proposed a single-window approach in which all of the agencies are represented in some form at the border. This can take the form of a virtual presence through the use of ICT. The inspection requirements should be enumerated in an integrated database that also contains the duties and taxes for each type of commodity. This would be part of a website accessible to traders and transporters as well as the agencies. The information in the database would then be used to initiate communications between relevant agencies regarding inspection activities, and the status of the cargo would be tracked through messages between customs and other border management agencies. Alternatively, many of these inspection activities can be moved behind the border to a location where there are proper facilities for testing. This can be further improved by allowing inspections to be performed at the source or during the movement to the border.

In the case of transit cargo, border management has the additional task to monitor the incoming cargo until it exits the country. In many countries, communications between border crossings is limited and the tracking is limited to issuing and collecting permits at the point of entry. Monitoring can be improved by limiting the transit movement to a specific time. This involves noting the time of entry listed on the transit permit at the point of exit or, where possible, notifying the officials at the intended exit point prior of the expected time of arrival of the cargo. More intrusive approaches, such as convoys or global positioning system (GPS) tracking, are generally avoided because of the high costs of implementation and the additional staff requirements they would imply.

Conclusions

Trade between South and East Asia can be facilitated in three ways: (i) development of transport infrastructure, (ii) improvement in logistics services, and (iii) modification of border-crossing procedures. The development of infrastructure involves public sector investment to complete the linkages in the Northern Land Corridor, improving the cargo handling facilities in the Central Air Corridor airports and the Southern Ocean Corridors ports, and developing inland corridors providing connections to the Southern Ocean Corridor. This requires the introduction of integrated planning for multimodal corridors development and refinement of the public–private partnership arrangements for these investments.

Improvements in logistics services involve improvements in the responsiveness of the private sector to the demands of shippers. The policy environment should encourage competition in the provision of logistics services, and at the same time allow for the vertical integration of services. The latter will allow the formation of a second tier of integrated logistics service providers who can offer value-added services. Public sector support is also needed to develop privately operated facilities that will improve logistics services, including intermodal terminals, ICDs, bonded warehouses, and SEZs.

There are reforms in the border-crossing procedures that need to be sustained. The ongoing efforts are directed toward

- the simplification of cargo clearance and inspection procedures at the borders;
- the integration of the activities of the agencies involved in border management;
- the transfer of these procedures away from the border;
- the development of a regime for the movements of goods under custom bond; and
- the improvement and simplification of the inspection and certification procedures, particularly for food products.

Development of Infrastructure

The major infrastructure investment underway is the construction of the Asian Highway. The links for completing that portion of the Asian Highway essential for supporting trade between South and East Asia are estimated to cost about $3 billion. Many of these investments will be completed as part of the national programs of affected countries, but for links passing through less-populated areas external funding may be required. Even with adequate financial support, it is unclear how much traffic will be diverted to this corridor since it passes through unpopulated areas and much of the route is far from the major economic centers. However, it does provide an opportunity to open trade between the less developed areas in the southwestern PRC, northern Thailand, and northeastern India. It is unlikely that the infrastructure for this route will be completed within the next 10–15 years, but the essential portions of it could be operational within 5–10 years.

Efforts to develop the Asian Highway have so far produced very little in the way of infrastructure improvements, but this program has created a focal point for discussions about developing common procedures for border crossings. Without an international agreement that will expedite the movement of vehicles and cargo across borders on this corridor,[17] it may not be able to compete with the Southern Ocean Corridor in terms of time and cost savings.

The development of the Trans-Asian Railway would also require more substantial capital investment. More importantly, it will require rail yards at the intersections between different track gauges to transfer cargo efficiently between trains. Given the limited success of national railroads in capturing market share for domestic container movements, it is unlikely that the railway will be effective in competing with the Asian Highway for anything other than long-distance movement of bulk cargo. While the railway's north-south routes are more likely to be successful in capturing cargo—particularly those connecting the PRC to the Russian Federation and Singapore—there will be little demand for the east-west route.

Since the primary route for trade between South and East Asia will continue to be the Southern Ocean Corridor, it is important to continue investing in infrastructure that improves and expands access. This includes

---

[17] This implies developing protocols for temporary admission of vehicles and guarantee systems for the duties and taxes for which the cargo would be liable if it did not exit the country. Negotiations related to these routes have already succeeded in introducing standards for vehicles that would be allowed to cross the borders.

gateway seaports and airports and the multimodal corridors linking these gateways with major markets and production centers. Ongoing efforts to upgrade the national highway networks in Pakistan, India, Thailand, and PRC should provide efficient access to these gateways. However, Bangladesh, Nepal, and Bhutan will continue to have problems because of difficulties posed by topography, and the fact that Nepal and Bhutan are landlocked. Upgrading the national rail networks presents a more difficult problem because of high capital costs and declining modal share. In contrast, developing gateways is less difficult because of the increased roles of public–private partnerships for providing not only equipment and superstructure but also basic infrastructure. This strategy should ensure adequate capacity and throughput in the countries that have adopted it.

The problems of developing efficient multimodal corridors are less technical or financial than they are political. The planning, budgeting, and execution of public investment in transport infrastructure continues to be done by ministries, authorities, departments, or government corporations responsible for individual modes of transport. Recent efforts to establish inter-ministerial committees to address the development of intermodal corridors have provided the first step in developing a permanent capability for corridor development. These include initiatives by India to develop the Mumbai–Delhi freight corridor and by Pakistan to develop the Lahore–Karachi freight corridor. The PRC has tried to develop a multimodal corridor along the coast from Qingdao to Guangzhou.[18] ADB and other multinational lenders can adjust their lending practices to support this type of planning.

Logistics Services

To promote trade between South and East Asia in the short term, it will be necessary to develop efficient supply chains for the trade in products that are most likely to be successful. Included in this group is the trade in fresh and semiprocessed seafood and agricultural goods, parts and equipment, textiles, and intermediate goods. The logistics required are not substantially different from those used in trade with the rest of the world. As a result, most of the initiatives to facilitate Southeast Asian trade are consistent with initiatives currently being undertaken to promote international trade in general.

For the transport components of logistics, investment in infrastructure needs to be sustained, as does competition in the provision of transport services and cargo handling at the seaports, airports, and border crossings.

---

[18] There are also a number of useful examples of corridors in Europe and elsewhere in the world as discussed in a recent World Bank paper, TP-13.

There is a need to promote the further evolution of the public–private partnership arrangements through appropriate regulation.

The Southern Ocean Corridor is well served by a highly competitive container-shipping market and the quasi-perfect market conditions for bulk shipping. However, there are some constraints on feedering activities, such as India's treatment of feedering from Indian transshipment ports as cabotage. The Central Air Corridor will likewise benefit from a highly competitive airfreight industry, although access to this market can be improved through an increase in the use of fifth and sixth freedoms or negotiations toward an open skies policy. The Northern Land Corridor benefits as well from substantial competition in the domestic trucking industries of all countries. However, this competition is limited by current restrictions on cross-border movements of commercial vehicles, such as constraints on foreign vehicles entering a country as well as difficulties in securing a return load for multi-country long-haul movements. For railroads, they continue to operate as public monopolies and are primarily focused on passenger operations as they generally lack the commercial management necessary to attract a significant share of the freight transport market. Efforts to increase the role of the private sector in freight train operations and to increase the rail capacity allocated to freight traffic are prerequisites for any effort to develop competition in this mode.

Cargo-handling operations in the major ports have benefited from the transition from public monopoly to private operation, with a resulting increase in efficiency and capacity. However, many of the Asian countries have not yet addressed the problems of overstaffed national port authorities regulating and managing the ports. A similar concern has been expressed with regard to the concentration of private container terminal operators. However, competition among private container terminal operators has recently begun to thrive because of (i) the growing role of local operators, (ii) increasing competition among ports, and (iii) an increase in the size of ports, permitting multiple operators. Nevertheless, effective policies are required to ensure that both interport competition and cargo-handling efficiency continue to increase.

For non-transport activities, the logistics industry is almost entirely private and highly competitive throughout Asia. In nearly all cases, it is client-driven, focused on providing services rather than developing fixed assets. As such, it remains both flexible and innovative. The industry tends to be lightly regulated, as government control is largely limited to issues of safety and competitiveness. The industry has a made attempts at self-regulation but these are more often directed at limiting competition rather than improving standards. Improvement in the range of services offered and the quality of the services is achieved through competitive forces, where it is mostly industry leaders driving innovation. As such, there is limited role for the public sector in improving quality of service or promoting value-added services. Instead, this will occur in response to the demands of exporters and importers and through increasing competition between local and international logistics service providers. At present, the logistics service industry is highly fragmented both in terms of the size of individual firms and the range of services offered. It is anticipated that a second tier of service will develop with integrators offering a range of logistics services to meet the supply-chain needs, particularly of their larger clients. In addition, larger companies will spin off their supply-chain activities, creating specialized integrated logistics service providers.

Because logistics industry is a service industry and has relatively little interest in investing in fixed capital, the public sector can contribute to sector efficiency by providing land and the basic infrastructure for facilities that support logistics services. These include ICDs, truck terminals, multimodal freight terminals, and logistics hubs that are located within SEZs and customs-bonded areas.

Regulatory Constraints

There are some important conclusions that can be reached with regard to the role of logistics in promoting trade between South and East Asia. The first is that the basic concerns regarding facilitation of trade and transport between South and East Asia are the same as those that apply to trade and transport between these regions and North America and Europe. Where there are differences, they originate with differences in scale and degree of integration in both the production and retail sectors. While final goods dominate extra-Asian trade, the growth in trade between South and East Asia is expected to involve exchange in raw materials and intermediate goods. This is expected to grow not only because of similarities in the type of goods produced but also because of the trend toward spreading production along the supply chain to take advantage of differences in production costs and to undertake assembly in manufacturing locations closer to the end market.

Efforts to address trade facilitation have largely focused on customs reform. Most countries in South and East Asia are now signatories to the Kyoto convention for simplification and harmonization of customs procedures (1999) and have undertaken steps to implement the practices and procedures outlined in the convention. In most countries, this effort has been complemented by unilateral tariff liberalization and the simplification of the overall tariff regime through the reduction in the number of tariff categories and tariff bands.

The other important area for reform is risk management. This includes the development of risk profiling systems so as to limit physical inspections to shipments that have the greatest likelihood of anomalies. This has led to the establishment of green channels and gold card services, which is now being extended to more importers through post-clearance audits and computerization of the entire risk management process. The need for face-to-face contact during the payment of duties and certification of customs documents is also being eliminated through the use of electronic banking and electronic signatures.

The implementation of these reforms varies by country. Thailand, Malaysia, Japan, and Korea have come closest to completing the current round of reforms, while the PRC and India are halfway through the process, having initiated most of the necessary changes in their large international seaports and airports. However, the implementation of these improvements at the land borders is expected to require some time.

Even where the countries have been successful in reforming their own customs, considerable improvements in protocols and procedures are required to allow goods from other countries to move in transit. Effective transit regimes require

- a guarantee system for customs duties,
- simplification of the documentation for transit permits,
- techniques for securing cargo moving under customs bond,
- non-invasive methods for enforcing security at the border, and
- tracking systems for recording the entry and exit of transit cargo.

Efforts to develop a system similar to that of the European TIR carnet have so far been unsuccessful. It is necessary to determine the nature of the difficulties encountered in the application of alternative systems.

The use of ICT for trade facilitation has allowed simplification of cargo clearing procedures and documentation; it has also improved coordination among providers, users, and regulators of logistics services, leading to significant reductions in transit time and increases in reliability. Efforts to extend use of trade-related technologies within individual countries are progressing, albeit at a gradual pace.

Mobilizing Local Expertise

There is considerable diversity in the variety, efficiency, and complexity of the logistics services available in Asia, especially in Southeast Asia. Efforts to improve logistics services and supply chains between East and South Asia should take advantage of existing experience, particularly those made in the area of integrated logistics services; trade-related information systems; and organization of distribution centers in Singapore and, to a lesser extent, in Malaysia. The PRC has been a pioneer in developing SEZs and thus provides a useful business model for the development of these zones. India, on the other hand, has the most experience in developing a network of rail-based ICDs linked by rail services, while both India and Pakistan have begun developing modalities for planning intermodal corridors. Thailand has gone the furthest in customs reforms and in the development of national retail networks. Unfortunately, none of these countries has any significant experience with the operation of efficient land borders or the establishment of effective trade protocols and guarantees. For this, the EU's experience could prove to be illustrative.[19]

---

[19] While there have been significant efforts by the Greater Mekong Subregion (GMS) and Association of Southeast Asian Nations (ASEAN) to develop a similar capacity and there are some pilot projects underway, these do not get provide a useful working model for efficient movement of goods in transit across international borders.

APPENDIX TABLES

Table A6.1   Freight Rates for PRC and Thai Ports

	PRC Ports		Laem Chabang	
	Freight rates ($/TEU)	Transit time (days)	Freight rates ($/TEU)	Transit time (days)
Mediterranean (Marseilles)	2,500	19–30		
Northern Europe (Rotterdam)	2,240	26–32	1,800	26
East Coast US (Charleston)	3,250	26–35**		
West Coast US (Los Angeles)	1,800	12–18	3,200	
Middle East (Dubai/Salalah)	1,250–1,450	15–20	1,400	18
West Coast India (Mumbai)	2,500	18–30	1,600	13
East Asia (Yokohama)	520*	4		

PRC = People's Republic of China, TEU = 20-foot equivalent unit, US = United States, $ = US dollar.

* Subject to Bunker Adjustment Factor/Yen Appreciation Surcharge/Emergency Bunker Surcharge; Assumption: 10 TEU/month.
** Shorter times by landbridge or Panama Canal.

Source: Author's estimates.

Table A6.2 Typical Transit Times within Asia, Days

	Singapore	Laem Chabang	Xingang	Hong Kong, China	Shanghai	Chennai	Chittagong	Nhava Sheva	Colombo
Singapore		3	9	3	7	6	5	7	6
Laem Chabang	3		19	5	14	20	12		14
Xingang	12	15		9	5		22		16
Hong Kong, China	3	11	7		2	15	16	10	7
Shanghai	6	15		2		18	19	12	10
Chennai	7	16		12	15		13		2
Chittagong	5	9		16	14	8			4
Nhava Sheva	6			14	14				6
Colombo	6	15	20	8	10	2	16		

Source: Maersk Shipping.

Table A6.3   Hierarchical Port Structure

Port Status	Transship	Regional	Feeder
Pakistan		Karachi, Qasim	Gwadar
India		Mumbai, Chennai	Kolkata, Haldia, Visak, Kamdla, Mundra, Tuticorin, Cochin
Bangladesh			Chittagong
Sri Lanka	Colombo		
Thailand		Laem Chabang, Klong Toey	Songkla
Viet Nam			Ho Chi Minh City, Hai Phong, Da Nang
PRC	Hong Kong, China; Shanghai	Quingdao, Dahlian, Tianjin, Shenzhen, Guangzhou, Xiamen	
East Asia	Singapore, Kaoshiung Busan, Keelung	Tokyo, Yokohama, Inchon, Kwangyang	

PRC = People's Republic of China.

Source: Author's compilation.

Table A6.4   Container Facilities in South and East Asia

Location	Terminal	No. of Berths	Length (m)	Quay Cranes	TEUs (millions)	Draft
South Asia						
Jawaharlal Nehru	JNPT	3	680	8	1.30	13.5
	Maersk	3				
	NSICT	3	600	8	1.30	13.5
Kolkata		2	417	0	0.29	7.8
Haldia		2	440	7	0.14	
Chennai		4	885	4		11.0–12.0
Karachi		4				11.3– 14
Qasim		3	600	2		11.0–13.0
Chittagong		2	450			
Colombo	Jaya Container	6	1,292	14		12.0–15.0
	South Asia Gateway	3	940		2.20	15.0
	Unity Container	2		3		9.0–11.0
East Asia						
Laem Chabang		8	2,350	3	3.80	14.0
Ho Chi Minh City		9	1,311	10	2.30	10.0
Port Kelang	North Port	12	2,678		5.20	10.5–15.0
	West Port	7	2,033	44		
Tianjin		13	3,332			9.2–11.2
Hong Kong, China		24	8,530		23.00	15.5
Shanghai		24	4,461			9.0–10.5

JNPT = Jawaharlal Nehru Port Trust, m = meter, NSICT = Nhava Sheva International Container Terminal, TEU = 20-foot equivalent unit.

Source: Author's compilation.

Table A6.5   Country Data for Asian Highway

Country	Length (km)	Number of Lanes (km)					
		1	2	4	6	8	10
Bangladesh	1,774	–	1,131	30	27	–	–
PRC	26,699	69	19,220	1,369	6,067	16	–
India	11,432	46	10,656	747	18	24	–
Myanmar	3,003	1,531	1,299	93	80	–	–
Nepal	1,321	–	1,317	4	–	–	–
Sri Lanka	650	113	477	49	11	–	–
Pakistan	5,377	1	3,585	1,440	364	8	101
Thailand	5,108	1	1,879	2,980	56	112	101
Subtotal	55,364	1,761	39,564	6,712	6,623	160	101
		3%	71%	12%	12%	0%	0%

	Length (km)	Surface Type (km)				
		AC	CC	DBST	CG	G
Bangladesh	1,774	918	–	854	–	2
PRC	26,699	26,157	–	–	542	–
India	11,432	1,375	–	10,057	–	–
Myanmar	3,003	144	–	2,341	344	126
Nepal	1,321	342	–	953	26	–

continued next page

Table A6.5 continued

Surface Type (km)

		AC	CC	DBST	CG	G
Pakistan	5,377	2,147	–	3,230	–	–
Thailand	5,108	4,195	758	155	–	–
Subtotal	55,364	35,693	758	17,825	912	128
		64%	1%	32%	2%	0%

Surface Condition (km) and Toll Road (km)

		Good	Fair	Bad	Unknown	Toll	Free
Bangladesh	1,774	1,462	231	81	–	38	1,736
PRC	26,699	26,157	–	542	–	6,849	19,850
India	11,432	–	–	–	11,432	–	11,432
Myanmar	3,003	1,389	1,614	–	–	533	–
Nepal	1,321	916	371	34	–	–	1,321
Sri Lanka	650	415	177	58	–	–	650
Pakistan	5,377	631	1,602	3,144	–	488	4,889
Thailand	5,108	4,017	1,023	68	–	182	4,926
Subtotal	55,364	34,987	5,018	3,927	11,432	8,090	44,804
		63%	9%	7%	21%	15%	81%

AC = asphalt concrete, CC = cement concrete, CG = compacted gravel, DBST = double bituminous surface treatment, G = gravel, PRC = People's Republic of China, – = not available.

Source: United Nations Economic and Social Commission for Asia and the Pacific.

Table A6.6 Capital Investment Requirements for Asian Highway

Country	AH No	Section	Km	$ Mn
	2	Improvement of Sibi–Sariab	160	68
	2	Lakpass Tunnel		9
	2	Improvement of Dalbandin–Naushki section	167	34
	4	Dualization of Hassanabdal–Abbottabad–Mansehra	90	51
	7	Hub–Uthal	80	27
Pakistan	51	Improvement of Kuchlac–Zhob	306	60
	Other	Gwadar–Turbat–Hoshab–Awaran–Khuzdar section	650	271
	Other	Hyderabad–Mirpurkhas–Umarkot–Khokhropar	222	50
	Other	Sehwan–Dadu–Ratodero	199	103
	Other	National Highway N-70 (Multan–Muzaffargarh, Muzaffargarh Bypass, Muzaffargarh and Bewatta)	202	103
		Total	2,076	776
	1	Shillong–Dwaki	70	6
	2	India–India/Nepal border	10	1
India	2	Siliguri–Fulbari Mod–Border of Bangladesh 1	16	2
	43	Madurai–Dhanushkodi	19	2
		Total	115	11

continued next page

Table A6.6 continued

Country	AH No	Section	Km	$ Mn
	2	New Koshi bridge at Chatara and widening of bridges in Pathalaiya–Dhalkebar	170	31
Nepal	42	Naubise–Thankot (Tunnel)–Kathmandu–Kodari improvement and upgrading	48	24
	42	Kathmandu–Birgunj inland container depot link road	110	80
		Total	328	135
	41	Four laning of Daukandi–Chittagong	246	191
	41	Chittagong–Cox's Bazar–Ramu–Gundam	186	144
Bangladesh	2	Beldanga–Panchagarh	77	9
	41	Dasuria–Paksey–Kushtia	38	4
	41	Jhenaidah–Jessore	45	5
		Total	592	353
Bhutan	Potential	Phuentsholing–Thimphu double laning	179	60
		Total	179	60
	1	Myawadi (Border of Thailand)–Kawkareik	40	19
Myanmar	1	Monywa–Kalay/Kalewa	184	40
	2	Kyaing Tong–Takaw–Loilem–Taunggyi	450	23
		Total	674	82
Lao PDR	Link to 13	Oudomaxay–Muangkhua–Tai Chang	202	40
	Link to 11	Phiafai–Attapeu (NH18A)	114	23
		Total	316	63

continued next page

Table A6.6 continued

Country	AH No	Section	Km	$ Mn
Viet Nam	14	Ha Noi–Hai Phong Expressway (4–6 lanes)	100	410
	1	Bien Hoa–Vung Tau Expressway (4–6 lanes)	90	600
	16	Da Nang–Quang Ngai (4 lanes)	140	700
	1	Sai Gon–Long Thanh–Dau Day (4–6 lanes)	55	350
	14	Ha Noi–Lao Cai Expressway	290	600
	15	Vinh–Cau Treo rehabilitation	85	44
		Total	760	2,704
PRC	3	Jinghong–Mohan	343	1,160
	3	Jinghong–Daluo	60	60
	4	Kashi–Honqiraf	360	70
	42	Lhasa–Zhangmu	680	140
		Total	1,443	1,430
		Grand Total	6,483	5,614

AH = Asian Highway, km = kilometer, Lao PDR = Lao People's Democratic Republic, PRC = People's Republic of China, $ Mn = million of US dollars.

Source: Author's compilation.

Table A6.7   Comparison of Road and Rail Transport Time and Cost

From Shanghai to		Distance (km)	Rail Transport		Road Transport	
City	Province		CNY per TEU	Transit time (days)	CNY per 15-ton truck	Transit time (days)
Beijing		1,490	1,334	5	1,676	3
Lanzhou	Gansu	2,190	1,994	7	2,502	3
Shijiazhuang	Hebei	1,338	1,156	4	1,448	2
Taiyuan	Shanxi	~1,550	1,346	5	1,689	3
Wulumqi	Shaanxi	4,120	3,734	12	4,661	6
Xi'an	Henan	1,500	1,384	5	1,727	3
Yinchuan	Ningxia	1,310	2,426	8	3,035	4
Zhengzhou	Henan	1,090	914	4	1,143	2

CNY = yuan, km = kilometer, TEU = 20-foot equivalent unit.

Source: Author's compilation.

Table A6.8   Asian Highway Route Connecting New Delhi and Shanghai

Route AH	Province/State	City/Town Start Point	City/Town End Point	Number of Lanes (km)				
				Length	1	2	4	6
1	Haryana/Delhi	New Delhi	Palwal	61	0	0	61	0
1	Uttar Pradesh/Haryana	Palwal	Mathura	87	0	0	87	0
1	Uttar Pradesh	Mathura	Agra	49	0	30	19	0
1	Uttar Pradesh	Agra	Etawah	124	0	124	0	0
1	Uttar Pradesh	Etawah	Sikandara	75	0	75	0	0
1	Uttar Pradesh	Sikandara	Bara	33	0	33	0	0
1	Uttar Pradesh	Bara	Kanpur	25	0	25	0	0
1	Uttar Pradesh	Kanpur	Fatehpur	77	0	77	0	0
1	Uttar Pradesh	Fatehpur	Allahabad	110	0	110	0	0
1	Uttar Pradesh	Allahabad	Varanasi	145	0	145	0	0
1	Bihar/Uttar Pradesh	Varanasi	Mohania	71	0	71	0	0
1	Bihar	Mohania	Aurangabad	96	0	96	0	0
1	Bihar	Aurangabad	Dhobi	55	0	55	0	0
1	Bihar	Dhobi	Barhi	60	0	60	0	0
1	Bihar	Barhi	Gobinpur	127	0	127	0	0
1	West Bengal/Bihar	Gobinpur	Asansol	32	0	32	0	0

continued next page

Table A6.8 continued

Route AH	Province/State	City/Town Start Point	City/Town End Point	Number of Lanes (km)				
				Length	1	2	4	6
1	West Bengal	Asansol	Burdwan	127	0	127	0	0
1	West Bengal	Burdwan	Kolkata	113	0	113	0	0
1	West Bengal	Kolkata	Barasat	23	0	23	0	0
1	West Bengal	Barasat	Bangaon (India)	60	0	60	0	0
1	Meghalaya	Dwaki (Bangladesh)	Shillong	83	0	83	0	0
1	Meghalaya	Shillong	Jorabat	80	0	80	0	0
1	Assam	Jorabat	Nagaon	103	0	103	0	0
1	Assam	Nagaon	Dimapur	17	0	17	0	0
1	Nagaland	Dimapur	Kohima	76	0	76	0	0
1	Manipur/Nagaland	Kohima	Imphal	137	0	137	0	0
1	Manipur	Imphal	Tengnoupal	70	0	70	0	0
1	Manipur	Tengnoupal	Moreh (India)	40	8	32	0	0
1	Sagaing	Tamu (Myanmar)	Kalemyo	144	0	144	0	0
1	Magway/Sagaing	Kalemyo	Gangaw	180	180	0	0	0
1	Sagaing/Magway	Gangaw	Pale	135	135	0	0	0
1	Sagaing	Pale	Chaung-U	69	69	0	0	0
1	Sagaing	Chaung-U	Ondaw	33	0	33	0	0
1	Sagaing	Ondaw	Sagaing	24	0	24	0	0

continued next page

Table A6.8 continued

Route AH	Province/State	City/Town Start Point	City/Town End Point	Length	Number of Lanes (km)			
					1	2	4	6
1	Mandalay/Sagaing	Sagaing	Mandalay	19	0	19	0	0
1	Mandalay	Mandalay	Myittha	78	0	78	0	0
1	Mandalay	Myittha	Meiktila	89	0	89	0	0
14	Shan/Mandalay	Pyin U Lwin	Kyaykme	106	0	106	0	0
14	Shan	Kyaykme	Lashio	104	0	104	0	0
14	Shan	Lashio	Hsenwi	52	0	52	0	0
14	Shan	Hsenwi	Muse (Myanmar)	124	0	124	0	0
14	Yunnan	Ruili (PRC)	Luxi	106	0	106	0	0
14	Yunnan	Luxi	Baoshan	188	0	188	0	0
14	Yunnan	Baoshan	Dali	166	0	0	166	0
14	Yunnan	Dali	Chuxiong	178	0	0	178	0
14	Yunnan	Chuxiong	Kunming	197	0	157	40	0
3	Yunnan	Kunming	Qujing	130	0	0	0	130
3	Guizhou/Yunnan	Qujing	Guanling	341	0	341	0	0
3	Guizhou	Guanling	Anshun	76	0	76	0	0
3	Guizhou	Anshun	Guiyang	92	0	0	0	92
3	Guizhou	Guiyang	Majiang	143	0	143	0	0

continued next page

Table A6.8 continued

Route AH	Province/State	City/Town Start Point	City/Town End Point	Length	Number of Lanes (km)			
					1	2	4	6
3	Guizhou	Majiang	Kaili	55	0	55	0	0
3	Hunan/Guizhou	Kaili	Huaihua	306	0	306	0	0
3	Hunan	Huaihua	Shaoyang	251	0	251	0	0
3	Hunan	Shaoyang	Xiangtan	174	0	174	0	0
3	Hunan	Changsha	Liuyang	70	0	0	0	70
3	Jiangxi/Hunan	Liuyang	Wanzai	168	0	168	0	0
3	Jiangxi	Wanzai	Nanchang	184	0	184	0	0
3	Jiangxi	Nanchang	Yingtan	136	0	136	0	0
3	Jiangxi	Yingtan	Shangrao	106	0	106	0	0
3	Zhejiang/Jiangxi	Shangrao	Changshan	100	0	100	0	0
3	Zhejiang	Changshan	Quzhou	50	0	50	0	0
3	Zhejiang	Quzhou	Hangzhou	259	0	259	0	0
3	Shanghai/Zhejiang	Hangzhou	Shanghai	166	0	0	0	166
			Total	6,955	392	5,554	551	458

AH = Asian Highway, km = kilometer, PRC = People's Republic of China.

Source: United Nations Economic and Social Commission for Asia and the Pacific.

Table A6.9   Growth in Traffic for IATA Carriers

		Growth (%)	
	Number 2004	5-yr Trend	10-yr Trend
International			
Scheduled Services			
Freight Tons Carried ('000)	25,198	4.10	5.70
Freight (including Express)	126,598	4.60	5.70
All-Cargo Flights (included above)			
Kilometers Flown (millions)	1,225	7.40	7.40
Freight Tons Carried ('000)	12,429	7.70	9.30
Freight (including Express)	67,675	7.30	7.80
Domestic			
Scheduled Services			
Freight Tons Carried ('000)	14,310	4.00	3.30
Freight (including Express)	22,511	4.00	3.30
All-Cargo Flights (included above)			
Freight Tons Carried ('000)	8,923	5.60	4.80
Freight (including Express)	14,547	4.70	4.50
All Services			
Ton-Kilometers Performed (millions)	121,585	2.00	2.70

Source: International Air Transport Association (IATA).

Table A6.10   Characteristics of Major Regional Airports

Airport	Airport Tonnage 2004 ('000 tons)	Passengers (million)	No. of Runways	Total Runway Length ('000 meters)	Aircraft Movements ('000)
Karachi-QIAP		~ 6.0	2	6.60	~ 50.0
Bombay IA	402		2	6.41	155.0
Delhi IA	344		2	7.79	–
Chennai IA	186	19.5	2	5.69	67.0
Kolkata	70		2	6.03	43.0
Colombo IA*	147	2.8	1	3.35	25.0
Bangkok IA**	700	39.0	2	7.20	160.0
Singapore	1,780	32.4	3	10.75	–
Beijing IA	782	41.0	2	7.50	342.0
Shanghai Pudong	1,872	23.6	2	8.00	205.0
Hong Kong IA	3,400	40.3	2	7.60	263.4
Guangzhou	600	23.5	2	6.70	211.0

IA = International Airport, QIAP = Quaid-e-Azam International Airport, – = not available.

* 2002, ** Jan–Sep 2005.

Sources: International Air Transport Association, Airports Council International, www.caac.gov.cn, www.karachiairport.com/, http://en.wikipedia.org/wiki/, www.changiairport.com, www.hongkongairport.com, www.aci-asia.org/, www.airportsindia.org.in

Table A6.11   Distance between Major Airports, Miles

	KHI	BOM	DEL	MAA	CAL	CMB	BKK	SIN	SZB	PEK	SHA
Mumbai	543										
Delhi	664	707									
Chennai	1,180	642	1,090								
Kolkata	1,350	1,040	815	861							
Colombo	1,490	948	1,490	402	1,210						
Bangkok	2,300	1,870	1,810	1,370	999	1,480					
Singapore	2,940	2,430	2,580	1,820	1,790	1,710	897				
Kuala Lumpur	2,730	2,220	2,370	1,610	1,600	1,510	743	213			
Beijing	3,010	2,950	2,350	2,880	2,020	3,190	2,030	2,770	2,700		
Shanghai	3,300	3,130	2,640	2,900	2,110	3,140	1,770	2,380	2,320	662	
Hong Kong, China	2,970	2,670	2,340	2,320	1,530	2,510	1,060	1,650	1,570	1,220	770

BKK = Suvarnabhumi Airport, BOM = Chhatrapati Shivaji International Airport, CAL = Calcutta International Airport, CMB = Bandaranayake International Airport, DEL = Indira Gandhi International Airport, KHI = Karachi International Airport, MAA = Chennai International Airport, PEK = Beijing Capital Airport, SHA = Shanghai Airport, SIN = Changi Airport, SZB = Sultan Abdul Aziz Shah Airport.

Source: Author's compilation.

Table A6.12 Weekly Flights between Major Airports in South and East Asia

From	To	KHI	BOM	DEL	MAA	CMB	BKK	SIN	PEK	SHA	HKG
Karachi	Direct		2	0	0	2	5	2	1	0	2
	Indirect		44	46	42	35	42	46	43	45	44
Mumbai	Direct	1		47	20	4	7	6	0	1	4
	Indirect	40		0	22	34	43	30	41	36	34
Delhi	Direct	0	48		10	4	5	7	2	3	3
	Indirect	45	0		29	36	36	30	39	36	32
Chennai	Direct	0	19	10		6	5	5	0	0	0
	Indirect	43	24	31		36	38	29	35	31	32
Colombo	Direct	1	4	4	8		4	8	1	0	3
	Indirect	33	32	39	35		34	28	32	36	26
Bangkok	Direct	5	10	5	4	4		27	4	9	24
	Indirect	38	37	41	45	29		17	38	28	7
Singapore	Direct	2	6	5	5	8	25		8	8	16
	Indirect	43	30	41	32	23	17		25	25	17

continued next page

Table A6.12 continued

To / From		KHI	BOM	DEL	MAA	CMB	BKK	SIN	PEK	SHA	HKG
Beijing	Direct	1	0	4	0	1	4	8		40	39
	Indirect	41	38	39	34	29	22	28		0	0
Shanghai	Direct	0	1	3	0	0	9	9	32		31
	Indirect	38	39	31	34	31	22	26	0		7
Hong Kong,	Direct	2	7	4	0	3	23	16	38	31	
China	Indirect	36	28	29	31	28	10	14	0	8	

BKK = Suvarnabhumi Airport, BOM = Chhatrapati Shivaji International Airport, CAL = Calcutta International Airport, CMB = Bandaranayake International Airport, DEL = Indira Gandhi International Airport, HKG = Hong Kong International Airport, MAA = Chennai International Airport, PEK = Beijing Capital Airport, SHA = Shanghai Airport, SIN = Changi Airport.

Source: Amadeus.net

Table A6.13 Transit Time Flying Directly between Major Airports

From \ To	KHI	BOM	DEL	MAA	BKK	SIN	PEK	SHA	HKG	CMB
Karachi		1:50			5:00	6:00	6:20		9:00	5:20
Mumbai	1:40		1:55	1:45	4:15	5:20		12:05	8:00	2:20
Delhi		1:55		2:30	3:50	5:30	6:30	6:15	5:15	3:25
Chennai		1:45	2:30		3:00	4:05				1:20
Bangkok	5:00	4:00	4:00	3:15		2:20	4:30	4:10	2:45	3:15
Singapore	6:15	5:00	5:30	4:00	2:20		6:00	5:10	3:45	3:40
Beijing	7:30		6:45		4:30	6:00		2:00	3:30	9:05
Shanghai		12:15	6:30		4:20	5:15	1:50		2:40	
Hong Kong, China	9:00	8:00	5:30		2:40	3:40	3:10	2:25		7:05
Colombo	5:05	2:25	3:35	1:20	3:30	4:00	9:05		7:20	

BKK = Suvarnabhumi Airport, BOM = Chhatrapati Shivaji International Airport, CAL = Calcutta International Airport, CMB = Bandaranayake International Airport, DEL = Indira Gandhi International Airport, HKG = Hong Kong International Airport, MAA = Chennai International Airport, PEK = Beijing Capital Airport, SHA = Shanghai Airport, SIN = Changi Airport.

Source: Amadeus.net

Table A6.14   Top 30 Airports

Airport	Passengers (millions)	Increase (%)	Airport	Freight ('000 ton)	Increase (%)
Atlanta (ATL)	85.9	2.8	Memphis (MEM)	3,599	1.2
Chicago (ORD)	76.5	1.3	Hong Kong, China (HKG)	3,433	9.9
London (LHR)	67.9	0.8	Anchorage (ANC)	2,554	13.4
Tokyo (HND)	63.3	1.6	Tokyo (NRT)	2,291	(3.5)
Los Angeles (LAX)	61.5	1.3	Seoul (ICN)	2,150	0.8
Dallas (DFW)	59.2	(0.4)	Paris (CDG)	2,010	7.2
Paris (CDG)	53.8	5.0	Frankfurt (FRA)	1,963	6.7
Frankfurt (FRA)	52.2	2.2	Los Angeles (LAX)	1,938	1.3
Amsterdam (AMS)	44.2	3.8	Shanghai (PVG)	1,857	13.1
Las Vegas (LAS)	44.0	6.0	Singapore (SIN)	1,855	3.3
Denver (DEN)	43.4	2.6	Louisville (SDF)	1,815	4.3
Madrid (MAD)	41.9	8.4	Miami (MIA)	1,755	(1.4)
New York (JFK)	41.9	8.9	Taipei,China (TPE)	1,705	0.3
Phoenix (PHX)	41.2	4.3	New York (JFK)	1,661	(2.6)
Beijing (PEK)	41.0	17.5	Chicago (ORD)	1,546	4.8
Hong Kong, China (HKG)	40.3	9.7	Amsterdam (AMS)	1,496	2.0
Houston (IAH)	39.7	8.7	London (LHR)	1,390	(1.6)
Bangkok (BKK)	39.0	2.7	Dubai (DXB)	1,315	12.5
Minneapolis (MSP)	37.6	2.4	Bangkok (BKK)	1,141	7.8
Detroit (DTW)	36.4	3.2	Indianapolis (IND)	985	5.7
Orlando (MCO)	34.1	8.4	Newark (EWR)	950	(3.5)
Newark (EWR)	34.0	3.3	Osaka (KIX)	869	(2.1)
San Francisco (SFO)	32.8	2.0	Tokyo (HND)	799	3.2
London (LGW)	32.8	4.2	Beijing (PEK)	782	17.0

continued next page

Table A6.14 continued

Airport	Passengers (millions)	Increase (%)	Airport	Freight ('000 ton)	Increase (%)
Singapore (SIN)	32.4	6.8	Atlanta (ATL)	768	(10.8)
Philadelphia (PHL)	31.5	10.5	Guangzhou (CAN)	751	18.7
Tokyo (NRT)	31.5	1.3	Luxembourg (LUX)	743	4.2
Miami (MIA)	31.0	2.8	Dallas (DFW)	742	(0.1)
Toronto (YYZ)	29.9	4.5	Oakland (OAK)	673	0.0
Seattle (SEA)	29.3	1.7	Brussels (BRU)	661	5.2

( ) = figures in parentheses represent decrease in growth.

Source: Airports Council International.

Table A6.15   Major Features of Revised Kyoto Convention

General Features of Modern Customs Administration
- Maximum use of automated systems
- Risk management techniques (including risk assessment, selectivity)
- Pre-arrival information to drive programs of selectivity
- Electronic funds transfer
- Coordinated interventions with other agencies
- Ready availability of information on customs requirements
- A system of appeals in customs matters
- Formal consultative relationships with the trade

Technical Issues Addressed in the Annexes
- Temporary storage of goods
- Customs warehouses and free zones
- Customs warehouses
- Free zones
- Transit, transship, and carriage of goods coastwise
- Duty drawback and temporary admission
- Rules and documentary evidence of origin

Important Annexes
- E - the procedures for goods in transit and goods being transshipped
- F - both inward and outward processing
- G - temporary admission
- K - rules of origin

Source: Author's compilation.

7

REGIONAL INTEGRATION IN ASIA: THE ROLE OF INFRASTRUCTURE

Joseph Francois, Miriam Manchin, and Annette Pelkmans-Balaoing

Introduction

The rapid growth of intra-Asian trade, especially in the last couple of decades, represents both a marked shift in export orientation and an increasing integration of regional markets. In 2005, half of total Asian exports were destined for regional consumption, and a further rise can only be expected given the high growth rates of intraregional trade, peaking at 25% in 2004 (World Trade Organization [WTO] 2006). Against such a backdrop, the surge of regionalism in Asia today comes as no surprise. Nowhere in the world is the proliferation of regional integration arrangements (RIAs) more evident than in Asia today. As of September 2006, the individual East and South Asian countries considered in this study were involved in 301 free trade negotiations or signed agreements. While political and security motives are also influential, the economic imperative to further feed the market's appetite for more regional trade is clearly driving policy agents along the track toward free trade agreements (FTAs).

The reduction of most-favored nation (MFN) tariffs following the widespread unilateral liberalization in Asia in the 1990s, however, has narrowed the trade-enhancing space for preferential tariff arrangements. In Association of Southeast Asian Nations (ASEAN), for instance, products with preferential margins above 5% constitute 15% of total regional imports in 2001 and 13% in 2003 (Manchin and Pelkmans-Balaoing 2007a). Preferences are obviously more important among tariff-peak products, but the presence of nontariff barriers (NTBs) and complex rules of origin ensure that high tariff discounts do not erode the protection of politically sensitive products, not even within a limited regional market. This implies that the utility of FTAs as a means of expanding intraregional trade largely via tariff liberalization may be fast approaching its limits.

439

Negotiations are thus increasingly shifting toward the possible employ-ment of collective policy tools to reduce transaction costs, including those related to infrastructural constraints.[1] This may prove to yield more trade creation gains. A study conducted by the Asia-Pacific Economic Coopera-tion (APEC) on trade facilitation (1996), in fact, showed that economic benefits originating from trade facilitation measures could account for about 0.26% of real gross domestic product (GDP) for APEC members, compared to those from trade liberalization which could be in the magni-tude of 0.14% of real GDP. More recent efforts to quantify the trade and growth impact of trade facilitation measures only further strengthen and support these findings. A 2002 World Bank study considered four aspects of trade facilitation: ports, customs, regulations, and e-business, and found that increasing performance across the APEC region even halfway up the average could lead to a 10% increase in intraregional exports, with about half of that gain being due to increased efficiency in port logistics (Wilson et al 2004). Nordas and Piermartini (2004) focused on the link between quality of infrastructure and trade performance, and likewise drew evidence pointing to port efficiency as having the greatest impact on trade performance. The determinant role of infrastructure on overall trade costs have also been emphasized by Limao and Venables (2001), showing how poor infrastructure accounts for 40% of predicted transport costs for coastal countries and up to 60% for landlocked countries. In a study of trade, infrastructure, and transaction costs in selected Asian countries, De (2006) finds that differentials in transaction costs and infrastructure facilities indeed strongly determine regional trade flows and variations thereof. Trade elasticities with respect to reduction in transaction costs are in the neighborhood of 84%, while those related to improvement in infrastructure register high rates of 100% (exporting countries) and 180% (importing countries).

In this paper we further examine the trade and infrastructure nexus in East and South Asia, looking not only at how transaction costs and other institutional factors affect trade, but also at the role they play in explain-ing why trade does or does not occur between two partner countries. We are thus interested in the so-called threshold effects, thereby empha-sizing those cases where bilateral country pairs do not actually trade. Recent related work involving thresholds, zeros in bilateral trade, and

---

[1] Trade facilitation issues have long figured in various regional cooperation agen-da, however. Asia-Pacific Economic Cooperation (APEC), since its inception in 1989, for instance, has initiated trade facilitation projects among members, cul-minating in a trade facilitation action plan (TFAP) geared to reduce business transaction costs by 5% in 2003.

trade growth along extensive and intensive margins, includes Hummels and Klenow (2005), Evenett and Venables (2003), and Felbermayr and Kohler (2004).

Our results indicate that while the evidence on institutions is somewhat mixed, variation in infrastructure relative to the expected values for a given income cohort is strongly linked to exports. Indeed, sample variation in basic infrastructure (communications and transportation) explains substantially more of the overall sample variation in exports than does the trade barriers faced by developing countries.

The paper is organized as follows. A section examines the nature of infrastructure in Asia given our data and related literature. The data sources as well as the estimation framework are presented in the next section, the results of which are given in the succeeding section. To gauge the importance of infrastructure in regional trade, we further explore the trade cost equivalents of the infrastructure quality. The final section summarizes our results and concludes.

Infrastructure in the Asian Economies

Asia has witnessed a fast pace of infrastructural growth during the period covered by the data used in this paper. Average indexes for physical and communication infrastructure during the period 1998–2003 were calculated for Asia, European Union (EU), and United States (US), on freight of air transport (million tons per kilometer), number of fixed and mobile telephone subscribers (per 1,000 people), number of mobile phones (per 1,000 people), and the number of telephone mainlines (per 1,000 people). A comparison of Asia's performance vis-à-vis performances in the EU and the US in Table 7.1, however, reveals considerable scope for catch-up.

Within Asia, wide income disparities are mirrored by the qualitative and quantitative differentials in the region's infrastructure facilities. Table 7.2 reports some selected infrastructure indicators for East and South Asia, making evident the large gap between these subregions (Annex A7.1 provides further data on the evolution of infrastructure quality for individual countries).

To better assess the general quality of both physical and communications infrastructure, we constructed summary indexes using principal component analysis. This method allows us to combine several indicators of infrastructure quality (such as those presented in Table 7.2) into summary indexes that are not correlated with each other. Ideally, principal component analysis identifies patterns in data, and based on these patterns it reduces the number of dimensions of the data without a lot of loss of information. The process involves the generation of weights, which when applied to the individual values of infrastructure facilities per country allows us to extract the necessary summary index.

Table 7.1   Evolution of Communications and Physical Infrastructure

Region	Year	Air transport (million tons/kilometer)	Fixed phone subscribers (per 1,000 inhabitants)	Mobile phones (per 1,000 inhabitants)	Telephone mainlines (per 1,000 inhabitants)
Asia	1998	1,975	312	118	194
	1999	2,175	367	167	200
	2000	2,316	427	219	208
	2001	2,193	473	264	209
	2002	2,439	511	303	208
	2003	2,499	554	346	208
European Union	1998	1,709	826	280	546
	1999	1,819	1,004	446	557
	2000	2,064	1,222	649	573
	2001	1,956	1,351	775	575
	2002	2,015	1,407	831	575
	2003	2,069	1,442	899	549
United States	1998	25,758	907	252	655
	1999	27,292	970	310	660
	2000	30,166	1,054	389	664
	2001	27,920	1,121	451	671
	2002	31,762	1,134	488	646
	2003	34,206	1,164	543	621

Asia is the average of indexes for Australia; Bangladesh; Cambodia; People's Republic of China; Hong Kong, China; India; Indonesia; Japan; Lao People's Democratic Republic; Malaysia; Myanmar; New Zealand; Pakistan; Philippines; Republic of Korea; Singapore; Thailand; and Viet Nam. Cambodia is not included in the air transport figures.

Source: World Bank, *World Development Indicators* and the authors' own calculations.

Table 7.2 Comparative Infrastructure Indicators in East and South Asia

Major Access Indicators	East Asia	South Asia
Electricity (% of population with access to network)	88	43
Roads (% of rural population living within 2 km of an all-season road)	95	65
Teledensity (fixed-line and mobile subscribers per 1,000 people)	357	61

km = kilometer, % = percent.

Compiled from *World Bank (2005): Infrastructure* and the *World Bank: A Progress Report, Infrastructure Vice-Presidency*, 6 September.

Table 7.3. Principal Components Weighting Factors for Infrastructural Indexes

Variable	Component 1	Component 2
Log of air transport	0.0534	0.6629
Log of fixed and mobile telephone subscribers	0.4626	(0.0378)
Log of mobile phones	0.3016	0.1661
Log of roads paved	0.3470	(0.1105)
Log of telephone mainlines	0.4595	(0.0466)
Log of telephone mainlines in the city	0.4356	(0.0069)
Log of telephone mainlines per employee	0.4097	0.0822
Log of roads total network	(0.0545)	0.7144
Cumulative proportion	0.5670	0.7714

( ) = negative value.

Source: Authors' calculations.

The first and the second components of the principal component analysis using the full sample[2] are shown in Table 7.3. These first two components reflect between 70% and 77% of variation in the sample. We then

---

[2] See a detailed description on the sample in Data and Methodology, on page 447.

Table 7.4   Infrastructure Components for Asian Economies

	1st infrastructure component proxying communication infrastructure	2nd infrastructure component proxying physical infrastructure
Japan	22.231	8.881
Hong Kong, China	21.754	0.847
Korea, Republic of	18.100	3.517
Singapore	17.733	1.148
Australia	10.356	5.928
New Zealand	10.342	2.139
Malaysia	5.409	2.463
Thailand	3.248	2.393
Indonesia	0.787	3.479
Philippines	0.665	2.905
Pakistan	0.345	2.543
India	0.339	5.375
Viet Nam	0.234	1.533
Lao People's Democratic Republic	0.055	0.358
Myanmar	0.044	0.497
Cambodia	0.040	0.744
Bangladesh	0.037	2.329

Source: Authors' calculations.

utilize these weights to construct two types of infrastructure indexes: the first pertaining to communication facilities, and the second to the physical transport system.

The average values of these two infrastructure measures for the period 1998–2003 are presented separately in Table 7.4.[3] The Asian countries in the table are ranked based on the first infrastructure component, which proxies the quality of communication infrastructure. The most developed countries in the region in terms of their communication infrastructure are

[3] See Annex 7.2 which presents the same infrastructure data for all Asian countries in our sample over the period 1998–2003.

Japan and Hong Kong, China followed by Republic of Korea (henceforth Korea) and Singapore. Most of the countries that have good-quality communication infrastructure also possess good-quality physical infrastructure. The disparity in the quality of infrastructure between countries is quite evident here, with the imbalance being more pronounced in communication facilities.

Data and Methodology

When examining the global pattern of bilateral trade flows, one striking feature of the landscape is that many country pairs do not trade. In our full sample, including 19 Asian economies and other non-Asian countries,[4] 42% of importer-exporter pairings had zero bilateral trade. Thus, apart from analyzing the effects of different factors on worldwide trade, we also attempt to unravel the factors that could explain why trade does not occur at all. While some factors might be expected to be important in the decision on how much to import, the same factors may be differentially important when the trader decides whether he or she will import at all. And yet, these two decisions clearly are linked. Only if the trader decides to import can trade volumes be observed and hence examined. Analyzing the determinants of trade flows without taking into account potential trade that does not take place between country pairs may bias results. At a minimum, unobserved trade may contain information about the factors driving bilateral trade relationships.

In this section we elaborate upon our estimation strategy. This involves specifying a sample selection model. Employing a sample selection model allows us to take account of the censoring process that leads to zero or missing bilateral trade flows. More precisely, in our estimating framework the outcome variable (the dependent variable in the second stage equation) is only observed if the defined selection criterion is met. In our case, the amount of trade can only be observed if trade occurs at all. We therefore employ sample selection estimation, combining the analysis of the probability of trade flows with the analysis of trade volumes. (Similarly, Felbermayr and Kohler [2004] employ a Tobit estimator to examine bilateral zeros).

Data

We work with a panel of bilateral trade, trade policy, geographic characteristics, and income data spanning 1988–2002. Our trade and tariff data were obtained from the United Nations (UN)/World Bank World Integrated Trade Solution (WITS) system. The countries included in the sample are

---

[4] See the list of all countries included in our sample in Annex A7.3.

listed in annex A7.3.[5] There are several country combinations for which trade is not reported. Following the recent literature, we assume that these missing observations from the database represent zero trade (Coe et al 2002, Felbermayr and Kohler 2004, Santos and Tenreyro 2006). We use import data as it is likely to be more reliable than export data since imports constitute a tax base and governments have an incentive to track import data. Whenever import data was missing we used mirrored export data if it was available (this represented only half a percentage point of the observations). Trade data is deflated using the reporter country's GDP deflator. Income and population are taken from the *World Development Indicators* database. Geographic data, together with dummies for same language and colonial links, are taken from Clair et al (2004).[6] The distance data is calculated following the great circle formula, which uses latitudes and longitudes of the relevant capital cities.

We are ultimately interested in the role of infrastructure and we also consider the importance of institutions. Our data include indexes produced by the World Bank for infrastructure, and by the Fraser Institute for institutions. To measure infrastructure, we have taken data from the *World Development Indicators* database. This includes data on the percentage of paved roads out of total roads, on the number of fixed and mobile telephone subscribers (per 1,000 people), on the number of telephone mainlines (per 1,000 people), on telephone mainlines in largest city (per 1,000 people), telephone mainlines per employee, mobile phones (per 1,000 people), and freight of air transport (million tons per kilometer). Interpolation is used for years where no data was available.

The institution indexes are from the Economic Freedom of the World database.[7] These indexes are themselves based on several sub-indexes designed to measure the degree of economic freedom in five areas: (i) size of government (expenditures, taxes, and enterprises); (ii) legal structure and protection of property rights, (iii) access to sound money (inflation rate, possibility to own foreign currency bank accounts); (iv) freedom to trade internationally (taxes on international trade, regulatory trade barriers, capital market

---

[5] While trade data are available for a wide range of country pairs, the available tariff data are more limited. For this reason, we utilize a standard World Integrated Trade Solutions (WITS) procedure of matching the nearest adjacent year to represent otherwise missing tariff data. Interpolation is then used for wider gaps. A further complication is when tariff data are never reported for a country pair. To obtain an approximate tariff value applicable between these country pairs, we use the average applied tariff for the reporting countries for a given year.

[6] Available at www.cepii.fr/anglaisgraph/bdd/distances.htm

[7] Available at www.freetheworld.com/download.html.efw

controls, difference between official exchange rate and black market rate); and (v) regulation of credit, labor, and business. Each index ranges from 0 to 10, reflecting the distribution of the underlying data. Notionally, a low value is bad, and a higher value is good. We work with indexes for 1985, 1990, 1995, 2000, 2001, and 2002, with interpolated values for years without values.

Since the institutional indexes are highly correlated, we have used again principal component analysis to produce a set of summary indexes. The results are reported in Table 7.5. From these results, we take the first two components to produce two institutional indexes. These reflect 70–77% of variation in the sample. From these weights, we can interpret the first institutional index as measuring general correspondence with the market-oriented legal and institutional orientation flagged by the Fraser indexes (in a sense the correspondence to the Anglo–US socioeconomic model). The second institutional index then measures less interventionist systems with lower taxes and more market-friendly regulations (deviations toward the Anglo–US social model).

Table 7.5   Principal Components Weighting Factors of Institutional Variables

Institutions Variable	Component 1	Component 2
Size of government	(0.1893)	0.7096
Legal system property rights	0.6728	(0.1431)
Sound money	0.3245	0.3724
Freedom to trade internationally	0.6203	0.0401
Regulation	0.1466	0.5794
Cumulative proportion	0.3485	0.6966

( ) = negative value.

Source: Authors' calculations.

The Empirical Model

We work with Heckman's selection model (Heckman 1979, Greene 2003), where we estimate the probability of trade occurring jointly with the determinants of the level of trade using maximum likelihood methods. This is based on the following two latent variable submodels:

$$M_1 = \alpha'X + u_1 \tag{1}$$

$$M_2 = \beta'Z + u_2 \tag{2}$$

where X is a k-vector of regressors, Z is an m-vector of regressors, and u1 and u2 are the error terms which are jointly normally distributed, independently of X and Z, with zero expectations. The variable M1 is only observed if M2 > 0. The variable M2 takes the value of one if M1 is observed, while it is 0 if the variable M1 is missing. In our regressions, M1 is the value of imports, while M2 is a dummy variable taking the value one if trade occurs while zero otherwise. The first equation shows how the value of imports is affected by different factors, while the second gives some insight into why trade occurs at all between two partner countries.

In specifying the underlying structure of equation (1), or identically the right-hand side variables that make up X, we follow the gravity-model based literature. (See Evenett and Keller 2002, Anderson 1979, Anderson and Marcoullier 2002, Anderson and van Wijncoop 2003, and Deardorff 1988). These can be interpreted as a reflection of first-order conditions given an equilibrium dataset for goods trade. Interpreted this way, the gravity equation maps relative variations in bilateral trade flows to the determinants of relative variations in price. Price determinants in the empirical literature include bilateral variables like tariffs, geographic distance, as well as country-specific factors for both importer and exporter. At a macroeconomic level, models of bilateral trade based on constant elasticity of substitution (CES) preferences, like the Obstfeld-Rogoff model, lead immediately to such a relationship (Obstfeld and Rogoff 1995). So do CES-based multisector models based on either firm or national product differentiation (Hertel 1997). In formal terms, if we start with CES preferences defined over r regions as in equation (3)

$$Q = \left[\sum_{i=1}^{r} \alpha_i M_i^\phi \right]^{1/\phi} \qquad 1 > \phi > 0 \tag{3}$$

then it follows immediately from first-order conditions that import demand will be as defined by equation 4

$$M_i = Q \left(\frac{\alpha_i}{P_i} \right)^\sigma P^{\sigma-1} \tag{4}$$

where $\sigma = 1/(1-\phi)$. Similarly, under monopolistic competition with firm level differentiation and standard assumptions about symmetry and large group competition (Francois and Roland-Holst 1997), then with nr firms located in each of r regions, the CES aggregator can be written as in equation (5):

$$Q = \left[\sum_{i=1}^{r} \alpha_i n_i \bar{x}_i^{\phi} \right]^{1/\phi} = \left[\sum_{i=1}^{r} \left(\alpha_i n_i^{1-\phi} \right) M_i^{\phi} \right]^{1/\phi} = \left[\sum_{i=1}^{r} \gamma_i M_i^{\phi} \right]^{1/\phi} \qquad (5)$$

In equation (5), the term reflects a combination of CES weights and number of firms, aggregated by country, while $\bar{x}_i$ is the average quantity consumed from each firm in a region. The number will be fixed or given in a particular cross-section, as we are then working with an actual (particular) market outcome. A comparison of equations (3) and (5) should make it clear that in both cases we can work with equation (4). Starting with equation (4), if we take logs we have the following representation of import demand:

$$\ln M_i = \ln Q + \sigma \ln \alpha_i - \sigma \ln P_i + (\sigma - 1) \ln P. \qquad (6)$$

Defining the free on board (FOB) price from country i as P_i^*, then the landed or cost, insurance, or freight (CIF) price will then be

$$P_i = P_i^* (1+\tau) G. \qquad (7)$$

In equation (7), the term τ represents trade taxes, while the term G represents factors linked to the cost of trade, such as administrative burdens, and also transport and communications costs linked to physical infrastructure and physical distance. We can make a substitution of equation (7) into equation (6) to then get the basic gravity equation:

$$\ln M_i = \ln Q_j + \sigma \ln \alpha_{i,j} - \sigma \ln P_i^* - \sigma \ln(1+\tau_{i,j}) + \sigma \ln G_{i,j} \qquad (8)$$
$$= D_j + D_i - \sigma \ln(1+\tau_{i,j}) - \sigma \ln G_{i,j}$$

In arriving at the final version of equation (8) we have introduced indexing by source and destination, while also imposing similar preferences (i.e., similar CES weights) across importers with respect to exporters. Importer and exporter effects (our dummy variables Di and Dj) sweep up a range of country specific effects, like free-on-board (FOB) price, the linkage between income level and total demand Q, and the linkage in firm level differentiation models between size of total output in a country and the number of firms included in the term. Note that when we interpret the gravity model as following from first-order conditions, we can hold these various country-specific effects as fixed as we are working with data reflecting a particular set of actual market outcomes. This lets us focus on the determinants of bilateral variations in import demand. For this reason, an extremely reduced-form gravity model can be useful for estimating trade-cost related effects linked to variables like distance, customs union membership, and bilateral tariff rates. When we replace the summary exporter and importer dummies (as we will do here) by explicit measures of country specific variables like GDP, country size, governance, infrastructure, and the like, we are then also able to quantify their impact on trade flows as well.

Equation (8) is relatively general, and is used in much of the current literature. This includes Mtys (1997) and Francois and Woerz (2006). For our purposes, however, we cannot use both fixed importer and exporter effects in our panel regressions. This is because we want to work with time-varying country-specific variables related to institutions and infrastructure, which precludes the use of time-varying country dummies. Instead, we include time- and reporter-(importer) country-specific dummies.[8] This forces us to include variables that are likely to be important determinants of the reduced-form exporter effects dummies in equation (8). From the gravity literature, we expect trade flows to be a function of importer and exporter size and income, as well as of determinants of bilateral trade costs like distance and tariffs. We also include variables of interest for the present exercise.

These are measures of infrastructure and institutional aspects of importers and exporters that we expect to impact on trading costs. In terms of our sample selection model, we specify the following:

$$
\begin{aligned}
\ln M_{i,j,t} = \beta_0 &+ \beta_1 p\_pcGDP_{j,t} + \beta_2 r\_pcGDP_{j,t} + \beta_3 pPOP_{j,t} \\
&+ \beta_4 rPOP_{i,t} + \beta_5 T_{i,j,t} + \beta_6 dist_{i,j} + \beta_7 landlocked_i. \\
&+ \beta_8 comlang\_ethno_{i,j,t} + \beta_9 colony_{i,j} \\
&+ \beta_{10} INF1_{j,t} + \beta_{11} INS1_{j,t} + \beta_{12} INF2_{j,t} \\
&+ \beta_{13} INS2_{j,t} + u_1
\end{aligned}
\tag{9}
$$

---

[8] Since for several countries the indexes measuring institutional quality or infrastructure quality do not change importantly during the period, to avoid multicollinearity we include reporter-fixed effects and do not include partner-fixed effects.

and for the selection estimation we assume that Mi,j,t is observed when we have

$$
\beta_0 + \beta_1 p\_pcGDP_{j,t} + \beta_2 r\_pcGDP_{j,t} + \beta_3 pPOP_{j,t} \tag{10}
$$
$$
+ \beta_4 rPOP_{i,t} + \beta_5 dist_{i,j} + \beta_6 landlocked_i
$$
$$
+ \beta_7 comlang\_ethno_{i,j} + \beta_8 colony_{i,j}
$$
$$
+ \beta_9 INF1_{j,t} + \beta_{10} INS1_{j,t} + \beta_{11} INF2_{j,t}
$$
$$
+ \beta_{12} INS2_{j,t} + u_1 > 0
$$

In equation (10), u1 has correlation ρ. Equation (10) assesses the determinants of the bilateral trade and shows the main factors influencing the amount of trade, given trade occurred between the two trading partners. Equation (11) sets out the selection criteria and provides information on the factors that determine whether or not we observe trade between country pairs.

Table 7.6 Regression Model Variable Description

ln p_pcGDP	log of per capita GDP of partner
ln r_pcGDP	log of per capita GDP of reporter
ln pPOP	log of population of partner
ln rPOP	log of population of reporter
ln T	log of tariff: (1+t)
ln dist	the log of distance (km, great circle method)
landlocked	landlocked partner
comlang_ethno	shared linguistic/cultural heritage
colony	reporter and partner had colonial relations
ln INF1	partner infrastructure index 1
ln INS1	partner institution index 1
ln INF2	partner infrastructure index 2
ln INS2	partner institution index 2

GDP = gross domestic product, km = kilometer.

Source: Authors' compilation.

All of our right-hand-side variables are summarized in Table 7.6. Mi,j,t is country i's imports from country j at time t. As a proxy for market potential, POP is included for partner (exporter) and reporter countries, as well as per capita income pcGDP. These are standard gravity variables, as is distance *dist* and tariffs T. For bilateral import protection, we use applied tariffs, $\ln T_{ijt} = \ln(1+\tau_{ijt})$, where τ_{ijt} indicates the applied tariff rate offered by importer i to exporter j in period t. As reporter-specific fixed effects (non-time-varying) are included in the regressions and these are highly correlated with the tariff data, we regressed the log of the tariffs on the reporter dummies and retained the residuals. These residuals are used for the regressions and provide a measure of the effects of bilateral tariffs given other reporter specific characteristics. Distance is well established in the gravity equation literature (see for example Disidier and Head 2003, and Anderson and van Wijncoop 2003). The dummy landlocked takes the value of one if the importing country is landlocked and zero otherwise. Landlocked countries are expected to have higher transportation costs than countries with similar characteristics not being landlocked. Limão and Venables (2001) estimate that a representative landlocked country has transport costs approximately 50% greater than does a representative coastal economy.

To capture historical and cultural linkages between trading partners several zero-one type dummy variables are included in the estimating equation. The variable *colony* takes the value of 1 if the exporting country j was a colony of the partner country i. A separate dummy, *comlang_ethno*, captures whether the traders of the two partner countries can speak the same language or generally share the same linguistic heritage.

Since both the factor proxying institutional quality of the partner country and the factor measuring the availability of infrastructure are highly correlated with income per capita and population, we regress our indexes against per capita income and population and take the residuals as representative of deviations from income-conditional expected values for each of the four indexes.

$$\ln INDEX_{k,j,t} = \alpha_{k,0} + \alpha_{k,1} pcGDP_{j,t} + \alpha_{k,2} \ln POP_{j,t} + e_{j,t}, k = 1.4 \qquad (11)$$

These deviations ej,t then correspond to the index values in equations (10) and (11). Ordinary least-squares (OLS) estimates of equation (12) are reported in Table 7.7. Both the first infrastructure variable, mapping to communications infrastructure, and the second variable, capturing physical transportation, are highly correlated with income. Roughly half of the variations in the institutional variables can be represented by income levels.

Table 7.7   OLS Regressions of Principal Components on GDP per Capita

	Infrastructure 1	Infrastructure 2	Institution 1	Institution 2
lGDP95 percapita	1.198 (0.018)***	0.293 (0.008)***	0.648 (0.011)***	0.187 (0.013)***
lpPOP	0.079 (0.016)***	0.516 (0.007)***	0.039 (0.011)***	-0.024 (0.013)*
Constant	-9.609 (0.204)***	-7.001 (0.092)***	-5.11 (0.141)***	-0.85 (0.174)***
Observations	2015	2015	1766	1766
R-squared	0.69	0.76	0.67	0.11

GDP = gross domestic product, OLS = ordinary least-squares.

Standard errors in parentheses, * significant at 10%; ** significant at 5%; *** significant at 1%.

Source: Authors' estimates.

Results

Estimation results are reported in Table 7.8 where we report marginal effects from ML-based Heckman selection model regressions. For the full sample, the communications infrastructure (INF1) is significant with the expected sign. This holds both for the first equation (probability of trading or not) and for the second equation (the value of trade given that trade does occur). Again, there is a broad correspondence with priors. Transport infrastructure matters significantly, both for trade volumes and for the probability that trade occurs at all. The quality of the general governance has a positive effect on both trade and the probability that trade occurs. Moreover, countries with lower degrees of government intervention in the economy have higher exports than otherwise. The economic magnitudes of these effects are actually quite significant, as we will further investigate shortly.

In the remaining columns of the table, we turn to various sample splits on our full sample. The aim is to ascertain the extent to which institutions and infrastructure could impact on trade flows at the margin, depending on the level of development. The second column of Table 7.8 focuses on South exports to the North, the third on least-developed country (LDC) exports to the North, and the last on South–South trade. The exporters in the last three sets of results are therefore restricted to low and lower-middle-income countries according to World Bank definitions, and hence exclude high-income countries. The importers exclude low and lower-

Table 7.8 Regression Results

Variable	Full Sample		North–South		North–LDC		South–South	
	OLS	Probit	OLS	Probit	OLS	Probit	OLS	Probit
lpGDP95pop	1.068***	0.114***	1.077***	0.052***	0.061	0.019	0.592***	0.154***
	-0.004	-0.001	-0.012	-0.002	-0.058	-0.014	-0.006	-0.002
lrGDP95pop	2.611***	-0.032***	0.799***	-0.033*	0.694***	0.235***	2.012***	-0.066***
	-0.051	-0.008	-0.126	-0.013	-0.024	-0.006	-0.057	-0.014
lppop	1.021***	0.100***	1.118***	0.076***	0.725***	0.171***	0.564***	0.164***
	-0.004	-0.001	-0.009	-0.001	-0.023	-0.006	-0.005	-0.001
lrpop	1.333***	-0.348***	0.43	-0.285***	0.597***	0.094***	3.357***	-0.519***
	-0.115	-0.023	-0.257	-0.035	-0.012	-0.002	-0.143	-0.039
ldist	-1.311***	-0.127***	-1.335***	-0.069***	-0.865***	-0.085***	-0.909***	-0.193***
	-0.007	-0.002	-0.017	-0.003	-0.043	-0.01	-0.009	-0.003
partnerlandlocked	-0.259***	-0.031***	-0.471***	-0.028***	-0.415***	-0.078***	-0.071***	-0.051***
	-0.016	-0.003	-0.031	-0.005	-0.049	-0.012	-0.018	-0.005
comlang_ethno (d)	0.618***	0.033***	0.605***	0.040***	0.619***	0.130***	0.381***	0.117***
	-0.016	-0.003	-0.032	-0.004	-0.066	-0.012	-0.019	-0.005
colony (d)	0.372***	-0.142***	0.489***	-0.139***	1.025***	0.175***	0.516***	-0.360***
	-0.046	-0.018	-0.101	-0.032	-0.167	-0.058	-0.034	-0.022

continued on next page

Table 7.8 continued

Variable	Full Sample		North–South		North–LDC		South–South	
	OLS	Probit	OLS	Probit	OLS	Probit	OLS	Probit
Partner_einfr	0.176***	0.038***	0.183***	0.031***	0.02	0.030***	0.061***	0.053***
	-0.006	-0.001	-0.012	-0.002	-0.031	-0.008	-0.007	-0.002
Partner_einst	0.202***	0.018***	0.048**	-0.008**	0.183***	0.023*	0.088***	0.055***
	-0.008	-0.002	-0.017	-0.003	-0.041	-0.009	-0.01	-0.003
Partner_einfr2	0.178***	0.057***	0.334***	0.005	0.04	0.051***	0.081***	0.075***
	-0.01	-0.002	-0.019	-0.003	-0.054	-0.014	-0.011	-0.003
Partner_einst2	0.171***	0.033***	0.287***	0.055***	-0.303***	0	-0.013	0.058***
	-0.006	-0.001	-0.013	-0.002	-0.046	-0.011	-0.007	-0.002
Tariffs	-0.942***		-1.197***		-2.901***		-0.770***	
	-0.079		-0.211		-0.376		-0.076	
Observations	209,528	209,528	50,266	50,266	13,674	13,674	127,697	127,697

LDC = least-developed country.

Source: Authors' calculations. Marginal effects are presented in the table. Standard errors in parentheses. significant at 10%; ** significant at 5%; *** significant at 1%.

middle-income countries in the second and third sets of results, high income in the fourth. For developing countries overall, the message is again that infrastructure, both physical and communications, matters.[9]

General governance has a positive effect on trade, and a smaller presence by the state in the economy of the exporter does increase exports somewhat. However, the governance result changes to some extent for the poorest countries. We will explore this point further when we develop interaction terms. An important point to make at this juncture is that relative to the average level for its income cohort, increased regulation and size of government improved performance for LDCs. This points to an undersupply of government services at the lowest income levels in the sample. This is further manifested when we turn to the South–South sample split, where we find that the involvement of the state in the economy has an ambiguous impact on trade. An activist government positively influences the probability of trading, but affects export values negatively. Then again, the positive impact of infrastructure is consistent all throughout our sample. It is a significant determinant of trade both for the probit results, and for the observed trade volumes.

If we move from statistical significance to economic relevance, what do our coefficient estimates tell us? We address this question in Table 7.9. The table reports estimated percentage variation in expected trade related to a one-standard deviation variation in infrastructure and institutions around mean values. Values are normalized (and so can be gauged as rough measures of the contribution to overall sample variation in exports, measured by the coefficient of variation.) In general, the combination of institutional and infrastructure variation is much more important to the pattern of bilateral trade volumes than is bilateral protection. In the North–South sample split, for example, infrastructure variation implies marginal variations in the volume of trade of roughly 11% around the mean for communications and 7% for transport, compared to 2% for tariffs. For the LDCs, transport is more important than communications linkages. For the North–LDC sample, however, it is tariffs that are more determinant, although even here the combined effect of infrastructure and institutions implies 2.5 times more variation in the sample than those associated with tariff deviations. Turning finally to South–South trade, tariff and infrastructure effects are roughly similar to those observed in the full sample split.

---

[9] This confirms the pioneering results of Boatman (1992). Boatman found that not only general export levels, but also the technology composition of exports, hinges critically on the quality of the telecommunications system. In a world with globally integrated production systems, this result is intuitively appealing.

Table 7.9 Contributions of Variations in Infrastructure and Institutions to Overall Variation in Expected Exports

	Full Sample	North–South	North–LDC	South–South
ln INF1	0.09	0.11	0.05	0.11
ln INF2	0.04	0.07	0.11	0.07
ln INS1	0.06	0.02	0.11	0.08
ln INS2	0.1	0.13	0.05	0.05
ln T	0.05	0.02	0.12	0.04
coefficient of variation for exports	1.3	1.15	2.88	3.14

LDC = least-developed country.

Note: calculated using estimated coefficients and one standard deviation in variable, for marginal effects on E(ln(M)).

To further understand what is driving the differences detected in the results from the various sample splits, we conduct a full sample regression that includes an interaction term for each index (INF1, INF2, INS1, INS2) with respect to per capita income. Table 7.10 reports the corresponding results, while the associated marginal effects are shown in Figures 7.1 and 7.2. Given the combination of level and interaction effects, and variations in sign, it is hard to interpret the results without some knowledge of the range of income linked to the coefficient estimates. For this reason, in Figures 7.1 and 7.2 we plot estimated marginal effects from the coefficients reported in Table 7.10 linked to variations in institutions and infrastructure. Given the underlying model, these marginal effects can be interpreted as variations relative to the mean value at a given income level. In other words, they quantify the observed improvement in export performance when a country has better transport infrastructure, for example, relative to other countries at the same income level.

From the figures, variations in basic transportation are much more important at low-income levels in explaining variations in trade performance than at higher-income levels. The opposite holds for communications, which grow increasingly important, particularly as a country reaches the middle-income range. We also get a mixed message with institutions. While at high incomes, the combination of a larger size of government and greater regulation is bad for exports, the effect is more benign at lower-income levels. This is consistent with the North–LDC results from the split sample regressions reported in Table 7.8.

Table 7.10   Interactions

Variable	Interaction Infrastructure		Interacting Institutions	
	OLS	Probit	OLS	Probit
lpGDP95pop	1.081***	0.120***	1.068***	0.113***
	(0.004)	(0.001)	(0.004)	(0.001)
lrGDP95pop	2.610***	-0.032***	2.619***	-0.032***
	(0.051)	(0.008)	(0.051)	(0.008)
lppop	1.030***	0.102***	1.025***	0.099***
	(0.004)	(0.001)	(0.004)	(0.001)
lrpop	1.367***	-0.353***	1.294***	-0.339***
	(0.114)	(0.023)	(0.115)	(0.023)
ldist	-1.311***	-0.126***	-1.320***	-0.126***
	(0.007)	(0.002)	(0.008)	(0.002)
partnerlandlocked	-0.261***	-0.035***	-0.257***	-0.041***
	(0.016)	(0.003)	(0.016)	(0.004)
comlang_ethno (d)	0.622***	0.034***	0.605***	0.037***
	(0.016)	(0.003)	(0.016)	(0.003)
colony (d)	0.358***	-0.147***	0.365***	-0.149***
	(0.045)	(0.018)	(0.046)	(0.018)
Partner_einfr	0.070*	-0.033***	0.176***	0.040***
	(0.030)	(0.006)	(0.006)	(0.001)
Partner_einst	0.194***	0.017***	0.226***	0.102***
	(0.008)	(0.002)	(0.041)	(0.009)
Partner_einfr2	1.165***	0.199***	0.181***	0.055***
	(0.048)	(0.010)	(0.010)	(0.002)
Partner_einst2	0.165***	0.034***	-0.090**	0.224***
	(0.006)	(0.001)	(0.033)	(0.007)

continued on next page

Table 7.10 continued

Variable	Interaction Infrastructure		Interacting Institutions	
	OLS	Probit	OLS	Probit
	(0.079)	(0.000)	(0.079)	(0.000)
pe_infr1gdppop	0.017***	0.010***		
	(0.004)	(0.001)		
pe_infr2gdppop	-0.111***	-0.017***		
	(0.005)	(0.001)		
pe_inst2gdppop		0.032***	-0.024***	
			(0.004)	(0.001)
pe_inst1gdppop		-0.003	-0.011***	
			(0.005)	(0.001)
Observations	209,528	209,528	209,528	209,528

Marginal effects with std errors in parentheses; * significant at 10%; ** significant at 5%; *** significant at 1%.

Source: Authors' estimates.

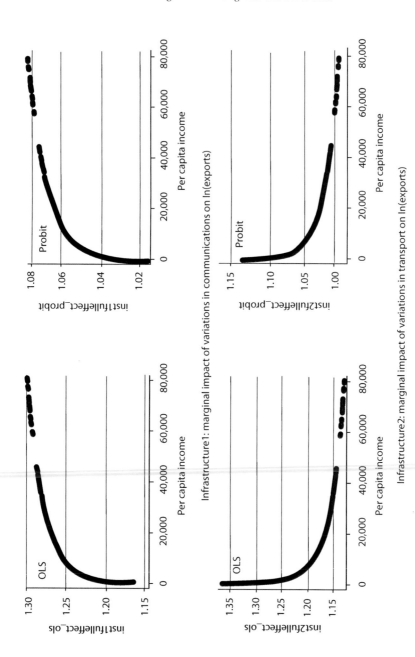

Figure 7.1   Marginal Impact of Variations in Communications and Transportation

OLS = ordinary least-squares, Probit = a regression model.

Source: Authors' estimates.

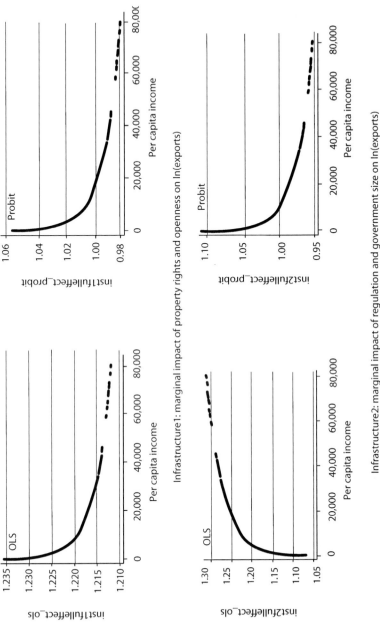

Infrastructure1: marginal impact of property rights and openness on In(exports)

Infrastructure2: marginal impact of regulation and government size on In(exports)

Figure 7.2   Marginal Impact of Institutions

OLS = ordinary least-squares, Probit = a regression model.

Source: Authors' estimates.

Importance of Infrastructure in Intra-Asian Trade

To what extent does the under-provision of infrastructure hamper region-al trade? For answers, we turn to the results of our Heckman estimates and use them to calculate the trade costs reductions corresponding to 1% improvement in infrastructure quality for each of the Asian countries in our sample. Furthermore, we also calculate the impact of 1% improve-ment of infrastructure on trade volumes. We do this taking into account their current levels of communication and physical infrastructure and given their current levels of per capita income. Table 7.11 illustrates effect of a 1% improvement in both physical and communication infrastructure on trade volumes. The effect of a 1% improvement in communication infrastructure on trade volumes is rather similar between countries in the region and it leads to about 0.2–0.3% higher trade. A 1% improvement in physical infrastructure has more diversified and often higher effect on countries' trade ranging from 0.1% to 0.5%.

Table 7.12 presents the trade-cost equivalent of a 1% change in both communication and physical infrastructure quality on trade-given income. The trade-cost equivalents of a 1% change for the amount of goods traded are shown in the first two columns. For most of the countries, better physi-cal infrastructure would have a more important contribution in reduc-ing trade costs than would communication infrastructure; nevertheless, both improvements in physical and communication infrastructure could importantly reduce trade costs. There are important differences between countries regarding to what extent costs for traders could be reduced through improvements to infrastructure. Those countries that are lagging behind in terms of infrastructure in the region could gain more than those that already have relatively good infrastructure. For example, the trade-cost equivalent of a 1% change in the quality of physical infrastructure is 13.7% for Cambodia, 19.5% for the Lao People's Democratic Republic (Lao PDR), and only 0.2% for Australia. In other words, improving the quality of infrastructure in the Lao PDR by 1% would have the same effect on trade as abolishing a 19.5% tariff on trade.

It is also apparent from the table that for most of the Asian countries sampled, an improvement in infrastructure quality increases significantly not only the actual amount of goods traded but also the probability of trading although the infrastructure effect is larger on the former. When considering the average for all Asian countries sampled, a 1% improve-ment in the quality of physical infrastructure, given income per capita, would decrease the trade-cost equivalents for the amount traded by almost 4.5% and for the probability of trading by 0.4%. On the other hand, a

Table 7.11   Analysis of 1% Infrastructure Improvement

	Trade cost reduction (% of value)		Impact on trade volumes (%)	
	Communication infrastructure	Physical infrastructure	Communication infrastructure	Physical infrastructure
Full sample	0.2	0.2	0.2	0.2
North–South sample	0.2	0.3	0.2	0.3
Country estimates				
Australia	0.3	0.1	0.2	0.1
Bangladesh	0.2	0.6	0.2	0.5
Cambodia	0.2	0.5	0.2	0.5
Hong Kong, China	0.3	0.1	0.2	0.1
India	0.2	0.5	0.2	0.5
Indonesia	0.2	0.4	0.2	0.4
Japan	0.3	0.0	0.3	0.0
Korea, Republic of	0.2	0.1	0.2	0.1
Lao PDR	0.2	0.5	0.2	0.5
Malaysia	0.2	0.3	0.2	0.2
New Zealand	0.2	0.1	0.2	0.1
Pakistan	0.2	0.5	0.2	0.5
Philippines	0.2	0.4	0.2	0.4
Singapore	0.3	0.1	0.2	0.1
Thailand	0.2	0.3	0.2	0.3
Viet Nam	0.2	0.6	0.2	0.5

Lao PDR = Lao People's Democratic Republic, % = percent.

Source: Authors' estimates.

similar 1% improvement in communication infrastructure would have a smaller, but still important, positive effect by decreasing the trade cost equivalent for the amount traded by 1.5% and for the probability of trading by 0.3%.

Table 7.12   Trade Cost Equivalents of a 1% Change

	Amount traded communication infrastructure	Amount traded physical infrastructure	Probability of trade communication infrastructure	Probability of trade physical infrastructure
Australia	0.779	0.197	0.470	0.130
Bangladesh	3.106	7.068	0.180	0.615
Cambodia	3.084	13.709	0.171	0.611
Hong Kong, China	0.475	0.312	0.411	0.177
India	1.814	3.762	0.129	0.618
Indonesia	1.609	3.232	0.173	0.491
Japan	0.493	(0.044)	0.580	0.093
Korea, Rep. of	0.513	0.598	0.292	0.220
Lao PDR	2.910	19.495	0.178	0.642
Malaysia	0.923	1.608	0.227	0.297
New Zealand	0.762	0.423	0.390	0.151
Pakistan	1.872	5.431	0.145	0.564
Philippines	1.738	3.269	0.196	0.438
Singapore	0.555	0.279	0.422	0.153
Thailand	1.094	2.226	0.204	0.382
Viet Nam	1.915	9.762	0.117	0.664
Average change	1.478	4.458	0.268	0.390

Lao PDR = Lao People's Democratic Republic, ( ) = negative value.

Source: Authors' estimates.

Summary

In recent years, the reduction of transaction costs has figured prominently in the agenda of policy makers, especially as they negotiate the final contours of various discriminatory trading agreements. This is partly because of the creeping realization that tariff liberalization alone may not be sufficient to generate the needed trade expansion in the region. An even more immediate reason is the binding constraint posed by infrastructural limitations on over-all growth in Asia, especially after a period of rapid catch-up even among the lower-income countries such as India, Bangladesh, Pakistan, People's Republic of China (PRC), and Viet Nam.

In this paper, we traced the evolution of trade across a panel spanning the bilateral trade flows from 1988 to 2002. Our aim was not only to explain what is driving the trade flows that are observed, but also the determinants of non-trade. Using a selection model with maximum likelihood techniques, we then estimate the probability of a bilateral trade occurring as well as the determinants of these exchanges. We were particularly interested in gauging the possible influences of trading costs that originate from insufficiencies in infrastructure and other institutional facilities. A gravity model has therefore been employed, where the standard right-hand-side variables have been expanded to include indexes of both physical infrastructure and institutional development.

While our results indicate somewhat mixed evidence on the effects of institutions, the strong links of infrastructure performance with exports has been clearly established. By using interaction terms between institutional and infrastructure quality indicators, we derived the tariff equivalents of marginal variation in infrastructure relative to the expected values for a given income cohort. These measures demonstrate the significant trade dividends generated by any improvement in the provision of infrastructure. In addition, we find on the basis of split sample regressions that for the least-developed countries in the region, a broad three-part complementarity exists between (i) better communication and transport infrastructures, (ii) greater involvement of the government in the domestic economy, and (iii) improved export performance.

Using our estimation results, we calculated the trade-cost equivalents of the infrastructure quality for Asian economies. The trade-cost equivalents indicate that, although there are important differences between countries, several countries impose important barriers for traders by having less-developed infrastructure than do other countries with similar characteristics. Furthermore, calculations indicate that, when considering the average for all Asian countries sampled, a 1% improvement in physical infrastructure quality given income per capita is equivalent to having a 4.5% tariff when considering the amount traded. On the other hand, a similar 1% improvement in communication infrastructure is the equivalent of 1.5% tariffs.

There has already been much progress in regional cooperation in the development of regional and subregional networks such as the Greater Mekong Subregion initiative linking Cambodia, PRC, Lao PDR, Myanmar, Thailand, and Viet Nam. The results of this paper only further strengthen the case for a regional approach in overcoming the infrastructure constraints that significantly obstruct not only current but also potential intra-Asian trade and the integration of Asian region into the world economy.

ANNEXES

Annex A7.1: Evolution of Selected Infrastructure Variables Over Time

Name	Year	Air transport	No. of fixed mobile subscribers	No. of mobile phones	No. of telephone main lines
Australia	1998	1,904	772	263	509
	1999	1,693	849	333	515
	2000	1,731	987	447	540
	2001	1,678	1,115	574	541
	2002	1,545	1,178	640	539
	2003	1,355	1,262	719	542
Bangladesh	1998	145	4	1	3
	1999	143	5	1	3
	2000	194	6	2	4
	2001	170	8	4	4
	2002	172	13	8	5
	2003	179	16	10	5
Cambodia	1998		7	5	2
	1999		10	7	2
	2000		12	10	2
	2001		19	17	2
	2002	4	30	28	3
	2003	3	38	35	3
China, People's Republic of	1998	2,474	89	19	70
	1999	3,295	120	34	86
	2000	3,900	178	66	112
	2001	4,232	248	110	137
	2002	5,014	328	161	167
	2003	5,651	424	215	209

continued on next page

Annex A7.1: continued

Name	Year	Air transport	No. of fixed mobile subscribers	No. of mobile phones	No. of telephone main lines
Hong Kong, China	1998	4,151	1,055	485	570
	1999	4,546	1,233	647	586
	2000	5,112	1,406	817	589
	2001	5,066	1,439	859	580
	2002	5,715	1,507	942	565
	2003	5,781	1,638	1,079	559
Indonesia	1998	429	32	5	27
	1999	362	40	11	30
	2000	413	50	18	32
	2001	424	66	31	35
	2002	406	92	55	37
	2003	424	127	87	39
India	1998	531	23	1	22
	1999	531	28	2	27
	2000	548	36	4	32
	2001	519	44	6	38
	2002	546	52	12	40
	2003	580	71	25	46
Japan	1998	7,514	908	374	534
	1999	8,226	1,006	449	557
	2000	8,672	1,112	526	586
	2001	7,614	1,164	588	576
	2002	8,183	1,195	637	558
	2003	7,985	1,151	679	472
Korea, Republic of	1998	7,290	751	309	442
	1999	8,098	962	513	449
	2000	7,651	1,060	583	477
	2001	6,827	1,106	621	486

continued on next page

Annex A7.1: continued

Name	Year	Air transport	No. of fixed mobile subscribers	No. of mobile phones	No. of telephone main lines
Korea, Republic of	2002	7,897	1,168	679	489
	2003	8,312	1,239	701	538
Lao People's Democratic Republic	1998	2	7	1	6
	1999	2	9	2	7
	2000	2	10	2	8
	2001	2	15	5	10
	2002	2	21	10	11
	2003	2	32	20	12
Myanmar	1998	7	5	0	5
	1999	6	6	0	6
	2000	1	6	0	6
	2001	1	7	0	6
	2002	2	8	1	7
	2003	2	8	1	7
Malaysia	1998	1,376	303	101	202
	1999	1,425	340	137	203
	2000	1,864	419	220	199
	2001	1,775	510	313	197
	2002	1,924	567	377	190
	2003	2,176	624	442	182
New Zealand	1998	826	697	212	485
	1999	856	860	372	489
	2000	817	893	408	485
	2001	763	1,076	599	477
	2002	688	1,070	622	448
	2003	801	1,097	648	448
Pakistan	1998	402	22	2	21
	1999	332	24	2	22

continued on next page

Annex A7.1: continued

Name	Year	Air transport	No. of fixed mobile subscribers	No. of mobile phones	No. of telephone main lines
Pakistan	2000	340	24	3	22
	2001	371	29	6	23
	2002	347	34	8	25
	2003	351	44	18	27
Philippines	1998	185	58	24	34
	1999	241	77	38	39
	2000	290	124	84	40
	2001	264	198	155	42
	2002	275	233	191	42
	2003	274	311	270	41
Singapore	1998	4,724	732	279	453
	1999	5,451	888	413	475
	2000	6,005	1,168	684	484
	2001	5,774	1,196	724	471
	2002	6,772	1,258	796	463
	2003	6,683	1,303	852	450
Thailand	1998	1,522	118	33	85
	1999	1,671	126	39	87
	2000	1,713	143	50	92
	2001	1,669	222	123	99
	2002	1,824	365	260	105
	2003	1,764	499	394	105
Viet Nam	1998	96	25	3	22
	1999	99	31	4	27
	2000	117	42	10	32
	2001	135	53	15	38
	2002	151	72	23	48
	2003	165	88	34	54

Source: World Bank, *World Development Indicators.*

Annex A7.2:   First and Second Infrastructure Components, Measuring
Communication and Physical Infrastructure, 1998–2003

Name	Year	First infrastructure component	Second infrastructure component
Australia	1998	11.827	6.584
	1999	11.990	6.170
	2000	14.024	6.318
	2001	14.660	6.289
	2002	15.225	6.203
	2003	19.029	6.276
Bangladesh	1998	0.052	2.641
	1999	0.061	2.706
	2000	0.077	2.976
	2001	0.098	2.900
	2002	0.124	2.937
	2003	0.139	2.979
Cambodia	1998	0.076	0.658
	1999	0.096	0.649
	2000	0.120	0.636
	2001	0.153	0.570
	2002	0.206	0.499
	2003	0.185	0.385
Hong Kong, China	1998	22.031	1.005
	1999	23.914	1.027
	2000	24.682	1.060
	2001	29.311	1.106
	2002	35.266	1.184
	2003	33.968	1.181
Indonesia	1998	1.660	3.682
	1999	2.097	3.559
	2000	2.500	3.719
	2001	3.008	3.806
	2002	3.547	3.851
	2003	4.218	3.939

continued on next page

Annex A7.2: continued

Name	Year	First infrastructure component	Second infrastructure component
India	1998	0.700	6.118
	1999	0.901	6.304
	2000	1.155	6.543
	2001	1.438	6.662
	2002	1.659	7.352
	2003	2.046	7.581
Japan	1998	30.062	9.713
	1999	31.755	9.994
	2000	34.514	10.242
	2001	35.372	10.059
	2002	35.786	10.288
	2003	33.859	10.338
Korea, Republic of	1998	24.199	4.241
	1999	27.434	4.386
	2000	29.536	4.407
	2001	31.741	4.366
	2002	37.092	4.662
	2003	30.542	4.510
Myanmar	1998	0.084	0.717
	1999	0.092	0.718
	2000	0.097	0.474
	2001	0.109	0.496
	2002	0.138	0.604
	2003	0.148	0.620
Malaysia	1998	8.440	2.630
	1999	9.356	2.688
	2000	10.677	2.855
	2001	12.615	2.848
	2002	13.589	2.886
	2003	14.504	2.948

continued on next page

Annex A7.2: continued

Name	Year	First infrastructure component	Second infrastructure component
Pakistan	1998	0.562	2.765
	1999	0.632	2.710
	2000	0.667	2.790
	2001	0.788	2.964
	2002	0.903	2.978
	2003	1.131	3.097
Philippines	1998	1.643	3.000
	1999	2.191	3.241
	2000	2.437	3.423
	2001	3.754	3.400
	2002	3.151	3.786
	2003	3.511	3.878
Singapore	1998	22.661	1.274
	1999	26.171	1.337
	2000	30.256	1.389
	2001	28.784	1.374
	2002	30.101	1.433
	2003	31.125	1.441
Thailand	1998	5.789	2.595
	1999	6.183	2.666
	2000	7.042	2.615
	2001	9.674	2.638
	2002	12.724	2.705
	2003	14.924	2.678
Viet Nam	1998	0.375	1.602
	1999	0.506	1.648
	2000	0.710	1.765
	2001	0.945	1.858
	2002	1.278	1.927
	2003	1.474	1.962

Source: Authors' calculations.

Annex A7.3:   Countries Included in the Sample

Albania	Germany	Morocco
Algeria	Ghana	Namibia
Argentina	Greece	Nepal
Australia	Guatemala	New Zealand
Austria	Guinea-Bissau	Nicaragua
Bahamas, The	Guyana	Niger
Bangladesh	Honduras	Nigeria
Barbados	Hong Kong, China	Norway
Belgium	Hungary	Oman
Benin	Iceland	Poland
Bolivia	India	Portugal
Botswana	Indonesia	Romania
Brazil	Iran, Islamic Rep.	Russian Federation
Bulgaria	Ireland	Rwanda
Cameroon	Israel	Senegal
Central African Republic	Italy	Singapore
Chad	Jamaica	Slovak Republic
Chile	Japan	Slovenia
Colombia	Jordan	South Africa
Congo, Rep.	Kenya	Spain
Costa Rica	Korea, Rep.	Sri Lanka
Cote d'Ivoire	Kuwait	Sweden
Croatia	Latvia	Syrian Arab Republic
Cyprus	Lithuania	Tanzania
Czech Republic	Luxembourg	Thailand
Dominican Republic	Madagascar	Togo
Ecuador	Malawi	Trinidad and Tobago
Egypt, Arab Rep.	Malaysia	Tunisia
El Salvador	Mali	Turkey
Estonia	Malta	Uganda
Finland	Mauritius	Ukraine
Gabon	Mexico	United States

continued on next page

Annex A7.3: continued

Uruguay

Venezuela

Zambia

Zimbabwe

Only partner countries:

Fiji

Haiti

Sierra Leone

United Arab Emirates

Annex A7.4:   Trade-Cost Equivalents of a 1% Change, Elasticities Over Time

Full period		Infrastructure 1 Full effect (OLS) (%)	Infrastructure 2 Full effect (OLS) (%)	Infrastructure 1 Full effect (probit) (%)	Infrastructure 2 Full effect (probit) (%)
Australia	1988	0.237	0.074	0.065	0.032
	1989	0.238	0.072	0.065	0.032
	1990	0.237	0.074	0.065	0.032
	1991	0.237	0.075	0.065	0.032
	1992	0.238	0.072	0.065	0.032
	1993	0.238	0.069	0.066	0.031
	1994	0.239	0.066	0.066	0.031
	1995	0.239	0.062	0.066	0.030
	1996	0.240	0.060	0.067	0.030
	1997	0.240	0.056	0.067	0.029
	1998	0.241	0.052	0.067	0.028
	1999	0.241	0.049	0.068	0.028
	2000	0.241	0.048	0.068	0.028
	2001	0.242	0.045	0.068	0.027
	2002	0.242	0.043	0.068	0.027
	2003	0.242	0.042	0.068	0.027
Bangladesh	1988	0.165	0.546	0.023	0.104
	1989	0.165	0.545	0.023	0.104
	1990	0.166	0.542	0.023	0.103
	1991	0.166	0.540	0.023	0.103
	1992	0.167	0.537	0.024	0.103
	1993	0.167	0.533	0.024	0.102
	1994	0.167	0.531	0.024	0.102
	1995	0.168	0.528	0.025	0.101
	1996	0.168	0.524	0.025	0.101
	1997	0.169	0.521	0.025	0.100
	1998	0.170	0.517	0.026	0.100
	1999	0.170	0.513	0.026	0.099
	2000	0.171	0.509	0.026	0.098

continued on next page

Annex A7.4: continued

Full period		Infrastructure 1 Full effect (OLS) (%)	Infrastructure 2 Full effect (OLS) (%)	Infrastructure 1 Full effect (probit) (%)	Infrastructure 2 Full effect (probit) (%)
Bangladesh	2001	0.171	0.505	0.027	0.098
	2002	0.172	0.502	0.027	0.097
	2003	0.172	0.498	0.027	0.097
Cambodia	1988	0.070	1.172	(0.033)	0.199
	1989	0.070	1.172	(0.033)	0.199
	1990	0.070	1.172	(0.033)	0.199
	1991	0.070	1.172	(0.033)	0.199
	1992	0.070	1.172	(0.033)	0.199
	1993	0.166	0.537	0.024	0.103
	1994	0.167	0.531	0.024	0.102
	1995	0.168	0.527	0.025	0.101
	1996	0.168	0.525	0.025	0.101
	1997	0.169	0.520	0.025	0.100
	1998	0.168	0.525	0.025	0.101
	1999	0.170	0.516	0.026	0.099
	2000	0.171	0.511	0.026	0.099
	2001	0.171	0.507	0.026	0.098
	2002	0.172	0.503	0.027	0.097
	2003	0.173	0.496	0.027	0.096
China, People's Republic of	1988	0.169	0.521	0.025	0.100
	1989	0.169	0.519	0.025	0.100
	1990	0.170	0.516	0.026	0.099
	1991	0.171	0.508	0.026	0.098
	1992	0.173	0.494	0.028	0.096
	1993	0.175	0.481	0.029	0.094
	1994	0.177	0.469	0.030	0.092
	1995	0.178	0.460	0.031	0.091
	1996	0.180	0.450	0.031	0.089
	1997	0.181	0.442	0.032	0.088
	1998	0.182	0.435	0.033	0.087

continued on next page

Annex A7.4: continued

Full period		Infrastructure 1 Full effect (OLS) (%)	Infrastructure 2 Full effect (OLS) (%)	Infrastructure 1 Full effect (probit) (%)	Infrastructure 2 Full effect (probit) (%)
China, People's Republic of	1999	0.183	0.428	0.033	0.086
	2000	0.184	0.421	0.034	0.085
	2001	0.185	0.413	0.035	0.084
	2002	0.187	0.405	0.036	0.083
	2003	0.188	0.396	0.036	0.081
Hong Kong, China	1988	0.237	0.075	0.065	0.032
	1989	0.237	0.073	0.065	0.032
	1990	0.238	0.072	0.066	0.032
	1991	0.238	0.067	0.066	0.031
	1992	0.239	0.061	0.067	0.030
	1993	0.240	0.056	0.067	0.029
	1994	0.241	0.051	0.067	0.028
	1995	0.241	0.050	0.067	0.028
	1996	0.241	0.050	0.067	0.028
	1997	0.242	0.046	0.068	0.028
Hong Kong, China	1998	0.241	0.052	0.067	0.029
	1999	0.241	0.050	0.067	0.028
	2000	0.243	0.040	0.068	0.027
	2001	0.243	0.040	0.068	0.027
	2002	0.243	0.039	0.068	0.027
	2003	0.243	0.036	0.069	0.026
Indonesia	1988	0.181	0.443	0.032	0.088
	1989	0.182	0.435	0.033	0.087
	1990	0.183	0.427	0.034	0.086
	1991	0.184	0.420	0.034	0.085
	1992	0.185	0.414	0.035	0.084
	1993	0.186	0.408	0.035	0.083
	1994	0.187	0.401	0.036	0.082
	1995	0.188	0.394	0.037	0.081

continued on next page

Annex A7.4: continued

Full period		Infrastructure 1 Full effect (OLS) (%)	Infrastructure 2 Full effect (OLS) (%)	Infrastructure 1 Full effect (probit) (%)	Infrastructure 2 Full effect (probit) (%)
Indonesia	1996	0.189	0.387	0.037	0.080
	1997	0.190	0.383	0.037	0.079
	1998	0.187	0.401	0.036	0.082
	1999	0.187	0.401	0.036	0.082
	2000	0.188	0.397	0.036	0.081
	2001	0.188	0.395	0.036	0.081
	2002	0.189	0.393	0.037	0.081
	2003	0.189	0.389	0.037	0.080
India	1988	0.167	0.533	0.024	0.102
	1989	0.168	0.529	0.024	0.101
	1990	0.168	0.525	0.025	0.101
	1991	0.168	0.526	0.025	0.101
	1992	0.169	0.522	0.025	0.100
	1993	0.169	0.519	0.025	0.100
	1994	0.170	0.513	0.026	0.099
India	1995	0.171	0.507	0.026	0.098
	1996	0.172	0.501	0.027	0.097
	1997	0.173	0.498	0.027	0.097
	1998	0.173	0.493	0.028	0.096
	1999	0.174	0.487	0.028	0.095
	2000	0.174	0.485	0.028	0.095
	2001	0.175	0.481	0.029	0.094
	2002	0.176	0.478	0.029	0.094
	2003	0.177	0.471	0.030	0.093
Japan	1988	0.249	0.000	0.072	0.021
	1989	0.250	(0.006)	0.072	0.020
	1990	0.250	(0.011)	0.073	0.019
	1991	0.251	(0.014)	0.073	0.018
	1992	0.251	(0.015)	0.073	0.018
	1993	0.251	(0.015)	0.073	0.018

continued on next page

Annex A7.4: continued

Full period		Infrastructure 1 Full effect (OLS) (%)	Infrastructure 2 Full effect (OLS) (%)	Infrastructure 1 Full effect (probit) (%)	Infrastructure 2 Full effect (probit) (%)
Japan	1994	0.251	(0.016)	0.073	0.018
	1995	0.251	(0.017)	0.074	0.018
	1996	0.252	(0.021)	0.074	0.017
	1997	0.252	(0.023)	0.074	0.017
	1998	0.252	(0.021)	0.074	0.017
	1999	0.252	(0.021)	0.074	0.017
	2000	0.252	(0.024)	0.074	0.017
	2001	0.252	(0.024)	0.074	0.017
	2002	0.252	(0.024)	0.074	0.017
	2003	0.253	(0.027)	0.074	0.016
Korea, Republic of	1988	0.222	0.177	0.056	0.048
	1989	0.222	0.172	0.057	0.047
	1990	0.224	0.163	0.057	0.046
	1991	0.225	0.155	0.058	0.044
	1992	0.226	0.150	0.058	0.043
	1993	0.227	0.145	0.059	0.043
	1994	0.228	0.137	0.060	0.042
	1995	0.229	0.127	0.061	0.040
	1996	0.230	0.121	0.061	0.039
	1997	0.231	0.117	0.061	0.039
	1998	0.229	0.126	0.061	0.040
	1999	0.231	0.116	0.061	0.038
	2000	0.232	0.108	0.062	0.037
	2001	0.233	0.105	0.063	0.037
	2002	0.234	0.098	0.063	0.036
	2003	0.234	0.096	0.063	0.035
Lao People's Democratic Republic	1988	0.166	0.543	0.023	0.104
	1989	0.168	0.531	0.024	0.102

continued on next page

Annex A7.4: continued

Full period		Infrastructure 1 Full effect (OLS) (%)	Infrastructure 2 Full effect (OLS) (%)	Infrastructure 1 Full effect (probit) (%)	Infrastructure 2 Full effect (probit) (%)
Lao People's Democratic Republic	1990	0.168	0.526	0.025	0.101
	1991	0.168	0.524	0.025	0.101
	1992	0.169	0.520	0.025	0.100
	1993	0.170	0.516	0.026	0.100
	1994	0.171	0.511	0.026	0.099
	1995	0.171	0.508	0.026	0.098
	1996	0.172	0.503	0.027	0.098
	1997	0.172	0.499	0.027	0.097
	1998	0.173	0.497	0.027	0.097
	1999	0.173	0.492	0.028	0.096
	2000	0.174	0.488	0.028	0.095
	2001	0.175	0.484	0.028	0.095
	2002	0.175	0.481	0.029	0.094
	2003	0.175	0.479	0.029	0.094
Myanmar	1988	0.070	1.172	(0.033)	0.199
	1989	0.070	1.172	(0.033)	0.199
	1990	0.070	1.172	(0.033)	0.199
	1991	0.070	1.172	(0.033)	0.199
	1992	0.070	1.172	(0.033)	0.199
	1993	0.070	1.172	(0.033)	0.199
	1994	0.070	1.172	(0.033)	0.199
	1995	0.070	1.172	(0.033)	0.199
	1996	0.070	1.172	(0.033)	0.199
	1997	0.070	1.172	(0.033)	0.199
	1998	0.070	1.172	(0.033)	0.199
	1999	0.070	1.172	(0.033)	0.199
	2000	0.070	1.172	(0.033)	0.199
	2001	0.070	1.172	(0.033)	0.199
	2002	0.070	1.172	(0.033)	0.199
	2003	0.070	1.172	(0.033)	0.199

continued on next page

Annex A7.4: continued

Full period		Infrastructure 1 Full effect (OLS) (%)	Infrastructure 2 Full effect (OLS) (%)	Infrastructure 1 Full effect (probit) (%)	Infrastructure 2 Full effect (probit) (%)
Malaysia	1988	0.205	0.285	0.046	0.064
	1989	0.206	0.279	0.047	0.063
	1990	0.207	0.273	0.047	0.062
	1991	0.208	0.265	0.048	0.061
	1992	0.209	0.259	0.049	0.060
	1993	0.210	0.251	0.049	0.059
	1994	0.211	0.244	0.050	0.058
	1995	0.212	0.236	0.051	0.057
	1996	0.214	0.229	0.051	0.056
	1997	0.214	0.223	0.052	0.055
	1998	0.213	0.235	0.051	0.056
	1999	0.213	0.231	0.051	0.056
	2000	0.214	0.224	0.052	0.055
	2001	0.214	0.226	0.052	0.055
	2002	0.214	0.224	0.052	0.055
	2003	0.215	0.221	0.052	0.054
New Zealand	1988	0.234	0.094	0.064	0.035
	1989	0.234	0.095	0.063	0.035
	1990	0.234	0.097	0.063	0.035
	1991	0.233	0.100	0.063	0.036
	1992	0.233	0.100	0.063	0.036
	1993	0.234	0.094	0.064	0.035
	1994	0.235	0.090	0.064	0.034
	1995	0.235	0.087	0.064	0.034
	1996	0.236	0.085	0.064	0.034
	1997	0.236	0.085	0.064	0.034
	1998	0.236	0.085	0.064	0.034
	1999	0.236	0.080	0.065	0.033
	2000	0.237	0.078	0.065	0.033

continued on next page

Annex A7.4: continued

Full period		Infrastructure 1 Full effect (OLS) (%)	Infrastructure 2 Full effect (OLS) (%)	Infrastructure 1 Full effect (probit) (%)	Infrastructure 2 Full effect (probit) (%)
New Zealand	2001	0.237	0.075	0.065	0.032
	2002	0.238	0.072	0.066	0.032
	2003	0.238	0.071	0.066	0.031
Pakistan	1988	0.173	0.493	0.028	0.096
	1989	0.174	0.490	0.028	0.095
	1990	0.174	0.488	0.028	0.095
	1991	0.174	0.485	0.028	0.095
	1992	0.175	0.480	0.029	0.094
	1993	0.175	0.481	0.029	0.094
	1994	0.175	0.479	0.029	0.094
	1995	0.176	0.477	0.029	0.093
	1996	0.176	0.474	0.029	0.093
	1997	0.176	0.476	0.029	0.093
	1998	0.176	0.476	0.029	0.093
	1999	0.176	0.474	0.029	0.093
	2000	0.176	0.472	0.030	0.093
	2001	0.176	0.472	0.030	0.093
	2002	0.176	0.472	0.030	0.093
	2003	0.177	0.468	0.030	0.092
Philippines	1988	0.188	0.394	0.037	0.081
	1989	0.189	0.390	0.037	0.080
	1990	0.189	0.389	0.037	0.080
	1991	0.189	0.393	0.037	0.081
	1992	0.188	0.395	0.036	0.081
	1993	0.188	0.395	0.036	0.081
	1994	0.189	0.393	0.037	0.081
	1995	0.189	0.390	0.037	0.080
	1996	0.190	0.386	0.037	0.080
	1997	0.190	0.383	0.038	0.079

continued on next page

Annex A7.4: continued

Full period		Infrastructure 1 Full effect (OLS) (%)	Infrastructure 2 Full effect (OLS) (%)	Infrastructure 1 Full effect (probit) (%)	Infrastructure 2 Full effect (probit) (%)
Philippines	1998	0.190	0.386	0.037	0.080
	1999	0.190	0.385	0.037	0.079
	2000	0.190	0.381	0.038	0.079
	2001	0.190	0.380	0.038	0.079
	2002	0.191	0.378	0.038	0.078
	2003	0.191	0.375	0.038	0.078
Singapore	1988	0.235	0.091	0.064	0.034
	1989	0.236	0.083	0.064	0.033
	1990	0.237	0.078	0.065	0.033
	1991	0.237	0.074	0.065	0.032
	1992	0.238	0.070	0.066	0.031
	1993	0.240	0.060	0.067	0.030
	1994	0.241	0.052	0.067	0.028
	1995	0.242	0.046	0.068	0.028
	1996	0.242	0.042	0.068	0.027
	1997	0.243	0.037	0.069	0.026
	1998	0.242	0.041	0.068	0.027
	1999	0.243	0.035	0.069	0.026
	2000	0.245	0.027	0.070	0.025
	2001	0.244	0.033	0.069	0.026
	2002	0.244	0.030	0.069	0.025
	2003	0.244	0.031	0.069	0.025
Thailand	1988	0.196	0.343	0.041	0.073
	1989	0.198	0.332	0.042	0.071
	1990	0.199	0.322	0.043	0.070
	1991	0.201	0.315	0.044	0.069
	1992	0.202	0.307	0.044	0.068
	1993	0.203	0.300	0.045	0.066
	1994	0.204	0.291	0.046	0.065
	1995	0.206	0.282	0.047	0.064

continued on next page

Annex A7.4: continued

Full period		Infrastructure 1 Full effect (OLS) (%)	Infrastructure 2 Full effect (OLS) (%)	Infrastructure 1 Full effect (probit) (%)	Infrastructure 2 Full effect (probit) (%)
Thailand	1996	0.206	0.276	0.047	0.063
	1997	0.206	0.278	0.047	0.063
	1998	0.204	0.292	0.046	0.065
	1999	0.205	0.288	0.046	0.065
	2000	0.205	0.283	0.046	0.064
	2001	0.206	0.282	0.047	0.064
	2002	0.206	0.277	0.047	0.063
	2003	0.207	0.270	0.048	0.062
Viet Nam	1988	0.160	0.581	0.020	0.109
	1989	0.161	0.576	0.020	0.109
	1990	0.161	0.572	0.021	0.108
	1991	0.162	0.568	0.021	0.107
	1992	0.163	0.561	0.022	0.106
	1993	0.164	0.555	0.022	0.105
	1994	0.165	0.548	0.023	0.104
	1995	0.166	0.539	0.023	0.103
	1996	0.167	0.531	0.024	0.102
	1997	0.168	0.524	0.025	0.101
	1998	0.169	0.520	0.025	0.100
	1999	0.170	0.516	0.026	0.099
	2000	0.171	0.510	0.026	0.099
	2001	0.172	0.504	0.027	0.090
	2002	0.173	0.498	0.027	0.097
	2003	0.174	0.491	0.028	0.096

OLS = ordinary least-squares, probit = a regression model.

Source: Authors' calculation.

8

Pan-Asian Integration: Economic Implications of Integration Scenarios

Joseph Francois and Ganeshan Wignaraja

Introduction

An alphabet soup of regional trade agreements has proliferated in recent years. Such agreements include the North American Free Trade Agreement (NAFTA), the European Free Trade Association (EFTA), the European Union (EU), the Southern Common Market (MERCOSUR), Association of Southeast Asian Nations (ASEAN), and the South Asian Free Trade Agreement (SAFTA). Some of these regional initiatives have been very successful in integrating markets for goods and services, while others have gone through cycles of periodic collapse and revival. The most successful regional initiatives have been in North America and Europe. Success has been more limited in Asia. There is interest, though, in pursuing deeper regional integration across Asia. This includes subregional initiatives in East and South Asia, both through deepening of existing agreements and the creation of new ones.[1]

In this paper we explore the implications of a broad-based pan-Asian regional initiative spanning East and South Asia. We do this in the context of a global general equilibrium model of the world economy, benchmarked to a projected 2017 set of trade and production patterns. Working with the model, we also examine regionally narrow and broad agreements. For the narrow assessments, we examine the extension of the reach of ASEAN to include free trade agreements (FTAs) with combinations of the Northeast Asian economies (People's Republic of China [PRC], Japan, Republic

---

[1] In this volume, East Asia includes the 10 members of the Association of Southeast Asian Nations (ASEAN) (Brunei Darussalam, Cambodia, Indonesia, Lao People's Democratic Republic [Lao PDR], Malaysia, Philippines, Singapore, Thailand, and Viet Nam); Japan; People's Republic of China (PRC); Republic of Korea; Hong Kong, China; and Taipei,China. South Asia includes Bangladesh, Bhutan, India, Maldives, Nepal, Pakistan, and Sri Lanka.

of Korea [henceforth Korea]) and also the South Asian economies. We also examine various South Asian options. We focus on a stylized FTA that includes goods, services, and some aspects of trade-cost reduction through trade facilitation and related infrastructure improvements. This is a broader coverage scope than that used in existing studies and provides more comprehensive insights into economic implications.

We emphasize on the alternative prospects for insider and outsider countries. Interestingly, we find that with a true pan-Asian focus, the insiders benefit substantively in terms of trade and income while the aggregate impact on outside countries is negligible. Broadly speaking, an Asian regional FTA would appear to cover enough countries, with a great enough diversity in production and incomes, to actually allow for regional gains without a price measured in substantive third-country losses. Realizing such potential, however, requires overcoming a proven regional tendency to circumscribe trade concessions with rules of origin, nontariff barriers (NTBs), and exclusion lists. The more likely outcome—a web of bilateral agreements—involves outsider costs within and outside the region.

In the wake of the effective suspension of the Doha Round of trade talks, a myriad of possible bilateral and regional combinations is now on the table. Indeed, even if the World Trade Organization (WTO) talks conclude successfully, it is unlikely they would yield any substantive impact on Asia protection patterns (see Francois, van Meijl, and van Tongeren 2005). This has increased the momentum behind Asian negotiations. As reviewed below, the existing Asian FTA literature is focused on goods. In this regard, its piecemeal nature means that it offers a fragmented assessment of the general regional policy landscape. Given the importance of services and trade facilitation in ongoing FTA discussions, along with the piecemeal nature of the existing collection of assessments, there is a need for a comprehensive exploration, within a common framework, of current alternative FTA scenarios for pan-Asian integration. This is our goal in this paper. We offer a comprehensive examination of regional and subregional FTA pairings, inclusive not only of tariffs but also of trade facilitation and services liberalization. Both our facilitation and services experiments are built from gravity-based econometric estimates of trade costs. Because the collective impact of a set of FTAs can contrast sharply with what assessments of individual FTAs imply (Francois, McQueen, and Wignaraja, 2005), the comprehensive approach offered here also provides insight into the differential impact of individual Asian FTAs, a collective wave of such FTAs, and a comprehensive regional approach to liberalization.

The paper is organized as follows. As background, we provide a summary of the existing literature on FTAs (actual and prospective) in the region. A section offers an overview of the model and database, followed by policy scenarios, linking them to the underlying patterns of production and trade. This paper ends with a conclusion.

Background

There is a growing body of literature on the impact of FTAs in Asia using global computable general equilibrium (CGE) models. This interest can be attributed to the proliferation of bilateral and plurilateral FTAs in Asia in recent years. Table 8.1 provides a broad overview of this literature. From the table, it can be discerned that the bulk of the research attention in the literature has been devoted to FTAs covering East Asian economies. The literature on FTAs involving South Asian economies or pan-Asian FTAs between East and South Asian economies is more limited. The existing literature raises question such as: will an East Asia FTA, a South Asian FTA, or even a Pan-Asian FTA create gains for members? Will non-FTA members lose? And what sectors will gain or lose among members and non-members? There is currently intense debate in Asian policy circles on these questions and possible adjustment strategies needed to deal with countries and sectors that may lose though FTA formation.

By relying on a simulation approach that combines data and prospective scenarios in a structured manner to analyze the economic effects of policy changes on due to the formation of an East Asia FTA, CGE models have emerged as the tool of choice for shedding light on these issues. The CGE models used have varied somewhat in their underlying economic structure, behavior of agents, and focus, but commonly they build on the Global Trade Analysis Project (GTAP) database. The primary focus of such policy scenarios has been on the removal of price distortions against imports that arise from existing trade barriers (in particular merchandise tariffs). Most studies have used the standard GTAP model with constant returns to scale in production, perfect competition, and the Armington assumption (or some variant of GTAP). A few, by contrast, have adopted CGE models with firm-level imperfect competition.

Four major findings from the formation of an East Asian FTA emerge from this literature (for a selection see Ballard and Cheong 1997, Urata and Kyota 2003, Gilbert et al 2004, Lee et al 2004, Zhang et al 2006, and Mohanty and Pohit 2007): (i) all the East Asian countries involved would collect welfare gains, (ii) the countries that are excluded are much more likely to suffer welfare losses, (iii) production of sectors with a comparative advantage increases, and (iv) an East Asian FTA is a step toward multilateral liberalization.

Table 8.1   Selected Studies on the Impact of Asian FTAs

Study	Model and Baseline	Parameters and Assumptions	Impact of FTA Scenarios	Notes
Ballard and Cheong (1997)	GTAP Model Base year of 1992	Uses 1994 GTAP database; data disaggregated into nine regions and five sectors. Assumes removal of all tariffs and NTBs between all members of FTA. Uses two models with different assumptions: (i) perfect competition (costs explained by Armington assumption), and (ii) firm-level imperfect competition.	Welfare effects of East Asian and APEC FTAs, and global liberalization scenarios from perfectly-competitive model (EV as % of GDP under each scenario): • ASEAN countries—0.54, 0.92, 1.41 • PRC—0.45, 1.40, 1.72 • Japan—0.02, 0.97, 1.08 • Newly industrialized economies (NIEs)—1.12, 3.72, 3.75 • Rest of the world—(0.02), (0.06), 0.33 • US—(0.03), 0.13, 0.15 Welfare effects of East Asian FTA, APEC FTA, and global liberalization scenarios from the imperfectly-competitive model (EV as % of GDP under each scenario): • ASEAN countries—3.49, 3.06, 2.36 • PRC—6.68, 3.07, 1.98 • Japan—(2.40), 2.71, 2.19 • NIEs—7.58, 13.35, 12.78 • Rest of the world—(0.15), (0.29), 1.35 • US—(0.13), 0.42, (0.04)	ASEAN countries include Indonesia, Malaysia, Philippines, and Thailand only. NIEs include Hong Kong, China; Republic of Korea; Singapore; and Taipei,China. East Asia FTA includes ASEAN countries, PRC, NIEs, and Japan.

continued on next page

Table 8.1: continued

Study	Model and Baseline	Parameters and Assumptions	Impact of FTA Scenarios	Notes
Urata and Kiyota (2003)	GTAP Model Base year of 1997	Uses GTAP database (version 5); data disaggregated into 20 countries and 21 sectors. Assumes removal of tariff and NTBs among East Asian economies.	Estimated effects of an East Asian FTA (EV as % of GDP): • Thailand—12.54 • Viet Nam—6.61 • Singapore—3.69 • PRC—0.64 • Japan—0.19 • US—(0.09) • EU—(0.02)	East Asia FTA covers all East Asian countries and economies.
Gilbert, Scollay, and Bora (2004)	GTAP Model Base year of 1997	Uses the pre-release version of GTAP database (version 5); data disaggregated into 26 regions and 20 commodities. Assumes removal of all import tariffs on a preferential basis between members, with each member maintaining its own initial extra-RTA tariffs.	Welfare effects of PRC–Japan–Korea FTA, ASEAN+3 FTA, and APEC FTA (EV as % of GDP under each scenario): • Thailand—(0.2), 1.6, 1.0 • Viet Nam—(0.6), 3.1, 4.8 • Singapore—(0.2), 2.5, 1.9 • PRC—0.0, 0.0, 0.2 • Japan—0.1, 0.1, 0.4 • Republic of Korea—0.7, 0.7, 0.7 • US—0.0, 0.0, 0.0 • EU—0.0, 0.0, 0.1	APEC FTA assumes MFN liberalization.

continued on next page

Table 8.1: continued

Study	Model and Baseline	Parameters and Assumptions	Impact of FTA Scenarios	Notes
Lee, Roland-Holst, and van der Mensbrugghe (2004)	LINKAGE Model Base year of 1997	Uses the GTAP database (version 5.2); data disaggregated into 9 regions and 18 sectors. Assumes gradual removal of bilateral tariffs and export subsidies of the relevant sectors among the member countries over the period 2005–2010.	Welfare effects of ASEAN+3 FTA in 2015 (EV in $ Bn): • ASEAN countries—41.8 • PRC and Hong Kong, China—102.3 • Taipei,China—(5.4) • Japan—66.3 • Republic of Korea—30.1 • US—(0.9) • EU-15—6.8 • Rest of the world—(9.8)	ASEAN countries include Indonesia, Malaysia, Philippines, Singapore, Thailand, and Viet Nam only. ASEAN+3 does not include Taipei,China
Zhang et al (2006)	GTAP Model Base year of 2001	Uses the GTAP database (version 6); data disaggregated into 87 regions and 57 sectors. Assumes elimination of all tariff and NTBs on trade in goods and some trade facilitation programs for the member countries.	East Asian FTA would increase overall GDP of East Asian countries by 1.2% and economic welfare by $104.6 billion. Welfare effects of East Asian FTA (EV in $ Bn): • ASEAN countries—37.6 • PRC, Japan, and Republic of Korea—66.9 • ASEAN+3—104.6	FTA scenarios assume tariff and NTB elimination for goods, combined with some trade facilitation

continued on next page

Table 8.1: continued

Study	Model and Baseline	Parameters and Assumptions	Impact of FTA Scenarios	Notes
Bandara and Yu (2003)	GTAP Model Base year of 1997	Uses 1997 GTAP database; data disaggregated into 12 regions and 17 industries. Performs two opposite policy simulations: (i) unilateral trade liberalization scenario assumes removal of all import tariff and export duties of all South Asian countries; and (ii) preferential trade liberalization scenario assumes removal of all tariffs and export duties between South Asian countries but not between other regions.	Welfare effects under unilateral trade liberalization scenario (EV in $ Mn): • ASEAN countries—94.6 • Japan—438.7 • India—2331.9 • Sri Lanka—83.9 • Bangladesh—173.9 • Rest of South Asia—(511.1) • NAFTA—(2509.0) • EU—1125.1 Welfare effects under SAFTA, South Asia–ASEAN, and multilateral trade liberalization scenario (EV in $ Mn under each scenario): • ASEAN countries—(70.1); 3,039.5; 7,324.3 • Japan—(156.6); (33.3); 33,638.1 • India—756.2; (1,313.4); 3,521.3 • Sri Lanka—4.1; (29.8); 274.4 • Bangladesh—(41.2); (151.9); 288.9 • Rest of South Asia—52.3; (791.1); 96.7 • NAFTA—(113.9); (42.2); (6,091.5) • EU—(169.9); (396.4); 9,097.4	SAFTA scenario assumes 100% tariff cut as opposed to actual tariff concessions given by SAFTA members during the final round of tariff reductions in 1998. GTAP database disaggregates South Asia into four regions: India, Sri Lanka, Bangladesh, and rest of South Asia.

continued on next page

Table 8.1: continued

Study	Model and Baseline	Parameters and Assumptions	Impact of FTA Scenarios	Notes
Mohanty, Pohit, and Roy (2004)	GTAP Model Base year of 1997	Uses GTAP database (version 5); data disaggregated into 14 regions and 26 sectors. Simulates three scenarios: (i) removal of tariff and NTBs between Japan, ASEAN, PRC, India, and Republic of Korea (JACIK) countries; (ii) free movement of investments within JACIK countries; and (iii) free movement of investments and skilled labor within JACIK countries.	Welfare effects under Scenarios 1, 2, and 3 (EV in $ Mn): • Thailand—4,409.8; 4,594.7; 5,799.7 • Singapore—2,292.5; 1,786.7; 1,741.4 • Indonesia—3,760.3; 3,993.9; 6,968.1 • PRC—6,326.5; 7,100.0; 16,327.7 • Japan—107,625.7; 111,807.0; 150,695.2 • Republic of Korea—13,042.9; 13,317.4; 14,075.7 • India—6,971.3; 7,378.6; 9,937.0 • JACIK—147,417.6; 153,155.7; 210,440.9 • Rest of South Asia not shown	GTAP database disaggregates South Asia into two regions: India and rest of South Asia. ASEAN includes Indonesia, Malaysia, Philippines, Singapore, and Thailand only.

continued on next page

Table 8.1: continued

Study	Model and Baseline	Parameters and Assumptions	Impact of FTA Scenarios	Notes
Mohanty and Pohit (2007)	GTAP Model	Uses GTAP database (version 6); data disaggregated into 11 out of the 16 regions and 26 sectors. Simulates 3 FTA scenarios: (i) ASEAN+3, (ii) ASEAN+4, and (iii) ASEAN+6, where each scenario is simulated according to three levels of economic liberalization: (i) FTA, (ii) FTA+investment, and (iii) FTA+investment+services.	Welfare effects under Scenarios 1, 2, and 3 (absolute change in welfare, in $ Mn) under FTA+investment+services economic liberalization: • Indonesia—13,004; 15,806; 22,300 • Malaysia—1,692; 1,956; 2,670 • Philippines—1,179; 1,383; 2,005 • Singapore—698; 755; 1,164 • Thailand—1,958; 2,520; 3,765 • Japan—40,236; 61,313; 91,029 • Republic of Korea—6,503; 7,650; 10,976 • PRC—11,561; 17,193; 30,128 • India—3,428; 5,026; 6,462 • Australia—1,477; 5,369; 5,962 • New Zealand—224; 655; 1,667 • South Asia—634; 2,295; 3,336	
Plummer and Wignaraja (2006)	GEMAT Model Base year of 2001	Uses GTAP database (version 6); data disaggregated into 19 countries and 14 sectors. Assumes removal of tariff barriers between FTA members.	Welfare effects of multiple bilateral FTAs in Asia, Asia-wide FTA, and APEC FTA scenarios (EV in $ Mn under each scenario): • ASEAN—8,869; 10,907; 8,341 • Northeast Asia—(1,219); 35,713; 56,734 • Rest of Asia—(101), 1,355, (1,560) • US—(1,371); 3,263; 12,035 • EU—(1,021), (1,413), (3,047)	ASEAN includes Indonesia, Malaysia, Philippines, Singapore, Thailand, and Viet Nam only.

continued on next page

Table 8.1: continued

Study	Model and Baseline	Parameters and Assumptions	Impact of FTA Scenarios	Notes
Siriwardana (2003)	GTAP Model Base year of 1997	Uses GTAP database (version 5); data disaggregated into 11 regions and 20 sectors. Performs two liberalization scenarios: (i) assumes removal of all bilateral tariffs between South Asian countries but not between other countries; (ii) creation of customs union by eliminating all tariffs between South Asian regions and adopting common external tariff against all other countries in the world.	Welfare effects under South Asia FTA and South Asia Customs Union scenarios (EV in \$ Mn): • PRC—(680.55), (743.40) • Japan—(4,008.51), (4,111.84) • India—3,046.62; 4,995.84 • Sri Lanka—261.96; 1,466.11 • Bangladesh—90.47; 1,043.15 • Rest of South Asia—579.83; 4,062.39 • NAFTA—(6,434.40), (24,333.60) • EU—(6,434.40), (18,950.50)	GTAP database disaggregates South Asia into four regions: India, Sri Lanka, Bangladesh, and rest of South Asia.
Bchir and Fouquin (2006)	MIRAGE Model	Uses GTAP database (version 6). Performs two policy experiments: 1) assumes that ASEAN removes its tariffs bilaterally with PRC, India, Japan, and Republic of Korea (with and without exclusion of sensitive products); and 2) assumes removal of tariffs between ASEAN, PRC,	Welfare effects under bilateral agreements between ASEAN and PRC, India, Japan, and Republic of Korea in 2015, without exclusion (EV as % change from baseline):	

continued on next page

Table 8.1: continued

Study	Model and Baseline	Parameters and Assumptions	Impact of FTA Scenarios	Notes
		India, Japan, and Republic of Korea (with or without exclusion of sensitive products).	• ASEAN—2.18 • PRC—(0.12) • Japan—0.18 • Republic of Korea—(0.40) • India—(0.32) • South Asia—(0.05) • US—0.00 • EU-25—(0.01) Welfare effects under a single global agreement between ASEAN and PRC, India, Japan, and Republic of Korea in 2015, without exclusion (EV as % change from baseline): • ASEAN—1.43 • PRC—(0.27) • Japan—0.41 • Republic of Korea—1.64 • India—(0.37) • South Asia—(0.12) • US—0.00 • EU-25—(0.02)	

APEC = Asia-Pacific Economic Cooperation, ASEAN = Association of Southeast Asian Nations, CGE = computable general equilibrium, EU = European Union, EV = equivalnet value, FTA = free trade agreement, GDP = gross domestic product, GEMAT = General Equilibrium Model for Asia's Trade, GTAP = Global Trade Analysis Project, MFN = most favored nation, NAFTA = North American Free Trade Agreement, NTB = nontariff barrier, PRC = People's Republic of China, SAFTA = South Asian Free Trade Agreement, US = United States, $ Bn = billions of US dollars, $ Mn = millions of US dollars, ( ) = negative value.

Source: Various sources as shown column 1.

Studies, however, differ in their estimates of welfare gains to members and losses to non-members from an East Asia FTA, depending on the type of CGE model used, data source, and baseline year. An early study by Ballard and Cheong (1997), using a CGE model with firm-level imperfect competition, indicated that both an Asia-Pacific Economic Cooperation (APEC) FTA and an East Asian FTA would generate gains for all members even without the participation of the United States (US) or Japan. They also estimate that developing nations in Asia are expected to gain more when the US joins the FTA than when Japan joins. Urata and Kyota (2003) estimate from GTAP simulations that an East Asia FTA will generate welfare gains for members from the highest of 12.5% of gross domestic product (GDP) for Thailand and 6.6% for Viet Nam to the lowest of 0.19% for Japan and 0.64% for the PRC. They find modest welfare loses for non-members of -0.02% for EU, -0.09% for US, and -0.29% for Australia and New Zealand. Also using GTAP, Gilbert et al (2004) find that an East Asia FTA will produce higher welfare gains for members than a narrower PRC–Japan–Korea FTA indicating that broadening FTAs brings benefits. They report lower welfare gains from an East Asia FTA for Viet Nam (3.1%) and Thailand (1.6%) than do Urata and Kyota (2003). Most recently, Zhang et al (2006) report GTAP simulations confirming the common result that all members gain from an East Asian FTA. They estimate that such an FTA would increase the overall GDP of East Asian countries by 1.2% and economic welfare by $104.6 billion. From their LINKAGE CGE model, Lee et al (2004) show significantly higher welfare gains from an East Asia FTA for the PRC and Hong Kong, China (4.0%) and Japan (1.6%), notable gains for Korea (3.7%) and ASEAN as a group (4.0%), and welfare losses for the rest of the world of under -0.2%.

By comparison, the available studies suggest mixed views about the impact of an FTA involving only South Asian economies and one between selected East and South Asian countries. Using GTAP, Siriwardena (2003) compares the effects of an FTA and a customs union for South Asian countries. He finds that the South Asian FTA scenario (with full trade liberalization internally) brings gains to all members and losses to non-members but that the customs union entails bigger gains for members as well as bigger loses to non-members. Not surprisingly, perhaps, the region's largest and most competitive economy—India—gains the most ($3.1 billion in the FTA scenario). However, Bandara and Yu (2003) (also using GTAP) find lower gains for India ($756 million) from a South Asia FTA scenario, negligible gains for Sri Lanka and the rest of South Asia, and losses for Bangladesh. Likewise, Bandara and Yu (2003) provide a pessimistic assessment of an ASEAN–South Asia FTA. ASEAN as a whole is likely to see modest gains ($3 billion) and all the South Asian economies including India incur welfare loses. Non-members (e.g., the EU and the US) also lose.

With an opposite result, Mohanty, Pohit, and Roy (2004) argue that an East Asia–India FTA (Japan, ASEAN, PRC, India, and Korea [JACIK]) will bring gains to members of $147.4 billion (liberalization of trade barriers only scenario) to $210.4 billion (liberalization of barriers to trade, investment, and labor). In their scenarios, all members benefit, with Japan witnessing the largest gains ($108.0 billion), followed by the PRC and India (under $7.0 billion each). The Philippines benefits the least ($1.0 billion).[2] In a follow-up study, Mohanty and Pohit (2007) show reduced gains for members from an East Asia–India FTA ranging from $52.3 billion for a simple FTA (liberalization of trade barriers only) to $113.6 billion for a more comprehensive FTA (liberalization of barriers to trade, investment, and services). In the FTA scenario, both members and non-members gain. The work of Bchir and Fouquin (2006) on an East Asia–India FTA, relying on the MIRAGE CGE (also relying on GTAP data), suggest that non-members see small loses ranging from -0.02% for the EU, -0.12% for the rest of South Asia, and -0.16% for Russian Federation. Interestingly, they also find that Asia's giant economies—the PRC (-0.27%) and India (-0.37%)— lose from an East Asia–India FTA, while ASEAN, Japan, and Korea gain.

Finally, drawing on a GEMAT CGE model (a variant of the LINKAGE model), Plummer and Wignaraja (2006) investigate the relative economic effects of various possible FTA scenarios: (i) a fragmented scenario of bilateral FTAs and ASEAN to depict the current East Asian policy reality; (ii) an Asia-wide FTA (including Northeast Asia, ASEAN, and South Asia); and (iii) an APEC FTA. Compared to the others, the fragmented FTA scenario leads to lower welfare for all. An Asia-wide FTA generates gains of $48 billion for the region. All members gain, but Northeast Asian economies gain disproportionately. Meanwhile, the APEC FTA generates larger gains of $64 billion for Asia. As expected, Northeast Asia and US members gain but non-members like South Asia and the EU lose.

---

[2] Interestingly, the authors do not provide details of how the normally technically difficult barriers to investment and labor are incorporated into their model. Nor do they provide estimates for the effects of (Japan, ASEAN, PRC, India, and Republic of Korea [JACIK]) an East Asia-India Free Trade Agreement on non-members.

The Model and Data

We turn to a brief overview of the global CGE model used here. As is standard in the literature (Hertel et al 1997), the model is characterized by a global input-output structure (based on regional and national input-output tables) that explicitly links industries in a value-added chain from primary goods over continuously higher stages of intermediate processing to the final assembling of goods and services for consumption. Intersectoral linkages are direct, like the input of steel in the production of transport equipment, and indirect, via intermediate use in other sectors. The model captures these linkages by modeling firms' use of factors and intermediate inputs. In terms of structure, the model is a version of the basic one employed by Francois, van Meijl, and van Tongeren (2005) to assess the Doha Round. The data, however, reflects a more current (and projected) economic landscape. The most important aspects of the model can be summarized as follows: (i) it covers all world trade and production, (ii) it includes intermediate linkages between sectors (see Hertel et al 1997), and (iii) it allows for trade to affect capital stocks through investment effects. The last point means we model medium to long-run investment effects (see Francois, McDonald, and Nordstrom 1997).

Model Data and the Benchmark

Our data come from a number of sources. Data on production and trade are based on national social accounting data linked through trade flows (see Reinert and Roland-Holst 1997). These social accounting data are drawn directly from the GTAP dataset version 6.3. (Dimaranan and McDougall 2002). The GTAP version 6 dataset is benchmarked to 2001, and includes detailed national input-output, trade, and final demand structures. The basic social accounting and trade data are supplemented with trade policy data, including additional data on tariffs and NTBs. We have projected the database to 2007, and through to 2017, using macroeconomic projections from the World Bank (circulated through the GTAP consortium) combined with macroeconomic outlook data from the International Monetary Fund (IMF).

The 2007 projection includes the phase-out of the Agreement on Textiles and Clothing (ATC) quotas in 2005, as well as remaining WTO commitments under the Doha Round and the enlargement of the EU from 15 to 27 members. The data on tariffs is taken from the WTO's integrated database, with supplemental information from the World Bank's recent assessment of detailed pre- and post-Uruguay Round tariff schedules and from the United Nations Conference on Trade and Development (UNCTAD)/World Bank's World Integrated Trade Solution (WITS) dataset. All of this tariff information has been mapped to activity sectors. Services trade barriers are based on the gravity model estimates described in the annex. These estimates are also discussed in the next section. We also work with the schedule of the PRC's WTO accession commitments. While the basic GTAP dataset is benchmarked to 2001, and reflects applied tariffs actually in place in 2001, we of course want to work with a representation of a post-Uruguay Round world. We also want to include the accession of the PRC and the enlargement of the EU, as part of the baseline. Our 2017 projection is based on the 2007 policy baseline. The social accounting data has been aggregated into 35 sectors and 36 regions. The sectors and regions for the 35 x 36 aggregation of the data are given in table 8.2.

Table 8.2   Model Region and Sectoring Scheme

Model Regions	Model Sectors
1 Australia	1 Grains
2 New Zealand	2 Horticulture
3 Other Oceania	3 Oil seeds
4 PRC	4 Sugar
5 Hong Kong, China	5 Cotton
6 Japan	6 Beef
7 Korea, Republic of	7 Dairy
8 Taipei,China	8 Vegetable oils
9 Other East Asia	9 Other primary agriculture
10 Cambodia	10 Other processed foods
11 Indonesia	11 Beverages and tobacco
12 Malaysia	12 Forestry
13 Philippines	13 Fisheries
14 Singapore	14 Mining
15 Thailand	15 Textiles
16 Viet Nam	16 Clothing
17 Other Southeast Asia	17 Leather
18 Bangladesh	18 Lumber
19 India	19 Paper, pulp, and printing
20 Pakistan	20 Petrochemicals

continued on next page

Table 8.2: continued

Model Regions	Model Sectors
21 Sri Lanka	21 Chemicals, rubber, and plastics
22 Other South Asia	22 Iron and steel
23 Central Asia	23 Non-ferrous metals
24 Canada	24 Motor vehicles
25 United States	25 Electrical machinery
26 Mexico	26 Other machinery
27 Latin America	27 Other manufactures
28 EU-27	28 Utilities
29 EFTA	29 Construction
30 Turkey	30 Trade services
31 Russia	31 Transport services
32 Other Europe	32 Communications
33 North Africa and Middle East	33 Financial services
34 South Africa	34 Insurance
35 Sub-Saharan Africa	35 Other business services
	36 Other services

EFTA = European Free Trade Agreement, EU = European Union, PRC = People's Republic of China.
Source: Global Trade Analysis Project database.

Theoretical Structure

We turn next to the basic theoretical features of the model. In all regions, there is a single representative, composite household in each region, with expenditures allocated over personal consumption and savings (future consumption) and over government expenditures. The composite household owns endowments of the factors of production and receives income by selling them to firms. It also receives income from tariff revenue and rents accruing from import/export quota licenses (when applicable). Part of the income is distributed as subsidy payments to some sectors, primarily in agriculture.

On the production side, in all sectors, firms employ domestic production factors (capital, labor, and land) and intermediate inputs from domestic and foreign sources to produce outputs in the most cost-efficient way that technology allows. Perfect competition is assumed, while products from different regions are assumed to be imperfect substitutes, in accordance with the so-called Armington assumption.

Prices on goods and factors adjust until all markets are simultaneously in (general) equilibrium. This means that we solve for equilibria in which all markets clear. While we model changes in gross trade flows, we do not model changes in net international capital flows. Rather, our capital market closure involves fixed net capital inflows and outflows. This does not preclude changes in gross capital flows. To summarize, factor markets are competitive, and labor and capital are mobile between sectors but not between regions. All primary factors—labor, land, and capital—are fully employed within each region.

We also include a dynamic link, whereby changes in investment, following from policy changes, lead to changes in installed capital stocks and ultimately to production and trade volumes. This is based on the Solow model approach, as outlined in Francois, McDonald, and Nordstrom (1997). Conceptually, as we are working with a projected baseline, these dynamic effects can be thought of as including induced investment effects along an alternative path to the 2017 benchmark, wherein we have implemented the policy changes in time for investment effects to be realized in the 2017 equilibrium.

Policy Landscape, Scenarios, and Discussion

We next turn to our analysis of regional integration initiatives between East and South Asia. This includes a broad overview of trade structure and policy in the region, our scenarios, and the impact of those scenarios on our baseline.

Trade and Trade Policy in the Region

The regional share of international trade in Asia varies widely across regions. This was true in 2001 and also holds in our projected 2007 and 2017 benchmarks. Tables 8.3 and 8.4 provide detailed information of this pattern. The countries of East Asia (including Northeast and Southeast Asia) are in general much more integrated, in a regional sense, than are the countries of South Asia. Indeed, the difference is striking. For most countries in the region, more than 40% of their exports are destined for Asian markets. From table 8.3, it is clear that most of this trade is destined for East Asia. Indeed, for many countries in the region, this share is projected to rise. Oceania (primarily Australia and New Zealand), while not technically part of the region geographically, is closely tied economically, with the vast majority of its exports going to the region. With projected economic growth through 2017, this dependence only increases.

Table 8.3   Direction of Exports, % of total export value

	2001		2007		2017	
	East Asia	South Asia	East Asia	South Asia	East Asia	South Asia
Australia	46.0	2.9	49.9	3.7	61.4	5.9
New Zealand	33.6	1.3	37.2	1.9	44.0	2.9
Other Oceania	33.6	0.8	36.0	0.8	42.5	0.8
PRC	36.5	1.4	34.8	1.3	33.6	1.2
Hong Kong, China	38.9	1.4	42.2	1.3	44.7	1.2
Japan	37.9	1.0	38.8	0.9	40.2	0.9
Korea, Rep. of	40.9	1.9	41.8	1.7	41.3	1.5
Taipei,China	43.1	1.6	44.6	1.6	46.3	1.6
Other East Asia	26.7	1.5	29.3	1.5	35.4	1.2
Cambodia	14.5	0.6	16.5	0.6	15.5	0.6
Indonesia	48.2	3.8	46.0	3.6	49.1	4.0
Malaysia	47.0	3.4	48.6	3.5	51.0	4.5
Philippines	47.2	0.4	47.8	0.4	46.1	0.4
Singapore	47.0	3.9	49.1	3.5	50.6	2.9
Thailand	43.4	2.1	44.2	1.9	45.9	1.6
Viet Nam	41.7	0.5	43.8	0.5	46.5	0.4
Other Southeast Asia	52.7	7.5	54.8	6.0	59.6	4.1
Bangladesh	6.8	1.4	8.3	1.6	7.3	1.5
India	20.6	3.9	21.6	3.7	24.9	3.2
Pakistan	16.5	4.2	12.6	3.2	11.0	2.8
Sri Lanka	10.0	3.1	10.4	3.3	7.9	3.0
Other South Asia	12.7	20.5	12.0	22.2	12.2	30.9

PRC = People's Republic of China.

Source: Computed from Global Trade Analysis Project database.

Table 8.4   Source of Imports, % of total export value

	2001		2007		2017	
	East Asia	South Asia	East Asia	South Asia	East Asia	South Asia
Australia	39.1	1.1	41.5	1.3	46.8	1.8
New Zealand	26.6	1.1	29.1	1.1	36.6	1.6
Other Oceania	30.3	1.0	32.6	1.2	39.8	1.6
PRC	53.7	1.0	53.2	1.1	51.6	1.5
Hong Kong, China	63.4	1.3	63.9	1.6	65.1	2.4
Japan	38.0	1.0	40.7	1.1	45.3	1.2
Korea, Rep. of	40.0	1.1	40.4	1.1	40.9	1.2
Taipei,China	51.1	0.7	52.8	0.7	56.7	1.0
Other East Asia	61.8	2.6	61.9	2.7	62.8	3.4
Cambodia	84.4	1.1	84.7	1.2	83.2	1.5
Indonesia	49.1	2.1	49.3	2.2	50.4	2.5
Malaysia	57.4	1.5	58.7	1.7	61.4	2.1
Philippines	53.4	1.0	53.1	1.0	56.1	1.7
Singapore	54.2	1.3	58.5	1.5	65.6	2.3
Thailand	52.7	1.7	54.5	1.8	57.5	2.6
Viet Nam	51.8	1.6	52.1	1.7	53.6	2.1
Other Southeast Asia	75.5	2.0	76.8	2.2	77.5	2.6
Bangladesh	50.2	13.7	50.1	14.0	49.8	16.0
India	27.8	1.3	28.1	1.4	28.6	1.6
Pakistan	28.0	3.3	27.8	3.1	25.8	3.1
Sri Lanka	43.7	11.5	44.0	11.8	45.7	13.9
Other South Asia	35.3	18.7	34.7	19.3	35.9	21.7

PRC = People's Republic of China.

Source: Computed from Global Trade Analyis Project database.

In contrast to East Asia, South Asian economies are much less closely tied to one another. Trade shares with Asia are generally well below 30%. From tables 8.3 and 8.5, it is also clear that most of this trade is not actually with South Asia. Ironically, while there have been regional initiatives in South Asia—and not so much between South and East Asia—the bulk of South Asian regional exports go to East Asia rather than to South Asia. This points both to a relatively low degree of integration within the region, and also to the potential for gains from liberalization initiatives that span the two subregions.

Table 8.5 provides a breakdown of most-favored nation (MFN) protection as of 2004/05 (from the WITS database) on a trade-weighted basis. This provides a sense of the scope for gains from liberalization in merchandise trade. In general, import protection is higher in South Asia than it is in East Asia. This explains in part why East Asian trade relationships are deeper and why South Asian trade is biased toward East Asia. Of course, the relative size of the economies in the two regions also helps to explain this regional bias.

Table 8.5   MFN Protection, 2004/05

	Average MFN tariff	MFN tariff*	Energy share of imports
Bangladesh	55.8	54.9	0.1
Nepal	14.6	14.7	0.2
India	13.9	15.4	0.3
Pakistan	12.2	13.1	0.2
Sri Lanka	7.3	7.9	0.1
Thailand	5.4	6.5	0.2
PRC	4.9	5.3	0.1
Singapore	0.0	0.0	0.2

MFN = most favored nation, PRC = People's Republic of China.

* Less energy.

Source: World Integrated Trade Solution database.

Table 8.6 provides a similar picture, only for services. These tables are based on our estimates of services trade barriers for cross-border trade, as discussed in the annex. Unlike goods, services see little regional difference

Table 8.6 Services Trade Barriers

Estimated Coefficients

	Producer Services	Other Non-trade Services
PRC	25.2	11.2
Hong Kong, China	0.0	0.0
Japan	27.0	20.6
Korea, Republic of	15.7	20.6
Taipei,China	14.3	10.7
Other East Asia	11.9	10.8
Cambodia	20.8	36.1
Indonesia	12.5	12.2
Malaysia	8.3	9.3
Singapore	0.0	0.0
Philippines	8.3	12.8
Thailand	6.6	5.6
Viet Nam	20.8	36.1
Other Southeast Asia	46.3	46.4
Bangladesh	25.2	29.0
India	26.0	32.6
Pakistan	30.0	34.5
Sri Lanka	22.0	20.9
Other South Asia	7.4	9.4

PRC = People's Republic of China.

Source: Authors' estimates.

in the pattern of protection. In general, our estimates are that protection is much higher for goods than for services, and that this holds for countries in East Asia as well as South Asia.

The broad picture that emerges from this overview of the trade and trade protection data is (i) East Asia is more integrated than South Asia, (i) South Asia itself has deeper trade ties with East Asia than with itself, and (iii) import protection for merchandise explains part of this pattern. We now turn to an assessment of a set of stylized regional integration schemes.

Scenarios

In most of what follows we examine three cores scenarios as follows.

- Scenario 1: ASEAN+3 FTA. An FTA encompassing the members of ASEAN as well as PRC, Japan, and Korea;
- Scenario 2: ASEAN+3 and India FTA. Extends scenario 1's FTA to include India. South Asia's largest economy is included but the rest of South Asia is excluded.
- Scenario 3: ASEAN+3 and South Asia FTA. Extends scenario 2 to include the rest of South Asia and implements full free trade across South Asia itself.

We will also (in less detail) look at subregional scenarios involving South Asia. All three core scenarios involve free trade in merchandise goods (i.e., tariffs as represented in table 8.5), free trade in services (based on estimates in table 8.6), and trade-cost reductions equal to 2.5% of the cost of trade. Trade-cost reductions can follow from trade facilitation measures that streamline the administrative cost of clearing goods across borders. Recent estimates place these costs at anywhere from 6% to 30% of the costs of goods traded. (Francois, Hoekman, and Manchin 2006; Manchin and Pelkmans-Balaoing 2007). They can also follow from improvements to trade-related infrastructure. Indeed, recent estimates suggest that for North–South trade, variations in trade-related infrastructure explain more of the sample variations in goods trade than does trade policy itself (Francois and Manchin 2007). Table 8.7 reports estimates of the trade cost savings that would follow from a 1% and 5% improvement in the general quality of trade-related infrastructure, based on Francois, Manchin, and Pelkmans-Balaoing (2008). From the estimates in the table, a 5% improvement would yield a 2.5% trade cost savings, on average. Broadly speaking, the 2.5% trade cost reduction in our scenarios is meant to capture a regional trade initiative that includes both administrative improvements (so that goods move more quickly and with less paperwork) and some investment in physical infrastructure in the poorer countries in the region. Japan, in particular, has emphasized the infrastructure potential of regional schemes. From Manchin and Pelkmans-Balaoing (2007), this seems a conservative estimates of the benefits from a simple streamlining of administrative barriers in the region, let alone other measures to reduce the costs of trade.

Broad Welfare and Trade Effects

Tables 8.8 to 8.17 summarize the results of our three core experiments. All results are reported relative to the 2017 baseline simulation. Broadly speaking, the scenario with the widest regional FTA coverage implies global income gains of $260.9 billion in 2001 dollars, or approximately 0.5% of

Table 8.7 Trade Cost Impact of Infrastructure Improvement

Estimated coefficients

	Trade Cost Elasticities (equivalent as % of value)		Total for 1% improvement	Total for 5% improvement
	Communication	Transport		
Full Sample	0.19	0.19	0.37	1.87
North-South Sample	0.15	0.28	0.43	2.15
Country Estimates				
Australia	0.25	0.06	0.32	1.58
Bangladesh	0.18	0.55	0.73	3.65
Cambodia	0.18	0.55	0.72	3.62
PRC	0.19	0.48	0.67	3.36
Hong Kong, China	0.25	0.06	0.31	1.55
India	0.18	0.53	0.71	3.56
Indonesia	0.20	0.43	0.62	3.12
Japan	0.27	-0.02	0.25	1.23
Korea, Republic of	0.24	0.14	0.38	1.90
Lao PDR	0.18	0.53	0.71	3.57
Malaysia	0.22	0.26	0.48	2.40
New Zealand	0.25	0.09	0.34	1.70
Pakistan	0.18	0.50	0.69	3.45
Philippines	0.20	0.41	0.61	3.04
Singapore	0.25	0.05	0.31	1.54
Thailand	0.21	0.31	0.53	2.63
Viet Nam	0.18	0.57	0.74	3.71

Lao PDR = Lao People's Democratic Republic, PRC = People's Republic of China.

Source: Francois, Manchin, and Pelkmans-Balaoing (2008).

global income. This follows from a $263.9-billion gain for insiders, and a loss of $3 billion for outsiders. Interestingly, for the narrower FTAs there are losses for South Asian economies in the range of -0.3 to -0.5% of GDP, while for regional outsiders in all cases the extra-regional losses are generally quite small. This suggests a pattern that we will see in the sections on sector effects and on regional direction of trade, of apparent dominance of the results by trade creation and gains from trade, rather than trade diversion and losses, under our broad FTA scenario. In other words, while the narrower scenarios imply losses for the (South Asian) outsiders, a broad pan-Asian initiative appears to imply only minimal third-country effects and substantial gains across the regional participants.

Scenario 1: ASEAN+3 FTA. From table 8.8, the ASEAN+3 FTA yields the bulk of the gains realized across all the scenarios for East Asia. This should not surprise us, given the trade shares reported earlier. In absolute terms, the primary winners from the ASEAN+3 scenario are Japan ($74.8 billion, or 1.5% of baseline 2017 GDP), Korea ($49.4 billion, or 6.2% of 2017 GDP), PRC ($41.5 billion, or 1.3% of 2017 GDP), and Malaysia ($10.4 billion, or 5.5% of 2017 GDP). Expressed as a percentage of baseline income, the greatest gains under this scenario are realized in Thailand (12.1%), Viet Nam (7.4%), and Korea (6.2%). The ASEAN+3 scenario also has negative implications, linked to trade diversion, for Australia (-0.4% of GDP), New Zealand (-0.3%), and Taipei,China (-2.0% of GDP).

Broad effects on trade can be seen in tables 8.9 and 8.10. These tables report the impact on overall exports, as well as the impact on terms of trade. There are dramatic increases in exports for the PRC (12.4%), Korea (12.9%), and Japan (7.1%). These results relate to a mix of improved market access and an opening up of own markets. In addition to the benefits to the biggest three East Asian economies, reductions in trade costs and services liberalization also benefit exporters across Southeast Asia, including Viet Nam (34.1%), Thailand (22.3%), Philippines (7.6%), and Indonesia (7.4%). The impact on the terms of trade is mixed across the region. The impact on outsider countries is mixed and generally negative, with India and Pakistan both seeing a drop in exports of over 1% and a worsening terms of trade. This also implies a drop of income of -0.3% in India and -0.5% in Pakistan.

Scenario 2: ASEAN+3 and India FTA. When the ASEAN+3 FTA scenario is expanded to include India, some additional gains are visible for East Asia. Interestingly, PRC, Korea, and Japan collectively witness a $7.2-billion gain from the inclusion of India in an East Asia FTA. ASEAN economies also gain roughly $5.7 billion more than under the first scenario, with Thailand, Malaysia, and Singapore, benefiting somewhat more than others as a percentage of 2017 baseline GDP (12.8%, 6.4%, and 5.6%, respectively). India gains strongly—$17.8 billion per annum, or 2.2% of baseline income. Furthermore, the negative effects on its South Asian

Table 8.8 National Income Effects

Compared to 2017 baseline (at constant 2001 prices), in $ Mn and in %

	ASEAN+3 FTA		ASEAN+3 and India FTA		ASEAN+3 and South Asia FTA	
	$ Mn	%	$ Mn	%	$ Mn	%
Australia	(2,376)	(0.4)	(2,946)	(0.5)	(2,987)	(0.5)
New Zealand	(216)	(0.3)	(183)	(0.2)	(169)	(0.2)
Other Oceania	(8)	0.0	13	0.1	7	0.0
PRC	41,502	1.3	43,289	1.3	43,454	1.3
Hong Kong, China	(1,051)	(0.3)	(1,713)	(0.5)	(1,811)	(0.6)
Japan	74,825	1.5	78,080	1.6	78,650	1.6
Korea, Rep. of	49,393	6.2	51,545	6.5	52,100	6.5
Taipei,China	(10,493)	(2.0)	(10,770)	(2.1)	(10,997)	(2.1)
Other East Asia	(105)	(0.2)	(115)	(0.3)	(161)	(0.4)
Cambodia	107	1.2	106	1.2	79	0.9
Indonesia	7,884	2.6	8,818	2.9	9,090	3.0
Malaysia	10,391	5.5	12,014	6.4	12,376	6.6
Philippines	3,177	2.6	3,521	2.9	3,495	2.9
Singapore	7,943	4.8	9,285	5.6	9,717	5.9
Thailand	26,728	12.1	28,220	12.8	28,534	12.9
Viet Nam	5,293	7.4	5,449	7.6	5,428	7.5
Other Southeast Asia	661	0.6	483	0.4	374	0.3
Bangladesh	(297)	(0.3)	(355)	(0.3)	1,874	1.7
India	(2,371)	(0.3)	17,779	2.2	18,240	(2,3)
Pakistan	(824)	(0.5)	(862)	(0.6)	298	0.2
Sri Lanka	(117)	(0.4)	(123)	(0.4)	631	2.0
Other South Asia	(12)	0.0	(240)	(0.6)	1,380	3.7
Central Asia	(159)	(0.1)	(165)	(0.1)	(181)	(0.1)
Canada	1,796	0.2	2,137	0.2	2,295	0.2
United States	(4,966)	0.0	(3,214)	0.0	(1,924)	0.0

continued on next page

Table 8.8: continued

Compared to 2017 baseline (at constant 2001 prices), in $ Mn and in %

	ASEAN+3 FTA		ASEAN+3 and India FTA		ASEAN+3 and South Asia FTA	
	$ Mn	%	$ Mn	%	$ Mn	%
Mexico	2,935	0.3	3,982	0.4	4,116	0.4
Latin America	(2,082)	(0.1)	(1,423)	(0.1)	(1,905)	(0.1)
EU27	6,786	0.1	9,248	0.1	10,300	0.1
EFTA	1,089	0.2	1,211	0.2	1,309	0.3
Turkey	(538)	(0.2)	(468)	(0.2)	(652)	(0.2)
Russian Fed.	(197)	0.0	(165)	0.0	(126)	0.0
Other Europe	(52)	(0.1)	(61)	(0.1)	(74)	(0.1)
North Africa and Middle East	(1,083)	(0.1)	(1,275)	(0.1)	(2,016)	(0.1)
South Africa	(44)	0.0	(284)	(0.2)	(330)	(0.2)
Sub-Saharan Africa	396	0.1	544	0.1	493	0.1
TOTAL	213,919	0.4	251,363	0.5	260,907	0.5

ASEAN+3 = Association of Southeast Asian Nations plus People's Republic of China (PRC), Japan, and Republic of Korea; EFTA = European Free Trade Agreement, EU = European Union, FTA = free trade agreement, $ Mn = millions of US dollars, % = percent, ( ) = negative value.

Source: Authors' estimates.

Table 8.9   Export Effects, % of 2017 baseline exports

	ASEAN+3 FTA	ASEAN+3 and India FTA	ASEAN+3 and South Asia FTA
Australia	(0.91)	(1.03)	(1.06)
New Zealand	(0.43)	(0.45)	(0.47)
Other Oceania	(0.93)	(1.03)	(1.11)
PRC	12.38	13.14	13.19
Hong Kong, China	(0.80)	(0.96)	(1.00)

continued on next page

Table 8.9: continued

	ASEAN+3 FTA	ASEAN+3 and India FTA	ASEAN+3 and South Asia FTA
Japan	7.08	7.31	7.34
Korea, Republic of	12.87	13.32	13.38
Taipei,China	(2.70)	(2.72)	(2.74)
Other East Asia	(1.67)	(1.74)	(2.18)
Cambodia	7.55	7.62	6.80
Indonesia	7.37	8.15	8.42
Malaysia	6.04	6.79	6.95
Philippines	7.56	8.41	8.43
Singapore	2.64	2.89	3.03
Thailand	22.31	23.57	23.85
Viet Nam	34.07	35.28	35.36
Other Southeast Asia	4.10	5.30	4.78
Bangladesh	(0.89)	(1.14)	51.65
India	(1.01)	21.36	22.73
Pakistan	(1.26)	(1.34)	7.03
Sri Lanka	(0.45)	(0.44)	5.84
Other South Asia	(0.25)	(2.16)	19.86
Central Asia	(0.34)	(0.39)	(0.42)
Canada	0.02	0.04	0.04
United States	(0.90)	(0.95)	(0.95)
Mexico	0.58	0.74	0.76
Latin America	(0.34)	(0.33)	(0.38)
EU27	(0.08)	(0.08)	(0.08)
EFTA	(0.27)	(0.27)	(0.27)
Turkey	(0.19)	(0.16)	(0.20)
Russian Federation	(1.05)	(1.12)	(1.15)
Other Europe	(0.22)	(0.25)	(0.28)
North Africa and Middle East	(0.87)	(0.99)	(1.10)
South Africa	(0.38)	(0.69)	(0.75)

continued on next page

Table 8.9: continued

	ASEAN+3 FTA	ASEAN+3 and India FTA	ASEAN+3 and South Asia FTA
Sub-Saharan Africa	(0.43)	(0.49)	(0.56)
TOTAL	2.62	3.09	3.26

ASEAN+3 = Association of Southeast Asian Nations plus People's Republic of China (PRC), Japan, and Republic of Korea; EFTA = European Free Trade Agreement, EU = European Union, FTA = free trade agreement, $ Mn = millions of US dollars, % = percent, ( ) = negative value.

Source: Authors' estimates.

Table 8.10   Terms of Trade Effects, % change in export/import price ratio

	ASEAN+3 FTA	ASEAN+3 and India FTA	ASEAN+3 and South Asia FTA
Australia	(0.79)	(1.19)	(1.21)
New Zealand	(0.17)	(0.15)	(0.12)
Other Oceania	0.71	0.81	0.83
PRC	(1.29)	(1.18)	(1.17)
Hong Kong, China	(0.21)	(0.28)	(0.33)
Japan	2.86	2.95	2.95
Korea, Republic of	1.65	1.75	1.79
Taipei,China	(1.78)	(1.88)	(1.93)
Other East Asia	(0.28)	(0.31)	(0.52)
Cambodia	(0.9)	(1.04)	(1.48)
Indonesia	(0.16)	0.22	0.27
Malaysia	(0.2)	0.11	0.16
Philippines	(1.06)	(1.14)	(1.16)
Singapore	0.6	0.78	0.86
Thailand	(0.89)	(0.91)	(0.91)
Viet Nam	(1.87)	(1.98)	(2.07)
Other Southeast Asia	0.01	0.5	0.66
Bangladesh	(0.64)	(0.82)	(6.18)

continued on next page

Table 8.10: continued

	ASEAN+3 FTA	ASEAN+3 and India FTA	ASEAN+3 and South Asia FTA
India	(0.9)	(2.08)	(2.29)
Pakistan	(1.64)	(1.82)	(2.20)
Sri Lanka	(0.49)	(0.65)	(0.18)
Other South Asia	(0.08)	(1.98)	7.85
Central Asia	(0.03)	(0.03)	(0.03)
Canada	0.24	0.26	0.27
United States	(0.44)	(0.45)	(0.43)
Mexico	0.17	0.11	0.09
Latin America	(0.02)	(0.09)	(0.11)
EU27	(0.06)	(0.09)	(0.09)
EFTA	0.29	0.29	0.32
Turkey	(0.26)	(0.29)	(0.37)
Russian Federation	0.38	0.40	0.41
Other Europe	0.10	0.09	0.08
North Africa and Middle East	0.41	0.40	0.38
South Africa	0.02	(0.11)	(0.14)
Sub-Saharan Africa	0.48	0.53	0.52

ASEAN+3 = Association of Southeast Asian Nations plus People's Republic of China (PRC), Japan, and Republic of Korea; EFTA = European Free Trade Agreement, EU = European Union, FTA = free trade agreement, $ Mn = millions of US dollars, % = percent, ( ) = negative value.

Source: Authors' estimates.

neighbors (like Pakistan and Sri Lanka) are magnified relative to the first scenario. For example, in other South Asian countries, primarily Nepal, the loss is 0.6% of GDP. India's exports see a tremendous boost, equal to 21.3% of baseline exports, while there is a negative impact on other subregional exporters. Again, the results illustrate the consistent pattern of gains for insiders, losses for Asian outsiders, and minimal negative effects outside (with the exception of Australia and New Zealand).

Scenario 3: ASEAN+3 and South Asia FTA. Finally, our broadest scenario bridges ASEAN+3 and all the South Asian economies. Under this scenario, we see substantial gains for Sri Lanka (2.0% of base income); Bangladesh (1.7% of base income); India (2.3% of base income); and other South Asian countries, including Nepal (3.7% of base period income). Pakistan, with a trade pattern more oriented outside Asia, realizes smaller income gains (0.2%). India and Pakistan are projected to see exports rise by 22.7% and 7.0% respectively. Bangladesh and other South Asian countries see exports rise by 51.7% and 19.9%, respectively. In other South Asian countries, there is also a slight deterioration in terms of trade under this last scenario.

In comparing the last scenario with the previous two, it is clear that while the broad FTA is the only one to consistently generate gains for South Asia, it matters little for most of the East Asian economies. With a few exceptions (Malaysia, Singapore, and Thailand), East Asian economies gain most from integration within the region. For the East Asian countries that geographically bridge the two regions, the gains are more substantial. As such, South Asian inclusion in the last scenario benefits not only South Asia but also the countries that share the Malay Peninsula: Malaysia, Singapore, and Thailand. It is also clear that to the East Asian parties in these scenarios, it is the India component of the East–South Asia scenario that really matters. This is true for both trade and income effects.

Wage Effects

The estimated wage effects for unskilled workers (see table 8.11) can be taken as a rough measure of the distributional impacts of the three scenarios. The gains for unskilled workers are more or less linked to the welfare gains for members under the three scenarios. Accordingly, in the ASEAN+3 FTA scenario, Korea, Malaysia, and Thailand—with relatively large income effects—witness relatively large unskilled wage increases. For fast-growing poor countries such as Cambodia and Viet Nam, the effects are mixed (gains for Viet Nam, losses for Cambodia). As a mature, developed economy with limited unskilled labor, Japan experiences an increase in unskilled worker wages in line with income effects. The inclusion of India in the basic scenario sees a significant increase in the wages for unskilled Indian workers (in excess of 2.5%) compared to the ASEAN+3 scenario. In the ASEAN+3 and South Asia FTA scenario, India sees an improvement in wages for unskilled workers while Pakistan and Sri Lanka record drops. This is reversed in the broadest FTA scenario. As the membership base widens, we have real wage gains for unskilled workers in India, Pakistan, Sri Lanka, and Bangladesh of 2–3%. Workers in other South Asia (i.e., Nepal) lose with the increased orientation of South Asia toward East Asia.

Table 8.11 Labor Wage Effects in Asia and the Pacific, % change

	ASEAN+3 FTA	ASEAN+3 and India FTA	ASEAN+3 and South Asia FTA
Unskilled workers			
Australia	(0.69)	(0.74)	(0.75)
New Zealand	(0.60)	(0.56)	(0.57)
Other Oceania	(0.49)	(0.50)	(0.55)
PRC	1.83	1.78	1.75
Hong Kong, China	(0.62)	(0.80)	(0.87)
Japan	1.79	1.86	1.87
Korea, Republic of	9.33	9.66	9.74
Taipei,China	(1.97)	(2.05)	(2.10)
Other East Asia	(0.44)	(0.51)	(0.69)
Cambodia	(1.07)	(1.09)	(1.13)
Indonesia	1.67	1.47	1.43
Malaysia	4.91	4.99	5.08
Philippines	0.65	0.68	0.64
Singapore	4.64	5.41	5.69
Thailand	11.07	11.84	12.00
Viet Nam	7.96	8.19	8.27
Other Southeast Asia	(0.53)	(1.45)	(1.63)
Bangladesh	0.44	0.18	3.01
India	(0.19)	2.67	2.78
Pakistan	(0.15)	(0.15)	0.66
Sri Lanka	(0.26)	(0.37)	1.91
Other South Asia	0.00	(0.32)	(2.54)
Skilled workers			
Australia	(0.54)	(0.62)	(0.63)
New Zealand	(0.39)	(0.37)	(0.37)
Other Oceania	(0.31)	(0.29)	(0.32)
PRC	1.42	1.37	1.34

continued on next page

Table 8.11: continued

	ASEAN+3 FTA	ASEAN+3 and India FTA	ASEAN+3 and South Asia FTA
Hong Kong, China	(0.37)	(0.56)	(0.59)
Japan	1.87	1.94	1.95
Korea, Republic of	9.24	9.56	9.63
Taipei,China	(1.98)	(2.05)	(2.08)
Other East Asia	(0.23)	(0.32)	(0.42)
Cambodia	(2.48)	(2.53)	(2.37)
Indonesia	1.65	1.39	1.37
Malaysia	4.70	4.66	4.71
Philippines	0.99	1.06	1.04
Singapore	4.74	5.51	5.78
Thailand	9.00	9.73	9.90
Viet Nam	4.51	4.57	4.61
Other Southeast Asia	(0.55)	(1.67)	(1.80)
Bangladesh	0.58	0.32	1.59
India	(0.03)	1.98	2.06
Pakistan	(0.01)	(0.03)	0.63
Sri Lanka	(0.16)	(0.31)	1.87
Other South Asia	0.07	0.00	(3.30)

ASEAN+3 = Association of Southeast Asian Nations plus People's Republic of China (PRC), Japan, and Republic of Korea; FTA = free trade agreement; ( ) = negative value.

Source: Authors' estimates.

Trade and Production Effects by Sectors

We turn next to trade and output effects by sector. We will focus here on discussing our broadest scenario, although the tables include the narrower scenarios as well. The output and sector export results are reported in tables 8.12 to 8.17. On the output side, it is worth noting that we consistently see increases in service-sector output across the region for all FTA insiders. Indeed, in some cases, this expansion is quite dramatic: Viet Nam sees a 15.9% increase; Thailand, 13.1%; Singapore, 4.9%;

Table 8.12 Change in Output across Broad Sectors in Asia of ASEAN+3 FTA Scenario, %

	Japan	Korea, Rep. of	PRC	Hong Kong, China	Taipei, China	Other East Asia	Cambodia	Indonesia	Malaysia	Philippines	Singapore	Thailand	Viet Nam	Other Southeast Asia	Bangladesh	India
Agriculture and Food	(0.9)	11.4	0.40	0.1	0.5	(0.91)	30.4	(0.3)	(1.5)	0.1	21.3	(0.4)	(4.3)	0.4	0.3	0.2
Other Primary	1.1	0.7	0.1	0.2	1.7	0.3	0.2	0.3	0.4	0.5	0.1	0.4	0.3	0.2	0.4	0.1
Manufactures	0.3	5.0	2.1	(9.6)	(2.2)	(1.1)	52.3	2.2	2.5	10.4	(3.1)	7.3	48.6	(0.9)	(0.6)	(2.4)
Textiles and clothing	5.5	24.9	1.3	(12.7)	(16.5)	(3.5)	(3.0)	1.8	(1.5)	17.3	31.3	1.3	61.3	(1.8)	0.4	(1.7)
Metals	5.9	9.4	(1.6)	(5.4)	2.7	(0.7)	(0.3)	(5.4)	13.0	(2.5)	(8.8)	12.9	12.3	(5.1)	0.3	(0.9)
Electrical machinery	(8.6)	2.8	13.0	(21.4)	(5.0)	(7.4)	(18.1)	8.7	0.3	1.5	1.7	25.0	10.7	6.3	(6.2)	(5.1)
Motor vehicles	(0.6)	1.1	(5.5)	1.9	0.4	1.2	(7.4)	(5.6)	(3.8)	(19.7)	(28.0)	8.6	(28.6)	(1.4)	(2.0)	0.2
Services	1.1	5.5	2.3	0.5	0.7	0.7	2.8	3.0	4.4	3.6	3.9	12.3	15.6	0.7	(0.1)	(0.1)

ASEAN+3 = Association of Southeast Asian plus People's Republic of China (PRC), Japan, and Republic of Korea; FTA = free trade agreement; ( ) = negative value.

Source: Authors' estimates.

Table 8.13 Change in Exports across Broad Sectors in Asia of ASEAN+3 FTA Scenario, %

	Japan	Korea, Rep. of	PRC	Hong Kong, China	Taipei, China	Other East Asia	Cambodia	Indonesia	Malaysia	Philippines	Singapore	Thailand	Viet Nam	Other Southeast Asia	Bangladesh	India
Agriculture and Food	71.8	170.7	191.1	(1.6)	6.1	3.7	(23.7)	(9.2)	(13.9)	59.7	12.0	55.6	(32.5)	10.7	10.5	2.3
Other Primary	15.1	(14.7)	13.5	2.5	16.7	1.7	0.3	(10.1)	(8.5)	(3.9)	0.1	(40.4)	(28.9)	1.6	(10.1)	1.3
Manufactures	6.1	10.0	12.7	(18.5)	(3.7)	(4.4)	47.9	4.7	3.2	13.1	(4.4)	13.5	85.2	29.7	(2.3)	(7.0)
Textiles and clothing	82.3	37.6	21.0	(18.2)	(18.8)	(4.5)	(0.2)	3.9	1.31	13.6	(21.3)	10.5	85.0	1.4	0.7	(3.1)
Metals	21.3	20.6	12.5	(9.4)	1.7	(7.7)	(1.0)	0.8	11.0	(9.4)	(11.3)	14.9	(4.1)	(7.2)	2.9	(4.4)
Electrical machinery	(5.7)	3.9	18.3	(22.4)	(5.4)	(13.0)	(10.1)	10.9	0.3	1.4	1.7	25.8	11.3	246.3	(9.8)	(10.8)
Motor vehicles	(1.0)	0.9	21.9	(1.7)	0.9	2.2	(1.7)	(14.8)	35.0	(32.0)	(31.9)	24.3	49.6	10.3	(14.6)	(1.1)
Services	(4.2)	(8.9)	3.3	2.0	8.5	3.3	(3.0)	1.9	(2.6)	2.8	(0.5)	0.2	3.3	4.9	2.7	2.9

ASEAN+3 = Association of Southeast Asia plus People's Republic of China (PRC), Japan, and Republic of Korea; FTA = free trade agreement; ( ) = negative value.

Source: Authors' estimates.

Table 8.14 Changes in Output across Broad Sectors in Asia of ASEAN+3 and Indian FTA Scenario, %

	Japan	Korea, Rep. of	PRC	Hong Kong, China	Taipei, China	Other East Asia	Cambodia	Indonesia	Malaysia	Philippines	Singapore	Thailand	Viet Nam	Other Southeast Asia	Bangladesh	India
Agriculture and Food	(0.9)	11.6	0.5	0.5	0.5	(0.91)	(4.1)	(0.3)	(1.9)	0.2	21.7	0.5	(4.6)	1.0	0.5	0.7
Other Primary	1.3	0.8	0.3	0.4	1.8	0.4	0.2	0.4	0.6	0.5	0.3	0.5	0.4	0.2	0.3	0.3
Manufactures	0.3	5.3	2.2	(9.9)	(2.2)	(1.2)	(3.3)	2.6	6.4	7.3	1.7	8.8	49.2	(2.7)	(1.2)	4.6
Textiles and clothing	5.6	26.2	1.6	(12.6)	(17.4)	(3.4)	(17.4)	2.5	3.8	14.0	(14.3)	3.0	61.8	(3.4)	0.4	(1.5)
Metals	6.5	11.7	(1.2)	(6.1)	2.6	(1.2)	6.7	(1.8)	25.1	(60.1)	17.0	21.9	12.9	(7.6)	(0.8)	13.6
Electrical machinery	(8.8)	2.3	13.1	31.3	(4.5)	(7.2)	(17.7)	7.3	(0.2)	(75.0)	1.3	25.6	11.6	5.8	(6.4)	0.8
Motor vehicles	(0.6)	1.3	(5.6)	1.9	0.5	1.2	(7.2)	(5.6)	(3.4)	(85.0)	(26.6)	10.5	(28.1)	(1.7)	(1.9)	(2.7)
Services	1.1	5.8	2.3	0.2	(1.5)	(0.1)	2.9	2.9	4.6	4.0	4.6	12.9	15.9	0.3	0.1	3.9

ASEAN+3 = Association of Southeast Asian plus People's Republic of China (PRC), Japan, and Republic of Korea; FTA = free trade agreement; ( ) = negative value.

Source: Authors' estimates.

Table 8.15 Changes in Exports across Broad Sectors in Asia of ASEAN+3 and India FTA Scenario, %

	Japan	Korea, Rep. of	PRC	Hong Kong, China	Taipei, China	Other East Asia	Cambodia	Indonesia	Malaysia	Philippines	Singapore	Thailand	Viet Nam	Other South-east Asia	Bangladesh	India
Agriculture and Food	72.7	171.3	189.1	(1.5)	6.1	4.4	(23.1)	27.3	(8.7)	61.4	14.6	53.0	(11.2)	27.3	8.3	7.3
Other Primary	18.3	(14.8)	37.3	2.9	16.6	1.6	(3.4)	3.4	(11.7)	(5.1)	0.3	(41.5)	(27.5)	1.8	(27.5)	17.0
Manufactures	6.3	10.4	13.1	(18.6)	(3.7)	(4.5)	48.8	4.8	5.5	13.4	(1.0)	15.9	85.6	23.5	(3.2)	35.5
Textiles and clothing	82.9	39.5	21.6	(18.2)	(19.8)	(4.5)	(0.3)	5.0	3.6	13.8	(21.6)	12.9	84.7	(0.8)	0.4	6.7
Metals	23.5	25.0	22.0	(10.0)	1.5	(8.5)	54.3	(3.7)	26.0	18.8	21.4	29.3	5.7	(9.7)	(43.3)	58.5
Electrical machinery	(6.2)	3.4	18.3	(22.1)	(4.9)	(13.0)	(9.7)	9.4	(0.2)	1.9	1.3	26.4	12.4	247.8	(10.1)	41.5
Motor vehicles	(1.0)	(1.01)	21.6	(14.33)	0.1	2.1	(1.5)	(14.3)	35.7	(26.8)	430.4	30.4	50.0	10.7	(14.5)	17.9
Services	(4.2)	(9.4)	3.2	1.9	8.7	3.2	(2.9)	0.8	(3.9)	2.8	(1.3)	(0.2)	3.8	4.1	2.9	8.6

ASEAN+3 = Association of Southeast Asian plus People's Republic of China (PRC), Japan, and Republic of Korea; FTA = free trade agreement; ( ) = negative value.

Source: Authors' estimates.

Table 8.16 Changes in Output Across Broad Sectors in Asia of ASEAN+3 and South Asia FTA Scenario, %

	Japan	Korea, Rep. of	PRC	Hong Kong, China	Taipei, China	Other East Asia	Cambodia	Indonesia	Malaysia	Philippines	Singapore	Thailand	Viet Nam	Other Southeast Asia	Bangladesh	India
Agriculture and Food	(0.9)	11.6	(0.9)	0.1	0.5	6.30	(3.3)	50.3	(1.5)	0.3	193.9	0.9	(4.6)	1.0	(6.3)	0.1
Other Primary	1.3	0.8	0.4	0.4	1.9	0.4	0.2	0.4	0.7	0.5	0.4	0.5	0.4	0.3	(3.0)	0.3
Manufactures	0.3	5.3	2.0	(10.4)	(2.3)	59.3	59.3	2.7	7.7	7.8	3.2	9.5	48.7	(3.1)	(14.0)	4.9
Textiles and clothing	5.7	28.3	0.8	(14.0)	(20.8)	(4.9)	(20.8)	1.7	5.6	8.7	(7.8)	3.9	60.8	(4.5)	16.4	(3.7)
Metals	6.4	11.4	(1.5)	(6.0)	2.9	(1.0)	69.5	(1.0)	24.9	2.1	18.4	22.4	13.0	(6.8)	(7.2)	14.2
Electrical machinery	(8.8)	2.1	12.9	(20.9)	(42.81)	(6.4)	(14.2)	7.1	(0.6)	2.1	1.1	25.6	11.8	5.8	(42.8)	1.3
Motor vehicles	(0.7)	1.1	(5.7)	2.0	0.5	1.5	(5.5)	(5.5)	(3.4)	(16.1)	(26.6)	10.8	(28.0)	(1.9)	(16.3)	(2.3)
Services	1.2	5.8	2.3	0.3	(1.5)	0.20	2.8	3.0	4.7	4.0	4.9	13.1	15.9	0.2	0.2	3.9

ASEAN+3 = Association of Southeast Asian plus People's Republic of China (PRC), Japan, and Republic of Korea; FTA = free trade agreement; ( ) = negative value.

Source: Authors' estimates.

Table 8.17   Changes in Exports across Broad Sectors in Asia of ASEAN+3 and South Asia FTA Scenario, %

	Japan	Korea, Rep. of	PRC	Hong Kong, China	Taipei, China	Other East Asia	Cambodia	Indonesia	Malaysia	Philippines	Singapore	Thailand	Viet Nam	Other South-east Asia	Bangladesh	India
Agriculture and Food	(0.4)	0.5	(6.6)	(1.4)	0.7	33.6	(19.9)	7.8	(10.8)	62.4	11.0	53.0	(11.2)	33.6	10.7	19.6
Other Primary	(6.6)	0.2	(1.2)	2.7	(4.0)	(8.0)	(3.0)	3.3	(12.6)	(4.9)	0.4	(41.5)	(27.7)	2.1	214.6	21.4
Manufactures	(0.6)	(0.60)	(2.1)	(19.6)	43.4	(0.4)	55.4	4.4	3.4	10.3	0.6	15.9	85.6	23.3	4.5	36.4
Textiles and clothing	(1.7)	(2.2)	(2.3)	(20.3)	(2.0)	(21.3)	(19.1)	4.4	1.3	10.1	(19.1)	12.9	84.7	(3.5)	45.9	3.9
Metals	(2.2)	(0.2)	(3.3)	(9.9)	(2.5)	(11.9)	69.1	(3.5)	26.0	18.7	22.9	29.3	5.7	(8.4)	203.1	64.6
Electrical machinery	0.1	0.5	(1.8)	(21.9)	0.3	(23.8)	(4.3)	9.5	(0.6)	2.1	1.1	26.4	12.4	249.5	(26.2)	42.5
Motor vehicles	0.2	0.2	(1.1)	(1.1)	0.7	(1.8)	1.4	(13.9)	35.5	(26.0)	(30.4)	30.4	50.0	12.0	40.8	19.9
Services	0.1	0.2	0.5	2.0	0.1	2.7	0.10	0.7	(4.1)	3.0	(1.7)	(0.2)	3.8	4.7	(18.0)	8.6

ASEAN+3 = Association of Southeast Asian plus People's Republic of China (PRC), Japan, and Republic of Korea; FTA = free trade agreement; ( ) = negative value.

Source: Authors' estimates.

Malaysia, 4.7%; and Philippines, 4.0%. In some cases, services sector growth follows a general increase in economic activity. As can be seen in table 8.8, this is clearly the case for Thailand, Viet Nam, Singapore, and Malaysia. In other cases, especially India, this appears to follow from increased exports of services. Hence, we see service-sector expansion across the region driven by a mix of increased overall economic activity and increased export opportunities.

On the manufacturing side, the greatest positive effects are seen in Cambodia (59.3% increase in output), Viet Nam (48.7%), and Sri Lanka (21.6%). In all these cases, the expansion involves a mix of electrical machinery and metals production. There is overall contraction of manu-facturing in Pakistan; Hong Kong, China; Bangladesh; and the regional outsiders (Taipei,China and other Northeast Asian economies). For the politically sensitive motor-vehicle sector, there is some contraction (2–5% range) in three of the four big Asian economies (PRC, India, and Japan) and expansion in the fourth (Korea). Thailand also sees dramatic increase in production for export.

Direction of Trade

We turn next to the impact of FTA implementation on the direction of trade. This is summarized in tables 8.18 and 8.19. These tables summa-rize the Asia-orientation of exports both for insider countries (those that benefit from improved market access under the various scenarios) and the pure outsiders (those that are left out of market access gains). The first, fourth, and seventh data columns provide export shares in the 2017 base-line. The corresponding right-hand columns report the same shares after the experiments. This is followed in the third, sixth, and ninth data col-umns by changes in these shares. The insider-outsider picture in the table provides a broad sense of the extent to which countries outside the region lose market access, and the extent to which those inside the region reorient exports away from third countries and toward Asia. Combined with the income effects above, these estimates of the direction of trade indicate the extent to which the diversion of trade away from third countries has led to a destruction of overall trade (and gains from trade), and alternatively the extent to which new trade opportunities may have boosted income and overcome these diversion effects.

In table 8.18, there is a significant reorientation of trade shares away from third-countries and toward the region. For example, Thailand sees a ten-percentage-point increase (47.5% to 57.5%) in the share of goods and services exports destined for Asia. Korea's regional exports increase substantially as well. In the baseline, 42.8% of goods and services exports

Table 8.18   Impact on Insiders of ASEAN+3 and South Asia FTA Scenario

Direction of Trade, shares in %

	Export Share to East Asia			Export Share to South Asia			Total (exports to East Asia and South Asia)			Total Exports, % change
	2017 baseline	Post-experiment	Change	2017 baseline	Post-experiment	Change	2017 baseline	Post-experiment	Change	
PRC	33.6	37.3	3.7	1.2	3.2	2.0	34.8	40.5	5.7	13.2
Hong Kong, China	44.7	48.3	3.7	1.2	1.0	(0.2)	45.9	49.3	3.4	(1.0)
Japan	40.2	52.5	12.4	0.9	1.9	1.0	41.1	54.5	13.4	7.3
Korea, Rep. of	41.3	59.1	17.9	1.5	3.4	1.8	42.8	62.5	19.7	13.4
Cambodia	15.5	15.1	(0.5)	0.6	0.8	0.2	16.2	15.9	(0.2)	6.80
Indonesia	49.1	53.6	4.5	4.0	6.8	2.8	53.1	60.4	7.3	8.4
Malaysia	51.0	52.3	1.3	4.5	6.1	1.6	55.5	58.3	2.9	7.0
Philippines	46.1	53.3	7.1	0.4	0.7	0.4	46.5	54.0	7.5	8.4
Singapore	50.6	56.1	5.4	2.9	3.7	0.7	53.5	59.7	6.2	3.0
Thailand	45.9	54.8	8.9	1.6	2.7	1.2	47.5	57.5	10.0	23.9
Viet Nam	46.5	56.1	9.6	0.4	0.5	0.1	46.9	56.6	9.7	35.4
Other Southeast Asia	59.6	46.0	(13.6)	4.1	7.7	3.7	63.7	53.8	(9.9)	4.8
Bangladesh	7.3	5.4	(1.9)	1.5	2.3	0.8	8.8	7.7	(1.1)	51.7

continued on next page

Table 8.18: *continued*

Direction of Trade, shares in %

	Export Share to East Asia			Export Share to South Asia			Total (exports to East Asia and South Asia)			Total Exports, % change
	2017 baseline	Post-experiment	Change	2017 baseline	Post-experiment	Change	2017 baseline	Post-experiment	Change	
India	24.9	32.6	7.7	3.2	3.8	0.6	28.2	36.4	8.3	22.7
Pakistan	11.0	20.2	9.2	2.8	7.2	4.4	13.8	27.4	13.6	7.0
Sri Lanka	7.9	11.7	3.8	3.0	7.7	4.7	10.9	19.4	8.5	5.8
Other South Asia	12.2	11.1	(1.1)	30.9	49.8	18.9	43.2	61.0	17.8	19.9

ASEAN+3 = Association of Southeast Asian Nations plus People's Republic of China (PRC), Japan, and Republic of Korea; FTA = free trade agreement; ( ) = negative value.

Source: Authors' estimates.

Table 8.19 Impact on Outsiders of ASEAN+3 and South Asia FTA Scenario

Direction of Trade, shares in %

	Export Share to East Asia			Export Share to South Asia			Total (exports to East Asia and South Asia)			Total Exports, % change
	2017 baseline	Post-experiment	Change	2017 baseline	Post-experiment	Change	2017 baseline	Post-experiment	Change	
Australia	61.4	56.5	(4.9)	5.9	12.5	6.6	67.4	69.0	1.6	(1.1)
New Zealand	44.0	47.8	3.8	2.9	6.0	3.1	47.0	53.8	6.8	(0.5)
Other Oceania	42.5	36.4	(6.1)	0.8	0.6	(0.3)	43.3	37.0	(6.3)	(1.1)
Taipei,China	46.3	42.2	(4.1)	1.6	0.9	(0.7)	47.9	43.1	(4.8)	(2.7)
Other East Asia	35.4	31.4	(4.1)	1.2	0.7	(0.5)	36.7	32.1	(4.5)	(2.2)
Rest of Central Asia	9.7	9.5	(0.3)	1.2	0.9	(0.3)	10.9	10.3	(0.6)	(0.0)
Canada	10.8	7.8	(2.9)	0.7	0.5	(0.2)	11.4	8.3	(3.1)	0.3
United States	26.0	26.0	(0.1)	1.0	0.8	(0.2)	27.0	26.7	(0.3)	(0.4)
Mexico	3.0	2.2	(0.8)	1.9	0.3	(1.6)	4.9	2.5	(2.4)	0.1
Other Americas	16.8	14.4	(2.3)	4.3	0.9	(3.4)	21.1	15.4	(5.7)	(0.1)

continued on next page

Table 8.19: continued

Direction of Trade, shares in %

	Export Share to East Asia			Export Share to South Asia			Total (exports to East Asia and South Asia)			Total Exports, % change
	2017 baseline	Post-experiment	Change	2017 baseline	Post-experiment	Change	2017 baseline	Post-experiment	Change	
EU27	11.1	11.2	0.1	0.9	0.6	(0.2)	11.9	11.8	(0.2)	(0.1)
EFTA	11.3	12.0	0.7	0.9	0.6	(0.3)	12.1	12.6	0.4	0.3
Turkey	8.0	9.2	1.3	0.8	0.6	(0.2)	8.7	9.8	1.1	(0.4)
Russian Federation	11.5	19.9	8.3	0.6	0.7	0.1	12.1	20.5	8.4	0.4
Other Europe	9.6	9.7	0.2	0.6	0.4	(0.1)	10.2	10.2	0.0	0.1
North Africa and Middle East	43.0	27.8	(15.2)	5.5	2.7	(2.7)	48.5	30.6	(17.9)	0.4
South Africa	25.4	20.8	(4.6)	4.3	2.5	(1.8)	29.7	23.3	(6.4)	(0.1)
Sub-Saharan Africa	21.9	18.3	(3.6)	3.6	3.3	(0.3)	25.5	21.6	(3.9)	0.5

ASEAN+3 = Association of Southeast Asian Nations plus People's Republic of China (PRC), Japan, and Republic of Korea; EFTA = European Free Trade Agrement; EU = European Union; ( ) = negative value.

Source: Authors' estimates.

go to Asia. In the full East Asia–South FTA scenario, this increases 19.7% to 62.5%. The PRC shifts 5.7% of exports away from third countries and back toward Asia. Some countries are actually projected to reorient away from the region slightly—Bangladesh, Cambodia, and other Southeast Asian countries. Overall, however, under the widest free-trade scenario we have Asian exports estimated to rise by 11.3%, with this export growth generally being targeted within the region.

Clues as to the fate of third countries are provided in tables 8.8 and 8.19. In table 8.18, third-country income effects are relatively small. In fact, the losses amount to -0.01% of baseline national income, or $3.0 billion. This is fully consistent with the estimated trade effects. In table 8.19, under the widest free-trade scenario, the rest of the world is virtually unaffected, with trade volumes falling by 0.15% in total. For individual countries, there is a varied pattern of trade reorientation, but there is not a consistent, discernable global drop in trade and incomes. Rather, the widest of our free-trade scenarios implies broad-based trade and income growth across Asia with little effect on for the rest of the world. Indeed, exports from some middle- and low-income countries and regions (Africa, Turkey, Russian Federation) benefit slightly, filling the gap in supplying third-country markets while Asia turns inward.

Subregional Schemes—The Example of South Asia

Finally, in table 8.20, we turn to impacts on South Asia of alternative bilateral agreements between ASEAN and PRC, Japan, and Korea. We

Table 8.20   South Asian Effects, Alternative Subregional Schemes

Real income effects compared to 2017 baseline (at constant 2001 prices), in %

	ASEAN-PRC FTA	ASEAN-Japan FTA	ASEAN-Korea FTA	South Asia FTA	ASEAN+3 and India FTA
Bangladesh	(0.08)	(0.06)	(0.04)	0.31	(0.31)
India	(0.10)	(0.08)	(0.05)	0.14	2.23
Pakistan	(0.11)	(0.06)	(0.06)	0.42	(0.58)
Sri Lanka	(0.07)	(0.05)	(0.07)	1.08	(0.40)
Other South Asia	0.05	(0.01)	(0.01)	3.37	(0.65)

ASEAN+3 = Association of Southeast Asian Nations plus People's Republic of China (PRC), Japan, and Republic of Korea; FTA = free trade agreement; ( ) = negative value.

Source: Authors' estimates.

also highlight the impact of a geographically limited subregional (i.e., South Asia) agreement. The table demonstrates the point that, depending on trade orientation, a subregional scheme is not necessarily of equal interest to all economies in the subregion. For Sri Lanka and other South Asian countries, particularly Nepal, for example, it is indeed subregional integration, or the subregional component of broad agreements, that matter most. For India, the regional scheme offers relatively little compared to the implications of initiatives targeting East Asia. The varied regional impacts in the table illustrate why, overall, it is the broader approach under our core experiments that leads to the most balanced result across countries. This is because the different countries in the region have different trade orientations vis-à-vis East and South Asia.

Conclusions

In this paper we have examined the economic implications of pan-Asian integration schemes. We have examined three core scenarios: ASEAN+3 FTA, ASEAN+3 and India FTA, and ASEAN+3 and South Asia FTA. The results of the scenarios follow from the underlying patterns of Asian protection. What matters most for East Asia is that PRC, Japan, and Korea be brought into any scheme for deeper regional integration. This alone drives most of the income and trade effects in the East Asia region across all our scenarios. Of secondary importance is the inclusion of India, which some gains by bridging East and South Asia and by its focus on the countries that share the Malay Peninsula.

For South Asia, the results again reflect relative trade and protection patterns. The economies of South Asia already have trade patterns directed toward East Asia. This reflects the higher incomes in East Asia and the greater absolute size of the export markets in East Asia. This means that for most of the economies of South Asia, deeper integration with East Asia has the potential to bring modest income gains (roughly 2–4% of GDP) along with associated export growth.

Interestingly, the one regional player in South Asia that seems to matter to East Asian exporters in terms of improved market access is India. Most of the East Asian gains from any initiative that includes South Asia follow directly from Indian participation. The other players in the region have a limited impact on East Asia. Yet if India looks east, South Asian economies need to be part of the program as well. Hence, the politics of any regional scheme will be complex with the East Asian countries gaining most from access to India, while the South Asian economies standing to gain if India makes sure the full region is included.

Finally, our results also provide a lesson on third-country effects. As long as Asia aims to include all countries in the various subregions, an Asian FTA has the potential to boost regional trade and incomes without substantive adverse effects on the terms of trade. This may follow partially from our emphasis on reducing trade costs and services barriers, both of which involve relatively large savings on deadweight transaction costs. Recent experience, however, suggests that the institutional barriers to any real progress (like rules of origin, failure to implement trade facilitation agreements that have already been agreed, and NTBs) can be substantial. These pose a formidable challenge, though the potential benefits in dismantling them appear to be substantial.

ANNEX

Trade and Transportation Costs and Services Barriers

International trade is modeled as a process that explicitly involves trading costs, which include both trade and transportation services. These trading costs reflect the transaction costs involved in international trade, as well as the physical activity of transportation itself. Those trading costs related to international movement of goods and related logistic services are met by composite services purchased from a global trade services sector, where the composite "international trade services" activity is produced as a Cobb-Douglas composite of regional exports of trade and transport service exports. Trade-cost margins are based on reconciled free-on-board (FOB) and cost, insurance, and freight (CIF) trade data, as reported in version 6.2 of the Global Trade Analysis Project (GTAP) dataset.

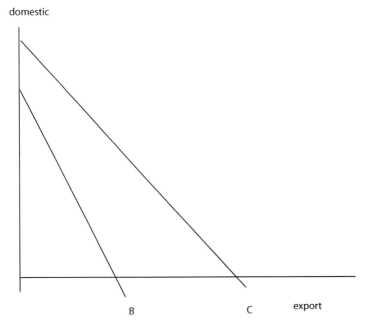

Figure A8.1 Linear transformation technology between domestic and export goods and services.

A second form of trade cost is referred to in the literature as a frictional trading cost. These are implemented in the service sector. They are also implemented as costs for trading goods, so that we can examine the impact of trade facilitation. They represent real resource costs associated with producing a good or service for sale in an export market instead of the domestic market. Conceptually, we have implemented a linear transformation technology between domestic and export goods and services. This technology is represented in annex figure A.81. The straight line AB indicates, given the resources necessary to produce a unit of services for the domestic market, the feasible amount that can instead be produced for export using those same resources. If there are no frictional barriers to trade in services, this line has slope of -1. This free-trade case is represented by the line AC. As we reduce trading costs, the linear transformation line converges on the free trade line, as indicated in the figure.

The basic methodology for estimating services barriers involves the estimation of an equation where import demand is a function of the size of the economy (as measured by gross domestic product [GDP]) and its income level (per capita income). We have also included dummy variables by sector, and country-specific dummies (with Hong Kong, China and Singapore being the base case). Our import data is on a sector basis by country with respect to the world, and is at the same level of aggregation as the CGE model data. Formally, our estimating equation is

(1) $$M_{i,j} = a_i + a_j \ln(GDP)_j - a_2 \ln(PCI)_j + \varepsilon_j$$

where Mi,j represents imports in sector i by Country J, a_i and a_j are sector and country effect variables, GDP_j represents national GDP (taken in logs), PCI_j is per capita income (again taken in logs), and ε is an error term. This is an improvement on the approach in Francois, ven Meijl, and van Tongeren (2005) as under this approach we have several points for estimating each national restriction index (the a_j coefficient). Adjusted by the import substitution elasticity, these national coefficients provide an estimate of the trade-cost equivalent of existing barriers in services as an average across service sectors.

(2) $$a_j = -\sigma \ln(T_j)$$

Here, T_j is the power of the tariff equivalent $(1+t_j)$ such that in free trade $T = 1$, and σ is the trade substitution elasticity relative to domestic production (taken to be the substitution elasticity used in the computable general equilibrium (CGE) model.

Regression results from this approach are reported in Annex Tables A8.1 and A8.2. This involves a two-stage regression. In the first stage, we estimate equation (1) without the dummy term a_j that captures trade barriers. We include average distance from the world in the first stage. We work with trade data from the benchmark dataset (i.e., 2001 services trade from the International Monetary Fund's balance of payments data). The second stage then involves regression of error terms against country dummies (with several sectors pooled) to estimate average barriers across a set of service sectors, as identified in the tables. Resulting barrier estimates for the model application are reported in Table 8.6 on page 507.

Table A8.1   First Stage Regression Result

	All Services		Producer Services		Other Non-Trade Services	
	Estimated Coefficients	t-values	Estimated Coefficients	t-values	Estimated Coefficients	t-values
lnpop	0.84	44.48	0.84	27.3	0.86	26.93
lnpcGDP	1.00	44.21	1.02	27.48	0.93	24.12
lnWDIST	(0.63)	(5.48)	(0.53)	(2.80)	(0.79	(4.02)
Electricity	(2.10)	(14.33)				
Gas distribution	(10.86)	(74.03)				
Water	(5.34)	(36.41)				
Construction	(3.25)	(22.13)			(2.22)	(15.91)
Trade	(0.72)	(4.89)			0.34	2.45
Water transport	(2.48)	(6.80)				
Airtransport	(1.20)	(8.08)				
Other transport	(1.47)	(9.27)				
Communications	(2.18)	(14.86)	(2.17)	(16.12)		
Other financial services	(2.14)	(14.60)	(2.14)	(15.88)		
Insurance and real estate	(1.86)	(12.64)	(1.85)	(13.73)		
Personal services	(1.37)	(9.35)			(0.30)	(2.17)
Public services	(1.06)	(7.21)				

continued on next page

Table A8.1: continued

	All Services		Producer Services		Other Non-Trade Services	
	Estimated Coefficients	t-values	Estimated Coefficients	t-values	Estimated Coefficients	t-values
Intercept	1.82	1.59	0.70	0.37	2.67	1.38
Observations, first stage		1,165		364.0		364
F, (Pr>F), first stage		770.72, (0)		280.28, (0)		263.00, (0)
R^2 from corresponding OLS regression note: default case is business services		0.750		0.839		0.807

References

Adlung, R. 2006. Services Negotiations in the Doha Round: Lost in Flexibility? *Journal of International Economic Law* 9(4): 865–893. December.

Ahn, S., and J. W. Lee. 2007. Integration and Growth in East Asia. *Institute for Monetary and Economic Studies, Bank of Japan Discussion Paper Series* 07-E-14.

Ahluwalia, M.S. 2002. Economic reforms in India since 1991: Has gradualism worked? *Journal of Economic Perspectives* 16(3): 67–88.

Alburo, F. 2004. *Promoting Trade in SASEC: A Report on Non-Tariff and Non-Trade Barriers* (TA 6090). Manila: Asian Development Bank.

Anderson, J. 1979. A Theoretical Foundation for the Gravity Equation. *American Economic Review* 69(1): 106–116. March.

Anderson, J., and D. Marcouiller. 2002. Insecurity and the Pattern of Trade: An Empirical Investigation. *The Review of Economics and Statistics* 84(2): 342–352. March.

Anderson, J., and E. van Wijncoop. 2003. Gravity with Gravitas: A Solution to the Border Puzzle. *American Economic Review* 93(1): 170–192. March.

Arnold, J. R. 2009. The Role of Transport Infrastructure, Logistics, and Trade Facilitation in Asian Trade. In this volume.

Arnold, J. R., R. Banomyong, and N. Ritthironk. 2002. Logistics Development and Trade Facilitation in Lao PDR. Mimeo, Washington, DC: World Bank.

Arnold, J. R., and M. Lord. 2007. *BIMSTEC Logistics Study.* Paper prepared for the Asian Development Bank (ADB). Manila: ADB.

Arnold, J. R., and J. Stone. 2002. Viet Nam: Logistics Development Trade Facilitation and the Impact on Poverty Reduction. Paper prepared for East Asia Transport Unit of the World Bank. Washington, DC: World Bank.

Arnold, J. R., and T. Villareal. 2002. Philippines Logistics Study. Paper prepared for the World Bank. Washington, DC: World Bank.

Asher, M. G., and R. Sen. 2005. India-East Asia Integration: A Win-Win for Asia. *Research and Information Systems for the Non-Aligned and Other Developing Countries (RIS) Discussion Paper 91/2005.*

Asian Development Bank (ADB). 2001. *Report and Recommendation to the President on Proposed Loan to India for West Bengal Corridor Development Project.* Manila: ADB.

————. 2002. *Asian Development Outlook 2002.* Manila: ADB.

————. 2004. SAARC Regional Transport Connectivity Review. Mimeo, Manila, ADB.

————. 2005a. *Quarterly Economic Update: Bangladesh.* Manila: ADB.

————. 2005b. *Project Completion Report on Bangladesh: Jamuna Bridge Railway Link Project.* Manila: ADB.

————. 2005c. *People's Republic of China: Dali-Lijiang Railway Project.* Manila: ADB.

————. 2005d. *Preparing the Market Access and Productivity Growth for the Private Sector: Identifying Nepal's Emerging Comparative Advantage.* Manila: ADB.

————. 2006a. *Asian Development Outlook 2006.* Manila: ADB.

————. 2006c. *Central Asia: Increasing Gains from Trade Through Regional Cooperation in Trade Policy, Transport and Customs Transit.* Manila: ADB.

————. 2006d. SAARC Regional Multimodal Transport Study. Mimeo, Manila: ADB.

————. 2006e. *Regional Cooperation and Integration Strategy.* Manila: ADB.

————. 2008a. Free Trade Agreement Database for Asia. Asia Regional Integration Center. Available: www.aric.adb.org

————. 2008b. *Emerging Asian Regionalism: A Partnership for Shared Prosperity.* Manila: ADB.

————. 2008c. *National Strategies for Regional Integration: South and East Asian Case Studies.* Manila: ADB.

Asia-Pacific Economic Cooperation. 1996. *1996 Report to Economic Leaders.* APEC Business Advisory Council. Available: www.apec.org

Baig, M. A., and S. C. Saxena. 2003. Monetary Cooperation in South Asia: Potential and Prospects. RIS (New Delhi) / SACEPS (Dhaka) Workshop on Monetary Cooperation in South Asia: Potential and Prospects, 23 December, Research and Information Systems for the Non-Aligned and other Developing Countries (RIS), New Delhi.

Bajracharya, P. 2005. *SAARC Regional Multimodal Transport Study – Final Report for Nepal.* Manila: ADB.

Balasubramanyam, V. N., and A. Balasubramanyam. 1997. International Trade in Services: The Case of India's Computer Software. *The World Economy* 20(6): 829–843. September.

Baldwin, R. 1997. The Causes of Regionalism. *The World Economy* 20(7): 865–888. November.

————. 2007. Managing the Noodle Bowl: The Fragility of East Asian Regionalism. *ADB Working Paper Series on Regional Economic Integration* 7. February. Manila: ADB.

Ballard, C. L., and I. Cheong. 1997. The Effects of Economic Integration in the Pacific Rim: A Computational General Equilibrium Analysis. *Journal of Asian Economics* 8(4): 505–524. Autumn.

Bandara, J., and W. Yu. 2003. How Desirable is the South Asian Free Trade Area? *The World Economy* 26 (9): 1293–1323. September.

Barro, R., and X. Sala-i-Martin. 2004. *Economic Growth.* Cambridge: MIT Press.

Batra, A. 2004. India's Global Trade Potential: The Gravity Model Approach. *Indian Council for Research on International Economic Relations (ICRIER) Working Paper* 151.

Batra, A., and Z. Khan. 2005. Revealed Comparative Advantage: An Analysis for India and China. *ICRIER Working Papers* 168. New Delhi: ICRIER.

Bay of Bengal Initiative for MultiSectoral Technical and Economic Cooperation (BIMSTEC). 2006. Free Trade Agreement. Available: www.bimstec.org/free_trade_ agreement.asp

Bayoumi, T., and B. Eichengreen. 1999. Is Asia an Optimal Currency Area? Can It Become One? Regional, Global, and Historical Perspectives on Monetary Relations. In *Exchange Rate Policies in Emerging Asian Countries, edited by S. Collignon, J. Pisani-Ferry, and Y.C. Park*. London: Routledge.

Bayoumi, T., B. Eichengreen, and P. Mauro. 1999. On Regional Monetary Arrangements for ASEAN. Prepared for the ADB/Centre d'etudes Prospectives et d'Informations Internationales/KIEP Conference on Exchange Rate Regimes in Emerging Economies, Tokyo, 17–19 December.

Baysan, T., et al. 2004. *Pakistan: Growth and Export Competitiveness Report 31394-BR*. Washington, DC: World Bank.

————. 2004. *Bangladesh: Growth and Export Competitiveness Report 31394-BR*. Washington, D.C.: International Bank for Reconstruction and Development (IBRD).

————. 2006. *Pakistan: Growth and Export Competitiveness*. Washington, DC: IBRD.

Bchir, M. H., and M. Fouquin. 2006. Economic Integration in Asia: Bilateral Free Trade Agreements versus Asian Single Market. *CEPII Working Paper* 2006-15. Paris: CEPII.

Bearing Point. 2006. *Legal Review of the Indian Special Economic Zone Regime: Prepared for Reliance Industries Limited*. Available: www.bearingpoint.com

Bergsten, F. 2000, 15 July. Towards a Tripartite World. *The Economist*. Available: www.economist.com

—————. 2007. Toward a Free Trade Area of the Asia-Pacific. *Policy Briefs International Economics* 07-2. February. Washington, DC: Peter G. Peterson Institute for International Economics.

Bhagwati, J. 1978. *Anatomy and Consequences of Exchange Control Regimes*. Cambridge, Massachusetts: Ballinger Publishing Co. for the National Bureau of Economic Research (NBER).

Bhagwati, J., D. Greenaway, and A. Panagariya. 1998. Trading Preferentially: Theory and Policy. *The Economic Journal* 108 (449): 1128–1148. July.

Bhattacharya, S. K., and B. N. Bhattacharyay. 2006. Prospects and Challenges of Cooperation and Integration in Trade, Investment and Finance in Asia: An Empirical Analysis on BIMSTEC Countries and Japan. *CESifo Working Paper* 1725. Munich.

Boatman, K. T. 1992. *Telecommunications System Quality and Export Performance*. Doctoral dissertation. University of Maryland, College Park.

Boeing Co. 2004. *World Air Cargo Forecast 2004/2005*. Available: www. boeing.com

Bonapace, T. 2005. Regional Trade and Investment Architecture in Asia-Pacific: Emerging Trends and Imperatives. *RIS Discussion Papers 92*.

—————. 2006. New Age Regionalism and Multilateralism: Systemic Issues and the Evolving Trade Architecture. Paper presented at the United Nations Economic and Social Commission for Asia and the Pacific.

Bonapace, T., and M. Mikic. 2005. *Multilateralizing Regionalism: Towards and Integrated and Outward-Looking Asia-Pacific Economic Area*. Bangkok: United Nations Economic and Social Commission for Asia and the Pacific (UNESCAP).

Bougheas, S., P. O. Demetriades, and E. L. W. Morgenroth. 1999. Infrastructure, transport costs and trade. *Journal of International Economics* 47(1): 169–189. February.

Burki, S. J. 1980. *Pakistan: A Nation in the Making.* Boulder, Colorado: Westview Press.

Candelon, B., J. Piplack, and S. Straetmans. 2008. On Measuring Synchronization of Bulls and Bears: The Case of East Asia. Forthcoming, Journal of Banking and Finance.

Carruthers, R., and J. Bajpai. 2002. Trends in Trade and Logistics: An East Asian Perspective. *World Bank East Asia Transport Unit Working Paper* 2. Washington, DC: World Bank.

Carruthers, R., J. Bajpai, and D. Hummel. 2003. Trade and Logistics in East Asia: A Development Agenda. *World Bank East Asia Transport Unit Working Paper* 3. Washington, DC: World Bank.

Center for International Economic Studies. 2006. Impediments to Trade in the Priority Sectors. Draft prepared for AADCP-REPSF Project 06/001, An Investigation into the Measures Affecting the Integration of ASEANs Priority Sectors (Phase 2): Workshop 1, Singapore, 9–10 September.

Chakraborty, C., and P. Nunnenkamp. 2006. Economic Reforms, Foreign Direct Investment and its Economics Effects in India. *Institut für Weltwirtschaft, Kiel Working Paper* 1272. March.

Chanda, R. 2001. Trade in Health Services. *Bulletin of the World Health Organization* 80: 158–163. Geneva: World Health Organization.

Chang, R., L. Kaltani, and N. Loayza. 2005. Openness Can Be Good for Growth: The Role of Policy Complementarities. *World Bank Policy Research Working Paper* 3763. September. Washington, DC: World Bank.

Cheong, I. 2003. Regionalism and Free Trade Agreements in East Asia. *Asian Economic Papers* 2(2): 145–180. Massachusetts: MIT Press.

Chirathivat, S., and C. Sabhasri. 2009. Thailand. In *National Strategies for Regional Integration: South and East Asian Case Studies*, edited by J. Francois, P. Rana, and G. Wignaraja. Manila: ADB.

Clair, G., G. Gaulier, T. Mayer, and S. Zignago. 2004. Notes on CEPII's Distances Measures. Paris: CEPII.

Clark, X., D. Dollar, and A. Micco. 2001. Maritime Transport Costs and Port Efficiency. *World Bank Policy Research Working Paper Series* 2781. Washington, DC: World Bank.

Click, R., and M. Plummer. 2005. Stock Market Integration in ASEAN after the Asian financial crisis. *Journal of Asian Economics* 16(1): 5–28. February.

Coe, D. T., A. Subramanian, and N. T. Tamirisa. 2002. The Missing Globalisation Puzzle. *International Monetary Fund (IMF) Working Paper* 02/171. Washington, DC: IMF.

Containerisation International. 2006a. *Services between Asia and Northern Europe on 01/05/06 (Capacity and TEU).* July. Available: www.ci-online.co.uk/

————. 2006b. *Freight Rate Indicators: 2003–2006.*

————. 2006c. *Key Numbers: North-South Trade Cargo Analysis: 2003–2006.*

————. 2006d. *Regional Review: Hong Kong in Southern China: Plugging into IT.* March.

————. 2006e. *Top 30 Container Ports in 2005 by TEU Throughput.* March.

————. 2006f. *Under the Spotlight: Regional Review of Hong Kong in Southern China.* March.

————. 2006g. *3 PLs Not Moving with the Times.* March.

————. 2005. *On the Move.* November.

————. 2003. *Regional Review: India Subcontinent: Making Colombo Move.* December.

Daniels, P. W. 1998. Economic Development and Producer Services Growth: The APEC Experience. *Asia Pacific Viewpoint* 39(2): 145–159.

Das, G. 2002. *India Unbound: The Social and Economic Revolution from Independence to the Global Information Age.* New York: Anchor Books.

Dasgupta, A., and N. M. Maskay. 2003. Financial Policy Cooperation in SAARC: A First Step toward Greater Monetary Integration in South Asia. *South Asian Economic Journal* 4(1): 133–143.

De, P. 2004. Transaction Costs as Barriers to Economic Integration in Asia: An Empirical Exploration. *RIS Discussion Paper 77.* New Delhi: RIS.

————. 2006. Regional Trade in Northeast Asia: Why Do Trade Costs Matter? *CESifo Working Paper* 1809. September. Munich: CESifo.

De, P., and B. Ghosh. 2003. How Do Infrastructure Facilitates Affect Regional Income? An Investigation with South Asian Countries. *RIS Discussion Paper* 66. New Delhi: RIS.

Dennis, D. J., and Z.A. Yusof. 2003. Developing Indicators of ASEAN Integration – A Preliminary Survey for a Roadmap. *Regional Economic Policy Support Facility Project 02/001, Final Report.* August.

Deardorff, A. 1998. Determinants of Bilateral Trade: Does Gravity Work in a Neoclassical World? In *Regionalization of the World Economy,* edited by J. Frankel. Chicago: The University of Chicago Press.

Dee, P. 2004. Services Trade Liberalization in South East European Countries. Study prepared for the Organisation for Economic Co-operation and Development (OECD). January (revised).

————. 2005a. *A Compendium of Barriers to Services Trade.* Prepared for the World Bank. Washington, DC: World Bank.

————. 2005b. East Asian Economic Integration and its Impact in Future Growth. *Pacific Economic Papers No. 350.* Australia-Japan Research Center and Asia Pacific School of Economics and Government.

Dee, P., and C. Findlay. 2006. Services – A Dealmaker in the WTO? Mimeo.

Dee, P., K. Hanslow, and T. Phamduc. 2003. Measuring the Cost of Barriers to Trade in Services. In *Services Trade in the Asia-Pacific Region*, edited by T. Ito and A. Kruegen. Chicago: The University of Chicago Press.

De Grauwe, P. 2005. *The Economics of Monetary Union*. Oxford: Oxford University Press.

De Wulf, L., and J. B. Sokol. 2005. *Customs Modernization Handbook*. Washington, DC: World Bank.

Dent, C. 2003. Networking the Region? The Emergence and Impact of Asia-Pacific Bilateral Free-trade Agreement Projects. *The Pacific Review* 16(1): 1–28. March.

Depken II, C. A., and R.J. Sonora. 2005. Asymmetric Effects of Economic Freedom on International Trade Flows. *International Journal of Business and Economics* 4(2): 141–155.

Dimaranan, B. V., and R. A. McDougall. 2002. Global Trade, Assistance, and Production: The GTAP 5 Data Base. Indiana: Center for Global Trade Analysis, Purdue University.

Disdier, A. C., and K. Head. 2003. Exaggerated Reports on the Death of Distance: Lessons from a Meta-Analysis. Mimeo, TEAM Universite de Paris I Pantheon Sorbonne.

Dobson, W. 2001. Deeper Integration in East Asia: Regional Institutions and the International Economic System. *The World Economy* 24 (8): 995–1018. August.

Dollar, D., and A. Kraay. 2002. Institutions, Trade, and Growth. *Journal of Monetary Economics*. 50: 133–162.

————. 2004. Trade, Growth, and Poverty. *Economic Journal* 114: F22–F49. February.

Doove, S., O. Gabbitas, D. Nguyen-Hong, and J. Owen. 2001. Price Effects of Regulation: International Air Passenger Transport, Telecommunications, and Electricity Supply. *Productivity Commission Staff Research Paper* 1682. Canberra: Ausinfo.

Drysdale, P. 2005. Regional Cooperation in East Asia and FTA Strategies. *Pacific Economic Papers* 344. Canberra: Australian National University.

Dungey, M., R. Fry, B. Gonzales-Hermosillo, and V. M. Martin. 2004. Empirical Modeling of Contagion: A Review of Methodologies. *IMF Working Paper* 04/78. May. Washington, DC: IMF.

East Asian Study Group. 2001. Towards an East Asian Community report to the ASEAN Plus Three Summit. ASEAN+3. Brunei Darussalam.

—————. 2002. Final Report of the East Asia Study Group for ASEAN Plus Three Summit. ASEAN+3. Phnom Penh.

Edwards, S. 1993. Openness, Trade Liberalization, and Growth in Developing Countries. *Journal of Economic Literature* 31(3): 1358–1393.

Estevadeordal, A., and K. Suominen. 2004. Rules of Origin: A World Map and Trade Effects. Presented at conference on Rules of Origin in Regional Trade Agreements: Conceptual and Empirical Approaches. Washington, DC: Inter-American Development Bank (IADB).

Evenett, S. J., and W. Keller. 2002. On Theories Explaining the Success of the Gravity Equation. *Journal of Political Economy* 110(2): 281–316.

Evenett, S., and A. J. Venables. 2003. Export Growth in Developing Countries: Market Entry and Bilateral Trade. Mimeo.

Felbermayr, G. J., and W. Kohler. 2004. Exploring the Intensive and Extensive Margins of World Trade. *CESifo Working Paper Series* 1276. Munich: CESifo.

Feridhanusetyawan, T. 2005. Preferential Trade Agreements in the Asia-Pacific Region. *IMF Working Paper* 05/149. Washington, D.C: IMF.

Findlay, C., and S. Guo. 2007. Foreign Direct Investment in Services: The Experiences of India and China. Paper prepared for the International Workshop on Intra-Asian FDI Flows: Magnitude, Trends, Prospects, and Policy Implications. New Delhi, 25–26 April.

Findlay, C., R. Ochiai, and P. Dee. 2009. Integrating Services Market. In this volume.

Francois, J. F., B. Hoekman, and M. Manchin. 2006. Preference Erosion and Multilateral Trade Liberalization. *World Bank Economic Review* 20(2): 197–216.

Francois, J. F., and M. Manchin. 2007. Institutions, Infrastructure, and Trade. Center for Economic Policy Research *(CEPR) Discussion Paper* 6068. London: CEPR.

Francois, J. F., M. Manchin, and A. Pelkmans-Balaoing. 2009. Regional Integration in Asia: The Role of Infrastructure. In this volume.

Francois, J. F., B. McDonald, and H. Nordstrom. 1997. Capital Accumulation in Applied Trade Models. In *Applied Methods for Trade Policy Analysis: A Handbook,* edited by J. F. Francois and K. Reinert. Cambridge: Cambridge University Press.

Francois, J. F., M. McQueen, and G. Wignaraja. 2005. EU–Developing Country FTAs: Overview and Analysis. *World Development* 33(10): 1545–1566.

Francois, J. F., and D. Roland-Holst. 1997. Scale Economies and Imperfect Competition. In *Applied Methods for Trade Policy Analysis: A Handbook,* edited by J.F. Francois and K. Reinert. Cambridge: Cambridge University Press:

Francois. J. F., H. van Meijl, and F. van Tongeren. 2005. Trade Liberalization in the Doha Development Round. *Economic Policy* 20(42): 349–391. April.

Francois, J. F., and G. Wignaraja. 2009. Pan-Asian Integration: Economic Implications of Integration Scenarios. In this volume.

Francois, J. F., and J. Woerz. 2006. Rags in the High Rent District: The Evolution of Quota Rents in Textiles and Clothing. *CEPR Discussion Paper.* London: CEPR.

Frankel, J., and A. Rose. 1998. The Endogenity of the Optimum Currency Area Criteria. The *Economic Journal* 108(449): 1009–1025(17).

———. 2000. Estimating the Effects of Currency Unions on Trade and Output. *NBER Working Paper No. 7857.* Massachusetts: NBER.

Frankel, J., and S. J. Wei. 1995. European Integration and the Region-alization of World Trade and Currencies: The Economics and the Politics. *Center for International and Development Econom-ics Research Working Papers* C95-053, University of California at Berkeley.

Frankel, J., and S. Wei. 1998. Regionalization of World Trade and Cur-rencies: Economics and Politics. In *The Regionalization of the World Economy*, edited by J. A. Frankel. Chicago: University of Chicago Press.

Frankel, J., E. Stein, and S. Wei. 1995. Trading Blocs and the Americas: The Natural, the Unnatural and the Super Natural. *Journal of Devel-opment Economics* 47 (1): 61–95.

Freund, C., and B. Bolaky. 2002. Trade, Regulations, and Growth. *World Bank Policy Research Working Paper* 3255. November. Washington, DC: World Bank.

Gauthier, J. P. 2004. An Enabling Environment and Economic Zones for Private Sector Development in Bangladesh: Free Zones: Performance, Lessons Learned, and Implications for Zone Development. Presenta-tion by FIAS. IBRD. December.

Gilbert, J., R. Scollay, and B. Bora. 2004. New Regional Trading Devel-opments in the Asia-Pacific. In *Global Change and East Asian Pol-icy Initiatives*, edited by S. Yusuf, M.A. Talaf, and K. Nabeshima. Washington, DC: World Bank and New York: Oxford University Press.

Gill, I., and H. Kharas. 2007. *An East Asian Renaissance*. Washington, DC: World Bank.

Glick, R., and A. K. Rose. 1999. Contagion and Trade: Why Are Currency Crises Regional? *Journal of International Money and Finance* 18(4): 603–17.

———. 2001. Does a Currency Union Affect Trade? The Time Series Evidence. *NBER Working Paper* 8396. Massachusetts: NBER.

Gonenc, R., and G. Nicoletti. 2000. Regulation, Market Structure and Performance in Air Passenger Transport. *OECD Working Paper* 254. Paris: OECD.

Gordon, J., and P. Gupta. 2003. Understanding India's Services Revolution. Paper prepared for the IMF–NCAER Conference, A Tale of Two Giants: India's and China's Experience with Reform, New Delhi, 14–16 November.

Greenaway, D., W. Morgan, and P. Wright. 2002. Trade Liberalization and Growth in Developing Countries. *Journal of Development Economics* 67: 229–244.

Greene, W. H. 2003. *Econometric Analysis: 5th Edition.* Prentice Hall: New Jersey.

Grubel, H. 2006. The Economics of Monetary Unions: Traditional and New. Paper presented at the joint Fraser Institute and Kiel Institute of World Economics conference, The Economics of Regional Monetary Integration, 24–26 September, Kiel, Germany.

Gwartney, J., and R. Lawson. 2005. *Economic Freedom of the World: 2005 Annual Report.* Vancouver: The Fraser Institute. Available: www.freetheworld.com

Havemann, J., and D. Hummels. 2004. Alternative Hypotheses and the Volume of Trade: the Gravity Equation and the Extent of Specialization. *Canadian Journal of Economics* 37 (1): 199–218.

Heckman, J. 1979. Sample Selection Bias as a Specification Error. *Econometrica* 47: 153–161.

Hejmadi, S. 2004. An Enabling Environment and Economic Zones for Private Sector Development in Bangladesh: Best Practice in Public Free Zones: the UAE Free Zone Model and Its Economic Impact. FIAS, IBRD. Washington, DC: IBRD.

Hertel, T. W., ed. 1997. *Global Trade Analysis: Modeling and Applications.* Cambridge: Cambridge University Press.

Hertel, T. W., E. Ianchovichina, and B. J. McDonald. 1997. Multi-Region General Equilibrium Modeling. In *Applied Methods for Trade Policy Analysis: A Handbook,* edited by J. F. Francois and K.A. Reinert. Cambridge: Cambridge University Press.

Hew, D., ed. 2005. *Roadmap to an ASEAN Economic Community.* Singapore: Institute of Southeast Asian Studies (ISEAS).

Hirantha, S. W. 2004. From SAPTA to SAFTA: Gravity Analysis of South Asia Free Trade. Department of Commerce, Faculty of Management Studies and Commerce, University of Jayewardenpura, Sri Lanka. Mimeo.

Hiratsuka, D. 2005. An East Asian Spontaneous Economic Activity Space and the RTA/FTA Architecture: Does Japan Take a Right Way? Presented at PECC Trade Forum and APEC Study Center joint conference, Jeju, Republic of Korea, 22–25 May.

Hummels, D., and P. J. Klenow. 2005. The Variety and Quality of a Nation's Exports. *The American Economic Review* 95 (3): 704–723.

Indicus Analytics. 2006. Service Sector Reforms. Available: www.indicus. net/fileadmin/Studies/Service_sector_reforms.pdf

Inoue, K., M. Murayama, and M. Rahmatullah. 2004. Subregional Relations in the Eastern South Asia: With Special Focus on Bangladesh and Bhutan. *Institute of Developing Economics (IDE)- Japan External Trade Organization (JETRO) Joint Research Program Series No. 132.* Japan: IDE.

International Civil Aviation Organization. 2005. *World Air Transport Statistics 49th Edition.* Available: www.icao.int

IMF. 2006. *Balance of Payments Statistics* CD-ROM. April.

————. 2006. *Direction of Trade Statistics* CD-ROM. July.

————. 2007. *Direction of Trade Statistics* CD-ROM. June.

International Union of Railways. 2004. *International Railway Statistics.* Paris.

Jayasuriya, S., N. Maskay, D. Weerakoon, Y. R. Khatiwada, and S. Kurukulasuriya. 2003. *Monetary Cooperation in South Asia.* Mimeo, South Asia Network of Economic Research Institutes (SANERI) Kathmandu, Nepal.

Kalirajan, K. 2000. Restrictions on Trade in Distribution Services. *Productivity Commission Staff Research Paper*. Canberra: Ausinfo.

Karmacharya, B. 2002. Nepal's Informal Trade with India. Report prepared for SANERI.

Karmacharya, B., and N. Maskay. 2009. Nepal. In *National Strategies for Regional Integration: South and East Asian Case Studies*, edited by J. Francois, P. Rana, and G. Wignaraja. Manila: ADB.

Kaufmann, D., A. Kraay, and M. Mastruzzi. 2005. Governance Matters IV: Governance Indicators for 1996–2004. *World Bank Policy Research Working Paper Series No. 3630*. Washington, DC: World Bank.

Kawai, M. 2002. Exchange Rate Arrangements in East Asia: Lessons from the 1997-98 Currency Crisis. *Monetary and Economic Studies* 20(S1): 167–204.

———. 2005a. East Asian Economic Regionalism: Progress and Challenges. *Journal of Asian Economics* 16: 29–55.

———. 2005b. Trade and Investment Integration and Cooperation in East Asia: Empirical Evidence and Issues. In *Asian Economic Cooperation and Integration: Progress, Prospects, and Challenges*. Manila: ADB.

———. 2008. Toward A Regional Exchange Rate Regime in East Asia. *Pacific Economic Review* 13(1): 83–103.

Kawai, M., and S. Takagi. 2005. Towards regional monetary cooperation in East Asia: lessons from other parts of the world. *International Journal of Finance and Economics* 10(2): 97–116. April.

Kawai, M., and G. Wignaraja. 2008. EAFTA or CEPEA: Which Way Forward? *ASEAN Economic Bulletin*, 25(2): 113–139.

Kemal, A., R. Musleh-udDin, Klabe Abbas, and Usman Kadir. 2000. A Plan to Strengthen Regional Trade Cooperation in South Asia. Study prepared for SAMEI-I Project, Islamabad: Pakistan Institute of Development Economics (PIDE).

Kim, S., J. W. Lee, and K. Shin. 2006. Regional and Global Financial Integration in East Asia. *Institute of Economic Research, Korea University Discussion Paper Series* 0602. Seoul: Institute of Economic Research.

Kim, S., A. Kose, and M. Plummer. 2002. Contagion or Simple Transmission of Business Cycles? In *The Post-Financial Crisis Challenges for Asian Industrialization*, edited by R. Hooley and J. H. Yoo. New York: Elsevier.

Kochar, K., P. Loungani, and M. Stone. 1998. The East Asian Crisis: Macroeconomic Developments and Policy Lessons. *IMF Working Paper No. 98/128*. Washington, DC: IMF.

Kose, A., S. Kim, and M. Plummer. 2003. Dynamics of Business Cycles in Asia: Differences and Similarities. *Review of Development Economics*, 7 (3): 462–477.

Krueger, A. O. 1978. *Foreign Trade Regimes and Economic Development: Liberalization Attempts and Consequences*. Massachusetts: Ballinger Publishing Co. for the NBER.

Krueger, E., R. C. Bastos Pinto, V. Thomas, and T. To. 2004. Impacts of the South Asia Free Trade Agreement. Policy Analysis Workshop, Public Affairs 869. Wisconsin: University of Wisconsin-Madison.

Kumar, N., K. Kesavapany, and Y. Chaocheng. 2007. *Asia's New Regionalism and Global Role: Agenda for the East Asia Summit*. New Delhi: RIS and Singapore: ISEAS.

Kumar, N., R. Sen, and M. G. Asher. 2006. India-ASEAN Economic Relations: Meeting the Challenges of Globalization. *Asian-Pacific Economic Literature* 20 (2): 84–84.

Kumar, N. and Sharma. 2009. India. In *National Strategies for Regional Integration: South and East Asian Case Studies*, edited by J. Francois, P. Rana, and G. Wignaraja. Manila: ADB.

Kuroda, H., and M. Kawai. 2003. Strengthening Regional Financial Cooperation in East Asia. *East Asian Bureau of Economic Research, Finance Working Papers* 483.

Kwan, C. H. 2001. *Yen Bloc: Toward Economic Integration in Asia*. Washington, DC: Brookings Institution Press.

Kwan, Y. K., and L. D. Chiu. 2003. The ASEAN Plus Three Trading Bloc. Hong Kong, China. Mimeo.

Lee, H., D. Roland-Holst, and D. van der Mensbrugghe. 2004. China's Emergence and the Implications of Prospective Free Trade Agreements in East Asia. Kobe: Kobe University. Mimeo.

Lee, J. W., and I. Park. 2005. Free Trade Areas in East Asia: Discriminatory or Non-Discriminatory? *World Economy* 28 (1): 21–48.

Lee, J. W. and K. Shin. 2006. Does regionalism lead to more global trade integration in East Asia?. *The North American Journal of Economics and Finance* 17 (3): 283–301. December.

Lee, J. W., and P. Swagel. 1997. Trade Barriers and Trade Flows Across Countries and Industries. *The Review of Economics and Statistics* 79 (3): 372–382. August.

Levchenko, A. 2004. Institutional Quality and International Trade. *IMF Working Paper 04/231*. Washington, DC: IMF.

Li, Y. 2005. Preliminary Findings from Study of Legal Regimes for International Land Transport. Presentation at National Workshop and Advisory Services on Trade and Transport Facilitation, ESCAP.

Limao, N., and A. J. Venables. 2001. Infrastructure, Geographical Disadvantage, Transport Costs and Trade. *World Bank Economic Review* 15: 451–479. Washington, DC: World Bank.

Logistics Consulting Group. 2006. Pakistan Logistics Cost Study: Final Draft Report. April.

Low, L. 2004. A Comparative Evaluation and Prognosis of Asia Pacific Bilateral and Regional Trade Arrangements. *Asian-Pacific Economic Literature* 18 (1): 1–11.

Madani, Z. 1999. A Review of the Role and Impact of Export Processing Zones. *Policy Research Working Paper 2238*. Washington, DC: IBRD.

Malik, M. 2006. The East Asia Summit. *Australian Journal of International Affairs* 60 (2): 207–211.

Manchin, M., and A. Pelkmans-Balaoing. 2007a. Rules of Origin and the Web of East Asian FTAs. *World Bank Policy Research Working Paper Series*, 4273. July. Washington, DC: World Bank.

————. 2007b. Clothes without an Emperor: Analysis of the Preferential Tariffs in ASEAN. *Centro Studi Luca D'Agliano Development Studies Working Papers No. 223*. January.

Maskay, N.M. 2003. Patterns of Shocks and Regional Monetary Cooperation in South Asia. *IMF Working Papers* 03/240.

Mattoo, A. 2003. China's Accession to the WTO: The Services Dimension *Journal of International Economic Law* 6: 299–339.

Mattoo, A., R. Rathindran, and A. Subramaniam. 2006. Measuring Services Trade Liberalization and its Impact on Economic Growth: An Illustration. *Journal of Economic Integration*, 21 (1): 64–98.

McGuire, G., and M. Schuele. 2000. Restrictiveness of International Trade in Banking Services. In *Impediments to Trade in Services, Measurement and Policy Implications*, 201–214, edited by C. Findlay and T. Warren. London and New York: Routledge.

McKibbin, W. 2004. Which Exchange Rate Regime for Asia? *Brookings Discussion Papers in International Economics, No. 158*. February. Washington, DC: Brookings Institution.

McKibbin, W., J. W. Lee, and I. Cheong. 2004. A dynamic analysis of the Korea-Japan free trade area: simulations with the G-cubed Asia-Pacific model. Korean International Economic Association. 18(1): 3–32. March.

Ministry of Foreign Affairs, Thailand. 2006. BIMSTEC Free Trade Area Framework Agreement. Available: www.mfa.go.th/bimstec/bimstecweb/html/fta.html

Ministry of Trade, Singapore. 2005. Singapore's FTA Network. Available: http://app.fta.gov.sg/asp/index.asp

Mishra, S. K. 2006. SAARC Regional Multimodal Transport Study – India (draft) ADB RETA 6187. January.

Mohanty, S. K., and S. Pohit. 2007. Welfare Gains from Regional Economic Integration in Asia: ASEAN+3 or EAS. *RIS Discussion Paper* 126. Delhi: RIS.

Mohanty, S. K., S. Pohit, and S. Roy. 2004. Towards Formation of Close Economic Cooperation among Asian Countries. *RIS Discussion Papers* 78. Delhi: RIS.

Mtys, L. 1997. Proper Econometric Specification of the Gravity Model. *The World Economy* 20: 363–368.

Mukherji, I. N. 2005. The Bangkok Agreement: A Negative List Approach to Trade Liberalization in Asia and the Pacific. *Asia Pacific Trade and Investment Review* 1 (2). November.

———. 2000. Charting a Free Trade Area in South Asia: Instruments and Modalities. Nepal: SANERI.

Mukherji, I. N., T. Jayawardhana, and S. Kelegama. 2004. Indo–Sri Lanka Free Trade Agreement: An Assessment of Potential Impact. Nepal: SANERI.

Munakata, N. 2002. Whither East Asian Economic Integration. *RIETI Discussion Paper Series* 02-E-007. Tokyo: Research Institute for Economy Trade and Industry (RIETI).

Mundell, R. 1961. A Theory of Optimum Currency Areas. *American Economic Review* 51: 657–65.

Muni, S. 1992. *India and Nepal: A Changing Relationship*. New Delhi: Konark.

Murthy, N. 2004. The Impact of Economic Reforms on Industry in India: A Case Study of the Software Industry. In *India's Emerging Economy: Performance and Prospects in the 1990's and Beyond*, edited by K. Basu. Massachusetts: MIT Press.

Nath, V. 2004. Nepal-India Trade Treaty and WTO Compatibility. In *Implications of the WTO Membership on Nepalese Agriculture*, edited by P. Sharma, and M.K. Karkee, Nepal: Food and Agriculture Organisation (FAO), United Nations Development Programme (UNDP), and Ministry of Agriculture and Cooperatives.

National Association of software and services companies (Nasscom). 2006. Factors and Policies Influencing the Expansion of Services Trade – Experiences of the Indian IT-BPO Sector. Available: http://siteresources.worldbank.org/INTRANETTRADE/Resources/WBI-Training/288464-1161888800183/S2b2_Singh_En.pdf

National Bureau of Statistics of the People's Republic of China. 2005. *China Statistical Yearbook*. Beijing: China Statistics Press.

Nicolas, F. 1999. Is There a Case for a Single Currency within ASEAN? *The Singapore Economic Review* 44 (1): 1–25.

Nordas, H. K., and R. Piermartini. 2004. "Infrastructure and Trade". *WTO Staff Working Paper ERSD-2004-04*. Geneva: World Trade Organization (WTO).

Obstfeld, M., and K. Rogoff. 1995. Exchange Rate Dynamics Redux. *Journal of Political Economy* 102: 624–660 June.

OECD. 2004. *The Economy-Wide Effects of Services Trade Barriers in Selected Developing Countries*. TD/TC/WP (2004) 42. Paris: OECD.

Ogawa, E., and J. Shimizu. 2006. Progress towards a Common Currency Basket System in East Asia. *RIETI Discussion Paper Series* 07-E-002. November. Japan: RIETI.

Padeco Consultants. 2005. *SASEC: Subregional Corridor Operational Efficiency Study* (TA 6112-REG.) Manila: ADB.

———. 2005. GMS Transport Sector Strategy—Draft Final Report. November.

Panagariya, A. 2007. Why India Lags Behind China and How it Can Bridge the Gap. *World Economy* 30 (2): 229–248.

———. 1999. The WTO Trade Policy Review of India, 1998. *World Economy 1999*. 799–824.

———. 1999. Trade Policy in South Asia: Recent Liberalization and Future Agenda. *The World Economy* 22 (3): 353–378.

Pangestu, M., and C. Findlay. 2004. Service sector reform options: the experience of China. Mimeo, University of Adelaide.

Pelkmans-Balaoing, A. 2006. *The Web of East Asian FTAs and the Resulting Labyrinth of Origin Rules* (PhD dissertation). Rotterdam: Erasmus University.

Petri, P. 2006. Is East Asia Becoming More Independent? Prepared for the Session on European and Asian Integration: Trade and Monetary Issues organized by the American Economic Association and American Committee on Asian Economic Studies, 8 January 2006, Boston, Massachusetts, United States.

Plummer, M. 2007. Harnessing Productivity and Competitiveness in East Asia. Paper presented at Integrating Asian Economies: Ten Years after the Crisis, 18 July, Bangkok.

Plummer, M., and G. Wignaraja. 2006. The Post-Crisis Sequencing of Economic Integration in Asia: Trade as a Complement to a Monetary Future. *Economie Internationale* 107: 59–85.

—————. 2009. Integration Strategies for ASEAN: Alone, Together, or Together with Neighbors? In this volume.

Pradhan, J. P. 2003. Rise of Service Sector Outward Foreign Direct Investment from India: Trends, Patterns and Determinants. *RIS Discussion Papers* 63/2003. New Delhi: RIS.

Radelet, S., J. Sachs, and J. W. Lee. 2001. The Determinants and Prospects of Economic Growth in Asia. *International Economic Journal, Korean International Economic Association* 15 (3): 1–29. October.

Railway Gazette International. 2005. Railway Directory. Available: www.railwaygazette.com

Rajan, R., and S. M. Thangavelu. 2009. Singapore. In *National Strategies for Regional Integration: South and East Asian Case Studies,* edited by J. Francois, P. Rana, and G. Wignaraja. Manila: ADB.

Rana, P. B. 2005. Economic Relations between South and East Asia: The Evolution of Pan-Asian Integration. Paper prepared for the High Level Conference on Asian Economic Integration, New Delhi, 18–19 November.

————.2006. Economic Integration in East Asia: Trends, Prospects, and a Possible Roadmap. *Working Paper Series on Regional Economic Integration* 2. Manila: ADB.

Rana, P. B., and J. M. Dowling. 2009. Economic Integration in South Asia and Lessons from East Asia. In this volume.

Ranjan, P. and J. Y. Lee. 2003. Contract Enforcement and the Volume of International Trade in Different Types of Goods. Mimeo, University of California-Irvine.

Rashid, M. 2008. Bangladesh. In *National Strategies for Regional Integration: South and East Asian Case Studies*, edited by J. Francois, P. Rana, and G. Wignaraja. Manila: ADB.

Reinert, K. A., and D. W. Roland-Holst. 1997. Social Accounting Matrices. In *Applied Methods for Trade Policy Analysis: A Handbook*, edited by J. F. Francois and K. A. Reinert. Massachusetts: Cambridge University Press.

Roberts, M. J., and J. R. Tybout. 1997. The Decision to Export in Colombia: An Empirical Model of Entry with Sunk Costs. *The American Economic Review* 87(4): 545–564. September.

Robinson, S., and K. Thierfelder. 1999. Trade Liberalization and Regional Integration: The Search for Large Numbers. *International Food Policy Research Institute Discussion Paper* 34. Washington, DC.

Rodriguez, F. and D. Rodrik. 1999. Trade Policy and Economic Growth: A Skeptic's Guide to the Cross-National Evidence. *CEPR Discussion Paper* 2143. London: CEPR.

Rodrik, D., A. Subramanian, and F. Trebbi. 2004. Institutions Rule: The Primacy of Institutions over Geography and Integration in Economic Development. *Journal of Economic Growth* 9(2): 131–165. June.

Rose, A. K., and C. Engel. 2002. Currency Unions and International Integration. *Journal of Money, Credit and Banking* 34 (4): 1067–1089. November.

Roy, J. 2005. South Asian Regional Trade Agreements: Perspectives, Issues and Options. Presented at an international trade roundtable entitled The WTO at 10 Years: The Regional Challenge to Multilateralism. Brussels, 27 June.

Sally, R., and R. Sen. 2005. Whither Trade Policies in Southeast Asia? The Wider Asian and Global Context. *ASEAN Economic Bulletin* (22)1: 92–115.

Santos Silva, J. M. C., and S. Tenreyro. 2006. The Log of Gravity. *Review of Economics and Statistics* 88(4): 641–658. November.

Saxena, S. C. 2002. Is the Euro Area a Role Model for Asia? Mimeo, University of Pittsburgh.

————. 2003. India's Monetary Integration with East Asia: A Feasibility Study. *RIS Discussion Paper* 64. New Delhi: RIS.

Scollay, R. 2001. The Changing Outlook for Asia-Pacific Regionalism. *World Economy* 24 (9): 1135–1160. September.

————. 2005. East Asia and the Evolution of Preferential Trading Arrangements. In *Asia-Pacific Region: A Stocktake in New East Asian Regionalism*, edited by C. Harvie, F. Kimura, and H. H. Lee. Cheltenham: Edward Elgar.

————. 2006. East Asian Regionalism: Undermining or Underpinning Asia Pacific Integration? In *Reshaping the Asia Pacific Economic Order*, edited by C. Findlay and H. Soesastro. London: Routledge.

Scollay, R., and A. Pelkmans-Balaoing. 2009. Current Patterns of Trade and Investment. In this volume.

Sheng, L. 2003. China–ASEAN Free Trade Area: Origins, Developments, and Strategic Motivations. *ISEAS Working Paper International Politics and Security Series* 1. Singapore: ISEAS.

Shoban, R. 2000. *Rediscovering the Southern Silk Road. Integrating Asia's Transport Infrastructure*. Dhaka: University Press Ltd.

Shrestha, G. R. 2003. Nepal-India Bilateral Trade Relations: Problems and Prospects. *RIS Discussion Paper No. 54*. New Delhi: RIS.

Siriwardana, M. 2003. Trade Liberalization in South Asia: Free Trade Area or Customs Union. *Journal of South Asian Studies* XXVI (3): 309–329.

Soesastro, H. 2003. *Dynamics of Competitive Liberalization in RTA Negotiations: East Asian Perspectives.* Singapore: Pacific Economic Cooperation Council.

————. 2005. Realizing the East Asian Vision. *Economics Working Paper Series.* Jakarta: Center for Strategic and International Studies.

South Asia Subregional Economic Cooperation (SASEC). 2005. *SAARC Regional Multimodal Transport Study.* Manila: ADB.

————. 2004. *SAARC Regional Multimodal Transport Study—Final Report for Bangladesh.* Manila: ADB.

————. 2005. *SAARC Regional Multimodal Transport Study—Country Report for Sri Lanka.* Manila: ADB.

Srinivasan, T. N. 1994. Regional Trading Arrangements and Beyond: Exploring Some Policy Options for South Asia. *World Bank Report* IDP42.

Stahl, C. 1999. Trade in Labor Services and Migrant Worker Protection with Special Reference to East Asia. *International Migration* 37 (3): 545–568.

Suzuki, S. 2004. East Asian Cooperation through Conference Diplomacy: Institutional Aspects of the ASEAN Plus Three Framework. *IDE APEC Study Center Working Paper Series 03/04 No. 4.* Tokyo: IDE.

Taneja, N., and S. Pohit. 2002. India's Informal Trade with Bangladesh and Nepal: A Qualitative Assessment. *ICHER Working Paper* 58. New Delhi.

Taneja, N., B. Sarvananthan, B. Karmacharya, and S. Pohit. 2004. India's Informal Trade with Sri Lanka and Nepal: An Estimation. *South Asia Economic Journal* 5 (1): 27–54.

Tang, H. C. 2006. An Asian Monetary Union? *Center for Applied Macroeconomic Analysis Working Paper* 13/2006. Australian National University.

Ul Haque, N. and Ghani, E. 2009. Pakistan. In *National Strategies for Regional Integration: South and East Asian Case Studies,* edited by J. Francois, P. Rana, and G. Wignaraja. Manila: ADB.

UNESCAP. 2004. *Traders' Manual For Least Developed Countries: Bangladesh.* Bangkok: UNESCAP.

————. 2006a. *Project Profile of Priority Projects Along the Asian Highway: Tables for Bangladesh, Myanmar, India, Pakistan, Nepal, China, Thailand, and the Lao People's Democratic Republic.* Bangkok: UNESCAP.

————. 2006b. Emerging Issues in Transport: Item 5(b) of the Provisional Agenda: Regional Cooperation in Infrastructure Development for an International Integrated Intermodal Transport System in Asia. Presentation at Meeting of Senior Government Officials. Busan, Republic of Korea.

United Nations Conference on Trade and Development (UNCTAD). 1987. *Trans-country Power Exchange and Development.* Bangkok: UNESCAP.

————. 2006a. *Transport Newsletter No. 32.* Available: www.unctad.org/transportnews

————. 2006b. Simplification of Trade Documentation using International Standards. *Technical Note No. 13.* Geneva.

United States Agency for International Development. 2005. *South Asia Free Trade Area: Opportunities and Challenges.* Washington, DC.

Urata, S., and K. Kiyota. 2003. Impacts of an East Asian FTA on Foreign Trade in East Asia. *NBER Working Paper Series, 10173.* Massachusetts: NBER.

Venables, A., and N. Linao. 1999a. Geographical Disadvantage: A Hecksher-Olin-Von Thunen Model of International Specialization. *World Bank Policy Research Working Paper* 2256. Washington, DC.

————. 1999b. Infrastructure, Geographical Disadvantage and Transport Costs. *World Bank Policy Research Working Paper* 2257. Washington, DC.

Vucetic, V. 2004. South Asia Regional Energy Trade: Opportunities and Challenges. Presentation to the World Bank/IMF Annual Meetings, Washington, DC, October.

Wacziarg, R., and K. H. Welch. 2003. Trade Liberalization and Growth: New Evidence. *NBER Working Paper 10152.* December. Massachusetts: NBER.

Wangyal, T. 2005. SAARC Regional Multimodal Transport Study – Draft Final Report for Bhutan. Paper prepared for ADB (RETA 6187). Manila: ADB.

Warren, T. 2000. The Impact on Output of Impediments to Trade and Investment in Telecommunications Services. In *Impediments to Trade in Services: Measurement and Policy Implications*, edited by C. Findlay and T. Warren. London and New York: Routledge.

Weerakoon, D. 2009. Sri Lanka. In *National Strategies for Regional Integration: South and East Asian Case Studies*, edited by J. Francois, P. Rana, and G. Wignaraja. Manila: ADB.

Wickramasinghe, U. 2000. Services Trade as a "New Frontier" in South Asia: Is the Optimism Warranted? *South Asia Economic Journal* 1(2): 1–23.

Wignaraja, G. 1991. Industrialization and Social Development: Some Comparisons of South Asia with the East Asian NICS. In *Participatory Development: Learning from South Asia* of P. Wignaraja, A. Hussain, H. Sethi, and G. Wignaraja. Tokyo: United Nations University Press and Karachi: Oxford University Press.

————. 1998. *Trade Liberalization in Sri Lanka: Exports, Technology and Industrial Development*. Basingstoke, United Kingdom: MacMillan Press.

————. 2003. Competitiveness Analysis and Strategy. In *Competitiveness Strategy in Developing Countries*, edited by G. Wignaraja. London: Routledge.

————. 2008a. Foreign Ownership, Technological Capabilities, and Clothing Exports in Sri Lanka, *Journal of Asian Economics* 19 (1): 29–39. February.

————. 2008b. FDI and Innovation as Drivers of Export Behaviour: Firm-level Evidence from East Asia, *UNU-MERIT Working Paper Series* 2008–061.

Wignaraja, G., and D. Joiner. 2006. Can small states compete in manufacturing? In *WTO at the Margins: Small States and the Multilateral*

Trading System, edited by R. Grynberg. Cambridge: Cambridge University Press.

Wignaraja, G., and F. Nixson. 2006. Export Performance and Nontariff Measures: Lessons from India's Pharmaceutical Sector. In *Trade, Aid and Development*, edited by M. B. Saad and M. Leen. Dublin: University College Dublin Press.

Wignaraja G., M. Lezama, and D. Joiner. 2004. *Small States in Transition: From Vulnerability to Competitiveness*. London: Commonwealth Secretariat.

Wignaraja, G., and C. Oman. 1991. *The Postwar Evolution of Development Thinking*. New York: St. Martin's Press.

Wignaraja, G., and A. Taylor. 2003. Benchmarking Competitiveness: A First Look at the MECI. In G. Wignaraja (ed.), *Competitiveness Strategy in Developing Countries*. London: Routledge.

Wilson, J. S., C. L. Mann, and T. Otsuki. 2004. Assessing the Potential Benefit of Trade Facilitation: A Global Perspective. *World Bank Working Paper* 3224. Washington, DC: World Bank.

Winters, L. A., and S. Yusuf. 2007. *Dancing with Giants: China, India, and the Global Economy*. Washington, DC: World Bank.

World Bank.1987. *World Development Report 1987*. New York: Oxford University Press and Washington, DC: World Bank.

————.1993. *East Asian Miracle*. Washington, DC.

————. 2001. Trade and Transport Facilitation: A Toolkit for Audit, Analysis and Remedial Action, *World Bank Discussion Paper 427*. Washington, DC.

————. 2004. Trade Policies in South Asia: An Overview *Report No. 29929*. Washington, DC.

————. 2006a. *An East Asian Renaissance: Ideas for Economic Growth*. Mimeo, Washington, DC.

————. 2006b. *Global Economic Prospects 2006: Economic Implications of Remittances and Migration.* Available: www.worldbank.org.

————. 2006c. *Pakistan: Transport Competitiveness in Pakistan,* Analytic Underpinning for National Trade Corridor Improvement Program. Washington, DC.

————. 2006d. *Doing Business 2007.* Washington, DC.

————. 2006e. *South Asia Growth and Regional Integration.* Washington, DC.

————. 2007. Transport and Trade Facilitation in South Asia (Annexes: Bangladesh, India, Nepal and Pakistan). Mimeo. Washington, DC.

————. 2007. World Development Indicators Online. Available: http://devdata.worldbank.org/data-query/

World Trade Organization. 2006a. *WTO Annual Report.* Geneva.

————. 2006b. *International Trade Statistics.* Geneva.

Yap, J. T. 2005. Economic Cooperation and Regional Integration in East Asia: A Pragmatic View. *Philippine Institute for Development Studies Discussion Paper Series* 2005.32. Manila.

Yip, W. K. 2001. Prospects for Closer Economic Integration in East Asia. *Stanford Journal of East Asian Affairs* 1 (Spring): 106–111.

Zhai, F. 2006. Preferential Trade Agreements in Asia: Alternative Scenarios of Hub and Spoke. *Economics and Research Department (ERD) Working Paper Series* 83. Manila: ADB.

Zhang, Y. 2009. People's Republic of China. In *National Strategies for Regional Integration: South and East Asian Case Studies,* edited by J. Francois, P. Rana, and G. Wignaraja. Manila: ADB.

Zhang, Y. et al. 2006. *Towards an East Asia FTA: Modality and Road Map.* A Report by Joint Expert Group for Feasibility Study on EAFTA. Jakarta: Association of Southeast Asian Nations.

List of Websites Used

Airports Authority of India. www.airportsindia.org.in

Airports Council International. www.aci-asia.org/

Airports Council International. www.airports.org/cda/aci/display/main/aci_content.jsp?zn=aci&cp=1-5-212-219_9_2__

APL. www.apl.com/routes/html/asia_north_america.html

Asia Regional Integration Center – Asian Development Bank. www.aric.adb.org

Automated System for Customs Data. www.asycuda.org

Changi Airport, Singapore. www.changiairport.com

People's Republic of China Maps. www.maps-of-china.com/ and http://www.maps-of-china.net/g_highways_china.html

China Railway Statistics. www.railwaysofchina.com/statistics.htm

China Supply Chain Council. www.supplychain.cn/

City Population, Denmark. www.citypopulation.de/China.html#Stadt_alpha

Container Corporation of India, Ltd. www.concorindia.com

DHL. www.dhl-usa.com/tasclient/HandlerServlet?CLIENT=TD_DISPLAY_HANDLER

Dpiterminals.com—DPWorld.http://dpiterminals.com/subpages.asp?PSID=1&PageID=21

Financial Express Capital One. www.financialexpress-bd.com

General Administration of Civil Aviation in China. www.caac.gov.cn

Global Facilitation Partnership for Transportation and Trade. www.gfptt.org/Entities/ContributionRequestProfile.aspx?list=all&id=c818e494-38a9-4c4b-b48c-b7e6d9e5aa6e

Greenwich Meantime. www.greenwichmeantime.com/time-zone/asia/china/province/index.htm

The Hindu Business Line. www.blonnet.com

Hong Kong International Airport. www.hongkongairport.com www.unece.org/trade/workshop/geneva_oct06/presentations/Session2_SITPRO.ppt

Infoplease: Encyclopedia, Almanac, Atlas, Biography, Dictionary, Thesaurus. www.infoplease.com/ipa/A0759496.html

Intermodal Association of North America. www.intermodal.org/fact.html

ITP Division, Ministry of External Affairs, India. www.indiainbusiness.nic.in/trade-india/importclear.htm

Karachi International Airport. www.karachiairport.com/

Kintetsu World Express Inc. www.kwe.co.jp/service/china/eng/businfo/distance.html

La Em Chabang World Class Port. www.laemchabangport.com/lcp/Internet/directory.fairplay.co.uk/

Maersks Line Shipping Containers Worldwide. www.maersksealand.com/HomePage/appmanager/?_nfpb=true&_pageLabel=schedules&_nfls=false

Maps of India. www.mapsofindia.com/maps/india/sea-ports.htm

Mediterranean Shipping Company. www.mscgva.ch/schedule.html

MOL Power.com -Profit in Motion. www.molpower.com/htm/default.htm

NYK Logistics and Megacarrier. www2.nykline.com/nykinfo/liner_services/con_serv/index.html

Railway Directory: A Railway Gazette Publication. www.railwaydirectory.net

Rediff.com India Limited. www.in.rediff.com/money/2005/sep/27china.htm

Special Economic Zones in India, Ministry of Commerce and Industry, Department of Commerce. www.sezindia.nic.in/faq.asp

World Bank. www.devdata.worldbank.org/data-query/

Time and Date.Com www.timeanddate.com/worldclock/distances.html?n=237

Trade and Transport Facilitation in Southeast Europe Program. www.ttfse.org/

Trade Gallery of Asia.www.asiatradehub.com/world_ports.asp

Tradenic Online, India. www.tradenic.nic.in/tfo.htm

Transport Corporation of India Ltd. www.tcil.com/

United Nations Conference on Trade and Development. www.unctad.org/ttl/technical-notes/TN13_Document%20Simplification.pdf

United Nations Economic Commission for Europe. www.unece.org/trade/kyoto/; and www.unece.org/statistics/tradetable.html

United Nations Statistics Division. www.unstats.un.org/unsd/comtrade/mr/rfCommoditiesList.aspx?px=H1&cc=60

University of Texas at Austin Libraries. www.lib.utexas.edu/maps/middle_east_and_asia/china_industry_83.jpg
www.lib.utexas.edu/maps/middle_east_and_asia/india_pop_1973.jpg

Wikipedia. www.en.wikipedia.org/wiki/

World Bank. web.worldbank.org/wbsite/external/countries/southasiaext/extsarregtoptransport/0,,menuPK:579621~pagePK:51065911~piPK:64171011~theSitePK:579598,00.html

World Customs Organization www.wcoomd.org/ie/En/Topics_Issues/FacilitationCustomsProcedures/Kyoto_New/Content/body_content.html; www.wcoomd.org/ie/En/Conventions/conventions.html; www.wcoomd.org/ie/En/en.html

World News Network. www.distances.com/

World Trade Organization. www.wto.org/English/thewto_e/whatis_e/tif_e/org6_e.htm

Index